All in One

Recommended by Teachers Trusted by Toppers

COMPUTER SCIENCE

Class 11

EVERYTHING YOU NEED TO SCORE

- Simplified Theory
- Topic & Chapter Exercises
- Solved NCERT Exercise
- All Types of Exam Pattern Questions
- CBQs; MCQs, A-R, Case Based
- Sample Question Papers

CBSE Exams 2026

Authors
Lalita Kaler,
Abhishek

arihant
SUCCESS AND NOTHING LESS

arihant
SUCCESS AND NOTHING LESS

ARIHANT PRAKASHAN

(School Division Series)

卐 *ADMINISTRATIVE & PRODUCTION OFFICES*

Regd. Office

'Ramchhaya' 4577/15, Agarwal Road, Darya Ganj, New Delhi -110002
Tele: 011- 47630600, 43518550; Fax: 011- 23280316

卐 *Head Office*

Kalindi, TP Nagar, Meerut (UP) - 250002, Tel: 0121-7156203, 7156204

卐 *SALES & SUPPORT OFFICES*

Agra, Ahmedabad, Bengaluru, Bareilly, Chennai, Delhi, Guwahati, Hyderabad, Jaipur, Jhansi, Kolkata, Lucknow, Nagpur & Pune.

PO No : TXT-XX-XXXXXXX-X-XX

Published By Arihant Publications (India) Ltd.

For further information about the books published by Arihant, log on to www.arihantbooks.com or e-mail at info@arihantbooks.com

Follow us on

卐 *PRICE* ₹350.00

PRODUCTION TEAM

Publishing Managers	*Cover Designer*	*Inner Designer*
Mahendra Singh Rawat & Keshav Mohan	Rakesh Rawat	Ankit Tyagi
Project Head	*Page Layouting*	*Proof Reader*
Shruti Aggarwal	Ravinder Kumar	Sumit Rawat

Index *cum* Study Planner

Studied | Revised | Exam ready

Latest Course *Structure*

1. Learning Outcomes

Student should be able to

(a) develop basic computational thinking

(b) explain and use data types

(c) appreciate the notion of algorithm

(d) develop a basic understanding of computer systems - architecture, operating system.

(e) explain cyber ethics, cyber safety and cybercrime

(f) Understand the value of technology in societies along with consideration of gender and disability issues

2. Distribution of Marks:

Unit No.	Unit Name	Marks
I	Computer Systems and Organisation	10
II	Computational Thinking and Programming - 1	45
III	Society, Law and Ethics	15
	TOTAL	70

3. UNITWISE SYLLABUS

UNIT I Computer Systems and Organisation

- **Basic Computer Organisation** Introduction to computer system, hardware, software, input device, output device, CPU, memory (primary, cache and secondary), units of memory (Bit, Byte, KB, MB, GB, TB, PB)
- **Types of Software** system software (operating systems, system utilities, device drivers), programming tools and language translators (assembler, compiler & interpreter), application software
- **Operating System (OS)** functions of operating system, OS user interface
- **Boolean Logic** NOT, AND, OR, NAND, NOR, XOR, truth table, De Morgan's laws and logic circuits
- **Number System** Binary, Octal, Decimal and Hexadecimal number system; conversion between number systems.
- **Encoding Schemes** ASCII, ISCII and UNICODE (UTF8, UTF32)

UNIT II Computational Thinking and Programming - 1

- **Introduction to Problem Solving** Steps for problem solving (analysing the problem, developing an algorithm, coding, testing and debugging) representation of algorithms using flow chart and pseudo code, decomposition
- **Familiarization with the Basics of Python Programming** Introduction to Python, features of Python, executing a simple "hello world" program, execution modes: interactive mode and script mode, Python character set, Python tokens (keyword, identifier, literal, operator, punctuator), variables, concept of l-value and r-value, use of comments
- **Knowledge of Data Types** number (integer, floating point, complex), boolean, sequence (string, list, tuple), none, mapping (dictionary), mutable and immutable data types
- **Operators** arithmetic operators, relational operators, logical operators, assignment operator, augmented assignment operators, identity operators (is, is not), membership operators (in, not in)
- **Expressions, Statement, Type Conversion & Input/Output** precedence of operators, expression, evaluation of expression, type conversion (explicit & implicit conversion), accepting data as input from the console and displaying output
- **Errors** syntax errors, logical errors, runtime errors
- **Flow of Control** introduction, use of indentation, sequential flow, conditional and iterative flow
- **Conditional Statements** if, if-else, if-elif-else, flowcharts, simple programs: e.g.: absolute value, sort 3 numbers and divisibility of a number
- **Iterative Statements** for loop, range function, while loop, flowcharts, break and continue statements, nested loops, suggested programs: generating pattern, summation of series, finding the factorial of a positive number etc
- **Strings** introduction, string operations (concatenation, repetition, membership & slicing), traversing a string using loops, built-in functions: len(), capitalize(), title(), lower(), upper(), count(), find(), index(), endswith(), startswith(), isalnum(), isalpha(), isdigit(), islower(), isupper(), isspace(), lstrip(), rstrip(), strip(), replace(), join(), partition(), split()
- **Lists** introduction, indexing, list operations (concatenation, repetition, membership & slicing), traversing a list using loops, built-in functions: len(), list(), append(), extend(), insert(), count(), index(), remove(), pop(), reverse(), sort(), sorted(), min(), max(), sum(); nested lists, suggested programs: finding the maximum, minimum, mean of numeric values stored in a list; linear search on list of numbers and counting the frequency of elements in a list
- **Tuples** introduction, indexing, tuple operations (concatenation, repetition, membership & slicing), built-in functions: len(), tuple(), count(), index(), sorted(), min(), max(), sum(); tuple assignment, nested tuple, suggested programs: finding the minimum, maximum, mean of values stored in a tuple; linear search on a tuple of numbers, counting the frequency of elements in a tuple
- **Dictionary** introduction, accessing items in a dictionary using keys, mutability of dictionary (adding a new item, modifying an existing item), traversing a dictionary, built-in functions: len(), dict(), keys(), values(), items(), get(), update(), del, clear(), fromkeys(), copy(), pop(), popitem(), setdefault(), max(), min(), sorted(), suggested programs : count the number of times a character appears in a given string using a dictionary, create a dictionary with names of employees, their salary and access them
- **Introduction to Python Modules** Importing module using 'import <module>' and using from statement, Importing math module (pi, e, sqrt(), ceil(), floor(), pow(), fabs(), sin(), cos(), tan()); random module (random(), randint(), randrange()), statistics module (mean(), median(), mode())

UNIT III Society, Law and Ethics

- Digital Footprints
- **Digital Society and Netizen** net etiquettes, communication etiquettes, social media etiquettes
- **Data Protection** Intellectual Property Right (copyright, patent, trademark), violation of IPR (plagiarism, copyright infringement, trademark infringement), open source softwares and licensing (Creative Commons, GPL and Apache)
- **Cyber-Crime** definition, hacking, eavesdropping, phishing and fraud emails, ransomware, cyber trolls and bullying.
- **Cyber Safety** safely browsing the web, identity protection, confidentiality.
- **Malware** viruses, trojans, adware
- **E-waste Management** proper disposal of used electronic gadgets
- Information Technology Act (IT Act)
- **Technology & Society** Gender and disability issues while teaching and using computers

4. Practical

S.No.	Unit Name	Marks (Total = 30)
1	**Lab Test (12 marks)**	
	Python program (60% logic + 20% documentation + 20% code quality)	12
2	**Report File + Viva (10 marks)**	
	Report file: Minimum 20 Python programs	7
	Viva voce	3
3	**Project** *(that uses most of the concepts that have been learnt)*	8

5. Suggested Practical List

Python Programming

- Input a welcome message and display it.
- Input two numbers and display the larger/smaller number.
- Input three numbers and display the largest/smallest number.
- Generate the following patterns using nested loop.

Pattern-1	Pattern-2	Pattern-3
*	1 2 3 4 5	A
* *	1 2 3 4	A B
* * *	1 2 3	A B C
* * * *	1 2	A B C D
* * * * *	1	A B C D E

- Write a program to input the value of x and n and print the sum of the following series:

  - $1+x+x^2+x^3+x^4+ \dots\dots\dots x^n$
  - $x+\frac{x^2}{2}+\frac{x^3}{3}+\frac{x^4}{4}+ \dots\dots\dots \frac{x^n}{n}$
  - $1-x+x^2-x^3+x^4- \dots\dots\dots x^n$
  - $x+\frac{x^2}{2!}+\frac{x^3}{3!}+\frac{x^4}{4!}+ \dots\dots\dots \frac{x^n}{n!}$

- Determine whether a number is a perfect number, an armstrong number or a palindrome.
- Input a number and check if the number is a prime or composite number.
- Display the terms of a Fibonacci series.
- Compute the greatest common divisor and least common multiple of two integers.
- Count and display the number of vowels, consonants, uppercase, lowercase characters in string.
- Input a string and determine whether it is a palindrome or not; convert the case of characters in a string.
- Find the largest/smallest number in a list/tuple.
- Input a list of numbers and swap elements at the even location with the elements at the odd location.
- Input a list/tuple of elements, search for a given element in the list/tuple.
- Create a dictionary with the roll number, name and marks of n students in a class and display the names of students who have scored marks above 75.

01 CHAPTER

Computers are an integral part of our daily lives, shaping how we communicate, work, learn, and solve problems. This chapter provides a foundational understanding of computers, their evolution, components, and the role they play in the digital world.

YOUR STUDY GOALS

1.1 Evolution of Computer
1.2 Functional Units of Computer
1.3 Basic Units of Measurement
1.4 Data Transfer between Memory and CPU

YOUR PRACTICE GOAL

- Objective Type Questions (34 Qs ; MCQs, True or False, Fill in the Blanks, Assertion and Reason)
- Subjective Type Questions (51 Qs ; VSA, SA, LA)
- Case Study Based Questions-4

Computer Overview

A computer is an electronic device that can be programmed to accept data (input), process it according to a set of instructions, and generate meaningful results (output). It performs complex calculations, stores information, and automates various tasks efficiently.

A computer, along with additional hardware components such as a monitor, keyboard, mouse, printer, and storage devices, as well as software like operating systems and application programs, together form a complete computer system.

Computer systems are used in various fields, including education, healthcare, business, research, and entertainment, making them an essential part of modern life.

Data and Information

Data In terms of computers, data means raw facts and figures.

For example, +, 3, 8, 11, =, etc.

Data can be classified into three types

1. **Structured Data** Organized in a defined format, such as tables. Examples include attendance records or sales transactions.
2. **Unstructured Data** Data without a specific format, like audio, video, and social media posts.
3. **Semi-structured Data** Data with internal tags for separating elements, such as emails or CSV files.

Whereas **Information** is the meaningful content which is extracted from data i.e., raw facts and figures.

For example, $3 + 8 = 11$ is the information.

The process of converting data into information is known as **Information Processing Cycle** or **Input Process Output Cycle**.

Basic Computer Operations

A computer system performs five essential operations to convert raw input data into meaningful information. These operations are:

1. **Input** This is the process of entering data and instructions into the computer. For example, typing on a keyboard or clicking with a mouse.
2. **Store** The computer stores the data and instructions for easy access during processing. This includes saving information in memory (e.g., RAM or hard drive).
3. **Process** The computer performs arithmetic (e.g., addition, subtraction) or logical operations (e.g., comparing values) on the input data to transform it into useful information.
4. **Output** After processing, the computer produces results or information for the user, such as displaying on the screen or printing a report.
5. **Control** The control operation manages the order in which all the above operations are carried out, ensuring everything happens in the correct sequence.

Characteristics of Computer

Some characteristics of computer are as follows:

1. The **speed** of a computer is much faster than human beings. A computer can perform the amount of work, in few seconds that a human being can do in a number of days. A powerful computer is capable of performing (10 to 40 million approx) arithmetic calculations in a second.
2. Computer provides a high degree of **accuracy**. The accuracy obtained from calculations depends on using bug-free computer chips as well as the quality of the input.
3. The **storage capacity** of a computer is very high. Once, the data is stored in the computer, it can be retrieved at any time without any error.
4. Computers are highly consistent as compare to human beings. These are immune to tiredness and boredom or fatigue. Hence, they are **more reliable than human beings.**
5. **Flexibility** Unlike televisions, refrigerators, or typewriters, computers can do various tasks.

Limitations of Computer

Computers have some limitations, which are the strength of human beings. These limitations are given below

1. An user gives the instructions to computer to do some specific task, but if the instructions are not designed properly, then the task will not be performed correctly. Hence, **computer is not able to ascertain the correctness of the results.**
2. Computer has **no capability of thinking to take a correct decision as a human being.**

1.1 Evolution of Computer

Computing devices have come a long way, from simple calculators to powerful computers.

This rapid evolution is shown in the below timeline figure

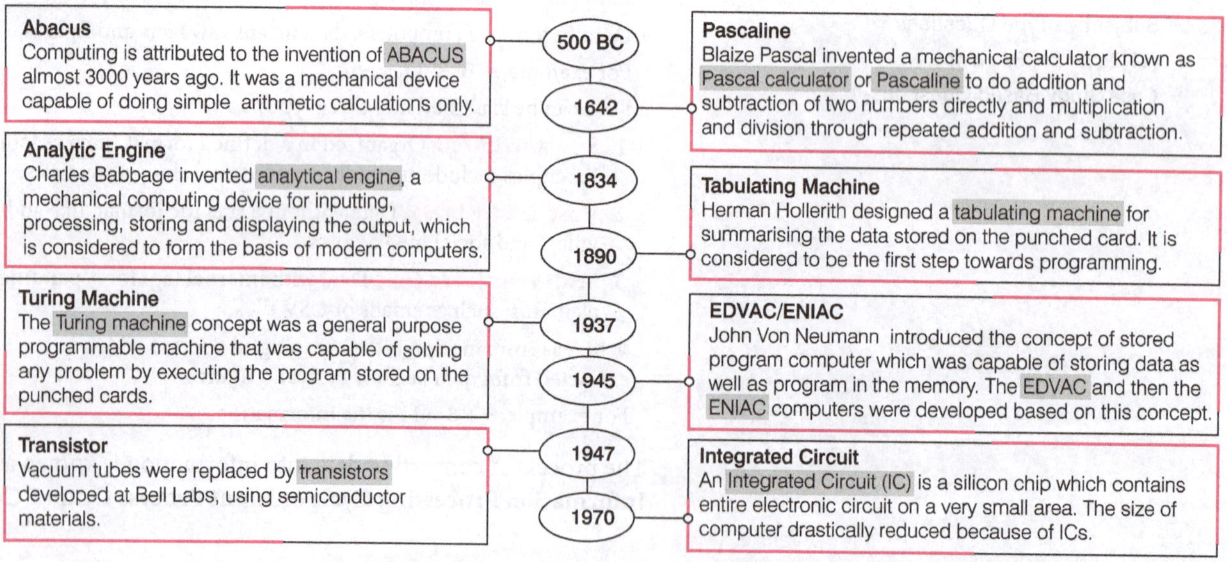

- In the **1970s**, Large Scale Integration (LSI) enabled entire CPUs on single chips, known as microprocessors. Moore's Law predicted exponential growth in transistor density.
- By the **1980s**, Very Large Scale Integration (VLSI) allowed around 3 million components on a chip, advancing to Super Large Scale Integration (SLSI) with over 1 million components per IC.
- IBM introduced its first PC in **1981**, and Apple launched Macintosh in **1984**. Graphical User Interfaces (GUI) replaced command-line systems, boosting PC popularity. The **1990s** saw the rise of the World Wide Web (WWW), making computers essential.
- Laptops, smartphones, and tablets enhanced portability and accessibility, driven by processor miniaturization and high-speed connectivity. Wearable gadgets like smartwatches and IoT-enabled smart appliances now utilize Artificial Intelligence (AI), shaping the next wave of computing.

1.2 Functional Units of Computer

The basic organization of computer system includes four major functional units; Input unit, Output unit, CPU and computer memory/memory unit. The block diagram of basic computer system is shown below

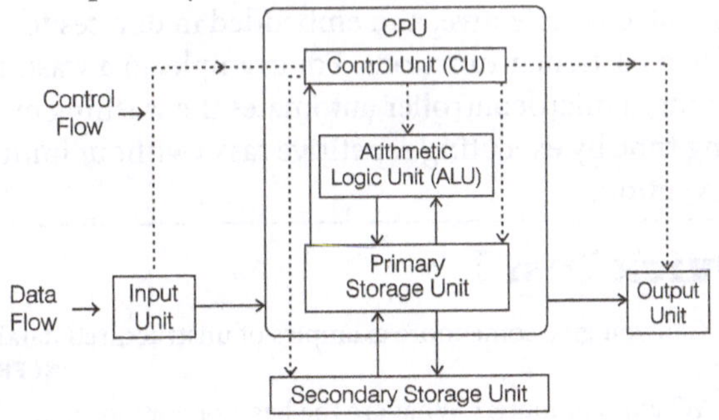

Input Unit (Device)

The devices used to send control signals to a computer are called **input devices.**

The following functions are performed by an input unit

(i) It accepts (or reads) the instructions and data from the outside world.

(ii) It converts these instructions and data in computer acceptable form (i.e., binary form) because a computer can understand only binary symbols (i.e., 0 and 1).

(iii) It supplies the converted instructions and data to the computer system for further processing.

Some of the commonly used input devices:

- **Keyboard** Keyboard is used for typing text and entering commands.
- **Mouse** Mouse is used for navigating the screen and selecting options.
- **Scanner** Scanner is used for digitizing physical documents.
- **Touchscreen** It is used for direct interaction with the screen.

Note *Specially designed braille keyboards are also available to help the visually impaired for entering data into a computer.Besides, we can now enter data through voice, for example, we can use Google voice search to search the web where we can input the search string through our voice.*

Output Unit (Device)

The devices that receive data from a computer for display, printing, or other physical outputs are called **output devices.**

The following functions are performed by an output unit

(i) It accepts the results produced by the computer, which are in coded form (i.e., in binary form), and hence, can't be easily understood by us.

(ii) It converts these coded results to human acceptable (readable) form.

(iii) It supplies the converted result to the outside world.

Some of the commonly used output devices:

- **Monitor** Monitor is used for displaying visual information to the user.
- **Printer** Printer produce hard copies of documents.
- **Speakers** It is used for producing sounds.
- **Projector** Projector display images on a large screen.

3D Printers

Now-a-days 3D printers are widely accessible, used across various industries for prototyping, creating custom parts, and even producing finished products. Advancements allowing for higher print quality, faster speeds, and a wider range of materials, made have them valuable tools in fields like engineering, healthcare, manufacturing, education, and even consumer markets, where people can print items at home for personal use.

Central Processing Unit (CPU)

Sometimes CPU is only referred as the central processor, but more commonly called only processor, the CPU is the brain of the computer where all or most of the calculations take place. In terms of computing power, the CPU is the most important element of a computer system.

Two typical components of a CPU are the following

(i) The **Arithmetic Logic Unit (ALU)**, performs arithmetic and logical operations.

(ii) The **Control Unit (CU)**, extracts instructions from memory and decodes then executes them.

Arithmetic Logic Unit (ALU)

The ALU of a computer system is the place, where the actual execution of the instructions takes place, during the processing operation. To be more precise, all the arithmetic (+, –, ×, /) and logical (<, >, ==, < =, > =) operations are performed in the ALU.

The data and instructions, stored in the primary storage before processing are transferred as and when needed to the ALU, where processing takes place.

No processing is done in the primary storage unit. Intermediate results generated in the ALU are temporarily transferred back to the primary storage, until needed later.

Control Unit (CU)

It does not perform any actual processing on the data, the control unit acts as a central nervous system, for the other components of the computer system. It manages and co-ordinates the entire computer system.

Also it controls and guides the operations like a **supervisor**. It obtains instructions from the program stored in main memory, interprets the instructions, and issue signals which cause other units of the system to execute them.

> **Register**
>
> It is the internal part of CPU which give special purpose location to arithmetic logic unit and control unit. These are used to store intermediate results obtained during the execution of instructions.

Microprocessor

In the past, a computer's CPU occupied large spaces, but advancements in technology have reduced its size to a single microchip, known as a microprocessor. Today, microprocessors perform data processing, arithmetic, and logical operations, and are made up of millions of components like resistors, transistors, and diodes. Over time, microprocessors have become faster, smaller, and cheaper, now capable of processing millions of instructions per millisecond.

Characteristics of Microprocessor

- **Word Size** The maximum number of bits a microprocessor can process at once. It has increased from 8 bits to a range of 16 to 64 bits today.
- **Memory Size** RAM size depends on the word size, ranging from small capacities (4MB) to large ones (up to 16 Exabytes).
- **Clock Speed** Indicates how fast a computer executes instructions, measured in Gigahertz (GHz), representing billions of pulses per second.
- **Cores** Refers to the basic computation units. Early processors had one core, while modern processors (dual-core, quad-core, octa-core) can perform multiple tasks simultaneously, enhancing performance.

Microcontroller

A microcontroller is a small computing device that integrates a CPU, RAM, ROM, and other peripherals on a single chip, unlike a microprocessor, which only has a CPU. Examples of microcontrollers include keyboards, mice, washing machines, digital cameras, and remote controllers. Designed for specific tasks, microcontrollers are small, cost-effective, and embedded in devices to perform particular functions. For example, in a washing machine, a microcontroller automates the washing cycle, saving time by executing repetitive tasks without human intervention.

Quick Test 1

1. Can you give some more examples of unstructured data? **NCERT**
2. What is computer? What are the basic operations of a computer?
3. What is the difference between input and output devices?
4. What is the role of the control unit in a computer?
5. What are the five functional units of a computer system?
6. What is the primary function of the arithmetic logic unit (ALU)?
7. The maximum memory size of microprocessors of different generations are given as 1KB, 1MB, 16MB, 4GB, 64GB. Represent each of the memory size in terms of power of 2. **NCERT**

Memory

Memory is the storage area (internal or external), which holds the data and instructions during processing in the form of binary numbers.

Memory Hierarchy

Memory hierarchy is a system of arranging memory components based on their speed and cost. The faster memory components, like registers and cache, are smaller and more expensive, while slower but larger memory components, like main memory and secondary storage, are cheaper.

This hierarchy structure allows computers to balance performance and cost-effectiveness.

The memory is characterised on the basis of two key factors: capacity and access time.

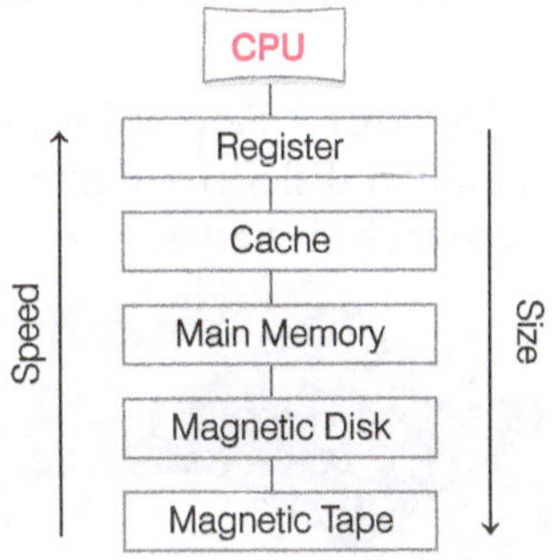

Classification of Computer Memory

Computer memory mainly classified into two categories shown below

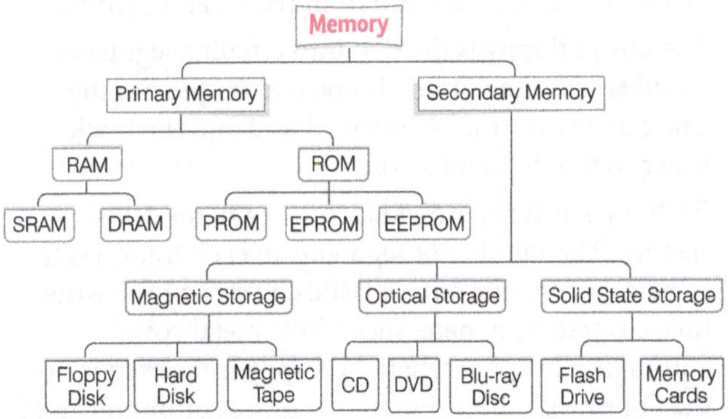

Primary Memory

Primary memory is a essential part of a computer system. Programs and data must be loaded into it before processing.

The CPU directly interacts with primary memory to perform read and write operations.

There are two types of primary memory

Random Access Memory (RAM)

RAM (Random Access Memory) is a type of computer memory that allows for both **reading** and **writing** of data. It is faster than other types of memory, such as hard drives, and is used to store data that the computer is actively working with. However, RAM is volatile, meaning that its contents are lost when the power is turned off.

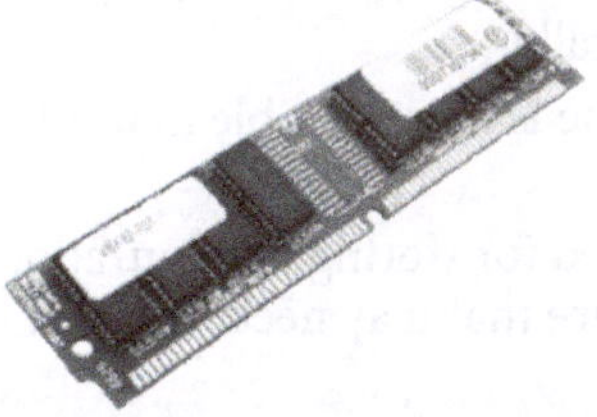

There are two main types of RAM:

(i) **SRAM (Static RAM)** is a type of memory that requires a constant power supply in order to hold the data and information. SRAM is faster but more expensive and is often used for cache memory.

(ii) **DRAM (Dynamic RAM)** stores the information and data in a cell containing a capacitor and transistor, these cells may be refreshed with electric pulses in few milliseconds. DRAM is slower but cheaper, and the most common type of RAM used in computers.

Read Only Memory (ROM)

ROM (Read Only Memory) is a type of computer memory that stores permanent information. It's a non-volatile memory means once data is written to ROM, it cannot be changed. It holds essential instructions for the computer's startup and basic operations.

ROM is further sub divided into following categories

(i) **PROM (Programmable Read-Only Memory)**
- Data is written to PROM once, typically during manufacturing.
- After programming, the data cannot be changed.
- It is used for storing firmware, device drivers, and other essential system software.

(ii) **EPROM (Erasable Programmable Read-Only Memory)**
- Data can be erased using ultraviolet light.
- Once erased, the EPROM can be reprogrammed.
- It is less flexible than EEPROM but more cost-effective.

(iii) **EEPROM (Electrically Erasable Programmable Read-Only Memory)**
- Data can be erased and reprogrammed electrically.
- This one is more flexible than EPROM but slower.
- It is used for storing configuration settings and firmware that may need updates.

Cache Memory

It is the type of memory which is very nearest to the CPU and all the recent instructions are stored in it. The cache memory stores the program (or its part) currently being executed or which may be executed within a short period of time. The cache memory also stores temporary data that the CPU may recently require for manipulation.

The capacity of the cache memory is too low in compare to memory and hard disk.

Characteristics of Cache Memory

(i) Cache memory is faster than main memory.
(ii) It consumes less access time as compared to main memory.
(iii) It stores the program that can be executed within a short period of time.
(iv) It stores data for temporary use.
(v) Cache memory has limited capacity.
(vi) It is very expensive.

Importance of Cache Memory

Cache memory is a high-speed memory that sits between the processor and main memory. It stores frequently accessed data, reducing the need to fetch data from the slower main memory.

A cache memory has an access time of 100ns (100 nano seconds) while the main memory may have an access time of 700ns. This significantly improves the overall performance of the computer by bridging the speed gap between the processor and main memory.

Secondary Memory

Secondary memory/storage, also known as **auxiliary memory**, is a slower and cheaper form of memory compared to primary memory. It is a permanent storage device and **non-volatile** in nature, i.e. the information cannot be erased even power is switched OFF. CPU does not access the secondary memory directly.

Some secondary memories are described below

Magnetic Storage

Magnetic storage is a storage medium commonly used for large volumes of data (**For example**, video, image, or remote sensing data). Some points related to magnetic storage medium are given below:

(i) It uses magnetic head to read and write the data.
(ii) It gets the data from a magnetisable medium. The medium may be a plastic tape coated with fine particles of a metal.
(iii) It can store lots of data, but this data is slower to access.

This storage device includes floppy disk drives, tape drives and hard drives. Some of them are described below:

- **Floppy Disk** (Diskette) A Floppy Disk Drive or FDD in short, is a computer disk drive that enables a user to save data on removable diskettes.

This portable storage device is a rewritable media and can be reused a number of times. It is round in shape and is covered by square **plastic jacket**. The data inside the floppies are stored in tracks and sectors.

The entire floppy is divided into circular segments called **tracks.** Each track is given a unique number. The outermost track is referred as 0 and the track inner to that is 1 and so on.

Each track is further divided into segments called **sectors**. The number of segments in each track has the same capacity. The outer plastic cover has read/write hole covered by a metal sheet. This metal cover automatically opens when the floppy is inserted inside the floppy disk drive. Floppy disks are commonly used to move files between different computers. The first widely used floppy disk drives were the 8 inch, $5\frac{1}{4}$ inch, which were later replaced with $3\frac{1}{2}$inch.

Note *Floppy disks were a popular storage medium from the 1970 s to the early 2000s but their use has declined significantly since then.*

- **Hard Disk Drive** Hard Disk Drive or HDD is a non-volatile, random access digital storage device. It is a data storage device used for storing and retrieving information using rotating disks (platters) coated with magnetic material.

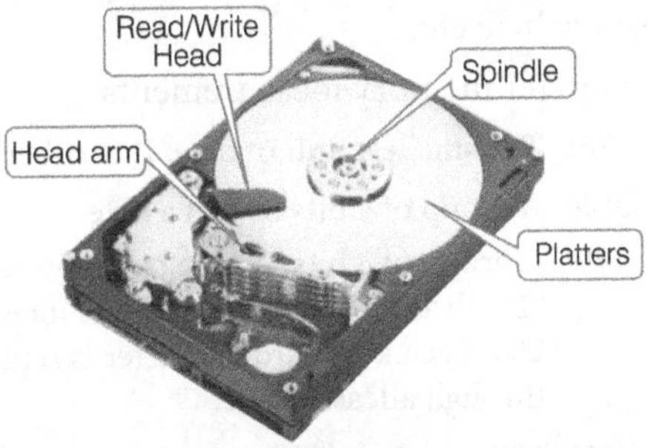

It consists of a spindle that holds non-magnetic flat circular disks, called **platters**, which hold the recorded data. Each platter requires two read/write heads, that are used to read and write the information from a platter. The information is stored in bands; each band of information is called a **track**. Each platter has the same number of tracks, and a track location that cuts across all platters is called a **cylinder**. The tracks are divided into pie-shaped sections known as **sectors**.

- **Magnetic Tape** It is a medium of data storage, made up of a magnetic material. It is a storage medium on a large open reel or in a smaller cartridge or cassette (like a music cassette).

  Physically, the tape medium is a plastic ribbon, which is usually 1/2 inch or 1/4 inch wide and 50 to 2400 feet long. The tape itself is a strip of plastic, coated with magnetic recording medium.

  Data are recorded on the tape in the form of tiny invisible magnetized and non-magnetized spots on its coated surface. Tape ribbon is stored in reels or cassette or cartridge.

  Magnetic tapes are cheaper storage media. They are sequential access devices, *i.e.*, the tape need to rewind or move forward of the location where the requested data is stored. Due to this sequentially data access nature, they are not suitable for data files that need to be revised or updated often. They are generally used to store back up data that is not frequently used or to transfer data from one system to another.

Optical Storage

Optical media are storage media that hold content in digital form. Some point related to optical storage are as follows

(i) It uses a laser to read and write data.

(ii) In optical storage media, the data is stored in the form of pits that are prepared by using a laser beam. This process is known as **burning** data onto a disk.

(iii) The data on the storage media is read by bouncing the laser beam off the surface of the media. If the beam hits a dot, it is reflected back, then records the pit as a 1, otherwise records the pit as 0.

(iv) Optical disc capacity ranges up to 8GB.

(v) It tends to be slower than typical hard drive speeds.

(vi) Examples of optical storage devices include CDs, DVDs etc.

Some of the optical storage are described below

(i) **Compact Disc** (CD) CD is an optical media that is used to store digital data.

It consists of a circular disc, which is coated with a thin metal that is highly reflective. Laser beam technology is used for recording/reading of data on the disk. It is also known as **laser disc** or **optical laser disc**, due to the use of laser beam technology. It provides random access medium for high capacity secondary storage. The diameter of the CD ranges from 10 cms to 30 cms. One CD can store 600 MB to 750 MB.

Compact discs are categorized into three parts

(a) Compact Disc-Read Only Memory (CD-ROM)
(b) Compact Disc-Recordable (CD-R)
(c) Compact Disc-Rewritable (CD-RW)

(ii) **Digital Video Disc** (DVD) DVD is also known as **Super Density Disc** (SDD) or **Digital Versatile Disc** (DVD). A DVD is an optical disc storage media manufactured by **Philips, Sony, Toshiba** and **Panasonic** in 1995. DVDs offer higher storage capacity than compact disc while having the same dimensions. It has capacity of 4.7 GB to 9.4 GB.

DVDs come in three varieties

(a) DVD ROM (DVD-Read Only Memory).
(b) DVD-R (DVD-Recordable).
(c) DVD-RW (DVD-Rewritable).

(iii) **Blu-ray Disc** It is an optical disc storage medium designed to re-capture the data normally in DVD format. Blu-ray disc (BD) contains 25 GB (23.31 GB) per layer space.

The name Blu-ray disc refers to the blue laser used to read the disc, which allows information to be stored at a greater density than the longer- wavelength red laser used in DVDs.

Blu-ray can hold almost 5 times more data than a single layer DVD.

The variations in the formats are as follows

(a) BD-ROM (Read only)
(b) BD-R (Recordable)
(c) BD-RW (Rewritable)
(d) BD-RE (Rewritable)

Solid State Storage

The term solid state essentially means **no moving parts.** Solid- state storage devices are based on electronic circuits with no moving parts.

It stores persistent data on flash memory. A solid state disk is a high-performance plug-and-play storage device. Examples of solid-state storage include pen drive, memory card etc.

Some of solid state storage are described below

(i) **Flash Drive/Pen Drive** A flash drive is a portable data storage device that includes flash memory with an integrated Universal Serial Bus (USB) interface.

Flash drives are typically removable, rewritable and physically much smaller than a floppy disk (as same as the size of your thumb).

Today flash drives are available in various storage capacities, 256 MB, 512 MB, 1 GB, 2 GB, 4 GB, 8 GB, 16 GB, 64 GB upto.

(ii) **Memory Cards** These are the data storage devices in a chip shaped which can store the data in it. They are commonly used in many electronic devices, including digital cameras, mobile phones, laptop computers. They are small, re-recordable, easily portable and very light weighted.

TEACHER TIP

Relate the concept of memory to real-life examples like human memory. For instance, short-term memory can be compared to RAM, and long-term memory can be compared to secondary storage.

1.3 Basic Units of Measurement

When you use a RAM, ROM, floppy disk or hard disk, the data is measured using some unit. In computer terminology, they are called Nibble, Bit, Byte, Kilobyte, Megabyte, Gigabyte etc.

Units of computer memory measurements

Bit The smallest unit of data. It is either 0 or 1.

Nibble A group of 4 bits or half a byte.

Byte A group of 8 bits. A byte can represent 256 (2^8) distinct values, such as the integers 0 to 255. Each keyboard character is represented through atleast 1 byte.

KiloByte (KB) It is actually 2^{10} bytes or 1 KB = 1024 bytes.

MegaByte (MB) It is actually 2^{20} bytes or 1 MB = 1024 KB.

GigaByte (GB) It is actually 2^{30} bytes or 1 GB = 1024 MB.

TeraByte (TB) It is actually 2^{40} bytes or 1 TB = 1024 GB.

PetaByte (PB) It is actually 2^{50} bytes or 1 PB = 1024 TB.

ExaByte (EB) It is actually 2^{60} bytes or 1 EB = 1024 PB.

ZettaByte (ZB) It is actually 2^{70} bytes or 1 ZB = 1024 EB.

YottaByte (YB) It is actually 2^{80} bytes or 1 YB = 1024 ZB.

BrontoByte It is actually 2^{90} bytes or 1 BrontoByte = 1024 YB.

GeopByte It is actually 2^{100} bytes or 1 GeopByte = 1024 BrontoByte.

Here, GeopByte is the highest memory measurement unit.

Hardware

Hardware refers to the physical components of a computer system that can be seen and touched. It includes input devices (keyboard, mouse), output devices (monitor, printer), storage devices (HDD, SSD), and processing units (CPU, RAM). Hardware is essential for running software and performing computing tasks. It is broadly classified into:

- **Input Devices** Devices like a keyboard, mouse, or scanner used to enter data into a computer.
- **Processing Unit** The CPU (Central Processing Unit) is the brain of the computer, responsible for executing instructions.
- **Memory** Includes Primary Memory (RAM, Cache) for temporary storage and Secondary Memory (HDD, SSD) for permanent storage.
- **Output Devices** Devices like a monitor, printer, and speakers that display or output processed data.

Hardware and software work together to make a computer functional.

1.4 Data Transfer between Memory and CPU

Data transfer is an essential process in a computer system. It happens between the CPU and primary memory, as well as between primary memory and secondary storage. The bus is a set of physical wires used for transferring data between different components of the computer.

For example, a bus is used to transfer data between a USB port and a hard disk or between the hard disk and main memory.

There are three types of buses:

1. **Data Bus** Transfers data between different components.
2. **Address Bus** Transfers memory addresses between the CPU and main memory. The CPU specifies the memory location it wants to read or write using this bus.
3. **Control Bus** Transfers control signals between different components.

Together, these three buses are known as the **system bus** as shown in given figure.

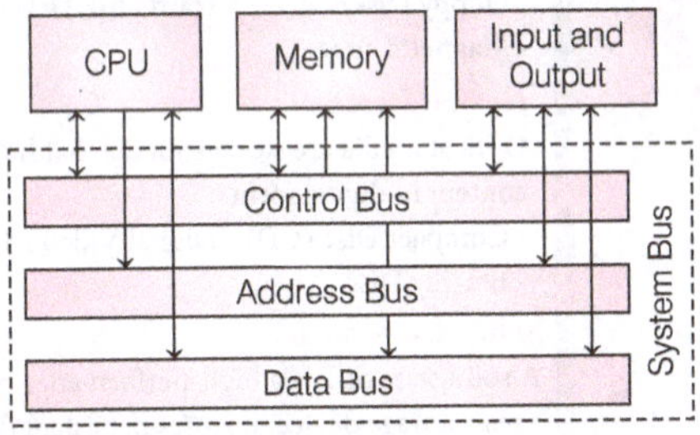

When the CPU processes data

- Any data entered through an input device or retrieved from the hard disk is first loaded into the main memory.
- The CPU interacts directly with the main memory through the system bus.

Data Transfer Steps

1. The CPU places the memory location's address on the **address bus** to indicate where it wants to read or write data.
2. Using the **control bus**, the CPU sends a control signal to specify whether it's a read or write operation.
3. The **data bus**, which is bidirectional, transfers the actual data:
   - For writing, the CPU places data on the data bus to store it at the specified address.
   - For reading, the memory controller retrieves data from the specified address and places it on the data bus for the CPU to access.

Key Features of Buses

- **Data Bus** Bidirectional (used for both reading and writing).
- **Address Bus** Unidirectional (CPU to memory).
- **Control Bus** Unidirectional (CPU to other components).

The **memory controller** ensures that data flows correctly between the main memory and other components, managing read and write operations efficiently.

Quick Test 2

1. Which memory is the fastest?
   (a) RAM (b) Cache (c) Hard disk (d) SSD
2. What is primary memory and how is it different from secondary memory?
3. What is the difference between SRAM and DRAM?
4. Define cache memory.
5. What is the smallest unit of data in a computer?
   (a) Byte (b) Bit (c) Nibble (d) Word

Mind Map

Input Unit (Device)

The devices used to send control signals to a computer are called **input devices**. e.g. Keyboard, Mouse, Scanner, Touchscreen, etc.

Output Unit (Device)

The devices that receive data from a computer for display, printing, or other physical outputs are called **output devices.** e.g. Monitor, Printer, Speakers, Projector, etc.

Central Processing Unit (CPU)

It is the primary component of a computer that processes instructions and data.

Arithmetic Logic Unit (ALU) It handles arithmetic and logical operations.

Control Unit (CU) It manages and coordinates the entire computer system.

Note

Register *is the internal part of CPU which give special purpose location to arithmetic logic unit and control unit.*

In the past, a computer's CPU occupied large spaces, but advancements in technology have reduced its size to a single microchip, known as a ***microprocessor****.*

Functional Units of Computer

Memory

Memory is the storage area, which holds the data and instructions during processing in the form of binary numbers.

Primary Memory

Programs and data must be loaded into primary memory before processing.

CPU directly interacts with primary memory to perform read and write operations.

Random Access Memory (RAM)

Stores data you are currently working on.

- SRAM (Static RAM) - DRAM (Dynamic RAM)

Read Only Memory (ROM) Holds instructions for computer's startup and basic operation.

- PROM (Programmable Read-Only Memory)
- EPROM (Erasable Programmable Read-Only Memory)
- EEPROM (Electrically Erasable Programmable Read-Only Memory)

Secondary Memory

It is a permanent storage device and non-volatile in nature, i.e. the information cannot be erased even power is switched OFF.

Magnetic Storage

Magnetic storage is a storage medium commonly used for large volumes of data (For example, video, image, or remote sensing data).

- Floppy Disk - Hard Disk Drive
- Magnetic Tape

Optical Storage

Optical media are storage media that hold content in digital form.

- Compact Disc (CD) - Digital Video Disc (DVD)
- Blu-ray Disc

Solid State Storage

A solid state disk is a high-performance plug-and - play storage device. It stores persistent data on flash memory.

- Flash Drive/Pen Drive - Memory Cards

Note

Cache memory is a temporary storage space in a computer that holds frequently used data and instructions.

COMPUTER OVERVIEW

Basic Computer Operations

- **Input** This is the process of entering data and instructions into the computer.
- **Store** The computer stores the data and instructions for easy access during processing.
- **Process** The computer performs arithmetic or logical operations on the input data to transform it into useful information.
- **Output** After processing, the computer produces results or information for the user.
- **Control** The control operation manages the order in which all the above operations are carried out, ensuring everything happens in the correct sequence.

Basic Units of Measurement

Bit	The smallest unit of data. It is either 0 or 1.
Nibble	A group of 4 bits or half a byte.
Byte	A group of 8 bits. A byte can represent 256 (2^8) distinct values, such as the integers 0 to 255. Each keyboard character is represented through atleast 1 byte.
KiloByte (KB)	It is actually 2^{10} bytes or 1 KB = 1024 bytes.
MegaByte (MB)	It is actually 2^{20} bytes or 1 MB = 1024 KB.
GigaByte (GB)	It is actually 2^{30} bytes or 1 GB = 1024 MB.
TeraByte (TB)	It is actually 2^{40} bytes or 1 TB = 1024 GB.
PetaByte (PB)	It is actually 2^{50} bytes or 1 PB = 1024 TB.
ExaByte (EB)	It is actually 2^{60} bytes or 1 EB = 1024 PB.
ZettaByte (ZB)	It is actually 2^{70} bytes or 1 ZB = 1024 EB.
YottaByte (YB)	It is actually 2^{80} bytes or 1 YB = 1024 ZB.
BrontoByte	It is actually 2^{90} bytes or 1 BrontoByte = 1024 YB.
GeopByte	It is actually 2^{100} bytes or 1 GeopByte = 1024 BrontoByte.

System Bus

A system bus is a set of electronic cables that connects a computer is main components, such as the CPU, memory and input/output devices.

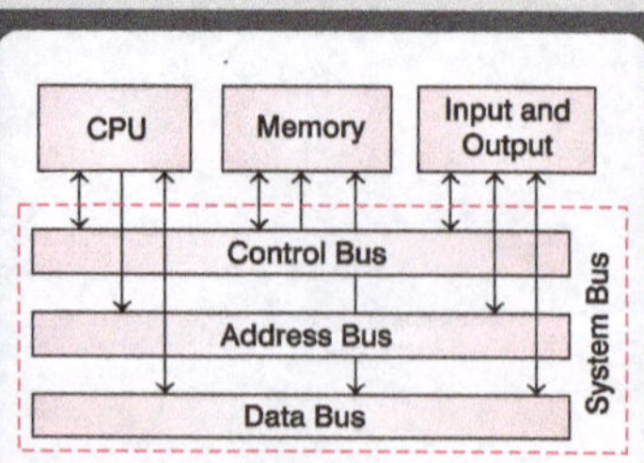

NCERT Folder

1. What is the need of RAM? How does it differ from ROM?

Ans. RAM is used for quickly accessing a data.

RAM is temporary and volatile memory, used for active programs and data whereas ROM is permanent and non-volatile memory, storing essential system instructions.

2. What is the need for secondary memory?

Ans. Secondary memory (like hard drives, SSDs) provides non-volatile storage for programs and data when the computer is OFF.

3. How do different components of the computer communicate with each other?

Ans. Components of computer communicate with each other using the system bus, which consists of:

- **Data Bus** It transfers the data between components.
- **Address Bus** It specifies the memory locations.
- **Control Bus** It synchronizes the data transfers and controls operations.

4. Draw the block diagram of a computer system. Briefly write about the functionality of each component.

Ans. Refer to text on page 3-8 (Functional Units of Computer)

5. What is the primary role of system bus? Why is data bus is bidirectional while address bus is unidirectional?

Ans. The system bus connects components which allows the data and control signals to flow between them.

The data bus needs to transfer data in both the directions as a result it is bidirectional while the address bus only needs to specify memory locations hence it's unidirectional.

6. Write the main difference between microcontroller and microprocessor. Why do smart home appliances have a microcontroller instead of microprocessor embedded in them?

Ans. Microprocessor is a general-purpose processor capable of executing a wide range of instructions whereas Microcontroller is a specialized processor designed for specific tasks, often embedded in devices.

Microcontrollers is used for smart home appliances for various reasons some of them are mentioned below:

- Microcontrollers are **cost-effective** (cheap) and more power-efficient than microprocessors.
- They are designed for **specific tasks**, making them ideal for controlling appliances like lights, security systems etc.
- Microcontrollers have a **smaller footprint**, making them suitable for compact devices.

7. Mention the different types of data that you deal with while browsing the internet.

Ans. Articles, Blog posts, photos, graphics, podcasts, voice recordings, TV shows, YouTube videos etc.

8. Categorize the following data as structured, semi-structured and unstructured:

(a) Newspaper
(b) Cricket Match Score
(c) HTML Page
(d) Patient records in a hospital

Ans. (a) Semi-structured (b) Structured
(c) Semi-structured (d) Structured

9. Name the input and output device used to do the following:

(a) To output audio
(b) To enter textual data
(c) To make hard copy of a text file
(d) To display the data or information
(e) To enter audio-based command
(f) To build 3D models
(g) To assist a visually-impaired individual in entering data

Ans. (a) Speaker, headphones (b) Keyboard
(c) Printer (d) Monitor
(e) Microphone (f) 3D mouse, 3D pen
(g) Braille keyboard

EXAM PATTERN QUESTIONS

Objective Type Questions

Multiple Choice Questions

1. **The set of instructions given to a computer is called:**
(a) Program (b) ALU (c) CU (d) Storage

2. **A computer takes ____ then ____ it and returns ____.**
(a) Process, input, output (b) Input, output, process
(c) Input, process, output (d) None of these

3. **User communicates with a computer with the help of which device?**
(a) Input device (b) Output device
(c) Software device (d) Both (a) and (b)

4. **The device that used to give single or multiple colored image and drawings are______**
(a) Monitors (b) Printers (c) Plotters (d) VDUs

5. **Which among the following is an important circuitry in a computer system that directs the operation of the processor?**
(a) Memory (b) Address Bus
(c) Accumulator (d) Control unit

6. **A computer science student is analyzing the factors affecting the speed of program execution. They observe that a specific component within the CPU temporarily holds data and instructions, allowing faster access compared to other storage types. Which component is responsible for this function?** **Competency Based Que.**
(a) Register (b) Cache
(c) Control Unit (d) ALU

7. **During a system startup, a technician notices that the computer loads essential firmware before the operating system begins. This firmware is stored in a type of non-volatile memory that retains data even when the system is powered off. Which type of memory is used for this purpose?** **Competency Based Que.**
(a) DRAM (b) SRAM
(c) ROM (d) Cache memory

8. **Which of the following statements about DRAM is true?**
(a) It is faster than SRAM.
(b) It retains data as long as power is supplied.
(c) It needs to be refreshed periodically.
(d) It is used in specialized applications.

9. **........ acts as temporary high speed holding area between the memory and the CPU thereby improving processing capabilities.**
(a) ROM (b) RAM
(c) Temporary memory (d) Cache memory

10. **Which of the following is not a characteristic of secondary memory?**
(a) It is volatile.
(b) It is used to store data permanently.
(c) It is slower than main memory.
(d) It can transfer data between devices.

11. **A disc's content that is recorded at the time of manufacture and that cannot be changed or erased by the user is**
(a) memory only (b) write only
(b) once only (d) read only

12. **Which of these is not optical media?**
(a) CDs (b) Blue ray Disc
(c) DVDs (d) Flash memory

13. **........... is a collection of wires through which data is transmitted from one part of the computer to another.**
(a) Bus (b) Car (c) Traffic (d) ALU

14. **Which bus is called expansion Bus?**
(a) Internal (b) External
(c) Parallel (d) None of these

15. **1 TB is equivalent to ____ bytes.**
(a) 1024 (b) $(1024)^2$ (c) $(1024)^3$ (d) $(1024)^4$

Fill in the Blanks

16. The devices through which control signals are sent to a computer are termed as ______ devices. These devices convert the input data into a digital form that is acceptable by the computer system.

17. Data entered through input devices is temporarily stored in the ______ (also called RAM) of the computer system. For permanent storage, data is stored in ______ memory.

18. During the 1970s, Large Scale Integration (LSI) of electronic circuits allowed integration of complete ______ on a single chip, called microprocessor.

19. Cache memory helps bridge the speed gap between the ______ and ______, providing faster data access than RAM.

20. Secondary memory is ______ and has a larger storage capacity than primary memory, but it is ______ and cannot be directly accessed by the CPU.

State Whether True or False

21. The timeline indicates that the development of the Integrated Circuit was a crucial step in making computers smaller and more powerful.
22. The Central Processing Unit (CPU) uses its local memory, called registers, to temporarily store data, instructions, or intermediate results during processing.
23. The Arithmetic Logic Unit (ALU) is responsible for both fetching instructions from memory and carrying out the arithmetic and logical operations on the data.
24. Microprocessors and microcontrollers are essentially the same thing, with the main difference being that microcontrollers are smaller in size.
25. EEPROM is more flexible than EPROM because it can be erased and reprogrammed electrically.
26. Cache memory is faster than main memory and has a limited capacity compared to main memory.
27. The Address Bus is bidirectional, meaning it can transfer data in both directions between the CPU and memory.
28. A Kilobyte (KB) is equivalent to 2^{10} bytes, which is exactly 1000 bytes.

Assertion and Reason Based Questions

Assertion (A) and Reason (R) Type questions. Choose the correct option as:

(a) Both Assertion (A) and Reason (R) are true, and Reason (R) is the correct explanation of Assertion (A).
(b) Both Assertion (A) and Reason (R) are true, but Reason (R) is not the correct explanation of Assertion (A).
(c) Assertion (A) is true, but Reason (R) is false.
(d) Assertion (A) is false, but Reason (R) is true.

29. **Assertion (A)** A computer converts raw data into meaningful information through the Information Processing Cycle (IPC).
Reason (R) The Input Process Output (IPO) cycle involves processing data using the Arithmetic Logic Unit (ALU) of the CPU.
30. **Assertion (A)** Computers are highly accurate and reliable because they can perform operations without errors.
Reason (R) Computers depend on human input and programming to perform tasks accurately.
31. **Assertion (A)** A CPU's Control Unit manages the flow of data between the CPU and other components.
Reason (R) The Arithmetic Logic Unit (ALU) of the CPU is responsible for controlling the sequence of operations.
32. **Assertion (A)** Cache memory is faster than main memory.
Reason (R) Cache memory stores programs or data that the CPU is likely to access soon, reducing the need to fetch data from main memory.
33. **Assertion (A)** ROM is a type of volatile memory.
Reason (R) ROM retains data even when the power is turned OFF.
34. **Assertion (A)** Solid-state drives (SSDs) are slower than traditional hard disk drives (HDDs).
Reason (R) SSDs use flash memory, which has no moving parts, making them faster and more reliable than HDDs.

Answers

1. (a) Program
2. (c) Input, process, output
3. (a) Input device
4. (c) Plotters
5. (d) Control unit
6. (a) Register
7. (c) ROM
8. (c) It needs to be refreshed periodically.
9. (d) Cache memory
10. (a) It is volatile.
11. (d) read only
12. (d) Flash memory
13. (a) Bus
14. (b) External
15. (d) $(1024)^4$
16. input
17. main, secondary
18. CPU
19. CPU, RAM
20. non-volatile, slower
21. True
22. True
23. False
24. False
25. True
26. True
27. False
28. False
29. (a) Both Assertion (A) and Reason (R) are true, but Reason (R) is the correct explanation of Assertion (A).
30. (b) Both Assertion (A) and Reason (R) are true, but Reason (R) is not the correct explanation of Assertion (A).
31. (c) Assertion (A) is true, but Reason (R) is false.
32. (a) Both Assertion (A) and Reason (R) are true, and Reason (R) is the correct explanation of Assertion (A).
33. (d) Assertion (A) is false, but Reason (R) is true.
34. (d) Assertion (A) is false, but Reason (R) is true.

Subjective Type Questions

Very Short Answer Type Questions

1. What is computer?

Ans. Computer is an electronic device, which manipulates the data according to the list of instructions.

2. (a) What was the first mechanical computing device?

(b) Which invention led to the miniaturization of computers?

Ans. (a) The first mechanical computing device was Abacus.

(b) Integrated Circuit (IC)

3. Which unit in a computer is responsible for decoding and executing instructions?

Ans. Control unit is responsible for decoding and executing instructions.

4. Give the name of the basic functional unit of a digital computer system.

Ans. Computer organisation displays the four major building blocks of a digital computer system.

- Input Unit
- Output Unit
- Central Processing Unit
- Memory

5. What is input unit?

Ans. The unit that takes input from the users and converts it into computer understandable form is called input unit.

6. Write about the most commonly used input device.

Ans. Keyboard is used to enter text information into the computer. It is the most commonly used input device which can also be used to type commands directing the computer to perform certain actions.

7. What is the use of output unit?

Ans. Output unit converts the coded results to human acceptable form.

8. What role does the control unit play in the instruction cycle?

Ans. The control unit initiates and coordinates the fetch-decode-execute cycle.

9. Name the three components of the central processing unit.

Ans. Control unit (CU), Arithmetic logic unit (ALU) and the main/primary memory are the three components of the CPU.

10. What is register?

Ans. Register is the internal part of the CPU which is used to store intermediate results obtained during the execution of instructions.

11. (a) What is a microprocessor?

(b) What is the difference between a microprocessor and a microcontroller?

Ans. (a) A microprocessor is a CPU implemented on a single microchip.

(b) A microprocessor contains only the CPU on a single chip, while a microcontroller includes the CPU, RAM, ROM, and other peripherals on a single chip.

12. A software developer is optimizing a computer system for faster data access. They need to understand how memory is structured to efficiently manage data storage and retrieval. Based on this, how is the main memory organized, and why is this organization important for system performance?

Competency Based Que.

Ans. The main memory is organized into memory locations, each with a unique address. It consists of RAM (for temporary data storage and quick access) and ROM (for permanent instructions). This organization ensures efficient data retrieval and processing, improving system performance.

13. List the two basic types of RAM.

Ans. (i) Static RAM (SRAM) (ii) Dynamic RAM (DRAM).

14. Can RAM retain data when computer is switched OFF?

Ans. No, RAM cannot retain data when computer is switched OFF because it is temporary storage.

15. Define static RAM.

Ans. Static RAM or SRAM is a type of RAM that holds the data and information in static form, i.e., as long as the power supply is ON.

16. A technician is troubleshooting a computer that is failing to boot properly. They suspect an issue with the system firmware stored in ROM. Can they modify the data stored in ROM? If not, what alternatives are available for updating system firmware?

Competency Based Que.

Ans. No, data in ROM (Read-Only Memory) cannot be directly modified. However, firmware updates can be made using Flash ROM or EEPROM, which allow rewriting data under special conditions.

17. (a) What is the primary function of cache memory?

(b) Name the types of ROM used in a computer system.

Ans. (a) The primary function of cache memory is to speed up data access by storing frequently used data from the main memory.

(b) (i) PROM (Programmable ROM)
(ii) EPROM (Erasable Programmable ROM)
(iii) EEPROM (Electrically Erasable programmable ROM).

18. (a) Name four secondary storage devices.
(b) Give one difference between primary and secondary memory.

Ans. (a) (i) Floppy disk (ii) Hard disk
(iii) Compact disc (iv) Magnetic tape.

(b) Primary memory is volatile in nature and has limited storage capacity, whereas secondary memory is non-volatile in nature and store huge amount of data.

19. What are the two advantages of using floppy disks?

Ans. (i) They are quite cheap.
(ii) They allow to copy files from one computer to another.

20. (a) What are tracks?
(b) What are sectors?

Ans. (a) A magnetic disk is divided into concentric circles known as tracks.
(b) The track on the disk surface is divided into invisible segments known as sectors.

21. What component is responsible for reading and writing data on a magnetic disk?

Ans. Read/Write heads are the components that facilitate the process of reading and writing data on a magnetic disk.

22. Which unit is used to store information on optical disc?

Ans. In optical disc, information is stored in bits that are prepared by using a laser beam.

23. Name the varieties of DVD.

Ans. (i) DVD ROM (ii) DVD-R
(iii) DVD-RW

24. How can we read the content of memory card?

Ans. Content of memory card can read by connecting the device having the card to your computer or by using a USB card reader.

25. What are the three types of buses used in a computer system?

Ans. Data bus, Address bus, Control bus

26. What is the function of the address bus?

Ans. The address bus transfers addresses between the CPU and main memory.

27. Define the term byte. What is the difference between a bit and byte?

Ans. A binary digit either 0 or 1 is called a bit. A combination of 8 bits is called a byte and is a unit of computer storage.

Short Answer Type I Questions

28. Describe the types of inputs are given to the computer.

Ans. Two types of inputs are given to the computer, data and instructions.

- Data may be in the form of numbers, characters, pictures, graphics, etc.
- Instructions can be in the form of a computer program/software or it may be just a single instruction.

29. Distinguish between input unit and output unit.

Ans.

Input Unit	Output Unit
It accepts the data and instructions from the outside world.	It accepts the result produced by the computer.
It converts the accepted instruction and data in computer acceptable form.	It converts the results, which are in coded form to human readable form.
It supplies the converted instruction and data to the computer system for further processing.	It supplies the converted results to the user.

30. What is the purpose of input and output devices in a computer system?

Ans. Input and output devices enable communication between the computer and the user. Input devices allow users to provide data and instructions to the computer, while output devices display the results of computations or other information to the user.

31. What are the functions of Arithmetic Logic Unit (ALU)?

Ans. Arithmetic logic unit performs all the arithmetic and the logical operations. i.e. all the calculations take place in this unit. Arithmetic instructions include addition, subtraction, multiplication and division operations, while logic instructions include Boolean comparisons, such as AND, OR, XOR and NOT operations. The numbers on which the operations have to be done are taken from the memory and after operation is done then the result is again sent to the memory.

32. Write the characteristics based on which microprocessors are differentiated.

Ans. Characteristics of Microprocessor

- **Word Size** The maximum number of bits a microprocessor can process at once. It has increased from 8 bits to a range of 16 to 64 bits today.
- **Memory Size** RAM size depends on the word size, ranging from small capacities (4MB) to large ones (up to 16 Exabytes).
- **Clock Speed** Indicates how fast a computer executes instructions, measured in Gigahertz (GHz), representing billions of pulses per second.

- **Cores** Refers to the basic computation units. Early processors had one core, while modern processors (dual-core, quad-core, octa-core) can perform multiple tasks simultaneously, enhancing performance.

33. Imagine you are using a video editing software on your computer. While editing a high-resolution video, the software processes multiple frames, applies effects, and temporarily stores data before saving the final video.

How does the computer's memory contribute to the smooth functioning of such tasks, and why is it essential for real-time processing? Competency Based Que.

Ans. The computer's memory acts as a temporary storage area, holding data, intermediate results, and final outputs to ensure smooth and efficient performance. It allows quick access to frequently used data, which is crucial for processing-intensive tasks like video editing.

34. What is the primary function of RAM, and how does it differ from ROM?

Ans. RAM, or Random Access Memory, is a volatile memory used for temporary storage of data and instructions that are currently being used by the CPU. It allows for rapid access to data. ROM, or Read-Only Memory, is a non-volatile memory that stores permanent data and instructions. Unlike RAM, ROM retains its data even when the power is turned OFF.

35. How does SRAM store data?

Ans. SRAM stores data using flip-flops, which are electronic circuits that can store a single bit of information. As long as the device has power, the flip-flops retain the stored data.

36. How does DRAM maintain data over time?

Ans. DRAM uses a technique called refreshing to maintain data. Since DRAM cells lose their charge over time, the memory controller periodically recharges these cells to prevent data loss.

37. Why we use cache memory in a computer system.

Ans. Cache memory is the reserved section of main memory (RAM) that is used to enhance performance of a CPU. It is located between the main memory and the CPU. Cache memory is used to hold data and instructions that are transferred to and from main memory.

38. Which memory is slower among the following memories:

(i) Primary Memory

(ii) Secondary Memory.

Explain the slower memory.

Ans. Secondary memory is the slower memory. It is the memory which is not directly accessible by the central processing unit of a computer system. It is non-volatile in nature and is used to store large amount of data on permanent basis.

39. Differentiate between volatile and non-volatile memory.

Ans.

Volatile Memory	Non-Volatile Memory
Volatile memory needs power to work and to keep the data in it.	Non-volatile memory does not needs power to keep data in it.
Once the power is OFF, the volatile memory loss the data in it.	Once the power is OFF, the non-volatile memory does not loss the data in it.
Volatile storage affects system performance.	Non-volatile storage affects storage capacity.
For example, RAM	For example, ROM

40. Secondary storage is also known as auxiliary memory. Explain it.

Ans. Secondary storage is also known as auxiliary memory because it is a part of external memory and used to store a large amount of data at less cost per-byte than primary memory. The secondary storage devices were used to overcome the problems with primary memory.

41. A small business owner needs to store large amounts of customer data, financial records, and software applications on their computer. They are looking for a cost-effective and reliable storage solution.

Why would a hard disk drive (HDD) be a suitable choice for their storage needs compared to other storage options? Competency Based Que.

Ans. A hard disk drive (HDD) is suitable because it offers large storage capacity, fast access to files, and is cost-effective compared to other storage media.

This makes it ideal for storing extensive business data while keeping expenses low.

Short Answers Type II Questions

42. Explain the various characteristics of computer.

Ans. Refer to text on page no. 2. (Characteristics of Computer)

43. A school is planning to set up a digital learning system where students can access online study materials, submit assignments, and interact with teachers through video conferencing. To ensure smooth operation, the school administrator needs to understand how computers process data, execute instructions, and manage storage.

How do the basic operations of a computer (input, processing, storage, and output) help in managing the digital learning system efficiently? Explain with examples. Competency Based Que.

Ans. Refer to text on page no. 2. (Basic Computer Operations)

44. What role does central processing unit play in the computer system?

Ans. A Central Processing Unit (CPU) plays a vital role in the functioning of a computer system. It is termed as 'brain of a computer' because its primary function is to execute programs. In terms of computing power, the CPU is the most important element of a computer system.

Two typical components of a CPU are the following

(i) **Arithmetic Logic Unit (ALU)** ALU performs all the arithmetic (+, -, *, /) and logical (<, >, =, < =, > =, <>) operations. It is the place, where the actual execution takes place, during the processing operation. The data and instructions, stored in memory before processing are transferred as and when needed to the ALU, where processing takes place.

(ii) **Control Unit (CU)** A control unit guides the flow of work or procedure which takes place in CPU. Control unit is just like a circuitry that directs operations within the computer's processor by directing the input and output of a computer system.

Control unit co-ordinates various operations of the computer like,

(i) It directs the sequence of operations.

(ii) It interprets the instructions of a program in storage unit and produces signals to execute the instructions. It directs the flow of data and instructions in the computer system.

45. Explain main memory and its types.

Ans. Main memory, also known as primary memory, is a crucial component of a computer system. It serves as a temporary storage area for data and instructions that the CPU needs to access quickly.

There are two primary types of main memory:

1. **Random Access Memory (RAM)**
   - **Volatile Memory** It is volatile in nature means data stored in RAM is lost when the power is turned OFF.
   - **Fast Access**: RAM allows for rapid access to data, making it ideal for storing currently running programs and data.
   - **Types of RAM**
     - **DRAM (Dynamic RAM)** The most common type of RAM, it requires periodic refreshing to retain data. It's relatively cheap but slower than SRAM.
     - **SRAM (Static RAM)** Faster and more expensive than DRAM. It doesn't require constant refreshing, making it suitable for cache memory.
2. **Read-Only Memory (ROM)**
   - **Non-Volatile Memory** It is non-volatile in nature means data stored in ROM persists even when the power is turned OFF.
   - **Read-Only** Data can only be read from ROM, not written to.
   - **Types of ROM**
     - **PROM (Programmable ROM)** Can be programmed once, typically during manufacturing.
     - **EPROM (Erasable Programmable ROM)** Can be erased and reprogrammed using ultraviolet light.
     - **EEPROM (Electrically Erasable Programmable ROM)** Can be erased and reprogrammed electrically.

46. What do you mean by secondary memory and give a brief note on any of its two types?

Ans. Secondary memory is the memory which is not installed inside the computer system. These memories are used to store the data, so that the internal memory could be made free and the speed of the computer system could be enhanced. This secondary memory uses many memory devices known as secondary storage devices.

Two of them are described below

(i) **Hard Disk Drive** Hard Disk Drive or HDD is a non-volatile, random access digital storage device. It is a data storage device used for storing and retrieving information using rotating disks (platters) coated with magnetic material.

It consists of a spindle that holds non-magnetic flat circular disks, called **platters**, which hold the recorded data. Each platter requires two read/write heads, that are used to read and write the information from a platter. The information is stored in bands; each band of information is called a **track**. Each platter has the same number of tracks, and a track location that cuts across all platters is called a **cylinder**. The tracks are divided into pie-shaped sections known as **sectors**.

(ii) **Compact Disc** (CD) CD is an optical media that is used to store digital data.

It consists of a circular disc, which is coated with a thin metal that is highly reflective. Laser beam technology is used for recording/reading of data on the disk. It is also known as **laser disc** or **optical laser disc**, due to the use of laser beam technology. It provides random access medium for high capacity secondary storage. The diameter of the CD ranges from 10 cms to 30 cms. One CD can store 600 MB to 750 MB.

47. Explain the evolution of computers from early mechanical devices to modern computing.

Ans. Refer to text on page no. 9. (Data transfer between Memory and CPU).

Long Answer Type Questions

48. What is keyboard? Also, write types of keys on keyboard.

Ans. It is one of the most common input devices. The user can type text and command using this device. The layout of the keyboard was borrowed from the regular typewriter with some additional keys.

Keyboard is used to enter data or information in a computer system, which may be in numeric form or alphabetic form. When key is pressed, keyboard interacts with a keyboard controller and keyboard buffer. Keyboard controller stores the code of pressed key in keyboard buffer. There are different types of keyboard such as QWERTY, DVORAK and AZERTY.

The keys are categorised under the following groups

1. **Alphanumeric Keys** include the alphabet keys (A, B, C, ..., Z) and number keys (0, 1, 2, 3, ..., 9).
2. **Numeric Keys** are located at the right hand side of the keyboard. They consist of digits and mathematical operators.
3. **Function Keys** are the programmable keys, i.e. the programs can assign some specific actions. They are numbered from F1 to F12.
4. **Cursor Control Keys** include four directional (left, right, up, down) arrow keys that are arranged in a inverted T formation between the alphanumeric and numeric keypad. Above the arrow keys there are four more keys to control the cursor. *These are as follows*
   (i) Home (ii) End
   (iii) Page Up (iv) Page Down
5. **Other Keys** A keyboard contains some other keys such as follows
   (i) **Control Key** It performs a special operation with the combination of other keys.
   (ii) **Enter Key** It is used to finish an entry and begin the new entry in a document. Enter key is an alternative to press ok button.
   (ii) **Shift Key** Some keys on the keyboard like numeric keys have a symbol printed on their upper portion. Shift key is used to print these symbols. This key is also called combination key.
   (iii) **Escape Key (Esc)** It allows a user to cancel or abort operations, which are executing at present. It opens Start menu with the combination of Ctrl key.
   (iv) **Backspace Key** It is used to erase anything typed.
   (v) **Delete Key** It is used to erase information from the computer's memory and characters on the screen.
   (vi) **Caps Lock Key** It is used to type the alphabet in capital letters. It enables or disables all the letters from being typed in capital letters. When this key is enable, the alphabet would be in capital letters and when it is disabled, the alphabet would be in small letters.
   (vii) **Num Lock Key** It is used to enable and disable the numeric keypad.
   (viii) **Windows Key** It is used to open the Start menu.
   (ix) **Spacebar Key** It provides a space between two words. It is the longest key on the keyboard.
   (x) **Tab Key** It is used to move the cursor over to the right to a pre-set point. In Word document, tab is used to indent a paragraph.

49. What is monitor? Also, explain its popular types in detail.

Ans. It is also known as Visual Display Unit (VDU). The monitor is provided along with the computer to view the display result. A monitor is of two kinds; monochrome display monitor and colour display monitor.

A monochrome display monitor uses only one colour to display text and colour display monitor can display 256 colours at a time. An image on the monitor is created by a configuration of dots, also known as pixels. The refresh rate of monitor is measured in Hertz (Hz).

The popular types of monitor are as follows

1. **Cathode Ray Tube** (CRT) It is a typical rectangular shaped monitor that you see on a desktop computer. The CRT works in a same way as a television. CRT has a vacuum tube. CRT works by moving an electron beam back and forth across the back of the screen. A screen covered with a fine layer of phosphorescent elements, called phosphores.
2. **Liquid Crystal Display** (LCD) These screens are used in laptops and notebook sized PCs. A special type of liquid is sandwiched between two plates. It is a thin, flat and light weight screen made up of any number of colour or monochrome pixels arranged in front of a light source.
3. **Liquid/Light Emitting Diode** (LED) It is an electronic device that emits light when electrical current is passed through it. LEDs usually produce red light, but today's LEDs can produce RGB (Red, Green and Blue) light, and white light as well.
4. **3-D Monitor** It is a television that conveys depth perception to the viewer. 3-D describes an image that provides the perception of length. When 3-D images are made interactive then user feels involved with the scene and this experience is called **virtual reality**.
5. **Thin Film Transistor** (TFT) TFT and Active-Matrix LCD (AMLCD) is a Liquid Crystal Display (LCD). With active-matrix displays, each pixel is controlled by one to four transistors that can make the screen faster, brighter, more colorful than passive-matrix and capable of being viewed at different angles.
   Because of this improved technology, active-matrix screens are often more expensive.

50. What is printer? Explain its types.

Ans. A printer prints information and data from the computer onto a paper. It can print documents in color as well as in black and white. The quality of a printer is determined by the clarity of a print.

The speed of a printer is measured in Characters Per Second (CPS), Lines Per Minute (LPM) and Pages Per

Minute (PPM). Printer resolution is a numerical measure of print quality that is measured in *Dots Per Inch* (DPI).

Printers are divided into two basic categories

Impact Printer This type of printer strikes paper and ribbon together to form a character, like a typewriter. Impact printer can print a character or an entire line at a time. They use pins or hammers that pressed an inked ribbon against the paper. They are less expensive, fast and can make multiple copies with multipart paper.

There are four types of impact printer

1. **Dot Matrix Printer** It forms characters using rows of pins which impact the ribbon on top of the paper therefore also called pin printers. Dot matrix printers print one character at a time. It prints characters and images as a pattern of dots. Many dot matrix printers are bi-directional, that is they can print the characters from either direction, i.e. left or right.
2. **Daisy Wheel Printer** In daisy wheel printers, characters are fully formed on the *petals*, like typewriter keys. These printers produce high resolution output and are more reliable than dot matrix.
3. **Line Printer** It is a high-speed printer capable of printing an entire line of text at once instead of one or more characters at a time. These are impact shaped character printers which print one line at a time. Print quality of line printer is not high.
4. **Drum Printer** An old line printer technology that uses formed character images around a cylindrical drum as its printing mechanism. When the desired character for the selected position rotated around the hammer line, the hammer hit the paper from behind and pushed it into the ribbon and onto the character.

Non-Impact Printer This type of printer uses electrostatic chemicals and inkjet technologies. They do not hit or impact a ribbon to print.

It can produce high quality graphics and often a wide variety of fonts than impact printers. There are following types of non-impact printer

1. **Inkjet Printer** It is a printer that places extremely small droplets of ink onto paper to create an image. It sprays ink onto paper to form characters and prints high quality text and graphics.
2. **Thermal Printer** It uses heat on chemically treated paper to form characters. Fax machines that use rolls of paper are also of thermal printers type. It is relatively slow, expensive and requires special paper.
3. **Laser Printer** It provides the highest quality text and images for personal computer. They can print in different fonts that is, type styles and sizes. Laser printer uses laser beam onto photo sensitive surface for printing. It prints high quality graphics and more expensive than impact printers.
4. **Electromagnetic Printer** Electrographic or electro-photographic printers are very fast printers and they fall under the category of page printers. The electrographic technology have developed from the paper copier technology.
5. **Electrostatic Printer** These printers are generally used for large format printing. They are favoured by large printing shops because of their ability to print fast and making low cost.

51. Which memory allows only to read the data? Explain that memory with its types?

Ans. ROM is a type of memory that normally can only be read. The two main reasons why the read-only memory is used for certain functions within the PC are

Permanent The values stored in ROM are always there, whether the power is ON or not.

A ROM can be removed from the PC, stored for an indefinite period of time, and then replaced, and the data it contains will still be there. For this reason, it is called non-volatile storage. A hard disk is also non-volatile, for the same reason, but regular RAM is not.

Security The fact that ROM cannot easily be modified, provides a measure of security against accidental (or malicious) changes to its contents. There are no possible ways that the virus can affect the true ROMs. Read only memory is most commonly used to store system-level programs that we want to make available to the PC at all times. It contains the programs that are used to start up the computer and bring the operating system into main memory. This memory is set at the factory and usually never changed.

ROMs are of three types namely

(i) **PROM (Programmable Read-Only Memory)**
- Data is written to PROM once, typically during manufacturing.
- After programming, the data cannot be changed.
- It is used for storing firmware, device drivers, and other essential system software.

(ii) **EPROM (Erasable Programmable Read-Only Memory)**
- Data can be erased using ultraviolet light.
- Once erased, the EPROM can be reprogrammed.
- It is less flexible than EEPROM but more cost-effective.

(iii) **EEPROM (Electrically Erasable Programmable Read-Only Memory)**
- Data can be erased and reprogrammed electrically.
- This one is more flexible than EPROM but slower.
- It is used for storing configuration settings and firmware that may need updates.

Case Study Based Questions

Case Study 1

Shreya got an assignment from her teacher for a school project. She has written the following lines on a chart paper.

A computer is a versatile and powerful machine that can perform a wide range of tasks. It consists of various components working together to process information. The central processing unit (CPU) is the brain of the computer, responsible for executing instructions and performing calculations. The memory unit stores data and instructions, while the input and output units allow communication with the user.

But her younger sister has some doubts on the concepts of computer system.

(i) **Which of the following is the brain of the computer?**
(a) Memory (b) Input unit
(c) Output unit (d) Central Processing Unit

(ii) **Which component is responsible for storing data and instructions?**
(a) CPU (b) Memory unit
(c) Input unit (d) Output unit

(iii) **Which of the following is not a core component of a computer system?**
(a) Central Processing Unit (CPU)
(b) Input/Output Devices
(c) Memory
(d) Power supply unit

(iv) **What is the primary function of the CPU?**
(a) Store data
(b) Display information
(c) Execute instructions
(d) Input data

(v) **Which of the following is an example of an output device?**
(a) Keyboard (b) Mouse
(c) Monitor (d) Joystick

(vi) **What is the role of input device in a computer system?**
(a) Process data
(b) Store data
(c) Display information
(d) Enter data into the computer

Ans. (i) (d) Central Processing Unit
(ii) (b) Memory unit
(iii) (d) Power supply unit
(iv) (c) Execute instructions
(v) (c) Monitor
(vi) (d) Enter data into the computer

Case Study 2

Input and output devices facilitate interaction with the computer. Input devices, such as keyboards and mice, allow users to enter data and commands. Output devices, like monitors and printers, display information and generate tangible results.

(i) **Which of the following is an input device?**
(a) Monitor (b) Printer
(c) Keyboard (d) Speaker

(ii) **Which of the following is not an output device?**
(a) Monitor (b) Printer
(c) Keyboard (d) Speaker

(iii) **Which input device is used to control the movement of a cursor on a computer screen?**
(a) Keyboard (b) Mouse
(c) Scanner (d) Microphone

(iv) **Which output device is used to produce hard copies of documents?**
(a) Monitor (b) Printer
(c) Speaker (d) Projector

(v) **What is the function of a scanner?**
(a) To input audio data
(b) To input video data
(c) To input printed text and images
(d) To output sound

Ans. (i) (c) Keyboard
(ii) (c) Keyboard
(iii) (b) Mouse
(iv) (b) Printer
(v) (c) To input printed text and images

Case Study 3

Memory is the electronic holding place for the instructions and data that a computer needs to access quickly. It is where information is stored for immediate use. Memory is one of the fundamental components of a computer because, without it, the system would not function properly. Additionally, memory is utilized by a computer's operating system, hardware, and software.

There are two main types of computer memory: primary memory and secondary memory. The term memory is often used as a synonym for primary memory or as an abbreviation for a specific type of primary memory called random access memory (RAM). This type of memory is located on microchips that are physically close to a computer's microprocessor.

Answer the following questions:

(i) The boot sector files of the system are stored in which type of computer memory?
(a) RAM (b) ROM
(c) Cache (d) Register

(ii) Which memory acts as a buffer between the CPU and main memory?
(a) RAM (b) ROM
(c) Cache (d) Storage

(iii) Which of the following is the smallest unit of data in a computer?
(a) Bit (b) KB
(c) Nibble (d) Byte

(iv) Where does your PC store your programs when the power is off?
(a) DRAM (b) Cache
(c) ROM (d) Hard Disk Drive

(v) What is the name of the storage device used to compensate for the difference in data transfer rates between two devices?
(a) Cache (b) Concentrator
(c) Buffer (d) I/O device

Ans. (i) (b) ROM (ii) (c) Cache
(iii) (a) Bit (iv) (d) Hard Disk Drive
(v) (c) Buffer

Case Study 4

Computing devices have come a long way from simple counting tools to powerful digital processors. The journey started with early mechanical devices like the Abacus, followed by Pascaline, and later Charles Babbage's Analytical Engine, which introduced the concept of a general-purpose computing machine. The invention of the Turing Machine provided a theoretical model for modern computers. The Von Neumann Architecture, used in ENIAC, laid the foundation for binary-programmed computers.

The development of transistors (1947) and integrated circuits (1970s) led to the creation of microprocessors, allowing complete CPUs to be built on a single chip.

With the introduction of personal computers (IBM PC in 1981, Apple Macintosh in 1984) and Graphical User Interfaces (GUI), computers became more user-friendly and accessible to the masses. The growth of the World Wide Web (WWW) in the 1990s further accelerated the widespread use of computers.

Today, computing devices have evolved into portable gadgets like laptops, tablets, and smartphones. The rise of Artificial Intelligence (AI) and the Internet of Things (IoT) has paved the way for smart appliances and wearable technology, making computing more integrated into daily life.

Based on the above information, answer the following questions:

(i) Which of the following was one of the earliest computing devices used for arithmetic calculations?
(a) ENIAC (b) Pascaline
(c) Transistor (d) Turing Machine

(ii) Which computing model introduced the concept of storing a program in memory for execution?
(a) Abacus
(b) Von Neumann Architecture
(c) Turing Machine
(d) Analytical Engine

(iii) What was the key technological advancement in the 1970s that allowed complete CPUs to be built on a single chip?
(a) Vacuum Tubes
(b) Super Large Scale Integration (SLSI)
(c) Large Scale Integration (LSI)
(d) Artificial Intelligence (AI)

(iv) Which company introduced the first personal computer (PC) for home users in 1981?
(a) Microsoft (b) IBM
(c) Apple (d) Intel

(v) Which of the following best describes the latest trend in computing technology?
(a) Command-line interface
(b) Use of vacuum tubes
(c) Wearable gadgets and IoT devices
(d) Only desktop computing

Ans. (i) (b) Pascaline
(ii) (b) Von Neumann Architecture
(iii) (c) Large Scale Integration (LSI)
(iv) (b) IBM
(v) (c) Wearable gadgets and IoT devices

SELF ASSESSMENT TEST

Multiple Choice Questions

1. **Which unit of computer helps in communication between the memory and the arithmetic logical unit?**

(a) CMU (b) CCU
(c) UPS (d) CPU

2. **A device, which is used for making drawings, graphics and for menu selection.**

(a) Keyboard (b) Mouse
(c) Touch screen (d) Light Pen

3. **Which of the following printers, are you sure, will not to use if your objective is to print on multi carbon forms?**

(a) Daisy wheel (b) Dot matrix
(c) Laser (d) Thermal

Fill in the Blanks

4. The CPU (Central Processing Unit) is known as the ______ of the computer.

5. RAM (Random Access Memory) is an example of ______ memory, which provides fast access to data but is volatile.

6. 1 Byte consists of ______ bits.

State Whether True or False

7. The CPU is responsible for processing data and instructions in a computer system.

8. Secondary memory is faster than primary memory and is used to store temporary data.

Assertion and Reason Based Questions

Assertion (A) and Reason (R) Type questions. Choose the correct option as:

(a) Both Assertion (A) and Reason (R) are true, and Reason (R) is the correct explanation of Assertion (A).

(b) Both Assertion (A) and Reason (R) are true, but Reason (R) is not the correct explanation of Assertion (A).

(c) Assertion (A) is true, but Reason (R) is false.

(d) Assertion (A) is false, but Reason (R) is true.

9. **Assertion (A)** The Central Processing Unit (CPU) is known as the brain of the computer.

Reason (R) The CPU controls all operations of a computer, processes data, and executes instructions.

10. **Assertion (A)** Secondary memory is faster than cache memory.

Reason (R) Cache memory is located closer to the CPU and stores frequently accessed data for quick retrieval.

Very Short Answer Type Questions

11. The word computer has been derived from which of the language?

12. What do you mean by function keys of the keyboard?

13. Explain the types of impact printer.

14. Give relation between byte and gigabyte.

15. What does a bus mean?

Short Answer Type Questions

16. What is the hardware ?

17. A company is planning to have a video conference. In its video conferencing area, there are some microphones, speakers and webcams. Describe the purpose of each of the devices.

Long Answer Type Questions

18. Explain hard disk drive with its advantages and disadvantages.

19. Describe the functioning of a computer.

Case Study Based Questions

20. **Ravi is a high school student who recently bought a new computer for his studies. He is curious about how different components work together in a computer system. His teacher explains that a computer has hardware and software components.**

The hardware includes the CPU, memory, and input/output devices, while software enables users to perform tasks. Ravi also learns about different types of memory, such as primary, cache, and secondary storage, and the various units of memory measurement.

Answer the following given questions

(i) **Which of the following is NOT a type of computer memory?**
(a) Primary memory
(b) Cache memory
(c) Virtual memory
(d) Mechanical memory

(ii) **Ravi wants to store large files, such as movies and software programs, on his computer. Which type of memory should he use?**
(a) Cache memory
(b) Primary memory
(c) Secondary memory
(d) Register memory

(iii) **The CPU is often referred to as the "brain" of the computer. Which of the following is NOT a function of the CPU?**
(a) Processing data
(b) Storing long-term files
(c) Controlling input and output devices
(d) Executing instructions

(iv) **Ravi notices that his computer's speed slows down when he runs multiple applications at once. His teacher explains that an essential component of the CPU helps in faster data access. Which component is responsible for this?**
(a) Cache memory (b) Hard disk
(c) USB storage (d) DVD-ROM

Answers

1. (d) 2. (d) 3. (c) 4. Brain 5. Primary
6. 8 7. True 8. False 9. (a) 10. (c)
20. (i) → (d), (ii) → (c), (iii) → (b), (iv) → (a)

02

CHAPTER

Software is a generic term for programs, scripts and applications that run on a device.

YOUR STUDY GOALS

2.1 System Software
2.2 Programming Tools
2.3 Application Software
2.4 Proprietary or Free and Open Source Software

YOUR PRACTICE GOAL

- Objective Type Questions (38 Qs ; MCQs, True or False, Fill in the Blanks, Assertion and Reason)
- Subjective Type Questions (48 Qs ; VSA, SA, LA)
- Case Study Based Questions-4

Software Concepts

The concept of software is fundamental to modern computing, serving as the bridge between hardware and user interaction. Software encompasses a wide range of programs, applications, and systems that enable a computer to perform specific tasks, from simple calculations to complex data processing like video editing, online shopping, document creating and editing etc.

Classification of Software

Depending on the mode of interaction with hardware and functions to be performed, the software can be broadly classified into three categories.

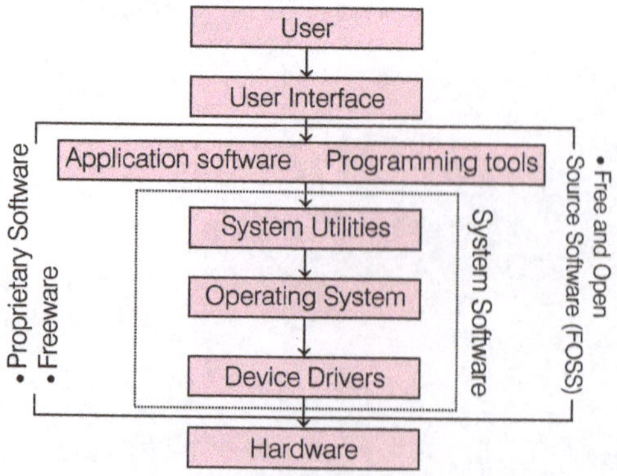

2.1 System Software

It is a program that manages and supports the computer resources and operations of a computer system while the computer executes its various tasks such as processing data and information, controlling hardware components, and allowing users to use application software.

System software is the invisible backbone of a computer system. It's the software that manages all the internal operations, making it possible for us to interact with the computer and run our favorite applications.

Without system software, our computers would be useless.

Examples of system software include:

Operating system, Device drivers, Utility software

1. Operating System

An Operating System (OS) is the fundamental software that controls your computer. It's like the brain of your computer, managing everything from **hardware** resources to **software applications**.

The OS ensures smooth operation, handles tasks like memory allocation, input/output operations, and file management. It creates a user-friendly interface, allowing you to interact with your computer effortlessly.

An operating system is a collection of softwares or a series of programs which performs various types of functions in order to manage and organize files.

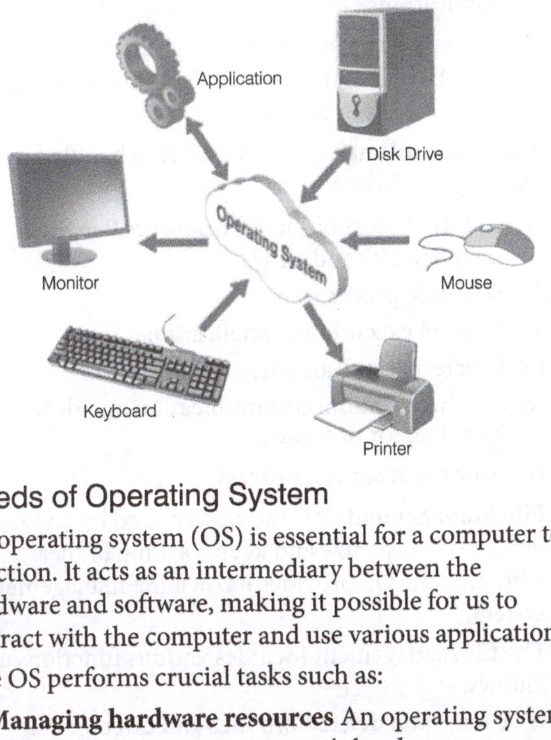

Needs of Operating System

An operating system (OS) is essential for a computer to function. It acts as an intermediary between the hardware and software, making it possible for us to interact with the computer and use various applications.

The OS performs crucial tasks such as:

- **Managing hardware resources** An operating system efficiently manages a computer's hardware resources, including memory, CPU, and input/output devices. It allocates memory to running processes, schedules CPU time for different tasks, and controls the flow of data between the computer and external devices.
- **Providing a user-friendly interface** The OS provides a user-friendly interface, such as a graphical user interface (GUI) or a command-line interface, allowing users to interact with the computer easily. It simplifies complex tasks and makes the computing experience more simple.
- **Executing user commands** The OS translates user commands into machine-understandable instructions, enabling the computer to execute tasks. It interprets user input, whether it's a mouse click, keyboard input, or voice command, and converts it into a sequence of instructions that the CPU can process.
- **Coordinating system activities** The OS manages all the processes running on the computer, ensuring smooth and efficient operation. It manages the scheduling of tasks, handles resource allocation, and coordinates the interaction between different software components.

TEACHER TIP
An Operating System (OS) is the first program that is loaded into the computer's main memory, when a computer is switched ON.

Types of Operating System

At present, operating systems come in various types, each designed for specific purposes.

1. **Batch Processing OS** Batch processing OS groups jobs submitted on punch cards into batches based on similar requirements. The processor executes these batches together, improving efficiency and ensuring smooth task execution. Users don't need to interact with the computer directly as the system manages the job execution automatically
2. **Multi-Programing Operating Systems**
   Multi-Programing OSs allow multiple users to access and utilize a computer's resources simultaneously. They are commonly used in server environments and large organizations. These systems manage user accounts, allocate resources, and ensure that multiple users can work efficiently without interfering with each other. Examples include Unix and Linux.
3. **Time-Sharing Operating System** Time-sharing OSs allow multiple users to share a single computer

system. Each user gets a specific time slot to use the CPU and other resources. This enables efficient resource utilization and cost-effective computing in large organizations.

4. **Multi-tasking Operating Systems (Multitasking OS)** The OS that allows you to run multiple programs at once, even though the processor can only handle one at a time. They efficiently switch between tasks, creating the illusion of simultaneous operation. Examples include Windows and macOS.

   Multi-tasking OS can be classified as

   (i) **Preemptive Multitasking** It is a type of multitasking that allows computer programs to share operating system and underlying hardware resources.

   It divides the overall operating and computing time between processes, and the switching of resources between different processes occurs through predefined criteria. OS/2, Windows 95, Window NT, Amiga operating system and UNIX use preemptive multitasking.

   (ii) **Cooperative Multitasking** It is the simplest form of multi-tasking. In it, each program can control the CPU for as long as it need it. If a program is not using the CPU, however it can allow another program to use it temporarily.

   For example Mac OS, MS Window 3-x etc.

5. **Real-Time Operating Systems (RTOS)** RTOS are designed for systems that require strict timing constraints.

   They prioritize tasks and ensure timely responses to events. This makes them suitable for applications like industrial control systems, medical devices, and robotics. Linux OS is an example of real-time operating system.

   Real-time operating system can be classified as

   (i) **Hard Real-Time OS** An OS that can absolutely guarantee a maximum time for the operations it performs, is referred to as hard real-time OS.

   (ii) **Soft Real-Time OS** An OS that cannot absolutely guarantee a maximum time for operations it performs, is referred to as soft real-time OS.

6. **Single-User Operating Systems** As the name suggests a Single-user OSs are designed for individual use on personal computers. They provide a user-friendly interface and are commonly used for tasks like browsing the internet, word processing, and playing games. Examples include Windows, macOS, and Linux distributions like Ubuntu.

7. **Distributed Operating System** Distributed OSs distribute computing tasks across multiple interconnected computers. This allows for increased processing power, improved reliability, and scalability. By sharing resources and workload, distributed systems can handle complex tasks and large datasets efficiently.

Functions of Operating System

An operating system (OS) is like a manager that manages the smooth functioning of a computer. It performs various crucial tasks in which some of them are as follows:

1. **Process Management** A process is an application or program in running state. Process management is the important part of an operating system which involves managing and scheduling the execution of different programs or applications.

   The two crucial issues are given below.

   (i) The operating system should distribute processor time evenly among all running applications.

   (ii) The operating system aims to keep the processor busy by efficiently scheduling tasks, which can be processes or threads.

   The processor management activities handled by an OS are given below.

   (i) Control access of shared resources like file, memory, I/O and CPU.

   (ii) Schedule process.

   (iii) Control execution of applications.

   (iv) Create, execute and delete a process.

   (v) Synchronization, communication and deadlock handling for processes.

   (vi) Abort or resume a process.

2. **File Management** It is the system used by an OS or program to organize and keep tracking of files. Although the OS provides its own file management system.

   The file management includes various functions as follows.

   (i) Create and delete both files and directories.

   (ii) Easy access to files.

   (iii) Allocate space for files.

(iv) Keep back-up of files.
(v) Secure files.
(vi) Keeps track of files, its location, use, status etc.

3. **Memory Management** It is the act of managing computer memory. When an operating system manages the computer's memory, there are two broad tasks to be accomplished
   (i) Each process must have sufficient memory to execute and it cannot run into the memory space of another process.
   (ii) The different types of memory in the system must be used properly, so that each process can run most effectively.

   Computers can be upgraded with more memory, like RAM, to improve performance. However, it's important to remember that most of the memory is often idle, not actively used by applications. This suggests that there's potential for more efficient memory usage.

   The memory management activities handled by an operating system are given below.
   (i) Keeps track of the memory.
   (ii) Decides which process gets memory and when it gets it and how much it gets.
   (iii) Allocates the memory when the process requests it.
   (iv) De-allocates the memory when the process has been terminated.
4. **Storage Management** Storage management is the process of efficiently storing and managing data on computer systems.

   It involves techniques like virtualization, replication, and compression to optimize storage usage and performance.

   Secondary storage devices, such as hard drives, are essential for storing data when the computer is turned OFF or for programs that require more memory than the main memory can provide. The operating system plays a crucial role in managing this storage process.
5. **Device Management** In a computer system, there is a tremendous speed mismatch between the CPU and the I/O devices.

   The job of an operating system is to maintain a balance between the two I/O devices and has to keep the CPU busy, i.e. achieved through overlapped processing.

   Basically, an operating system as a device manager performs the following tasks as follows.
   - Keeps track of devices, channels and control units.
   - Decides what is an efficient way to allocate the device.
   - Allocates device and initiate input/output operation.
   - De-allocates the device.

User Interface

The user interface is one of the most important parts of any operating system. It allows users to easily access and communicate with the applications and the hardware.

The user can interact with the computer by using these kinds of interfaces:

1. **Command-based or Character User Interface (CUI)** It is a means of interacting with computer program where the user issues commands to the program in the form of successive lines of text (command lines). It was used by DOS. It is also known as command line interface.
2. **Graphical User Interface (GUI)** It is a program interface that takes advantage of the computer's graphics capability to make the program easier to use.

   In this interface, the commands are given by selecting or clicking on the options, which can be identified with the small figures that appear with them.

   The first graphical user interface was designed by Xerox Corporation in 1970s. GUIs can be found in handheld devices such as MP3 players, portable media players, gaming devices, etc.
3. **Touch-based Interface** Today, phones, tablets, and computers let us do things just by touching the screen.

   When we touch the screen, the computer understands what we want, like opening an app, closing it, calling someone, or scrolling through apps. Popular systems like Android, iOS, Windows 8.1, and Windows 10 work well with touchscreens.
4. **Voice-based Interface** Today's computers are made to work for everyone, even people who need special

help or want to use their computer or phone while doing other things. For people who can't use a mouse, keyboard, or touchscreen, modern computers let you use your voice to control them. Some operating systems, like iOS (with Siri), Android (with Google Now or "OK Google"), and Windows 10 (with Cortana), let you do this.

5. **Gesture-based Interface** Some phones and computers, like those using Android and iOS, let you control them with gestures, like waving, tilting, moving your eyes, or shaking the device. This technology is getting better and could be really useful for games, medicine, and other things.

Booting

Booting is starting up a computer or computer appliance until it can be used. It can be initiated by hardware such as a Start button or by software command. There are two types of booting:

- **Cold Booting** When a computer is turned ON after it has been completely shutdown.
- **Warm Booting** When a computer is restarted by pressing the combination of Ctrl + Alt + Del keys or by restart button.

Quick Test 1

1. What are the core functions of an operating system?
2. Explain the concept of multitasking and multiprogramming in operating systems.
3. Differentiate between a GUI and a CUI.
4. What are the key differences between batch operating systems, time-sharing operating systems, and real-time operating systems?
5. When a computer is turned ON, who brings the OS into RAM from the secondary storage? NCERT

2. Device Drivers

Device drivers are specific programs that enable the computer to communicate with hardware devices. They act as intermediaries, translating data between the device and the operating system. Without device drivers, a computer would be unable to recognize and utilize connected hardware devices, such as printers, scanners, sound cards, or even input devices like keyboards and mouse.

Key Functions of Device Drivers

- **Hardware Initialization** Device drivers initialize hardware devices upon system startup, ensuring they are ready to operate.
- **Input/Output Operations** They manage the transfer of data between the device and the system's memory.
- **Error Handling** Device drivers detect and handle errors that may occur during device operations, such as paper jams in printers or disk read/write errors.
- **Resource Allocation** They allocate system resources, such as memory and interrupt requests, to the device.
- **Configuration** Device drivers allow users to configure device settings, such as printer resolution or sound card volume.
- **Power Management** They can help manage power consumption by devices, especially in laptops and mobile devices.

TEACHER TIP

Consider device drivers as the language translators between the Operating system and hardware devices.

3. Utility Software

Utility software is a category of system software designed to enhance the performance, security, and maintenance of a computer system. Unlike application software, which is used to perform specific tasks, utility software works behind the scenes to optimize system performance, protect data, and troubleshoot issues.

Here are some of the most common types of utility software:

Antivirus Software

Antivirus software is essential for protecting computers from malicious software, such as viruses, worms, and malware. It scans the system for threats, removes existing infections, and prevents future attacks.

To remove viruses, follow the following steps

- Buy or download an antivirus software.
- Install it.
- Update it with the latest virus definitions.
- Do a complete scan.

Some basic functions of an antivirus tool are

- Scans specific files or directories for any malware or unknown malicious patterns.
- Allows you to schedule your scan timings.
- Malicious code can infect files. You may be notified and asked to clean the infected file, or it might be cleaned automatically by other programs.
- Displays health of your computer system.

Disk Defragmenter

Disk defragmentation is a process that reorganizes fragmented files on a hard drive, improving access time and overall system performance. By bringing scattered file fragments together, the disk defragmenter reduces the time it takes for the computer to access data. To start disk defragmenter tool, follow the following steps

Click Start → All Programs → Accessories → System Tools → Disk Defragmenter.

Backup Utility

Backup utilities create copies of important data, allowing for data recovery in case of hardware failures, accidental deletions, or malicious attacks. Regular backups are crucial for data protection and business continuity.

You can run backup option to backup or restore files from settings of your computer system as follows

Click Start → All Programs → Accessories → System Tools → Backup. After that, you will be guided to Backup or Restore Wizard. Press two times Next button.

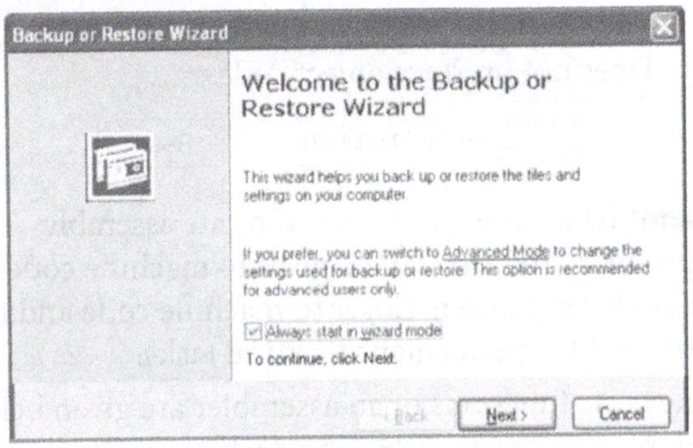

Backup or Restore Wizard Window

Select a place and press Next button again. Click Finish to take backup.

Compression Utility

Compression utilities reduce the size of files, making them easier to store, transmit, and download. This is particularly useful for large files, such as videos and images. It is a technique used to reduce the size of data by eliminating redundancy. This process results in compressed data, which can be significantly smaller than the original data.

Decompression is the reverse process, restoring the compressed data to its original form. Compression can be applied to both data content and transmission units, leading to substantial reductions, especially in text files, which can be compressed by up to 50%.

Popular compression tools include Disk double, Superstar Pro, Double Disk Gold, Xtra Drive, and WinZip.

Disk Cleaner

Disk cleaner utilities identify and remove unnecessary files, such as temporary files, system logs, and old downloads, freeing up disk space and improving system performance.

You can start disk cleanup tool as

Click Start → All Programs → Accessories → Systems Tools → Disk Cleanup.

File Management Tools

File management tools help users organize and manage files and folders on their computer. They provide features like searching, sorting, and copying files, making it easier to find and access data.

Files are collections of information stored on a disk and accessed by a name. A file manager organizes and maintains these files within directories. The most common operations performed on files or group of files are create, open, edit, view, print, delete, copy, paste, etc.

Mistake Alert!

Student can ignore utility software but it plays a crucial role in system maintenance.

Quick Test 2

1. Locate any two device drivers installed on your computer. **NCERT**
2. Explain the concept of utility software and provide examples of common utility programs.
3. How do system utilities like disk defragmenters and antivirus software contribute to system performance and security?
4. Discuss the role of compression utilities in efficient data storage and transmission.

2.2 Programming Tools

To make a computer perform tasks, we provide instructions in the form of programs. These instructions are written using computer languages. Since computers understand machine language, human-written programs in high-level languages must be converted to machine language using translators. Additionally, code editors, like IDLE for Python, are used for writing instructions.

1. Classification of Programming Languages

Programming languages are developed to simplify coding, as writing in machine language (**1s and 0s**) is difficult. These languages are divided into two categories:

- **Low-level languages**, such as machine language and assembly language, are machine-dependent. Machine language uses binary instructions directly understood by computers, while assembly language uses English-like words but is still CPU-specific.
- **High-level languages**, like C++, Java, and Python, are machine-independent and use English-like syntax. These languages require translators to convert code into machine language.

2. Language Translators (Language Processor)

Language translators bridge the gap between human-readable programming languages and machine code.

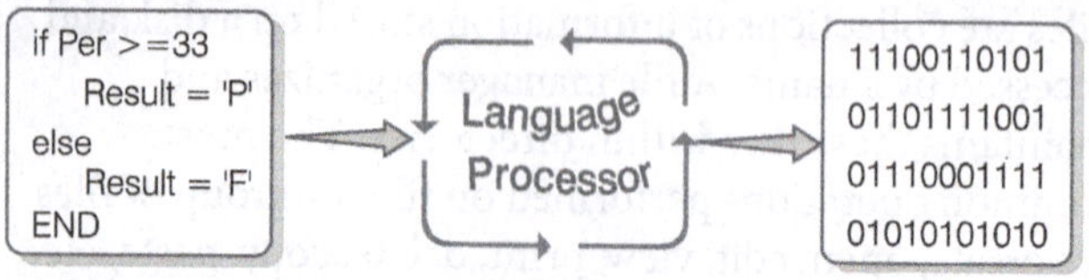

Program Translator

This language is extremely difficult to learn for a general programmer and thus there is a need for some special language which is easy to learn and understand for the programmer in order to interact with the computer system. These special languages or set of commands are collectively known as programming languages or High Level Languages (HLL).

In other words, **'Language processor is a program that performs tasks, such as translating and interpreting, required for processing a specified programming language.'**

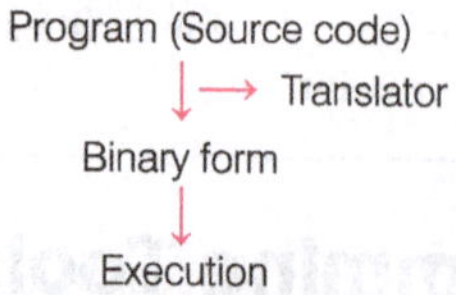

The language translator is of three types as shown below

- **Compilers** These programs translate entire high-level language programs into machine code before execution. This pre-compilation process results in faster execution.

  It converts the entire high level language program in one go and reports all the errors of the program along with the line numbers.

  Some basic functions of a compiler are given below.

  (i) Checks the code line-by-line to find syntax errors.

  (ii) If object code is error free, then it translates the whole program into machine language (object code). If there is any error, the computer generates a printout of the errors it has detected. This action is known as **diagnostics**.

- **Interpreters** These programs translate and execute high-level language programs line by line, without creating an executable file.

  This provides flexibility but can be slower than compiled programs.

  Some basic functions of an interpreter are given below.

  (i) Translates one instruction at a time.

  (ii) It checks the execution of an instruction line-by-line.

  (iii) Does not produce object code.

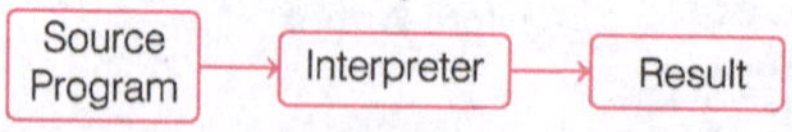

- **Assemblers** These programs translate assembly language, a low-level language, into machine code. Assembly language is closer to machine code and is often used for performance-critical tasks.

  Some basic functions of an assembler are given below.

  (i) Replaces mnemonic codes by machine codes.

  (ii) Replaces symbolic addresses by numeric addresses.

  (iii) Determines machine representation for constants.

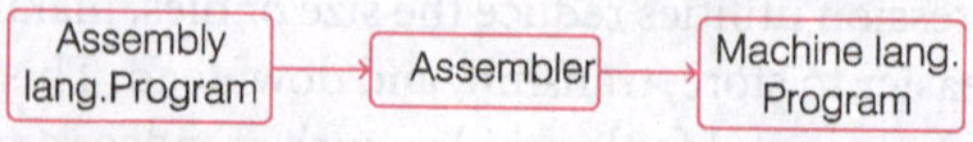

Mistake Alert!

Student can misunderstand the difference between compilers and interpreters.

Specifically regarding which one translates the code completely & which one translates it line-by-line.

3. Program Development Tools

To write a program, a text editor is used to create and store the source code. A translator then converts it into object code for execution.

Integrated Development Environments (IDEs) like Python IDLE, NetBeans, and Eclipse simplify the process, offering text editors, build tools, and debuggers for writing, compiling, and debugging code. Debuggers help detect and fix errors in the source code.

2.3 Application Software

Application software is a category of software designed to perform specific tasks for users.

It can be broadly categorized into two types:

1. General-Purpose Application Software

General-purpose application software refers to software that can be used for a wide range of tasks and is not specific to a particular industry or job function. It often provides essential tools for productivity, creativity, and communication.

There are several good reasons for using general purpose software and some of them are given below

- These are relatively cheap.
- Easily available.
- Thoroughly tested.
- Easily handleable.

Some of the general purpose softwares are:

- **Word Processors** These applications are used to create, edit, and format text documents. Today, the Word processor is one of the most frequently used programs or online services used on a computer system.
  Examples include Microsoft Word and LibreOffice Writer.
- **Presentation Tools** These tools help create visually appealing presentations with slides, images, text, and multimedia elements.

  It has three major functions

  (i) An editor that allows text to be inserted or formatted.

  (ii) A method for inserting and manipulating graphic images.

  (iii) A slide-show system to display the content.

  Popular examples are Microsoft PowerPoint and LibreOffice Impress.
- **Spreadsheet Software** These applications allow users to organize data in rows and columns, perform calculations, and generate charts and graphs.

  In a spreadsheet application, each value exists in a cell, and user can define what type of data is in each cell and how different cells depend upon one another. The relationships between the cells are called **'Formulas'** and the names of the cells are called **'Labels'**. Each cell is labeled according to its placement.

  Some basic functions of a spreadsheet package are as follows

  - It creates and manipulates simple databases.
  - Establishes a relationship between numerical data.
  - Represents datasets in graphical or chart form.
  - It create simple lists and tables of alphabetic or numerical data.

  Microsoft Excel and LibreOffice Calc are widely used spreadsheet software.
- **Database Management Systems (DBMS)** DBMS software helps manage and organize large amounts of data. It enables a user to define, create and maintain the database and provide controlled access on it.

  Database management system provides several additional features as

  - Remove data redundancy
  - Elimination of data inconsistency
  - Data sharing
  - Data integration
  - Data security.

  Examples include Microsoft Access and LibreOffice Base.
- **Desktop Publishing Package (DTP)** is a digital process that involves creating documents using page layout software on a computer. It combines text and graphics to produce high-quality printed materials. Before DTP, printing was a manual and time-consuming process. With the introduction of DTP software, the process has become significantly more efficient and accessible.

  Popular DTP software includes Adobe PageMaker, CorelDraw, and iStudio Publisher.

2. Special-Purpose Application Software

These software applications are personalized to specific needs and industries. They are often developed to automate tasks or solve particular problems. Some examples include:

- **Inventory Management Systems** These systems help businesses track and manage their inventory, including stock levels, purchase orders, and sales.

  The transactions possible in an inventory management system are

  (a) Receipts/Purchase of items
  (b) Issues an item
  (c) Purchase return
  (d) Issue return

- **Payroll System** Payroll software helps streamline the payroll process by automating tasks like calculating pay, deducting taxes, and generating paychecks. This reduces errors and saves time compared to manual methods.

  In a payroll system, there are two important modules

  (a) Earnings calculation module.
  (b) Deduction calculation module.

  The broad objectives of a payroll system are as follows

  (a) Preparation of wages slip giving details of all earnings and deductions of an employee's wages together with the net salary payable for the month.
  (b) Preparation of a currency analysis to facilitate distribution of salary by the employer.
  (c) Reports generation- Monthly.
  (d) Preparation of annual summaries.

- **Financial Accounting Systems** These systems help businesses manage their finances, including accounting, budgeting, and financial reporting.

  All the business organizations maintain the following books of accounting

  (a) Sales book
  (b) Journal
  (c) Creditors ledger
  (d) Advance to staff
  (e) Purchases book
  (f) Cash book
  (g) Debtor's ledger
  (h) General ledger.

- **Hotel Management Systems** These systems help hotels manage reservations, room assignments, billing, and other operations.

  In hotel management there is another system of restaurant billing. The reports can be viewed completely and the head of the management daily or weekly or monthly can review it. The proposed system will be interactive, faster and user friendly for the end users.

- **Reservation Systems** These systems are used to book various services, such as airline tickets, hotel rooms, and restaurant tables.

  There are different types of reservation systems running in various organizations as follows

  (a) Railway reservation system
  (b) Hotel reservation system
  (c) Central reservation system.

- **Weather Forecasting Systems** These systems use complex algorithms and data to predict weather patterns. Numerical Weather Prediction (NWP) is a scientific method that uses computer models to forecast future weather conditions. It involves collecting current weather data, processing it through complex models, and generating predictions for various meteorological elements.

Advantages of Special-Purpose Software

- Special-purpose software can be designed to fit the exact needs of an organization, improving efficiency and productivity.
- By automating tasks and streamlining workflows, special-purpose software can significantly improve operational efficiency.
- Unique software solutions can give businesses a competitive edge by providing features and capabilities that competitors may lack.
- Special-purpose software can be designed with strong security measures to protect sensitive data.
- Special-purpose software can be easily scaled to accommodate future growth and changing business needs.

Note *A computer system can work without application software, but it cannot work without system software. For example, we can use a computer even if no word processing software is installed, but if no operating system is installed, we cannot work on the computer. In other words, the use of computer is possible in the absence of application software.*

2.4 Proprietary or Free and Open Source Software

Software developers sometimes share their code freely, allowing others to improve it. This type of software is called **Free and Open Source Software (FOSS)**.

For example, Ubuntu, a popular operating system, allows anyone to modify its code. Other FOSS examples include Python, LibreOffice, OpenOffice, and Mozilla Firefox.

Some software is free to use but does not share its code. This is called **freeware**. Examples include Skype and Adobe Reader.

Other software must be purchased from the company that created it. This is called **proprietary software**. Examples include Microsoft Windows, Tally, and QuickHeal.

Quick Test 3

1. What is the main difference between a compiler and an interpreter?
2. What is the difference between general-purpose and special-purpose application software?
3. Which of the following is an example of general-purpose application software?
   (a) Word processor
   (b) Spreadsheet
   (c) Web browser
   (d) All of the above
4. Which of the following is an example of special-purpose application software?
   (a) Accounting software (b) CAD software
   (c) Medical software (d) All of these

NCERT Folder

1. Name the software required to make a computer functional. Write down its two primary services.

Ans. **Operating System (OS)** OS manages the hardware and the software resources, It provides a user interface.

Primary services include Process management, Input/Output management.

System Software System Software includes device drivers, utilities, and compilers/interpreters which requires to make any computer functional.

Primary services include Language processors, System tools.

2. How does the computer understand a program written in high level language?

Ans. A compiler or interpreter translates high-level code into machine code (binary instructions) that the computer can execute.

3. Why is the execution time of the machine code less than that of source code?

Ans. Machine code is directly executable by the CPU, which eliminates the need for translation at runtime, leading to faster execution.

4. Differentiate between proprietary software and freeware software. Name two software for each type.

Ans.

Proprietary Software	Freeware Software
These software is commercially licensed.	No licensing fees are required for these software tools.
In proprietary software we often requires purchase.	Freeware software is distributed free of charge
Example include Microsoft Office, Adobe Photoshop.	**Example include** VLC Media player, Notepad++.

5. Identify the category (system, application, programming tool) of the following software:
(a) Compiler
(b) Assembler
(c) Ubuntu
(d) Text editor

Ans. (a) Programming tool
(b) Programming tool
(c) System software
(d) Application software

Mind Map

SOFTWARE CONCEPTS

System Software

It is a set of programs that manage a computer's hardware and resources. It also provides a platform for running application software.

Operating System (OS)

It allows users to interact with their computer's hardware. It performs basic tasks like memory management, file management, and controlling devices like printers and disk drives.

Device Driver

It allows computer to communicate with hardware devices. Device drivers act as a bridge between the operating system and hardware, allowing the two to interact.

Utility Software

It helps maintain and analyze a computer's performance. It can help with tasks like disk space management, file organization, and backup.

Types of Utility Software

- **Disk Cleanup** – Removes unused files to free up disk space
- **Disk Defragmenter** – Rearranges scattered files into contiguous spaces to improve disk performance
- **Text Editor** – It refers to a computer program that allows users to create, edit, and manipulate plain text files
- **Antivirus** – It helps protect your computer from viruses, malware, and other threats. It can also help prevent identity theft and phishing.
- **Backup** – It is a software that copies data from a computer or network to a storage medium.

Application Software

It is a computer program that helps users perform tasks on their computer. It can be used for personal, professional, or educational purposes.

General Purpose Application Software

It can perform a variety of tasks. It's often used at home and school. e.g., Word processors, Spreadsheets, Web browsers , Multimedia software ,Accounting and finance software,etc.

Special Purpose Software

It is designed to perform a specific task or set of tasks. It is often created to meet the needs of a specific business, organization, or user. e.g., Camera application, Chess game ,Scientific calculator , Accounting software ,Medical billing software , Engineering design tools , Airline reservation systems, etc.

Language Processor

It is a software program that translates programming languages into machine language so that computers can understand and execute them.

Compilers

Read entire source codes and translate them into machine code object files

Assemblers

Translate assembly language into machine code

Interpreters

Read and translate source code line by line before executing each line

Proprietary or Free and Open Source Software

Proprietary software is software that is owned by a company or individual, and is not free to use. It is also known as closed-source software

EXAM PATTERN QUESTIONS

Objective Type Questions

Multiple Choice Questions

1. Which of the following is not a type of software?

(a) System software (b) Application software
(c) Utility software (d) Hardware software

2. System software

(a) allows the user to diagnose and troubleshoot the device
(b) is a programming language
(c) is a part of productivity suite
(d) helps the computer manage internal resources

3. What type of software is used to manage computer hardware and software resources?

(a) Application software (b) System software
(c) Utility software (d) Firmware

4. It is the set of programs that enables your computer's hardware device and application software to work together.

(a) Management (b) Processing
(c) Utility (d) System software

5. A company is setting up a new office and needs to install software that manages hardware resources and provides a platform for running other software. Which type of software should they install first? **Competency Based Que.**

(a) Application Software
(b) System Software
(c) Programming Tools
(d) Language Translators

6. Which of the following is the type of software that controls the internal operations in the computer and controls how the computer works well all its parts?

(a) Shareware
(b) Public domain software
(c) Application software
(d) Operating system software

7. What is the primary function of an operating system?

(a) To run application software
(b) To manage hardware and software resources
(c) To create documents
(d) To play games

8. A mobile phone requires special software to allow the operating system to communicate with its touchscreen and camera hardware. Which type of software performs this function? **Competency Based Que.**

(a) Assembler (b) Device Driver
(c) Programming Language (d) Compiler

9. Which of the following is not an example of a device driver?

(a) Printer driver (b) Keyboard driver
(c) Mouse driver (d) Web browser

10. A user installs an antivirus program to scan and remove malware from their computer. This type of software falls under which category? **Competency Based Que.**

(a) Application Software (b) System Utility
(c) Language Translator (d) Operating System

11. What is the purpose of disk defragmentation?

(a) To remove viruses from the computer
(b) To compress files to save space
(c) To reorganize files on the hard drive
(d) To translate code into machine language

12. .... helps in converting programming language to machine language.

(a) Operating system (b) Device driver
(c) Language translator (d) Linker

13. A software developer writes a program in a high-level language. To convert this code into machine language for execution, which of the following software tools is required? **Competency Based Que.**

(a) Device Driver (b) Operating System
(c) Compiler (d) System Utility

14. Software designed for a specific purpose/ application such as pay calculations, processing of examination result etc., are known as

(a) utility software (b) system software
(c) application software (d) customized software

Fill in the Blanks

15. ______ represents set of programs that govern operations of a computer system.

16. A set of instructions given to a computer is called ____.

17. ______ is the collection of programs that. coordinates the operation of computer hardware and software.

18. ______ are the graphical representations of the programs on the desktop.

19. CLI stands for ______.

20. ______ programs perform specific tasks, usually related to managing a computer, its devices or its programs.

21. ______ utility is used to create copy of complete data on a disk.

22. Language translators are used to convert ______ to ______.

23. ______ converts one line of a high level language program to machine code at a time.

State Whether True or False

24. A Real-Time Operating System (RTOS) is designed for systems where strict timing constraints are not critical, such as desktop computers.

25. A Multitasking Operating System allows a computer to execute multiple programs or tasks concurrently.

26. The first graphical user interface (GUI) was developed by Apple in the 1970s.

27. Device drivers are responsible for allocating system resources such as memory and interrupt requests to the device they manage.

28. Anti-virus software can only detect and remove existing malware infections, and cannot prevent future attacks.

29. Application software, like Microsoft Word, is considered general-purpose software because it can be used for a wide range of tasks.

30. An interpreter translates the entire high-level language program into machine code before execution, resulting in faster execution compared to compilers.

31. An Integrated Development Environment (IDE) provides a set of tools that can help with various stages of software development, such as code editing, debugging, and building.

32. Open-source software is freely available to use, modify, and distribute, even for commercial purposes.

Assertion and Reason Based Questions

Assertion (A) and Reason (R) Type questions. Choose the correct option as

(a) Both Assertion (A) and Reason (R) are true, and Reason (R) is the correct explanation of Assertion (A).
(b) Both Assertion (A) and Reason (R) are true, but Reason (R) is not the correct explanation of Assertion (A).
(c) Assertion (A) is true, but Reason (R) is false.
(d) Assertion (A) is false, but Reason (R) is true.

33. **Assertion** (A) System software manages the hardware and software resources of a computer system.
Reason (R) System software directly interacts with the user to perform specific tasks.

34. **Assertion** (A) An operating system is a type of system software.
Reason (R) An operating system manages the hardware and software resources of a computer system.

35. **Assertion** (A) An operating system provides a user interface for interacting with the computer.
Reason (R) The command-line interface is a type of user interface.

36. **Assertion** (A) Device drivers are software programs that enable communication between hardware devices and the operating system.
Reason (R) Device drivers are a type of application software.

37. **Assertion** (A) An interpreter translates and executes each line of code one at a time.
Reason (R) Interpreted programs generally run faster than compiled programs.

38. **Assertion** (A) Application software is designed to perform specific tasks for users.
Reason (R) Word processors, spreadsheets, and web browsers are examples of application software.

Answers

1. (d) Hardware software
2. (d) helps the computer manage internal resources
3. (b) System software
4. (d) System software
5. (b) System Software
6. (d) Operating system software
7. (b) To manage hardware and software resources
8. (b) Device Driver
9. (d) Web browser
10. (b) System Utility
11. (c) To reorganize files on the hard drive
12. (c) Language translator
13. (c) Compiler
14. (c) application software

15. Software
16. Program
17. Operating System
18. Icons
19. Command Line Interface
20. Utility
21. Backup
22. HLL, Machine language
23. Interpreter
24. False
25. True
26. False
27. False
28. False
29. True
30. False
31. True
32. True
33. (c) Assertion (A) is true, but Reason (R) is false.
34. (a) Both Assertion (A) and Reason (R) are true, and Reason (R) is the correct explanation of Assertion (A).
35. (a) Both Assertion (A) and Reason (R) are true, and Reason (R) is the correct explanation of Assertion (A).
36. (c) Assertion (A) is true, but Reason (R) is false.
37. (c) Assertion (A) is true, but Reason (R) is false.
38. (a) Both Assertion (A) and Reason (R) are true, and Reason (R) is the correct explanation of Assertion (A).

Subjective Type Questions

Very Short Answer Type Questions

1. Name the set of instructions that directs the computer to process the information.

Ans. Software

2. How many types of softwares are there? Name them.

Ans. There are three types of software

(i) System Software (ii) Application Software

(iii) Programming tools

3. What is the difference between system software and application software?

Ans. System software manages the computer's hardware and software resources, while application software performs specific tasks for users.

4. What are the main components of system software?

Ans. Operating system, device drivers, system utilities.

5. What purpose does the operating system serve to the computer and the user?

Ans. The operating system reduces the gap between the user and computer by receiving and interpreting user's request and then get this work done with the help of hardware.

6. A computer technician is setting up a new system. When the computer is switched ON, a specific program is loaded first into memory to manage hardware and software resources. Identify this program and explain its role. **Competency Based Que.**

Ans. Operating System.

7. Write the example of Android operating system.

Ans. Android operating system is basically designed for touch screen mobile devices like tablets, smart phone etc.

8. What is the difference between command-line interface and a graphical user interface?

Ans. A command-line interface requires users to type commands, while a graphical user interface uses icons and menus for interaction.

9. How are device drivers installed in a computer system?

Ans. Device drivers are usually installed from a CD or downloaded from the manufacturer's website.

10. Define a utility software.

Ans. A utility software is a kind of software designed to help analyze, configure, optimize and maintain a computer system.

11. Which program carries out some of the common tasks needed when using a computer?

Ans. A utility program carries out some of the common tasks needed when using a computer.

12. Name three utility softwares.

Ans. Text editor, Antivirus program and Compression tool.

13. Which utility software is used to free the disk space?

Ans. Disk cleanup.

14. Why is it important to regularly update antivirus software?

Ans. Regular updates protect against new viruses and threats.

15. Why is backup utility used in the computer system?

Ans. Backup utility is used to keep the backup of stored data in computer.

If the original files are lost or damaged, this data can be used. This backup can be used after the event of a disaster also.

16. A travel company wants to automate its railway ticket booking process. They are considering different types of software. Would a utility software be suitable for this task? Justify your answer. **Competency Based Que.**

Ans. No, a railway reservation system is not a utility software because it does not analyze, configure, or maintain a computer system.

It is an application software designed for booking and managing reservations.

17. **Write the method, which is used to remove viruses?**

Ans. Antivirus software is the method which is used to remove viruses.

18. **Why application software is required in computer system?**

Ans. Application software is required because system software cannot carry out the routine jobs performed by the user which application software can easily do.

19. **Write the name of three application softwares.**

Ans. Word processor, DBMS and railway reservation system.

20. **A recent graduate wants to create a professional and visually appealing resume. Which application software should they use, and why?** **Competency Based Que.**

Ans. A word processor (e.g., MS Word, Google Docs) is the best choice as it allows formatting, text editing, and adding design elements to make the resume attractive.

21. **Which records are maintained by the financial accounting software?**

Ans. Budget, General Ledger, Balance sheet, Profit & Loss statement.

22. **Explain hotel management system.**

Ans. Hotel management system refers to the management techniques used in the hotel sector. These can include hotel administration accounts, billing, marketing, housekeeping etc.

Short Answer Type I Questions

23. **Name the types of software with examples for each.**

Ans. There are three types of software, i.e., system software, application software and programming tool. Operating systems, etc., are system softwares. Payroll system, financial accounting etc., are application softwares. Translators, program development tools etc., are programming tool.

24. **Which type of operating system is used in palmtop computers? Explain that operating system.**

Ans. In palmtop computers, single user (with single task) operating system is used. This type of operating system is designed for use by a single user for a stand-alone single computer for performing a single task. Operating systems for personal computers are single user operating systems.

25. **A company is developing a new range of compact handheld devices for business professionals. Which type of operating system should they integrate to ensure smooth functioning? Justify your answer.** **Competency Based Que.**

Ans. The company should use a mobile operating system (like android or IOS) because these systems are designed for portability touch interaction, and have a wide range of bussiness applications available.

26. **Which activities are performed by an operating system as a resource manager?**

Ans. As a resource manager operating system performs the following activities.

(i) Monitors the different resources.
(ii) Allocates the resources.
(iii) Reclaims the resources.
(iv) Decides which resource get what, when and for how much time.

27. **When a disk is said to be fragmented and also write one disadvantage of a fragmented disk.**

Ans. A disk is said to be fragmented when some of the files are divided into pieces and are scattered around the disk. Fragmentation occurs naturally when you use a disk frequently, creating, deleting, and modifying files.

Disadvantage At some point, the operating system needs to store parts of a file in non-contiguous clusters. This is entirely invisible to users, but can slow down the speed at which data is accessed. This is the main disadvantage of disk fragmentation.

28. **(a) What are programming tools and why are they necessary?**

(b) What are the functions of an interpreter?

Ans. (a) Programming tools are software applications that assist in the development, debugging, and maintenance of computer programs.

They bridge the gap between human-readable programming languages and machine code. These tools are essential for converting high-level code into machine-executable instructions, enabling efficient and effective software development.

(b) An interpreter is a program that translates and executes code line by line.

Key Functions

1. **Translates Code** Converts high-level code into machine code one statement at a time.
2. **Executes Immediately** Runs the code as it translates, without creating a separate executable file.
3. **Error Detection** Stops execution and displays errors when encountered.
4. **Platform Independence** Allows running code across different systems without compilation.

Examples Python Interpreter, JavaScript Engine.

29. **What are HLLs? Give example of some HLLs.**

Ans. HLLs (High-Level Languages) are programming languages that are closer to human language and easier to understand compared to low-level languages.

They are designed to be user-friendly and portable across different hardware.

Examples of HLLs:

- Python
- Java
- C++
- JavaScript
- Ruby

30. What is application software? Why it is required?

Ans. Application software is a type of software designed to perform specific tasks for users, such as word processing, web browsing, or data management.

Application software are required for such reasons

- It helps users accomplish specific tasks efficiently.
- Enhances productivity in various fields like business, education, and entertainment.
- Provides a user-friendly interface to interact with computer hardware.

Examples: MS Word, Google Chrome, Tally, Photoshop.

31. A travel agency wants to automate its booking process to improve efficiency and customer experience. What system should they use, and how will it benefit their business? **Competency Based Que.**

Ans. The travel agency should implement a reservation system (Central Reservation System - CRS). This computerized system helps store and retrieve booking information for air travel, hotels, car rentals, and other activities. By using CRS, businesses can streamline transactions, provide real-time availability, and offer customers easy online booking options through platforms like www.yatra.com and www.makemytrip.com.

32. What kind of software is used to manipulate images, text, sound, animation, and video sequences?

Ans. Graphics software refers to computer programs designed to create, edit, and manipulate digital images. These tools allow users to work with a wide range of visual elements, including photographs, illustrations, animations, and 3D models. They offer a variety of features such as image editing, color correction, special effects, and the ability to combine text, graphics, and multimedia elements. Popular graphics software examples include Adobe Photoshop, GIMP, and CorelDraw.

Short Answer Type II Questions

33. What are operating systems and utility software, and how do they contribute to computer functionality?

Ans. An operating system (OS) serves as the fundamental software layer that bridges the gap between a computer's hardware components and the user. It handles essential tasks such as managing files, allocating memory, executing processes, and controlling input/output devices like printers and disk drives.

Utility software, often integrated into the OS, complements the core functions of the operating system. These tools are designed to optimize, maintain, and troubleshoot computer systems.

They encompass a wide range of functions, including disk defragmentation, virus scanning, data backup, system optimization, and network configuration.

34. What is the role of memory management of an operating system?

Ans. Memory management is the process of managing the computer memory which consist of primary memory or secondary memory. It keeps track of each and every memory location, regardless of either it is allocated to some process or it is free. It checks how much memory is to be allocated to processes.

Memory management activities handled by an operating system are as follows.

- Keeps track of the memory.
- Decides which process gets memory and when it gets it and how much it gets.
- Allocates the memory when the process requests it.
- De-allocates the memory when the process has been terminated.

35. Differentiate between system software and application software? Give examples of each type of software.

Ans. Differences between system software and application software are

System Software	Application Software
Enables the computer to function properly.	Enables users to work efficiently with documentation such as letters, accounting reports and presentation.
Compulsory-each computer must have a system software to function.	Optional-depends on usage and needs. Without an application software, the computer is still able to function.
Independent system software can function without an application software.	Dependent-application software cannot work without system software.
Provides the environment in which the applications run.	Provides the environment to enable users to accomplish specific tasks.
e.g. Operating system, compiler, interpreter, etc.	e.g. Payroll system, word processor, database management system, etc.

36. What are the different types of software that can be used to convert human-readable code into machine-executable instructions?

Ans. Language translators are specialized software programs designed to bridge the gap between human-readable programming languages and machine code. They fall into three primary categories:

Assembler Translate assembly language to machine code. This process involves a one-to-one mapping between assembly instructions and machine instructions.

Interpreter An interpreter executes source code line by line, translating and executing each instruction before proceeding to the next.

Compiler A compiler translates entire source code programs into machine code in a single process.

37. How does assembly language offer advantages over machine language in terms of programming efficiency and ease of use?

Ans. Assembly language provides several key advantages over machine language:

- **Improved Readability** Assembly language uses mnemonics (like ADD, SUB, etc.) to represent machine instructions, making code more readable than binary code.
- **Enhanced Debugging** Assembly language allows for more precise debugging as programmers can examine individual instructions and their effects.
- **Easier Maintenance** Modifying assembly language code is generally simpler than directly manipulating machine code, reducing maintenance costs and effort.
- **Optimal Performance for Specific Tasks** Assembly language offers fine-grained control over hardware, allowing optimization for specific tasks, especially in real-time and embedded systems.

Long Answer Type Questions

38. What are the key differences between compilers and interpreters in terms of performance, error detection, and execution environment?

Ans. Compilers and interpreters are two fundamental approaches to translating high-level programming languages into machine code. While both serve the same purpose, they exhibit distinct advantages and disadvantages.

Advantages of Compilers

(a) **Faster execution** Compiled code is directly executable by the machine, resulting in significantly faster performance compared to interpreted code.

(b) **Standalone execution** Compiled programs can be executed independently, without the need for the compiler or interpreter to be present.

Disadvantages of Compilers

(a) **Slower development cycle** Any modification to the source code requires a complete recompilation process.

(b) **Less immediate feedback** Syntax errors are typically detected only after the entire program has been compiled.

Advantages of Interpreters

(a) **Faster development cycle** Changes to the source code can be tested immediately, without the need for recompilation.

(b) **Immediate error detection** Syntax errors are identified as soon as the interpreter encounters them, allowing for quick corrections.

Disadvantages of Interpreters

(a) **Slower execution** Interpreted code is executed line by line, which can be significantly slower than compiled code.

(b) **Dependency on interpreter** The interpreter must be present on the target machine to run the program.

39. Mr. X has recently installed a new operating system on his computer. **Competency Based Que.**

(i) Describe the main functions of an operating system.

(ii) Identify two utility programs used by an operating system.

(iii) What does command-driven user interface mean?

Ans. (i) The main functions of an operating system are

1. **Resource Management**
   - **Memory Management** Allocates memory to programs, ensuring they have enough space to run without interfering with each other.
   - **CPU Scheduling** Manages the CPU's time, allowing multiple programs to seem like they are running simultaneously.
   - **Device Management** Controls and coordinates input/output devices like keyboards, mice, printers, and monitors.
   - **File Management** Organizes and manages files and folders, enabling users to create, access, and store data efficiently.
2. **Task Management**
   - **Process Management** Creates, schedules, and terminates programs running on the computer.
   - **Multitasking** Enables multiple programs to run concurrently, giving the illusion of simultaneous execution.
   - **Multi-user Support** Allows multiple users to share a single computer system.
3. **User Interface** Provides a way for users to interact with the computer, typically through a graphical user interface (GUI) or a command-line interface.
4. **Security** Implements security measures to protect the computer system from unauthorized access and malicious software.

5. **Hardware Abstraction** Creates a layer of abstraction between the hardware and software, making it easier for programmers to develop applications.

(ii) Two examples of utility programs used by an operating system are:

- **Disk Defragmenter** Rearranges fragmented files on a hard drive to improve disk performance and access speed.
- **Backup and Restore** Creates backups of system files, user data, and applications, allowing for recovery in case of data loss.

(iii) A command-driven user interface is a type of user interface where users interact with the computer by typing commands or instructions at a prompt. It requires users to remember specific commands and their syntax. Compared to graphical user interfaces (GUIs) with icons and menus, command-driven interfaces are less user-friendly for beginners but can be more efficient for experienced users.

40. A school is setting up a computer lab, and the administrator needs to ensure that all computers function efficiently. They must install a system that manages hardware, provides a user-friendly interface, and coordinates all activities.

Based on this scenario, explain why an operating system is necessary and how it helps in managing computer resources effectively. **Competency Based Que.**

Ans. An Operating System (OS) is essential for a computer to function as it acts as a bridge between hardware and software, ensuring smooth operation.

1. **Managing Hardware Resources** The OS efficiently allocates memory, schedules CPU tasks, and controls input/output operations, optimizing system performance.
2. **Providing a User-Friendly Interface** It offers interfaces like GUI or CLI, making it easier for users to interact with the computer.
3. **Executing User Commands** The OS translates user inputs (mouse clicks, keyboard strokes, or voice commands) into machine-readable instructions for execution.
4. **Coordinating System Activities** It manages multiple processes, ensuring smooth execution of tasks and efficient resource utilization.

41. Operating system is an important component of computer system. Various types of operating systems are available.

(i) What kind of software is an operating system?

(ii) Why operating system is important?

(iii) Name any three types of operating systems.

Ans. (i) An operating system is a type of system software. This means it's a program that controls the inner workings of the computer. It makes sure that the hardware (like the processor and memory) works together properly and allows other software (like games or word processors) to run.

(ii) The operating system is like the brain of the computer. It makes the computer work effectively and allows you to use it easily.

(iii) There are many different types of operating systems, each designed for a specific purpose. Here are a few examples:

- **Batch systems** These systems run programs one after the other, like a line of people waiting to use a machine.
- **Multiprogramming systems** These systems can run multiple programs at the same time, making the computer more efficient.
- **Real-time systems** These systems are used in situations where timing is critical, like in medical equipment or self-driving cars. They need to respond very quickly to events.

42. Reena got an assignment on the topic Word processing software. Help her to solve the assignment. **Competency Based Que.**

(i) What is Word processing software?

(ii) Which type of software is Word processor?

(iii) Give some examples equivalent to type of Word processing software.

Ans. (i) Word processing software is a type of computer program that allows you to create, edit, and format text documents. It makes writing and manipulating text easier and more efficient than using a typewriter.

(ii) Word processors belong to the category of application software. Application software is designed to perform specific tasks for users, such as creating documents, browsing the web, or editing images.

(iii) Here are some other examples of application software:

- Spreadsheets (like Excel)
- Presentation software (like PowerPoint)
- Image editing software (like Photoshop)
- Media players (like VLC)
- Web browsers (like Chrome)
- Email clients (like Outlook)

43. Name a software that can be used to display the information in the form of a slide show. Explain that software.

Ans. Presentation tool is the general-purpose application software which is used to display the information in the form of a slide show. Presentation is the practice of showing and explaining the content of a topic to audience or learner visually. A presentation tool involves graphics and animation packages.

It has three major functions

(i) An editor that allows text to be inserted or formatted.

(ii) A method for inserting and manipulating graphic images.

(iii) A slide-show system to display the content.

Presentation tool is used by users to create professional looking visual aids for an audience to make the information easily understandable.

For example, marketing managers use presentation tool to present new marketing strategies to their superiors, and students use it to create high quality class presentations.

Some of the examples of presentation tool include Microsoft PowerPoint, Corel presentations, Lotus Freelance Graphics etc.

44. What is an inventory control system name any two entities or tables that could be a part of this system?

Ans. An inventory control system is a crucial aspect of any business that deals with the management of goods. It's a structured approach to tracking and monitoring the movement of stock within a company. This includes everything from the moment goods are received to when they are sold or used in production

Key Functions of an Inventory Control System:

- **Keeps track of what you have** It tells you how much of each item is in your store at any given time.
- **Predicts what you'll need** It helps you guess how much of each item you'll need to sell in the future.
- **Orders more when needed** It helps you place orders to get more items when you're running low.
- **Manages your storage space** It helps you organize your storage area so that you can find things easily.
- **Tells you how much your inventory is worth** This is important for your business finances.
- **Helps prevent losses** It helps you keep track of any items that might be lost, stolen, or damaged.
- **Makes it easy to ship orders** It helps you quickly find and pack the items customers order.

Two Entities/Tables in an Inventory Control System are

- **Product List** This list has all the information about each item you sell, like its name, how it's measured (like "each" or "kilograms"), who you buy it from, how much it costs, and how much you sell it for.
- **Transaction Log** This keeps a record of every time something happens to your inventory, like when you receive a new shipment, sell an item, or find that something is missing.

These two parts work together to give you a clear picture of your inventory and help you make smart decisions about your business.

45. Explain system software in detail along with its types.

Ans. System software is a program that manages and supports the computer resources and operations of a computer system while it executes various tasks such as processing data and information, controlling hardware components, and allowing users to use application software, i.e., system software functions as a bridge between computer system hardware and the application software.

The system software is made up of many control programs, including the operating system. There are many kinds of computers these days. Some of them are easier to learn than others.

Some of them perform better than others. The system software contains those programs that control and support the computer system and its data processing applications. It includes

(i) **Operating System** An Operating System (OS), is a software program that enables the computer hardware to communicate and operate with the computer software. Without an operating system, a computer would be useless.

(ii) **Device Drivers** It ensure the proper functioning of hardware by acting as an interface between the device and the operating system.

(iii) **Utility Software** Software used for maintaining and configuring the computer system, such as disk defragmentation, antivirus and disk cleaner tools.

46. Differentiate between GUI and CUI.

Ans.

GUI (Graphical User Interface)	CUI (Character User Interface)
Uses graphical elements like icons, menus, and windows	Uses text-based commands and prompts
Generally easier to learn and use	Requires more technical knowledge and command-line syntax
More intuitive and user-friendly	Can be more efficient for experienced users
Often requires more system resources (CPU, memory)	Less resource-intensive
Offers more flexibility for customization	Less customization options
Can be slower due to graphical elements	Generally faster due to direct command execution
Less precise for complex tasks	More precise for specific tasks
Windows, macOS, Linux desktop environments	Command prompt, terminal, DOS

47. Discuss the features of electronic spreadsheets that make it useful?

Ans. (i) It provides facilities of cutting, pasting, moving, copying data values of formulae or formats etc.

(ii) Spreadsheets cannot represent only data values but their relationship also.

(iii) Data can be represented graphically.

(iv) The relationships between cells are called 'Formulae' and the names of the cells are called 'Labels'.

(v) Spreadsheet accepts data in a tabular form.

(vi) Numerous built-in functions are available in spreadsheets.

(vii) The user of the spreadsheet can make changes in any stored value and observe the effects on calculated values.

(viii) We can sort data to find individual data easily.

(ix) Spreadsheets replaced paper-based systems throughout the business world.

(x) Calculations such as net present value or standard deviation can be applied to tabular data with a pre-programmed function in a formula.

48. What is utility software, and what are some common types of utility software?

Ans. Utility software is a category of system software designed to optimize, maintain, and troubleshoot computer systems. These tools are essential for ensuring efficient and reliable computer operation.

Common types of utility software include:

(i) **Disk Compression Utilities** These tools reduce the size of files and directories on a hard drive, freeing up valuable storage space. By compressing data, these utilities can significantly increase the effective storage capacity of a drive.

(ii) **Backup Utilities** Backup utilities create copies of important data, protecting it from accidental deletion, hardware failures, or natural disasters. These tools allow users to restore files and entire systems to their previous state in case of data loss.

(iii) **Disk Defragmentation Utilities** Over time, file fragments can become scattered across a hard drive, leading to slower performance.
Disk defragmentation utilities reorganize these fragments, improving access times and overall system responsiveness.

(iv) **Virus Scanning and Removal Utilities** Antivirus software protects computers from malicious software, such as viruses, worms, and malware. These utilities scan files and systems for threats, remove infections, and provide real-time protection.

(v) **Data Recovery Utilities** Data recovery software can recover lost or deleted files from hard drives, USB drives, and other storage devices. These tools can be invaluable in recovering important data after accidental deletion or system failures.

Case Study Based Questions

Case Study 1

Software is the intangible set of instructions, data, and programs that tell a computer how to function. It acts as the brain of the computer, dictating its actions and guiding its operations. Unlike hardware, which refers to the physical components of a computer, software is a collection of digital instructions that enable the hardware to perform specific tasks.

There are two main types of software:

1. **System Software** This category forms the foundation for all computer operations. It includes core functions like operating systems (e.g., Windows, macOS, Android), disk management tools, utilities (e.g., antivirus software, disk defragmenters), and hardware management tools. System software acts as the intermediary between the user and the hardware, providing the essential services needed to run applications and manage resources.
2. **Application Software** As the name suggests, application software (often called apps) helps users accomplish specific tasks. This broad category encompasses a wide range of programs, including office productivity suites (e.g., Microsoft Office, Google Workspace), data management software (e.g., databases), media players (e.g., VLC Media Player), and security programs (e.g., firewalls). Applications also extend to the web and mobile world, with tools for shopping (e.g., Amazon), social networking (e.g., Facebook), and photo sharing (e.g., Instagram).

(i) What refers to the set of instructions that tell a computer how to function?

(a) Hardware
(b) Software
(c) Data
(d) User Interface

(ii) Which of the following is an example of application software?
(a) Operating System
(b) Word Processing Software (e.g., Microsoft Word)
(c) Device Drivers
(d) Memory Management Tools

(iii) What type of software provides core functions like managing files and memory?
(a) User Interface Software
(b) System Software
(c) Development Tools
(d) Entertainment Software

(iv) Which software acts as the intermediary between the user and the computer hardware?
(a) Software in general
(b) Application Software
(c) Hardware Drivers
(d) Programming Languages

(v) What program loads executable files into memory for execution?
(a) Compiler (b) Interpreter
(c) Linker (d) Loader

(vi) What software helps protect your computer from viruses and malware?
(a) Operating System (b) System Utilities
(c) Security Software (d) Productivity Tools

(vii) Which type of software allows users to create and edit digital images?
(a) Multimedia Software
(b) System Management Tools
(c) Communication Software
(d) Web Browsers

Ans. (i) (b) Software
(ii) (b) Word Processing Software (e.g., Microsoft Word)
(iii) (b) System Software
(iv) (a) Software in general
(v) (d) Loader
(vi) (c) Security Software
(vii) (a) Multimedia Software

Case Study 2

A User Interface (UI) serves as a bridge between a user and an application. It can be either a Graphical User Interface (GUI) or a Command Line Interface (CLI). GUIs utilize visual elements such as icons and menus, allowing users to interact with the application through a mouse or touchscreen. CLIs, on the other hand, rely on text-based commands entered by the user via a keyboard, providing feedback in the form of text output.

(i) Which of the following is an example of a GUI element?
(a) A text prompt in a terminal window
(b) A clickable icon on a desktop
(c) A command-line argument
(d) A machine code instruction

(ii) What is the primary difference between a GUI and a CLI?
(a) GUIs are faster, CLIs are slower
(b) GUIs are more complex, CLIs are simpler
(c) GUIs use visual elements, CLIs use text commands
(d) GUIs are newer, CLIs are older

(iii) Which of the following devices is essential for a GUI to function?
(a) Keyboard
(b) Mouse or touchpad
(c) Printer
(d) Scanner

(iv) What is the primary input method in a CLI?
(a) Voice commands (b) Keyboard
(c) Touchscreen (d) Mouse

(v) Which type of interface is typically used by system administrators and programmers?
(a) GUI (b) CLI
(c) Both (a) and (b) (d) Neither (a) nor (b)

(vi) A user interface that displays information and allows interaction through visual elements like icons and menus is called
(a) Command-line interface
(b) Graphical user interface
(c) Text-based interface
(d) None of the above

(vii) A user interface that relies on text commands to interact with a computer system is called:
(a) Graphical user interface
(b) Command-line interface
(c) Text-based interface
(d) None of the above

Ans. (i) (b) A clickable icon on a desktop
(ii) (c) GUIs use visual elements, CLIs use text commands
(iii) (b) Mouse or touchpad
(iv) (b) Keyboard
(v) (b) CLI
(vi) (b) Graphical user interface
(vii) (b) Command-line interface

Case Study 3

Operating system is a program that acts as an interface between the user and the hardware (i.e. for all computer resources). An operating system is an important component of a computer system, which controls and co-ordinates all other components of it. It activates all devices that make them ready for work. It also performs all internal management functions and ensures systematic functioning of a computer system.

The operating system performs the following functions:

- **It recognises input from keyboard and sends output to the display screen.**
- **It makes sure that the programs running simultaneously do not interfere with each other.**
- **It is also responsible for security and ensuring that unauthorised users cannot access the System e.g. MS-DOS, Windows 95, Windows XP, Windows Vista etc.**

Based on the above information, answer the following questions.

(i) What is the primary role of an operating system?

(a) To develop software applications

(b) To act as an interface between the user and hardware

(c) To provide internet access

(d) To create and edit documents

(ii) Which of the following is NOT a function of an operating system?

(a) Managing hardware resources

(b) Controlling and coordinating system components

(c) Developing new programming languages

(d) Ensuring security from unauthorized access

(iii) How does an operating system handle multiple programs running at the same time?

(a) By shutting down the computer

(b) By ensuring programs do not interfere with each other

(c) By deleting unnecessary programs

(d) By allowing only one program to run at a time

(iv) Which of the following is an example of an operating system?

(a) MS Word (b) Windows XP

(c) Google Chrome (d) Python

(v) What function of an OS ensures that unauthorized users cannot access the system?

(a) Memory management

(b) Device activation

(c) Security management

(d) File editing

Ans. (i) (b) To act as an interface between the user and hardware

(ii) (c) Developing new programming languages

(iii) (b) By ensuring programs do not interfere with each other

(iv) (b) Windows XP

(v) (c) Security management

Case Study 4

Software is a set of computer programs, procedures and associated documentation concerned with the operation of a data processing system. Software commonly known as programs, consists of all required instructions that tell the hardware how to perform a task. It is not basic requirement of a computer system, but it makes a computer more powerful and useful.

Software can be broadly classified into two major categories as follows:

1. System software 2. Application software

Based on the above information, answer the following questions.

(i) What is the term used to describe intangible instructions that tell the computer what to do?

(a) Hardware (b) Software

(c) Database (d) Network

(ii) What is software?

(a) A set of physical computer components

(b) A type of hardware device

(c) A collection of programs and procedures for operating a system

(d) A storage device for data

(iii) Which of the following are examples of software?

(a) CPU and RAM (b) MS Word and Windows

(c) Monitor and Keyboard

(d) Printer and Scanner

(iv) The primary purpose of software is to turn data into what?

(a) Hardware (b) Programs

(c) Information (d) Network

(v) A set of instructions that tell the computer how to perform a task is called?

(a) Algorithm (b) Software

(c) Database (d) Hardware

Ans. (i) (b) Software

(ii) (c) A collection of programs and procedures for operating a system

(iii) (b) MS Word and Windows

(iv) (c) Information (v) (b) Software

SELF ASSESSMENT TEST

Multiple Choice Questions

1. This type of software works with end-users, application software and computer hardware to handle the majority of technical details.

(a) Communications software (b) Application software
(c) Utility software (d) System software

2. It is the program that manages the hardware of the computer system including the CPU, memory storage devices and input/output devices.

(a) Software (b) Operating system
(c) Hardware (d) System software

3. The primary purpose of the Windows operating system is

(a) to make the most efficient use of the computer hardware
(b) to allow people to use the computer
(c) to keep systems programmer's employed
(d) to make computers easier to use

Fill in the Blanks

4. Since computers understand __________ language, human-written programs in high-level languages must be converted using translators.

5. __________ translate entire high-level language programs into machine code before execution, making them faster than interpreters.

6. High-level languages like C++, Java, and Python are __________ and require translators to convert code into machine language.

7. Integrated Development Environments (IDEs) like __________ simplify the coding process by offering text editors, build tools, and debuggers.

State Whether True or False

8. Device drivers are not necessary for a computer to recognize and use connected hardware like printers and keyboards.

9. Compression utilities reduce the size of files to make storage and transmission more efficient.

10. A disk defragmenter deletes unnecessary files from the system to free up storage space.

Assertion and Reason Based Questions

Assertion (A) and Reason (R) Type questions. Choose the correct option as

(a) Both Assertion (A) and Reason (R) are true, and Reason (R) is the correct explanation of Assertion (A).
(b) Both Assertion (A) and Reason (R) are true, but Reason (R) is not the correct explanation of Assertion (A).
(c) Assertion (A) is true, but Reason (R) is false.
(d) Assertion (A) is false, but Reason (R) is true.

11. Assertion (A) A Multi-Tasking Operating System allows multiple programs to run simultaneously by efficiently switching between tasks.

Reason (R) Multi-Tasking Operating Systems execute all processes at the same time using multiple CPUs.

12. Assertion (A) A Real-Time Operating System (RTOS) is used in time-critical applications like industrial control systems and medical devices.

Reason (R) A Real-Time Operating System (RTOS) ensures that every task gets executed within a specific time constraint.

Very Short Answer Type Questions

13. What is software? How softwares are classified?

14. Explain the term operating system?

15. What is language processor?

16. What is system software? How is it different form application software?

17. Which tool is used to reduce the size of data?

Short Answer Type Questions

18. Explain the need of operating system in computer.

19. Distinguish between single-task and multi-task operating system.

20. Distinguish between freeware and proprietary software.

21. Describe Windows and mobile operating system.

22. What do you mean by inventory management system?

Long Answer Type Questions

23. Explain disk management tools with its example.

24. Explain Word processor.

25. Briefly explain the hotel management system.

26. Explain the following terms
(i) BOSS (ii) Symbian
(iii) iOS

27. Describe the open source concepts in detail.

Case Study Based Questions

28. Rahul is a computer science student working on a school project. He needs to write and test a program in Python, but he also wants to ensure that his system is secure and optimized for smooth performance. To do this, he installs an Integrated Development Environment (IDE) for coding, an antivirus program for protection, and a disk cleaner to remove unnecessary files. Additionally, he learns about different types of software such as system software, application software, and utility software to understand their roles in a computer system.

Based on the above scenario, answer the following multiple-choice questions:

(i) **Which type of software does Rahul use to write and test his Python program?**
(a) System Software
(b) Utility Software
(c) Programming Software
(d) Application Software

(ii) **The antivirus software Rahul installs is an example of:**
(a) System Software (b) Utility Software
(c) Application Software (d) Firmware

(iii) **Rahul's disk cleaner helps remove unnecessary files to free up space. This software is classified as:**
(a) System Software
(b) Utility Software
(c) Application Software
(d) Real-Time Software

(iv) **Which of the following is an example of system software?**
(a) Microsoft Word
(b) Windows Operating System
(c) Photoshop
(d) VLC Media Player

(v) **Rahul wants to create a presentation for his project. Which type of software should he use?**
(a) System Software
(b) Programming Software
(c) Application Software
(d) Firmware

Answers

1. (d) 2. (b) 3. (a) 4. Machine
5. Compilers 6. human-readable
7. visual studio
8. False 9. True 10. False
11. (c) 12. (a)
28. (i) → (c), (ii) → (b), (iii) → (b), (iv) → (b), (v) → (c)

03

CHAPTER

A number system in a computer is a way of representing numbers using digits or symbols. Computers use number systems to store, process and transmit data.

YOUR STUDY GOALS

YOUR PRACTICE GOAL

- Objective Type Questions (37 Qs ; MCQs, True or False, Fill in the Blanks, Assertion and Reason)
- Subjective Type Questions (30 Qs ; VSA, SA, LA)
- Case Study Based Questions-2

Data Representation

Data representation refers to the methods used to represent information stored internal to a computer. Computers store lots of different types of information such as numbers, text, graphics, sound, video, etc. In digital system, all this data are represented by equivalent strings of symbols where each symbol called a **bit** (binary digit), either 0 or 1. The two main categories of the data used in digital computers are

(i) Numbers (ii) Alphanumeric characters

Numbers are represented by number system and alphanumeric characters are represented by character encoding in the computer system.

3.1 Number System

A set of values used to represent different quantities is known as **number system**. When we enter data into the computer, it translates them in binary numbers (*i.e.*, 0 and 1) as computer can understand only 0 or 1. A computer can understand **positional number system** where only a few symbols, called **digits,** represent different values depending on the position they occupy in the number.

A value of each digit in a number can be determined using

- The digit.
- The position of the digit in the number.
- The base or radix of the number systems (where base or radix is defined as the number of distinct digits available in the number system).

The most common positional number systems used are decimal, binary, octal and hexadecimal systems.

The decimal number system is used in general. However, the digital computers use binary number system. The octal and hexadecimal number systems are also used in the computer. These number systems are described below

1. Binary Number System

Computers use binary number system for counting and arithmetic operations. This number system has base 2 as it uses 2 digits 0 and 1. A string which have any combination of these two digits is called binary number. A binary number showing its base would be written as $(11001)_2$.

Bits Weighting in Binary Number

Binary numbers are written as sequence of bits. Each bit in a binary number carry a special weight. The number $(101101.10110)_2$ has been represented in the following figure

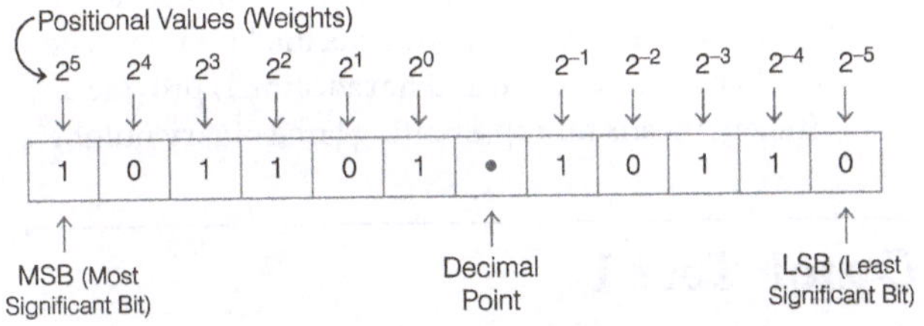

Positional values (weights) in binary number

- **Decimal Point** Any decimal fraction is also a string of the number (0 … 9), but with an embedded decimal point. The decimal point is used to separate the integer and fractional parts of the number.
- **Most Significant Digit (MSD)** The digit that has the maximum weight in the number, is called most significant digit. It is the leftmost digit in the number.
- **Least Significant Digit (LSD)** The digit that has the minimum weight in the number, is called least significant digit.

  It is the rightmost digit in the number. In general, any number is simply the sum of the products of each digit value and its weight (positional value).

2. Decimal Number System

The number system that we use in our day-to-day life is the decimal number system. It has base 10 as it uses 10 digits from 0 to 9 (*i.e.*, 0, 1, 2, 3, 4, 5, 6, 7, 8 and 9). Any decimal number is a string of any combination of these digits.

A decimal number showing its base would be written as

$$(257)_{10} \quad or \quad (257)_d$$

Where '10' and the small letter 'd' designate that it is a decimal number.

Digits Weighting in Decimal Number

The value of each digit of a decimal number depends on its relative position in the number. As it is a positional value system, where in each decimal digit has its own weight expressed as a power of 10.

In left before decimal point, this power increases in positive and in right (after decimal point), it increases in negative. The number $(967514.40032)_{10}$ has been represented in the following figure

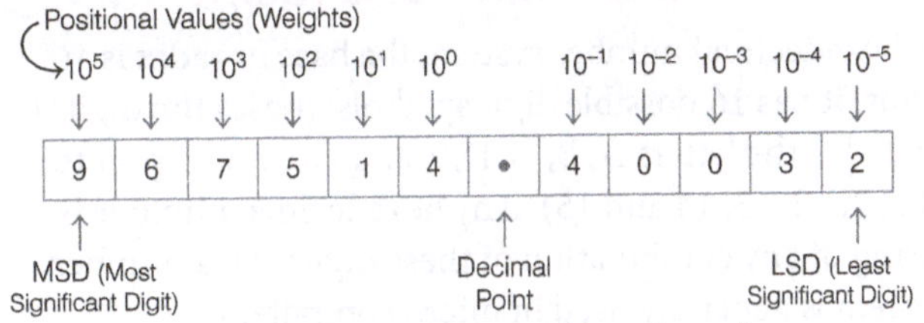

Positional values (weights) in decimal numbers

3. Octal Number System

The octal number system has a base of 8, as it uses 8 values 0, 1, 2, 3, 4, 5, 6 and 7. Thus each digit of an octal number can have any value from 0 to 7. Any octal number is a string of any combination of these digits.

An octal number showing its base would be written as $(2317)_8$.

Digits Weighting in Octal Number

The octal number system is a positional value system, where in each octal digit has its own weight expressed as a power of 8. The places to the left of the decimal point are positive powers of 8 and places to the right are negative powers of 8.

The number (613752.23657) has been represented in the following figure

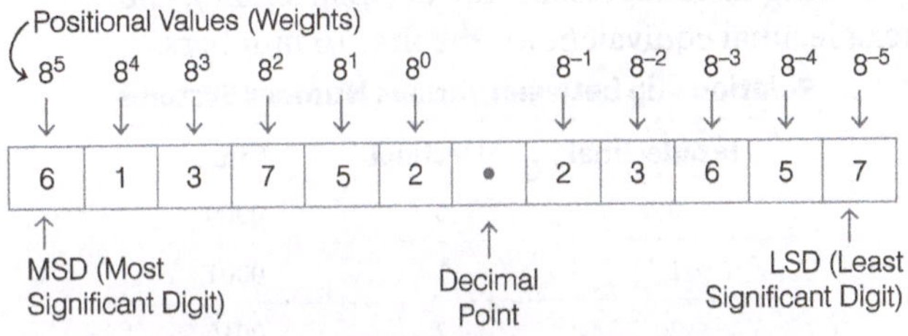

Positional values (weights) in octal numbers.

Following table represents the binary equivalent for the octal number.

Octal	Binary
0	000
1	001
2	010
3	011
4	100
5	101
6	110
7	111

4. Hexadecimal Number System

In hexadecimal number system, the base or radix is 16. Thus, it has 16 possible digit symbols. It uses the digits 0 to 9 plus the letters A, B, C, D, E and F (with respect to 10, 11, 12, 13, 14 and 15). Any hexadecimal number is a string of any combination of these digits. This number system is generally used in micro computers.

A hexadecimal number showing its base would be written as $(134BD)_{16}$.

Digits Weighting in Hexadecimal Number

Hexadecimal number system is also a positional value system, where in each hexadecimal digit has its own weight expressed as a power of 16.

The number (1B0982.A345F) has been represented in the following figure

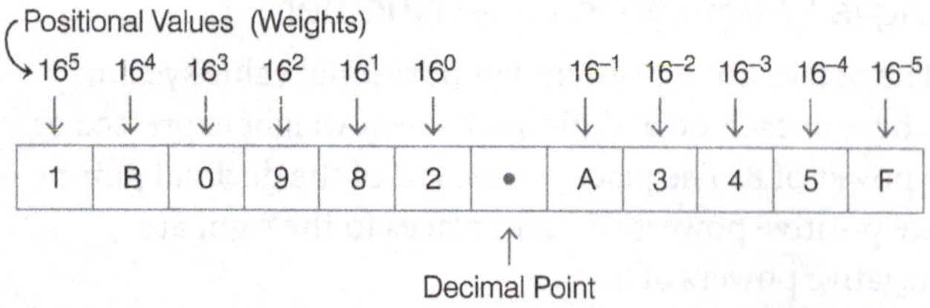

Positional values (weights) in a hexadecimal number

Following table represents the decimal, binary, and hexadecimal equivalent for the first 16 numbers.

Relationship between various Number Systems

Hexadecimal	Decimal	Binary
0	0	0000
1	1	0001
2	2	0010
3	3	0011
4	4	0100
5	5	0101
6	6	0110
7	7	0111
8	8	1000
9	9	1001
A	10	1010
B	11	1011
C	12	1100
D	13	1101
E	14	1110
F	15	1111

TEACHER TIP

We do not write the base on decimal numbers normally. If the base of any number is not displayed, the number is assumed to be a decimal number. The number systems (octal and hexadecimal) provide an efficient means for representing large binary numbers.

Quick Test 1

1. How many digits are there in the binary number system?
2. Which number system is used in daily life?
3. In which number system A is used in place of 10?
4. Briefly explain the binary number system?

3.2 Number System Conversion

Conversion of number systems is shown as follows

Binary to Decimal Conversion

Use the following steps to convert binary to decimal:

Step 1 Multiply all binary numbers by the power of 2.

Step 2 For integer, the power will be positive and for fraction, the power will be negative.

Step 3 Add all the multiplier numbers.

Example 1. $(1101.10)_2 = (?)_{10}$

Sol. $(1101.10)_2 = 1\times2^3+1\times2^2+0\times2^1+1\times2^0+1\times2^{-1}+0\times2^{-2}$

$= 8+4+0+1+0.5+0 = 13.5$

$\therefore \quad (1101.10)_2 = (13.5)_{10}$

Binary to Octal Conversion

Use the following steps to convert binary to octal:

Step 1 Create groups of three bits each from the right side of the given binary number.

Step 2 If required, zero digits can be added to the leftmost or rightmost side of the decimal point to complete the group of three bits.

Step 3 Then keep the octal digit value according to each group.

Example 2. $(1110111001.1000011)_2 = (?)_8$

Sol. To complete a group of three bits ↓ (leftmost) … To complete a group of three bits ↓ (rightmost)

001 110 111 001 . 100 001 100

1 6 7 1 . 4 1 4

$\therefore (1110111001.1000011)_2 = (1671.414)_8$

> ***Why 3 bits in a binary number are grouped together to get octal number?***
>
> The base value of octal number system is 8. Convert value 8 in terms of exponent of 2, i.e., $8 = 2^3$. Hence, three binary digits are sufficient to represent all 8 octal digits. Simply stated, count all possible combinations of three binary digits, which are $2 \times 2 \times 2 = 8$. Therefore, 3 bits are sufficient to represent any octal digit. Hence, 3-bit groups in a binary number are formed to get equivalent octal number.

Binary to Hexadecimal Conversion

Use the following steps to convert binary to hexadecimal

Step 1 Create groups of four bits each from the right side of the given binary number.

Step 2 If necessary, zero digits can be added to the leftmost or rightmost side of the decimal point to complete the group of four bits.

Step 3 Then keep the hexadecimal value according to each group.

Example 3. $(110011011101.10110011)_2 = (?)_{16}$

Sol.

1100	1101	1101	.	1011	0011
12 = C	13 = D	13 = D		11 = B	3

$\therefore (110011011101.10110011)_2 = (CDD.B3)_{16}$

> ***Why 4 bits in a binary number are grouped together to get hexadecimal number?***
>
> The base value of hexadecimal number system is 16. Write value 16 in terms of exponent of 2 i.e. $16 = 2^4$. Hence, four binary digits are sufficient to represent all 16 hexadecimal symbols.

Decimal to Binary Conversion

Use the following steps to convert decimal to binary

Step 1 To convert decimal to binary number, divide the decimal number by the base 2 of the binary number.

Step 2 The remainder obtained from this is written on the right side and the quotient obtained is again divided by 2. After that the same process is repeated.

Step 3 The process continues until the quotient becomes zero.

Step 4 The obtained remainders are written in the order from bottom to top. This remainder is the binary number equivalent to the given decimal number.

Example 4. $(43)_{10} \rightarrow (?)_2$

Sol.

		Remainder
2	43	1 → LSB
2	21	1
2	10	0
2	5	1
2	2	0
2	1	1 → MSB
	0	

(remainders read upward ↑)

$\therefore (43)_{10} \rightarrow (101011)_2$

Decimal to Octal Conversion

The method of converting an integer into octal is exactly the same as converting a decimal number into binary.

The only difference is that while to convert a decimal number to binary, we divide it repeatedly by 2, while to convert it to octal, we divide it repeatedly by 8.

The following steps should be used to convert decimal to octal.

Step 1 To convert a decimal number with decimal point to octal number, we multiply the decimal number by octal base 8.

Step 2 Write the obtained integer (1 or 0) on the right side and multiply the fraction by 8 again. After that the same process is repeated.

Step 3 The same process continues until either fraction remains 0 or the bits are filled to the desired locations.

Step 4 These integers are written in the order from top to bottom after the decimal point.

Example 5. $(423.03125)_{10} = (?)_8$

Sol. 423 ↓ Integer   0.03125 ↓ Fraction

Converting integer$(423)_{10}$ part to octal

$423 \div 8 = 52$ remainder 7

$52 \div 8 = 6$ remainder 4

$6 \div 8 = 0$ remainder 6 ↑

writing the remainders from bottom to top

$(423)_{10} = (647)_8$ ...(i)

and converting the fraction(0.03125) part to octal

$0.03125 \times 8 = 0.25$ integer 0

$0.25 \times 8 = 2.00$ integer 2 ↓

∴ $(0.03125)_{10} = (0.02)_8$ ...(ii)

By adding Eqs. (i) and (ii) we get

∴ $(423.03125)_{10} = (647.02)_8$

Decimal to Hexadecimal Conversion

The method of converting an integer from decimal to hexadecimal is exactly the same as converting a decimal number to binary. The only difference is that instead of 2, division is done repeatedly by 16.

Following steps should be used to convert decimal to hexadecimal.

Step 1 To convert a decimal number with decimal point to hexadecimal number, we multiply the decimal number by the base 16 of hexadecimal.

Step 2 Write the obtained integer (1 or 0) on the left side and write the fraction on the right side.
Let's multiply by 16 again. After that the same process is repeated.

Step 3 This process continues until either the fraction remains 0 or the bits are filled to the desired locations.

Step 4 These integers are written in the order from top to bottom after the decimal point.

Example 6. $(2863.225)_{10} = (?)_{16}$

Sol. 2863 (Integer)   0.225 (Fraction)

Conversion of integer part$(2863)_{10}$ to hexadecimal

$2863 \div 16 = 178$ remainder 15 = F

$178 \div 16 = 11$ remainder 2

$11 \div 16 = 0$ remainder 11 = B ↑

∴ $(2863)_{10} = (B2F)_{16}$ ...(i)

And conversion of fraction part$(0.225)_{10}$ to decimal

$0.225 \times 16 = 3.6$ integer 3

$0.6 \times 16 = 9.6$ integer 9 ↓

∴ $(0.225)_{10} = (0.39)_{16}$ ...(ii)

By adding Eqs. (i) and (ii), we get

∴ $(2863.225)_{10} = (B2F.39)_{16}$

Octal to Binary Conversion

The conversion of octal to binary is extremely simple. In place of each octal digit, its equivalent binary group of three bits is written.

Example 7. $(325.614)_8 = (?)_2$

Sol.

3	2	5	.	6	1	4
011	010	101		110	001	100

∴ $(325.614)_8 = (011010101.110001100)_2$

Octal to Decimal Conversion

Use the following steps to convert octal to decimal.

Step 1 Multiply each digit of the octal number by a power of 8.

Step 2 These powers will be positive for the integer part and the negative for the fractional part.

Step 3 Add all the digits.

Example 8. $(327.4)_8 \longrightarrow (?)_{10}$

Sol. $(327.4)_8 = 3\times8^2 + 2\times8^1 + 7\times8^0 + 4\times8^{-1}$

$= 3\times64 + 2\times8 + 7\times1 + 4/8$

$= 192 + 16 + 7 + 0.5$

$= 215.5$

∴ $(327.4)_8 \longrightarrow (215.5)_{10}$

Octal to Hexadecimal conversion

Use the following steps to Convert an Octal Number to a Hexadecimal Number

Step 1 Replace each octal digit with its equivalent 3-bit binary representation.

Step 2 Start grouping from the right. Add leading zeros if necessary to complete a group.

Step 3 Replace each 4-bit binary group with its corresponding hexadecimal value.

Example 9. $(756)_8 = (?)_{16}$

Sol. Convert Octal to Binary $(756)_8 = (111\ 101\ 110)_2$

111 101 110 → 0001 1110 1110 (Adding leading zeros)

0001	1110	1110
1	14=E	14=E

So, $(756)_8 = (1EE)_{16}$

Hexadecimal to Binary Conversion

Converting hexadecimal to binary is extremely simple. In this, in place of each hexadecimal value, its equivalent binary group of four bits is written.

Example 10. $(D7A)_{16} = (?)_2$

Sol. D = 13 7 A = 10

1101 0111 1010

or $(D7A)_{16} = (110101111010)_2$

Hexadecimal to Decimal Conversion

Use the following steps to convert hexadecimal to decimal.

Step 1 Multiply each digit of hexadecimal by a power of 16.

Step 2 These powers will be positive for the integer part and negative for the fractional part.

Step 3 Add all the multiplier digits.

Example 11. $(BC9.8)_{16} \longrightarrow (?)_{10}$

Sol. $(BC9.8)_{16} = B\times16^2+C\times16^1+9\times16^0+8\times16^{-1}$

$=11\times256+12\times16+9\times1+8/16$

$=2816+192+9+0.5=3017.5$

$\therefore$ $(BC9.8)_{16} \longrightarrow (3017.5)_{10}$

Hexadecimal to Octal Conversion

To convert a hexadecimal number to its octal equivalent, you can follow these two steps:

Step 1 Hexadecimal to Decimal

- Expand the hexadecimal number using powers of 16.
- Multiply each hexadecimal digit by its corresponding power of 16.
- Add the results to get the decimal equivalent.

Step 2 Decimal to Octal

- Repeatedly divide the decimal number by 8, noting the remainders.
- Read the remainders in reverse order to get the octal equivalent.

Example 12. $(A7C)_{16} = (?)_8$

Sol. ***Step 1*** Hexadecimal to Decimal

$(A7C)_{16} = A\times16^2+7\times16^1+C\times16^0$

$=10\times256+7\times16+12\times1$

$=2560+112+12=2684$

So, $(A7C)_{16}$ is equivalent to $(2684)_{10}$.

Step 2 Decimal to Octal

$2684 \div 8 = 335$ remainder 4

$335 \div 8 = 41$ remainder 7

$41 \div 8 = 5$ remainder 1

$5 \div 8 = 0$ remainder 5

Reading remainders upwards $(5174)_8$

Therefore, $(A7C)_{16} = (5174)_8$

Mistake Alert

When converting between number systems (Binary, Decimal, Octal, Hexadecimal), students often make mistakes that lead to incorrect answers. e.g.

- Incorrectly assigning place values when converting.
- Misinterpreting hex values.
- Wrong bit grouping when converting.
- Skipping valid digits due to leading zeros.
- Misplacing powers of -2, -3, etc.

Quick Test 2

1. Convert the following decimal numbers in the form understood by computer. **NCERT**
   (i) $(593)_{10}$ (ii) $(326)_{10}$ (iii) $(79)_{10}$
2. Express the following decimal numbers into octal numbers. **NCERT**
   (i) $(913)_{10}$ (ii) $(845)_{10}$ (iii) $(66)_{10}$
3. Convert the following numbers into decimal numbers.
   (i) $(110101)_2$ (ii) $(1703)_8$ (iii) $(C0F5)_{16}$ **NCERT**
4. While converting the fractional part of a decimal number to another number system, why do we write the integer part from top to bottom and not other way? **NCERT**
5. Write binary representation of the following numbers.
   (i) $(F018)_{16}$ (ii) $(172)_{16}$ (iii) $(613)_8$ **NCERT**

3.3 Encoding of Characters

All digital computers also stored alphanumeric characters which includes the english alphabet, the decimal numbers, and special characters. Each one of these letters need a unique binary code to represent.

These codes are called **alphanumeric codes** (or **computer codes**).

Some of the main computer codes are described below

1. ASCII Code

ASCII is acronym for the **American Standard Code for Information Interchange.** ASCII is a code for representing english alphabets, decimal numbers or special characters with a 7-bit binary number.

ASCII has been adopted by several American computer manufacturers as their computers internal code. This code is popular in data communications, is used almost exclusively to represent data internally in microcomputers, and is frequently found in the larger computers produced by some vendors.

ASCII is a 7-bit code. So, it is usually referred as ASCII-7. It allows 128 (2^7) code groups. The extended version of ASCII-7 is ASCII-8, which is an 8-bit code that allows 256 (2^8) code groups rather than 128.

The following table shows a partial listing of the ASCII-7 code. In addition to the binary code group for each character, the table gives the decimal, octal and hexadecimal equivalents.

Character	7-bit ASCII	Decimal	Octal	Hexadecimal
A	1000001	065	101	41
B	1000010	066	102	42
C	1000011	067	103	43
D	1000100	068	104	44
E	1000101	069	105	45
F	1000110	070	106	46
G	1000111	071	107	47
H	1001000	072	110	48
I	1001001	073	111	49
J	1001010	074	112	4A
K	1001011	075	113	4B
L	1001100	076	114	4C
M	1001101	077	115	4D
N	1001110	078	116	4E
O	1001111	079	117	4F
P	1010000	080	120	50
Q	1010001	081	121	51
R	1010010	082	122	52
S	1010011	083	123	53
T	1010100	084	124	54
U	1010101	085	125	55

Character	7-bit ASCII	Decimal	Octal	Hexadecimal
V	1010110	086	126	56
W	1010111	087	127	57
X	1011000	088	130	58
Y	1011001	089	131	59
Z	1011010	090	132	5A
0	0110000	048	060	30
1	0110001	049	061	31
2	0110010	050	062	32
3	0110011	051	063	33
4	0110100	052	064	34
5	0110101	053	065	35
6	0110110	054	066	36
7	0110111	055	067	37
8	0111000	056	070	38
9	0111001	057	071	39
blank	0100000	032	040	20
!	0100001	033	041	21
“	0100010	034	042	22
#	0100011	035	043	23
$	0100100	036	044	24
%	0100101	037	045	25
&	0100110	038	046	26
'	0100111	039	047	27
(	0101000	040	050	28
)	0101001	041	051	29
*	0101010	042	052	2A
+	0101011	043	053	2B
,	0101100	044	054	2C
—	0101101	045	055	2D
.	0101110	046	056	2E
/	0101111	047	057	2F
:	0111010	058	072	3A
;	0111011	059	073	3B
<	0111100	060	074	3C
=	0111101	061	075	3D
>	0111110	062	076	3E
?	0111111	063	077	3F
@	0100000	064	100	40
[	1011011	091	133	5B
\	1011100	092	134	5C
]	1011101	093	135	5D

Example 13. The following codes are given in ASCII format. Encode them in general form.

1001000 1000101 1001100 1001111 1010111

Sol. Convert these codes to their hexadecimal equivalents.

1001000 = 48, 1000101 = 45
1001100 = 4C, 1001111 = 4F
1010111 = 57

Now, locate their values in table.

48 = H, 45 = E, 4C = L, 4F = O, 57 = W

So, the actual value is HELOW.

2. ISCII Code

ISCII stands for **Indian Script Code for Information Interchange**. It is used for Indian languages. ISCII has been created by the Indian Standards Organisation (ISO). This is an eight bit code capable of coding 256 characters.

ISCII code retains all ASCII characters and offers coding for Indian scripts also. The ISCII code standard allows English and Indian script alphabets to be used simultaneously. It shall not be used in incompatible environments like that of IBM-PC, and with computers which do not allow 8-bit characters or which do not follow ISO code extension technique.

The following table shows the 8-bit ISCII code for the Indian script alphabets

		A	B	C	D	E	F
Hex	Dec	160	176	192	208	224	240
0	0		ओ	ढ	ऱ	◌े	EXT
1	1	◌ँ	औ	ण	ल	◌ै	१
2	2	◌ं	ऑ	त	ळ	◌ै	२
3	3	◌ः	क	थ	ऴ	◌ॅ	३
4	4	अ	ख	द	व	◌ा	४
5	5	आ	ग	ध	श	◌ो	५
6	6	इ	घ	न	ष	◌ौ	६
7	7	ई	ङ	ऩ	स	◌ॉ	७
8	8	उ	च	प	ह	◌्	८
9	9	ऊ	छ	फ	INV	◌़	९
A	10	ऋ	ज	ब	◌ा	।	
B	11	ऐ	झ	भ	ि◌		
C	12	ए	ञ	म	◌ी		
D	13	ऐ	ट	य	◌ु		
E	14	ऍ	ठ	य़	◌ू		
F	15	ओ	ड	र	◌ृ	ATR	

3. Unicode

Unicode is a computing standard for the consistent encoding, representation and handling of text expressed in most of the world's writing systems. It is a fully international alphanumeric code which can represent all the characters found in human languages. It can represents Katakana, Cyrillic, Latin, Green, Arabic, Hebrew, Hangul and many more character.

Unicode uses a 16 bit encoding that provides code point for more than 65000 characters (65536). Unicode standard assigns each character a unique numeric value and name.

Unicode is required by modern standards such as XML, Java, JavaScript, etc. It is supported by many operating systems, all modern browsers, and many other products.

The following table shows the Unicode for some character

Char	Code	Char	Code	Char	Code	Char	Code
	160	¡	161	¢	162	£	163
¤	164	¥	165	¦	166	§	167
¨	168	©	169		170	«	171
¬	172		173	•	174	¯	175
°	176	±	177	2	178	3	179
´	180	µ	181	¶	182	·	183
¸	184	1	185	º	186	»	187
¼	188	½	189	¾	190	¿	191
À	192	-	193	Â	194	Ã	195
Ä	196	Å	197	Æ	198	Ç	199
È	200	É	201	Ê	202	Ë	203
Ì	204	Í	205	Î	206	Ï	207
Ð	208	Ñ	209	Ò	210	Ó	211
Ô	212	Õ	213	Ö	214	××	215
Ø	216	Ù	217	Ú	218	Û	219
Ü	220	Ý	221	Þ	222	β	223
à	224	á	225	â	226	ã	227
ä	228	å	229	æ	230	ç	231
è	232	é	233	ê	234	ë	235
ì	236	í	237	î	238	ï	239
ð	240	ñ	241	ò	242	ó	243
ô	244	õ	245	ö	246	÷	247
ø	248	ù	249	ú	250	û	251
ü	252	ý	253	Þ	254	ÿ	255

Significance of Unicode

Unicode provides a unique number for every character, no matter what the platform, what the program and what the language. The importance of unicode are given below

- Incorporating unicode into client-server or multi-tiered applications and websites offers significant cost savings over the use of legacy character sets.
- Unicode enables a single software product or a single website to be targeted across multiple platforms, languages and countries without re-engineering. It allows data to be transported through many different systems without corruption.
- Unicode is required by modern standards such as XML, Java, JavaScript, etc. It is supported in many operating systems, all modern browsers, and many other product.

Unicode Encoding Scheme

The encoding scheme distributes a unicode code value's bit pattern across 1,2,3, or even 4 bytes. This encoding is a multi-byte encoding scheme.

Unicode encoding can be used to encode a character from any language in the world. Unicode encoding encompasses several encoding scheme

UTF-8

8-bit Unicode Transformation Format is a method for encoding unicode characters using 8-bit sequence. In this encoding, every code point from 0-127 is stored in a single byte. UTF-8 encoding is a variable sized encoding scheme to represent unicode code points in memory.

Variable size encoding means the code point are represented using 1,2,3 or 4 bytes depending on their size.

The following table shows the structure of the encoding.

Number of bytes	Bits for code point	First code point	Last code point	Byte 1	Byte 2	Byte 3	Byte 4
1	7	U+0000	U+007F	0xxxxxxx			
2	11	U+0080	U+07FF	110xxxxx	10xxxxxx		
3	16	U+0800	U+FFFF	1110xxxx	10xxxxxx	10xxxxxx	
4	21	U+10000	U+10FFFF	11110xxx	10xxxxxx	10xxxxxx	10xxxxxx

- A **1 byte encoding** is identified by the presence of 0 in the first bit

  0 XXXXXXX
  ↓
  First zero bit indicates 1 byte encoding

  For example, The english alphabet A has unicode code point U+0041 its, binary representation is 1000001. A is represented in UTF-8 encoding as 01000001.

- **2-byte encoding** is identified by the presence of the bit sequence 110 in the first byte and 10 in the second byte.

  110XXXXX 10XXXXXX

  For example, The letter a′ has unicode code point value U+00E1, or 225 in decimal. 225 in binary is 11100001. a′ is represented in UTF-8 encoding as 11000011 10100001.

- **3-byte encoding** is identified by the presence of the bit sequence 1110 in the first byte and 10 in the second and third bytes.

  For example, The latin character õ with code point value U+1E4D is represented using 3 byte encoding as it is larger than the maximum value that can be represented using 2-byte encoding. The binary value for the code point is 1111001001101. õ is represented in UTF-8 encoding as 11100001 10111001 10001101.

- **4-byte encoding** is identified by the presence of 11110 in the first byte and 10 in the subsequent second, third and fourth bytes.

  For example, The emoji 11 has unicode code point U+1F62D. The binary representation of this code point is 11111011000101101. Emoji 11 is represented in UTF-8 encoding as 11110000 10011111 10011000 10101101.

UTF-16

UTF-16 (16-bit Unicode Transformation Format) is a standard method of encoding unicode character data. UTF-16 has the capacity to encode all currently defined unicode characters.

It encodes characters into specific binary sequences using either one or two 16-bit sequences. UTF-16 encoding is a variable byte encoding scheme which used either 2 bytes or 4 bytes to represent unicode code points. Most of the characters for all modern languages are represented using 2-bytes.

For example, The latin alphabet ñ with code point U+00F1 and with binary value 11110001 is represented in UTF-16 encoding as 0000000011110001.

UTF-32

It is a fixed-length encoding, in contrast to all other unicode transformation formats, which are variable length encodings.

Each 32-bit value in UTF-32 represents one unicode code point and is exactly equal to that code points numerical value. UTF-32 uses 4 bytes to represent all code points.

For example, The English alphabet A has unicode code point value U+0041. It's binary representation is 1000001.

It is represented in UTF-32 encoding as 0000000000000000 0000000001000001.

Quick Test 3

1. Do we need to install some additional tool or font to type in an Indian language using UNICODE? **NCERT**
2. Explore and list down two font names for typing in any three Indian languages in UNICODE. **NCERT**
3. Why a character in UTF 32 takes more space than in UTF 16 or UTF 8? **NCERT**
4. Explain the concept of variable-length encoding in UTF-8.

NCERT Folder

1. Write base values of binary, octal, and hexadecimal number systems.

Ans. **Binary** Base 2 (uses digits 0 and 1)

Octal Base 8 (uses digits 0-7)

Hexadecimal Base 16 (uses digits 0-9 and letters A-F)

2. Give the full form of ASCII and ISCII.

Ans. **ASCII** American Standard Code for Information Interchange

ISCII Indian Standard Code for Information Interchange

3. Try the following conversions:

(i) $(514)_8 = (?)_{10}$ **(ii)** $(220)_8 = (?)_2$

(iii) $(76F)_{16} = (?)_{10}$ **(iv)** $(4D9)_{16} = (?)_{10}$

(v) $(11001010)_2 = (?)_{10}$

(vi) $(1010111)_2 = (?)_{10}$

Sol. (i) $(514)_8 = (5\times8^2)+(1\times8^1)+(4\times8^0) = 332$

(ii) $(220)_8 = (10010000)_2$

(iii) $(76F)_{16} = (7\times16^2)+(6\times16^1)+(15\times16^0) = (1903)_{10}$

(iv) $(4D9)_{16} = (4\times16^2)+(13\times16^1)+(9\times16^0) = (1241)_{10}$

(v) $(11001010)_2 = (1\times2^7)+(1\times2^6)+(0\times2^5)+(0\times2^4)+(1\times2^3)+(0\times2^2)+(1\times2^1)+(0\times2^0) = (202)_{10}$

(vi) $(1010111)_2 = (1\times2^6)+(0\times2^5)+(1\times2^4)+(0\times2^3)+(1\times2^2)+(1\times2^1)+(1\times2^0) = (87)_{10}$

4. Do the following conversions from decimal numbers to other number systems.

(i) $(54)_{10} = (?)_2$ **(ii)** $(120)_{10} = (?)_2$

(iii) $(76)_{10} = (?)_8$ **(iv)** $(889)_{10} = (?)_8$

(v) $(789)_{10} = (?)_{16}$ **(vi)** $(108)_{10} = (?)_{16}$

Sol. (i) $(54)_{10} = (110110)_2$ (ii) $(120)_{10} = (1111000)_2$

(iii) $(76)_{10} = (114)_8$ (iv) $(889)_{10} = (1571)_8$

(v) $(789)_{10} = (315)_{16}$ (vi) $(108)_{10} = (6C)_{16}$

5. Express the following octal numbers into their equivalent decimal numbers:

(i) 145 (ii) 6760 (iii) 455 (iv) 10.75

Sol. (i) $145 = (1\times8^2)+(4\times8^1)+(5\times8^0) = 101$

(ii) $6760 = (6\times8^3)+(7\times8^2)+(6\times8^1)+(0\times8^0) = 3568$

(iii) $455 = (4\times8^2)+(5\times8^1)+(5\times8^0) = 301$

(iv) $10.75 = (1\times8^1)+(0\times8^0)+(7\times8^{-1})+(5\times8^{-2}) = 8.953125$

6. Express the following decimal numbers into hexadecimal numbers:

(i) 548 (ii) 4052 (iii) 58 (iv) 100.25

Ans. (i)

Divisor	Number	Remainders
16	548	4 ↑
16	34	2
16	2	2
	0	

$(548)_{10} = (224)_{16}$

(ii)

Divisor	Number	Remainders
16	4052	4 ↑
16	253	D
16	15	F
	0	

$(4052)_{10} = (FD4)_{16}$

(iii)

Divisor	Number	Remainders
16	58	A ↑
16	3	3
	0	

$(58)_{10} = (3A)_{16}$

(iv) We convert the whole number and fractional parts separately and then combine the results.

The whole number part of 100.25 is 100. Divide this number repeatedly by 16 until the quotient becomes 0.

Divisor	Number	Remainders
16	100	4 ↑
16	6	6
	0	

The fractional part of 100.25 is 0.25. Multiply the fractional part repeatedly by 16 until it becomes 0.

$0.25\times16 = 4.00$

From top to bottom, write the integer parts of the results to the fractional part of the number in base 16.

$(0.25)_{10} = (0.4)_{16}$

Combine the whole number and fractional parts to obtain the overall result.

$(100.25)_{10} = (64)_{16} + (0.4)_{16} = (64.4)_{16}$

7. Express the following hexadecimal numbers into equivalent decimal numbers.

(i) 4A2 (ii) 9E1A (iii) 6BD (iv) 6C.34

Ans. (i) $(4A2)_{16} = (4\times16^2)+(10\times16^1)+(2\times16^0) = (1186)_{10}$

(ii) $(9E1A)_{16} = (9\times16^3)+(14\times16^2)+(1\times16^1) + (10\times16^0) = (40474)_{10}$

(iii) $(6BD)_{16} = (6\times16^2)+(11\times16^1)+(13\times16^0) = (1725)_{10}$

(iv) $(6C.34)_{16} = (6\times16^1)+(12\times16^0) + (3\times16^{-1})+(4\times16^{-2}) = (108.203125)_{10}$

8. Convert the following binary numbers into octal and hexadecimal numbers.

(i) 1110001000 (ii) 110110101
(iii) 1010100 (iv) 1010.1001

Ans. (i) $(1110001000)_2 = (1610)_8 = (388)_{16}$

(ii) $(110110101)_2 = (665)_8 = (1B5)_{16}$

(iii) $(1010100)_2 = (124)_8 = (54)_{16}$

(iv) $(1010.1001)_2 = (12.44)_8 = (A.9)_{16}$

9. Write binary equivalent of the following octal numbers.

(i) 2306 (ii) 5610 (iii) 742 (iv) 65.203

Ans. (i) 2306 = 10011000110
(ii) 5610 = 101110001000
(iii) 742 = 111100010
(iv) 65.203 = 110101.010000011

10. Write binary representation of the following hexadecimal numbers.

(i) 4026 (ii) BCA1 (iii) 98E (iv) 132.45

Ans. (i) 4026 = 100000000100110
(ii) BCA1 = 1011110010100001
(iii) 98E= 100110001110
(iv) 132.45 = 100110010.01000101

11. How does the computer understand the following text? Hint: 7-bit ASCII code

(i) HOTS (ii) Main (iii) CaSe

(Computer understands the following text by 7-bit ASCII code)

Ans. (i) **HOTS** Each letter in "HOTS" is represented by its 7-bit ASCII code. For example, "H" is 1001000, "O" is 1001111, "T" is 1010100, and "S" is 1010011.

(ii) **Main** Similarly, each letter in "Main" is represented by its 7-bit ASCII code.

(iii) **CaSe** Each letter in "CaSe" is represented by its 7-bit ASCII code.

12. The hexadecimal number system uses 16 literals (0-9, A-F). Write down its base value.

Ans. The base value of the hexadecimal number system is 16.

13. Let X be a number system having B symbols only. Write down the base value of this number system.

Ans. The base value of this number system is B.

14. Write the equivalent hexadecimal and binary values for each character of the phrase given below.

"हम सब एक"

Ans. The hexadecimal and binary codes for each letter in the phrase are listed below:

Symbol	Hexadecimal	Binary Code
ह	0939	100100111001
म	092E	100100101110
स	0938	100100111000
ब	092C	100100101100
ए	090F	100100001111
क	0915	100100010101

15. What is the advantage of preparing a digital content in Indian language using UNICODE font?

Ans. The advantages are as follow:

- Unicode allows for the representation of a wide range of characters from different languages, including Indian languages.
- Digital content prepared in Indian languages using Unicode fonts can be displayed and understood correctly across various devices and platforms.

16. Explore and list the steps required to type in an Indian language using UNICODE.

Ans. 1. **Install a Unicode font** Ensure you have a font installed on your device that supports the Indian language you want to type in.

2. **Enable Unicode input** Activate the Unicode input method in your operating system or software.

3. **Type the characters** Use the keyboard shortcuts or input methods provided by your system to type the desired Indian language characters.

17. Encode the word 'COMPUTER' using ASCII and convert the encode value into binary values.

Ans. C = 67 = 01000011
O = 79 = 01001111
M = 77 = 01001101
P = 80 = 01010000
U = 85 = 01010101
T = 84 = 01010100
E = 69 = 01000101
R = 82 = 01010010

Mind Map

DATA REPRESENTATION

Number System Conversion

Binary to Other Number Systems

Binary to Decimal

Multiply each binary digit by 2^n (where n is the position from right, starting at 0) and sum the results.

Binary to Octal

Group binary digits in sets of three (from right) and convert each group to its octal equivalent.

Binary to Hexadecimal

Group binary digits in sets of four (from right) and convert each group to its hexadecimal equivalent.

Octal to Other Number Systems:

Octal to Binary

Convert each octal digit into its 3-bit binary equivalent.

Octal to Decimal

Multiply each octal digit by 8^n (where n is the position from right, starting at 0) and sum the results.

Octal to Hexadecimal

- First, convert octal to binary.
- Group binary digits into 4-bit sections (from right) and convert to hexadecimal.

Hexadecimal to Other Number Systems

Hexadecimal to Binary

Convert each hex digit into its 4-bit binary equivalent.

Hexadecimal to Decimal

Multiply each hex digit by 16^n (where n is the position from right, starting at 0).

Hexadecimal to Octal

-First, convert hex to binary.

-Then, group the binary digits into sets of three (from right) and convert each group to octal.

Number System

Decimal Number System

It has base 10 as it uses 10 digits from 0 to 9 (0, 1, 2, 3, 4, 5, 6, 7, 8 and 9).

A decimal number showing its base would be written as $(257)_{10}$ or $(257)_d$

Binary Number System

It has base 2 as it uses 2 digits 0 and 1.

A binary number showing its base would be written as $(11001)_2$.

Octal Number System

It has a base of 8, as it uses 8 values 0, 1, 2, 3, 4, 5, 6 and 7. An octal number showing its base would be written as $(2317)_8$.

Hexadecimal Number System

It has 16 possible digit symbols. It uses the digits 0 to 9 plus the letters A, B, C, D, E and F (with respect to 10, 11, 12, 13, 14 and 15).

A hexadecimal number showing its base would be written as $(134BD)_{16}$.

Note

- *The point which is used to separate the integer and fractional part of the number, is called* ***decimal point.***
- *The leftmost bit carries the largest weight and hence, is called the* ***most significant bit.***
- *The rightmost bit carries the smallest weight and hence, is called the* ***least significant bit.***

Encoding of Characters

ASCII Code

ASCII (American Standard Code for Information Interchange) is a code for representing english alphabets, decimal numbers or special characters with a 7-bit binary number.

ISCII Code

ISCII (Indian Script Code for Information Interchange) used for Indian languages. ISCII has been created by the Indian Standards Organisation (ISO). This is an eight bit code capable of coding 256 characters.

Unicode

Unicode is a computing standard for the consistent encoding, representation and handling of text expressed in most of the world's writing systems. It is required by modern standards such as XML, Java, JavaScript, etc. **Unicode Encoding Scheme:** 8-bit, 16-bit, 32-bit

EXAM PATTERN QUESTIONS

Objective Type Questions

Multiple Choice Questions

1. In binary language, each letter of the alphabet, each number and each special character is made up of a unique combination of

(a) 8 bytes (b) 8 KB
(c) 8 characters (d) 8 bits

2. To perform calculation on stored data, computer uses ………… number system.

(a) decimal (b) hexadecimal
(c) octal (d) binary

3. The octal system

(a) needs less digits to represent a number than in the binary system
(b) needs more digits to represent a number than in the binary system
(c) needs the same number of digits to represent a number as in the binary system
(d) needs the same number of digits to represent a number as in the decimal system

4. A hexadecimal can be represented by

(a) three binary bits (b) four binary bits
(c) six binary bits (d) eight binary bits

5. Conversion of octal number $(540)_8$ to binary number is

(a) $(101100000)_2$ (b) $(100110000)_2$
(c) $(101010000)_2$ (d) $(101100100)_2$

6. Conversion of octal number $(352.56)_8$ to binary number is

(a) $(011101010.101110)_2$
(b) $(011010101.101110)_2$
(c) $(011101010.101010)_2$
(d) $(011010110.101110)_2$

7. Conversion of binary number $(101110)_2$ to hexadecimal is

(a) $(35)_{16}$ (b) $(46)_{16}$
(c) $(2E)_{16}$ (d) $(50)_{16}$

8. Conversion of Decimal number $(947568)_{10}$ to hexadecimal is

(a) $(C75E0)_{16}$ (b) $(E7570)_{16}$
(c) $(E7870)_{16}$ (d) $(D7570)_{16}$

9. The most widely used code that represents each character as a unique 8-bit code is

(a) ASCII (b) UNICODE
(c) BCD (d) EBCDIC

10. What is the primary purpose of UNICODE?

(a) To encrypt data for security
(b) To provide a unique code for every character across all languages
(c) To compress text files efficiently
(d) To convert numbers into text

11. Which of the following is a commonly used UNICODE encoding format?

(a) ASCII (b) UTF-8
(c) Binary Coded Decimal (d) Base-64

12. What is the decimal equivalent of the octal number $(321)_8$?

(a) 177 (b) 209
(c) 171 (d) 251

13. What is the smallest unit of data in a computer?

(a) Byte (b) Bit
(c) Nibble (d) Word

14. Which encoding scheme is a superset of ASCII and includes characters from all languages?

(a) UTF-8 (b) EBCDIC
(c) BCD (d) Morse Code

Fill in the Blanks

15. A set of values used to represent different quantities is called .....

16. The decimal equivalent of $(E)_{16}$ is ......

17. LSB stands for ...... Significant Digit.

18. The value of radix in hexadecimal number system is......

19. ISCII has .... possible code groups.

20. ASCII is used in most ....

21. ASCII is a ..... bit code while ISCII is a ...... bit code.

22. …… scheme is a predefined way of converting information character by character in a machine intelligible code.

State Whether True or False

23. A single binary digit is abbreviated as byte.

24. MSB stands for Mathematically Significant Digit.

25. Binary number system is a positional number system.

26. Octal is sometimes abbreviated as O.

27. Each alphabet or digit has its unique binary code.

28. ASCII stands for Asian Standard Code for Information Interchange.

29. Code space refers to all the codes that an encoding scheme uses.

30. Unicode code points are written as <code point number> + U.

31. The symbols have similar binary codes.

Assertion and Reason Based Questions

Assertion (A) and Reason (R) Type questions. Choose the correct option as:

(a) Both Assertion (A) and Reason (R) are true, and Reason (R) is the correct explanation of Assertion (A).

(b) Both Assertion (A) and Reason (R) are true, but Reason (R) is not the correct explanation of Assertion (A).

(c) Assertion (A) is true, but Reason (R) is false.

(d) Assertion (A) is false, but Reason (R) is true.

32. Assertion (A) Binary number system uses only two digits, 0 and 1.

Reason (R) Binary number system is the foundation of digital computers.

33. Assertion (A) ASCII is a character encoding standard that uses 7 bits to represent characters.

Reason (R) ASCII can represent characters from various languages, including Chinese and Japanese.

34. Assertion (A) Unicode is a character encoding standard that can represent a wide range of characters from different languages.

Reason (R) UTF-8 is a variable-length encoding scheme that can represent all Unicode characters.

35. Assertion (A) Converting a decimal number to binary involves repeated division by 2.

Reason (R) The remainders obtained during the division process form the binary equivalent.

36. Assertion (A) Octal numbers can be easily converted to binary numbers.

Reason (R) Each octal digit can be represented by three binary digits.

37. Assertion (A) ISCII is a character encoding standard used for Indian languages.

Reason (R) ISCII can represent all the characters of all Indian languages.

Answers

1. (*d*) 8 bits
2. (*d*) binary
3. (*a*) needs less digits to represent a number than in the binary system
4. (*b*) four binary bits
5. (*a*) $(101100000)_2$
6. (*a*) $(011101010.101110)_2$
7. (*c*) $(2E)_{16}$
8. (*b*) $(E7570)_{16}$
9. (*a*) ASCII
10. (*b*) To provide a unique code for every character across all languages
11. (*b*) UTF-8
12. (*b*) 209
13. (b) Bit
14. (a) UTF-8
15. Number system
16. 14
17. Least
18. 16
19. 256
20. Computers
21. 7, 8
22. Encoding
23. False
24. False
25. True
26. False
27. True
28. False
29. True
30. False
31. False
32. (a) Both Assertion (A) and Reason (R) are true, and Reason (R) is the correct explanation of Assertion (A).
33. (c) Assertion (A) is true, but Reason (R) is false.
34. (a) Both Assertion (A) and Reason (R) are true, and Reason (R) is the correct explanation of Assertion (A).
35. (a) Both Assertion (A) and Reason (R) are true, and Reason (R) is the correct explanation of Assertion (A).
36. (a) Both Assertion (A) and Reason (R) are true, and Reason (R) is the correct explanation of Assertion (A).
37. (c) Assertion (A) is true, but Reason (R) is false.

Subjective Type Questions

Very Short Answer Type Questions

1. Give the different types of information which a computer can store.

Ans. Numbers, text, graphics, sound, video etc.

2. Which number system is used in general?

Ans. Decimal number system.

3. What are the bases of decimal, octal, binary and hexadecimal number systems?

Ans. The bases of decimal, octal, binary and hexadecimal number systems are 10, 8, 2 and 16, respectively.

4. Which factors are used to determine the value of each digit in a number?

Ans. A value of each digit in a number can be determined using

(i) The digit (ii) The position of digit in the number

(iii) The base of the number system

5. Expand the following terms.

(i) ASCII (ii) ISCII

Ans. (i) **ASCII** American Standard Codes for Information Interchange.

(ii) **ISCII** Indian Script Code for Information Interchange.

6. Give the name of three computer codes.

Ans. ASCII, ISCII, UNICODE.

7. What is the equivalent binary number for the decimal number 43?

Ans. To find the equivalent binary number, we need to divide 43 by 2, until we get 0 as the result.

Therefore, $(43)_{10} = 101011_2$

8. How to convert $(30)_8$ into a decimal number?

Ans. $(30)_8 = (3 \times 8^1) + (0 \times 8^0) = 24$

9. How many types of number systems are there?

Ans. There are four types of number system

(i) Binary number system (ii) Decimal number system

(iii) Octal number system

(iv) Hexadecimal number system

10. Which language does the computer use internally to perform any work?

Ans. Computer uses binary language to do any work internally.

Short Answer Type I Questions

11. Write the octal number of binary number $(\underline{101}\ \underline{001}\ \underline{100})_2$.

Ans. $\underbrace{101}_{5}\ \underbrace{001}_{1}\ \underbrace{100}_{4}$

$(101001100)_2 = (514)_8$

12. Write the binary number of $(FA1)_{16}$.

Ans.

F A 1
↓ ↓ ↓
15 10 1
↓ ↓ ↓
1111 1010 0001

$(FA1)_{16} = (111110100001)_2$

13. Determine decimal equivalent of $(B14)_{16}$.

Ans. $B \times 16^2 + 1 \times 16^1 + 4 \times 16^0 = 11 \times 16^2 + 1 \times 16^1 + 4 \times 16^0$

$= 2816 + 16 + 4$

$= 2836$

Thus, the decimal equivalent of $(B14)_{16}$ is $(2836)_{10}$.

14. Determine decimal equivalent of $(456)_8$.

Ans. $4 \times 8^2 + 5 \times 8^1 + 6 \times 8^0 = 256 + 40 + 6 = 302$

Thus, the decimal equivalent of $(456)_8$ is $(302)_{10}$.

15. Write the decimal value of $(11010)_2$.

Ans. $(11010)_2 = (?)_{10}$

$(11010)_2 = 1 \times 2^4 + 1 \times 2^3 + 0 \times 2^2 + 1 \times 2^1 + 0 \times 2^0$

$= 1 \times 16 + 1 \times 8 + 0 \times 4 + 1 \times 2 + 0 \times 1$

$= 16 + 8 + 0 + 2 + 0$

$\therefore (11010)_2 = (26)_{10}$

16. Determine octal equivalent of $(010111)_2$.

Ans.

010 111
↓ ↓
2 7

Thus, the octal equivalent of $(010111)_2$ is $(27)_8$.

17. Determine binary equivalent of $(231)_8$.

Ans.

2 3 1
↓ ↓ ↓
010 011 001

Thus, the binary equivalent of $(231)_8$ is $(010011001)_2$.

18. Convert $(11011101.11010101)_2$ into its hexadecimal equivalent.

Ans.

1101 1101 . 1101 0101
↓ ↓ ↓ ↓
D D D 5

$(11011101.11010101)_2 = (DD.D5)_{16}$

Thus, the hexadecimal equivalent of $(11011101.1101\ 0101)_2$ is $(DD.D5)_{16}$.

19. Explain the difference between octal number system and hexadecimal number system.

Ans. The differences between octal number system and hexadecimal number system are as follows

Octal number system	Hexadecimal number system
Octal number system is a number system with base 8.	Hexadecimal number system is a number system with base 16.
There are 8 digits in this system, that is 0, 1, 2, 3, 4, 5, 6, 7	There are 16 digits in this system that is 0, 1, 2, 3, 4, 5, 6, 7, 8, 9, A, B, C, D, E, F

20. Define the following:

(a) Code space (b) Code point

Ans. (a) Code space refers to the range of possible code points that an encoding scheme can represent.

(b) A code point is a unique number assigned to a specific character in a character set.

21. What is a code unit?

Ans. A code unit is the smallest unit of storage used to represent a character in a particular encoding scheme. For example, in UTF-8, code units can be 1, 2, 3, or 4 bytes long, depending on the character being encoded.

22. Name any three encoding schemes and briefly explain one of them.

Ans. Three encoding schemes are ASCII, ISCII, and Unicode (UTF-8, UTF-32).

ASCII (American Standard Code for Information Interchange) It is a 7-bit encoding scheme that represents 128 characters, including English alphabets, digits, and symbols.

23. A computer system receives an input in hexadecimal format as $(2F3A)_{16}$. Convert this number into its equivalent binary and octal representations.

Ans.

Step 1 Convert Hexadecimal $(2F3A)_{16}$ to Binary

Each hexadecimal digit is converted into a 4-bit binary equivalent: 2=0010,F=1111,3=0011,A=1010

So, $(2F3A)_{16} = (0010\ 1111\ 0011\ 1010)_2$

Step 2 Convert Binary to Octal

Group binary digits into 3-bit sections from the right: $(001011110011101010)_2$

Convert each group to octal: 001=1,011=3,110=6,011=3,101=5,010=2

So, $(2F3A)_{16} = (136352)_8$

Binary $(0010111100111010)_2$

Octal $(136352)_8$

Short Answer Type II Questions

24. What do you understand by binary number system?

Ans. The binary number system is base-2 numeral system that uses only two digits : (0 and 1). It is a way of representing numbers using only these two digits, in contrast to the decimal system, which is a base-10 system using digits from 0 to 9.

In the binary system, each digit is called a bit (binary digit), and the position of each bit in a binary number determines its weight or value. The rightmost bit is the least significant bit (LSB) and the left most bit is the most significant bit (MSB). The value of each bit is a power of 2, with the rightmost bit having a value of 2^0, the next bit 2^1, the next bit 2^2 and so on.

25. Convert into decimal number.

(a) $(11101010)_2$ (b) $(11011101)_2$

Ans. (a) $(11101010)_2 = (?)_{10}$

$$= 1\times2^7 + 1\times2^6 + 1\times2^5 + 0\times2^4 + 1\times2^3 + 0\times2^2 + 1\times2^1 + 0\times2^0$$

$$= 128 + 64 + 32 + 0 + 8 + 0 + 2 + 0 = 234$$

Therefore, $(11101010)_2 = (234)_{10}$

(b) $(11011101)_2 = (?)_{10}$

$$= 1\times2^7 + 1\times2^6 + 0\times2^5 + 1\times2^4 + 1\times2^3 + 1\times2^2 + 0\times2^1 + 1\times2^0$$

$$= 128 + 64 + 0 + 16 + 8 + 4 + 0 + 1 = 221$$

Therefore, $(11011101)_2 = (221)_{10}$

26. What is the difference between ASCII and Unicode?

Ans. The difference between ASCII and Unicode are described below:

Feature	ASCII	Unicode
Character Set	Limited to English characters, numbers, and some special symbols	Supports a wide range of characters from various languages and scripts
Code Size	Fixed 7-bit or 8-bit	Variable-length encoding (UTF-8, UTF-16, UTF-32)
Efficiency	Less efficient for representing diverse languages	More efficient for representing text from multiple languages
Compatibility	Widely supported by older systems	More modern and widely supported, but older systems might require special handling

Long Answer Type Questions

27. What is number system? Explain the types of number system.

Ans. Refer to text on page no. 48-50. (Number System)

28. Complete the following octal numbers
365, 366, 367,—, —, —.

Ans. To complete the given sequence, first we find the equivalent decimal number of the given octal numbers.

$$(365)_8 = 3\times8^2 + 6\times8^1 + 5\times8^0$$

$$= 192 + 48 + 5 = (245)_{10}$$

$$(366)_8 = 3\times8^2 + 6\times8^1 + 6\times8^0$$

$=192+48+6=(246)_{10}$

$(367)_8=3\times8^2+6\times8^1+7\times8^0$

$=192+48+7=(247)_{10}$

In decimal form, the given sequence will be 245, 246, 247, 248, 249, 250.

To complete the sequence of octal number, we need to find the octal equivalent of 248, 249, and 250.

		Remainders
8	248	
8	31	0 ↑
8	3	7
	0	3

		Remainders
8	249	
8	31	1 ↑
8	3	7
	0	3

		Remainders
8	250	
8	31	2 ↑
8	3	7
	0	3

$\therefore\quad (248)_{10}=(370)_8$

$\therefore\quad (249)_{10}=(371)_8$

$\therefore\quad (250)_{10}=(372)_8$

So, the complete sequence of octal numbers will be 365, 366, 367, 370, 371, 372.

29. Convert the

(i) decimal number 456 to its binary equivalent.

(ii) binary number 11011.11 to its decimal equivalent.

(iii) octal number 567.3 to its binary equivalent.

Ans. (i) Decimal to Binary Conversion:

To convert 456 to binary, we repeatedly divide by 2 and note the remainders:

$456\div2=228$ remainder 0

$228\div2=114$ remainder 0

$114\div2=57$ remainder 0

$57\div2=28$ remainder 1

$28\div2=14$ remainder 0

$14\div2=7$ remainder 0

$7\div2=3$ remainder 1

$3\div2=1$ remainder 1

$1\div2=0$ remainder 1

Reading the remainders from bottom to top, we get the binary equivalent:

111001000_2

(ii) Binary to Decimal Conversion:

To convert 11011.11 to decimal, we multiply each binary digit by its corresponding power of 2 and sum the results:

$1\times2^4+1\times2^3+0\times2^2+1\times2^1+1\times2^0+1\times2^{-1}+1\times2^{-2}$

$=16+8+0+2+1+0.5+0.25$

$=27.75_{10}$

(iii) Octal to Binary Conversion:

To convert an octal number to binary, we convert each octal digit to its 3-bit binary equivalent:

$5_8=101_2$

$6_8=110_2$

$7_8=111_2$

$3_8=011_2$

Therefore, $(567.3)_8=(101110111.011)_2$

30. Suppose a number system has been designed with radix 10 with symbols (ordered from small to large) A, B, C, D, G, H, I, L, M, N. Convert the following number to equivalent hexadecimal number; $(\text{INDIAN})_{10}$

Ans. Given that A, B, C, D, G, H, I, L, M, N are the symbols of the number system of base 10 with order small to large.

That means A, B, C, D, G, H, I, L, M, N represent 0, 1, 2, 3, 4, 5, 6, 7, 8, 9 respectively of decimal number system (base 10) because the given number also has base 10.

$\Rightarrow (\text{INDIAN})_{10}=(693609)_{10}$

To find its hexadecimal equivalent, use the repeated-division method.

		Remainder
16	693609	
16	43350	9 (LSB) ↑
16	2709	6
16	169	5
16	10	9
	0	10 → A (MSB)

$\therefore\quad (693609)_{10}=(\text{A9569})_{16}$

Thus, $(\text{INDIAN})_{10}=(\text{A9569})_{16}$

Case Study Based Questions

Case Study 1

A number system is a set of symbols used to represent numerical values. The most common number system we use is the decimal system, which has a base of 10. This means it uses ten digits: 0, 1, 2, 3, 4, 5, 6, 7, 8, and 9. Other important number systems used in computer science include:

Binary Number System A base-2 system using only two digits: 0 and 1. It's the foundation of digital computers.

Octal Number System A base-8 system using eight digits: 0, 1, 2, 3, 4, 5, 6, and 7. It's often used as a shorthand for representing binary numbers.

Hexadecimal Number System A base-16 system using sixteen digits: 0, 1, 2, 3, 4, 5, 6, 7, 8, 9, A, B, C, D, E, and F. It's widely used in computer programming and hardware addressing.

(i) Which number system is used as the foundation of digital computers?

(a) Decimal (b) Octal
(c) Hexadecimal (d) Binary

(ii) Which of the following is not a valid digit in the octal number system?

(a) 0 (b) 7
(c) 8 (d) 5

(iii) What is the base of the hexadecimal number system?

(a) 2 (b) 8
(c) 10 (d) 16

(iv) What is the decimal equivalent of the binary number 1011?

(a) 11 (b) 13
(c) 15 (d) 17

(iv) What is the hexadecimal equivalent of the decimal number 255?

(a) FF (b) EE
(c) DD (d) CC

Ans. (i) (d) Binary (ii) (c) 8
(iii) (d) 16 (iv) (a) 11
(v) (a) FF

Case Study 2

Unicode is a computing standard for the consistent encoding, representation and handling of text expressed in most of the world's writing systems. It is a fully international alphanumeric code which can represent all the characters found in human languages. It can represents Katakana, Cyrillic, Latin, Greek, Arabic, Hebrew, Hangul and many more characters.

Unicode uses a 16 bit encoding that provides code point for more than 65000 characters (65536). Unicode standard assigns each character a unique numeric value and name.

Unicode is required by modern standards such as XML, Java, JavaScript, etc. It is supported by many operating systems, all modern browsers, and many other products.

Unicode encoding encompasses several encoding schemes as UTF -8, UTF -16, UTF -32.

Based on the above information, answer the following questions.

(i) What bit sequence is present in the first byte of 2-byte Unicode encoding?

(a) 101 (b) 110
(c) 100 (d) 111

(ii) How many encoding schemes are encompassed by Unicode encoding?

(a) 2 (b) 3
(c) 4 (d) 5

(iii) In UTF-8 encoding, every code point from which range is stored in a single byte?

(a) 0–255 (b) 0–64
(c) 0–127 (d) 0–1024

(iv) Which Unicode Transformation Format (UTF) method is used for encoding Unicode characters using an 8-bit sequence?

(a) UTF-16 (b) UTF-32
(c) UTF-8 (d) ASCII

Ans. (i) (b) 110 (ii) (b) 3
(iii) (c) 0–127 (iv) (c) UTF-8

SELF ASSESSMENT TEST

Multiple Choice Questions

1. What type of information system would be recognised by digital circuits?

(a) Hexadecimal system
(b) Binary system
(c) Both (a) and (b)
(d) None of the above

2. Modern computers represent characters and numbers internally using one of the following number systems.

(a) Octal (b) Penta
(c) Hexa (d) Binary

3. The coding system allows non-english characters and special characters to be represented

(a) ASCII (b) UNICODE
(c) EBCDIC (d) All of these

Fill in the Blanks

4. Each key on the keyboard is internally mapped to an _______ code following an encoding scheme.

5. The count of unique characters in a number system is called its _______ or base.

6. The decimal number system is known as the _______ system since it uses 10 digits (0 to 9).

State Whether True or False

7. ASCII was developed in the early 1980s to standardize character representation for computers.

8. ISCII is an 8-bit encoding scheme that retains all 128 ASCII codes and adds additional codes for Indian scripts.

9. Unicode is not compatible with ASCII because it represents characters differently.

Assertion and Reason Based Questions

Assertion (A) and Reason (R) Type questions. Choose the correct option as

(a) Both Assertion (A) and Reason (R) are true, and Reason (R) is the correct explanation of Assertion (A).
(b) Both Assertion (A) and Reason (R) are true, but Reason (R) is not the correct explanation of Assertion (A).
(c) Assertion (A) is true, but Reason (R) is false.
(d) Assertion (A) is false, but Reason (R) is true.

10. Assertion (A) The decimal number 25 is represented as 11001 in the binary number system.
Reason (R) Binary number system uses base 2 and consists of only two digits: 0 and 1.

11. Assertion (A) The hexadecimal number system is more efficient for representing large binary values.
Reason (R) Each hexadecimal digit represents four binary digits (bits), making it easier to read and convert between binary and hexadecimal.

12. Assertion (A) Unicode (UTF-8 and UTF-32) is an encoding scheme that supports multiple languages and symbols.
Reason (R) ASCII can represent all characters used in all languages.

Very Short Answer Type Questions

13. What is hexadecimal point ?

14. Explain the UTF-32 encoding system.

15. Explain data representation.

Short Answer Type Questions

16. What is number system ? Give the name of different types of number system.

17. How can you estimate the weight or positional value of a bit in binary number ?

18. Complete the sequence of following binary numbers : 1000, 1001, 1010, ——,——,——.

19. How can you represent unsigned integer into binary?

Long Answer Type Questions

20. Briefly describe decimal number system.

21. Which computer code is used for Indian languages ? Explain that code.

Case Study Based Questions

22. Rohan, a software developer, is building a cross-platform text editor that supports both numerical conversions and multiple language texts. In his project, he is implementing modules that can convert numbers among Binary, Octal, Decimal, and Hexadecimal systems.

For text encoding, he initially uses ASCII for English characters but soon realizes its limitations. To support Indian scripts, he adopts ISCII and later switches to Unicode (using UTF-8 and UTF-32) for broader compatibility and internationalization.

Based on this scenario, answer the following questions:

(i) When converting a decimal number to its hexadecimal equivalent, which base is used for the hexadecimal number system?
(a) 2
(b) 8
(c) 10
(d) 16

(ii) In a positional number system, the value of each digit depends on its position. For the decimal number 237, what is the positional value of the digit 3?
(a) 1 (i.e., 10^0)
(b) 10 (i.e., 10^1)
(c) 100 (i.e., 10^2)
(d) 3 (i.e., the digit itself)

(iii) Rohan is reviewing encoding schemes and recalls that the original ASCII encoding uses 7 bits. How many distinct characters can be represented using 7-bit ASCII?
(a) 64 (b) 128 (c) 256 (d) 512

(iv) To support Indian languages, Rohan opts for ISCII, an 8-bit encoding scheme. How many distinct characters can ISCII represent?
(a) 128 (b) 256
(c) 512 (d) 1024

(v) Rohan adopts Unicode (UTF-8 and UTF-32) for his text editor to ensure universal compatibility. Which of the following statements is true regarding the relationship between Unicode and ASCII?
(a) Unicode is a subset of ASCII.
(b) ASCII is a subset of Unicode.
(c) Unicode and ASCII are completely unrelated.
(d) Unicode uses only 7 bits for encoding.

Answers

1. (b) 2. (d) 3. (b) 4. ASCII 5. radix
6. base-10 7. False 8. True 9. False 10. (a)
11. (a) 12. (c)
22. (i) → (d), (ii) → (b), (iii) → (b), (iv) → (b), (v) → (b)

04 CHAPTER

Boolean algebra is widely used in designing logic circuits within computers, where transistors represent logical states.

YOUR STUDY GOALS

YOUR PRACTICE GOAL

- Objective Type Questions (30 Qs ; MCQs, True or False, Fill in the Blanks, Assertion and Reason)
- Subjective Type Questions (50 Qs ; VSA, SA, LA)
- Case Study Based Questions-2

Boolean Algebra

Boolean algebra was discovered by English mathematician George Boole, in 1854 named as **'An investigation of the Laws of Thought'** upon which the mathematical theories of logic and probabilities called boolean algebra was founded.

Boolean algebra is the sub-area of algebra in which the values of the boolean variables are the truth values, i.e. True and False, usually denoted by 1 and 0 (respectively). The values 1 and 0 are called **boolean constant**.

A **boolean variable** is a variable that can take only Yes/No or True/False or 1/0. It is also used in digital logic, computer programming, set theory and statistics.

4.1 Basic Logic Operations

Logic is the process of drawing reasonable conclusions from given information. Logical operations, which work on true or false values, are fundamental to understanding compound logical functions and operators. Before learning about these operations, you must know about compound logical functions and logical operators.

1. Logical Functions or Compound Statements

Compound statements are formed by combining simple logical statements using logical operators. These operators, such as **AND, OR**, and **NOT**, manipulate the truth values (true or false) of the statements.

For example

- **Simple statement** "It is raining."
- **Compound statement** "It is raining AND the sky is cloudy."

2. Logical Operators

Boolean algebra has three logical (or boolean) operators, which are as follows:

(i) NOT Operator

The NOT operator, also known as an **inverter**, is a unary operator that reverses the input value. It changes 0 to 1 and 1 to 0. It represented by a bar (¯) or a prime (').

The truth table of NOT operator

X	$F = \overline{X}$
0	1
1	0

where, X is an input and F is an output of its operation.

Note *A truth table is composed of one column for each input variable and one final column for all of the possible results of the logical operation. Each row of the truth table contains one possible combination of the input variables and the result of the operation for those values.*

(ii) AND Operator

It is a binary operator that operates on two or more than two variables and the operation performed by the AND operator is known as logical multiplication. The symbol for AND operator is dot(.).

Expression for AND operator is F = A.B where A and B are the two inputs and F is an output of its operation.

The truth table of AND operator for two variables:

A	B	$F = A.B$
0	0	0
0	1	0
1	0	0
1	1	1

The truth table of AND operator for three variables:

A	B	C	$F = A.B.C$
0	0	0	0
0	0	1	0
0	1	0	0
0	1	1	0
1	0	0	0
1	0	1	0
1	1	0	0
1	1	1	1

(iii) OR Operator

It is a binary operator that operates on two or more than two variables and the operation performed by OR operator is known as **logical addition.**

The symbol for OR operator is plus(+).

Expression for OR operator is $F = A+B$

where, A and B are the two inputs and F is a output of its operation.

The truth table of OR operator for two variables:

A	B	$F = A+B$
0	0	0
0	1	1
1	0	1
1	1	1

The truth table of OR operator for three variables:

A	B	C	$F = A+B+C$
0	0	0	0
0	0	1	1
0	1	0	1
0	1	1	1
1	0	0	1
1	0	1	1
1	1	0	1
1	1	1	1

Evaluation of Boolean Expression using Truth Tables

To evaluate a logical expression, create a table of values for the variables and then evaluate the expression for each of the possible combinations of variables.

Example 1. Evaluate the boolean expression $X + Y\overline{Z}$.

Step 1 The possible combinations of three variables X, Y and Z are:

X	Y	Z
0	0	0
0	0	1
0	1	0
0	1	1
1	0	0
1	0	1
1	1	0
1	1	1

Step 2 Z is complemented in the expression $X + Y.\overline{Z}$, so one column is added to the table.

X	Y	Z	$\overline{Z}$
0	0	0	1
0	0	1	0
0	1	0	1
0	1	1	0
1	0	0	1
1	0	1	0
1	1	0	1
1	1	1	0

Step 3 $Y.\overline{Z}$ column is added in the table.

X	Y	Z	$\overline{Z}$	$Y.\overline{Z}$
0	0	0	1	0
0	0	1	0	0
0	1	0	1	1
0	1	1	0	0
1	0	0	1	0
1	0	1	0	0
1	1	0	1	1
1	1	1	0	0

Step 4 Now, logical addition of the values of X to the values calculated from $Y.\overline{Z}$ is performed.

X	Y	Z	$\overline{Z}$	$Y.\overline{Z}$	$X+Y.\overline{Z}$
0	0	0	1	0	0
0	0	1	0	0	0
0	1	0	1	1	1
0	1	1	0	0	0
1	0	0	1	0	1
1	0	1	0	0	1
1	1	0	1	1	1
1	1	1	0	0	1

4.2 Basic Rules (Postulates) of Boolean Algebra

- If one input of OR gate is always 0 and other input is X, then the output is always the value of X.

i.e. $X+0 = X$ or $0+X = X$

When, $X = 1$, $X+0 = 1+0 = 1 = X$

$X = 0$, $X+0 = 0+0 = 0 = X$

Illustrated as

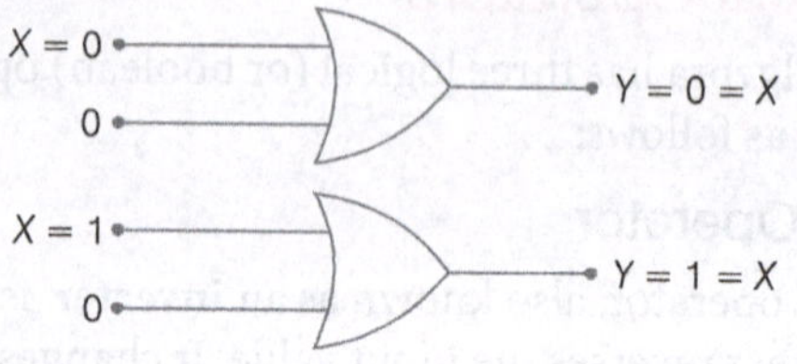

Truth Table

0	X	$Y = 0+X = X$
0	0	0
0	1	1

- If one input of OR gate is always 1, then output is always 1. i.e. $X+1=1$ or $1+X=1$

When, $X=0$, $X+1=0+1=1$

$X=1$, $X+1=1+1=1$

Illustrated as

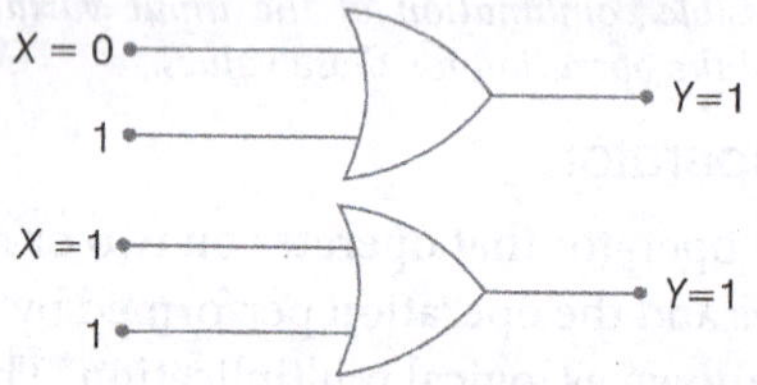

Truth Table

X	1	$Y = X+1=1$
0		1
1		1

- If one input of AND gate is 0, then output is always 0.

i.e. $X.0 = 0$

Illustrated as

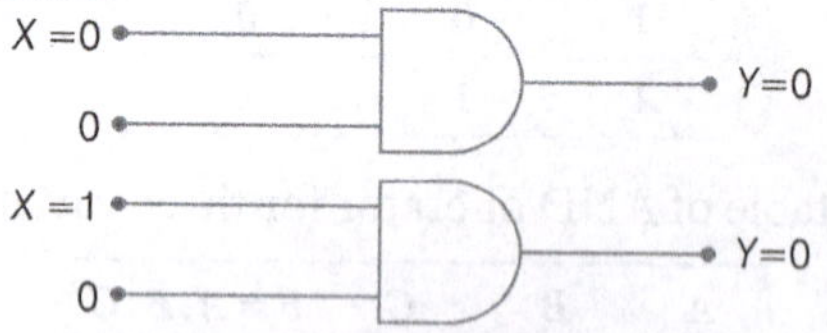

Truth Table

X	0	$Y = X.0 = 0$
0	0	0
1	0	0

- If one input of AND gate is variable X and other input is 1, then the output is always the value of X.

$\therefore$ $X.1 = X$

If $X = 0$, then $X.1 = 0.1 = 0 = X$

If $X = 1$, then $X.1 = 1.1 = 1 = X$

Illustrated as

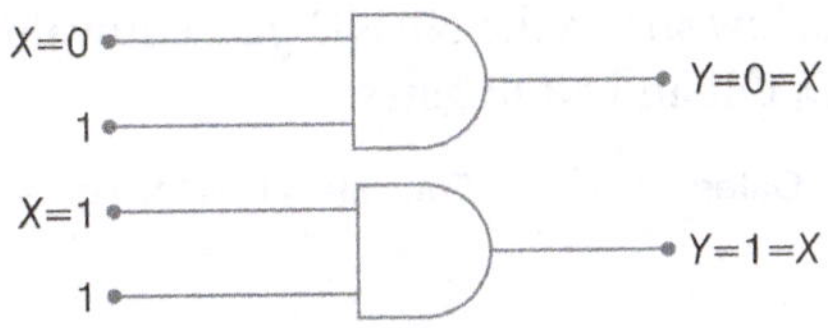

Truth Table

X	1	$Y = X.1 = X$
0	1	0
1	1	1

Duality Principle in Boolean Algebra

The Duality Principle states that if a Boolean equation is true, its dual equation is also true. The dual is obtained by swapping AND (•) with OR (+) and replacing 0 with 1 and vice versa.

Example:

Given: $1 \bullet 0 = 0$

Dual: $0 + 1 = 1$

This principle shows that the choice of symbols (0 and 1) is arbitrary in Boolean algebra.

Compliment is self-dual operation so, it is not changed.

4.3 Logic Gates

It is simply an electronic circuit, which operates on one or more input signals to produce an output signal.

Logic gates can be constructed from diodes, transistors and resistors connected in such a way that circuit output is the result of basic logic operations (OR, AND, NOT) performed on the inputs.

The three basic logic gates are

NOT Gate (Inverter)

It accepts one input and produces one output. It performs logical NOT operation on input.

The output is the complement of the given input. i.e. if input is 1, then output is 0 and *vice-versa*.

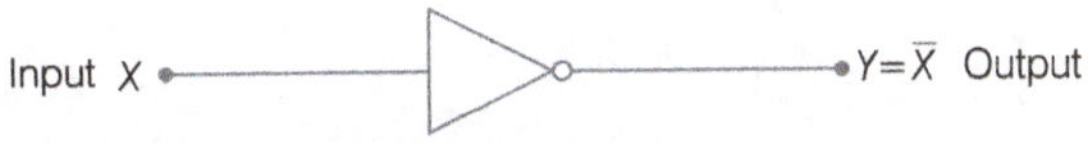

The truth table of NOT gate

X	$Y = \overline{X}$
0	1
1	0

AND Gate

It is a logic circuit that can have two or more than two inputs and produces only one output. It is a logic circuit that requires all inputs to be 1 at the same time in order for the output to be 1.

If any one input is 0 then output is also 0. Output of AND gate is equal to the AND product of logic inputs, i.e. $X = A.B$ (where, A and B are inputs and X is the output)

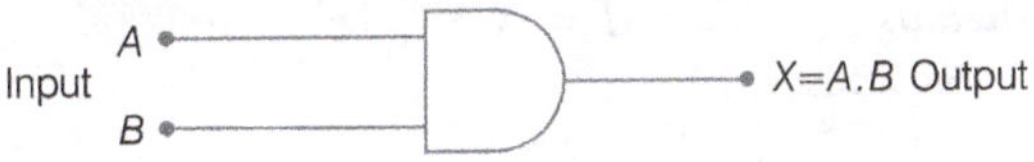

The truth table of AND gate for two variables

A	B	$X = A.B$
0	0	0
0	1	0
1	0	0
1	1	1

OR Gate

It is a logic circuit that can have two or more inputs and produces only one output. It performs logical OR operation on inputs.

The output of the OR gate is 1, when any of the input is 1, i.e. $X = A + B$ (where, A and B are inputs and X is the output).

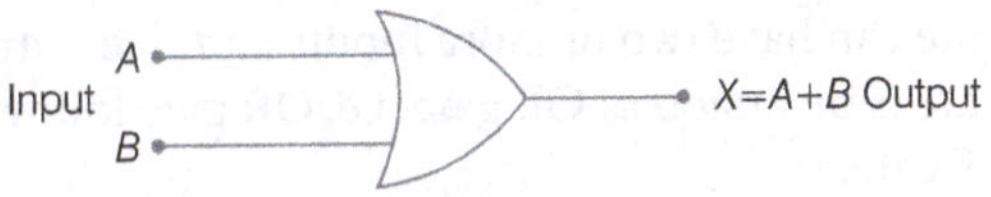

The truth table of OR gate for two variables

A	B	$X = A + B$
0	0	0
0	1	1
1	0	1
1	1	1

Quick Test 1

1. What is Boolean algebra? What are the basic Boolean operations?
2. Define a logic gate.
3. What is the difference between a truth table and a logic circuit?
4. What is the output of a NOT gate when the input is 1?

4.4 More Logic Gates

NAND Gate

This is the logic circuit that will produce the output 1, when any or all inputs are 0 and the output will be 0 only when all the inputs are 1. This gate can have two or more inputs and one output. NAND gate is constructed by using AND gate followed by NOT gate.

Illustrated as $F = \overline{X.Y}$

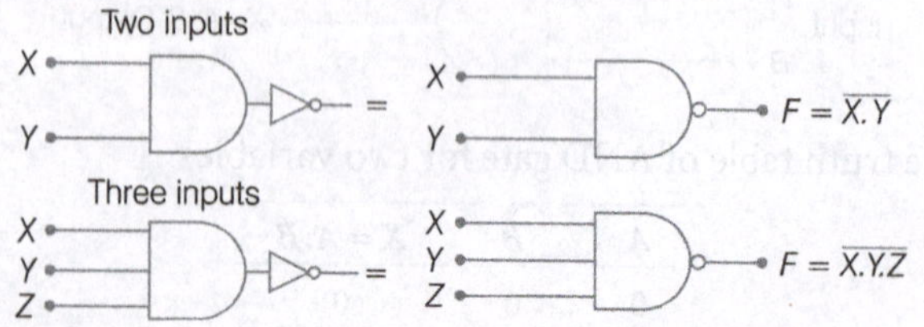

Truth Table

X	Y	$F = \overline{X \cdot Y}$
0	0	1
0	1	1
1	0	1
1	1	0

NOR Gate

This is a logic circuit, that will produce 1 output only when both inputs are 0. If any input is 1, then output will be 0.

NOR gate can have two or more inputs and one output. NOR gate is inversion of OR gate, i.e. OR gate followed by NOT gate.

Illustrated as $F = \overline{X + Y}$

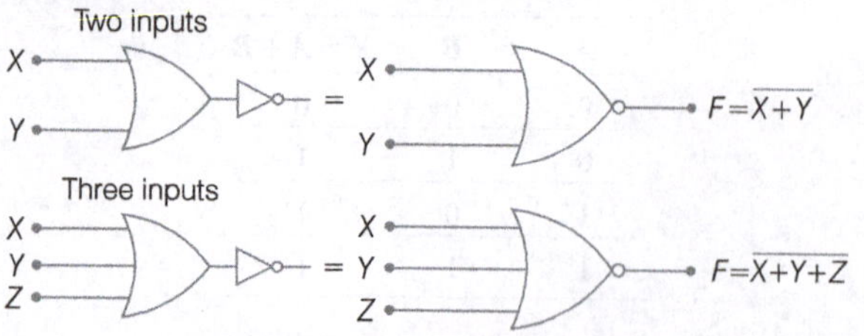

Truth Table

X	Y	$F = \overline{X + Y}$
0	0	1
0	1	0
1	0	0
1	1	0

***Note** NAND and NOR gates are also called Universal gates.*

NAND Gate Equivalents

The table below shows the NAND gate equivalents of NOT, AND, OR and NOR gates.

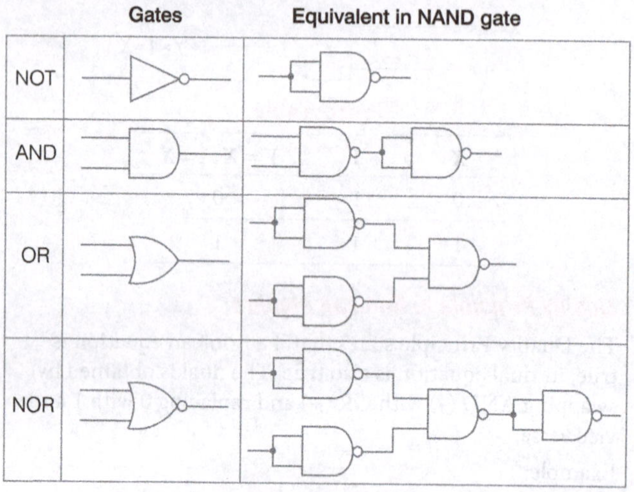

XOR Gate (Exclusive OR Gate)

This gate is widely used in digital circuits. It is not a basic operation but can be performed using basic gates AND, OR and NOT.

If the two inputs are same then output will be 0, otherwise 1.

Illustrated as $F = X \oplus Y = \overline{X}.Y + X.\overline{Y}$

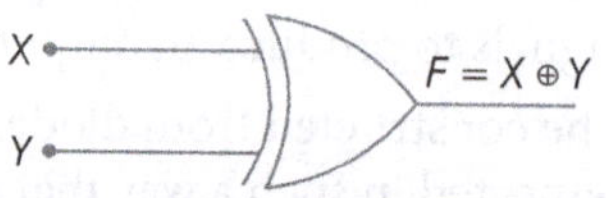

Truth Table

X	Y	$F = X \oplus Y$
0	0	0
0	1	1
1	0	1
1	1	0

The output expression $F = \overline{X}.Y + X.\overline{Y}$:

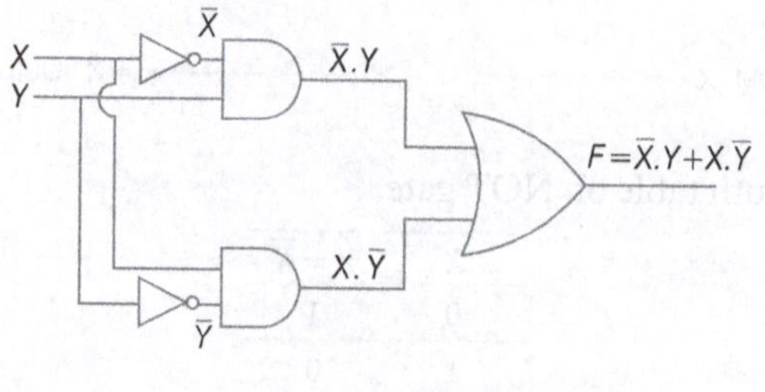

XNOR Gate (Exclusive NOR Gate)

This gate is completely opposite to the XOR gate. It means that if two inputs are different then output will be 0, otherwise 1.

Illustrated as

$$F = (X \odot Y) = \overline{X \oplus Y} = X.Y + \overline{X}.\overline{Y}$$

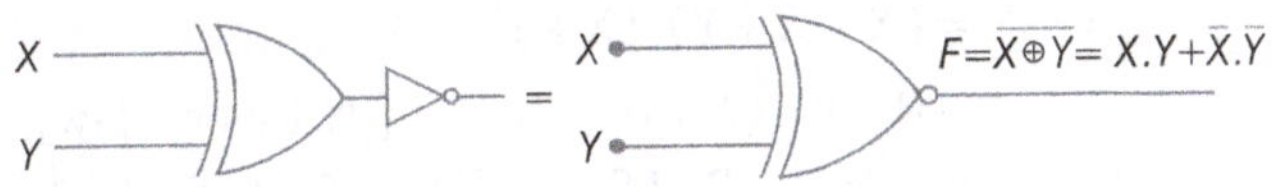

Truth Table

X	Y	$F = X \odot Y$
0	0	1
0	1	0
1	0	0
1	1	1

> **TEACHER TIP**
> Use truth tables to visualize the output of each gate for different input combinations.

4.5 Laws of Boolean Algebra

A set of rules or laws of boolean algebra expressions have been invented to reduce the number of logic gates needed to perform a particular logic operation resulting in a list of functions or theorems known as the laws of boolean algebra.

Boolean Algebra Laws are summarized in the following table

LAW	AND	OR
Properties of 0	A.0 = 0	A + 0 = A
Properties of 1	A.1 = A	A + 1 = 1
Commutative Law	A.B = B.A	A + B = B + A
Associative Law	A.(B.C) = (A.B).C	A + (B + C) = (A + B) + C
Distributive Law	A.(B + C) = A.B + A.C	A + (B.C) = (A + B).(A + C)
Identity Law	A.1 = A	A + 0 = A
Idempotent Law	A.A = A	A + A = A
Inverse/Complement Law	A.~A = 0	A + ~A = 1
Absorption Law	A.(A + B) = A	A + (A.B) = A
Double Negation or Involution Law	A" = A	

De Morgan's Theorems

Two of the most important theorems of boolean algebra were contributed by a great mathematician named **De Morgan**. De Morgan's theorems are extremely useful in simplifying expressions in which a product or sum of variables is inverted.

The two De Morgan's theorems are:

(i) $\overline{X\ .\ Y} = \overline{X} + \overline{Y}$

This theorem expressed as the complement of a product is equal to sum of complement, i.e. complement of two or more variables used in AND gate is same as the OR of the complement of each individual variable.

Illustrated as

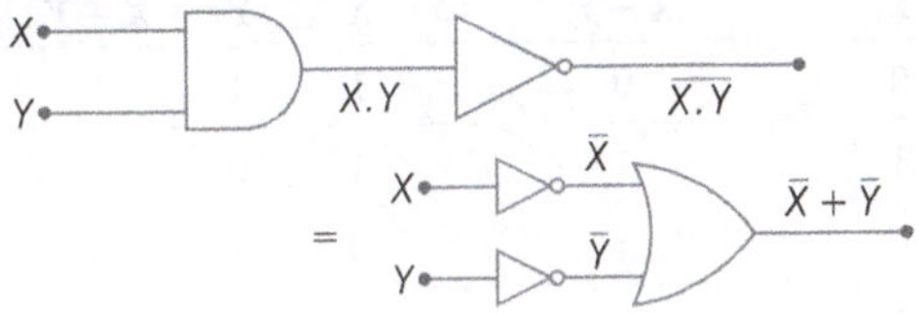

Truth Table

X	Y	$\overline{X}$	$\overline{Y}$	$X.Y$	$\overline{X.Y}$	$\overline{X}+\overline{Y}$
0	0	1	1	0	1	1
0	1	1	0	0	1	1
1	0	0	1	0	1	1
1	1	0	0	1	0	0

Both the columns $\overline{X.Y}$ and $\overline{X}+\overline{Y}$ are identical.

Hence Proved.

Example 2. We know that $\overline{X}+\overline{Y}$ is the complement of $X.Y$ so, (i) $X.Y+(\overline{X}+\overline{Y})=1$ and (ii) $X.Y.(\overline{X}+\overline{Y})=0$

Sol. (i) L.H.S $= X.Y+(\overline{X}+\overline{Y})$

$= (\overline{X}+\overline{Y})+X.Y$ [By Commutative law]

$= (\overline{X}+\overline{Y}+X).(\overline{X}+\overline{Y}+Y)$

[$\because X+Y.Z=(X+Y).(X+Z)$]

$= (X+\overline{X}+\overline{Y}).(\overline{X}+Y+\overline{Y})$

$= (1+\overline{Y}).(\overline{X}+1)$ [By Inverse law]

$= 1.1 = 1 =$ R.H.S [$\because 1+\overline{Y}=1, \overline{X}+1=1$]

Hence Proved.

(ii) L.H.S $= X.Y.(\overline{X}+\overline{Y})$

$= X.Y.\overline{X}+X.Y.\overline{Y}$ [$\because X.(Y+Z)=X.Y+X.Z$]

$= X.\overline{X}.Y+X.Y.\overline{Y}$

$= 0.Y+X.0$ [By Inverse law]

$= 0+0=0=$ R.H.S **Hence Proved.**

(ii) $\overline{X+Y} = \overline{X}.\overline{Y}$

This theorem expressed as the complement of sum is equal to the product of complements, i.e. complement of two or more variables used in OR gate is same as the AND of the complements of each individual variable.

Illustrated as

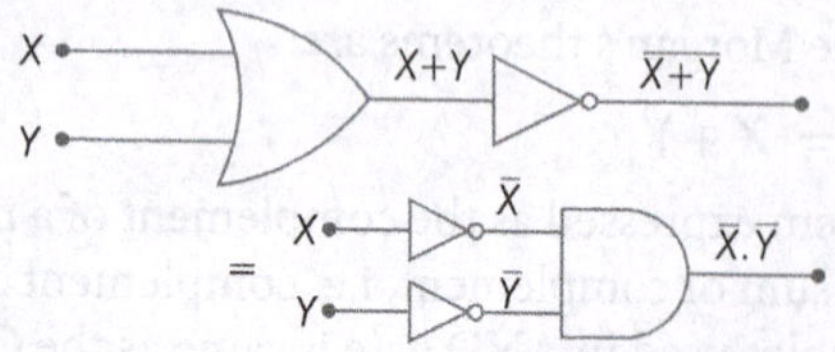

Truth Table

X	Y	$X+Y$	$\overline{X}$	$\overline{Y}$	$\overline{X+Y}$	$\overline{X}.\overline{Y}$
0	0	0	1	1	1	1
0	1	1	1	0	0	0
1	0	1	0	1	0	0
1	1	1	0	0	0	0

Both the columns $\overline{X+Y}$ and $\overline{X}.\overline{Y}$ are identical,

Hence Proved.

Example 3. We know that $X+\overline{X}=1$ and $X.\overline{X}=0$.

So, if $(\overline{X+Y}) = \overline{X}.\overline{Y}$ then:

(i) $(X+Y)+(\overline{X}.\overline{Y})=1$

(ii) $(X+Y).\overline{X}.\overline{Y}=0$

Sol. (i) L.H.S $= (X+Y)+\overline{X}.\overline{Y}$

$= ((X+Y)+\overline{X}).((X+Y)+\overline{Y})$

[$\because (X+Y).(X+Z) = X+Y.Z$]

$= (X+\overline{X}+Y).(X+Y+\overline{Y})$

$= (1+Y).(X+1)$ [By Inverse law]

$= 1.1 = 1 =$ R.H.S [$\because 1+Y=1,\ X+1=1$]

Hence Proved.

(ii) L.H.S $= (X+Y).\overline{X}.\overline{Y}$

$= \overline{X}.\overline{Y}.(X+Y)$ [$\because X\cdot Y = Y\cdot X$]

$= \overline{X}.\overline{Y}.X + \overline{X}.\overline{Y}.Y$ [By Inverse law]

$= 0.\overline{Y} + \overline{X}.0 = 0.0 = 0$ [$\because 0\cdot\overline{Y}=0,\ \overline{X}\cdot 0=0$]

$=$ R.H.S **Hence Proved.**

Quick Test 2

1. State De Morgan's laws.
2. How can you implement an OR gate using only NAND gates?
3. Create a truth table for a 2-input XOR gate.
4. Simplify the following boolean expression $\overline{A}B + A\overline{B}$

Mind Map

BOOLEAN ALGEBRA

Logical Gates

01 NOT Gate

It is a gate with only one input signal and one output signal the output state is always the opposite of input state.

02 AND Gate

The AND gate requires all inputs to be 1 for the output to be 1 and its output is the product of the input.

03 OR Gate

The OR gate output 1 when any input is 1 and its output is the sum of the inputs.

04 NAND Gate

This gate output 1 when any input is 0 and 0 only when all inputs are 1.

05 NOR Gate

This gate output 1 only when both input are 0 and is an inversion of the OR gate.

06 XOR Gate

This gate output 1 when the two inputs are different and 0 when they are the same

07 XNOR Gate

This gate is completely opposite to the XOR gate .It means that if two inputs are different then output will be 0,otherwise 1.

De Morgan's Theorems

(i) $\overline{X.Y} = \overline{X} + \overline{Y}$

(ii) $\overline{X+Y} = \overline{X}.\overline{Y}$

Logical Operator

NOT Operator

It reverse the input value, changing 0 to 1 and 1 to 0.

X	$F = \overline{X}$
0	1
1	0

AND Operator

It is a binary operator that performs logical multiplication , represented by a dot (.)

A	B	$F = A.B$
0	0	0
0	1	0
1	0	0
1	1	1

OR Operator

It is a binary operator that performs logical addition ,represented by a plus(+).

A	B	$F + A = B$
0	0	0
0	1	1
1	0	1
1	1	1

Note

*A **truth table** in Boolean algebra is a table that shows all possible input and output combinations. It's a mathematical tool used to determine the outcomes of logical expressions.*

Laws of Boolean Algebra

LAW	AND	OR
Properties of 0	A.0 = 0	A + 0 = A
Properties of 1	A.1 = A	A + 1 = 1
Commutative Law	A.B = B.A	A + B = B + A
Associative Law	A.(B.C) = (A.B).C	A + (B + C) = (A + B) + C
Distributive Law	A.(B + C) = A.B + A.C	A + (B.C) = (A + B).(A + C)
Identity Law	A.1 = A	A + 0 = A
Idempotent Law	A.A = A	A + A = A
Complement Law	A.~A = 0	A + ~A = 1
Absorption Law	A.(A + B) = A	A + (A.B) = A
Double Negation or Involution Law	A" = A	

EXAM PATTERN QUESTIONS

Objective Type Questions

Multiple Choice Questions

1. A smart home security system uses logic gates to control door access. To enhance security, the system needs to invert a signal when an unauthorized person tries to enter. Which operator should be used to achieve this? **Competency Based Que.**

(a) NOT (b) AND (c) OR (d) XOR

2. Which of the following Boolean operators is a unary operator?

(a) NOT (b) AND (c) OR (d) XOR

3. A traffic management system determines when to allow pedestrian crossings based on traffic conditions. The system follows a specific sequence of Boolean operations to prioritize decisions. Which order of precedence should be followed to ensure the correct logic is applied? **Competency Based Que.**

(a) OR→ AND→ NOT (b) AND→ OR→ NOT
(c) NOT→ AND→ OR (d) OR→ NOT→ AND

4. Two inputs A and B of NAND gate have 0 as output, if

(a) A is 0 (b) B is 0
(c) Both are zero (d) Both are 1

5. What is the Boolean expression for a NAND gate?

(a) A + B (b) A AND B
(c) NOT (A AND B) (d) NOT (A OR B)

6. A logic system with 'n' input binary values can have how many possible input combinations?

(a) n (b) n-1
(c) $2n^{-1}$ (d) 2^n

7. NOR gate is constructed by using OR gate followed by

(a) AND gate (b) XOR gate
(c) NAND gate (d) NOT gate

8. Which gate produces a high output only when both inputs are identical?

(a) AND (b) OR
(c) XOR (d) XNOR

9. Which law is represented by X +Y =Y + X

(a) Associative law (b) Commutative law
(c) Idempotent law (d) Involution law

10. Which laws do the following equations represent?

A + B = B + A; AB = BA

(a) Associative Laws (b) Commutative Laws
(c) Distributive Laws (d) Identity Laws

11. A + AB = A is stated as per

(a) Commutative law (b) Associative law
(c) Distributive law (d) None of these

12. The given logic circuit implements the following expression:

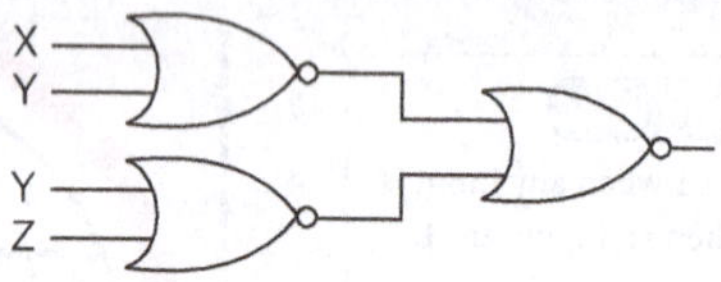

(a)(X'.Y) + (Y+Z)' (b) (X+Y) (Y+Z)
(c) (X.Y) (Y.Z) (d) (X.Y) + (Y+Z)'

13. Simplify the following Boolean expression: A + AB + ABC + ABCD + ABCDE + ...

(a) 1 (b) A (c) A + AB (d) AB

14. Simplify the Boolean expression (X+Y+XY) (X+Z):

(a) X+Y+Z (b) (X+Y) (Y+Z)
(c) X+YZ (d) XZ+Y

Fill in the Blanks

15. If the result of any logical statement or expression is always TRUE or 1 for all input combination. It is called _____.

16. The values which are stored in binary variables are known as ______.

17. ___________ gate give high output when all the inputs are 1.

18. (A'+B') = A' . B' is ______.

19. Dual of boolean expression (X+Y).(X'+Z').(Y+Z) is ________.

State Whether True or False

20. AND and OR gates are called Universal gates.

21. In Python, the AND operator returns True if at least one operand is True.

22. Not every boolean expression can have a dual.

23. Idempotent law state that: A + A = 1

24. The expression not (A and B) is equivalent to not A or not B according to De Morgan's law.

Assertion and Reason Based Questions

Assertion (A) and Reason (R) Type questions. Choose the correct option as:

(a) Both Assertion (A) and Reason (R) are true, and Reason (R) is the correct explanation of Assertion (A).

(b) Both Assertion (A) and Reason (R) are true, but Reason (R) is not the correct explanation of Assertion (A).

(c) Assertion (A) is true, but Reason (R) is false.

(d) Assertion (A) is false, but Reason (R) is true.

25. **Assertion (A)** A logic circuit can be implemented using only AND, OR, and NOT gates.
Reason (R) NAND and XOR gates are universal gates.

26. **Assertion (A)** A truth table lists all possible input combinations and corresponding output for a logic gate.
Reason (R) Truth tables are used to analyze the behavior of digital circuits.

27. **Assertion (A)** A NAND gate is a universal gate.
Reason (R) Any Boolean function can be implemented using only NAND gates.

28. **Assertion (A)** A NOR gate is the dual of an AND gate.
Reason (R) The output of a NOR gate is low only when all inputs are high.

29. **Assertion (A)** An XOR gate produces a high output only when the inputs are different.
Reason (R) An XOR gate is a special case of an OR gate.

30. **Assertion (A)** De Morgan's theorem states that the complement of the product of two variables is equal to the sum of their complements.
Reason (R) De Morgan's theorem is used to simplify complex Boolean expressions.

Answers

1. (a) NOT
2. (a) NOT
3. (c) NOT → AND → OR
4. (d) Both are 1
5. (c) NOT (A AND B)
6. (d) 2^n
7. (d) NOT gate
8. (d) XNOR
9. (b) Commutative law
10. (b) Commutative Laws
11. (d) None of these
12. (b) (X+Y) (Y+Z)
13. (b) A
14. (c) X+YZ
15. Tautology
16. Boolean Constants
17. AND
18. DeMorgan's theorem
19. (X.Y)+(X'.Z')+(Y.Z)
20. False
21. False
22. False
23. False
24. True
25. (c) Assertion (A) is true, but Reason (R) is false.
26. (a) Both Assertion (A) and Reason (R) are true, and Reason (R) is the correct explanation of Assertion (A).
27. (a) Both Assertion (A) and Reason (R) are true, and Reason (R) is the correct explanation of Assertion (A).
28. (a) Both Assertion (A) and Reason (R) are true, and Reason (R) is the correct explanation of Assertion (A).
29. (c) Assertion (A) is true, but Reason (R) is false.
30. (a) Both Assertion (A) and Reason (R) are true, and Reason (R) is the correct explanation of Assertion (A).

Subjective Type Questions

Very Short Answer Type Questions

1. What is a logic gate and what is its function?

Ans. A logic gate is an electronic circuit that implements a specific logical operation. It takes one or more binary inputs and produces a single binary output based on a predefined truth table. Logic gates are the building blocks of digital circuits.

2. (a) What is an OR gate?
(b) What is an inverter gate?

Ans. (a) An OR gate is a logic gate that produces a high output (1) if one or more of its inputs are high (1).

(b) An inverter gate is a fundamental logic gate that inverts the input signal. It has a single input and a single output. If the input is 0, the output is 1, and vice versa.

3. What is an AND gate?

Ans. An AND gate is a logic gate that produces a high output (1) only when all of its inputs are high (1).

4. Which logic gates implement logical OR, AND, and NOT operations?

Ans.
- **OR gate** Implements logical OR operation.
- **AND gate** Implements logical AND operation.
- **NOT gate** Implements logical NOT operation.

5. How can we express the logical OR operation using only logical AND and logical NOT operations?

Ans. $(A + B) = (\overline{A} + \overline{B}) = \overline{A} \cdot \overline{B} = \overline{(\overline{\overline{A}} + \overline{\overline{B}})} = \overline{\overline{A}} + \overline{\overline{B}} = A + B$

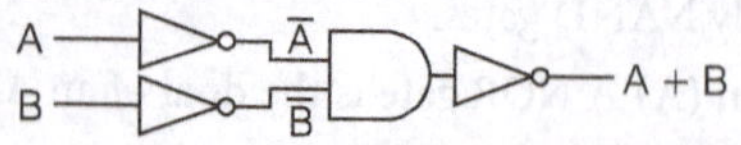

6. What are the fundamental values that logical variables can take on?

Ans. The fundamental values that logical variables can take on are true and false.

7. What kind of variable can only have two possible values, usually represented as 0 and 1?

Ans. A binary variable is a type of variable that can only assume two distinct values, typically represented as 0 and 1.

8. Represent F(a, b) = a.b using only NOT and OR gates.

Ans. The expression $F(a,b) = a.b$ using only NOT and OR gates is

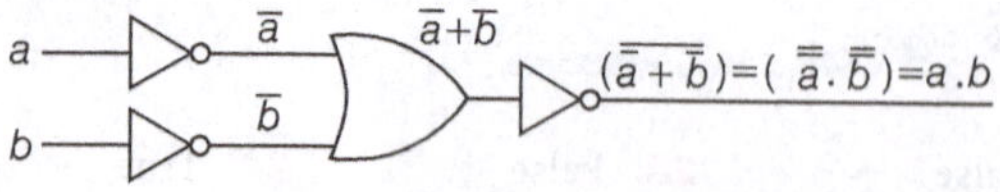

9. A smartphone uses logical operations to verify user authentication. If the system needs to deny access when a wrong password is entered and grant access when the correct password is provided, how many types of logical operators are commonly used in Boolean algebra for such decision-making? Competency Based Que.

Ans. Boolean algebra has three logical operators: NOT, AND, and OR.

10. Seven inverters are cascaded one after another. What is the output, if the input is 1?

Ans. The logic circuit is given

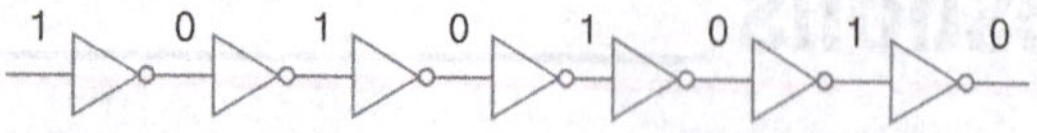

The output will be 0.

11. Why are NAND and NOR gates called Universal gates?

Or **Which gates are called Universal gates and why?**

Ans. NAND and NOR gates are easier to design and basic functions like AND, OR and NOT, etc., can be easily implemented using NAND/NOR gates. So, these gates are called Universal gates.

12. Implement the following Boolean expression using logic gates:

$Y=(A \cdot B)+C$

Ans.

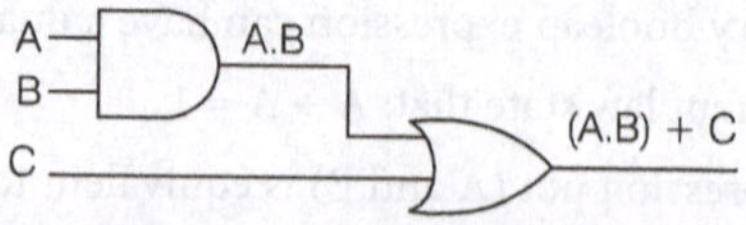

13. An elevator control system operates based on multiple sensor inputs (such as floor requests and weight sensors). If an elevator system has N input sensors, how many possible input combinations must be considered while designing its logic system? Competency Based Que.

Ans. The truth table will have 2^n input combinations.

14. Write the dual of the boolean expression.
$(A + 0) . (A . 1 . \overline{A})$

Ans. Using duality principle, changing (+) to (.) and *vice-versa* and by replacing 0's with 1's and 1's with 0's, the dual for the given expression is as follows. $(A.1) + (A + 0 + \overline{A})$

15. State the distributive laws of boolean algebra. How do they differ from the distributive laws of ordinary algebra?

Ans. Distributive laws of boolean algebra state that

(i) $X.(Y + Z) = X.Y + X.Z$

(ii) $X + Y.Z = (X + Y).(X + Z)$

Law $X.(Y + Z) = X.Y + X.Z$ satisfies ordinary algebra for all values, whereas $X + Y.Z = (X + Y).(X + Z)$ satisfies only for two values (0, 1) of X, Y and Z.

16. What is the dual of a Boolean expression?

Ans. The dual of a Boolean expression is obtained by interchanging the AND and OR operators and complementing all literals (variables). For example, the dual of (A + BC) is A · (B + C).

Short Answer Type I Questions

17. Verify the following using truth table:

(i) $X + 0 = X$ (ii) $X + \overline{X} = 1$

Ans. (i)

X	0	Y = X + 0
0	0	0
1	0	1

(ii)

X	$\overline{X}$	$Y = X + \overline{X}$
0	1	1
1	0	1

18. What is meant by a logic gate? State any one application of a logic gate circuit.

Ans. A logic gate is simply an electronic circuit which operates on one or more input signals to produce an output signal.

Logic gates can be constructed from diodes, transistors and resistors connected in such a way that circuit output is the result of a basic logic operations, performed on the input.

Logic gates are used in bitwise boolean operations. The most popular application of logic gate is a switch.

19. Represent the boolean expression $(X+\overline{Y})Z$ with the help of NAND gate only.

Ans. The boolean expression $(X+\overline{Y}).Z$ can be implemented as:

$(X+\overline{Y}).Z = \overline{\overline{X.Z+\overline{Y}.Z}} = \overline{\overline{X.Z}.\overline{\overline{Y}.Z}}$ [By DeMorgan's law]

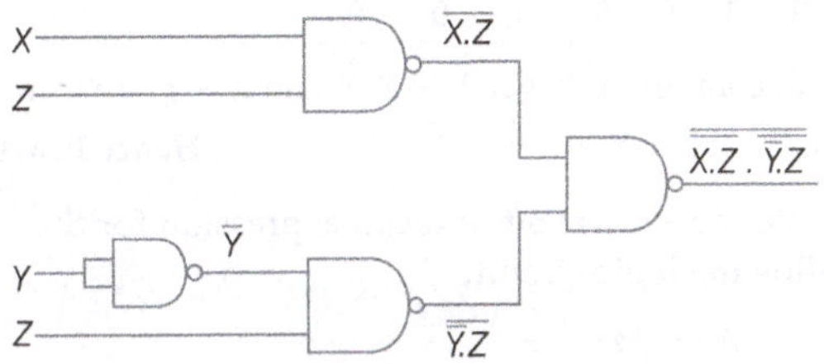

20. Define universal gates. Give one example and show how it works as an OR gate.

Ans. NAND and NOR gates are known as universal gates because all the other gates (AND, OR, NOT) can be constructed using only these two gates. Any Boolean or logic expression can be realised by using AND, OR and NOT gate.

e.g. NOR gate

OR gate can be replaced by NOR gate as

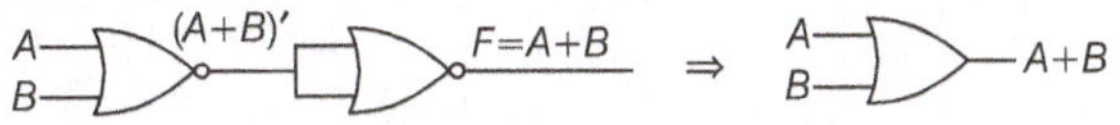

21. Using only NAND gates, draw the logic circuit diagram for $A'+B$.

Ans. Expression $A'+B$

Logic circuit diagram using NAND gates only

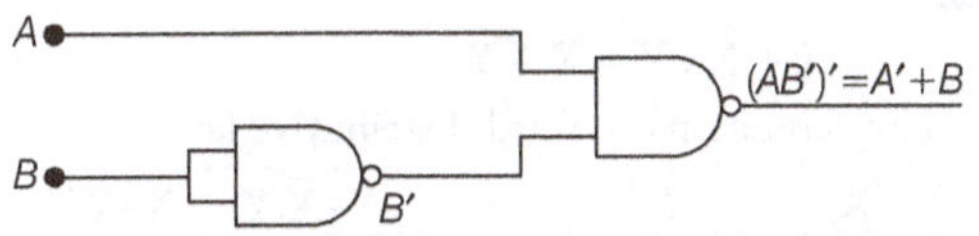

22. Answer the questions related to the circuit given below:

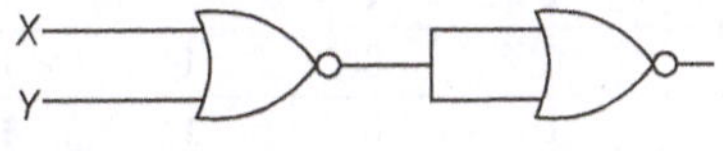

(i) Give the output if, X = 1 and Y = 0

(ii) Name the basic gate represented by the above diagram.

Ans. (i)

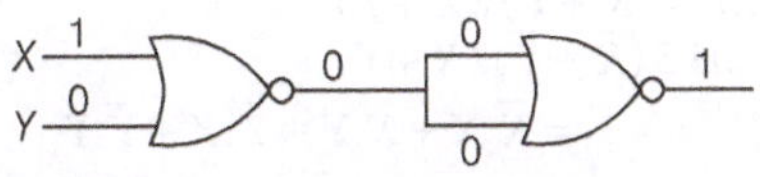

So, the output with $X=1$ and $Y=0$ is 1.

(ii) NOR gate.

23. Represent the boolean expression $X.\overline{Y}+Y.\overline{Z}$ using only NAND gate.

Ans. $X.\overline{Y}+Y.\overline{Z} = \overline{\overline{X.\overline{Y}+Y.\overline{Z}}}$ [using $\overline{\overline{A}} = A$]

$= \overline{\overline{X.\overline{Y}}.\overline{Y.\overline{Z}}}$

[By using DeMorgan's law, $\overline{A+B} = \overline{A}.\overline{B}$]

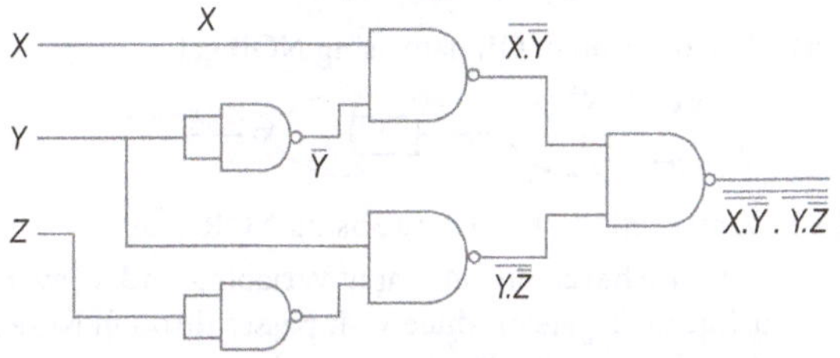

24. Draw the logic circuit of NOR using NAND gate only.

Ans.

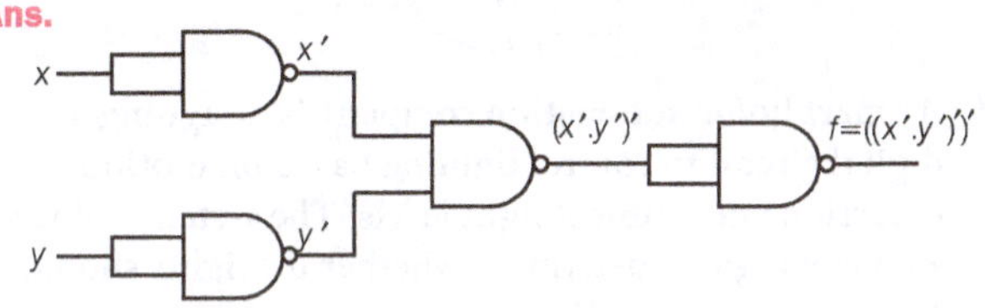

$F = ((x' \cdot y')')' = (x' \cdot y')$

$= (x+y)'$ (by involution law)

25. Prove that the complement of $A.(A+B).B(B+C')$ is a universal gate.

Ans. Given expression, say $X = A.(A+B).B(B+C')$

Its complement $X' = [A.(A+B).B(B+C')]'$

$= [(AA+AB).(BB+BC')]'$ [by distributive law]

$= [(A+AB).(B+BC')]'$ [by idempotent law]

$= [A(1+B) \cdot B(1+C')]'$

$= [A.B]'$ [by absorption law]

= NAND gate

Since, NAND is a universal gate. Hence, the complement of given expression is a universal gate.

26. Draw the logic gate diagram and truth table for XOR gate.

Ans.

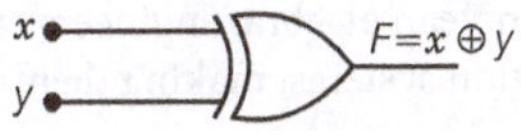

Here, x and y are two inputs and F represents the output of XOR. The truth table of XOR is:

x	y	$F = x \oplus y$
0	0	0
0	1	1
1	0	1
1	1	0

The algebraic expression is $F = x \oplus y = x'y + xy'$

27. Using NOR gates only, draw AND, OR and NOT gate.

Ans. (i) Construction of AND gate using NOR gate:

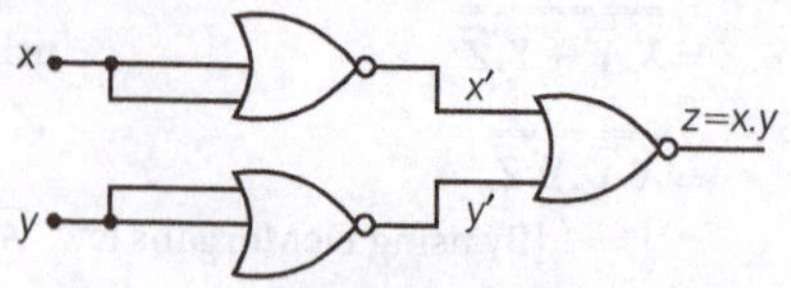

(ii) Construction of OR gate using NOR gate:

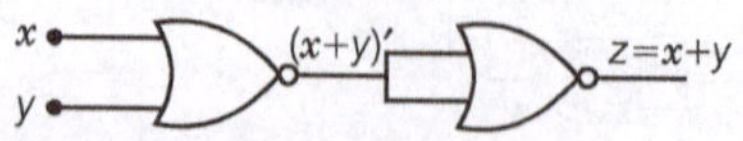

(iii) Construction of NOT gate using NOR gate

Here, we have only one input variable x and it inverse using NOT gate produce x'. It passes through NOR, then the output will be: $z = x'$

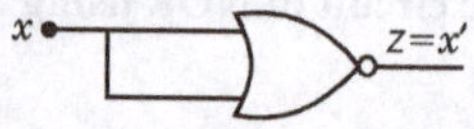

28. A smart home automation company is designing a digital circuit to control lighting based on motion detection and ambient light levels. The system follows Boolean logic to determine whether the lights should turn on or remain off. **Competency Based Que.**

Using Boolean algebra, the engineers simplify the logic circuit to ensure efficient operation.

How does Boolean algebra help in designing and optimizing digital circuits, such as those used in smart home automation? Explain its significance and state the key rules that guide Boolean algebra.

Ans. Boolean algebra helps in analyzing and simplifying digital circuits by representing logical conditions using binary values (0 and 1).

It ensures efficient circuit design by reducing the number of logic gates needed.

Key rules in Boolean algebra:

1. Variables can have only two values: 1 (High) and 0 (Low).
2. The complement of a variable is denoted by an overbar (‾). If B = 0, then B‾ = 1, and vice versa.

By applying Boolean algebra, engineers can optimize smart home automation systems, making them faster and more cost-effective.

29. Verify the following boolean expression using truth table.

(i) $X.\overline{X} = 0$ **(ii)** $X + 1 = 1$

Ans. (i) $X.\overline{X} = 0$

X	$\overline{X}$	$X.\overline{X}$
0	1	0
1	0	0

So, $X.\overline{X} = 0$

(ii) $X + 1 = 1$

X	1	$X+1$
0	1	1
1	1	1

As $X + 1 = 1$ **Hence Proved.**

30. Verify $\overline{X}.Y + X.\overline{Y} + \overline{X}.\overline{Y} = \overline{X} + \overline{Y}$ **using truth table.**

Ans. $\overline{X}.Y + X.\overline{Y} + \overline{X}.\overline{Y} = \overline{X} + \overline{Y}$

X	Y	$\overline{X}$	$\overline{Y}$	$\overline{X}.Y$	$X.\overline{Y}$	$\overline{X}.\overline{Y}$	$(\overline{X}.Y + X.\overline{Y} + \overline{X}.\overline{Y})$	$\overline{X}+\overline{Y}$
0	0	1	1	0	0	1	1	1
0	1	1	0	1	0	0	1	1
1	0	0	1	0	1	0	1	1
1	1	0	0	0	0	0	0	0

Both columns $\overline{X}.Y + X.\overline{Y} + \overline{X}.\overline{Y}$ and $\overline{X} + \overline{Y}$ are identical.

So, $\overline{X}.Y + X.\overline{Y} + \overline{X}.\overline{Y} = \overline{X} + \overline{Y}$ **Hence Proved.**

31. Write the equivalent boolean expression for the following logic circuit.

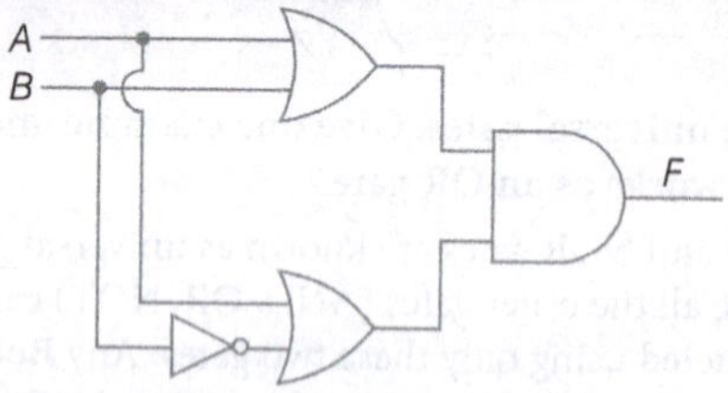

Ans.

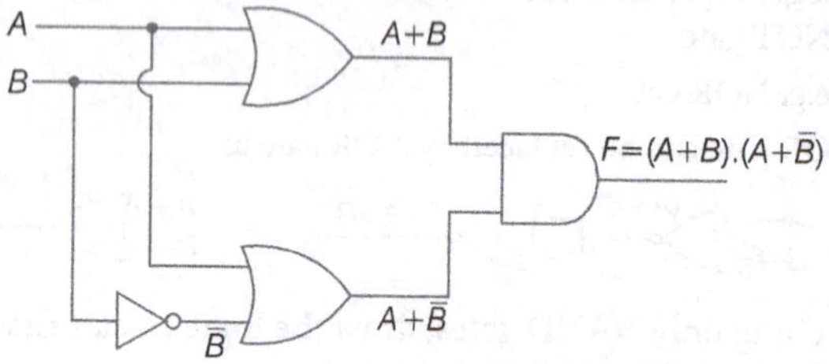

Hence, boolean expression $F = (A + B).(A + \overline{B})$

32. Name the law shown below and verify it using a truth table.

$$X + \overline{X}.Y = X + Y$$

Ans. This law is referring to third distributive law.

X	Y	$\overline{X}$	$X+\overline{X}.Y$	X+Y
0	0	1	0	0
0	1	1	1	1
1	0	0	1	1
1	1	0	1	1

33. Verify the following algebraically.

$$\overline{X}.Y + X.\overline{Y} = (\overline{X} + \overline{Y}).(X + Y)$$

Ans. $\overline{X}.Y + X.\overline{Y} = (\overline{X} + \overline{Y}).(X + Y)$

Taking R.H.S $(\overline{X} + \overline{Y}).(X + Y)$

$= \overline{X}.X + \overline{X}.Y + \overline{Y}.X + \overline{Y}.Y$

$= 0 + \overline{X}.Y + \overline{Y}.X + 0$ $[\because X.\overline{X} = 0, Y.\overline{Y} = 0]$

$= \overline{X}.Y + X.\overline{Y}$ $[X.\overline{Y} = \overline{Y}.X]$

= L.H.S **Hence Proved.**

34. State the dual for the following expression and also draw the logic gate diagram for the dual expression obtained using NOR gate only.

$$P = A.B + C.D$$

Ans. $P = A.B + C.D$

Dual of expression P is $(A + B).(C + D)$

The logic diagram for dual expression is:

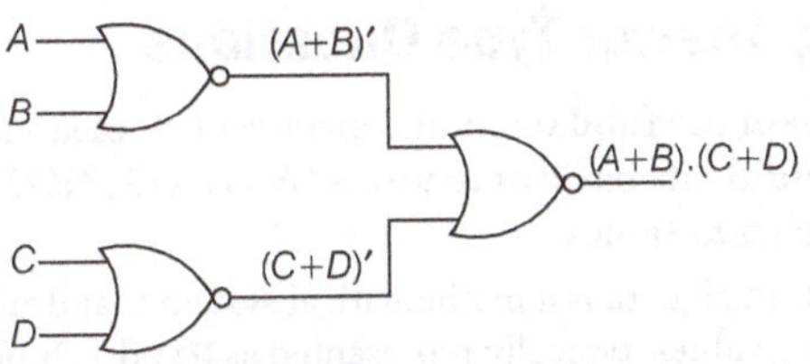

35. Given the following circuit:

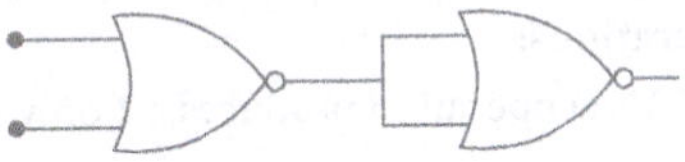

What is the output if,

(i) both inputs are false,

(ii) one is false and the other is true?

(iii) both inputs are true

Ans. (i) When both inputs are false:

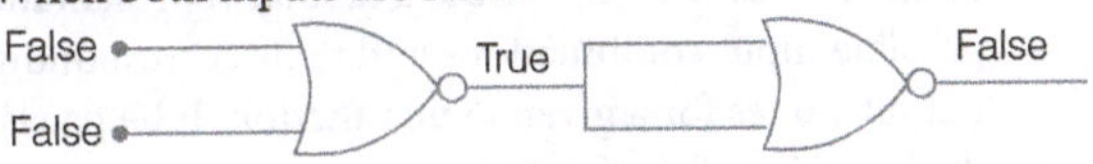

(ii) When one is false and the other is true:

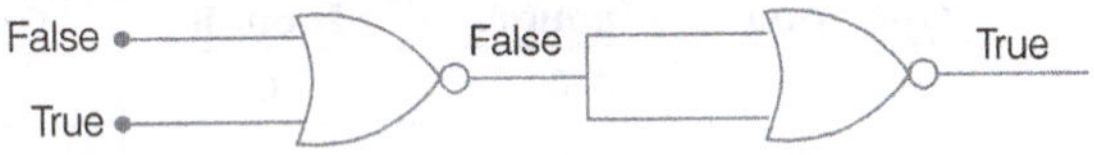

(iii) When both inputs are true

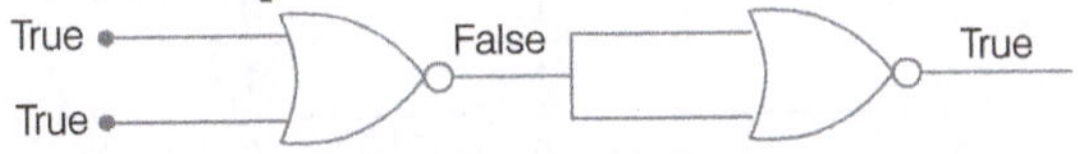

36. Write down the truth table for the Boolean Expression $(X + \overline{Y})$.

Ans.

X	Y	$\overline{Y}$	$(X+\overline{Y})$	$\overline{(X+\overline{Y})}$
0	0	1	1	0
0	1	0	0	1
1	0	1	1	0
1	1	0	1	0

Short Answer Type II Questions

37. What is Truth Table? Draw the truth table for the given Boolean expression (A + B')'.

Ans. A truth table is a tabular representation used in logic and mathematics to display all possible combinations of truth values (typically "1" or "0") for a given logical expression. Truth tables are particularly useful for evaluating the validity and behavior of logical propositions, such as logical operations (AND, OR, NOT) or complex logical statements. Given expression $(A + B')'$

Truth Table

A	B	B'	$A + B'$	$(A + B')'$
0	0	1	1	0
0	1	0	0	1
1	0	1	1	0
1	1	0	1	0

38. Draw the logic diagram of the given logic equation and also make its truth table.

$$Y = (A + B)(B + C)(A + C)$$

Ans. Logic diagram

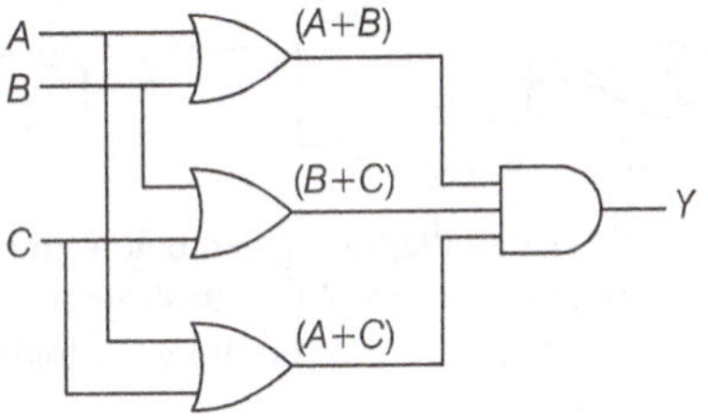

Truth table

A	B	C	$(A+B)$	$(B+C)$	$(A+C)$	$Y = (A+B)(B+C)(A+C)$
0	0	0	0	0	0	0
0	0	1	0	1	1	0
0	1	0	1	1	0	0
0	1	1	1	1	1	1
1	0	0	1	0	1	0
1	0	1	1	1	1	1
1	1	0	1	1	1	1
1	1	1	1	1	1	1

39. Draw the logic gate diagram for 2-input OR gate using NAND gates only. Show the expression at each step.

Ans.

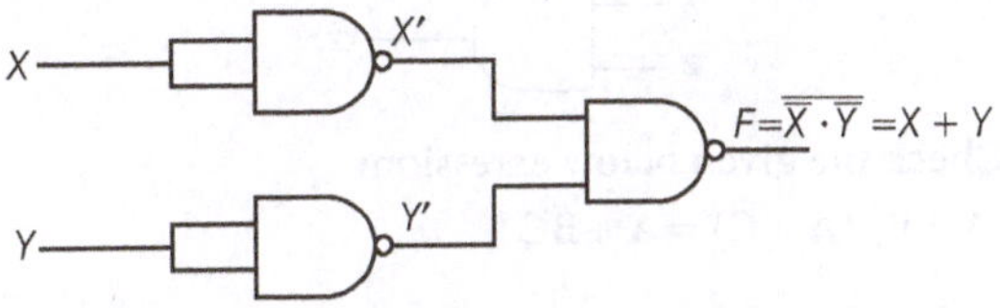

We implement this expression using three NAND gates

First NAND gate : $\overline{X}$

Second NAND gate : $\overline{Y}$

Third NAND gate : $\overline{\overline{X}\cdot\overline{Y}}$

So, the final expression using NAND gates is $= \overline{\overline{X}\cdot\overline{Y}}$

$= X + Y$

40. From the logic diagram given below, write the Boolean expression for (1) and (2). Also, derive the Boolean expression (F) and simplify it.

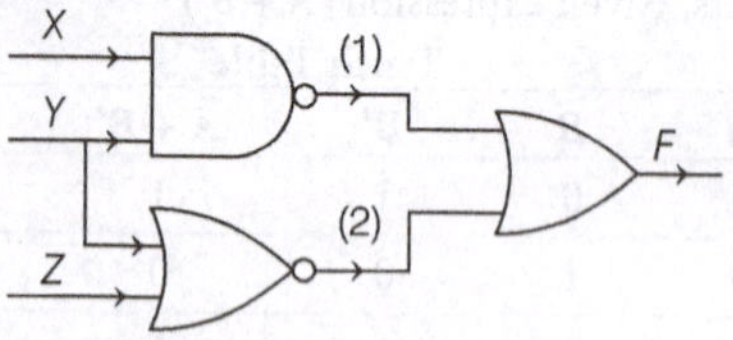

Ans. Boolean expression for (1) = $(XY)'$

Boolean expression for (2) = $(Y+Z)'$

Boolean expression for (F) = $(XY)' + (Y+Z)'$

41. Draw the circuit of two inputs XOR gate with the help of NOR gate.

Ans. XOR gate with the help of NOR gate

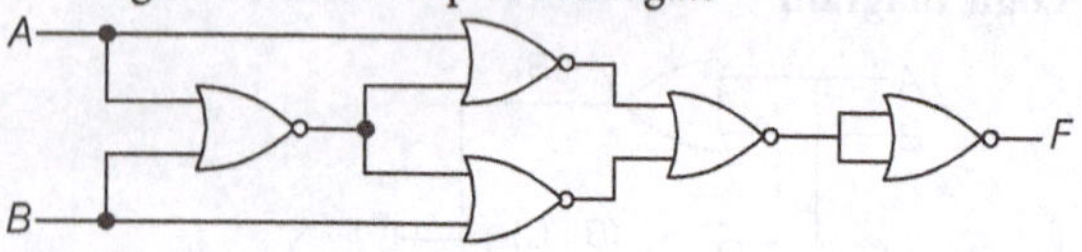

42. From the logic circuit diagram given below, derive the Boolean expression and simplify it to show that it represents a logic gate. Name and draw the logic gate.

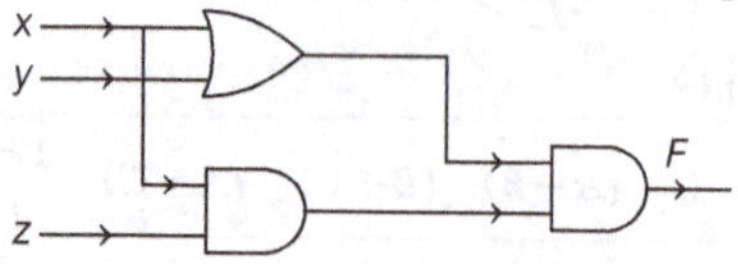

Ans.

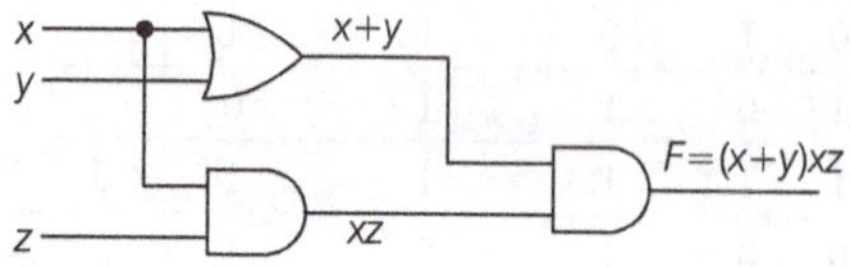

Final boolean expression = $(x+y)\,xz$

$\Rightarrow \quad xz + xyz$

$\Rightarrow \quad xz\,(1+y)$

$\Rightarrow \quad xz\,(1) \qquad [\because 1+y=1]$

$\Rightarrow \quad xz$

xz represents the AND gate and its logic gate is as follows

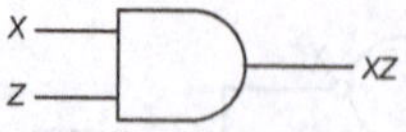

43. Check the given below exression:

(A + B) (A + C) = A + BC

Ans.

A	B	C	$A+B$	$A+C$	$(A+B)(A+C)$	BC	$A+BC$
0	0	0	0	0	0	0	0
0	0	1	0	1	0	0	0
0	1	0	1	0	0	0	0
0	1	1	1	1	1	1	1
1	0	0	1	1	1	0	1
1	0	1	1	1	1	0	1
1	1	0	1	1	1	0	1
1	1	1	1	1	1	1	1

Long Answer Type Questions

44. Explain the fundamental concepts of Boolean algebra, including its basic operations (AND, OR, NOT) and their truth tables.

Ans. Boolean algebra is a mathematical system that deals with binary values, typically represented as 0 and 1. It provides a formal framework for analyzing and simplifying digital circuits.

Basic Operations:

AND The AND operation produces a 1 only if all its inputs are 1.

OR The OR operation produces a 1 if at least one of its inputs is 1.

NOT The NOT operation inverts the input, changing 0 to 1 and 1 to 0.

Truth Tables A truth table is a tabular representation of all possible input combinations and their corresponding output values for a given logic function. It helps visualize the behavior of the function.

Operation	Input A	Input B	Output
AND	0	0	0
	0	1	0
	1	0	0
	1	1	1
OR	0	0	0
	0	1	1
	1	0	1
	1	1	1
NOT	**Input**	**Output**	
	0	1	
	1	0	

45. (a) Explain the different logical operators.

(b) What is a truth table? Explain the steps involved in creating a truth table for a given Boolean expression.

Ans. (a) Refer to text on page no. 69 (Logical Operators).

(b) A truth table is a tabular representation of all possible input combinations and their corresponding output values for a given Boolean expression.

If the output is always 1 (true), the expression is a tautology. Conversely, if the output is always 0 (false), it's a contradiction. The number of rows in a truth table is 2^n, where n is the number of input variables.

Steps to Construct a Truth Table:

1. **Identify the Input Variables** Determine the number of input variables in the Boolean expression.
2. **Determine the Number of Rows** Calculate the number of rows in the truth table using the formula 2^n, where n is the number of input variables.
3. **Create the Table**
   - **Input Columns** Create a column for each input variable.
   - **Output Column** Create a column for the output of the expression.
4. **Populate the Input Columns**
   - **Systematic Approach** Systematically list all possible combinations of 0s and 1s for the input variables.
   - **Binary Counting** You can use binary counting to fill the columns efficiently.
5. **Evaluate the Expression**
   - For each row of input values, evaluate the Boolean expression using the rules of Boolean algebra.
   - **Write the Output** Record the resulting output value in the output column of the corresponding row.

46. A smart home automation company is designing a security system that controls door access based on multiple conditions, such as a valid passcode and fingerprint authentication. The system uses electronic circuits that perform logical operations to process inputs and determine the output (grant or deny access).

How do logic gates help in designing such a system? Explain the different types of logic gates and their role in decision-making for electronic circuits.

Competency Based Que.

Ans. Refer to text on page no. 71-73. (Logic gates, More logic gates).

47. Compare and contrast NAND and NOR gates, including their symbols, Boolean expressions, and truth tables. Explain how they can be used as universal gates.

Ans.

NAND Gate	NOR Gate
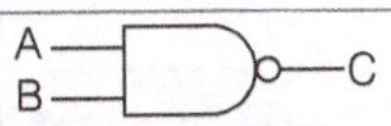 NAND Gate symbol	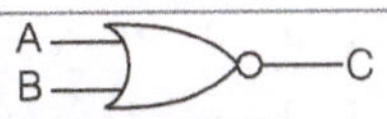 NOR Gate symbol
Boolean expression of NAND is (AB)'	Boolean expression of NOR is (A+B)'
Generates a false output only when both inputs are true.	Generates a true output only when both inputs are false.
It implements the logical function known as conjunction.	It implements the logical function known as dis-junction.

The truth-table of NAND gate:

A	B	Output
0	0	1
0	1	1
1	0	1
1	1	0

The truth-table of NOR gate:

A	B	Output
0	0	1
0	1	0
1	0	0
1	1	0

NAND and NOR gates are often referred to as universal gates because they can be combined to implement any Boolean function. This means that any complex digital circuit can be constructed using only NAND or NOR gates. To implement other logic gates using NAND gates, we can take advantage of De Morgan's theorem.

For example, to create an inverter, we can connect both inputs of a NAND gate together. To create an AND gate, we can invert the output of a NAND gate. Similarly, to create an OR gate, we can invert the inputs of a NAND gate and then invert the output. NOR gates can also be used as universal gates.

By connecting both inputs of a NOR gate together, we can create an inverter. To implement an OR gate, we can invert the output of a NOR gate. To implement an AND gate, we can invert the inputs of a NOR gate and then invert the output.

48. Differentiate between XNOR and XOR gates. Draw the truth table and logic diagrams of 3 input XNOR gates.

Ans. The differences between XNOR and XOR gate are as follows:

XNOR	XOR
XNOR gate is also known as Exclusive NOR gate. It is the complement of Exclusive OR and indicated by the ⊙ graphic symbol.	The *XOR* is also known as Exclusive OR gate. It is indicated by the ⊕ graphic symbol.

XNOR	XOR
The output of this gate is 1 only if both inputs are equal to 1 or both inputs are equal to 0, otherwise output will be zero.	The output of the *XOR* gate is 1 if any input is 1 but excludes the combination when both inputs are same.
Its algebraic expression is, $F = x \odot y = x'y' + xy$	Its algebraic expression is, $F = x \oplus y = xy' + x'y$

Truth Table of Three Inputs XNOR Gate

x	y	z	$F = x \odot y \odot z$
0	0	0	1
0	0	1	0
0	1	0	0
0	1	1	1
1	0	0	0
1	0	1	1
1	1	0	1
1	1	1	0

Logic diagram of XNOR for three-inputs is:

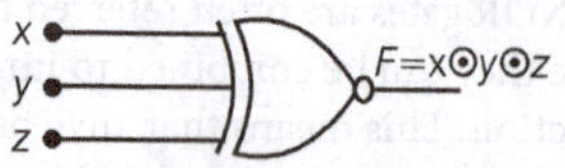

49. Design a circuit (3 inputs) which gives a high output only when there is even number of low or high inputs.

Ans. High output when even number of low inputs or even number of high inputs, i.e.

X	Y	Z	F
0	0	0	0
0	0	1	1
0	1	0	1
0	1	1	1
1	0	0	1
1	0	1	1
1	1	0	1
1	1	1	0

i.e. $F = \overline{X}.\overline{Y}.Z + \overline{X}.Y.\overline{Z} + \overline{X}.Y.Z + X.\overline{Y}.\overline{Z} + X.\overline{Y}.Z + X.Y.\overline{Z}$

Reducing it algebraically,

$= \overline{X}.\overline{Y}.Z + \overline{X}.Y.(\overline{Z} + Z) + X.\overline{Y}.(\overline{Z} + Z) + X.Y.\overline{Z}$

$= \overline{X}.\overline{Y}.Z + \overline{X}.Y + X.\overline{Y} + X.Y.\overline{Z}$ $[\because Z + \overline{Z} = 1]$

$= \overline{X}.Y + \overline{X}.\overline{Y}.Z + X.\overline{Y} + X.Y.\overline{Z}$

$= \overline{X}.(Y + \overline{Y}.Z) + X.(\overline{Y} + Y.\overline{Z})$

$= \overline{X}.(Y + \overline{Y}).(Y + Z) + X.(\overline{Y} + Y).(\overline{Y} + \overline{Z})$

$= \overline{X}.(Y + Z) + X.(\overline{Y} + \overline{Z})$ $[\because Y + \overline{Y} = 1]$

$= \overline{X}.Y + \overline{X}.Z + X.\overline{Y} + X.\overline{Z}$

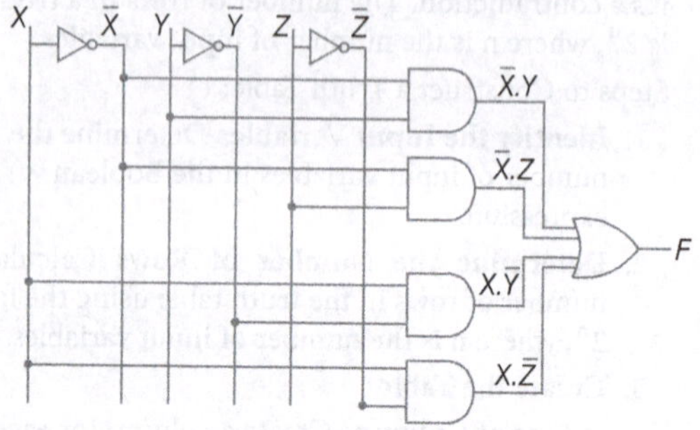

50. State and verify distributive law in boolean algebra.

Ans. Distributive law state that:

(i) $X.(Y + Z) = X.Y + X.Z$

(ii) $X + Y.Z = (X + Y).(X + Z)$

Verification:

(i) Truth table of: $X.(Y + Z) = X.Y + X.Z$

X	Y	Z	$Y+Z$	$X.(Y+Z)$	$X.Y$	$X.Z$	$X.Y+X.Z$
0	0	0	0	0	0	0	0
0	0	1	1	0	0	0	0
0	1	0	1	0	0	0	0
0	1	1	1	0	0	0	0
1	0	0	0	0	0	0	0
1	0	1	1	1	0	1	1
1	1	0	1	1	1	0	1
1	1	1	1	1	1	1	1

Both columns $X.(Y + Z)$ and $X.Y + X.Z$ are identical.

$\therefore$ $X.(Y + Z) = X.Y + X.Z$ **Hence Proved.**

(ii) Truth table for $X + Y.Z = (X + Y).(X + Z)$

X	Y	Z	$Y.Z$	$X+Y.Z$	$X+Y$	$X+Z$	$(X+Y).(X+Z)$
0	0	0	0	0	0	0	0
0	0	1	0	0	0	1	0
0	1	0	0	0	1	0	0
0	1	1	1	1	1	1	1
1	0	0	0	1	1	1	1
1	0	1	0	1	1	1	1
1	1	0	0	1	1	1	1
1	1	1	1	1	1	1	1

Both columns $X + Y.Z$ and $(X + Y).(X + Z)$ are identical.

$\therefore$ $X + Y.Z = (X + Y).(X + Z)$ **Hence Proved.**

Case Study Based Questions

Case Study 1

Boolean algebra, a branch of mathematics, deals with binary values, typically represented as 0 (false) and 1 (true). It provides a formal framework for analyzing and simplifying digital circuits. George Boole, a 19th-century mathematician, laid the foundation for this field.

Boolean algebra is fundamental to digital electronics and computer science. It allows us to represent and manipulate logical operations using symbols and rules. By understanding Boolean algebra, we can design and analyze digital circuits, from simple logic gates to complex computer systems.

Read the following text and answer the following questions on the basis of the same:

(i) **What is the primary purpose of Boolean algebra in digital electronics?**
(a) To design analog circuits
(b) To analyze continuous signals
(c) To represent and manipulate digital signals
(c) To study the properties of real numbers

(ii) **Which of the following is a fundamental operation in Boolean algebra?**
(a) Addition
(b) Subtraction
(c) Multiplication
(d) Logical OR

(iii) **The Boolean expression A + A' is equivalent to:**
(a) 0 (b) 1
(c) A (d) A'

(iv) **The Boolean expression A(A + B) is equivalent to:**
(a) A (b) B
(c) AB (d) A + B

(v) **The De Morgan's law for the expression (A + B)' is:**
(a) A' + B' (b) A'B'
(c) A + B' (d) A'B

(vi) **A logic gate that produces a high output only when all its inputs are high is called:**
(a) AND gate (b) OR gate
(c) NOT gate (d) XOR gate

(vii) **A logic gate that produces a high output when at least one of its inputs is high is called:**
(a) AND gate (b) OR gate
(c) NOT gate (d) XOR gate

(viii) **The Boolean expression for an AND gate with inputs A and B is:**
(a) A + B (b) A'B'
(c) AB (d) A' + B'

(ix) **The Boolean expression for a NOR gate with inputs A and B is:**
(a) (A + B)' (b) (AB)'
(c) A + B' (d) A'B

(x) **The Boolean expression for an XOR gate with inputs A and B is:**
(a) AB' + A'B (b) AB + A'B'
(c) (A + B)' (d) (AB)'

(xi) **Which of the following is a universal gate?**
(a) AND gate
(b) OR gate
(c) NAND gate
(d) XOR gate

Ans. (i) (c) To represent and manipulate digital signals
(ii) (d) Logical OR
(iii) (b) 1
(iv) (a) A
(v) (b) A'B'
(vi) (a) AND gate
(vii) (b) OR gate
(viii) (c) AB
(ix) (a) (A + B)'
(x) (a) AB' + A'B
(xi) (c) NAND gate

Case Study 2

Logic gate is simply an electronic circuit, which operates on one or more input signals to produce an output signal. Logic gates can be constructed from diodes, transistors and resistors connected in such a way that circuit output is the result of basic logic operations (OR, AND, NOT) performed on the inputs.

Three basic logic gates are

NOT Gate (Inverter) It accepts one input and produces one output. It performs logical NOT operation on input. The output is the complement of the given input. i.e. if input is 1, then output is 0 and vice-versa.

OR Gate It is a logic circuit that can have two or more inputs and produces only one output. It performs logical OR operation on inputs. The output of the OR gate is 1, when any of the input is 1.

AND Gate It is a logic circuit that can have two or more than two inputs and produces only one output. It is a logic circuit that requires all inputs to be 1 at the same time in order for the output to be 1. If anyone input is 0 then output is also 0.

Based on the above information, answer the following questions.

(i) What is the function of a logic gate?
(a) To store data
(b) To perform arithmetic operations
(c) To operate on input signals and produce an output
(d) To convert analog signals into digital signals

(ii) Which of the following logic gates produces an output that is the complement of the input?
(a) AND Gate
(b) OR Gate
(c) NOT Gate
(d) XOR Gate

(iii) What is the output of an OR gate when one of its inputs is 1 and the other is 0?
(a) 0
(b) 1
(c) Depends on the number of inputs
(d) Cannot be determined

(iv) In an AND gate, what must be the condition for the output to be 1?
(a) At least one input should be 1
(b) All inputs should be 1
(c) All inputs should be 0
(d) Any one input should be 0

(v) Logic gates are constructed using which of the following components?
(a) Capacitors and Resistors
(b) Inductors and Transformers
(c) Diodes, Transistors, and Resistors
(d) Switches and Batteries

Ans. (i) (c) To operate on input signals and produce an output
(ii) (c) NOT Gate
(iii) (b) 1
(iv) (b) All inputs should be 1
(v) (c) Diodes, Transistors, and Resistors

SELF ASSESSMENT TEST

Multiple Choice Questions

1. Using De Morgan's laws, how can the expression (A·B)' be rewritten?

(a) A+B (b) A'·B'
(c) A'+B' (d) A·B'

2. A logic circuit has inputs A and B. The output is 1 when both inputs are different but 0 otherwise. Which gate does this represent?

(a) NAND (b) NOR
(c) XOR (d) XNOR

3. Which Boolean equation correctly represents the given logic circuit with two inputs A and B, where the output is 0 only when both inputs are 1?

(a) A+B (b) (A·B)'
(c) A'·B'' (d) A'+B'

Fill in the Blanks

4. The Boolean expression for a NOR gate is the complement of the __ gate.

5. The logic gate that produces an output of 1 only when the inputs are different is called _____.

6. A logic circuit that performs a specific Boolean function using gates is called a _____.

State Whether True or False

7. The XOR gate produces a high (1) output only when both inputs are the same.

8. The NAND gate is the complement of the AND gate.

9. In a truth table, the number of rows is equal to 2^n, where n is the number of inputs.

Assertion and Reason Based Questions

Assertion (A) and Reason (R) Type questions. Choose the correct option as:

(a) Both Assertion (A) and Reason (R) are true, and Reason (R) is the correct explanation of Assertion (A).
(b) Both Assertion (A) and Reason (R) are true, but Reason (R) is not the correct explanation of Assertion (A).
(c) Assertion (A) is true, but Reason (R) is false.
(d) Assertion (A) is false, but Reason (R) is true.

10. **Assertion (A)** The NAND gate is called a universal gate.
Reason (R) Any Boolean function can be implemented using only NAND gates.

11. **Assertion (A)** XOR gate produces a high output when both inputs are high.
Reason (R) XOR gate follows the rule that output is high only when inputs are different.

Very Short Answer Type Questions

12. Explain the terms AND operator.

13. What do you mean by logic gates?

14. Give the dual of $(A+BC+\overline{A}B)$.

15. What is commutative law?

16. Give the symbol of NOR gate.

Short Answer Type Questions

17. Verify $X+Y.Z=(X+Y).(X+Z)$ using truth table.

18. Verify $X+Z=X+\overline{X}Z+YZ$ using boolean laws.

19. Draw the logic circuit diagram using NAND gate only for the following expression.

$$AB+\overline{A}B+\overline{AB}$$

20. Explain the NOR gate with its truth table and logic diagram.

Long Answer Type Questions

21. State the principle of duality. Give the dual of $(A\overline{B}+C\overline{A})\cdot D$.

22. Prove algebraically $X+\overline{X}Y=X+Y$.

23. State and verify identity law.

24. Show the following gates can be built using NAND gate.

(i) NOT gate
(ii) AND gate
(iii) OR gate
(iv) XOR gate

25. Prove the following boolean expression

(i) $\overline{A}B+AC+BC=\overline{A}B+AC$
(ii) $X.Y+(\overline{X}+\overline{Y})=1$
(iii) $\overline{XYZ}+\overline{XY}Z+X\overline{Y}Z=\overline{Y}(\overline{X}+Z)$
(iv) $(X+Y+Z)(\overline{X.Y.Z})=X\overline{Y}+Y\overline{Z}+Z\overline{X}$

Case Study Based Questions

26. **A digital circuit designer is working on a project that involves designing a secure access control system. The system processes multiple input signals to determine whether access should be granted. The designer uses Boolean logic gates such as AND, OR, and NOT to implement decision-making logic. Additionally, they apply De Morgan's laws to simplify expressions and optimize the circuit design.**

Answer the following questions:

(i) **Which logic gate produces an output of 1 only when all its inputs are 1?**

(a) NAND (b) AND
(c) XOR (d) NOR

(ii) **What is the output of a NOT gate if the input is 1?**

(a) 0
(b) 1
(c) Depends on other inputs
(d) Cannot be determined

(iii) **According to De Morgan's laws, the expression (A • B)' is equivalent to:**

(a) A' + B' (b) A' • B'
(c) (A + B)' (d) A + B

(iv) **Which gate produces an output of 1 only when the inputs are different?**

(a) XOR (b) AND
(c) NOR (d) NAND

(v) **What will be the output of a NAND gate if both inputs are 1?**

(a) 0
(b)
(c) Same as AND gate
(d) Cannot be determined

Answers

1. (c) 2. (c) 3. (b) 4. OR 5. XOR
6. Logic circuit 7. False 8. True 9. True
10. (a) 11. (d)
26. (i) → (b), (ii) → (a), (iii) → (a), (iv) → (a), (v) → (a)

05

CHAPTER

Computer Science is a science of abstraction creating the right model for a problem and devising the appropriate mechanizable techniques to solve it.

Introduction to Problem Solving

YOUR STUDY GOALS

5.1 Problem Solving Cycle
5.2 Algorithm
5.3 Flow Chart
5.4 Pseudocode
5.5 Decomposition

YOUR PRACTICE GOAL

- Objective Type Questions (27 Qs ; MCQs, True or False, Fill in the Blanks, Assertion and Reason)
- Subjective Type Questions (34 Qs ; VSA, SA, LA)
- Case Study Based Questions-2

Problem-solving is the process of identifying an issue, exploring solutions, and choosing the best approach to resolve it.

Problem-solving is a fundamental life skill that we use daily, often unconsciously. Whether at home, school, or work, we continuously encounter challenges that require us to identify solutions. This ability is crucial for navigating the complexities of everyday life.

Problem-solving is like a puzzle. We take a problem, break it down, and use our knowledge and skills to figure out how to fix it. We think carefully, choose the right tools, and find the best way to solve the puzzle. This helps us overcome challenges and find solutions in our daily lives.

5.1 Problem Solving Cycle

The Problem-Solving Cycle is a step-by-step process to find, analyze, and solve problems in business, technology, and daily life. It helps in making better decisions, improving productivity, and refining solutions through repetition.

Steps for Problem Solving

Problem solving begins with the precise identification of the problem and ends with a complete working solution in terms of a program or software.

Key steps required for solving a problem using a computer are discussed below:

Step 1 **Analyzing the Problem** Before we start fixing a problem, we need to understand what the problem is. If we don't know what we're trying to solve, we might end up with a solution that doesn't work. So, we should read the problem carefully, break it down into smaller parts, and decide what our solution should be.

Step 2 **Developing an Algorithm** Before we start writing computer code, we need to plan how to solve the problem. We create a step-by-step plan, like a recipe, called an algorithm. We start with a basic plan and keep improving it until it covers everything we want our solution to do.

Step 3 **Coding** Once we have our step-by-step plan (algorithm), we need to translate it into a language that computers understand. We use programming languages to write these instructions. Coding provides a structured approach to problem-solving, enhancing clarity and efficiency. It enables the review and refinement of solutions, which leads to improved outcomes.

Step 4 **Testing and Debugging** Once we've written our code, we need to test it to make sure it works correctly. We try it with different inputs and check if it gives the right outputs. If there are mistakes in how the code is written (syntax errors), it won't run at all. If the outputs are wrong, we look for mistakes in the logic of the code (logical errors). Software companies use special methods to test big programs, like unit testing, integration testing, and system testing. When we find errors, we fix them and test again until the program works perfectly.

5.2 Algorithm

An algorithm is like a recipe for solving a problem. It's a step-by-step plan that breaks down a complex task into smaller, easier steps. It's written in simple language, so anyone can follow it.

Algorithm is a stepwise solution written in simple English to fulfill a task. **"An algorithm is a set of instructions, sometimes called a procedure or a function that is used to perform a certain task"**. Algorithms help us solve problems efficiently and systematically.

Example 1. Write an algorithm to input two numbers and print their sum and also check whether they are equal or not.

Sol. *Step 1* Enter first number is A

Step 2 Enter second number is B

Step 3 C = A + B

Step 4 print C

Step 5 if (A == B)
print "Numbers are equal" else print "Numbers are not equal"

Step 6 Stop

Quick Test 1

1. What is problem-solving? Explain the concept with a real-world example.
2. Describe the problem-solving cycle. What are the key stages involved in this cycle?
3. Why is problem analysis a crucial step in problem-solving?
4. How do you identify the input, output, and constraints of a problem?
5. What is an algorithm? How does it differ from a program?

5.3 Flow Chart

A flowchart is like a visual map of an algorithm that shows the steps to complete a task.

It uses shapes like rectangles, diamonds, and circles connected by arrows to illustrate how information flows through a process. Flowcharts help us understand complex processes in a simple and visual way.

Some of the standard symbols along with respective functions that are used for making flowchart are as follows.

Symbols	Names
	Start/Stop Box
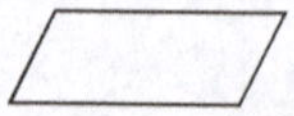	Input/Output Box
	Processing Box
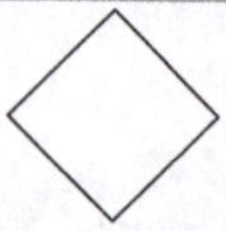	Decision Box
	Connectors
→	Flow lines

Rules for Constructing Flowcharts

- **Define the Problem Clearly** To create an effective flowchart, first, understand the specific task or process you want to visualize and identify its starting point, end point, and key decision points.
- **Break Down the Process** Divide the process into smaller, manageable steps, each with a clear beginning and end.
- **Choose the Right Symbols** Use standard flowchart symbols to represent different actions:
  - **Oval** Start or end point
  - **Rectangle** Process or action
  - **Diamond** Decision point
  - **Parallelogram** Input/output
  - **Arrow** Flow direction
- **Maintain a Logical Flow** Arrange the flowchart symbols in a logical sequence, typically from top to bottom and left to right, using arrows to indicate the flow of the process.
- **Keep it Simple** Avoid unnecessary complexity by focusing on the core steps and avoid overloading the flowchart with excessive detail.
- **Use Clear and Concise Labels** Label each symbol with a clear and concise description of the action or decision it represents and try to use simple language that is easy to understand.
- **Test Your Flowchart** Walk through the flowchart step-by-step to ensure it accurately represents the process and try to identify and correct any errors or inconsistencies.

TEACHER TIP
Draw the flowchart using a scale neatly. Flow lines should be neat and show the flow of control with an arrow use same case of same variable.

Example 2. Draw a flowchart to find the simple interest.

Sol.

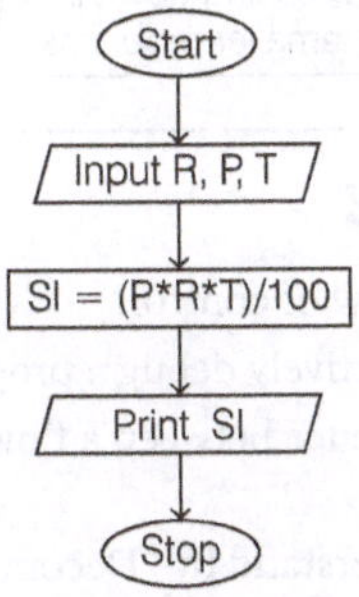

Example 3. Draw a flowchart to find the factorial of any number.

Sol.

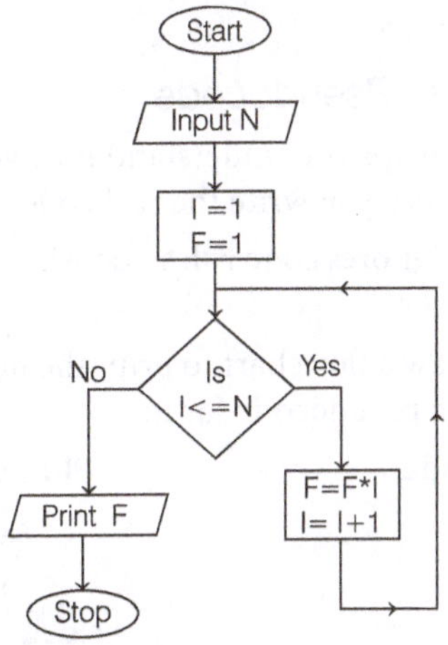

5.4 Pseudocode

Pseudocode is a simple, informal way to describe a computer program's logic without the strict rules of a programming language. It uses plain English statements and basic programming structures like loops and conditions, making it easier to understand and plan the program's flow.

General rules used in writing Pseudocodes are as follows:

1. **Imperative Sentences** The imperative sentences are used to show actions. It uses action words like "Start," "Input," "Process," "Output," and "End" to describe the steps.
2. **Operators** It uses arithmetic operators like +, -, *, /, and % for calculations, relational operators like =, >, <, >=, <=, and != for comparisons, and logical operators like AND, OR, and NOT for conditional statements.
3. **Decision Making** IF-THEN-ELSE and CASE statements are used for decision-making in algorithms. They help the program choose different actions based on specific conditions.
4. **Looping** FOR, FOR DO, ENDFOR, DO, DO WHILE, DO UNTIL, and END DO are used to repeat specific blocks of code, known as loops. These loops allow for efficient repetition of tasks based on certain conditions over a fixed number of times.

Example 4. Calculate area and perimeter of a rectangle using pseudocode.

Sol.

```
INPUT length
INPUT breadth
```

```
COMPUTE Area = length * breadth
PRINT Area
COMPUTE Perim = 2*(length+breadth)
PRINT Perim
```

Advantages of Pseudocode

- Pseudocode helps you understand how your program will work before you write the real code.
- Pseudocode ignores code rules, focusing on how the program works.

Example 5. Draw a flowchart to print the number from 1 to ∞ and write a pseudocode for it.

Sol. Pseudocode

```
START
INPUT N
I = 1
LOOP:
  IF I <= N THEN
    PRINT I
    I = I + 1
    GOTO LOOP
  ELSE
    STOP
  ENDIF
END
```

Flow Chart

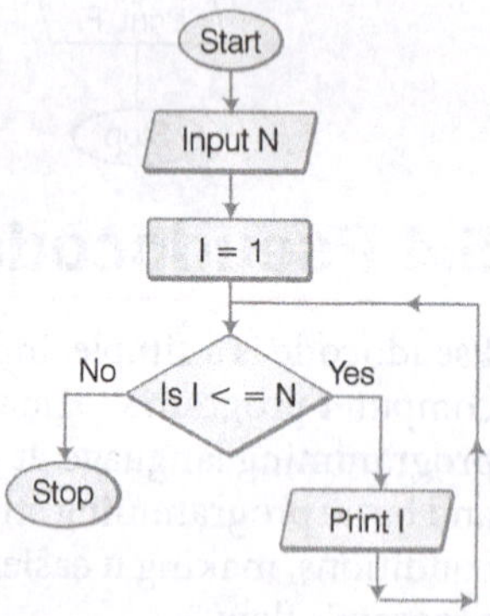

In the above example, "I" value is not at all incremented, so it will create an endless loop. This is also called an infinite loop.

Flow of Control

Flow of control refers to the order in which instructions are executed in a program. It can be simple, where instructions are followed one after the other, or more complex, involving branching (choosing different paths based on conditions) and looping (repeating a set of instructions).

(a) **Sequential flow** This means that the events happen in a specific order, and each event must finish before the next one can start.

(b) **Selective flow** This means that the program's path can split into two or more different directions, depending on the outcome of a specific condition. It's like a fork in the road, where the path you take depends on a certain choice.

(c) **Iterative flow** This means that a set of instructions is repeated multiple times, until a certain condition is no longer true. It's like doing the same thing over and over, until you reach a specific goal.

Comparison of Algorithms

The comparison of algorithms involves evaluating different algorithms to determine which one performs the best in terms of efficiency, speed, and resource usage. Key factors considered in comparison include:

- **Time Complexity** Measures the time an algorithm takes based on input size, using notations like Big O, Omega, and Theta.
- **Space Complexity** Refers to the memory an algorithm uses relative to the input size.

Verifying Algorithms

Verifying algorithms refers to the process of ensuring that an algorithm correctly solves the problem it's designed to address. It involves checking whether the algorithm produces the desired output for all valid inputs and that it meets specified requirements (like efficiency or termination).

5.5 Decomposition

Sometimes a problem can be too big and complicated to solve all at once. To make it easier, we break it down into smaller, simpler parts. For example, building a railway reservation system is a huge task.

Instead of trying to solve it all at once, we break it down into smaller parts like booking tickets, managing trains, and handling payments. By focusing on each smaller part, we can create a more efficient and effective solution. This approach of breaking down a big problem into smaller ones is called decomposition.

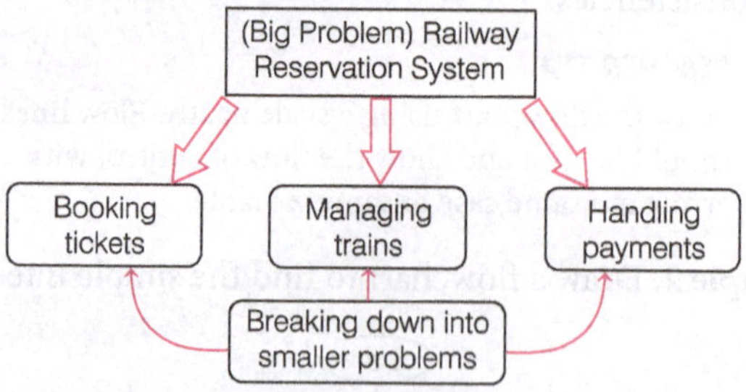

Quick Test 2

1. Briefly explain flow of control?
2. How can you effectively debug a program?
3. What is the difference between a flowchart and a pseudocode?
4. What do you understand by "Decomposition"?

Mind Map

Problem Solving Cycle

It is structured step-by-step approach where each stage builds on the previous one.

Steps of Problem Solving

- Analyzing the Problem
- Developing an Algorithm
- Coding
- Testing and Debugging

Algorithm

"An algorithm is a set of instructions, sometimes called a procedure or a function that is used to perform a certain task".

Pseudocode

Pseudocode is a simple, informal way to describe a computer program's logic without the strict rules of a programming language. It uses plain English statements and basic programming structures like loops and conditions.

Flow of Control

Flow of control refers to the order in which instructions are executed in a program.

- **Sequential flow**: This means that the events happen in a specific order, and each event must finish before the next one can start.
- **Selective flow**: This means that the program's path can split into two or more different directions, depending on the outcome of a specific condition.
- **Iterative flow**: This means that a set of instructions is repeated multiple times, until a certain condition is no longer true.

PROBLEM SOLVING

Flow Chart

A flowchart is like a visual map that shows the steps to complete a task. It uses shapes like rectangles, diamonds, and circles connected by arrows to illustrate how information flows through a process.

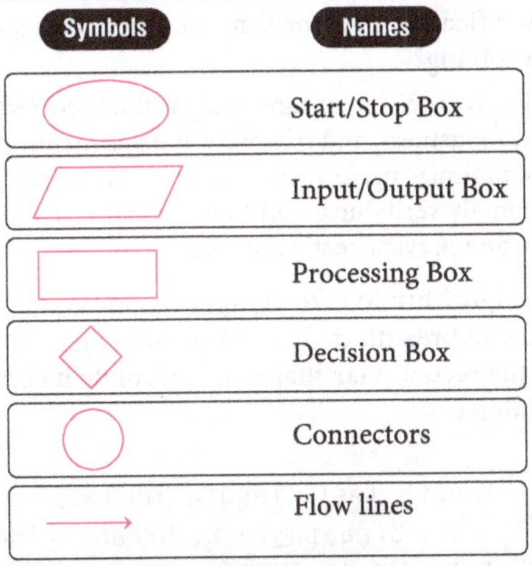

Decomposition

It breaks down complex problems into smaller , manageable parts.
e.g.

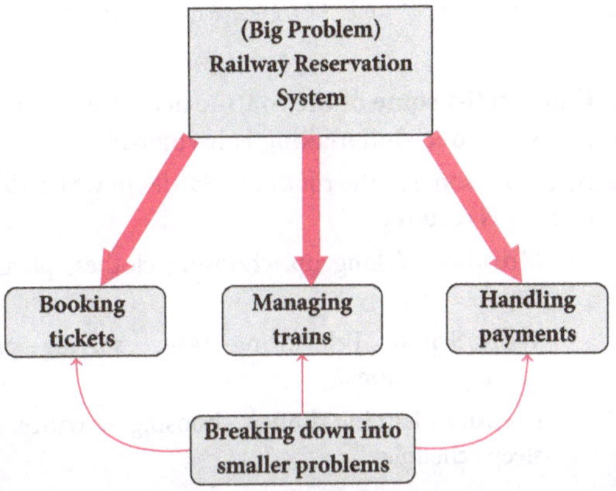

NCERT Folder

In-Text Questions

1. What sequence of steps will you follow to compute the LCM of two numbers?

Ans. Steps to compute the LCM of two numbers:

- Find the prime factors of both numbers.
- Identify common and unique prime factors.
- Multiply the common prime factors, taking the highest power from each number.
- Multiply the remaining prime factors, taking their powers from the original numbers.
- Multiply the results to get the LCM.

2. What will happen if an algorithm does not stop after a finite number of steps?

Ans. If an algorithm keeps running forever and never finishes, it's called an infinite loop. It won't give you an answer and will just waste your computer's energy and memory. This kind of algorithm is broken and not helpful.

3. Write a pseudocode for creating a scoreboard for a hockey match.

Ans.
```
Start
   Set TeamA_Score to 0
   Set TeamB_Score to 0
   Set Time_Left to 60 minutes
   While Time_Left > 0
      If TeamA scores
         Increase TeamA_Score by 1
      If TeamB scores
         Increase TeamB_Score by 1
      Decrease Time_Left by 1 minute
   End While
   Display final scores and winner
End
```

4. Can you list some of the routine activities in your daily life where decision making is involved?

Ans. Below are some of the routine activities in which decision making is required:

- **Morning** Waking up, choosing clothes, planning the day.
- **Work/School** Prioritizing tasks, solving problems, making decisions.
- **Evening** Planning dinner, choosing activities, setting a sleep schedule.

5. Can you list some of the routine activities in your daily life where repetition or iteration is involved?

Ans. Any activity that involves repeated actions or steps can be considered iterative. Below are some daily life activities where repetition or iteration is involved:

- **Daily Routine** Brushing teeth, showering, eating meals.
- **Work/School** Completing similar tasks, attending meetings, checking emails.
- **Learning** Practicing a skill, reviewing lessons, solving problems.
- **Hobbies** Playing video games, practicing a musical instrument, painting.

6. Let us answer the following questions using the pseudocode.

(i) What will the sum when input are 6, 7, 4, 8, 2, 5, 0, 3, 1.

(ii) What will be the value of count?

(iii) Why did we use the input statement to enter num twice?

(iv) Why did we divide sum by count?

(v) Can there be any other approach?

Ans. (i) The sum will be 36.

(ii) The value of count will be 9.

(iii) The first input is to initialize the loop. We need an initial value to check the condition of the while loop. The second input is inside the loop to get the next number and update the sum and count variables.

(iv) To calculate the average of the numbers.

(v) Yes, there are other ways to calculate the average. For example, you could use a for loop with a predefined number of iterations, or you could use a do-while loop to ensure at least one iteration.

7. Why is verification of algorithms an important step in problem solving?

Ans. Verification is crucial to ensure an algorithm's correctness, efficiency, robustness, and reliability. It helps identify and fix errors, optimize performance, and build confidence in the solution. By verifying algorithms, we can save time, resources, and prevent costly mistakes.

8. Write an algorithm to take as input the measurement of length and breadth in feet and inches (e.g., 5 ft 6 inch) of the rectangular shape and calculate its area and perimeter.

Ans.
```
Start
   Input length_feet, length_inches,
                breadth_feet, breadth_inches
   Convert length to inches:
```

```
   length_inches = length_feet * 12 +
                              length_inches
Convert breadth to inches:
   breadth_inches = breadth_feet * 12 +
                              breadth_inches
Calculate area in square inches:
   area_sq_inches = length_inches *
                              breadth_inches
Convert area to square feet:
   area_sq_feet = area_sq_inches / 144
Calculate perimeter in inches:
   perimeter_inches = 2 * (length_inches
                        + breadth_inches)
Convert perimeter to feet and inches:
   perimeter_feet = perimeter_inches / 12
   perimeter_inches = perimeter_inches % 12
Display area in square feet:
   Display "Area: ", area_sq_feet, " sq ft"
Display perimeter in feet and inches:
   Display "Perimeter: ", perimeter_feet,
      " ft ", perimeter_inches, " inches"
End
```

Exercise Questions

1. Write pseudocode that reads two numbers and divide one by another and display the quotient.

Ans.
```
Start
   Input number1, number2
   If number2 = 0
      Display "Error: Division by zero"
   Else
      Calculate quotient = number1 / number2

      Display "Quotient: ", quotient
   End If
End
```

2. Two friends decide who gets the last slice of a cake by flipping a coin five times. The first person to win three flips wins the cake. An input of 1 means player 1 wins a flip, and a 2 means player 2 wins a flip. Design an algorithm to determine who takes the cake?

Ans.
```
Start
   Initialize player1_wins = 0,
                       player2_wins = 0
   While player1_wins < 3 and player2_wins < 3
      Input flip_result
      If flip_result = 1
         player1_wins = player1_wins + 1
      Else
         player2_wins = player2_wins + 1
      End If
   End While
   If player1_wins = 3
      Display "Player 1 wins the cake!"
   Else
      Display "Player 2 wins the cake!"
   End If
End
```

3. Write the pseudocode to print all multiples of 5 between 10 and 25 (including both 10 and 25).

Ans.
```
Start
   For number = 10 to 25 Step 5
      Display number
   End For
End
```

4. Give an example of a loop that is to be executed a certain number of times.

Ans.
```
Start
   For i = 1 to 10
      Display i
   End For
End
```

5. Suppose you are collecting money for something. You need ` 200 in all. You ask your parents, uncles and aunts as well as grandparents. Different people may give either ` 10, ` 20 or even ` 50. You will collect till the total becomes 200. Write the algorithm.

Ans.
```
Start
   Initialize total_collected = 0
   While total_collected < 200
      Input amount_given
      total_collected = total_collected
                          + amount_given
   End While
   Display "Total collected: ",
                          total_collected
End
```

6. Write the pseudocode to print the bill depending upon the price and quantity of an item. Also print Bill GST, which is the bill after adding 5% of tax in the total bill.

Ans.
```
Start
   Input price, quantity
   Calculate total_bill = price * quantity
   Calculate bill_gst = total_bill * 1.05
   Display "Total Bill: ", total_bill
        Display "Bill with GST: ", bill_gst
End
```

7. Write pseudocode that will perform the following:

(a) Read the marks of three subjects: Computer Science, Mathematics and Physics, out of 100

(b) **Calculate the aggregate marks**

(c) **Calculate the percentage of marks**

Ans.
```
Start
  Input cs_marks, math_marks, phy_marks
  Calculate aggregate_marks = cs_marks
                  + math_marks + phy_marks
  Calculate percentage = (aggregate_marks
                              / 300) * 100
  Display "Aggregate Marks: ",
                           aggregate_marks
  Display "Percentage: ", percentage
End
```

8. Write an algorithm to find the greatest among two different numbers entered by the user.

Ans.
```
Start
  Input num1, num2
  If num1 > num2
    Display num1 as the greatest
  Else
    Display num2 as the greatest
  End If
End
```

9. Write an algorithm that performs the following: Ask a user to enter a number. If the number is between 5 and 15, write the word GREEN. If the number is between 15 and 25, write the word BLUE. if the number is between 25 and 35, write the word ORANGE. If it is any other number, write that ALL COLOURS ARE BEAUTIFUL.

Ans.
```
Start
  Input number
  If number >= 5 AND number <= 15
    Display "GREEN"
  Else If number > 15 AND number <= 25
    Display "BLUE"
  Else If number > 25 AND number <= 35
    Display "ORANGE"
  Else
    Display "ALL COLOURS ARE BEAUTIFUL"
  End If
End
```

10. Write an algorithm that accepts four numbers as input and find the largest and smallest of them.

Ans.
```
Start
  Input num1, num2, num3, num4
  // Find the largest
  largest = num1
  If num2 > largest
    largest = num2
  End If
  If num3 > largest
    largest = num3
  End If
  If num4 > largest
    largest = num4
  End If
  // Find the smallest
  smallest = num1
  If num2 < smallest
    smallest = num2
  End If
  If num3 < smallest
    smallest = num3
  End If
  If num4 < smallest
    smallest = num4
  End If
  Display "Largest number: ", largest
  Display "Smallest number: ", smallest
End
```

11. Write an algorithm to display the total water bill charges of the month depending upon the number of units consumed by the customer as per the following criteria:

- **for the first 100 units @ 5 per unit**
- **for next 150 units @ 10 per unit**
- **more than 250 units @ 20 per unit**

Also add meter charges of 75 per month to calculate the total water bill .

Ans.
```
Start
  Input units_consumed
  If units_consumed <= 100
    bill = units_consumed * 5
  Else If units_consumed <= 250
    bill = 500 + (units_consumed - 100) * 10
  Else
    bill = 1500 + (units_consumed - 250) * 20
  End If
    Calculate total_bill = bill + 75
    Display "Total water bill: ", total_bill
End
```

12. What are conditionals? When they are required in a program?

Ans. Conditionals are programming constructs that allow the flow of a program to be controlled based on certain conditions. They are used to make decisions and execute different code blocks depending on whether a specific condition is true or false.

Conditionals are required in programs when we want to:

- Make decisions based on input values
- Execute different code blocks under different circumstances
- Control the flow of a program's execution

13. **Match the pairs**

	Flowchart Symbol		Functions
(i)		(a)	Flow of Control
(ii)		(b)	Process Step
(iii)		(c)	Start/Stop of the Process
(iv)		(d)	Data
(v)		(e)	Decision Making

Ans. (i) → (c), (ii) → (d), (iii) → (b), (iv) → (e), (v) → (a)

14. **Following is an algorithm for going to school or college. Can you suggest improvements in this to include other options?**

Reach_School_Algorithm

(a) Wake up
(b) Get ready
(c) Take lunch box
(d) Take bus
(e) Get off the bus
(f) Reach school or college

Ans.
```
Start
  Wake up
  Get ready, Take lunch box
  If school/college is nearby
    Walk to school/college
  Else
    If public transport is available
      Take public transport
    Else
      Take private vehicle
    End If
  End If
  Reach school/college
End
```

15. **Write a pseudocode to calculate the factorial of a number (Hint: Factorial of 5, written as 5! = 5 × 4 × 3 × 2 × 1).**

Ans.
```
Start
  Input number
  Initialize factorial = 1
  For i = 1 to number
    factorial = factorial * i
  End For
  Display factorial
End
```

16. **Draw a flowchart to check whether a given number is an Armstrong number. An Armstrong number of three digits is an integer such that the sum of the cubes of its digits is equal to the number itself. For example, 371 is an Armstrong number since 3**3 + 7**3 + 1**3 = 371.**

Ans.

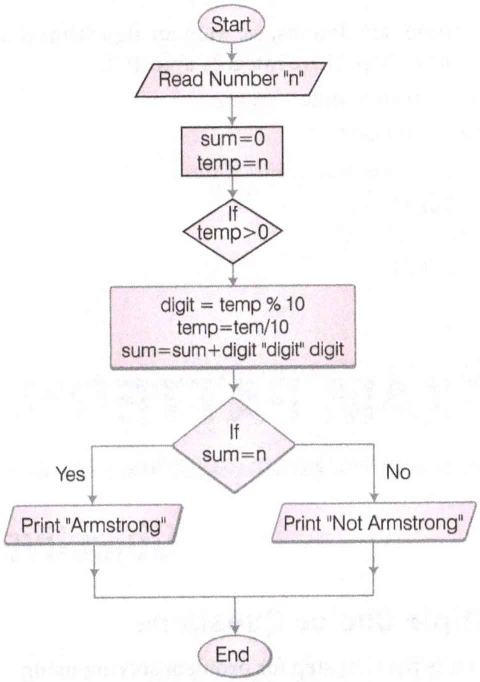

17. **Following is an algorithm to classify numbers as "Single Digit", "Double Digit" or "Big".**

Classify_Numbers_Algo
```
INPUT Number
IF Number < 9
  "Single Digit"
Else If Number < 99
  "Double Digit"
Else
  "Big"
```

Verify for (5, 9, 47, 99, 100, 200) and correct the algorithm if required.

Ans. The Issue:

The original algorithm uses IF Number < 9 to classify "Single Digit". This means that 9 itself does not fall into that category, as 9 is not less than 9.

The Correction:

We need to change the condition to include 9. We can do this by using "less than or equal to" (<=).

Classify_Numbers_Algo
```
  INPUT Number
  IF Number <= 9
```

```
    OUTPUT "Single Digit"
  ELSE IF Number < 99
    OUTPUT "Double Digit"
  ELSE
    OUTPUT "Big"
```

18. For some calculations, we want an algorithm that accepts only positive integers upto 100.

Accept_1to100_Algo

```
INPUT Number
IF (0<= Number) AND (Number <= 100)
  ACCEPT
Else
  REJECT
```

(a) On what values will this algorithm fail?

(b) Can you improve the algorithm?

Ans. (a) This algorithm will fail for negative numbers and numbers greater than 100.

(b) Yes, below are the improved algorithm:

```
Start
  Input number
  While number < 0 OR number > 100
    Display "Invalid input. Please
      enter a number between 1 and 100."
    Input number
  End While
  // Proceed with the rest of the algorithm
End
```

EXAM PATTERN QUESTIONS

Objective Type Questions

Multiple Choice Questions

1. What is the first step for problem solving using computer?

(a) Coding (b) Developing an algorithm
(c) Testing (d) Analyzing the problem

2. Which of the following is helpful when revisiting the programs at a later stage?

(a) testing (b) Coding
(c) Debugging (d) Algorithm

3. Which of the following is/are characteristic(s) of algorithm?

(a) Precision (b) Uniqueness
(c) Finiteness (d) All of these

4. Which of the following is a step by step process of solving a well-defined computational problem?

(a) Algorithm (b) Pseudocode
(c) Flowchart (d) Decision Table

5. A software developer is choosing an algorithm for a critical application. Which factor should they prioritize to ensure the application performs optimally and efficiently? **Competency Based Que.**

(a) Programmer's preference
(b) Ease of implementation
(c) Time and space efficiency
(d) Random selection

6. A step-by-step procedure to solve a problem is called a(n):

(a) Algorithm (b) Flowchart
(c) Program (d) Data Structure

7. Which of the following is NOT a common way to represent an algorithm?

(a) Flowchart (b) Pseudocode
(c) Assembly Language (d) Natural Language

8. Which of the following is characterized by the use of "special purpose symbols" to represent different operations and the flow of control within an algorithm?

(a) Algorithm (b) Pseudocode
(c) Flowchart (d) Decision Table

9. Which of the following are the primary control flow patterns in programming?

(a) Sequential and Iterative
(b) Sequential and Conditional
(c) Iterative and Conditional
(d) All of the above

Fill in the Blanks

10. ________ means removing errors that occur during a dry run of the algorithm.

11. ________ and ________ go hand in hand.

12. ______ uses sample inputs to check if the algorithm produces the desired output.

13. _______ keyword in a pseudocode is used to show data being input from the user.

14. An algorithm which has certain steps being repeated finite number of times is called ________.

State Whether True or False

15. The problem-solving cycle involves analyzing the problem, developing an algorithm, coding, and testing and debugging.

16. An algorithm is a set of instructions written in a specific programming language to solve a problem.

17. Flowcharts are visual representations of algorithms using shapes like rectangles, diamonds, and circles to show the flow of information.

18. Syntax errors occur when the code doesn't follow the rules of the programming language, while logical errors occur when the code produces incorrect results even though it runs without errors.

19. Pseudocode uses strict programming language rules and structures like English statements and basic programming logic to describe a program's flow.

20. Flowcharts and pseudocode are primarily used for visualizing and describing the design of hardware systems.

21. Decomposition is the process of breaking down a large problem into smaller, more manageable sub problems to make it easier to solve.

Assertion and Reason Based Questions

Assertion (A) and Reason (R) Type questions. Choose the correct option as:

(a) Both Assertion (A) and Reason (R) are true, and Reason (R) is the correct explanation of Assertion (A).

(b) Both Assertion (A) and Reason (R) are true, but Reason (R) is not the correct explanation of Assertion (A).

(c) Assertion (A) is true, but Reason (R) is false.

(d) Assertion (A) is false, but Reason (R) is true.

22. **Assertion (A)** The first step in problem-solving is to understand the problem.

Reason (R) A clear understanding of the problem is essential for developing an effective solution.

23. **Assertion (A)** Testing and debugging are crucial steps in the software development process.

Reason (R) They help to identify and fix errors in the code.

24. **Assertion (A)** An algorithm is a step-by-step procedure for solving a problem.

Reason (R) An algorithm can be represented using a flowchart or pseudocode.

25. **Assertion (A)** A flowchart is a visual representation of an algorithm.

Reason (R) A flowchart uses symbols to represent different operations and control flow.

26. **Assertion (A)** Pseudocode is a semi-formal language used to describe algorithms.

Reason (R) Pseudocode is more precise than natural language but less formal than a programming language.

27. **Assertion (A)** Decomposition is a technique for breaking down a complex problem into smaller, more manageable sub problems.

Reason (R) Decomposition helps to simplify the problem-solving process.

Answers

1. (d) Analyzing the problem
2. (d) Algorithm
3. (d) All of these
4. (a) Algorithm
5. (c) Time and space efficiency
6. (a) Algorithm
7. (c) Assembly Language
8. (c) Flowchart
9. (d) All of the above
10. Debugging
11. Testing and debugging
12. Testing
13. INPUT/ACCEPT
14. iterative
15. True
16. False
17. True
18. True
19. False
20. False
21. True
22. (a) Both Assertion (A) and Reason (R) are true, and Reason (R) is the correct explanation of Assertion (A).
23. (a) Both Assertion (A) and Reason (R) are true, and Reason (R) is the correct explanation of Assertion (A).
24. (a) Both Assertion (A) and Reason (R) are true, and Reason (R) is the correct explanation of Assertion (A).
25. (a) Both Assertion (A) and Reason (R) are true, and Reason (R) is the correct explanation of Assertion (A).
26. (a) Both Assertion (A) and Reason (R) are true, and Reason (R) is the correct explanation of Assertion (A).
27. (a) Both Assertion (A) and Reason (R) are true, and Reason (R) is the correct explanation of Assertion (A).

Subjective Type Questions

Very Short Answer Type Questions

1. Why is problem analysis important?

Ans. It helps in understanding the problem and identifying its requirements.

2. What is an algorithm?

Ans. A set of instructions which describes the steps to be followed to carry out an activity is called an algorithm.

3. Name one textual method for representing an algorithm.

Ans. Pseudocode

4. What is the role of finiteness characteristic in algorithm design?

Ans. The algorithm stops after a finite number of instructions are executed.

5. What is time complexity?

Ans. Measures the time taken by an algorithm to execute.

6. What is space complexity?

Ans. Measures the memory used by an algorithm.

7. What is a flowchart?

Ans. A flowchart is a diagrammatic representation of an algorithm, using symbols to depict different steps and their flow.

8. What is the purpose of a flowchart?

Ans. A flowchart helps visualize the logical flow of an algorithm, making it easier to understand and implement.

9. State the primary function of a connector in a flowchart.

Ans. Junction / Link / Connection

10. What do you mean by flow line?

Ans. In a flowchart, flow lines with arrowheads indicate the flow of operation, that is the exact sequence in which the instructions are to be executed

11. What are the basic symbols used in flowcharting?

Ans. Oval, rectangle, diamond, parallelogram, arrow.

12. What is pseudocode?

Ans. Pseudocode is a way to describe an algorithm using a combination of natural language and programming language elements. It helps in understanding and designing algorithms before writing actual code.

13. What is a dry run?

Ans. A dry run is a manual process of executing an algorithm using sample input values to check if it produces the correct output.

14. Give a one-word synonym for "decomposition" in the context of problem-solving.

Ans. Breakdown / Division / Partitioning / Separation

15. What are the control flow patterns in programming?

Ans. Sequential, iterative, and conditional.

Short Answer Type I Questions

16. Describe a real-life situation where you used problem-solving skills. Outline the steps you took to find a solution. Competency Based Que.

Ans. **Situation** My laptop suddenly wouldn't connect to the Wi-Fi.

Steps

Step 1 Identify: Noted the error message, checked router connection.

Step 2 Research: Searched online forums for similar issues.

Step 3 Hypothesis: Suspected outdated network drivers.

Step 4 Action: Updated drivers, restarted laptop.

Step 5 Test: Successfully connected to Wi-Fi.

17. What is coding?

Ans. Coding is the process of translating an algorithm (a step-by-step solution) into a specific programming language that a computer can understand and execute. It involves writing code statements using the syntax and keywords of the chosen language.

18. Imagine you've written a program that isn't producing the correct output. How does having a well-designed algorithm help you identify and fix the errors? Competency Based Que.

Ans. A well-designed algorithm acts as a blueprint. It breaks down the program's logic into clear, sequential steps. When your program has errors, you can compare the actual output to the expected outcome at each step of the algorithm.

19. How are algorithms evaluated?

Ans. Algorithms are compared based on their:

- **Time complexity** This measures the amount of time an algorithm takes to execute as the input size increases. Ideally, the algorithm with the least time complexity is preferred.
- **Space complexity** This measures the amount of memory an algorithm requires to run as the input size increases. Minimizing space complexity is also desirable.

20. Write the algorithm to find the perimeter of rectangle.

Ans. The algorithm is

Step 1 Start

Step 2 Enter the length (l) and breadth (b) of rectangle

Step 3 Calculate perimeter = 2 * (l+b)

Step 4 Print perimeter

Step 5 Stop

21. Write an algorithm to find out whether the given number is divisible by 3 or not.

Ans. The algorithm is

Step 1 Input "Enter a Number" N

Step 2 Let R = N % 3

Step 3 If R = 0, then "N is divisible by 3"

Step 4 If R! = 0, then "N is not divisible by 3"

Step 5 Stop

22. Write an algorithm to compute factorial of a given number.

Ans. The algorithm is

Step 1 Start

Step 2 Read a number N

Step 3 fact = 1

Step 4 i = 1

Step 5 while (i<=N)

fact = fact * i

i = i+1

Step 6 Print fact

Step 7 Stop

23. Why are these symbols used in flowcharts?

(a)  (b) 

Ans.

(a)	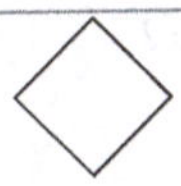	A decision box is used when the program needs to make a choice based on a specific condition. For example, if a number is greater than 10, the program might take one action, and if it's less than 10, it might take another.
(b)		A processing box represents an action or calculation that the program performs, such as adding two numbers or printing a message.

24. In your village many people are living. Draw a flowchart to enter the age of a person and find whether he can cast a vote or not. The minimum age limit is 18.

Ans.

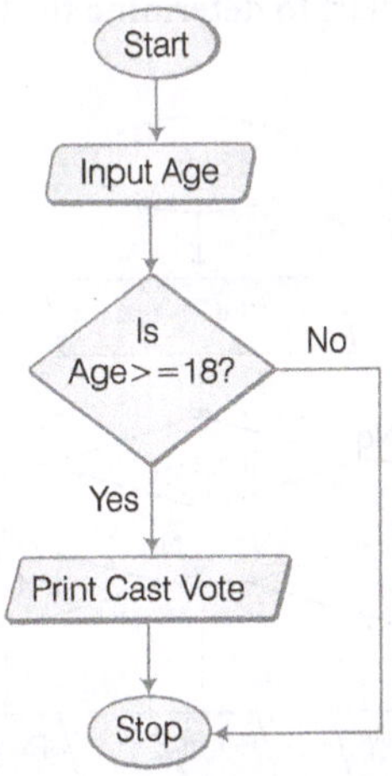

25. Draw a flowchart to find the compound interest of an amount for a certain period of time and total amount.

Ans.

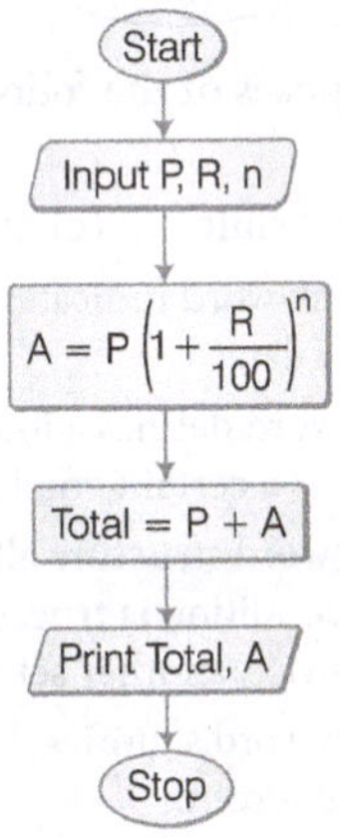

26. Draw a flowchart to find whether a number is even or odd.

Ans.

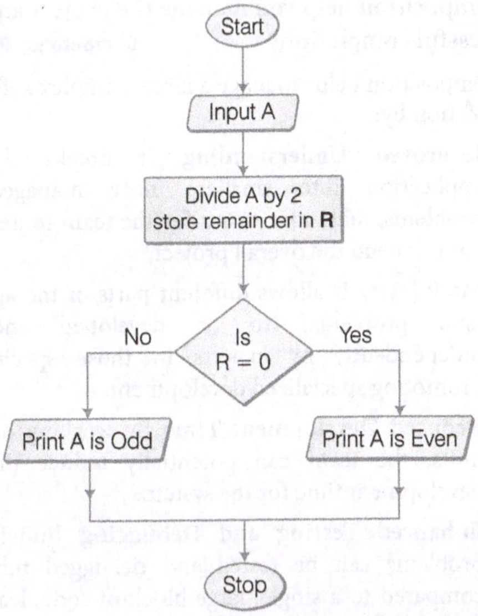

27. **Create a flowchart to determine the largest of three numbers.**

Ans.

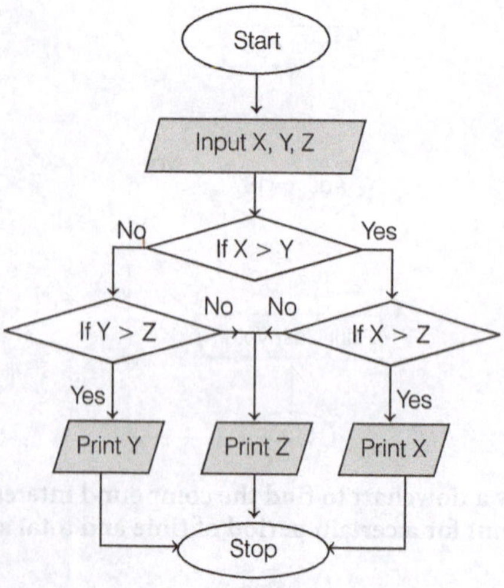

28. **What are the purposes of the following pseudocode keywords?**

(a) compute (b) while (c) if/else (d) display

Ans. (a) **compute** This keyword indicates a calculation or manipulation of data.

(b) **while** This keyword defines a loop that repeats a block of code as long as a certain condition remains true.

(c) **if/else** This keyword structure allows for conditional execution. If a condition is true, one set of code is executed; otherwise, another set of code is executed.

(d) **display** This keyword signifies displaying information or results on the screen.

29. **You're leading a team tasked with developing a large, complex software application. How does decomposition help you manage the project and ensure successful completion?** **Competency Based Que.**

Ans. Decomposition helps manage a large, complex software application by:

- **Improved Understanding** It breaks down the application into smaller, more manageable sub problems, making it easier for the team to analyze and comprehend the overall project.
- **Modularity** It allows different parts of the application (sub problems) to be developed and tested independently by experts in those specific areas, promoting specialized development.
- **Reduced Development Time** By working on smaller units, the team can potentially reduce the overall development time for the system.
- **Enhanced Testing and Debugging** Individual sub problems can be tested and debugged more easily compared to a single, large block of code, leading to a more robust and reliable application.

Short Answer Type II Questions

30. **Draw a flowchart to find the sum of squares of first N natural numbers.**

Ans.

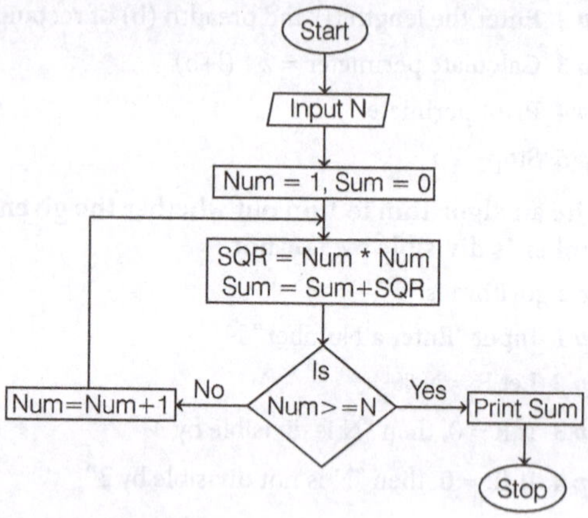

31. **Consider the flowchart shown below.**

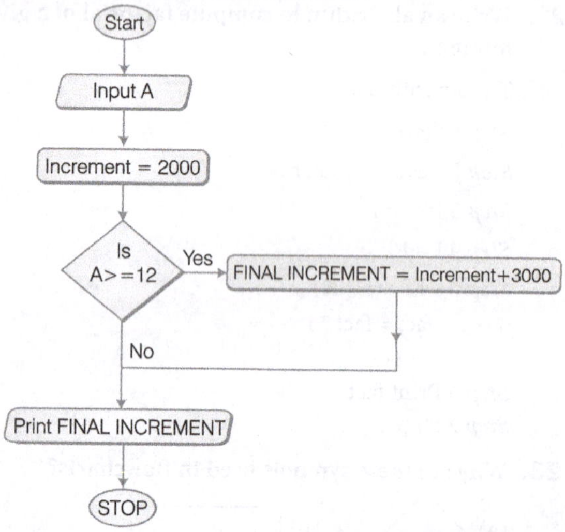

Give the value of Increment under the following condition

(i) A = 10 (ii) A = 12

Ans. (i) Value of A is given = 10.

This value will inputted in Step 2.

The value of increment is given = 2000 in Step 3. In Step 4, value of A is less than 12, so the Increment will be like

Increment = Increment + 3000

and the initial value of increment is 2000.

So, the final increment = 5000 in Step 5.

(ii) Value of A is given = 12. This value will inputted in Step 2. The value of increment is given = 2000 in Step 3.

In Step 4, the value of A is equal to 12, so the Increment is equal to 2000 in Step 4.

Hence, the value of FINAL INCREMENT is 2000 in Step 5.

32. What is the difference between a flowchart and pseudocode?

Ans.

Feature	Flowchart	Pseudocode
Representation	Flowchart is a visual representation of a problem's solution	Pseudocode is a textual representation of a problem's solution
Focus	It focuses on visualizing the flow of control	It describes the logic and steps
Level of Detail	It gives the high-level overview	It gives the detailed description
Complexity	It can become complex for large problems	It is more readable and easier to understand
Flexibility	This one is less flexible, requires specific symbols	This one is more flexible, can be adapted to different programming languages

Long Answer Type Questions

33. What is algorithm design? Explain its characteristics.

Ans. An algorithm is a step-by-step process that solves a problem or complete a task. If you follow the algorithm's steps correctly, you will arrive at a correct solution, even for different inputs. The algorithm design phase requires an analysis of each specific task, providing a step by step set of instructions on how to complete it.

Algorithm design is often based on the decomposition of a problem and the identification of patterns that help to solve the problem.

Characteristics of Algorithm Design

- **Precision** The steps are precisely defined.
- **Uniqueness** Result of each step are uniquely defined only depend on the input and the result of the preceding steps.
- **Finiteness** The algorithm steps often a finite number of instructions are executed.
- **Input** The algorithm receives input.
- **Output** The algorithm produces output.
- **Generality** The algorithm applies to a set of inputs.

34. A company provides sales commission to its salesman on monthly basis. There are 15 salesmen working in different areas.

The company provides the commission as

(i) Sales < 10000, no commission.

(ii) Sales > = 10000 and Sales < 30000, commission is 20% of sales.

(iii) Sales >=30000, commission is 25% of sales with ₹ 2000 bonus.

Draw flowchart for sales analysis.

Ans.

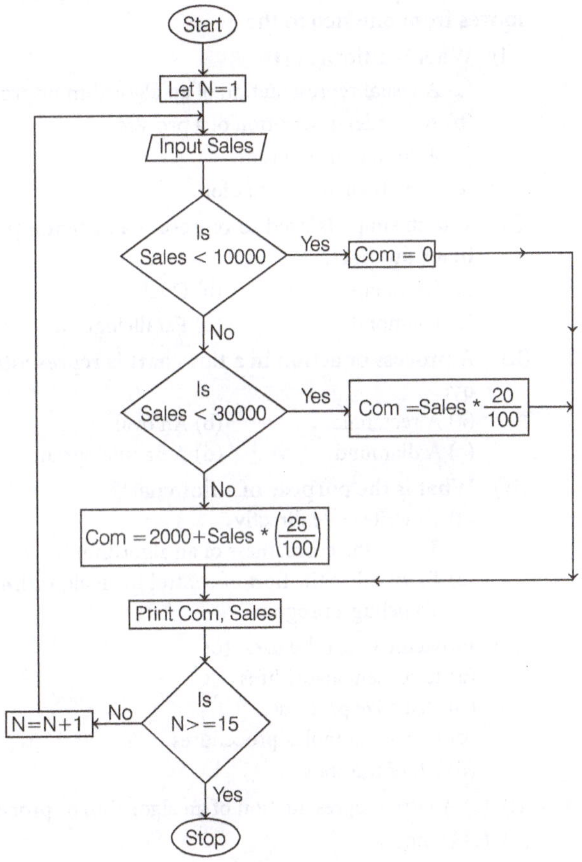

Case Study Based Questions

Case Study 1

Read the following paragraph and answer the following questions:

A flowchart is a visual tool that helps us understand and follow a process. It uses different shapes to represent different kinds of steps. A rectangle, for example, is used to show a process or action, while a diamond is used to represent a decision point. Arrows connect these shapes to show the flow of the process. By following the arrows, we can see how the process moves from one step to the next.

(i) **What is a flowchart?**
   (a) A visual representation of an algorithm or process.
   (b) A written description of a process.
   (c) A computer program.
   (d) A mathematical equation.

(ii) **Which shape is used to represent a decision point in a flowchart?**
   (a) Rectangle (b) Oval
   (c) Diamond (d) Parallelogram

(iii) **A process or action in a flowchart is represented by:**
   (a) A rectangle (b) An oval
   (c) A diamond (d) A parallelogram

(iv) **What is the purpose of a flowchart?**
   (a) To write code directly
   (b) To test the correctness of an algorithm
   (c) To visualize the flow of control in an algorithm
   (d) To debug a program

(v) **Flowcharts can be used to:**
   (a) Represent algorithms
   (b) Visualize processes
   (c) Explain complex procedures
   (d) All of the above

Ans. (i) (a) A visual representation of an algorithm or process
(ii) (c) Diamond
(iii) (a) A rectangle
(iv) (c) To visualize the flow of control in an algorithm
(v) (d) All of the above

Case Study 2

An algorithm is a set of step-by-step instructions that a computer follows to solve a problem. It's like a recipe, but for computers. Algorithms are essential in computer science and mathematics, helping computers perform tasks efficiently. Key components of an algorithm include:

Sequence Steps are executed one after another.

Selection Decisions are made based on conditions.

Iteration Steps are repeated until a certain condition is met.

Based on the above information, answer the following questions.

(i) **What is an algorithm?**
   (a) A type of computer hardware
   (b) A set of step-by-step instructions for solving a problem
   (c) A programming language
   (d) A database management system

(ii) **Which control structure is NOT a basic one in algorithms?**
   (a) Sequence (b) Selection
   (c) Iteration (d) Recursion

(iii) **What is NOT a characteristic of a good algorithm?**
   (a) Efficiency (b) Ambiguity
   (c) Finiteness (d) Precision

(iv) **What is a benefit of using algorithms?**
   (a) They make computers slower
   (b) They help computers perform tasks efficiently
   (c) They are only used in mathematics
   (d) They are difficult to understand

(v) **What is NOT a common error in algorithm design?**
   (a) Incorrect logic (b) Infinite loops
   (c) Syntax errors (d) Efficiency

(vi) **Why is it important to test an algorithm?**
   (a) To make the algorithm longer
   (b) To ensure the algorithm produces the correct output
   (c) To make the algorithm more complex
   (d) To avoid using a computer

Ans. (i) (b) A set of step-by-step instructions for solving a problem
(ii) (d) Recursion
(iii) (b) Ambiguity
(iv) (b) They help computers perform tasks efficiently
(v) (c) Syntax errors
(vi) (b) To ensure the algorithm produces the correct output

SELF ASSESSMENT TEST

Multiple Choice Questions

1. **................. is a cross between human language and a programming language.**
(a) Pseudocode
(b) Java
(c) Compiler
(d) Java Virtual Machine

2. **Which of the following is a graphical representation of the steps taken to reach a certain result?**
(a) Algorithm
(b) Flowchart
(c) Pseudocode
(d) Coding

3. **Symbols in flowchart are connected by arrows called**
(a) connectors
(b) start box
(c) flow lines
(d) processing

Fill in the Blanks

4. **A step-by-step procedure for solving a problem is called an ________.**

5. **Breaking down a complex problem into smaller, manageable parts is called ________.**

6. **The order in which instructions are executed in an algorithm is called ________.**

7. **________ is the process of translating an algorithm into a programming language.**

8. **________ is the process of checking if an algorithm produces the correct output for all valid inputs.**

State Whether True or False

9. **An algorithm must have a finite number of steps.**

10. **Decomposition involves combining multiple smaller problems into a larger one.**

11. **Flowcharts are a graphical representation of algorithms.**

12. **Coding is the process of defining the problem and its constraints.**

13. **Verifying algorithms ensures the algorithm solves the problem correctly.**

Assertion and Reason Based Questions

Assertion (A) and Reason (R) Type questions. Choose the correct option as:
(a) Both Assertion (A) and Reason (R) are true, and Reason (R) is the correct explanation of Assertion (A).
(b) Both Assertion (A) and Reason (R) are true, but Reason (R) is not the correct explanation of Assertion (A).
(c) Assertion (A) is true, but Reason (R) is false.
(d) Assertion (A) is false, but Reason (R) is true.

14. **Assertion (A)** Algorithms must be unambiguous.
Reason (R) Ambiguity leads to multiple interpretations and incorrect results.

15. **Assertion (A)** Flowcharts are the only way to represent an algorithm.
Reason (R) Pseudocode is a text-based method for representing algorithms that is less formal than programming code.

16. **Assertion (A)** Coding is the last step in problem-solving.
Reason (R) Coding involves translating the designed algorithm into a programming language.

17. **Assertion (A)** Decomposition helps in solving complex problems.
Reason (R) Decomposition involves breaking down a problem into smaller, more manageable sub-problems.

Very Short Answer Type Questions

18. **What is the difference between flowchart and algorithm?**

19. **What is the use of pseudocode?**

20. **Write one difference between pseudocode and algorithm.**

Short Answer Type Questions

21. **What is used to remove irrelevant information from a problem?**

22. **What are the logical constructs used in flowchart?**

23. **Explain the features of algorithm design.**

24. **What do you mean by algorithm design?**

25. Write an algorithm to find the sum of 3 numbers.

Long Answer Type Questions

26. How algorithm design is used to solve the problem?

27. Draw a flowchart to accept a number and print cube of that number.

Case Study Based Questions

28. The library is implementing a system for book returns. It starts by scanning the book's barcode to identify it. Then, the system verifies the member's ID to ensure they are authorized. Next, it calculates late fees based on the due date. Finally, it updates the book's availability in the database. The system aims to be efficient, accurate, and user-friendly, handling various scenarios like overdue books and different member types. This process needs careful planning and testing to ensure all steps work correctly.

(i) Which step in the problem-solving process would involve defining the specific tasks like barcode checking and fee calculation?

(a) Problem Definition (b) Algorithm Design
(c) Solution Evaluation (d) Implementation

(ii) Representing the sequence of tasks (barcode check, ID verification, fee calculation) would fall under which concept?

(a) Decomposition (b) Flow of Control
(c) Problem Definition (d) Coding

(iii) Breaking down the overall system into smaller, manageable parts (like barcode scanning module, fee calculation module) is an example of:

(a) Verifying Algorithms
(b) Comparison of Algorithms
(c) Decomposition
(d) Coding

(iv) Before implementing the system, the librarian tests the system with sample data to ensure that all the steps are working correctly. This is an example of:

(a) Coding
(b) Verifying Algorithms
(c) Comparison of Algorithms
(d) Algorithm Design

(v) Converting the designed algorithm into a specific programming language is:

(a) Problem Definition (b) Flow of Control
(c) Coding (d) Verifying Algorithms

Answers

1. (a) 2. (b) 3. (c) 4. Algorithm
5. Decomposition 6. Control flow 7. Coding
8. Testing 9. True 10. False 11. True 12. False
13. True 14. (a) 15. (d) 16. (d) 17. (a)
28. (i) → (b), (ii) → (b), (iii) → (c), (iv) → (b), (v) → (c)

06

CHAPTER

> Computer programming is an art, because it applies accumulated knowledge to the world, because it requires skill and ingenuity and especially because it produces objects of beauty.

▼ **YOUR STUDY GOALS**

6.1 Download and Installation of Python
6.2 Working in Python
6.3 Print "hello world" using command line

▼ **YOUR PRACTICE GOAL**

- Objective Type Questions (31 Qs ; MCQs, True or False, Fill in the Blanks, Assertion and Reason)
- Subjective Type Questions (32 Qs ; VSA, SA, LA)
- Case Study Based Questions-2

Python Overview

Python is a user-friendly programming language that lets you write code quickly and efficiently. It was created by **Guido Van Rossum** in **1991** and is now maintained by the **Python Software Foundation.**

Python is versatile, which means it can be used for various tasks, from simple scripts to complex software applications. It's easy to learn and understand, which makes it a great choice for both beginners and experienced programmers.

Python is based on two programming languages which are as follows:

- ABC language is an interactive programming and teaching language, originally intended as a good replacement for BASIC.
- Modula-3 supports interfaces, objects and generics.

Python interpreters are available for many operating systems such as Windows, MacOS etc.

Advantages of Python

Python is considered easy to learn and run almost anywhere, it is useful for a number of applications, including education, data analytics and web development. There are various advantages of Python as follows:

- **Easy to Use** Python's simple syntax and readability makes it easier for beginners to pick up and start coding quickly. Unlike many other programming languages, Python doesn't require complex syntax or strict rules, which can often be a barrier for new programmers.

- **Object-Oriented** Python supports both procedural and object-oriented programming paradigms, allowing for flexible and modular code. In object-oriented programming, code is organized into objects. Python's object-oriented features allow you to create classes, objects, and define relationships between them. By using object-oriented concepts like inheritance, polymorphism, and encapsulation, you can write more efficient and well-structured programs.
- **Productivity and Speed** Python's powerful features and integration capabilities enhance development speed and efficiency.
- **Portability** Python code can run on various platforms without significant modifications.
- **Open-Source** Python is freely available and open-source which promotes collaboration and innovation.
- **Extensive Libraries** Python comes with a built-in library that offers a vast collection of modules and functions for various tasks. This means you don't have to write code from scratch for common operations like file handling, network programming, data manipulation, and more. You can simply import the necessary modules and use their functions to perform these tasks efficiently. This significantly reduces development time and effort.
- **Interpreted** Python's interpreted nature makes it easier to debug and test code.
- **Integration** Python can integrate with other programming languages and systems which makes Python a versatile and powerful language.

Disadvantages of Python

There are some disadvantages of Python are as follows:

- **Slower Performance** Python is an interpreted language, which means that the code is executed line by line, one at a time. In contrast, compiled languages like C++ and Java are translated into machine code before execution, which can lead to faster performance. While Python's interpreted nature makes it easier to develop and debug code, it can sometimes result in slower execution times, especially for computationally intensive tasks.
- **Limited Mobile Applications** Python is less commonly used for mobile app development compared to languages like Java and Swift.
- **Runtime Errors** Python's dynamic typing can sometimes lead to unexpected errors if you accidentally assign a value of a different type to a variable. For example, if you try to perform arithmetic operations on a string, Python will raise a `TypeError`. To avoid such errors, it's important to be mindful of the data types you're working with and use appropriate type conversions when necessary.
- **Less Mature Database Access** Python's database access layers are not as mature as those in other languages, making it less suitable for large-scale enterprise applications.
- **Higher Memory Consumption** Python's dynamic typing allows for flexibility, but it can also impact memory usage. When you assign a value to a variable, Python allocates memory to store both the value and its type information. This can lead to higher memory consumption compared to statically typed languages where the type of a variable is determined at compile time.

Features of Python

Python's popularity stems from its numerous features and benefits:

- **Readability and Simplicity** Python's syntax is designed to be clear and concise, making it easy to learn and understand.
- **Interpreted Language** Python code is executed line by line, eliminating the need for compilation.
- **Dynamic Typing** Python automatically determines the data type of a variable at runtime, reducing the need for explicit type declarations.
- **Extensive Standard Library** Python comes with a vast standard library that provides modules for various tasks, including file I/O, network programming, regular expressions, and more.
- **Object-Oriented Programming** Python supports object-oriented programming principles, allowing you to create modular and reusable code.
- **Cross-Platform Compatibility** Python code can run on different operating systems (Windows, macOS, Linux) without significant modifications.
- **Large and Active Community** A large and active community provides extensive documentation, tutorials, and forums for help and collaboration.

6.1 Download and Installation of Python

Python is a versatile program that can run on many different computer systems, including those which used by servers that run websites and other online services.

Installing Python on a Windows server is pretty straightforward. All you need to do is download the setup program from the official Python website (Python.org) and run it on your server. It's that easy!

Downloading Python

To download a Python setup, follow the steps given below

(i) Enter Python.org in URL. A window will be appearing. Select Downloads tab, after this a pop-up will appear as shown below:

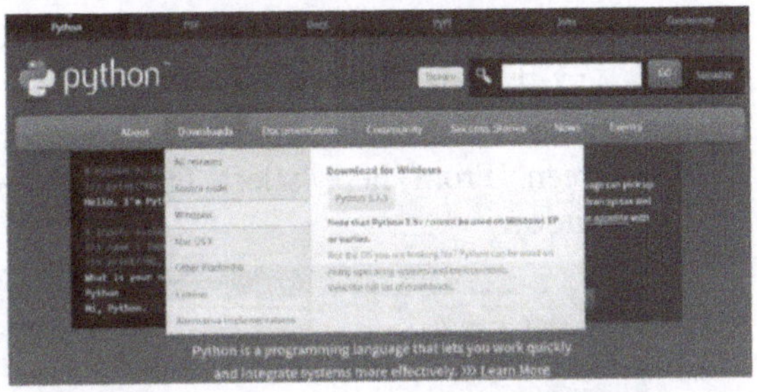

(ii) Click on Python 3.7.3 button to download.

The file named 3.7.3.exe should start downloading into your standard download folder.

(iii) Move this file to more permanent location, so that you can install Python.

Installing Python

To install Python, follow the steps given below:

(i) Open Downloads folder where Python setup was saved.Double click on the file python-3.7.3.exe.

(ii) An Open File-Security Warning dialog box will appear as shown below.

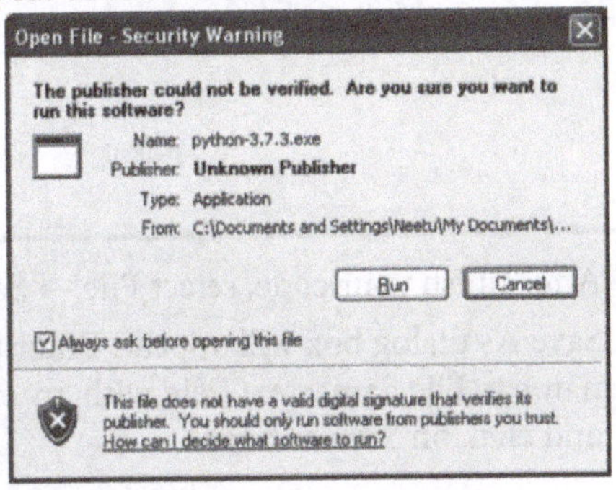

(iii) Click on Run button.

A Python 3.7.3 (32-bit) Setup pop-up window will appear.

(iv) Highlight the install now (or upgrade now) message and then click it. A user account control pop-up window will appear, that asked the question. Do you want to allow the following program to make changes to this computer?

(v) Click on Yes button.

A new Python 3.7.3 (32-bit) Setup pop-up window will appear, with a Setup Progress message and a progress bar.

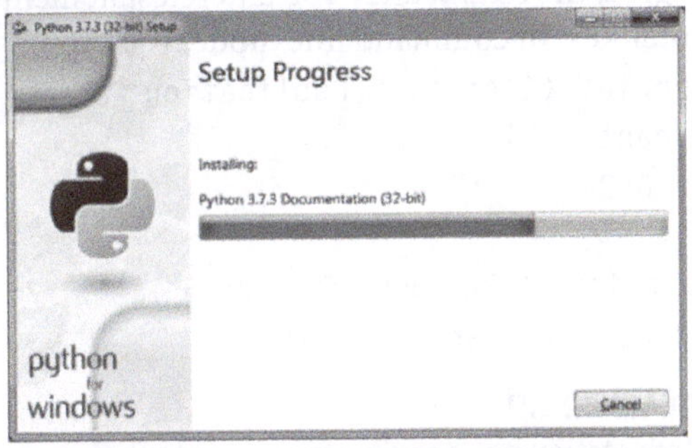

During installation, it will show the various components that are installing and move the progress bar towards completion. Soon, a new Python 3.7.3 (32 bit) Setup pop-up window will appear, with a "Setup was successful" message.

(vi) Click the Close button.

6.2 Working in Python

Programmers typically create individual programs, called scripts, that can work on their own without needing to be connected to something else. These scripts are saved with the ".py" extension, which tells both the computer and the programmer that the file contains Python code.Once you start the interpreter, it reads the script line by line and tells the computer what to do.

User can run a program with three ways in python

(i) Python (Command line)

You can run Python programs directly on your computer. To do this, you'll need to find the Python application on your computer, usually in the Start menu. Once you open it, a window will appear where you can type and run your Python code.

To start Python with command line, follow given step

Start → All Programs → Python 3.7 → Python 3.7 (32-bit).

Python 3.7 (32-bit) window will appear in your computer, where you can write code and execute it.

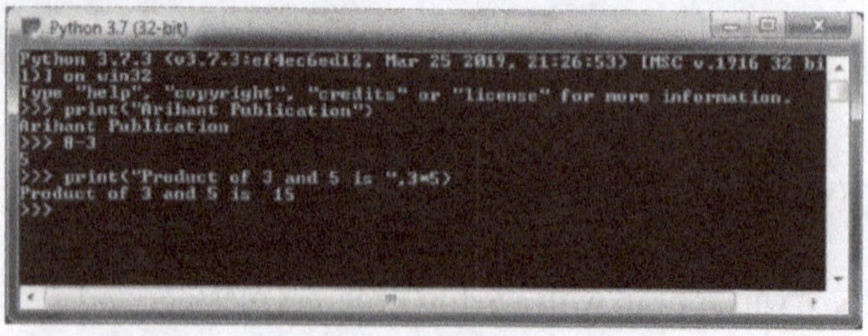

Python gives the output after you entered statement and press enter key. In command line mode, you type

```
>>>print (''Arihant Publication'')
Arihant Publication
>>> 8-3
5
>>> print (''Product of 3 and 5 is'',  3 * 5)
Product of 3 and 5 is 15
```

TEACHER TIP

Indentation plays a very crucial role in Python programming. If you give extra space, it will give syntax error.

(ii) Interactive Mode IDLE (Python GUI)

IDLE is a user-friendly tool that lets you write and run Python code in a window. You can use it to create and test your Python programs.

If you're having trouble setting up IDLE or Python, you can ask your system administrator for help. Make sure everything is set up correctly so you can start coding.

To start Python with IDLE, follow the given step

Start → All Programs → Python 3.7 → IDLE (Python 3.7 (32-bit)).

Python 3.7.3 Shell window will appear.

In that window, >>> sign will appear, here you can write your code and press Enter.

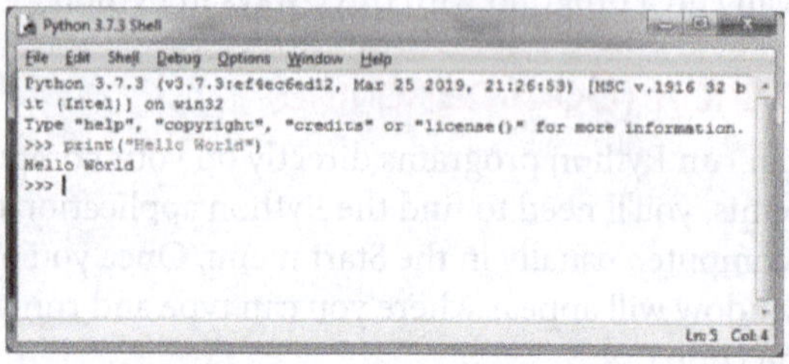

If you want to exit from the IDLE window, there are various options

Press Ctrl+D from keyboard

or Click File → Exit

or Click on cross ☒ button on title bar.

(iii) Python Script Mode

Python usually shows you the result as soon as you press Enter. However, if you want to see all the results at once after you've finished writing your code, you can use Python's script mode.

To work with Python script mode, you will have to follow given steps:

Step 1 Create Script/Program File

To create script/program file, follow the given instructions:

- Start button → All Programs → Python 3.7 → IDLE (Python 3.7 (32-bit)).
- Python 3.7.3 shell window will appear on your screen. From here select File → New File window.

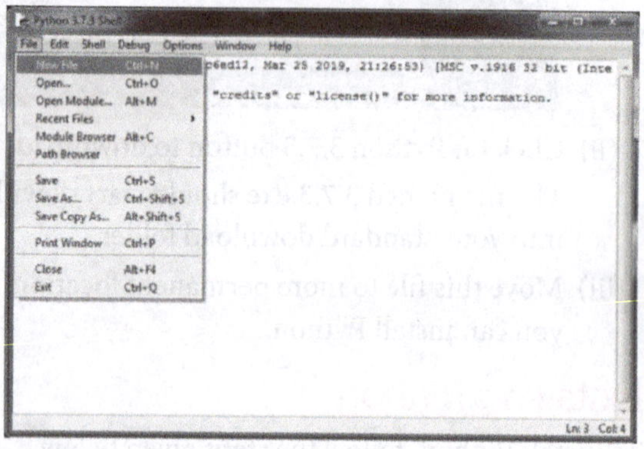

- An Untitled window will appear where you can write your code.

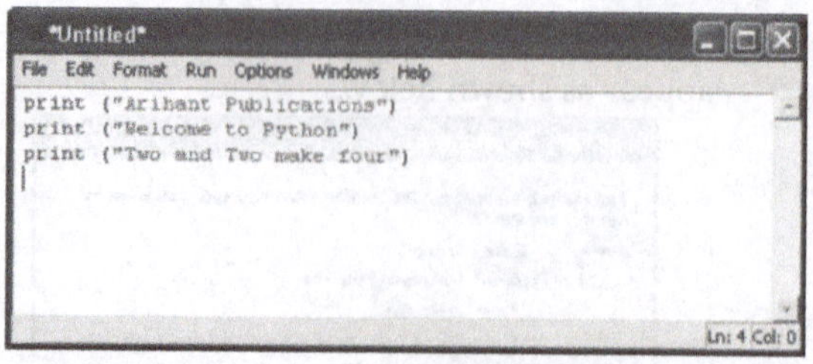

- After finish your code, select File → Save As.
- Save As dialog box will appear. Enter program name in File name: text field with .py extension and click on Save button.

Step 2 Run Script/ Program File

To run script/program file after creation of script, follow the given instructions:

- Now, open the IDLE file, which was opened in step1.
- Select File → Open and type file name in File name: box which file you want to open for executing.
- Click on Open button. Filename.py file will appear on your screen.
- Select Run → Run Module or press F5 key from keyboard.

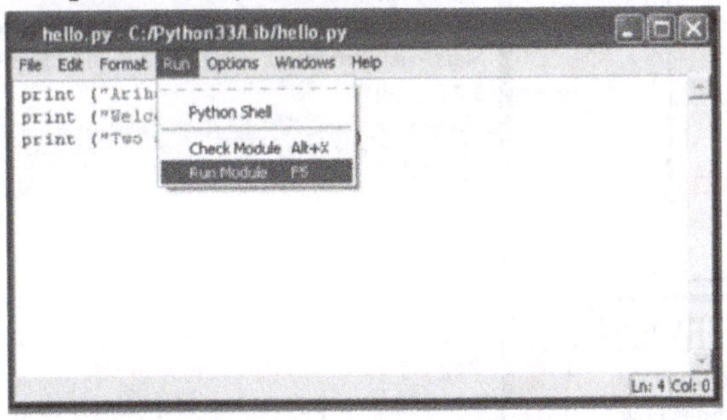

- It will execute and output will print in your IDLE window.

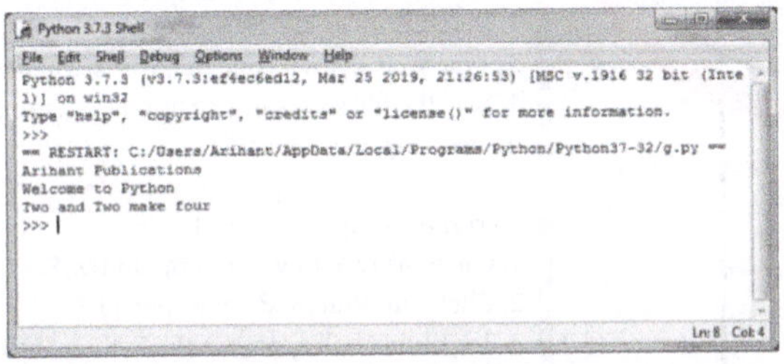

6.3 Print "hello world" using command line

You can easily write your first program by following these simple steps which are as follow:

1. Install Python

- Download the latest Python version from the official website (python.org).
- Follow the installation instructions for your operating system.

2. Open a Text Editor

- Use a simple text editor like Notepad (Windows), TextEdit (Mac), or a more advanced code editor like Visual Studio Code or PyCharm.

3. Write the Code

- Type the following line of code into the text editor:

```
print("hello world")
```

4. Save the File

- Save the file with a .py extension, like hello.py.

5. Run the Code

- **Using the Command Line**
  1. Open your terminal or command prompt.
  2. Navigate to the directory where you saved the file.
  3. Type python hello.py and press Enter.
- **Using an IDE**
  1. Open the file in your IDE.
  2. Click the "Run" button or use a keyboard shortcut to execute the code.

This will print "hello world" to your console as shown below.

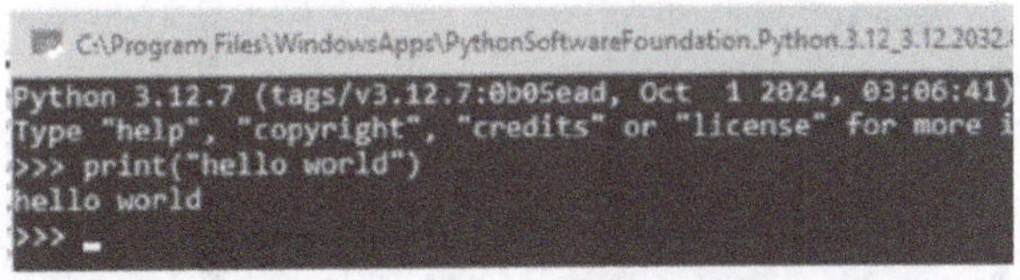

Mistake Alert

Students often make mistakes with indentation, which can lead to syntax errors in their Python code.

Mind Map

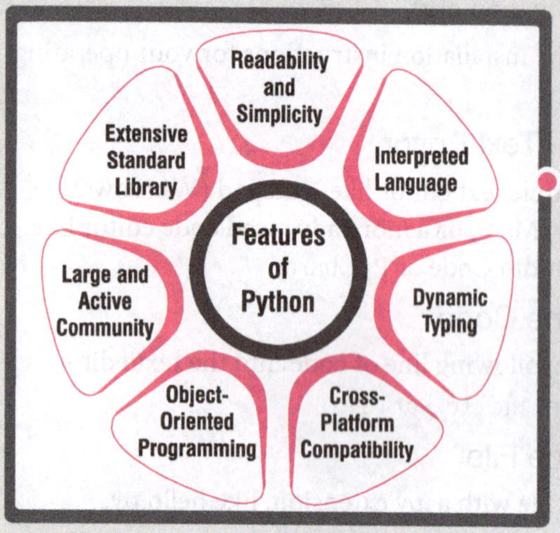

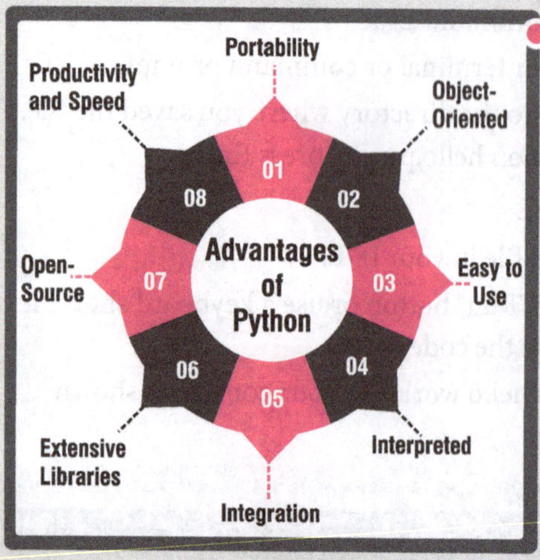

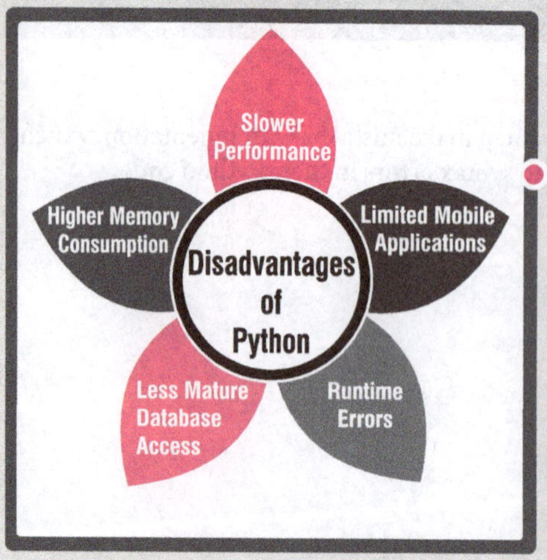

PYTHON OVERVIEW

It was created by **Guido Van Rossumin 1991** and is now maintained by the **Python Software Foundation.**

Working in Python

User can run a program with three ways in python

Command line

To start Python with command line, follow given step Start -> All Programs -> Python 3.7 -> Python 3.7 (32-bit).

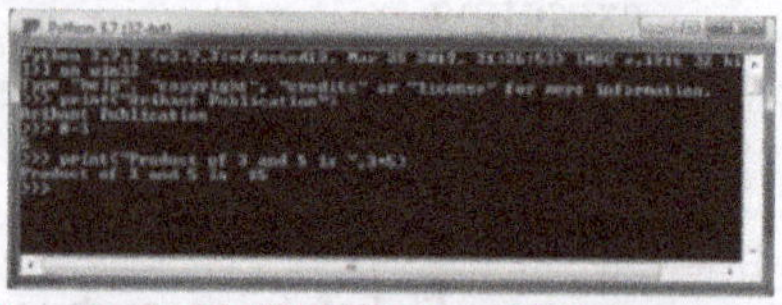

Interactive Mode IDLE (Python GUI)

To start Python with IDLE, follow the given step Start→All Programs→Python 3.7→IDLE (Python 3.7 (32-bit)).

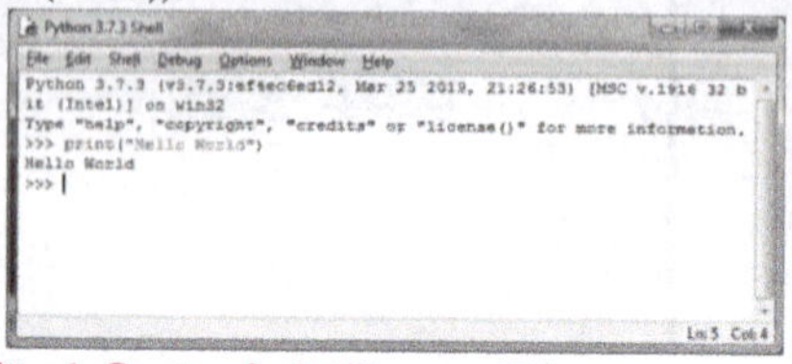

Step 1: Create a Script/Program File

To create a script/program file, follow these instructions:

1. Click on the Start button All Programs Python 3.7 IDLE (Python 3.7 (32-bit)).
2. In IDLE, go to File New File.
3. Type your Python code in the new window.
4. Save the file with a.py extension (e.g., program.py) by selecting File → Save As

Step 2: Run the Script/Program File

To run the script after creating it:

1. Open the saved Python script in IDLE.
2. Click Run Run Module (or press F5).
3. The output will appear in the Python Shell window.

Download and Installation of Python

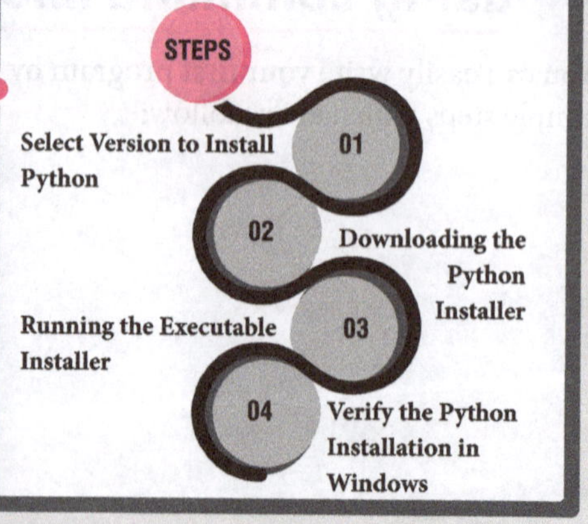

EXAM PATTERN QUESTIONS

Objective Type Questions

Multiple Choice Questions

1. What is Python?

(a) A programming language (b) A software application
(c) A hardware component (d) A network protocol

2. Python is based on

(a) ABC language (b) Modula 3
(c) Both (a) and (b) (d) None of these

3. Where can you download the latest Python installer?

(a) Python.org (b) GitHub
(c) SourceForge (d) Bitbucket

4. A developer is working on a Python project and notices they can assign different data types to the same variable during runtime. Which of the following features of Python enables this behavior? **Competency Based Que.**

(a) Dynamically typed
(b) Interpreted language
(c) Object-oriented programming
(d) Strongly typed

5. In which year was Python 3.0 released?

(a) 2000 (b) 2005
(c) 2008 (d) 2010

6. Python was initially designed by

(a) Guido Van Rossum (b) Charles Babbage
(c) Grace Hopper (d) Dennis Ritchie

7. Which of the following is/are advantage(s) of Python?

(a) Easy to use (b) Object oriented
(c) Portability (d) All of these

8. A developer is working on a Python application that requires efficient memory usage to prevent crashes. Which of the following approaches is Python designed to use for managing memory?

(a) Manual memory management
(b) Automatic garbage collection
(c) Hybrid memory management
(d) No memory management

9. The extension of Python files is

(a) .pyth (b) .python
(c) .py (d) .p

10. How do you check the python version in the command line?

(a) python - - version (b) python –v
(c) python version (d) version python

11. Python interpreters are available for operating system(s)

(a) Windows (b) MacOS
(c) Both (a) and (b) (d) None of these

12. A beginner programmer wants to start writing and running Python code directly within a user-friendly environment. Which tool would be MOST suitable for this purpose? **Competency Based Que.**

(a) To write and execute Python scripts
(b) To debug Python code
(c) To create Python GUIs
(d) To manage Python packages

Fill in the Blanks

13. Python is an example of a high-level, __________ programming language that is easy to read and write.

14. One of the key advantages of Python is its _________ syntax, which makes it beginner-friendly.

15. A disadvantage of Python is that it is slower in execution compared to ________ languages like C++ or Java.

16. Python provides different modes for working, such as __________ mode for running individual commands and script mode for executing an entire program.

17. ________ is the default IDE provided with Python, which allows you to write, edit, and run Python programs efficiently.

State Whether True or False

18. Python is a compiled language, which means that the code is translated into machine code before execution.

19. Python's dynamic typing can lead to runtime errors if you try to perform arithmetic operations on a string.

20. Python's standard library offers a vast collection of modules for various tasks, reducing the need to write code from scratch.

21. Python can only be installed on Windows servers.

22. Python scripts are typically saved with a ".py" extension.

23. Dynamically typed language means you do not need to declare variable before writing the code.

24. Indentation is not important in Python programming.

25. Python scripts can only be run within the IDLE environment.

Assertion and Reason Based Questions

Assertion (A) and Reason (R) Type questions. Choose the correct option as:

(a) Both Assertion (A) and Reason (R) are true, and Reason (R) is the correct explanation of Assertion (A).

(b) Both Assertion (A) and Reason (R) are true, but Reason (R) is not the correct explanation of Assertion (A).

(c) Assertion (A) is true, but Reason (R) is false.

(d) Assertion (A) is false, but Reason (R) is true.

26. Assertion (A) Python is a high-level programming language.
Reason (R) Python syntax is complicated and difficult to learn.

27. Assertion (A) Python is platform-independent.
Reason (R) Python code can be executed on different operating systems without modification.

28. Assertion (A) Python is slower compared to compiled languages like C or Java.
Reason (R) Python uses an interpreter to execute code.

29. Assertion (A) Python installation requires downloading it from python.org.
Reason (R) Python is pre-installed on all operating system.

30. Assertion (A) Python allows both interactive and script-based modes of programming.
Reason (R) Python does not support writing multiple lines of code in a script.

31. Assertion (A) You can print "Hello, world!" in Python using the command.
Reason (R) Python uses the echo command to print messages.

Answers

1. (a) A programming language
2. (c) Both (a) and (b) **3.** (a) Python.org
4. (a) Dynamically typed **5.** (c) 2008
6. (a) Guido Van Rossum **7.** (d) All of these
8. (b) Automatic garbage collection **9.** (c) .py
10. (a) python - - version **11.** (c) Both (a) and (b)
12. (a) To write and execute Python scripts
13. interpreted **14.** simple
15. compiled **16.** interactive
17. IDLE **18.** False **19.** True **20.** True
21. False **22.** True **23.** True **24.** False
25. False
26. (c) Assertion (A) is true, but Reason (R) is false.
27. (a) Both Assertion (A) and Reason (R) are true, and Reason (R) is the correct explanation of Assertion (A).
28. (a) Both Assertion (A) and Reason (R) are true, and Reason (R) is the correct explanation of Assertion (A).
29. (c) Assertion (A) is true, but Reason (R) is false.
30. (c) Assertion (A) is true, but Reason (R) is false.
31. (c) Assertion (A) is true, but Reason (R) is false.

Subjective Type Questions

Very Short Answer Type Questions

1. Who developed Python?

Ans. Python was initially designed by Guido Van Rossum in 1991 and developed by Python Software Foundation.

2. Python is which type of programming language?

Ans. Python is an object oriented programming language.

3. Is Python free and open source?

Ans. Yes, Python is both free and open-source. This means you can download, use, modify, and distribute it without any cost or licensing restrictions.

4. Python is based on which type of programming language?

Ans. Python is based on two types of programming languages as

- ABC language
- Modula-3

5. Name the core software component that enables Python's cross-platform capability.

Ans. Interpreter

6. List some advantages of Python.

Ans. Some advantages of Python are as follow:

- Easy to learn
- Expressive (can do a lot with few lines)
- Interpreted (no separate compilation step)
- Cross-platform (runs on many systems)
- Free and Open Source

7. Python can run "on any machine or platform." What single word describes this ability?

Ans. Portability

8. Why is Python easy to learn?

Ans. Python's simplicity, clear syntax, and extensive standard library make it easy to learn and use. Its object-oriented nature and cross-platform compatibility further enhance its appeal. A large and active community provides abundant resources for learning and support.

9. List two disadvantages of Python.

Ans. Two disadvantages of Python are as follow:

- Not as fast as compiled languages
- Not ideal for memory-intensive applications

10. What does IDLE stand for?

Ans. Integrated Development and Learning Environment

11. How to start Python from command prompt?

Ans. Type python on the search box and press enter

12. How can you start Python with a command line?

Ans. Start → All Programs → Python 3.7 → Python 3.7 (32-bit).

13. You need to display the message "Hello" on the screen. What Python command would you use?

Ans. `print("Hello")`

14. What is the extension of Python files?

Ans. Python files have extension .py.

15. What will be the output of the following code at the command line?

```
>>>print ("Sum of 10 and 20 is", 10+20)
```

Ans. Sum of 10 and 20 is 30.

16. Anurag is working on IDLE (Python GUI). He has finished his coding and now wants to exit from IDLE. How can he exit from IDLE? **Competency Based Que.**

Ans. Press Ctrl+D or File → Exit or Click on cross☒ button on title bar.

Short Answer Type I Questions

17. What is Python? Explain.

Ans. Python is a general purpose interpreted, interactive, object oriented and high level programming language. It was initially designed by Guido Van Rossum in 1991 and developed by Python Software Foundation.

18. Python is free and open source, what does it mean?

Ans. Python language is developed under an OSI-approved open source license, which makes it free to use and distribute, including for commercial purposes.

19. What is the difference between interactive mode and script mode in Python?

Ans. Interactive mode is used when a user wants to run one single line or one block of code. While script mode is used when the user is working with more than one single code or a block of code.

20. You're teaching Python to a group of beginners. Explain how Python's "readability" directly benefits them in learning the language.

Ans. Python code is like reading a simple story. This helps beginners understand how programs work without getting confused by complicated symbols. They can learn faster and focus on the main ideas of coding.

21. What is the role of indentation in python?

Ans. Indentation is used to define code blocks and determines the hierarchical structure of a program. Unlike many other programming languages that use curly braces to delimit code blocks, Python relies only on consistent indentation. This makes Python code more readable and visually appealing.

22. Give any three disadvantages of Python.

Ans. Three disadvantages of Python are as follows:

(i) **Speed Limitation** Python is interpreted language and slow as compared to C/C++ or Java, because interpreted languages are executed line by line.

(ii) **Weak in Mobile Computing** Python has made its presence on many desktop and server platforms, but it is seen as a weak language for mobile computing.

(iii) **Run-time Errors** Python programmers face several issues regarding the design of the language. This language requires more testing and also it has errors that only show up at run-time, this is because the language is dynamically typed.

23. How do you check the Python version in the command line?

Ans. To check the Python version, you can open your terminal or command prompt and type the following command:

Bash

```
python--version or python-V.
```

24. What do you mean by IDLE in Python?

Ans. IDLE (Integrated Development and Learning Environment) is Python's default integrated development environment. It provides a user-friendly interface for writing, running, and debugging Python code. It includes a text editor with syntax highlighting, an interactive shell, and debugging tools, making it a great tool for beginners.

25. How do you run a Python script named script.py from the command line?

Ans. To run the script, you can open your terminal or command prompt and type the following command:

Bash, `python script.py`

For Python 3, `python3 script.py`

Short Answer Type II Questions

26. What are the key features of Python that make it a popular programming language?

Ans. Python is a versatile and powerful language due to its following features:

- **Readability** Python's syntax is clean and easy to understand, making it a great language for beginners and experienced programmers alike.
- **Simplicity** Python reduces the complexity of programming tasks with its concise and intuitive syntax.
- **Cross-Platform Compatibility** Python code can run on various operating systems like Windows, macOS, and Linux without significant modifications.
- **Large Standard Library** Python's extensive standard library provides a wide range of modules for tasks such as file I/O, network programming, web development, and data science.
- **Object-Oriented Programming (OOP)** Python supports OOP principles, allowing for modular and reusable code.
- **Interactive Mode** Python's interactive mode enables testing and debugging code snippets directly in the interpreter.
- **Extensibility** Python can be extended with C/C++ modules for performance-critical tasks.
- **Community and Support** A large and active community provides extensive documentation, tutorials, and forums for learning and problem-solving.

27. How do you install Python and set up a development environment?

1. **Download the Installer** Go to the official Python website (https://www.python.org/downloads/) and download the latest Python installer for your operating system.
2. **Run the Installer** Follow the on-screen instructions to install Python.
3. **Verify Installation** Open your terminal or command prompt and type python --version. If it shows, it's version means we successfully installed python in our computer system.
4. **Set Up a Development Environment**
   - **Text Editor/IDE** Choose a suitable text editor or IDE like Visual Studio Code, PyCharm, or Sublime Text.
   - **Virtual Environments** Create virtual environments to isolate project dependencies. Use tools like venv or virtualenv.

28. How do you execute a Python script in IDLE?

Ans. To run a Python script in IDLE, follow these steps:

1. **Create a New File**
   - Open IDLE and go to File -> New File.
   - This will open a new window where you can write your Python code.
2. **Write Your Code**
   - Type your Python code into the new file.
3. **Save the File**
   - Go to File -> Save As and save the file with a .py extension (e.g., my_script.py).
4. **Run the Script**
   - You can run the script in two ways:
     - **Keyboard Shortcut** Press F5 on your keyboard.
     - **Menu Option** Go to Run -> Run Module.
5. **View the Output**
   - The output of your script will be displayed in the Python shell window.

29. How do you use Python's interactive mode and command-line interface?

Ans. Interactive Mode

- Open your terminal or command prompt.
- Type python and press Enter.
- You'll be in the Python interactive shell, where you can execute Python code line by line.

Command-Line Interface

- Write Python code in a .py file (e.g., hello.py).
- Open your terminal or command prompt.
- Navigate to the directory containing the script.
- Type python hello.py to execute the script.

30. Write a Python program to print "hello world" using command line.

Ans. Refer to text on page no. 111 (Print "hello world" using command line).

Long Answer Type Questions

31. Explain the concept of a programming language. How does Python work as a high-level programming language, and how does it differ from a compiler-based language?

Ans. A programming language is a set of instructions used to communicate with a computer to perform specific tasks. Since computers understand only machine language (binary code: 0s and 1s), programming languages provide a way for humans to write instructions in a structured and understandable format.

There are two main types of programming languages:

1. **Low-Level Languages** These include machine language and assembly language, which are closer to hardware but difficult for humans to read and write.
2. **High-Level Languages** These include Python, C++, Java, etc., which are easier to understand and write. They must be translated into machine language using a translator (compiler or interpreter).

Python Works as a High-Level Programming Language

Python is a high-level language that allows developers to write code in a simple, readable, and structured way. Here's how it works:

1. Python code is written in human-readable syntax and saved in a .py file.
2. Since the computer does not understand high-level code, Python uses an interpreter to translate it into machine language.
3. The interpreter executes Python statements line by line, making it easy to debug errors quickly.

Difference Between Python (Interpreter-Based) and Compiler-Based Languages

Python uses an interpreter, while some languages like C++ and Java use a compiler. The key differences are:

Feature	Interpreter (Python)	Compiler (C++, Java)
Execution Process	Translates and executes code line by line	Translates the entire program before execution
Speed	Slower due to step-by-step execution	Faster because the whole code is compiled first
Error Handling	Stops execution at the first error, making debugging easier	Shows all errors after compilation, requiring debugging later

32. Discuss the features of Python and its different execution modes. How do Interactive Mode and Script Mode work, and what are their advantages and limitations?

Ans. Python is a high-level, interpreted, and user-friendly programming language with several key features:

1. **Easy to Learn & Read** Simple syntax makes it beginner-friendly.
2. **Interpreted Language** Executes code line by line using an interpreter.
3. **Case-Sensitive** NUMBER and number are treated as different identifiers.
4. **Platform-Independent** Runs on various operating systems without modification.
5. **Rich Library Support** Provides built-in functions and modules for various tasks.
6. **Used in Web Development** Many web applications and services are built using Python.
7. **Uses Indentation** Defines code blocks using indentation instead of curly brackets {}.

Execution Modes in Python

Python code can be executed in two modes, depending on the use case.

1. **Interactive Mode**
   - Runs Python statements one by one in the Python shell (>>> prompt).
   - Provides instant execution, making it useful for quick testing and debugging.
   - Limitation: Code cannot be saved for future use and must be retyped.
2. **Script Mode**
   - Python code is written and saved in a .py file, then executed as a whole.
   - Suitable for writing full programs with multiple instructions.
   - Limitation: Debugging can be slower, as errors appear only after execution.

Case Study Based Questions

Case Study 1

Python, a versatile programming language, was conceived by Guido van Rossum in the late 1980s. It's renowned for its simplicity, readability, and powerful capabilities. Python's syntax is designed to resemble natural language, making it easy to learn and understand.

As an interpreted language, it executes code line by line, which aids in debugging and rapid development. Python's object-oriented nature allows for modular and reusable code, promoting efficient software development. It's widely used in various domains, including web development, data science, machine learning, and automation.

Based on the above paragraph answer the following questions

(i) Who is the creator of the Python programming language?

(a) Dennis Ritchie (b) James Gosling
(c) Guido van Rossum (d) Bjarne Stroustrup

(ii) Python is primarily a:

(a) Compiled language (b) Interpreted language
(c) Assembly language (d) Machine language

(iii) Python's syntax is often compared to:

(a) C++ (b) Java
(c) English (d) Assembly

(iv) One of the key strengths of Python is its:

(a) Complexity (b) Speed
(c) Readability (d) Low-level nature

(v) Python is used in which of the following fields?

(a) Web development (b) Data science
(c) Artificial intelligence (d) All of these

(vi) What is the correct file extension for a Python script?

(a) .txt (b) .py (c) .cpp (d) .java

Ans. (i) (c) Guido van Rossum
(ii) (b) Interpreted language
(iii) (c) English
(iv) (c) Readability
(v) (d) All of these
(vi) (b) .py

Case Study 2

In Python, comments are denoted by a hash symbol (#). They are ignored by the interpreter and are used to explain code or provide documentation. For example, # This is a comment. To print text to the console, we use the print () function. The code print ("Hello, world!") will give the output -> Hello, world!. To declare a variable in Python, we simply assign a value to it. For instance, x = 10 assigns the value 10 to the variable x. The if statement is used to execute a block of code conditionally. It checks a condition and executes the code within the block only if the condition is true. The for loop is used to iterate over a sequence of values. It repeatedly executes a block of code for each item in the sequence.

Based on the above paragraph answer the following questions

(i) Which is a valid Python comment?

(a) // This is a comment
(b) /* This is a comment */
(c) # This is a comment
(d) 'This is a comment'

(ii) What is the output of print ("Hello, world!")?

(a) "Hello, world!"
(b) Hello, world!
(c) 'Hello, world!'
(d) print ("Hello, world!")

(iii) How to declare a variable in Python?

(a) declare x = 10; (b) int x = 10;
(c) x := 10; (d) x = 10

(iv) What is the purpose of the if statement?

(a) To repeat a block of code
(b) To define a function
(c) To execute a block of code conditionally
(d) To declare a variable

(v) What is the purpose of the for loop?

(a) To define a function
(b) To execute a block of code conditionally
(c) To iterate over a sequence of values
(d) To declare a variable

Ans. (i) (c) # This is a comment
(ii) (b) Hello, world!
(iii) (d) x = 10
(iv) (c) To execute a block of code conditionally
(v) (c) To iterate over a sequence of values

SELF ASSESSMENT TEST

Multiple Choice Questions

1. Which of the following is not an advantage of Python?

(a) Interpreted
(b) Integration
(c) Memory consumption
(d) Extensive Support Libraries

2. User can run a program with .... ways in Python.

(a) two (b) three
(c) four (d) five

3. Python uses .... rather than curly brackets to delimit blocks.

(a) whitespace indentation
(b) square brackets
(c) parentheses
(d) None of the above

Fill in the Blanks

4. ________ is an interactive development environment for Python.

5. Python's ________ allows it to run on different operating systems.

6. The ________ is a disadvantage of Python that affects multithreaded performance.

7. To run a Python script from a file, you can use ________.

8. The command to print "hello world" in the command line is ________ or ________ when in the python shell.

State Whether True or False

9. Python is a compiled language.

10. Python is known for its readability and simple syntax.

11. The Global Interpreter Lock (GIL) in Python allows multiple threads to execute simultaneously.

12. IDLE is an integrated development environment for Python.

13. You can run Python code directly from the command line.

14. Python is not platform independent.

Assertion and Reason Based Questions

Assertion (A) and Reason (R) Type questions. Choose the correct option as:

(a) Both Assertion (A) and Reason (R) are true, and Reason (R) is the correct explanation of Assertion (A).
(b) Both Assertion (A) and Reason (R) are true, but Reason (R) is not the correct explanation of Assertion (A).
(c) Assertion (A) is true, but Reason (R) is false.
(d) Assertion (A) is false, but Reason (R) is true.

15. Assertion (A) Python is a dynamically typed language.
Reason (R) Python determines the data type of variables at runtime.

16. Assertion (A) Python is primarily a compiled language.
Reason (R) Python's extensive standard library makes it versatile for many applications.

17. Assertion (A) Python is only suitable for small scripting tasks.
Reason (R) Python is used in data science, web development, and machine learning.

18. Assertion (A) IDLE is a useful tool for learning Python.
Reason (R) IDLE provides an interactive environment for writing and testing Python code.

19. Assertion (A) IDLE is the only way to write python code.
Reason (R) Debugging is a crucial part of software development.

Very Short Answer Type Questions

20. In which year, Python was developed?

21. Python is an interpreted language. Explain.

22. Where can you install Python in your computer?

Short Answer Type Questions

23. How can you start Python with IDLE?

24. What is the output of the following statement?

```
>>> a = 25
>>> print (a)
```

25. Give any two advantages of Python Programming language.

26. Python is weak in mobile computing. Give reason.

27. How many ways can user run a program in Python?

28. Give output of the following code.

```
>>> print (''Hello world !!!'')
>>> print (''Python Program' )
>>> print (''Honesty is the best policy'')
```

Long Answer Type Question

29. What do you mean by script mode in Python?

Case Study Based Questions

30. A software development team needs to build a web application that works seamlessly across different operating systems (Windows, macOS, Linux). They are looking for a language that supports rapid development, has extensive libraries for web frameworks, and is easy to deploy. However, they are concerned about potential performance issues and the Global Interpreter Lock (GIL).

(i) Which programming language is a strong contender for this project, considering its cross-platform capabilities and extensive libraries?

(a) C# (b) Java
(c) Python (d) Swift

(ii) The team's concern about performance issues and the GIL highlights which aspect of Python?

(a) Advantages of Python
(b) Features of Python
(c) Disadvantages of Python
(d) Installation of Python

(iii) Using web frameworks like Django or Flask demonstrates which feature of Python?

(a) Dynamic Typing
(b) Extensive Libraries
(c) Interpreted Language
(d) Platform Independence

(iv) The team needs to ensure Python is installed on all target operating systems. This involves:

(a) Working in Python
(b) Download and Installation of Python
(c) IDLE, Python Script Mode
(d) Printing "hello world" using the command line

(v) To test a small snippet of code quickly, the team can use:

(a) Python Script Mode
(b) Command Line
(c) IDLE
(d) All of these

Answers

1. (c) 2. (b) 3. (a) 4. IDLE
5. Platform-independence
6. Global Interpreter Lock (GIL)
7. Python script mode
8. python -c 'print("hello world")', print("hello world")
9. False 10. True 11. False 12. True 13. True
14. False 15. (a) 16. (d) 17. (d) 18. (a)
19. (d)
30. (i) → (c), (ii) → (c), (iii) → (b), (iv) → (b), (v) → (d)

07
CHAPTER

Python is a high-level, interpreted programming language known for its simplicity and readability. It is widely used for web development, data science, artificial intelligence, automation, and more.

▼ **YOUR STUDY GOALS**

7.1 Python Character Set
7.2 Python Tokens
7.3 Function
7.4 Variables in Python
7.5 Input and Output in Python
7.6 Basic Structure of Python Program

▼ **YOUR PRACTICE GOAL**

- Objective Type Questions (30 Qs ; MCQs, True or False, Fill in the Blanks, Assertion and Reason)
- Subjective Type Questions (38 Qs ; VSA, SA, LA)
- Case Study Based Questions-2

Python Fundamental

We face the IPO cycle (Input, Process, Output) in our daily lives and computer activities. This cycle involves taking an input, processing it, and generating an output. To automate this process and transform input into useful output, we use programs.

These programs are written using various programming languages, and to effectively use a language, we need to understand its fundamental elements.

Python, for example, use character sets, tokens, expressions, statements, input/output functions, and more to construct programs.

7.1 Python Character Set

Python's character set is a collection of characters that can be used to create strings and other text-based data. It is a set of valid characters that a language can recognize. A character represents any digit, alphabet and special symbol. It primarily consists of:

ASCII Characters

- **Alphabetic characters** In alphabetic characters we have uppercase (A-Z) and lowercase (a-z) letters which allows us for creating words and identifiers.
- **Numeric characters** Numeric characters containing digits from 0 to 9 which are used to represent numbers and numeric values.

- **Punctuation marks** Punctuation marks such as commas, periods, colons, semicolons, and quotation marks are used to structure and format text.
- **Special Characters** A variety of special characters, including symbols like `@`, `#`, `$`, and `%`, as well as whitespace characters like spaces, tabs, and newlines, are used for various purposes, such as formatting, delimiting code blocks, and representing special characters.

Unicode Characters

Extended Character Set Python supports Unicode, which allows for a much wider range of characters, including characters from different languages and scripts.

Unicode Escape Sequences Unicode escape sequences are a way to represent Unicode characters within text, especially in programming languages. They typically consist of a backslash (\) followed by the letter 'u' and a four-digit hexadecimal code point. For example, the Unicode escape sequence for the character 'A' is '\u0041'.

7.2 Python Tokens

Tokens are the smallest individual units in a Python program. They are the building blocks of Python code. There are five main types of tokens in Python, these are as follow:

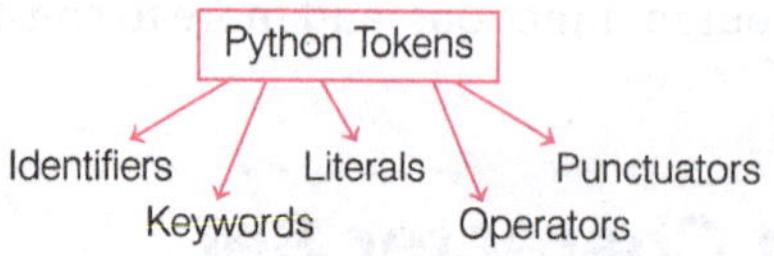

Identifiers

Identifiers are basically the names given to variables, functions, classes, and other entities in a Python program. It is a sequence of characters taken from Python character set.

The rules in Python for identifiers are

(i) Only alphabets, digits and underscores are allowed.
(ii) Identifier name cannot start with a digit.
(iii) Keywords cannot be used as identifier.
(iv) Uppercase and lowercase letters are distinct because Python is case sensitive language.
(v) Special characters are not allowed.

For example,

Following are the valid identifiers

Identifier	Explanation
Name	Capital letter with small letters are allowed
name	Small letters are allowed
name_1	Digits and underscore are allowed alongwith alphabets
_SUM	Underscore at the first position is allowed
sum_of_the _numbers	We can concatenate multiple words with underscore
PASS	Keywords are allowed but we have to change case of any letter or complete word
FirstName	Best style to concatenate multiple words (changing case of first letter of successive word).

Following are the invalid identifiers

Identifier	Explanation
global	Keywords name cannot be given to identifier
num^2	Special characters are not allowed
num 1	Spaces are not allowed in Python programming language for declaring identifier
2num	Digits are allowed but not as first character

Keywords

These are reserved words in Python that have special meanings. They cannot be used as variable names. Some commonly used keywords in Python, which are listed below

False	assert	del	for	in	or	while
None	break	elif	from	is	pass	with
True	class	else	global	lambda	raise	yield
and	continue	except	if	nonlocal	return	
as	def	finally	import	not	try	

Literals or Constants

Literals are the raw data values assigned to variables in a program. They represent fixed values that do not change during program execution. Python supports various types of literals:

- **Numeric literals** Numeric literals are immutable (unchangeable). Numeric literals can belong to three different numerical types as Integer, Float and Complex.

Integers like 10 and -5, floating-point numbers like 3.14, and complex numbers like 2+3j are all examples of numeric literals.

- **String literals** A series of characters enclosed in single quotes (' ') or double quotes (" ") is considered a string literal. These represent a sequence of zero or more characters enclosed by single/double quotes. It can also include blank spaces.

  Some valid string constants are

"j"	" ₹ 56,234.50 "	"computer"	'math'
"T"	"The result is: "	"Intel"	'2456'

Some invalid string constants are

No	Not enclosed in double quotes
"h'	Both quotes must be double or single quotes
"She said, "OK"	Number of double quotes must be even

The backslash (\) character is used to escape characters that have a special meaning, such as new line, backslash itself or the quote character.

The backslash can also help us type things we can't directly on the keyboard, like a new line or a tab. By using the backslash with specific codes, we can tell the computer to insert these invisible characters into our text.

Escape sequences in Python are as follows

Escape Sequence	Meaning
\\	backslash (\)
\'	single quote (')
\"	double quote (")
\a	ASCII Bell (BEL)
\b	ASCII Backspace (BS)
\f	ASCII Formfeed (FF)
\n	ASCII Linefeed (LF) or new line
\r	ASCII Carriage Return (CR)
\t	ASCII Horizontal tab (TAB)
\v	ASCII Vertical tab (VT)
\000	ASCII character with octal value 000
\xhh	ASCII character with hex value hh

- **Boolean literals** Boolean literals represent logical values, either `True` or `False`. They are used to express conditions and make decisions within a program.

  For example,

```
>>> a = 7
>>> b = 5
>>> a > 5
True
```

- **Special literal (None)** In Python, you have one special literal None. None is used to define a field that is not created. It is also used to indicate the end of lists in Python.

  For example,

```
>>> a = None
>>> if a == None:
    Print ("This is none")
This is none
```

  In the above program, we assigned None to a variable. You can use it anywhere in the program for conditions, loops, structures etc.

- **Literal Collections** In Python, you have literal collections like list, tuple, dictionary and set.

  We will discuss list, tuple and dictionary in forward chapters.

Operators

Operators are the symbols that perform operations on values. It is used in programs to operate on data and variables. Python carries a wide range of operators; these are as follows:

(i) Unary Operators

Those operators that work on single operand to form an expression are known as unary operators.

Following are some unary operators:

+	unary plus
–	unary minus
~	Bitwise complement
not	logical negation

(ii) Binary Operators

The operators that work upon two operands are known as binary operators. There are various types of binary operators in Python as follows:

- **Arithmetic operator** These operators are used to do arithmetic operations. These operators are

+	Addition
−	Subtraction
*	Multiplication
/	Division
%	Remainder / Modulus
**	Exponent (raise to power)
//	Floor division

- **Logical operators** These operators are used to make a decision on two conditions. Logical operators are typically used with boolean values and what they return is also a boolean value. These operators are

and	Logical AND
or	Logical OR

- **Relational operators** Relational operators compare two operands to one another. These operators are

<	less than
>	greater than
<=	less than or equal to
>=	greater than or equal to
==	equal to
!=	Not equal to

- **Assignment operators** Assignments operators are used to assign the value of an expression to a variable. These operators are

=	assignment
/=	assign quotient
+=	assign sum
*=	assign product
%=	assign remainder
−=	assign difference
**=	assign exponent
//=	assign floor division

- **Bitwise operators** Bitwise operators work on bits and perform bit by bit operation. These operators are

&	Bitwise AND
^	Bitwise XOR
|	Bitwise OR

- **Shift operators** These operators are used to shift value left or right. These operators are

<<	shift left
>>	shift right

- **Identity operators** These operators are

is	is the identity same ?
is not	is the identity not same?

- **Membership operators** These operators are

in	whether variable in sequence
not in	whether variable not in sequence

We will discuss operators in detail, in next chapter.

Punctuators

These are symbols used to structure and separate different parts of a Python program. They help the interpreter to understand the syntax and meaning of the code. The following characters are used as punctuators in Python:

' " # \ ( ) [ ] { } @ , : . ` =

Some of them are discussed below:

(i) **Brackets** [ ] indicate list.

(ii) **Parentheses** ( ) indicate tuples, function calls, function parameters for grouping expressions etc.

(iii) **Comma** (,) can be used as a separator in a function argument list or variable declaration.

(iv) **Colon** (:) indicates a labelled statement or conditional operator symbol.

(v) **Equal sign** (=) is used to initialize the value of variable i.e. used as assignment operator in an expression.

Delimiters

A delimiter is a sequence of one or more characters used to specify the boundary between separate, independent regions in plain text or other data streams.

e.g. ( ) { } [ ] , ; :

Quick Test 1

1. Which character set does Python use to represent characters internally?
2. Identify the type of token in the following Python statement: price = 99.99
3. Which category of tokens does the 'not' keyword belong to in Python?
4. What is the difference between a keyword and an identifier in Python?

7.3 Function

A function is a self-contained block of statements which are kept together to perform a specific task in related manner.

For example,

```
def add():
  a = int(input("Enter the first number: "))
  b = int(input("Enter the second number: "))
  return a + b
```

In above program, we have one function add ( ). All the statements which indented below add ( ) function are the part of add ( ). All statements below Add ( ) are executed by calling this function by following statement: add ( )

Blocks and Indentation

Blocks and indentation indicate the relationship between various statements and thus allow us to get a better picture of the overall organization and structure of the solution given in the program. It improves the readability of the program.

For example,

```
if (a == b):
    print ("Value of a is equal to b")
    print ("Finished")
```

This is block with all its statements same indentation. Python uses indentation while other programming languages such as C/C++, Java use curly braces { }.

7.4 Variables in Python

In python, variables are used to store data values. They act as containers that hold information.

Variables are like labeled boxes that we use to store information in our programs. We can give them names and use them to hold numbers, text, or other data. This makes our programs easier to read and understand.

Key points about variables in Python

- **No explicit declaration** Unlike many other programming languages, you don't need to declare the data type of a variable before using it. Python automatically determines the data type based on the value assigned to it.
- **Dynamic Typing** The ability of variables to change their data type during program execution. This means you don't need to explicitly declare the data type of a variable. Python automatically determines the data type based on the value assigned.
- **Case-Sensitive** Variable names are case-sensitive. This means that the computer distinguishes between uppercase and lowercase letters. For example, the variables `myVariable` and `MyVariable` are considered different.
- **Naming Conventions** Variable names should be descriptive and follow a consistent naming convention (often snake_case or camelCase).

  For example,

```
x = 10                # Integer variable
y = 3.14              # Floating-point variable
name = "Alice"        # String variable
is_student = True     # Boolean variable
print(x, y, name, is_student)
```

l-values and r-values in Python

In Python, the concepts of l-value and r-value are related to understanding how values are assigned and used in expressions. This concept is derived from the typical evaluation process on the left and right sides of an assignment statement.

l-value (Left-value)

An l-value, or left-value, in Python refers to a memory location that can be assigned to a value. It typically appears on the left side of an assignment operator (=). l-values represent variables that can be modified.

For example, in the statement `x = 10`, `x` is an l-value.

r-value (Right-value)

An r-value is simply a value that can be assigned to a variable. It could be a number like 5, a word like "hello", or the result of a calculation. r-values appear on the right side of an assignment operator.

For example, in the statement `x = 10`, `10` is an r-value.

Dynamic Typing

Python is a dynamically typed language, which means that you don't need to declare the type of a variable before using it. The type of a variable is determined at runtime based on the value assigned to it.

This makes Python more flexible and easier to learn, as you can focus on the logic of your code rather than worrying about specific data types.

Syntax `Type (variable_name)`

7.5 Input and Output in Python

When we run a program, it often requires us to input data, such as numbers or text. This data is stored in the computer's memory and processed according to the program's instructions.

The results of these calculations can then be displayed on the screen, saved to a file, or sent to another computer.

In essence, I/O operations enable computers to interact with users and other devices, making them essential for a wide range of tasks.

Input from User

Python has many built-in functions; one useful built-in function is `input ()`.

This function allows you to pause the program and ask the user to enter some information. The user's input is then stored in a variable, which can be used later in the program.

Python provides two build-in functions to read a line of text from standard input, which by default comes from the keyboard. These functions are as follows.

(i) input ( )

The input() function in Python allows you to get user input as text.

Python can then interpret this input as numbers, strings, or other data types. This makes input() a versatile tool for creating interactive programs.

Syntax

```
variable_name = input (< Message to be
displayed >)
```

e.g.
```
>>> a = input ("Enter a number: ")
Enter a number: 25
>>> print (a)
25
>>> name = input ("Enter your name: ")
Enter your name: Anurag
>>> print (name)
Anurag
```

(ii) raw_input ( )

In older versions of Python, like Python 2.x, the `raw_input()` function was used to get user input. This function takes whatever the user types and converts it directly into a string, regardless of its content.

Syntax

```
variable_name = raw_input ( < Message to be
displayed >)
```

e.g.
```
>>> n = raw_input ("Enter your hobbies: ")
Enter your hobbies: Reading novels
>>> print (n)
Reading novels
```

We can typecast and convert the string input from `raw_input()` to numeric types using `int()` or `float()`.

Syntax

```
variable_name = int (raw_input (Message))
```

e.g.
```
x = int (raw_input ("Enter your marks: "))
Enter your marks: 90
>>> print (x)
90
```

Output by print Statement

The `print()` function is used to display output on the screen. It can print numbers, text, or the results of calculations.

To print multiple items on the same line, you can separate them with commas.

Syntax

```
print (expression / constant / variable)
```

e.g.
```
>>> print ("Arihant")
Arihant
>>> print (5.65)
5.65
>>> print (10 * 3)
30
```

Using f-strings in Python

Python's f-strings (formatted string literals), introduced in Python 3.6, simplify string formatting by embedding expressions directly within {}.

They offer a concise and intuitive way to interpolate variables into strings.

Prefix a string with f to create an f-string. It allows embedding expressions directly within {}.

Example:

```
name = "Amit"
age = 25
print(f"My name is {name} and I am {age}
years old.")
```

Note *F-strings are faster than % formatting and str.format().*

7.6 Basic Structure of Python Program

Here, we will discuss the basic structure of Python program and terms which are used in it.

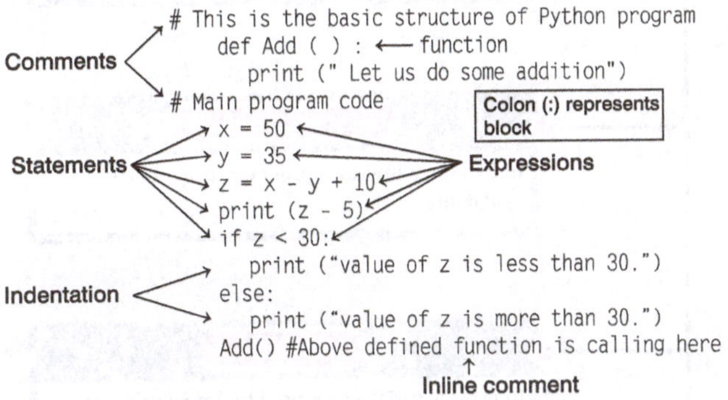

Above structure of Python program contains various components, which are discussed below:

Expressions

An expression is a combination of operators, constants and variables as per rule of the language. Any part in a program which can have a value, is an expression. It will have operands and operators together to produce a value.

e.g. `4 * i, x + y/10, (a < b) etc.`

From the above program, we have 5 expressions

`50, 35, x-y+10, (z-5), z < 30`

Statements

A statement in Python is a logical instruction, which Python interpreter can read and execute. In python, it could be an expression or assignment statement. The assignment statement is fundamental to Python.

e.g.
```
if x == y:
   print ("x is equal to y")
```

when expression will be evaluated, statement or group of statements executed.

Comments in Python

Comments are like notes you write to yourself or others to explain your code.

They help people understand what your code is doing, even if they don't know the programming language.

While they are ignored by the interpreter or compiler, they are crucial for human programmers to make sense of the code.

Types of comments in Python

- **Single-line Comments** Single-line comments are used to add short explanations or notes to a specific line of code. They start with a hash symbol (`#`) and continue until the end of the line. Anything after the `#` symbol on that line is ignored by the interpreter.

  For example, `# This is a single-line comment` will be ignored by the Python interpreter.

- **Multi-line Comments** Multi-line comments are used to add longer explanations or notes that span multiple lines of code. In Python, we use triple quotes ("""" ... """") for multi-line comments.

  Similarly, single triple quotes ('''...''') can also be used for the same purpose. We can also uses (#) in multiple lines, but triple quotes look much better.

  For example,
  ```
  """ This is a multi-line comment.
  It spans multiple lines.
  To explain a complex code block."""
  ```

Quick Test 2

1. In Python, what will be the output of the following code?
   ```
   x = 5
   y = x + (x := 10)
   print(y)
   ```
2. Identify the l-value and r-value in the statement below:
   a = b + 10
3. What concept of Python allows a variable to store different types of values at different times during execution?
4. What will be the output of the following code?
   ```
   print("5" + "5")
   ```
5. How does Python differentiate between an expression and a statement, and which of the two can be used inside function's return?

Mind Map

PYTHON FUNDAMENTAL

Python Character Set

Python's character set is a collection of characters that can be used to create strings and other text-based data. It is a set of valid characters that a language can recognize.

ASCII Characters
- Alphabetic characters
- Numeric characters
- Punctuation marks
- Special Characters

Unicode Characters
- Extended Character Set
- Unicode Escape Sequences

Tokens

Tokens are the smallest individual units in a Python program.

Identifiers

Identifiers are basically the names given to variables, functions, classes, and other entities in a Python program.

Valid identifiers	Name, name, name_1, _SUM, sum_of_the_numbers, PASS First Name
Invalid identifiers	global, num^2, num1, 2num

Keywords

These are reserved words in Python that have special meanings. They cannot be used as variable names.

Literals or Constants

Literals are the raw data values assigned to variables in a program. They represent fixed values that do not change during program execution.

Numeric literals	String literals	Boolean literals	Special literal	Literal Collections

Operators

Operators are the symbols that perform operations on values. It is used in programs to operate on data and variables.

- Unary Operators +,-,~, not
- Binary Operators
  - Arithmetic operator +, -, *, /, %, **, //
  - Logical operators AND, OR
  - Relational operators <, >, <=, >=, ==, !=
  - Assignment operators =, /=, +=, *=, %=, -=, **=, //=
  - Bitwise operators &, ^, |
  - Shift operators <<, >>
  - Identity operators is, is not
  - Membership operators in, not in

Punctuators

These are symbols used to structure and separate different parts of a Python program.

Function

A function is a self-contained block of statements which are kept together to perform a specific task in related manner.

Blocks and Indentation

In Python, it improves program structure and readability

Variable

In python, variables are used to store data values. They act as containers that hold information.

In Python, the concepts of **l-value** and **r-value** are related to understanding how values are assigned and used in expressions.

Input and Output in Python

- input() function in Python allows you to get user input as text.
- \`print()\` function is used to display output on the screen.

Basic Structure of Python Program

```
# This is the basic structure of Python program
def Add ( ) :          ← function
    print (" Let us do some addition")
# Main program code
x = 50
y = 35
z = x - y + 10
print (z - 5)
if z < 30:
    print ("value of z is less than 30.")
else:
    print ("value of z is more than 30.")
Add() #Above defined function is calling here
```

Comments: the lines beginning with #

Statements: x = 50, y = 35, z = x - y + 10, print (z - 5), if z < 30:

Expressions: x = 50, y = 35, z = x - y + 10, print (z - 5), if z < 30:

Colon (:) represents block

Indentation: the indented print statements under if and else

Inline comment: #Above defined function is calling here

EXAM PATTERN QUESTIONS

Objective Type Questions

Multiple Choice Questions

1. Which of the following is/are character set?

(a) Alphabets (b) Digits
(c) White spaces (d) All of these

2. Which of the following is a valid identifier in Python?

(a) 123number (b) my_variable
(c) @variable (d) class

3. What is the maximum length of an identifier in Python?

(a) 32 characters (b) 64 characters
(c) 128 characters (d) No fixed limit

4. Which of the following is not a valid identifier in Python?

(a) MyBook (b) @book
(c) _book (d) book23

5. What is the maximum possible length of an identifier in Python?

(a) 16 (b) 32
(c) 64 (d) None of these

6. Which of the following are the most obvious kind of constants?

(a) Keywords (b) Literals
(c) Variables (d) Identifiers

7. Which of the following is not a valid string literal in Python?

(a) "Hello World" (b) 'Python's Power'
(c) '''Multiline String''' (d) "12345"

8. Which of the following is not a valid string in Python?

(a) "Hello" (b) 'Hello'
(c) "Hello' (d) '''Hello'''

9. .... is a logical instruction which Python interpreter can read and execute.

(a) Expression (b) Statement
(c) Comment (d) Indentation

10. Find the punctuator(s) from the following options.

(a) Brackets (b) Parentheses
(c) Comma (d) All of these

11. Priya is writing a Python program and wants to display the values of a and b on the same line, separated by a space. Which syntax should she use? Competency Based Que.

(a) print(a, b) (b) print(a, end=" ", b)
(c) print(a, end="$", b) (d) print(a) print(b)

12. How are blocks of code defined in Python?

(a) Using curly braces {}
(b) Using keywords like BEGIN and END
(c) Using indentation
(d) Using parentheses ()

13. Rahul is learning Python and wants to add explanations to his code without affecting execution. He notices that some comments start with the # symbol. Which type of comment should he use? Competency Based Que.

(a) Double-line (b) Multi-line
(c) Single-line (d) All of these

Fill in the Blanks

14. Python uses the ________ character set to represent text and symbols.

15. The ______ operator in Python is used to calculate the remainder of a division.

16. In Python, a variable is created the moment you assign it a ______.

17. Python is a dynamically typed language, meaning you do not need to declare the _____ of a variable explicitly.

18. The function ______ is used to display output on the screen, while ______ is used to take input from the user.

State Whether True or False

19. The identifier "2name" is considered valid in Python.

20. Special characters like '@', '#', and '$' are allowed within identifiers.

21. Brackets "[ ]" are used to indicate a list in Python.

22. The "<<" operator is used to perform bitwise AND operation.

23. Indentation is used in Python to define blocks of code, similar to how curly braces are used in languages like C or Java.

24. In the Python statement y = x + 5, the variable y is an r-value, and the expression x + 5 is an l-value.

25. In Python, a statement like x = 5 is considered an expression.

26. A multi-line comment in Python can be started with # and ended with ##

Assertion and Reason Based Questions

Assertion (A) and Reason (R) Type questions. Choose the correct option as:

(a) Both Assertion (A) and Reason (R) are true, and Reason (R) is the correct explanation of Assertion (A).

(b) Both Assertion (A) and Reason (R) are true, but Reason (R) is not the correct explanation of Assertion (A).

(c) Assertion (A) is true, but Reason (R) is false.

(d) Assertion (A) is false, but Reason (R) is true.

27. **Assertion (A)** Python supports both ASCII and Unicode characters.

Reason (R) Unicode allows representing characters from multiple languages.

28. **Assertion (A)** Keywords, identifiers, literals, and operators are all tokens in Python.

Reason (R) Tokens are the smallest individual units in a Python program.

29. **Assertion (A)** Python uses indentation to define blocks of code.

Reason (R) Curly braces {} are mandatory to define blocks in Python.

30. **Assertion (A)** Variables in Python can hold values of any type due to dynamic typing.

Reason (R) Python variables must be declared with a specific data type before use.

Answers

1. (d) All of these
2. (b) my_variable
3. (d) No fixed limit
4. (b) @book
5. (d) None of these
6. (b) Literals
7. (b) 'Python's Power'
8. (c) "Hello"
9. (b) Statement
10. (d) All of these
11. (a) print(a, b)
12. (c) Using indentation
13. (c) Single line
14. Unicode
15. Modulus (%)
16. Value
17. Data type
18. print, input
19. False
20. False
21. True
22. False
23. True
24. False
25. True
26. False
27. (a) Both Assertion (A) and Reason (R) are true, and Reason (R) is the correct explanation of Assertion (A).
28. (a) Both Assertion (A) and Reason (R) are true, and Reason (R) is the correct explanation of Assertion (A).
29. (c) Assertion (A) is true, but Reason (R) is false.
30. (c) Assertion (A) is true, but Reason (R) is false.

Subjective Type Questions

Very Short Answer Type Questions

1. What is Python character set explaining in short?

Ans. Character set is a set of valid characters that a language can recognize. It represents any letter, digit or other sign.

2. What is token?

Ans. A smallest individual unit in a program is known as token.

3. How do different types of tokens in Python contribute to writing a structured and meaningful program? Competency Based Que.

Ans. Python has the following tokens

- Identifiers
- Keywords
- Punctuations
- Literals
- Operators

4. Can keywords be used as identifier?

Ans. No, keywords cannot be used as identifier.

5. While developing a payroll management system, a programmer tries to use the word class as a variable name but encounters an error. Explain why this happens and how reserved words impact programming in Python. Competency Based Que.

Ans. Reserved words also known as keywords are predefined by the programming language that have some special or predefined meanings.

6. Explain the concept of constants in Python.

Ans. Constants are the data values that can never change their values during program execution.

7. Write the name of any four punctuators used in Python program.

Ans. Brackets [ ], parentheses ( ), comma (,), colon (:)

8. Explain string literals.

Ans. The literal which is stored in a variable within double or single quotation mark is called string literal.

9. What are the different types of integer literals in Python?

Ans. The main integer constants in Python are decimal, octal and hexadecimal.

10. What is meant by \' in escape sequence?

Ans. \' represents single quote.

11. Define assignment operator?

Ans. An assignment operator is used to assign values to a variable or a constant.

12. Which symbol is represented the Bitwise OR?

Ans. (|) symbol is represented the bitwise OR.

13. Imagine you are developing a student management system where each student has a unique ID, name, and grade that can change over time. How would you use variables in Python to store and manage this information efficiently? **Competency Based Que.**

Ans. A variable is one which holds certain values.

14. Name the two values associated with the symbolic variable.

Ans. The two values associated with symbolic variables are

(i) r-value (ii) l-value

15. What is the output of following code?

```
>>> a = 10
>>> print ("Value of a is:", a + 10 * 2)
```

Ans. Value of a is: 30

Short Answer Type I Questions

16. Differentiate between identifier and keyword.

Ans. Differences between identifier and keyword are

Identifier	Keyword
Identifier consists any combination of letters, numbers and underscores.	Keyword must consist only letters.
It allows both uppercase and lowercase.	It allows only lowercase.
e.g. x, sum_5, _mul etc.	e.g. finally, continue, yield etc.

17. Which of the following are invalid names and why?

(i) PaidInterest **(ii) S_num**

(iii) Percent **(iv) 123**

(v) abc km **(vi) elif**

(vii) lambda

Ans. (i) Valid

(ii) Valid

(iii) Valid

(iv) Invalid, first character must be alphabet.

(v) Invalid, space is not allowed

(vi) Invalid, elif is a keyword.

(vii) Invalid, lambda is a keyword.

18. (a) Write the one example of following terms.

(i) Identifier **(ii) Punctuator**

(iii) Keyword **(iv) Constant**

(b) Identify the types of following literals.

False 'True' "False"

45345 00434 435.3

Ans. (a) (i) Identifier → Sum_1

(ii) Punctuator → Bracket ( )

(iii) Keyword → for

(iv) Constant → 'Neha'

(b)

False	Boolean
'True'	String
"False"	String
45345	Integer
00434	Integer (octal)
435.3	Floating point

19. What do you mean by special literal None ?

Ans. In Python, you have one special literal None. None is used to define a field that is not created.

e.g.
```
x = None
if x == None:
    print ('This is none')
```

20. Riya is writing a Python program to automate payroll processing. However, her code throws an indentation error, causing incorrect calculations. Why is indentation important in Python, and how does it impact code execution in real-world applications? **Competency Based Que.**

Ans. Indentation is used to define code blocks and determines the hierarchical structure of a program.

Unlike many other programming languages that use curly braces to delimit code blocks, Python relies only on consistent indentation. This makes Python code more readable and visually appealing.

21. Define the term r-value and l-value in Python?

Ans.
- **r-value** Pulls or fetches the value stored in a variable or constant.
- **l-value** The requirement that operand on the left side of the assignment operator is modifiable, usually a variable.

22. Find the errors in the following Python code:

(i) `a + 5 = b` (ii) `1 = 2 b + c * d`

(iii) `name = Aryan` (iv) `a = 20`
`print a;`

Ans. (i) `b = a + 5` (ii) `1 = 2 * b + c*d`

(iii) name = "Aryan" (iv) `a = 20`
`print (a)`

23. Imagine you are working on a team project where multiple developers contribute to the same Python codebase. How can using comments improve collaboration and code maintainability? Where should comments be placed for better readability? **Competency Based Que.**

Ans. The sequence of character which improves the readability of a program is called comment. It may start anywhere and do not require closing symbol.

24. What is the difference between statement and expression ?

Ans. Differences between statement and expression are as follows

Statement	Expression
A statement is a complete line of code that performs some action.	An expression is any section of the code that evaluates to a value.
Statements can only be combined vertically by writing one after another or with block constructs.	Expressions can be combined horizontally into larger expressions using operators.

25. Anurag is writing a Python program but is encountering an error. Can you identify the issue in the following code?

```
a = 10
b = 20
c = a + b
print ('The output is:", c)
```

Ans. The above code is having an indentation error and correct code is

```
a = 10
b = 20
c = a + b
 print ("The output is:", c)
```

26. What will be the output of the following code?

```
name = "Anurag"
rnk = 1
 print (name, "is a famous singer and his
 rank in India is", rnk)
```

Ans. Output

Anurag is a famous singer and his rank in India is 1.

27. What will be the output of the following code?

```
a, b = 10, 5
x, y = a + b, b - 2
z = x - y
print ( "x : " , x, "y:" , y, " z : " , z)
```

Ans. Output

x:15 y:3 z:12

28. Write a program to enter two numbers and print their difference.

Ans.
```
a = int(input("Enter first number : "))
b = int(input("Enter second number : "))
Difference = a - b
print (" Two numbers are :" , a, b)
print ("Difference is:", Difference)
```

Short Answer Type II Questions

29. What are identifiers? Also, give the rules in Python for identifiers.

Ans. Identifiers are the fundamental building blocks of a program which are used to give the name to data items included by the programmer. It is required in all programming languages, where the programmer has to include items like variables, objects, classes, functions, arrays, etc., to specify their names. The identifier is a sequence of characters taken from Python character set.

The rules in Python for identifiers are

(i) Only alphabets, digits and underscores are permitted.
(ii) Identifier name cannot start with a digit.
(iii) Keywords cannot be used as identifier.
(iv) Uppercase and lowercase letters are distinct because Python is case sensitive language.
(v) Special characters are not allowed.

30. Explain the process of declaring and assigning a variable in Python.

Ans. Creating of variables means providing an initial value when it is declared. A variable can be created anywhere in Python program.

e.g. x = 20
Subject = 'Mathematics'

Above code is an assignment statements which used to assign values to variables. The equal (=) sign causes the value on the right hand side of the variables to be assigned to the variables on the left..

31. A software company is developing a payroll system where employee salaries can be stored as integers, but bonuses may be represented as floating-point values. The system should handle both data types without explicit type declarations. **Competency Based Que.**

How does Python's dynamic typing feature help in this scenario? Provide an example.

Ans. A language is dynamically typed if the type is associated with run-time values and not named variables / fields etc.

Dynamic typing is used to know the type of variables. For which, type ( ) module is used.

e.g.
```
>>> x = 15
>>> type (x)
<class 'int'>
>>> a = 4.75
>>> type (a)
<class 'float'>
>>> n = 'Honesty'
>>> type (n)
<class 'str'>
```

32. Predict the output.

```
a,b=10,15
x=20
y=25
a=x+y-b
x=a+b-y+10
z=y+b*3+a
x=50
a=x+y+z
print("a:",a)
print("b:",b)
print("x:",x)
print("y:",y)
print("z:",z)
```

Ans. Output

a : 175
b : 15
x : 50
y : 25
z : 100

33. Correct the following code

(i)
```
x = 5
  print(x)
y = 10
  print(y)
a = x + y
  print(a)
```

(ii)
```
sub = Math
marks = 80
print("Value of subject and marks
are", sub + marks)
```

(iii)
```
x = 5
b = x + 5
x = "Try"
d = x/20
```

Ans. (i)
```
x = 5
print(x)
y = 10
print(y)
a = x + y
print(a)
```

(ii)
```
sub = "Math"
marks = 80
print("Value of subject and marks
are", sub, marks)
```

(iii)
```
x = 5
b = x + 5
#x = "Try"
d=x/20
```

Long Answer Type Questions

34. Determine which of the following identifiers are valid. If invalid, explain with reason.

(i) name_1
(ii) _SUM
(iii) $sum
(iv) num ^ 2
(v) Name

Ans. The valid identifiers are

Identifier	Reason
name_1	Digits and underscore is allowed along with alphabets
_SUM	Underscore at the first position is allowed
Name	Capital letter with small letters are allowed

The invalid identifiers are

Identifier	Reason
$sum	$ sign can be used in other programming languages for creating identifier, however Python does not support $ sign
num ^ 2	Special character are not allowed

35. What are literals in Python? Explain the different types of literals with examples.

Ans. Refer to text on page no. 122-123 (Literals or constants).

36. Discuss the various types of numeric literals.

Ans. Numeric literals are immutable (unchangeable). Numeric literals can belong to 3 different numerical types as

(i) **Integer Literals** Integers are whole numbers without any fractional part. The following rules are followed for constructing integer constant.

- A decimal point and comma is not allowed in an integer constant.
- It must have atleast one digit.
- Integer constants may have either positive or negative sign.
- In the absence of any sign, it is assumed to be positive.
- Blanks are not permitted in integer constants.

Integers literals can be further divided into three parts as

(a) **Decimal Integer Literals** These constants consist of a sequence of digits, taken from the set 0 to 9. e.g. 1024, +275 etc.

(b) **Octal Integer Literals** These constants are preceded by 0. The first digit must be 0, in order to identify the constant as an octal number. A octal value can contain only digits between 0 and 7. e.g. 01, 055 etc.

(c) **Hexadecimal Integer Literals** These literals must begin with either 0X or 0x. It can then be followed by any combination of digits taken from the set 0 to 9 and A to F. e.g. 0X0, 0x1, –0x523 etc.

(ii) **Floating Point Constants** Floating point literals are real numbers which hold a fractional part.

They express numbers with decimals and / or exponents. Its range is greater than the range of integer constant.

The rules for writing floating point constants in Python as

- It must have atleast one digit before and one digit after the decimal point.
- A floating point constant can be either positive or negative.
- Blanks and commas are not permitted.
- In the absence of any sign, it is assumed to be positive.

37. What do you understand by string literals? Explain.

Ans. The literal which is stored in a variable within single quotation mark or double quotation marks is called string literal.

These represent a sequence of zero or more characters enclosed by double quotes. It can also include blank spaces.

Some valid string constants are

'A'	"Science"	'560.50'	'The output is'
"24567"	"0.34"	'MP'	'Delhi'

Some Invalid string constants are

Neha	Not enclosed in double or single quotes
"Hello'	Number of quotes must be even either double or single.

There are two types of strings supported in Python:

(a) **Single Line String** Strings that are terminated within a single line are known as single line strings.

e.g. >>> value = 'Arihant'

(b) **Multiline String** A piece of text that is spread along multiple lines is known as multiple line string.

There are two ways to create multiline strings:

(I) Adding backslash at the end of each line

e.g.
```
>>> value = 'Arihant\
    Publication'
>>> value
'ArihantPublication'
```

(II) Using triple quotation marks

e.g.
```
>>> value = '''Welcome
    to
    Python '''
    >>> print (value)
    Welcome
    to
    Python
```

38. Write a Python program which calculate the cost of triangle area wise. Also, display its output.

Ans.
```
a = float(input('Enter first side: '))
b = float(input('Enter second side: '))
c = float(input('Enter third side: '))
# calculate the semi-perimeter
s = (a + b + c) / 2
# calculate the area
area = (s*(s-a)*(s-b)*(s-c)) ** 0.5
print('The area of the triangle is
%0.2f', area)
cost=float(input("Enter the cost per
meter square in rupees:`"))
Total_cost=area*cost
print("Total cost of triangle area
wise:`",Total_cost)
```

Output

Enter first side: 12
Enter second side: 13
Enter third side: 5
The area of the triangle is %0.2f 30.0
Enter the cost per meter square in rupees:`15.50
Total cost of triangle area wise:`465.0

Case Study Based Questions

Case Study 1

A variable in Python is a named storage location that holds a value. Unlike many other programming languages, Python is dynamically typed, meaning you don't need to declare a variable's data type explicitly. The interpreter automatically infers the type based on the assigned value. Variable names can be a combination of letters, numbers, and underscores, but they must start with a letter or an underscore.

(i) What is a variable in Python?
(a) A keyword (b) A data type
(c) A named storage location (d) A function

(ii) Is Python a statically typed or dynamically typed language?
(a) Statically typed (b) Dynamically typed
(c) Both (d) Neither

(iii) Which of the following is a valid variable name in Python?
(a) 123variable (b) my_variable
(c) @variable (d) class

(iv) How do you declare and initialize a variable named x with the value 10 in Python?
(a) int x = 10; (b) var x = 10;
(c) x = 10 (d) let x = 10;

(v) What happens if you try to use a variable that hasn't been assigned a value?
(a) The program will continue to run without any errors
(b) A NameError will be raised
(c) The program will crash
(d) The variable will be automatically assigned the value None

(vi) Can you change the data type of a variable after it's been assigned a value?
(a) Yes, Python is dynamically typed
(b) No, the data type is fixed once assigned
(c) It depends on the specific data type
(d) Only in certain cases

Ans. (i) (c) A named storage location
(ii) (b) Dynamically typed
(iii) (b) my_variable (iv) (c) x = 10
(v) (b) A NameError will be raised
(vi) (a) Yes, Python is dynamically typed

Case Study 2

Variable is a container object that stores a meaningful value that can be used throughout the program.

In a Python program, to store different types of values such as, name of a shop and quantities of items (goods) available in the shop during the run time. We require some sort of storage area called variables. Each variable has a specific type, which determines the size and layout of the variable's memory, the range of values that can be stored within that memory and the set of operations that can be applied to the variable.
A variable is an identifier that is used to represent specific data item. The data item may be a whole number, a fractional number, a sequence of characters, a single character, etc.

Based on the above information, answer the following questions.

(i) What is an identifier that is used to represent a specific data item?
(a) Function (b) Variable
(c) Operator (d) Statement

(ii) Which term is used to pull or fetch the value stored in a variable or constant?
(a) Assigning (b) Accessing
(c) Storing (d) Declaring

(iii) In Python, a data item may be represented by which type of character(s)?
(a) Whole number (b) Fractional number
(c) Sequence of characters (d) All of the above

(iv) Which sign is used to assign a value to a variable?
(a) == (b) =
(c) : (d) ->

(v) You can assign a single value to multiple variables using which statement?
(a) a = b = c = 10 (b) a, b, c = 10
(c) a == b == c == 10 (d) a -> b -> c = 10

(vi) How do you declare and assign a value to a variable in Python?
(a) int x = 10; (b) x = 10
(c) var x = 10 (d) declare x = 10

(vii) How do you swap the values of two variables in Python?
(a) temp = a; a = b; b = temp (b) a, b = b, a
(c) swap(a, b) (d) a = b, b = a

Ans. (i) (b) Variable
(ii) (b) Accessing
(iii) (d) All of the above
(iv) (b) =
(v) (a) a = b = c = 10
(vi) (b) x = 10
(vii) (b) a, b = b, a

SELF ASSESSMENT TEST

Multiple Choice Questions

1. The Python recognises these kind(s) of token

(a) identifier (b) keyword

(c) operator (d) All of these

2. Which of the following is invalid identifier?

(a) Name (b) num^2 (c) num 1 (d) _SUM

3. .... is a set of valid characters that a language can recognise.

(a) Variable (b) Datatype (c) Character set (d) Token

Fill in the Blanks

4. In Python, a token is the smallest unit of a program and includes categories like keywords, identifiers, literals, operators, and ________.

5. The input() function in Python always returns data in the ______ type, regardless of the user's input.

6. In Python, the print() function separates multiple arguments by a default separator, which is the _______ character.

7. Python uses ___________ typing, which means that the type of a variable is determined at runtime based on the assigned value.

State Whether True or False

8. Among Python's tokens, 'return' and 'global' are considered identifiers because they define names used in a program.

9. A floating-point literal in Python can contain an underscore (_) to improve readability, such as 1_000.25, without affecting its value.

10. The operators and, or, and not in Python are classified as special literals rather than keywords.

Assertion and Reason Based Questions

Assertion (A) and Reason (R) Type questions. Choose the correct option as:

(a) Both Assertion (A) and Reason (R) are true, and Reason (R) is the correct explanation of Assertion (A).

(b) Both Assertion (A) and Reason (R) are true, but Reason (R) is not the correct explanation of Assertion (A).

(c) Assertion (A) is true, but Reason (R) is false.

(d) Assertion (A) is false, but Reason (R) is true.

11. Assertion (A) In Python, an L-value refers to a memory location that can hold a value, whereas an R-value is any valid expression or literal that can be assigned to an L-value.

Reason (R) The expression 5 = x is a valid statement in Python because 5 is an L-value.

12. Assertion (A) Python uses dynamic typing, meaning a variable can hold different types of data at different times.

Reason (R) Once a variable is assigned a data type, it cannot change throughout the program.

Very Short Answer Type Questions

13. What is the meaning of ~ in Python?

14. Which escape sequence is represented the ASCII horizontal tab?

15. How many ways are there to write comments in Python program?

16. Write any two keywords which are used in Python.

Short Answer Type Questions

17. Differentiate between ** and //operators.

18. In how many ways can multiple assignments used in Python?

19. State the meaning of the following terms.

(i) ^

(ii) >>

(iii) \n

(iv) \b

20. Write the rules for writing the identifiers.

21. Distinguish between integer literals and floating point literals.

22. Explain the following terms.

(i) Operator

(ii) Indentation

(iii) Expression

23. Define the raw_input() function.

24. What are the comments ? What is the used of these in programming?

Long Answer Type Questions

25. Explain the basic structure of a Python program.

26. Write the short note.

(i) Boolean literal

(ii) Literal collection

(iii) Unary operator

(iv) Binary operator

27. Differentiate between input ( ) and raw_input ( ) with an example.

28. Correct the following code.

(i)
```
x = 10
  print(y)
y = 5
```

(ii)
```
x = 5
y = 10
print("Addition:" x +
y)
```

(iii)
```
sub = "Science"
code = 245
print ("Details:",
sub + code)
```

(iv)
```
a = 10
b = a + 10
b = "Hello"
c = b/20
```

Case Study Based Questions

29. Rahul is learning Python programming and wrote the following code:

```
name = input("Enter your name: ")
age = input("Enter your age: ")
age = age + 5
print("Hello", name, "You will be", age,
"years old in 5 years.")
```

However, when he runs the code, it throws an error. He is confused about Python's data types, input handling, and tokens. Help Rahul understand the concepts by answering the following questions.

Answer the following questions:

(i) Which type of error will Rahul encounter when he runs this code?

(a) SyntaxError (b) TypeError

(c) NameError (d) ValueError

(ii) What is the correct way to fix Rahul's error?

(a) Change age = input("Enter your age: ") to age = int(input("Enter your age: "))

(b) Change age = age + 5 to age = str(age) + "5"

(c) Use print("Hello" + name + "You will be" + str(age) + "years old in 5 years.")

(d) Remove the input() function and directly assign age = 20

(iii) In the given code, what kind of token will not print?

(a) Identifier (b) Keyword

(c) Operator (d) Function name

(iv) Which concept of Python is demonstrated when age is assigned a string first and later changed to an integer?

(a) Strong Typing (b) Static Typing

(c) Dynamic Typing (d) Explicit Casting

(v) What is the purpose of the input() function in Python?

(a) It takes user input and converts it into an integer automatically.

(b) It is used to display output on the screen.

(c) It takes user input as a string.

(d) It is used to define a variable.

Answers

1. (d) 2. (b) 3. (c) 4. punctuator
5. string 6. space 7. dynamic
8. False 9. True 10. False 11. (c) 12. (c)
29. (i) → (b), (ii) → (a), (iii) → (d), (iv) → (c), (v) → (c)

08

CHAPTER

Python data types are the classification or categorization of data items. It represents the kind of value that tells what operations can be performed on a particular data.

▼ YOUR STUDY GOALS

8.1 Data Types
8.2 Operators
8.3 Type Conversion
8.4 Expressions

▼ YOUR PRACTICE GOAL

- Objective Type Questions (34 Qs ; MCQs, True or False, Fill in the Blanks, Assertion and Reason)
- Subjective Type Questions (45 Qs ; VSA, SA, LA)
- Case Study Based Questions-2

Data Types and Operators

Before you start programming in Python, it's important to understand the basic building blocks of the language.

This includes learning about data types, operators and expressions used by Python to perform its various operations on different data types, which are used to perform calculations and manipulate data.

In this chapter, we'll explore these fundamental concepts and how they work in Python. We will learn about the order in which Python evaluates different operations.

This is determined by the type of operation and the number of values involved. Understanding operator precedence is crucial for writing correct and efficient Python code.

8.1 Data Types

Computers can process many different types of data. This data can be numbers (like 1, 2, 3.14), single letters (like 'A', 'b'), or groups of letters and numbers (like "Hello World 01 ").

To handle all these different types of data, programming languages use something called "data types."

A data type tells the computer what kind of data it's dealing with, so it can process and store it correctly.

Python has five standard data types which shown in figure below:

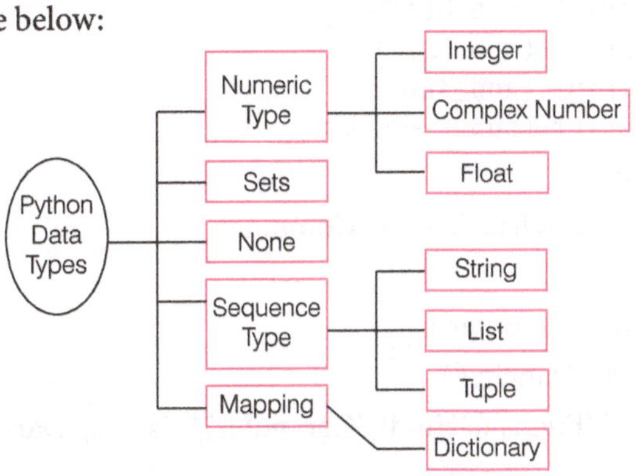

Numbers

Numbers data type contains only numeric values in Python. The types of numbers data type are as follows:

1. Integers

Integers are whole numbers, like 1, 2, 3, -1, -2, and so on having different storage ranges supported by a particular machine. They don't have any decimal parts. Integers can be both positive and negative.

There are two types of integers in Python as follows:

- **Integers (signed)** It is a simple whole number integers. In Python 3.x, integers are represented by any length and its length is limited depending on memory availability. It is a signed representation.
- **Boolean** data type, often termed as "bool," is a subtype of integer. It is a special kind of data that can only be one of two values: True or False. It's like a simple yes or no answer. "True" is represented by a non-zero value, while "False" is represented by zero.

2. Floating Point Numbers

A float is a number with a decimal point. For example, 3.14, 2.718, and 1.0 are all floats. Unlike integers, which are whole numbers, floats can represent fractional values. In Python, you use the float data type to store these kinds of numbers.

Floating point numbers can also be written in exponent notation.

e.g., 786.456 would be written as 7.86456E02.

```
>>> 1.1 + 1.1
2.2
>>> 4.2 % 2.1
0.0
```

Floating-point numbers are used to represent real numbers with decimal points. They're perfect for measuring things like distance, area, temperature, and weight, where precise values are important.

3. Complex Numbers

A complex number is a special kind of number that combines both real and imaginary numbers. It's written in the form a + bi, where 'a' is the real part and 'b' is the imaginary part. The letter 'i' represents the imaginary unit, which is the square root of -1.

So, a complex number is like a combination of two numbers, one real and one imaginary, working together.

e.g., 2 + 3i, 1 + 4i, 2 - 5i etc.

Here, you will learn about how to declare complex numbers in Python and extract their real and imaginary parts.

```
>>> a = complex (2,3)
>>> print (a)
(2 + 3i)
>>> a.real
2.0
>>> a.imag
3.0
```

Where, a.real will give the real part and a.imag will give the imaginary part of a complex number.

Sequence

Python sequences are like ordered lists of items. Each item has a specific position or index, which is a number. There are three main types of sequences in Python: strings, lists, and tuples. We'll explore each type in more detail later, but here's a quick overview:

1. Strings

Strings are collections of characters, like letters, numbers, or symbols. In Python, they are represented by the str data type. You can define a string by enclosing the characters within either single quotes (' ') or double quotes (" ").

e.g., "Anurag", 'ABC', "??\+", '$ABC' etc all are valid strings.

```
>>> print ("Arihant Publications")
Arihant Publications
>>> type("Arihant Publications")
<class 'str'>
```

A string in Python can contain as many characters as you want. The string limit depends on your machine's memory resources. A string can also be empty.

2. Lists

Lists are like versatile containers in Python. You can store a variety of items within them, such as numbers, text, or even other lists. To create a list, you enclose the items within square brackets [] and separate them with commas. Unlike some other data structures, lists are mutable, meaning you can add, remove, or modify elements after you've created the list.

e.g.,
```
x = [ ]
y = [1,2, 'Neha']
z = [23, 46, 52, 98]
```

Python lists start counting from zero. So, the first item in a list is at index 0, the second at index 1, and so on.

In IDLE Python,
```
value = [20, 25, 'Anurag', 42.6, 'Sharma']
value1 = ['Abhishek', 24, 3.75]
print (value)
print (value [2])
print (value [1: 3])
print (value1[0])
print (value1 * 2)
print (value + value1)
```

Output

[20, 25, 'Anurag', 42.6, 'Sharma']

Anurag

[25, 'Anurag']

Abhishek

['Abhishek', 24, 3.75, 'Abhishek', 24, 3.75]

[20, 25, 'Anurag', 42.6, 'Sharma', 'Abhishek', 24, 3.75]

If you want to change any element in list then follow this,
```
>>> value [3] = 'Harsh'
>>> value
[20, 25, 'Anurag', 'Harsh', 'Sharma']
```

3. Tuples

Tuples are similar to lists in that they are ordered collections of items. However, unlike lists, tuples are immutable, meaning they cannot be changed once they are created.

This makes them useful for protecting data that should not be altered. Tuples are often faster than lists because they are static and don't require dynamic memory allocation. To define a tuple, you enclose the items within parentheses ().

e.g.,
```
sub = ('Maths', 'English', 'Hindi', 'Computer')
add_sub = ('Games', 'Dancing')
print (sub)
print (sub [1])
print (sub [2:])
print (add_sub * 1)
print (sub + add_sub)
```

Output

('Maths', 'English', 'Hindi', 'Computer')

English

('Hindi', 'Computer')

('Games', 'Dancing')

('Maths', 'English', 'Hindi', 'Computer', 'Games', 'Dancing')

Set

A set is a collection of unique items, like a group of friends with no repeats. Unlike lists, sets don't have a specific order, and you can't have the same item appear multiple times. Once you create a set, you can't change its elements. Sets are defined using curly braces {}.

e.g.
```
#create a set
>>> set1 = {1, 12, 3.14, "New Delhi"}
>>> print(type(set1))
<class 'set'>
>>> print (set1)
{1, 12, 3.14, "New Delhi"}
#duplicate elements are not included in set
>>> set2 = {100,24,1,24}
>>> print (set2)
{100, 24, 1}
```

None

None is a special data type in Python that represents the absence of a value. It's different from zero or False. You can use it to indicate that a variable has no value assigned to it yet, or that a function hasn't returned a specific value. While it doesn't support many operations, it plays a crucial role in various programming scenarios.

e.g.
```
>>> myVar = None
>>> print (type(myVar))
<class 'NoneType'>
>>> print (myVar)
None
```

Mapping

A mapping data type in Python is a collection of items where each item is associated with a unique key. This allows you to efficiently store and retrieve values based on their corresponding keys. Currently, there is only one standard mapping data type in Python called a dictionary.

Dictionary

In Dictionaries, you can store information in key-value pairs. Each key is unique, and it's used to access the corresponding value.

For example, you could store a person's name as a key and their age as the value. Dictionaries are incredibly versatile and can be used to sort, search, and compare data.

You create a dictionary by enclosing key-value pairs within curly braces {}, separating each pair with a comma ,, and using a colon : to connect the key and value.

e.g.,
```
dict = ['Name' : 'Abhishek', 'Salary' : 80000,]
print (dict.keys())
print (dict.values())
print (dict ['Salary'])
```

Output
```
dict_keys(['Name', 'Salary'])
Dict_values(['Abhishek', 80000])
80000
```

Mutable and Immutable Data Types

Every variable in Python holds an instance of an object. There are two types of objects in Python as follows

1. Mutable Types

The values of mutable types can be changed after it is created. These are list, dictionary and sets.

e.g.
```
Subject = ['Maths', 'Hindi', 'English']
print (subject)
subject [0] = 'History'
subject [-1] = 'Economics'
print ("After change")
print (subject)
```

Output

['Maths', 'Hindi', 'English']
After change
['History', 'Hindi', 'Economics']

2. Immutable Types

The values of immutable cannot be changed after it is created. These are integer, float, boolean, string and tuple.

e.g.
```
tuple1 = ('Maths', 'English', 'Hindi')
tuple1 [1] = 'Computer'
print (tuple1)
```

Output

It will give an error message like tuple object does not support item assignment.

Quick Test 1

1. What are the basic data types in Python?
2. What is the difference between mutable and immutable data types?
3. What is the purpose of the None keyword in Python?
4. Explain the difference between a list and a tuple.
5. What is a dictionary in Python?

8.2 Operators

In Python, **operators** are symbols used to perform operations on values or variables. They can be classified as **unary** or **binary** based on the number of operands they operate on:

Unary Operators

Unary operators operate on a single operand. They are often used to perform operations like negation or to increment/decrement a value.

Common Unary Operators

1. **Unary Plus** (+) Indicates a positive value.
```
num = 5
print(+num) # Output: 5
```
2. **Unary Minus** (-) Negates the value of the operand.
```
num = 5
print(-num) # Output: -5
```

Binary Operators

Binary operators operate on two operands. They are used for arithmetic, comparison, logical, and other operations.

Arithmetic Operator

Arithmetic operators are symbols used to perform mathematical operations on numerical values. Arithmetic operators include addition (+), subtraction (-), multiplication (*), division (/), and modulus (%).

Operator	Description	Example
+	Adds two operands.	5 + 3 = 8
-	Subtracts the second operand from the first.	5 - 3 = 2
*	Multiplies two operands.	5 * 3 = 15
/	Divides the numerator by the denominator.	10 / 2 = 5.0
//	Divides and returns the integer part only.	10 // 3 = 3

Operator	Description	Example
%	Returns the remainder of the division.	10 % 3 = 1
**	Raises the first operand to the power of the second.	2 ** 3 = 8

Relational Operators

Relational operators compare two operands to one another. The relational operators are = =, ! =, <, >, <= and >= . When used in an expression, they all return a boolean value which states the result of comparison.

Relational operators are sometimes called comparison operators and expressions that contain relational operators are called relational expressions. Following table shows all the relational operators supported by Python language values of A and B are 5 and 9, respectively.

Operator	Name	Description	Example
= =	Equal to	Checks if the values of two operands are equal or not, if yes then condition becomes True.	(A= = B) is not True
! =	Not equal to	Checks if the value of two operands are equal or not, if values are not equal then condition becomes True.	(A ! = B) is True
>	Greater than	Checks if the value of left operand is greater than the value of right operand, if yes then condition becomes True.	(A>B) is not True
<	Less than	Checks if the value of left operand is less than the value of right operand, if yes then condition becomes True.	(A<B) is True
>=	Greater than or equal to	Checks if the value of left operand is greater than or equal to the value of right operand, if yes then condition becomes True.	(A>= B) is not True
<=	Less than or equal to	Checks if the value of left operand is less than or equal to the value of right operand, if yes then condition becomes True.	(A<=B) is True

In relational operators, use of equal to operator (= =) should be avoided with floating point numbers and it also be avoided with signed and unsigned values.

Logical Operators

Logical operators, like AND, OR, and NOT, are used to make decisions based on multiple conditions. They work with true/false values (Boolean values) and produce a true/false result.

These operators are often used to control the flow of a program, determining which parts of the code should be executed. You'll commonly find them in conditional statements like "if" and "while" to make choices based on different conditions.

Following table shows all the logical operators supported by the Python language. Assume variables A holds 5, B holds 7 and C holds 9, then

Operators	Name	Description	Example
and	Logical AND	It returns True, if both the conditions are True, otherwise returns False.	((A<B) and (C<B)) returns False
or	Logical OR	It returns True, if atleast one of the two conditions is True.	((A<B) or (C<B)) returns True
not	Logical NOT	It works on single operand. It is used to reverse the logical state of its operand. If a condition is True then logical NOT operator will make it False.	not ((A<B) or (C<B)) returns True

Bitwise Operators

Bitwise operators work on bits and perform bit-by-bit operation. These operators manipulate the values of data at bit level. These operators are generally used for testing and shifting of bits.

For example, if a = 44 and b = 12.

Now in binary format they will be as follows

a = 00101100

b = 00001100

A table is given to understand bitwise operators more precisely:

Operator	Description	Example
&	Binary AND operator copies 1 to the result if it exists in both operand otherwise copies 0.	(a & b) will give 12 which is 00001100
|	Binary OR operator copies 1 if it exists in either operand, otherwise copies 0.	(a|b) will give 44 which 00101100
^	Binary XOR operator copies 1 if it in one operand. If it is either in both operand or not in any operand the operator copies 0.	(a^b) will give 32 which 00100000
~	Binary one's complement operator is unary and has the effect of flipping bits.	(~a will give 211 which is 11010011)

Operator	Description	Example
<<	Binary left shift operator. The left operand value is moved left by the number of bits specifted by the right operand.	a<<2 will give 176 which is 10110000
>>	Binary right shift operator. The left operands value is moved right by the number of bits specified by the right operand.	a>>2 will give 11 which is 00001011

Assignment Operators

These operators are also known as shorthand operators.

These operators are used to assign the value of an expression to a variable.

The following lists are assignment operators:

Operator	Description	Example
+=	Add AND assignment operator, it adds right operand to the left operand and assigns the result to left operand.	c += a is equivalent to c = c + a
−=	Subtract AND assignment operator, it subtracts right operand from left operand and assigns the result to left operand.	c −= a is equivalent to c = c − a
*=	Multiply AND assignment operator, it multiplies right operand with left operand and assigns the result to the left operand.	c *= a is equivalent to c = c * a
/=	Divide AND assignment operator, it divides left operand with the right operand and assigns the result to left operand.	c /=a is equivalent to c = c /a
%=	Modulus AND assignment operator, it divides left operand with right operand and assigns the remainder to the left operand.	c %= a is equivalent to c = c % a
**=	Exponentiation AND assignment operator, it gives left operand raised to the power of right operand and assigns the value to the left operand.	c **= a is equivalent to c = c ** a
//=	Floor division AND assignment operator, it floor divides left operand with the right operand and assigns the result to the left operand.	c //= a is equivalent to c = c//a

Note *'=' and '==' are different things. '=' is used for assignment while '==' is used for relational operators.*

For example, x = 10 will assign 10 to variable x while if x = = 10 is given, it will test whether the value of x is equal to 10 or not? If it is True, then True else False will be returned.

Membership Operators

Membership operators are used to check if a value is a member of the given sequence or not. Python has two membership operators:

1. **in Returns** True if a sequence with the specified value is present in the object.
2. **not in Returns** True if a sequence with the specified value is not present in the object.

Identity Operators

Identity operators are used to check if two variables point to the same object in memory. They help us determine if two variables are essentially the same or if they represent different objects. Python has two identity operators:

1. **is** Checks if two variables refer to the same object.
2. **is not** Checks if two variables refer to different objects.

Operator Precedence in Python

Imagine you have a math problem with multiple operations, like addition, subtraction, multiplication, and division.

To solve it correctly, you follow a specific order: multiplication and division come before addition and subtraction. This order is called precedence.

In Python, operators also have a specific order of precedence. This order determines which operation is performed first when there are multiple operators in an expression.

A table of operators is given below according to their precedence from highest to lowest:

Precedence	Operator	Description
1.	( )	Parentheses
	**	Exponentiation
2.	+,−	Unary plus, unary minus
	not	Logical NOT
	~	Bitwise NOT
3.	*	Multiplication
	/	Division
	//	Floor division
	%	Modulus

Precedence	Operator	Description
4.	+	Addition
	−	Subtraction
5.	<<	Bitwise left shift
	>>	Bitwise right shift
6.	<,<=	Less than, less than or equal to
	>,>=	Greater than, greater than or equal to
7.	!=	Not equal to
	==	equal to
8.	&	Bitwise AND
9.	^	Bitwise XOR
10.	|	Bitwise OR
11.	and	Boolean AND
12.	or	Boolean OR
13.	=,+ =,− =,* =,/ =,% =	Assignment

- Logical OR operator and Logical AND operator have a low precedence than relational operators.
  e.g. (10 > 5) or (5 < 4)
  Here, relational operations will be performed first and then logical operations will be executed.
- Logical NOT operator has a higher precedence than relational and arithmetic operators.

Associativity of Python Operators

We can see in the above table that more than one operator exists in the same group. These operators have the same precedence. When two operators have the same precedence, associativity helps to determine the order of operations. Associativity is the order in which an expression is evaluated that has multiple operators of the same precedence. Almost all the operators have left-to-right associativity.

For example, multiplication and floor division have the same precedence. Hence, if both of them are present in an expression, the left one is evaluated first.

e.g.
```
>>> print (10 * 3 // 6)
```
Output 5
```
>>> print (10 * (3//6))
```
Output 0

8.3 Type Conversion

Sometimes we need to change the type of data in Python. For example, we might want to convert a string into a number for calculation purpose.

The below mentioned example will make you more understand:

```
string = input ("Enter a number: ")
number = int(string)
result = number * 3
print ("The result is:", result)
```

Output

Enter a number: 5
The result is: 15

Now, if the user enters "5" as text, the program will treat it as the number 5 and calculate the result, all because of type conversion. There are two ways to do this:

(i) Explicit Conversion

Explicit conversion, or type casting, is when we directly tell Python to change the data type of a value. We use special functions like int(), float(), and str() to do this. However, be careful when converting between data types, as you might lose information.

For example, converting a decimal number like 20.67 to an integer using int(20.67) will result in 20, as the decimal part is discarded.

(ii) Implicit Conversion

Implicit conversion, or coercion, is when Python automatically changes the data type of a value without explicit instruction from the programmer. This happens when Python can safely convert one data type to another, such as converting an integer to a float for calculations.

8.4 Expressions

An expression in Python is a combination of values, variables, and operators that, when evaluated, produces a result. It's like a mathematical equation where you combine numbers, letters, and symbols to get an answer.

For example, 2 + 3, x * y, and "Hello, " + "world!" are all expressions. The operators in an expression tell Python how to combine the values and variables to produce the final result.

Function	Description
int (x)	Converts x to an integer
float (x)	Converts x to a floating-point number
str (x)	Converts x to a string representation
chr (x)	Converts ASCII value of x to character
ord (x)	Returns the character associated with the ASCII code x

There are various types of expressions as follows.

Arithmetic Expression

These expressions are composed with operators, constants, variables etc. It can be either a pure integer expression, a floating point expression or complex numbers.

e.g.
```
a * b - 5 (integer expression)
x + y/10 (floating expression)
1 + 2i (complex number expression)
```

Logical Expression

Those expressions having logical operators in them are called logical expressions.

e.g. `x and b, a or not b, c or b`

Relational Expression

This type of expression includes relational operators.

e.g. `a == b, a <= b, a != b`

String Expression

This type of expression includes string operators with string operands and integers.

e.g. `>>> "Me" + "Cool"`

Output 'MeCool'

`>>> "Computer" * 2`

Output 'ComputerComputer'

TEACHER TIP

Use parentheses to explicitly control the order of operations.

Expression Evaluation

Evaluation means simplifying an expression down to a single numerical value. When a mixed expression evaluates, it is divided into sub-expressions. Expression evaluation is done from left-to-right and based on operator precedence.

e.g.
```
a = b = 10, c = 5
a = b * 3//4 + c//4 + 4-b + 5//6
  = 10*3//4 + 5//4 + 4-10 + 5//6
  = 7 + 5//4 + 4 - 10 + 5//6
  = 7 + 1 + 4 - 10 + 0
  = 12 - 10 + 0
  = 2 + 0
  = 2
```

Some Rules for Expressions

I. Arithmetic expressions may contain just one signed or unsigned variable/constant or it can have two or more variables or/and constants or two/more expressions joined by valid arithmetic operators. Two/more variables or operators should not occur in a continuous manner.

II. Logical expressions may contain just one signed or unsigned variable/constant or it can have two or more variables or/and constants or two/more expressions joined by valid relational and/or logical operators. Two/more variables or operators should not occur in a continuous manner.

Quick Test 2

1. What are the basic arithmetic operators in Python?
2. What is the difference between // and / operators?
3. What are relational operators in Python?
4. What is operator precedence in Python?
5. What is the purpose of the in and not in operators?

Mind Map

DATA TYPES AND OPERATORS

Data Types

Data types in programming defines how data is processed and stored by computer.

Numbers
It contains only numeric values in Python

Integers
These are whole numbers.e.g.,1, 2 , 3, -1, -2,.. and so on.

Floating Point Numbers
Float values are specified with decimal point.

Complex Number
A complex number is expressed in form of (a+ib).

Sequence
Python sequence are ordered list of items including String, List and Tuples.

String
String are collections of characters like letters , numbers or symbols.

List
A list is a mutable variable defined with [].

Tuples
It is an ordered , immutable sequence of items ,defined with ().

Set
A set is an unordered collection of unique items.

None
None in Python represents the absence of a value.

Mapping
It is a collection of items where each item is associated with a unique key.

Dictionary
In dictionary, you can store information in **key-value pairs.** Each key is unique and its used to access the corresponding value.

Note

The values of mutable types can be changed after it is created. These are list , dictionary and sets. The values of immutable types cannot be changed after it is created. These are integer, float, boolean, string and tuple.

Type Conversion

It is the process of converting a data type into another data type .

Implicit Conversion
Python ,automatically converts one data type to another .

Explicit Conversion
User convert the data type of an object to require data type .

Expression

Expressions are the combination of operators , constants ,variable ,etc.

01 Arithmetic Expression
02 Relational Expression
03 Logical Expression
04 String Expression
- Concatenation Operator (+)
- Replication Operator (*)

Operators

Operators are the symbols that perform operations on values. It is used in programs to operate on data and variables.

Unary Operators +,–,~, not

Binary Operators
- Arithmetic operator +, –, *, /, %, **, //
- Logical operators AND, OR
- Relational operators <, >, <=, >=, ==, !=
- Assignment operators =, /=, +=, *=, %=, –=, **=, //=
- Bitwise operators &, ^, |
- Shift operators <<, >>
- Identity operators is, is not
- Membership operators in, not in

Precedence of Python Operators
This is used in an expression with more than one operator with different precedence to determine which operation to perform first.

NCERT Folder

1. Which of the following identifier names are invalid and why?

(i) Serial_no.	(v) Total_Marks
(ii) 1st_Room	(vi) total-Marks
(iii) Hundred$	(vii) _Percentage
(iv) Total Marks	(viii) True

Ans. **Invalid Identifiers**

(i) **Serial_no** As we cannot use ‘ . ’ in variable names.

(ii) **1st_Room** Starts with a digit (1), which is not allowed. Identifiers must start with a letter or an underscore (_).

(iii) **Hundred$** Contains the special character '$', which is not allowed. Identifiers can only contain letters, digits, and underscores.

(iv) **Total Marks** As there are two separate words in the variable name.

(vi) **total-Marks** Contains the hyphen '-', which is not allowed. Identifiers can only contain letters, digits, and underscores.

(viii) **True** As it is a keyword.

2. Write the corresponding Python assignment statements:

(a) Assign 10 to variable length and 20 to variable breadth.

(b) Assign the average of values of variables length and breadth to a variable sum.

(c) Assign a list containing strings ‘Paper’, ‘Gel Pen’, and ‘Eraser’ to a variable stationery.

(d) Assign the strings ‘Mohandas’, ‘Karamchand’, and ‘Gandhi’ to variables first, middle and last.

(e) Assign the concatenated value of string variables first, middle and last to variable fullname. Make sure to incorporate blank spaces appropriately between different parts of names.

Ans. (a) Assigning values to length and breadth

```
length = 10
breadth = 20
```

(b) Calculating and assigning the average to sum

```
sum = (length + breadth) / 2
```

(c) Assigning a list to stationery

```
stationery = ['Paper', 'Gel Pen', 'Eraser']
```

(d) Assigning strings to variables

```
first = 'Mohandas'
middle = 'Karamchand'
last = 'Gandhi'
```

(e) Concatenating strings and assigning to fullname

```
fullname = first + ' ' + middle + ' ' + last
```

3. Write logical expressions corresponding to the following statements in Python and evaluate the expressions (assuming variables num1, num2, num3, first, middle, last are already having meaningful values):

(a) The sum of 20 and –10 is less than 12.

(b) num3 is not more than 24.

(c) 6.75 is between the values of integers num1 and num2.

(d) The string ‘middle’ is larger than the string ‘first’ and smaller than the string ‘last’.

(e) List Stationery is empty.

Ans. (a)
```
result_a = (20 + (-10)) < 12
print(result_a)
 #Output: False
```

(b)
```
result_b = not (num3 > 24)
print(result_b)
 #Output: True if num3 <= 24,
                otherwise False
```

(c)
```
result_c = (num1 < 6.75 < num2)
print(result_c)
 # Output: True if 6.75 lies between
          num1 and num2, otherwise False
```

(d)
```
result_d = (first < middle < last)
print(result_d)
 #Output: True if the string comparison
               holds, otherwise False
```

(e)
```
result_e = len(stationery) == 0
print(result_e)
 # Output: True if the list is empty,
                otherwise False
```

4. Add a pair of parentheses to each expression so that it evaluates to True.

(a) 0 == 1 == 2 (b) 2 + 3 == 4 + 5 == 7

(c) 1 < -1 == 3 > 4

Ans. (a) (0 == (1==2)) (b) (2 + (3 == 4) + 5) == 7

(c) (1 < -1) == (3 > 4)

5. Write the output of the following:

(a)
```
num1 = 4
num2 = num1 + 1
num1 = 2
print (num1, num2)
```

(b)
```
num1, num2 = 2, 6
num1, num2 = num2, num1 + 2
print (num1, num2)
```

(c)
```
num1, num2 = 2, 3
```

```
num3, num2 = num1, num3 + 1
print (num1, num2, num3)
```

Ans. (a) Output: 2 5

(b) Output: 6 4

(c) Output: 2 4 2

6. Which data type will be used to represent the following data values and why?

(a) Number of months in a year

(b) Resident of Delhi or not

(c) Mobile number

(d) Pocket money

(e) Volume of a sphere

(f) Perimeter of a square

(g) Name of the student

(h) Address of the student

Ans. (a) **Integer** The number of months in a year is a fixed integer value (12).

(b) **Boolean** This represents a true/false value (resident of Delhi or not).

(c) **String** Mobile numbers are sequences of digits, typically represented as strings.

(d) **Float** Pocket money can be a decimal value (e.g., 10.50).

(e) **Float** Volume of a sphere can be a decimal value.

(f) **Integer or Float** The perimeter can be a whole number or a decimal value, depending on the units used.

(g) **String** Names are sequences of characters.

(h) **String** Addresses are typically represented as text.

7. Give the output of the following when num1 = 4, num2 = 3, num3 = 2

(a)
```
num1 += num2 + num3
print (num1)
```

(b)
```
num1 = num1 ** (num2 + num3)
print (num1)
```

(c)
```
num1 **= num2 + num3
```

(d)
```
num1 = '5' + '5'
print(num1)
```

(e)
```
print(4.00/(2.0+2.0))
```

(f)
```
num1 = 2+9*((3*12)-8)/10
print(num1)
```

(g)
```
num1 = 24 // 4 // 2
print(num1)
```

(h)
```
num1 = float(10)
print (num1)
```

(i)
```
num1 = int('3.14')
print (num1)
```

(j)
```
print('Bye' == 'BYE')
```

(k)
```
print(10 != 9 and 20 >= 20)
```

(l)
```
print(10 + 6 * 2 ** 2 != 9//4 -3 and 29 >=
29/9)
```

(m)
```
print(5 % 10 + 10 < 50 and 29 <= 29)
```

(n)
```
print((0 < 6) or (not(10 == 6) and
(10<0)))
```

Ans. (a) 9 (b) 1024

(c) 1024 (d) 55

(e) 1.0 (f) 27.2

(g) 3 (h) 10.0

(i) Runtime error (j) False

(k) True (l) True

(m) True (n) True

8. A dartboard of radius 10 units and the wall it is hanging on are represented using a two-dimensional coordinate system, with the board's center at coordinate (0,0). Variables x and y store the x-coordinate and the y-coordinate of a dart that hits the dartboard. Write a Python expression using variables x and y that evaluates to True if the dart hits (is within) the dartboard, and then evaluate the expression for these dart coordinates:

(a) (0,0) **(b) (10,10)**

(c) (6, 6) **(d) (7,8)**

Ans.
```
import math
def is_hit(x, y):
    distance = math.sqrt(x**2 + y**2)
    return distance <= 10          # Test cases
print(is_hit(0, 0))    # Output: True
print(is_hit(10, 10)) # Output: False
print(is_hit(6, 6))   # Output: True
print(is_hit(7, 8))   # Output: False
```

9. Write a Python program to convert temperature in degree Celsius to degree Fahrenheit. If water boils at 100 degree C and freezes as 0 degree C, use the program to find out what is the boiling point and freezing point of water on the Fahrenheit scale. (Hint: T(°F) = T(°C) × 9/5 + 32)

Ans.
```
# Temperature in Celsius
celsius = float(input("Enter temperature
                          in Celsius: "))
# Convert Celsius to Fahrenheit
fahrenheit = (celsius * 9/5) + 32
print(f"{celsius}°C is equal to
                          {fahrenheit}°F.")
# Boiling and freezing points in Celsius
freezing_point_celsius = 0
boiling_point_celsius = 100
# Convert boiling and freezing points to
```

```
                                    Fahrenheit
freezing_point_fahrenheit =
        (freezing_point_celsius * 9/5) + 32
boiling_point_fahrenheit =
         (boiling_point_celsius * 9/5) + 32
print(f"The freezing point of water is
          {freezing_point_fahrenheit}°F.")
print(f"The boiling point of water is
           {boiling_point_fahrenheit}°F.")
```

10. Write a Python program to calculate the amount payable if money has been lent on simple interest. Principal or money lent = P, Rate of interest = R% per annum and Time = T years. Then Simple Interest (SI) = (P × R × T)/ 100.

Amount payable = Principal + SI.

P, R and T are given as input to the program.

Ans.

```
# Input the principal amount, rate of
                 interest, and time period
P = float(input("Enter the principal
                           amount (P): "))
R = float(input("Enter the rate of
                      interest (R) in %: "))
T = float(input("Enter the time period
                         (T) in years: "))
# Calculate simple interest (SI)
SI = (P * R * T) / 100
# Calculate total amount payable
Amount = P + SI
print(f"Simple Interest (SI) = {SI}")
print(f"The total amount payable =
                                {Amount}")
```

11. Write a program to calculate in how many days a work will be completed by three persons A, B and C together. A, B, C take x days, y days and z days respectively to do the job alone. The formula to calculate the number of days if they work together is xyz/(xy + yz + xz) days where x, y, and z are given as input to the program.

Ans.

```
# Input the number of days each person
           takes to complete the work alone
x = float(input("Enter the number of days
    A takes to complete the work alone: "))
y = float(input("Enter the number of days
    B takes to complete the work alone: "))
z = float(input("Enter the number of days
    C takes to complete the work alone: "))
# Calculate the number of days they will
         take to complete the work together
days_together = (x * y * z) / (x * y + y *
                                 z + x * z)
print(f"The work will be completed in
   {days_together} days if A, B, and C work
                                 together.")
```

12. Write a program to enter two integers and perform all arithmetic operations on them.

Ans.

```
num1 = int(input("Enter the first integer: "))
num2 = int(input("Enter the second integer: "))
addition = num1 + num2
subtraction = num1 - num2
multiplication = num1 * num2
division = num1 / num2
if num2 != 0:
   modulus = num1 % num2
else:
   modulus = "undefined (modulo by zero)"
if num2 != 0:
   division = num1 / num2
else:
   division = "undefined (division by zero)"
exponentiation = num1 ** num2
print(f"The sum of {num1} and {num2} is:
                               {addition}")
print(f"The difference of {num1} and {num2}
                        is: {subtraction}")
print(f"The product of {num1} and {num2}
                     is: {multiplication}")
print(f"The division of {num1} by {num2}
                           is: {division}")
print(f"The modulus of {num1} and {num2}
                            is: {modulus}")
print(f"{num1} raised to the power of
                {num2} is: {exponentiation}")
```

13. Write a program to swap two numbers using a third variable.

Ans.

```
# Input two numbers
num1 = float(input("Enter the first
                              number: "))
num2 = float(input("Enter the second
                              number: "))
# Swapping the numbers using a third
                                 variable
temp = num1
num1 = num2
num2 = temp
print(f"After swapping, the first number
                              is: {num1}")
print(f"After swapping, the second number
                              is: {num2}")
```

14. Write a program to swap two numbers without using a third variable.

Ans.
```
# Input two numbers
num1 = float(input("Enter the first
                           number: "))
num2 = float(input("Enter the second
                           number: "))
# Swapping the numbers without using a
                        third variable
num1 = num1 + num2
num2 = num1 - num2
num1 = num1 - num2
print(f"After swapping, the first
                    number is: {num1}")
print(f"After swapping, the second
                    number is: {num2}")
```

15. Write a program to repeat the string "GOOD MORNING" n times. Here 'n' is an integer entered by the user.

Ans.
```
n = int(input("Enter the number of times
                        to repeat: "))
for i in range(n):
print("GOOD MORNING")
```

16. Write a program to find the average of three numbers.

Ans.
```
# Input three numbers
num1 = float(input("Enter the first
                           number: "))
num2 = float(input("Enter the second
                           number: "))
num3 = float(input("Enter the third
                           number: "))
# Calculate the average
average = (num1 + num2 + num3) / 3
print(f"The average of the three
                numbers is: {average}")
```

17. The volume of a sphere with radius r is $4/3\pi r^3$. Write a Python program to find the volume of spheres with radius 7cm, 12cm, 16cm, respectively.

Ans.
```
import math
# Given radii
radius1 = 7
radius2 = 12
radius3 = 16
# Formula to calculate the volume of a
                 sphere: (4/3) * p * r³
volume1 = (4/3) * math.pi * (radius1 ** 3)
volume2 = (4/3) * math.pi * (radius2 ** 3)
volume3 = (4/3) * math.pi * (radius3 ** 3)
# Output the results
print(f"The volume of a sphere with radius
    {radius1} cm is: {volume1} cubic cm.")
print(f"The volume of a sphere with radius
    {radius2} cm is: {volume2} cubic cm.")
print(f"The volume of a sphere with radius
    {radius3} cm is: {volume3} cubic cm.")
```

18. Write a program that asks the user to enter their name and age. Print a message addressed to the user that tells the user the year in which they will turn 100 years old.

Ans.
```
# Input user's name and age
name = input("Enter your name: ")
age = int(input("Enter your age: "))
# Get the current year
current_year = 2025
# Calculate the year when the user will
                              turn 100
year_100 = current_year + (100 - age)
print(f"Hello, {name}! You will turn 100
        years old in the year {year_100}.")
```

19. The formula $E = mc^2$ states that the equivalent energy (E) can be calculated as the mass (m) multiplied by the speed of light (c = about 3×10^8 m/s) squared. Write a program that accepts the mass of an object and determines its energy.

Ans.
```
c = 3 * 10**8  # Speed of light in m/s
mass = float(input("Enter the mass of
                   the object in kg: "))
energy = mass * c**2
print("The equivalent energy is:",
                   energy, "joules")
```

20. Presume that a ladder is put upright against a wall. Let variables length and angle store the length of the ladder and the angle that it forms with the ground as it leans against the wall. Write a Python program to compute the height reached by the ladder on the wall for the following values of length and angle:

(a) 16 feet and 75 degrees

(b) 20 feet and 0 degrees

(c) 24 feet and 45 degrees

(d) 24 feet and 80 degrees

Ans.
```
import math
# Given values for length and angle
length1 = 16
angle1 = 75
length2 = 20
angle2 = 0
length3 = 24
angle3 = 45
length4 = 24
angle4 = 80
# Convert angles from degrees to radians
```

```
    and calculate the height for each case
height1 = length1 *
            math.sin(math.radians(angle1))
height2 = length2 *
            math.sin(math.radians(angle2))
height3 = length3 *
            math.sin(math.radians(angle3))
height4 = length4 *
            math.sin(math.radians(angle4))
print(f"The height reached by a {length1}
    -foot ladder at {angle1} degrees is:
                  {height1} feet.")
print(f"The height reached by a {length2}
    -foot ladder at {angle2} degrees is:
                  {height2} feet.")
print(f"The height reached by a {length3}
    -foot ladder at {angle3} degrees is:
                  {height3} feet.")
print(f"The height reached by a
  {length4}-foot ladder at {angle4} degrees
                  is: {height4} feet.")
```

EXAM PATTERN QUESTIONS

Objective Type Questions

Multiple Choice Questions

1. Which data type contains only numeric values in Python?
(a) Numbers (b) Strings (c) Lists (d) Tuples

2. In complex number, a + ib, where b represents as
(a) real part (b) imaginary part
(c) special part (d) None of these

3. A software company is developing a large-scale financial application where accuracy in calculations is crucial. The developers initially used the float data type for monetary values but noticed small precision errors. Which of the following data types is the most appropriate choice to handle financial transactions accurately in Python? **Competency Based Que.**
(a) float
(b) int
(c) decimal.Decimal
(d) complex

4. Which of the following are sequences of character data?
(a) Lists (b) Tuples
(c) Strings (d) Dictionaries

5. A data scientist is working with large datasets and wants to optimize memory usage. He needs a data type that is immutable and takes less memory compared to a list while still allowing indexing. Which of the following should he choose? **Competency Based Que.**
(a) list (b) tuple
(c) set (d) dict

6. Which operator is used to find the remainder of a division operation?
(a) / (b) // (c) % (d) *

7. How do you calculate the power of a number in Python, for example, 2 raised to the power of 3?
(a) 2^3 (b) pow (2, 3)
(c) 2**3 (d) 3^2

8. If x = 15 and y = 10, what will be the value of x after the operation x += y?
(a) 10 (b) 15 (c) 25 (d) 5

9. Consider the following Python expressions:

```
x = 5
y = 10
result = x < y == True
```

What will be the output of result and why? **Competency Based Que.**
(a) True, because < and == are evaluated from left to right.
(b) False, because comparison operators have different precedence levels.
(c) SyntaxError, because the comparison is invalid.
(d) True, because Python allows chaining of comparison operators.

10. Which data type can only store the values True or False?
(a) int (b) float (c) str (d) bool

11. Given the following Python expression:
a = True + 5 * False
What will be the value of a and why? **Competency Based Que.**

(a) True, because Boolean operations take precedence.
(b) 6, because True is treated as 1 and False as 0.
(c) 5, because multiplication is evaluated first.
(d) SyntaxError, because Booleans cannot be used in arithmetic operations.

12. These operators are used to make a decision on two conditions.
(a) Logical
(b) Arithmetic
(c) Relational
(d) Assignment

13. Which of the following is/are expressions?
(a) Arithmetic (b) Logical
(c) Relational (d) All of these

14. What will be the output of the following Python expression?

```
"hello" + " " + "world"
```

Use code with caution.
(a) hello world (b) "hello world"
(c) hello+world (d) Error

Fill in the Blanks

15. ______ data types can change their values in place.

16. Plain integers use ______ bytes to store a value.

17. ______ is an unordered set of key: value pairs where the keys are unique.

18. ______ are special symbols which perform some computations.

State Whether True or False

19. In Python, a string can only be defined using single quotes (') and cannot use double quotes (").

20. A complex number in Python is represented as a combination of two integers, where the first integer represents the real part and the second integer represents the imaginary part.

21. The unary minus operator changes the sign of a negative decimal value to positive.

22. The modulus operator can only be used with integer operands.

23. The logical OR operator returns True if both expressions are True, and False otherwise.

24. Relational operators have higher precedence than logical AND and logical OR operators.

25. The augmented assignment operator %= is equivalent to c = c % a, where c is the left operand and a is the right operand.

26. The **= operator (Exponentiation AND assignment) can only be used with integer operands.

Assertion and Reason Based Questions

Assertion (A) and Reason (R) based questions. Mark the correct choice as
(a) Both (A) and (R) are true and (R) is the correct explanation for (A).
(b) Both (A) and (R) are true but (R) is not the correct explanation for (A).
(c) Assertion (A) is true, but Reason (R) is false.
(d) Reason (R) is true, but Assertion (A) is false.

27. Assertion (A) Python is a strongly-typed language.
Reason (R) Variables in Python must be declared with a specific data type.

28. Assertion (A) Lists are mutable data structures.
Reason (R) Elements in a list can be changed, added, or removed after creation.

29. Assertion (A) Tuples are immutable data structures.
Reason (R) Once a tuple is created, its elements cannot be changed.

30. Assertion (A) The + operator can be used to concatenate strings.
Reason (R) String concatenation is the process of joining two or more strings together.

31. Assertion (A) Dictionaries are unordered collections of key-value pairs.
Reason (R) The order of elements in a dictionary is preserved.

32. Assertion (A) The % operator is used to calculate the remainder of a division operation.
Reason (R) It's known as the modulo operator.

33. Assertion (A) Operator precedence determines the order in which operations are performed in an expression.
Reason (R) Parentheses can be used to override the default precedence.

34. Assertion (A) Sets are unordered collections of unique elements.
Reason (R) Sets do not allow duplicate elements.

Answers

1. (a) Numbers
2. (b) imaginary part
3. (c) decimal.Decimal
4. (c) Strings
5. (b) tuple
6. (c) %
7. (c) 2**3
8. (c) 25
9, (d) True, because Python allows chaining of comparison operators.
10. (d) bool
11. (b) 6, because True is treated as 1 and False as 0.
12. (a) Logical
13. (d) All of these
14. (b) "hello world"
15. Mutable
16. 4
17. Dictionary
18. Operators
19. False
20. True
21. True
22. True
23. False
24. True
25. True
26. True
27. (c) Assertion (A) is true, but Reason (R) is false.
28. (a) Both Assertion (A) and Reason (R) are true, and Reason (R) is the correct explanation of Assertion (A).
29. (a) Both Assertion (A) and Reason (R) are true, and Reason (R) is the correct explanation of Assertion (A).
30. (a) Both Assertion (A) and Reason (R) are true, and Reason (R) is the correct explanation of Assertion (A).
31. (c) Assertion (A) is true, but Reason (R) is false.
32. (a) Both Assertion (A) and Reason (R) are true, and Reason (R) is the correct explanation of Assertion (A).
33. (a) Both Assertion (A) and Reason (R) are true, and Reason (R) is the correct explanation of Assertion (A).
34. (a) Both Assertion (A) and Reason (R) are true, and Reason (R) is the correct explanation of Assertion (A).

Subjective Type Questions

Very Short Answer Type Questions

1. What is the data type?

Or **What are some examples of mutable data types in Python?**

Ans. Data type is a term that is used to show the kind of data values or the type of data that is expected to be handled.

Or

Python offers only two data types that are mutable:

(1) Lists (e.g., [1, "hello", True])

(2) Dictionaries (e.g., {"name": "Alice", "age": 30})

2. Define the term operator.

Ans. Operators are symbols which take one or more operands to perform arithmetic or logical computations.

3. Explain unary operator.

Ans. A unary operator is an operator that performs its operation on only one operand.

4. Differentiate between / and % operators.

Ans. / operator is used to find the quotient while % operator is used to find the remainder.

5. The proper Python syntax for testing that value of A is between 2 and 9 inclusively is

(i) 2 < =A < = 9

(ii) 2> =A and A < = 9

(iii) A > = 2 and A < = 9

(iv) 2 < =A and A > = 9

Ans. (iii) A > = 2 and A < = 9

6. What is the use of a relational operator?

Ans. The relational operators are used for comparison between two or more operands.

7. Differentiate between = and = = operators.

Ans. = is an assignment operator whereas = = is a relational operator.

8. Write the augmented assignment operators used in Python.

Ans. + =,- =,* =,/ =,% =,// =,** =

9. What will be the output of the following code?

```
X= 2
Y= 6
X= X+Y/2 + Y//4
print(X)
```

Ans. 6.0

10. Name three logical operators.

Ans. (i) AND operator (and)

(ii) OR operator (or)

(iii) NOT operator (not)

11. What will be the result of the following expression?

```
-a <= 5
```

(i) if a = 5

(ii) if a = - 5

Ans. (i) True (ii) True

12. Write the value stored in the variable Num by each of the following statements.

(i) Num = 2 * 3 – 4

(ii) Num = 2+3-1*3

(iii) Num = (2+3)*2

Ans. (i) Num = 2

(ii) Num = 2

(iii) Num = 10

13. Convert the equation into corresponding Python statement $y = a^3 + b^2 + c + 2bc$

Ans. y = (a * *3 + b * *2 + c + 2 * b * c)

14. What are the two common string representations in Python?

Ans. Python supports two main string types: str(for text) and bytes(for binary data)

15. A bank maintains customer balances using Python. Consider the following code snippet:

Competency Based Que.

```
balance = 5000
withdrawal = "2000"
new_balance = balance - int(withdrawal)
print(type(new_balance))
```

What will be the output of type(new_balance)?

Ans. <class 'int'>

16. A scientist is performing calculations using Python and writes the following code:

```
x = 3 + 4.0 * 2 / 2 + 5 // 2
print(x)
```

What will be the output of x? **Competency Based Que.**

Ans. 9.0

17. An e-commerce platform records the number of items in a cart as a string:

```
items = "7"
price_per_item = 199.50
total_cost = float(items) * price_per_item
print(type(total_cost))
```

What will be the output of type(total_cost)?

Competency Based Que.

Ans. <class 'float'>

Short Answer Type I Questions

18. Imagine you are developing a banking application where account numbers, once assigned, should never be altered. Similarly, customer names should remain unchanged unless explicitly updated through a secure process.

Based on this scenario, explain why Python's immutable data types, such as strings and numbers, are useful in ensuring data integrity and security in applications. **Competency Based Que.**

Ans. Immutable data types in Python, like strings and numbers, prevent unintended changes, ensuring data integrity in applications like banking. Since modifying an immutable object creates a new one instead of altering the original, critical data (e.g., account numbers) remains secure and consistent, reducing risks in financial transactions.

19. Determine the Output.

```
x = -4
y = -x
print ("value of x =", x)
print ("value of y =", y)
x = 2
y = 3
z = x ** y + 3
x = y + 5
print("value of z =", z)
print ("value of x =", x)
```

Ans. value of x = -4

value of y = 4

value of z = 11

value of x = 8

20. How does the logical OR operator work when the operands are not relational expressions?

Ans. When using the logical OR operator (or) with non-relational operands in Python, it follows a specific evaluation process:

(a) **Evaluate the first operand** Python first evaluates the truth value of the first operand.

(b) **If the first operand is True** If the first operand is True, the entire expression is considered True, and the second operand is not evaluated.

(c) **If the first operand is False** If the first operand is False, Python evaluates the second operand. If the second operand is True, the entire expression is True. Otherwise, if the second operand is also False, the entire expression is False.

21. What is the difference between unary and binary operators?

Ans. **Unary** This operator works on a single operand. It negates the value of the operand. For example, -5 negates the number 5.

Binary This operator works on two operands. It subtracts the second operand from the first. For example, 10 - 5 subtracts 5 from 10.

22. Predict the output of the following code fragment.

```
b = 20
a = 90/b
print ("value of a is :", a)
```

Ans. value of a is : 4.5

23. Using the given values of x, y and z, evaluate the following.

```
(x >= y) and (not(z ==y)) or (z < x)
```

(i) x =5, y = 6, z = 20

(ii) x = 10, y = 4, z = 11

Ans. (i) False (ii) True

24. Predict the output of the following program.

```
a = 5
b = a = 15
c = (a < 15)
print ("a =", a)
print ("b =", b)
print ("c =", c)
```

Ans.
```
a = 15
b = 15
c = False
```

25. Write the corresponding Python expression for the following mathematical expression.

(i) $z = a / a + b - d^2$

(ii) $z = x^2 + y^3$

Ans. (i) z = a / (a + b) - (d * d)

(ii) z = (x * *2) + (y * *3)

26. Determine the hierarchy of operations and evaluate the following expression.

```
A = 3*4//5 + 5//7 + 8 - 2 + 4//2
```

Ans. The * operator will be performed before //. Though both have same priority but in this expression * is prior to //.

```
A = 12 //5 + 5//7 +8 - 2 + 4//2
  = 2 + 5//7 + 8 - 2 + 4//2
  = 2 + 0 + 8 - 2 + 4//2
  = 2 + 0 + 8 - 2 + 2
  = 2 + 0 + 6 + 2
  = 10
```

27. What will be the value of following if a = 2?

(i) (12 / + a)%3 **(ii) (21* + a)%9**

(iii) (21//+a)%3

Ans. (i) 0.0 (ii) 6 (iii) 1

28. Determine the hierarchy of operations and evaluate the following expression.

```
a = 2 *3//4 + 4//4 + 8 - 2 + 5//8
```

Ans.
```
a = 2*3//4 + 4//4 + 8 - 2 + 5//8
  = 6//4 + 4 //4 + 8 - 2 + 5//8    operation : *
  = 1 + 4//4 + 8 - 2 + 5//8        operation : //
  = 1 + 1 + 8 - 2 + 5//8           operation : //
  = 1 + 1 + 8 - 2 + 0              operation : //
  = 2 + 8 - 2 + 0                  operation : +
  = 10 - 2 + 0                     operation : + , -
  = 8 + 0 = 8                      operation : +
```

29. What value will be stored in different variables when the following Python statements are executed?

```
i = 10
j = i + 5
k = i + j/5
l = k + 1 + 4
m = l + 1 - i
n = k + m*l
print ("i: ", i)
print ("j: ", j)
print ("k: ", k)
print ("l: ", l)
print ("m: ", m)
print ("n: ", n)
```

Ans. i: 10

j: 15

k: 13.0

l: 18

m: 9

n: 175

Short Answer Type II Questions

30. How are strings stored and manipulated in Python?

Ans. A string in Python is an immutable sequence of characters enclosed in single (') or double (") quotes.

Example: text = "Hello, World!" assigns a string to the variable text.

Common operations include concatenation (+), repetition (*), and slicing ([:]).

Example: "Hello" + " World" results in "Hello World", and "Python"[0:3] gives "Pyt".

Since strings are immutable, modifying a string creates a new one instead of changing the original.

31. What is the difference between a list and a tuple in Python?

Ans.

List	Tuple
A list is a collection that is mutable, meaning its elements can be changed.	A tuple, on the other hand, is immutable, meaning once defined, it cannot be altered.
Lists are created using square brackets [], e.g., my_list = [1, 2, 3].	Tuples are created using parentheses (), e.g., my_tuple = (1, 2, 3).
Tuples are immutable, they are faster and preferred when data should not be changed.	Lists are commonly used for dynamic data, while tuples are for fixed collections.

32. What is the difference between set and dictionary in Python?

Ans. A set is an unordered collection of unique elements, whereas a dictionary stores key-value pairs.
Sets do not allow duplicate values and are created using curly braces {}: {1, 2, 3}.
Dictionaries store data in the form of key-value pairs, e.g., {'name': 'Alice', 'age': 25}.
In a dictionary, keys must be unique, but values can be duplicated.
Sets support operations like union, intersection, and difference for mathematical computations.
Dictionaries are widely used for mapping relationships, such as storing user details.

33. Determine which of the arithmetic expressions are valid. If invalid, explain the reason. [(a, b, c) are integers, (p, q, r) are float and (x, y, z) are float].

(i) p/q + a – c	(ii) q (a + b – z/4)
(iii) p/q + a – c	(iv) x/y + p * a/b
(v) a * + b	(vi) a//+b*c*2

Ans. (i) p/q + a – c valid
(ii) q (a + b – z/4) invalid because operator missing between q and a
(iii) p/q + a – c valid
(iv) x/y + p * a/b valid
(v) a * + b invalid because use of two operators together
(vi) a//+b*c*2 invalid

34. Write a program to calculate the GST.

Ans.
```
prod = int(input("Enter the original
                    amount of product:"))
gst = int(input("Enter the percentage of
                  GST on that product:"))
GST_Amount = (prod*gst)/100
Net_price = prod + GST_Amount
print ("Net Price:", Net_price)
```

35. The distance between two cities (in km) is input through the keyboard, write a Python program to convert this distance in meters.

Ans.
```
km = float (input ("Enter the distance
                     in km:"))
print ("Distance in km:", km)
meters = km * 1000
print ("Distance in meters :", meters)
```

Output

Enter the distance in km : 2.5
Distance in km : 2.5
Distance in meters : 2500.0

36. Write a Python program to find the perimeter of a rectangle.

Ans.
```
l = int (input ("Enter the length:"))
b = int (input ("Enter the breath:"))
print ("Length:", l)
print ("Breath:", b)
p = 2 * (l+b)
print ("Perimeter of the rectangle:", p)
```

Output

Enter the length : 6
Enter the breath: 4
Length : 6
Breath : 4
Perimeter of the rectangle : 20

Long Answer Type Questions

37. Write a Python program which input the time in seconds and convert it into days. Also, display its output.

Ans.
```
time = float (input("Enter the time in
                      seconds:"))
day = time // (24*3600)
time = time % (24* 3600)
hour = time // 3600
time %= 60
seconds = time
print ("Days:", day)
print ("Hours:", hour)
print ("Minutes:", minutes)
print ("Seconds:", seconds)
```

Output

Input time in seconds: 360425060
Days: 4171.0
Hours: 14.0
Minutes: 4.0
Seconds: 20.0

38. Write a program which input three sides of triangle and calculate its perimeter, semi perimeter and area.

Ans.
```
a = float (input("Enter the First side of
                  a Triangle:"))
b = float (input("Enter the Second side of
                  a Triangle:"))
c = float(input("Enter the Third side of
                 a Triangle:"))
  #calculate the Perimeter
Perimeter = a + b + c
  #calculate the semi-perimeter
s = (a+b+c)/2
  #calculate the area
Area = (s*(s-a)*(s-b)*(s-c)) ** 0.5
print ("\n The perimeter of Triangle =
        %.2f" %perimeter)
```

```
print ("The Semi Perimeter of Triangle
                              = %.2f" %s)
print ("The Area of a Triangle is %0.2f" %Area)
```

Output

Enter the First side of a Triangle: 13
Enter the Second side of a Triangle: 12
Enter the Third side of a Triangle: 5
The perimeter of Triangle = 30.00
The Semi Perimeter of Triangle = 15.00
The Area of a Triangle is 30.00

39. Evaluate the following expressions.

(a) A = 10*4//2 + 4 - 2//2 + 4 - 3 + 5//8
(b) A = 5 + 6//3 + 10*3//4 + 2 + 3//4
(c) A = 5*5 + 4 //5 + 15 - 9//2 + 10

Ans. (a) A =10*4//2 + 4 - 2//2 + 4 - 3 + 5//8
= 40//2 + 4 - 2//2 + 4 - 3 + 5//8
= 20 + 4 - 2//2 + 4 - 3 + 5//8
= 20 + 4 - 1 + 4 - 3 + 5//8
= 20 + 4 - 1 + 4 - 3 + 0
= 24 - 1 + 4 - 3 + 0
= 23 + 4 - 3
= 27 - 3
= 24

(b) A = 5 + 6//3 + 10*3//4 + 2 + 3//4
= 5 + 2 + 10*3//4 + 2 + 3//4
= 5 + 2 + 30//4 + 2 + 3//4
= 5 + 2 + 7 + 2 + 0
= 7 + 7 + 2
= 16

(c) A = 5*5 + 4//5 + 15 - 9//2 + 10
= 25 + 4//5 + 15 - 9//2 + 10
= 25 + 0 + 15 - 4 + 10
= 40 - 4 + 10
= 36 + 10
= 46

40. A software company stores employee details in a dictionary format, where each key represents an employee ID, and the values are stored as a list containing their name, age, and salary.

```
employees = {
    101: ["Ali", "28", "55000.50"],
    102: ["Bunny", "30", "62000.75"],
    103: ["Charu", "26", "48000.25"]
}
```

I. Identify the data types of age and salary values for each employee.

II. Convert the age to an integer type and the salary to a float type for all employees.

III. Calculate and display the average salary of all employees after conversion. **Competency Based Que.**

Ans. **Step I** Identifying Data Types Before Conversion

- The age values are stored as strings ("28", "30", "26").
- The salary values are also stored as strings ("55000.50", "62000.75", "48000.25").

Step II Converting age to int and salary to float:

```
for emp_id in employees:
  employees[emp_id][1] =
                    int(employees[emp_id][1])
# Convert age to int
    employees[emp_id][2] =
                float(employees[emp_id][2])
# Convert salary to float
```

Step III Calculating Average Salary

```
total_salary = sum([employees[emp_id][2]
                  for emp_id in employees])
average_salary = total_salary
                          / len(employees)
print(f"Average Salary: {average_salary}")
```

Output:

Average Salary: 55000.5

41. A company assigns bonus points to employees based on their performance scores. The formula for calculating bonus points is:

Bonus Points=(Performance Score×2+Experience in years)%7

The employee details are stored in a list of tuples, where each tuple contains:

```
employees = [
    ("Dev", 85, 5),
      # (Name, Performance Score, Experience)
    ("Mohit", 92, 3),
    ("Priya", 78, 7)
]
```

(i) Write Python code to calculate the Bonus Points for each employee using the given formula.

(ii) Identify the operator types used in the formula (*, +, %).

(iii) Determine which employee receives the highest Bonus Points and display their name. **Competency Based Que.**

Ans. Step (i) Calculate Bonus Points

```
bonus_points = {}
for emp in employees:
  name, score, experience = emp
  bonus = (score * 2 + experience) % 7
  bonus_points[name] = bonus
```

Step (ii) Identifying Operators in the Formula

- * (Multiplication): Arithmetic Operator
- + (Addition): Arithmetic Operator
- % (Modulus): Arithmetic Operator

Step (iii) Find the Employee with the Highest Bonus Points

```
max_bonus_employee = max(bonus_points,
key=bonus_points.get)
print(f"Employee with highest bonus points:
{max_bonus_employee}")
```

Output:

Employee with highest bonus points: Mohit

42. Write a program to calculate the volume of the sphere and hemisphere using math modules. Also, display the appropriate output.

Volume of sphere = $4/3\pi r^3$

Volume of hemisphere = $2/3\pi r^3$

Ans.
```
print ("Calculate the Volume of Sphere")
radius = int(input("Enter the radius of
                    a sphere:"))
print ("Radius of Sphere:", radius)
#Volume of sphere
volume = (4/3)*3.14*(radius**3)
print ("volume of sphere:", volume)
print ("\nCalculate the volume of
                    Hemisphere")
radius1 = int (input("Enter the radius of
                    a hemisphere:"))
print ("Radius of Hemisphere:", radius1)
#volume of hemisphere
volume1 = (2/3)*3.14*(radius**3)
print ("Volume of Hemisphere:", volume1)
```

Output

Calculate the Volume of Sphere
Enter the radius of a sphere: 5
Radius of Sphere: 5
Volume of Sphere: 523.3333333333334
Calculate the Volume of Hemisphere
Enter the radius of a hemisphere: 4
Radius of Hemisphere: 4
Volume of Hemisphere: 133.97333333333333

43. Predict the output:

(i)
```
a = 3
b = a *2
print(a*3+6+b)
```

(ii)
```
a, b = 12, 10
c = a//b + 4 * 2
d = c - 10
print(d)
```

(iii)
```
a = 5
b = 6
((a and b)
or (a > b))
```

(iv)
```
a = 4
b = 6
c = 10
(a >= b)
or ((c == b)
and (not(c < a)))
```

(v)
```
a = 4
b = 6
c = 10
(a <= b) and
((c == a)and
(not(c < b)))
```

(vi)
```
a = 60
b = 10
c = 85/b + a
print(c)
```

(vii)
```
a = 3
b = 4
c = a ** b + 5
print(c)
```

(viii)
```
b = 89
a = 78
c = (a <= b)
print(c)
```

Ans. (i) 21 (ii) −1
(iii) 6 (iv) False
(v) False (vi) 68.5
(vii) 86 (viii) True

44. Find the output

(i)
```
x = 20
y = 24
print('x > y  is',x>y)
print('x < y  is',x<y)
print('x == y is',x == y)
print('x != y is',x!=y)
print('x >= y is',x>=y)
print('x <= y is',x<=y)
```

(ii)
```
x = 19
y = 4
print('x + y =',x+y)
print('x - y =',x-y)
print('x * y =',x*y)
print('x / y =',x/y)
print('x // y =',x//y)
print('x ** y =',x**y)
```

Ans. (i) **Output**

x > y is False
x < y is True
x == y is False
x != y is True
x >= y is False
x <= y is True

(ii) **Output**

x + y = 23
x - y = 15
x * y = 76
x / y = 4.75
x // y = 4
x ** y = 130321

45. Describe the expressions in Python.

Ans. Refer to text on page no. 144-145 (Expressions).

Case Study Based Questions

Case Study 1

Operators are special symbols that perform specific operations on values or variables. They are the building blocks of expressions and form the core of programming logic. Python offers a wide range of operators, including arithmetic, comparison, assignment, logical, bitwise, membership, and identity operators.

Based on the above information, answer the following questions.

(i) Which operator is used to perform integer division in Python?

(a) / (b) // (c) % (d) **

(ii) What is the result of the expression 5 ** 2?

(a) 7 (b) 10 (c) 25 (d) 3

(iii) Which operator is used to check if two values are equal?

(a) == (b) != (c) > (d) <

(iv) What is the output of 10 % 3?

(a) 3 (b) 2 (c) 1 (d) 0

(v) Which operator is used to assign a value to a variable?

(a) = (b) == (c) := (d) ->

(vi) What is the result of the expression True and False?

(a) True (b) False (c) None (d) Error

Ans. (i) (b) // (ii) (c) 25
(iii) (a) == (iv) (c) 1
(v) (a) = (vi) (b) False

Case Study 2

Data Type The data that needs to be processed by a computer can be in various form. It can be numbers with or without decimal places or it can be just a single character or a sequence of characters.

The data to be handled by the computer can also be in group. All computer programming languages support wide variety of data that can be stored, processed and manipulated in a computer system.

Data type is a term that is used to show the kind of data values or the type of data that is expected to be handled. Python has five standard data types: Numbers, Strings, Lists, Tuples and Dictionaries.

Based on the above information, answer the following questions.

(i) Which data type contains only numeric values in Python?

(a) String (b) List
(c) Number (d) Dictionary

(ii) Which term is used to show the kind of data values?

(a) Variable (b) Data Type
(c) Operator (d) Function

(iii) Tuples are defined by which type of bracket?

(a) Square brackets [ ] (b) Curly braces { }
(c) Parentheses ( ) (d) Angle brackets < >

(iv) In Python, what are the uses of data types?

(a) To store data in different formats
(b) To define variables and their usage
(c) To perform specific operations on data
(d) All of the above

(v) Integer data type can be represented by which term(s)?

(a) int (b) float
(c) str (d) list

Ans. (i) (c) Number
(ii) (b) Data Type
(iii) (c) Parentheses ( )
(iv) (d) All of the above
(v) (a) int

SELF ASSESSMENT TEST

Multiple Choice Questions

1. These operators work on single operand

(a) Binary
(b) Unary
(c) Ternary
(d) None of these

2. Which of the following symbol is used for exponentiation?

(a) // (b) **
(c) * (d) ^^

3. Dictionary data types are created by using

(a) { } (b) [ ]
(c) ( ) (d) < >

Fill in the Blanks

4. In Python, the function _______ is used to check the data type of a variable, while the function _______ is used to explicitly convert a variable from one type to another.

5. The expression 5 + 3 * 2 ** 2 - 4 // 2 evaluates to _______, following Python's operator precedence rules.

State Whether True or False

6. In Python, the is operator checks whether two variables have the same value, similar to the == operator.

7. In Python, a set can contain both mutable and immutable data types as its elements.

Assertion and Reason Based Questions

Assertion (A) and Reason (R) Type questions. Choose the correct option as:

(a) Both Assertion (A) and Reason (R) are true, and Reason (R) is the correct explanation of Assertion (A).
(b) Both Assertion (A) and Reason (R) are true, but Reason (R) is not the correct explanation of Assertion (A).
(c) Assertion (A) is true, but Reason (R) is false.
(d) Assertion (A) is false, but Reason (R) is true.

8. **Assertion (A)** In Python, the int and float data types are both immutable.

Reason (R) Immutable data types in Python cannot be changed after they are created.

9. **Assertion (A)** The // operator in Python performs floor division and always returns an integer.

Reason (R) The // operator rounds the result towards zero.

10. **Assertion (A)** The + operator in Python can be used for both arithmetic addition and string concatenation.

Reason (R) Python allows operator overloading, enabling operators to perform different operations based on operand types.

Very Short Answer Type Questions

11. Which operator is used to connect relational expression?

12. What will be the value of z?

z = 2 * 3 + 4 – 3/2 * 4

13. Convert the equation into corresponding Python statement $a^3 + b^2 + 5c$.

Short Answer Type Questions

14. Define conditional operator with the help of an example.

15. Construct logical expression to represent the following condition

(i) a is odd.
(ii) age is less than 35 and greater than 18.

16. What will be the output of following program?

```
i = 4
j = -1
k = 0
w = i or j or k
x = i and j and k
print("w = ", w)
print("x = ", x)
```

17. Write the output of the following program:

```
x = 5
y = 3
z = ++ x + -- y
print ("z = ", - - z)
```

18. Evaluate the following expression and show their hierarchy

```
a = b * c/2 + 3/2 * c + 2 + d
(if b = 4, c = 1, d = 3.2)
```

Long Answer Type Questions

19. Any year is input through the keyboard. Write a program to determine whether the year is a leap year or not.

20. If a three digit number is input through the keyboard, write a program to reverse the number.

21. Write a Python program to input a number, if number is even print its cube otherwise print its square.

22. If the marks obtained by a student in five different subjects are input through the keyboard, find out the aggregate marks and percentage marks obtained by the student. Assume the maximum marks that can be obtained by a student in each subject is 100.

23. Ravish's basic salary is input through the keyboard. His dearness allowance is 40% of basic salary and house rent allowance is 20% of basic salary. Write a program to calculate his gross salary.

Case Study Based Questions

24. A software development company is designing an application that helps users analyze their monthly expenses. The application takes inputs for different expense categories, processes the data, and provides useful insights. The developer has implemented the following Python code to handle the data:

```
salary = 50000
rent = 12000
groceries = 8500
transport = 3200
utilities = 4100
savings = salary - (rent + groceries
                    + transport + utilities)
print("Remaining Balance:", savings)
print("Is rent greater than groceries?",
                           rent > groceries)
print("Total expenditure:", rent
      + groceries + transport + utilities)
print("Average expense per category:",
  (rent + groceries + transport + utilities)
                                        / 4)
```

Based on the above information, answer the following questions.

(i) What is the data type of the variable salary in the given Python code?

(a) int (b) float
(c) str (d) bool

(ii) What type of operator is used in the expression rent > groceries?

(a) Arithmetic Operator (b) Logical Operator
(c) Comparison Operator (d) Assignment Operator

(iii) What will be the output of the following expression: type(savings)

(a) <class 'int'> (b) <class 'float'>
(c) <class 'bool'> (d) <class 'str'>

(iv) Which of the following operators is used to calculate the average expense in the given code?

(a) + (Addition) (b) / (Division)
(c) - (Subtraction) (d) * (Multiplication)

(v) If the salary is changed to 50000.50, what will be the data type of savings?

(a) int (b) float
(c) str (d) bool

Answers

1. (b)	2. (b)	3. (a)	4. type()	5. 15
6. False	7. False	8. (a)	9. (a)	10. (a)

24. (i) → (a), (ii) → (c), (iii) → (a), (iv) → (b), (v) → (b)

09 CHAPTER

Conditional and Looping Statements

Programming is all about making decisions and automating repetitive tasks. Python provides powerful constructs for decision-making (conditional statements) and iteration (looping statements) that allow programmers to control the flow of execution efficiently.

▼ YOUR STUDY GOALS

9.1 Control Structure
- Sequence
- Selection
- Iteration

9.2 Programs

▼ YOUR PRACTICE GOAL

- Objective Type Questions (30 Qs ; MCQs, True or False, Fill in the Blanks, Assertion and Reason)
- Subjective Type Questions (39 Qs ; VSA, SA, LA)
- Case Study Based Questions-2

A computer program is a collection of instructions that tell a computer what to do. These instructions, or statements, are the building blocks of programs. The simplest statement is a null statement, which does nothing.

Compound statements are groups of statements that work together to perform a specific task. Control statements, like if, else, for, and while, determine the order in which these statements are executed.

This flow of control allows programmers to create complex programs with different execution paths.

9.1 Control Structure

A control structure is a programming language construct which affects the flow of the execution of a program.

Various types of control structure are described below.

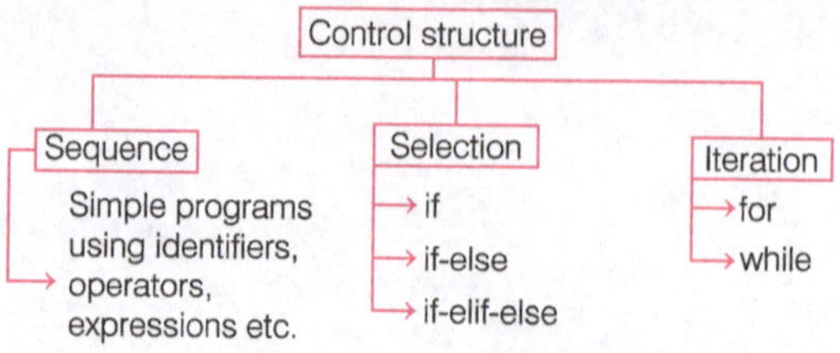

Sequence

Sequence control means the statements are being executed sequentially.

Sequence structure is also known as straight line path.

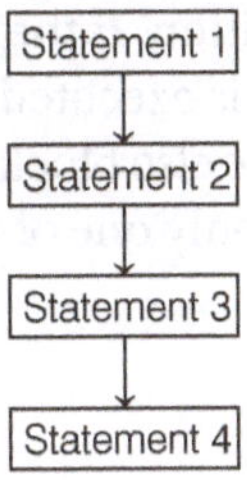

Sequence Statements

Sequence statements are instructions that are executed one after the other, in the order they appear in the program.

When a program runs, it follows a specific path, executing each **statement sequentially**. Simple programs often follow a straightforward, linear path, executing each instruction in order.

For example,

```
print ("A program which adds two integers\n")
x = int(input("Enter first integer:"))
y = int(input("Enter second integer:"))
sum = x + y
print ("Sum is :", sum)
```

Output

A program which adds two integers

Enter first integer: 5

Enter second integer: 5

Sum is: 10

Selection or Branching

When we want our program to make decisions and take different actions based on specific conditions, we use branching statements.

These statements allow us to control the flow of the program and execute different parts of the code depending on whether a certain condition is true or false.

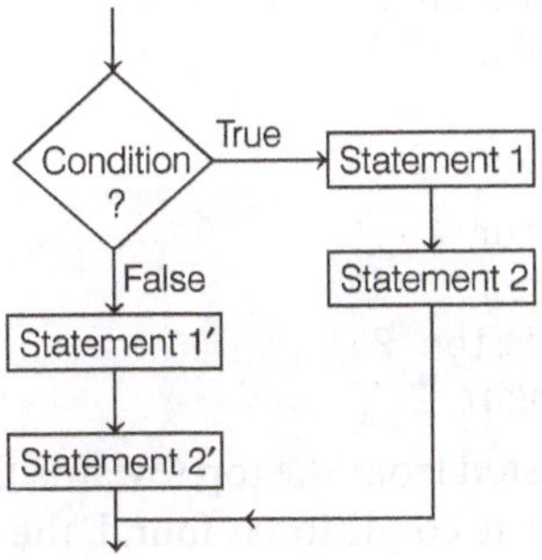

Selection Statements

Selection statements, also known as conditional statements or decision statements, allow a program to make choices.

They let us control the flow of the program by executing different blocks of code based on whether a certain condition is true or false.

This decision-making process is often based on the result of a boolean expression, which is a statement that evaluates to either true or false. Relational operators like ==, !=, <, >, <=, and >= are used to create these boolean expressions.

Python language provides the following selection statements

(i) if statement

(ii) if-else statement

(iii) if-elif-else statement

if Statement

The simplest and most common selection structure is the if statement. The if statement allows branch depending upon the value or state of variables.

If the condition evaluates true, an action is followed; otherwise, the action is ignored.

Syntax

```
if (conditional expression):
  statement(s)
```

Points to be remember

1. Logical statements in Python can only evaluate to either True or False.
2. In Python, any non-zero value (positive or negative) is considered True, while zero is considered False.
3. It's generally not recommended to use floating-point numbers to control conditional statements, as it can lead to unexpected behavior due to floating-point precision issues.

For example,

```
x = 1
y = 3
x = x + y
if (x > y):
  print ("x is greater")
```

In the above example, the conditional statement under if() will be always evaluated as True, i.e the output of the above code would be "x is greater".

Following flowchart illustrates if statement:

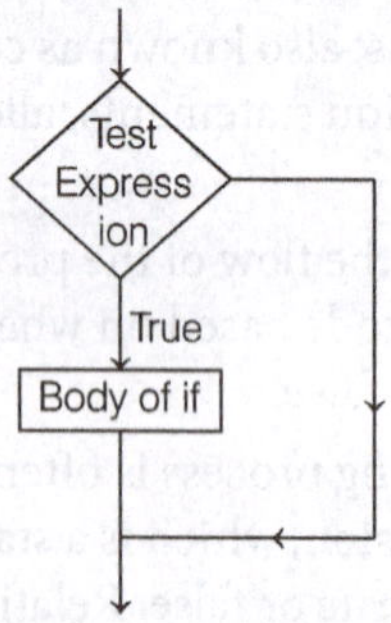

Some more examples of test conditions are

(i) Comparison with a literal
```
if(grade=='B'):
    print ("You did well")
```
(ii) Comparing two variables
```
if (x > y):
    print(" y is less than x")
```
(iii) Testing truth value of a variable
```
if (a):
    print("a is non-zero")
    print("It results into True")
```
(iv) Testing mathematical condition
```
if ((x> = 3) and (x< = 10)):
    print (" True")
```
(v) Return true when b is zero
```
if (not b):
    print(" b is zero ")
```
The value of not b will be True when b is zero.

if-else Statement

This statement also tests a conditional expression. If the condition is True, the entire block of statements following the if will be executed.

Otherwise, the entire block of statements following the else will be executed.

Syntax
```
if (conditional statement):
    statement(s)
else:
    statement(s)
```
Following flowchart illustrates if-else statement:

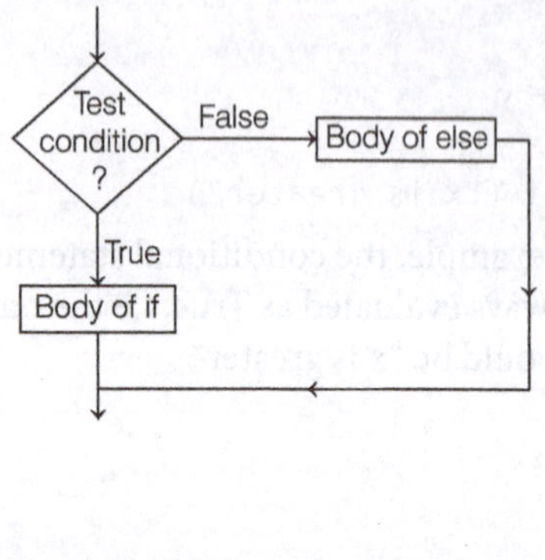

An if-else statement allows us to execute different code blocks based on a condition. If the condition is true, the code inside the if block is executed. If the condition is false, the code inside the else block is executed. It's important to note that only one of these blocks will be executed, not both.

e.g.,
```
x = 0
y = 3
x = x + y
if (x > y):
    print ("x is greater")
else:
    print ("we are in else part because x is
not greater")
```
The above code produces an output as "we are in the else part because x is not greater". Because the conditional statement under if ( ) evaluates as False x is not greater than y, it is the same as that of y.

Some of valid if-else statements are

(i)
```
if((ch>='a') and (ch<='z')):
    print(ch, "is a lowercase letter")
else:
    print(ch, "is not a lowercase letter")
```
(ii)
```
if((age==50) or (age==20)):
    print("You are old")
else:
    print("You are young")
```

if-elif-else statement

Sometimes, we need to make decisions based on multiple conditions. We can use a series of if-else statements to check each condition one by one.

If a condition is true, the corresponding code block is executed. If not, the next condition is checked, and so on. This allows us to create more complex decision-making processes.

Syntax
```
if (condition 1):
    statement 1
elif(condition 2):
    statement 2
else:
    statement 3
```
or
```
if(condition 1):
    statement 1
elif(condition 2):
    statement 2
```
Expression is tested from the top towards the downside. As soon as the true condition is found, the associated set of statement is executed.

e.g.
```
if((x % 5 = = 0) and (x % 8 = = 0)):
    print("Divisible by both 5 and 8")
elif(x % 8 = = 0):
    print("Divisible by 8")
elif (x % 5 = = 0):
    print("Divisible by 5")
else:
    print("Divisible by none")
```

For an if-elif-else

(i) Other than 0(zero), all other values are considered as True.

(ii) (==) must be used for comparision in the expression of if condition, if you use (=) the expression will always return True, because it performs assignment not comparison.

Nested if statement

A nested if statement is an if statement that is placed inside another if statement. It allows you to make more complex decisions by testing additional conditions after the first if condition is evaluated.

Syntax

```
if(condition 1):
   if(condition 2):
      statement 1
   else:
         statement 2
else:
      statement 3
```

e.g.
```
if(a > b):
   if(a > c):
      result = a
   else:
      result = c
else:
      if(b>c):
         result = b
      else:
         result = c
```

The nested if can have one of the following four forms:

(i) **if nested inside both, if part and else part**

```
if(condition 1):
   if(condition 2):
      statement 1
   else:
      statement 2
else:
      if(condition 3):
         statement 3
      else:
         statement 4
```

(ii) **if nested inside if part**

```
if(condition 1):
   if(condition 2):
      statement 1
   else:
      statement 2
else :
      statement 3
```

(iii) **if nested inside else part**

```
if(condition 1):
      statement 1
else:
      if(condition 2):
         statement 2
      else:
         statement 3
```

(iv) **One if inside another if statements**

```
if(condition 1):
   statement 1
   if (condition 2):
      statement 2
```

Quick Test 1

1. What is sequential flow in programming?
2. What is the purpose of conditional statements in programming?
3. Explain the difference between if, if-else and if-elif-else statements.
4. Write a Python program to sort three numbers in descending order.
5. Write a Python program to check if a number is divisible by 3 and 5.

Iteration

Iteration, or looping, is a way to repeat a block of code multiple times. We use it when we need to perform the same task over and over again until a certain condition is met. For example, if we want to print the numbers from 1 to 10, we can use a loop to repeat the printing process 10 times.

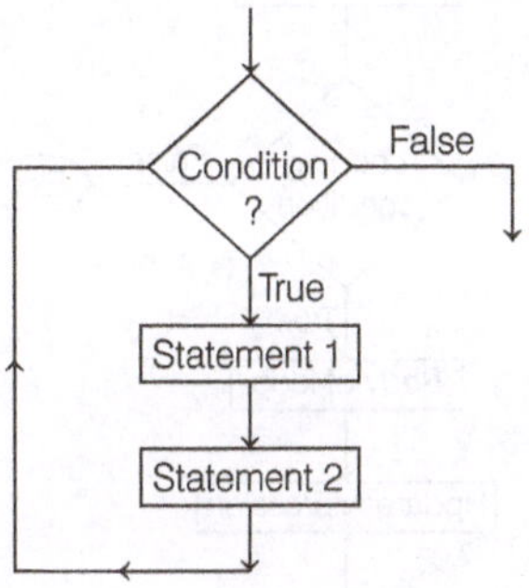

range( ) Function

The range( ) function is used to generate a sequence of numbers overtime. At its simplest, it accepts an integer and returns a range object (a type of iterable).

Syntax `range(start, stop, step)`

where,

- **start** This is where you want to begin your count. If you don't specify a number, it defaults to 0.
- **stop** This is where you want to end your count. You need to provide a number here (Required).
- **step** This tells you how much to increase the count each time. If you don't specify a number, it defaults to 1, meaning you'll count by ones.

e.g., if you set start to 2, stop to 10, and step to 2, you'll count: 2,4,6,8.

Iterative Statements

Loops in Python are used to repeatedly execute a block of code. This repetition is controlled by a condition, which is evaluated before each iteration. If the condition is true, the code block is executed. Once the condition becomes false, the loop terminates.

Python offers two main types of loops:

(i) for loop (ii) while loop

for loop

The for loop is a tool that lets you repeat a set of instructions a specific number of times. It iterates through a sequence (like a range, string, list, or tuple), processing each value. Once all items are processed, the loop ends, and control moves to the next statement.

Syntax
```
for variable in <sequence>:
        statement (s)
```

In general
```
for i in range(start, stop, step):
    statement (s)
```

Flowchart

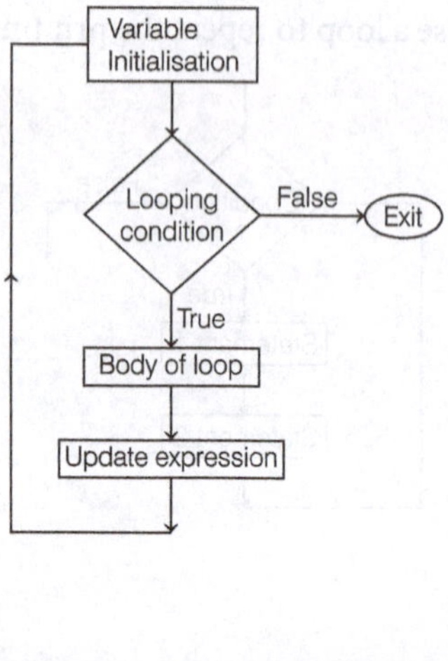

Example

(i)
```
for i in range (1,5):
    print("A")
    print("B")
```

Output

A
B
A
B
A
B
A
B

(ii)
```
a = "Arihant"
for i in a:
    print(i)
```

Output

A
r
i
h
a
n
t

while loop

A while loop is like a set of instructions that keeps repeating as long as a certain condition is true. Before it starts, it checks if the condition is true. If it is, it runs the instructions inside the loop.

Then it checks the condition again. If it's still true, it runs the instructions again, and so on. Once the condition becomes false, the loop stops.

Note *If the condition is false right at the beginning, the loop won't run even once. This is why it's called an "entry control loop."*

Syntax
```
while (loop-condition):
    statement (s)
```

Example
```
x = 5
sum = 0
while (x>0):
    sum = sum + x
    x = x - 1
print ("Sum is:", sum)
```

Output

Sum is: 15

In the above example, The loop keeps running as long as the value of x is more than 0. Once x reaches 0, the loop stops.

Inside the loop, we keep subtracting 1 from x with each repetition. At the same time, we add the current value of x to a total sum. This process continues until x becomes 0.

Let's understand the iterations of the above example with the help of a table.

Initial	Condition	Sum	x
Initial	–	0	5
1st Iteration	5 > 0 (True)	0 + 5 = 5	5 - 1 = 4
2nd Iteration	4 > 0 (True)	5 + 4 = 9	4 - 1 = 3
3rd Iteration	3 > 0 (True)	9 + 3 = 12	3 - 1 = 2
4th Iteration	2 > 0 (True)	12 + 2 = 14	2 - 1 = 1
5th Iteration	1 > 0 (True)	14 + 1 = 15	1 - 1 = 0
6th Iteration	0 > 0 (False)	*Loop ends*	

While loops aren't just for checking conditions; they can also use expressions. However, there are some things to avoid.

For example, you can't directly use assignments like x = x + 1 as conditions. This is because these assignments always result in a non-zero value (the new value of x), so the loop would run indefinitely.

Similarly, using decrement (n--) or increment (count += i) operations directly as conditions won't work as expected.

To make the loop exit, you'll need to have a condition that eventually becomes false.

TEACHER TIP
Always ensure that the loop condition will eventually become false.

Break and Continue

Loops are a great way to repeat tasks, but sometimes we need more control over when and how the loop runs. Python provides two special statements, break and continue, to help us with this.

break statement

The break statement is like a shortcut to exit a loop. When the program reaches a break statement, it immediately stops the loop and continues with the code that comes after the loop.

It's like saying, "I'm done with this loop, let's move on."

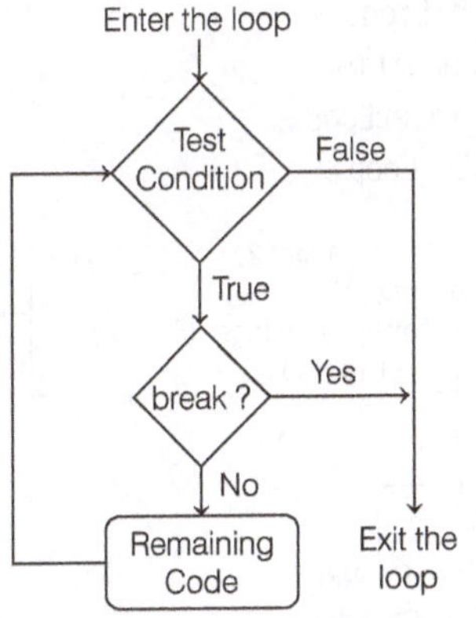

continue statement

The continue statement in Python is used to skip the current iteration of a loop and move to the next iteration.

It only affects the current loop cycle, and the remaining code in the loop for that iteration is not executed.

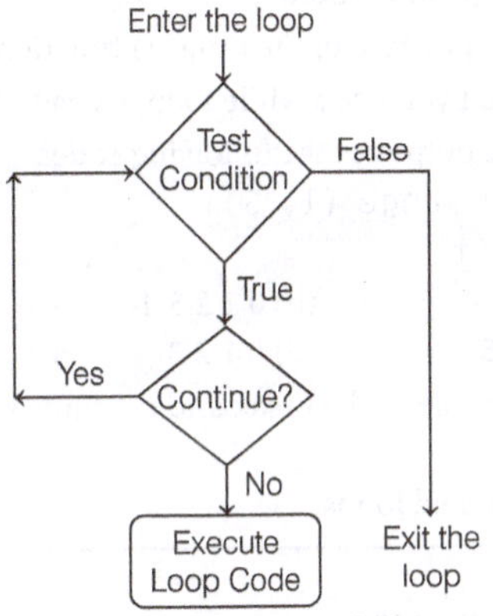

Nested Loops

A nested loop is a loop within a loop. Python has two main types of loops: for loops and while loops. We can combine these loops to create nested loops. It's a way to create more complex patterns of repetition.

Imagine a loop as a box. A nested loop is a smaller box inside the bigger one.

The inner loop runs completely for each iteration of the outer loop.

Syntax of Nested for loop

```
for outer_var in outer_sequence:
    for inner_var in inner_sequence:
        statement_innerLoop
    statement_outerLoop
```

Syntax of Nested while loop

```
while outer_condition:
   while inner_condition:
      statement_innerLoop
   statement_outerLoop
```

e.g.

```
for i in range(2):
  print(i)
  for j in range (10, 13):
    print(j)
```

Inner loop: `for j in range (10, 13): print(j)`; Outer loop: the whole code.

Output

```
0
10
11
12
1
10
11
12
```

Printed by outer loop: 0, 1. Printed by Inner loop: 10, 11, 12.

Quick Test 2

1. What is a loop in programming? What are the two main types of loops in Python?
2. What is the purpose of the range () function in Python?
3. When would you use a while loop instead of a for loop?
4. What is the output of the following code?
   ```
   for i in range (1, 5):
     print(i)
   ```
   (a) 1 2 3 4 (b) 0 1 2 3 4
   (c) 1 2 3 4 5 (d) 0 1 2 3
5. What is the role of the break and continue statements in loops?
6. What are nested loops?

9.2 Programs

1. For accepting an integer from user and checking if this integer is greater than 10.

Ans.

```
a = int(input ("Enter a number:"))
print ("Number is", a)
if (a>10):
   print (a, "is greater than 10")
```

Output

Enter a number: 56
Number is 56
56 is greater than 10

2. For adding a number to non-zero real number x.

Ans.

```
sum = 100.00
x = float (input("Please enter a real number:"))
print("Real number is",x)
if(x ! = 0.0):
  sum=sum + x
  print("The sum is:", sum)
```

Output

Please enter a real number: 45.9
Real number is 45.9
The sum is: 145.9

3. For asking a user to answer Yes or No to a question such as "Are you ready to provide your credit card number"?

Ans.

```
ans = input ("Are you ready to provide your credit card number (1=Yes/0 = No):")
print ("Your choice:", ans)
if(ans = = '1'):
   print ("Now we will continue the processing of transaction")
elif(ans = = '0'):
   print ("Now we will not continue the processing of transaction")
```

Output

Are you ready to provide your credit card number (1=Yes/0 = No):0
Your choice: 0
Now we will not continue the processing of transaction

4. To find the number is even or odd with compound statement.

Ans.

```
n = int(input("Enter a number:"))
print("The number is",n)
d = n%2
if(d= = 0):
   print ("Remainder on division by 2 is:", d)
   print ("The number is an even number.")
else:
   print("Remainder on division by 2 is:", d)
   print("The number is an odd number.")
```

Output

Enter a number:45
The number is 45
Remainder on division by 2 is: 1
The number is an odd number.

5. To accept a positive value from a user and prints the square of the number.

Ans.

```
n=int(input(" Enter a number:"))
if (n<0):
   print ("Number is negative")
else:
   print (" The square of " ,n, "is" ,n ** 2)
```

Output

Enter a number:6
The square of 6 is 36

6. To enter a character and print whether a given character is an alphabet, digit or any character.

Ans.

```
ch = input ("Enter a character:")
if (((ch>='A') and (ch<='Z')) or ((ch>='a')
and (ch<='z'))):
    print ("You entered an alphabet")
elif(ch>='0' and ch<='9'):
    print ("You entered a digit")
else:
    print ("You entered a character other than
    alphabets and digits")
```

Output

Enter a character:a
You entered an alphabet
>>>
Enter a character:2
You entered a digit

7. To print the largest number out of 3 numbers.

Ans.

```
i = int(input("Enter first number: "))
j = int(input("Enter second number: "))
k = int(input("Enter third number: "))
print("i =", i)
print("j =", j)
print("k =", k)
largest = i
if j > largest:
    largest = j
if k > largest:
    largest = k
print("The largest number is", largest)
```

Output

Enter first number: 78
Enter second number: 54
Enter third number : 23
i = 78
j = 54
k = 23
The largest number is 78

8. For fibonacci series using while loop.

Ans.

```
n=int(input("Enter the limit:"))
i = 1
a = 0
b = 1
while(i<=n):
    print(a)
    c = a+b
    a = b
    b = c
    i = i+1
```

Output

Enter the limit: 10
0
1
1
2
3
5
8
13
21

9. To find the factorial of a given number.

Ans.

```
num = int(input("Enter any number:"))
n = num
f = 1
while(n>0):
    f = f*n
    n = n - 1
print("The factorial of", num," is ", f)
```

Output

Enter any number:5
The factorial of 5 is 120

10. To display quotient and remainder.

Ans.

```
num = int(input("Enter Numerator:"))
den = int(input("Enter Denominator:"))
print("The Quotient is:", num//den)
print("The Remainder is:", num% den)
```

Output

Enter Numerator: 77
Enter Denominator: 2
The Quotient is: 38
The Remainder is: 1

11. Program to print all numbers in a range divisible by a given number.

Ans.

```
l = int(input("Enter lower range:"))
u = int(input("Enter upper range:"))
n = int(input("Enter the number to be divided
by:"))
for i in range (l, u+1):
    if (i% n= = 0):
        print (i)
```

Output

Enter lower range : 50
Enter upper range : 100
Enter the number to be divided by : 7
56
63
70
77
84
91
98

Mind Map

CONDITIONAL AND LOOPING STATEMENTS

Control Structure

Sequence

These statements refers to the instructions that are executed in the sequence.

Selection

Conditional statements executes specific action based on a given condition .

01 • **if Statement**

Syntax if(conditional expression):
    statement(s)

02 • **if-else Statement**

Syntax if(conditional expression):
    statement(s)
  else:
    statement(s)

03 • **if-elif-else Statement**

Syntax if(condition 1):
    statement 1
  elif(condition 2):
    statement 2
  else:
    statement 3

04 • **Nested if Statement**

Syntax if(condition 1):
    if(condition 2):
      statement 1
    else:
      statement 2
  else:
    statement 3

Jump Statements

It is used to break the normal flow of the program and jump onto a specific line of code in the program if the specific condition is true.

break Statement

```
for val in sequence
    # code
    if condition:
        break
    # code
```

```
while condition:
    #  code
    if condition:
        break
    # code
```

Continue Statement

```
for val in sequence
    # code
    if condition:
        continue
    # code
```

```
while condition:
    #  code
    if condition:
        continue
    # code
```

Iteration

It commonly known as loops, are statements in programming used to execute part of code repeatedly based on condition or set of conditions.

01 • **for Loop**

Syntax for variable in sequence:
    statements(s)

02 • **while Loop**

Syntax while expression:
    statement(s)

03 • **Nested Loop**

For nested for loop,

Syntax for iterator_var in sequence:
    for iterator_var in sequence:
      statements(s)
    statements(s)

For nested while loop,

Syntax while expression:
    while expression:
      statement(s)
    statement(s)

Note

range() function returns a sequence of numbers, starting from 0 by default, and increments by 1 (by default), and stops before a specified number.

Syntax range(*start, stop, step*)

NCERT Folder

Exercise Questions

1. What is the difference between else and elif construct of if statement?

Ans. (a) **else**

- Executes only when the condition of all preceding if and elif statements is False.
- It's a default block that runs if none of the previous conditions are met.
- There can be only one else block in an if statement.

(b) **elif**

- Short for "else if."
- It's used to check additional conditions after the initial if statement.
- Multiple elif blocks can be used to check different conditions sequentially.
- An elif block only executes if the preceding if and elif conditions are False, and its own condition is True.

2. What is the purpose of range() function? Give one example.

Ans. The range() function generates a sequence of numbers. It's commonly used in for loops to iterate over a specific range of values.

Example

```
for i in range(5):
    print(i)
```

3. Differentiate between break and continue statements using examples.

Ans.

break	continue
Immediately terminates the loop it's inside.	Skips the remaining code in the current iteration of the loop.
Execution jumps to the statement after the loop.	The loop then moves to the next iteration.

e.g.,
Python
`for i in range(10):`
`    if i == 5:`
`        break`
`    print(i)`
	e.g.,
	Python
	`for i in range(10):`
	`    if i % 2 == 0:`
	`        continue`
	`    print(i)`

4. What is an infinite loop? Give one example.

Ans. An infinite loop is a loop that continues to execute indefinitely because its termination condition is never met.

e.g.,
```
while True:
        print("This loop will run forever")
```

This loop will keep printing the message indefinitely because the condition True is always true.

5. Find the output of the following program segments:

(i)
```
a = 110
while a > 100:
    print(a)
    a -= 2
```

(ii)
```
for i in range(20,30,2):
    print(i)
```

(iii)
```
country = 'INDIA'
for i in country:
    print (i)
```

(iv)
```
i = 0; sum = 0
while i < 9:
    if i % 4 == 0:
        sum = sum + i
    i = i + 2
print (sum)
```

(v)
```
for x in range(1,4):
    for y in range(2,5):
        if x * y > 10:
            break
        print (x * y)
```

(vi)
```
var = 7
while var > 0:
    print ('Current variable value: ', var)
    var = var -1
    if var == 3:
        break
    else:
        if var == 6:
            var = var -1
            continue
    print ("Good bye!")
```

Ans. (i) **Output**

110
108
106
104
102

(ii) **Output**

20
22
24
26
28

(iii) **Output**

I

N
D
I
A

(iv) **Output**
4

(v) **Output**
6
8
9
10
12

(vi) **Output**
Current variable value: 7
Current variable value: 5
Current variable value: 4
Current variable value: 3
Good bye!

Programming Based Questions

1. Write a program that takes the name and age of the user as input and displays a message whether the user is eligible to apply for a driving license or not. (the eligible age is 18 years).

Ans.
```
name = input("Enter your name: ")
age = int(input("Enter your age: "))
if age >= 18:
    print(name, "is eligible to apply for
                        a driving license.")
else:
    print(name, "is not eligible to apply
                  for a driving license yet.")
```

2. Write a program that prints the minimum and maximum of five numbers entered by the user.

Ans.
```
num1 = int(input("Enter the first number: "))
num2 = int(input("Enter the second
                               number: "))
num3 = int(input("Enter the third
                               number: "))
num4 = int(input("Enter the fourth
                               number: "))
num5 = int(input("Enter the fifth
                               number: "))
numbers = [num1, num2, num3, num4, num5]
print("Minimum number:", min(numbers))
print("Maximum number:", max(numbers))
```

3. Write a program to check if the year entered by the user is a leap year or not.

Ans.
```
year = int(input("Enter a year: "))
if (year % 4 == 0) and (year % 100 != 0) or
                        (year % 400 == 0):
    print(year, "is a leap year.")
else:
    print(year, "is not a leap year.")
```

4. Write a program to generate the sequence: –5, 10, –15, 20, –25..... upto n, where n is an integer input by the user.

Ans.
```
n = int(input("Enter the value of n: "))
for i in range(1, n+1):
    if i % 2 == 1:
        print(-5 * i, end=",")
    else:
        print(10 * i, end=",")
```

5. Write a program to find the sum of 1+ 1/8 + 1/27......1/n^3, where n is the number input by the user.

Ans.
```
n = int(input("Enter the value of n: "))
sum = 0
for i in range(1, n+1):
    sum += 1 / (i ** 3)
print("The sum of the series is:", sum)
```

6. Write a program to find the sum of digits of an integer number, input by the user.

Ans.
```
num = int(input("Enter an integer: "))
sum_of_digits = 0
while num > 0:
    digit = num % 10
    sum_of_digits += digit
    num //= 10
print("Sum of digits:", sum_of_digits)
```

7. Write a program to print the following patterns:

(i)
```
  *
 * * *
* * * * *
 * * *
  *
```

(ii)
```
        1
      2 1 2
    3 2 1 2 3
  4 3 2 1 2 3 4
5 4 3 2 1 2 3 4 5
```

(iii)
```
1 2 3 4 5
  1 2 3 4
    1 2 3
      1 2
        1
```

(iv)
```
  *
 * *
*   *
 * *
  *
```

Ans. (i)
```
n = 3
for i in range(n):
    print(" " * (n - i) + "* " * (i + 1))
for i in range(n - 1, 0, -1):
    print(" " * (n - i + 1) + "* " * i)
print("\n")
```

(ii)
```
n = 5
for i in range(1, n + 1):
    print(" " * (n - i), end="")
    for j in range(i, 0, -1):
        print(j, end="")
    for j in range(2, i + 1):
        print(j, end="")
    print()
print("\n")
```

(iii)
```
n = 5
for i in range(n, 0, -1):
    for j in range(1, i + 1):
        print(j, end=" ")
    print()
print("\n")
```

(iv)
```
n = 3
for i in range(1, n + 1, 2):
    print(" " * (n - i) + "* " * i)
for i in range(n - 2, 0, -2):
    print(" " * (n - i) + "* " * i)
```

8. Write a program to find the grade of a student when grades are allocated as given in the table below.

Percentage of Marks	Grade
Above 90%	A
80% to 90%	B
70% to 80%	C
60% to 70%	D
Below 60%	E

Percentage of the marks obtained by the student is input to the program.

Ans.
```
percentage = float(input("Enter the
percentage of marks obtained: "))
if percentage > 90:
    grade = 'A'
elif percentage >= 80:
    grade = 'B'
elif percentage >= 70:
    grade = 'C'
elif percentage >= 60:
    grade = 'D'
else:
    grade = 'E'
print("The grade of the student is:", grade)
```

EXAM PATTERN QUESTIONS

Objective Type Questions

Multiple Choice Questions

1. Which Python construct allows you to repeat a block of code multiple times?

(a) Looping (b) Decision
(c) Condition (d) Sequence

2. When you use a for loop in Python, where does the counting usually start from?

(a) -1 (b) 0
(c) 1 (d) 10

3. Which statement is a sequence of more than one statements?

(a) Control statement (b) Compound statement
(c) Single statement (d) Sequence statement

4. Which function is used to generate a sequence of numbers overtime?

(a) range ( ) (b) len ( )
(c) limit ( ) (d) lim ( )

5. You are designing a program to simulate a game where players take turns making moves. The game continues until a player wins or a draw occurs. Which programming paradigm is most suitable for implementing the turn-based logic that repeats until a game-ending condition is met? **Competency Based Que.**

(a) Sequence programming
(b) Compound programming
(c) Single-statement programming
(d) Iterative programming

6. while loops are called as

(a) entry control loops
(b) exit control loops
(c) Both (a) and (b)
(d) None of the above

7. A computer program is a set of instructions and are also known as

(a) compounds (b) statements
(c) blocks (d) comments

8. Which Python keyword is often used as a placeholder, meaning "do nothing"?

(a) break (b) continue
(c) pass (d) jump

9. You are writing a program to determine if a student has passed an exam. The passing score is 60. You have a variable student_score that holds the student's score. Which if statement condition would correctly determine if the student has passed? **Competency Based Que.**

(a) if student_score < 60: (b) if student_score == 60:
(c) if student_score >= 60: (d) if student_score != 60:

10. Which Python statement allows you to choose between two options?

(a) if (b) for
(c) while (d) print

Fill in the Blanks

11. ________ is the simplest form of decision statement.

12. ______ is used to chain multiple conditions.

13. A set of statements is usually indented ______ spaces inside the if statement.

14. In a for loop, the ______ function is commonly used to generate a sequence of numbers.

15. A _______ statement skips the rest of the loop and jumps over to the statement following the loop.

16. ________ is the only way to figure out the level of nesting.

17. A loop that continues indefinitely without a condition to terminate it is called an ______ loop.

State Whether True or False

18. In Python, you can use the elif statement multiple times within an if-elif-else block. It allows you to check for multiple conditions sequentially.

19. The if statement can only be used to check for equality conditions.

20. You can use logical operators (and, or, not) within the conditions of if and elif statements.

21. A break statement can only be used within a for loop.

22. A continue statement in a loop will immediately terminate the loop and move to the next statement after the loop.

23. In nested loops, the inner loop completes all its iterations for each iteration of the outer loop.

Assertion and Reason Based Questions

Assertion (A) and Reason (R) Type questions. Choose the correct option as:

(a) Both Assertion (A) and Reason (R) are true, and Reason (R) is the correct explanation of Assertion (A).
(b) Both Assertion (A) and Reason (R) are true, but Reason (R) is not the correct explanation of Assertion (A).
(c) Assertion (A) is true, but Reason (R) is false.
(d) Assertion (A) is false, but Reason (R) is true.

24. Assertion (A) Indentation is crucial in Python to define code blocks.

Reason (R) Indentation helps the interpreter to understand the structure of the code.

25. Assertion (A) An if statement can exist without an accompanying else statement.

Reason (R) The else clause is mandatory when using an if statement to handle all possible conditions.

26. Assertion (A) The break statement can be used to exit a loop prematurely.

Reason (R) The break statement immediately terminates the innermost loop.

27. Assertion (A) A while loop is an entry-controlled loop.

Reason (R) The loop condition is checked at the end of each iteration.

28. Assertion (A) Nested loops can be used to create complex patterns and structures.

Reason (R) Nested loops involve one loop inside another, allowing for multiple levels of iteration.

29. Assertion (A) A for loop in Python is used when the number of iterations is known beforehand.

Reason (R) A for loop always executes at least once, even if the condition is false.

30. Assertion (A) The range() function in Python generates a sequence of numbers.

Reasong (R) range(5) generates the numbers 0,1,2,3, and 4.

Answers

1. (a) Looping	2. (b) 0
3. (b) Compound statement	4. (a) range ( )
5. (d) Iterative programming	6. (a) entry control loops
7. (b) statements	8. (c) pass
9. (c) if student_score >= 60:	
10. (a) if	11. if
12. if-elif	13. 4
14. range	15. break
16. indentations	17. infinite
18. True	19. False
20. True	21. False
22. False	23. True

24. (a) Both Assertion (A) and Reason (R) are true, and Reason (R) is the correct explanation of Assertion (A).
25. (c) Assertion (A) is true, but Reason (R) is false.
26. (a) Both Assertion (A) and Reason (R) are true, and Reason (R) is the correct explanation of Assertion (A).
27. (c) Assertion (A) is true, but Reason (R) is false.
28. (a) Both Assertion (A) and Reason (R) are true, and Reason (R) is the correct explanation of Assertion (A).
29. (c) Assertion (A) is true, but Reason (R) is false.
30. (a) Both Assertion (A) and Reason (R) are true, and Reason (R) is the correct explanation of Assertion (A).

Subjective Type Questions

Very Short Answer Type Questions

1. Define sequence statement.

Ans. Sequence statements refer to the instructions that are executed in the sequence in which they are written in the program.

2. What type of programming logic uses 'if' to decide what to do next? Competency Based Que.

Ans. Selection.

3. (a) Define iteration.
(b) What determines how a program runs?

Ans. (a) Iteration is a process of executing a statement or a set of statements repeatedly, until some specific condition is specified.
(b) Flow of control

4. (a) What is the minimum number of iterations that a while loop could make?
(b) What is looping?

Ans. (a) while loop could make minimum 0 iteration.

(b) Looping is also an iteration. It is the ability to perform the same set of operations repeatedly till a specific condition is met.

5. Explain entry controlled loop.

Ans. In an entry controlled loop, the loop control condition is evaluated at the entry point of the loop.

6. What must be defined for a loop to function correctly? **Competency Based Que.**

Ans. Body and exit condition.

7. For iterating over a list with a known length, which loop is most efficient? **Competency Based Que.**

Ans. for loop.

8. Give the output for the following program segment given below.

```
for i in range(-5, -7, -1):
  print (i + 1)
```

Ans. −4
−5

9. Find the output of the following code.

```
i = 1
while (i < 5):
  print (i)
  i = i * 2
```

Ans. Output

1

2

4

10. Write an appropriate loop for the condition-A loop is to be repeated 100 times.

Ans. for i in range (0, 100, +1):

11. List the two looping structures.

Ans. (i) for loop

(ii) while loop

12. What do flowcharts visualize?

Ans. Program flow

13. How does a flowchart typically read?

Ans. Top to bottom

14. How can you create an infinite loop using a while loop? Give an example.

Ans. To create an infinite while loop, use a condition that's always true.

For example,

```
while True:
  # Code to be repeated infinitely
```

15. What is the purpose of an else block in a try-except block?

Ans. The else block in a try-except runs only if no exceptions occur in the try block.

16. What are the three basic control flow structures in programming?

Ans. Sequence, Selection, Iteration

Short Answer Type I Questions

17. Write two different forms of if statement.

Ans. (i)
```
if (condition):
    statement (s)
```
(ii)
```
if (condition):
    statement 1
else:
    statement 2
```

18. What is the purpose of the `else` clause in a loop?

Ans. The `else` clause is executed only if the loop completes normally, without encountering a `break` statement.

19. What are loops and when do they end?

Ans. Loops are used to repeatedly execute a block of code. They continue as long as a certain condition remains true. Once the condition becomes false, the loop terminates.

20. (a) What is the difference between `for` and `while` loops?

(b) How does a `while` loop work?

Ans. (a) A `for` loop is used to iterate over a sequence of values, while a `while` loop continues as long as a given condition is true.

(b) A `while` loop repeatedly executes a block of code as long as the specified condition is true. Once the condition becomes false, the loop terminates.

21. Find the syntax error in the following program and underline after correct them.

```
w = 90:
while (w > 60)
  print(w)
  w = w - 50
```

Ans. Correct code is

```
w = 90
while (w > 60):
  print (w)
  w = w - 50
```

22. Construct logical expressions to represent the following conditions.

(i) Weight is greater than or equal to 115 but less than 125.

(ii) **Donation is in the range of 4000-5000 or Guest is 1.**

Ans. (i) (weight >=115 and weight < 125)

(ii) ((Donation > = 4000 and Donation <= 5000) or Guest = =1)

23. Write a python program to calculate simple interest and display it.

Ans.
```
p = int(input("Enter the principle:"))
r = int(input("Enter rate of interest:"))
t = int(input("Enter time:"))
si = (p*r*t)/100
print ("The simple interest is:", si)
```

Output

Enter the principle: 5000

Enter rate of interest: 10

Enter time: 2

The simple interest is 1000.0

24. Write a program to input three angles and determine if they make a triangle or not.

Ans.
```
a = float (input("Enter first angle:"))
b = float(input("Enter second  angle:"))
c = float(input("Enter third angle:"))
sum = a+b+c
if (sum == 180):
  print ("These angles will make a triangle")
else:
  print ("These angles will not make a
                                triangle"
```

Output

Enter first angle: 45.6

Enter second angle: 44.4

Enter third angle: 90.0

These angles will make a triangle

25. What happens when a `break` statement is encountered in a loop?

Ans. A `break` statement immediately terminates the loop, and the program continues with the next statement outside the loop.

Short Answer Type II Questions

26. Write a Python program that takes a number n as input and prints the first n Fibonacci numbers. However, for numbers in the Fibonacci sequence that are divisible by 3, print "Fizz", and for numbers divisible by 5, print "Buzz". If a number is divisible by both 3 and 5, print "FizzBuzz". **Competency Based Que.**

Ans.
```
n = int(input("Enter a number: "))
a, b = 0, 1
for i in range(n):
    if a % 3 == 0 and a % 5 == 0:
        print("FizzBuzz", end=" ")
    elif a % 3 == 0:
        print("Fizz", end=" ")
    elif a % 5 == 0:
        print("Buzz", end=" ")
    else:
        print(a, end=" ")
    a, b = b, a + b
```

27. Write a Python program that prints a right-angled triangle pattern of numbers. The number of rows should be taken as input, and the pattern should look like this for n=5: **Competency Based Que.**

```
1
2  3
4  5  6
7  8  9  10
11 12 13 14 15
```

Ans.
```
n = int(input("Enter the number of rows: "))
num = 1  # Start from number 1
for i in range(1, n+1):
    for j in range(i):
        print(num, end=" ")
        num += 1
    print()
```

28. Write a Python program that accepts a series of integers from the user and returns the second smallest odd number. If no odd number is found or if there is only one unique odd number, print "No second smallest odd number". The program should also ignore any negative numbers while processing the input. **Competency Based Que.**

Ans.
```
smallest_odd = float('inf')
second_smallest_odd = float('inf')
n = int(input("Enter the number of
                              integers: "))
for _ in range(n):
    num = int(input("Enter an integer: "))
    if num < 0:
        continue
    if num % 2 != 0:
        if num < smallest_odd:
            second_smallest_odd = smallest_odd
            smallest_odd = num
        elif num < second_smallest_odd and
                        num != smallest_odd:
            second_smallest_odd = num
```

```
if second_smallest_odd == float('inf'):
    print("No second smallest odd number")
else:
    print(f"The second smallest odd number
                is: {second_smallest_odd}")
```

Long Answer Type Questions

29. **Write a Python program that takes a list of integers and calculates the sum of all prime numbers in the list. The program should also find and print the largest prime number in the list. If no prime number is found, print "No primes found".** **Competency Based Que.**

Ans.
```
numbers = [10, 15, 7, 23, 19, 11, 4]
prime_sum = 0
largest_prime = -1
for num in numbers:
    if num <= 1:
        continue
    is_prime = True
    for i in range(2, int(num ** 0.5) + 1):
        if num % i == 0:
            is_prime = False
            break
    if is_prime:
        prime_sum += num
        if num > largest_prime:
            largest_prime = num
if largest_prime == -1:
    print("No primes found")
else:
    print(f"Sum of primes: {prime_sum}")
    print(f"Largest prime: {largest_prime}")
```

30. **An electricity board charges according to the following rules:**

- **For the first 100 units - 40 P per unit**
- **For the next 200 units - 50 P per unit**
- **Beyond 300 units - 60 P per unit**
- **All users have to pay a meter charge also, which is 50.**

Write a program to read the number of units consumed and print out the charges.

Ans.
```
units = int(input("Enter the number of
units consumed: "))
charges = 0.0
if units <= 100:
    charges = units * 0.4 + 50
elif units <= 300:
    charges = (units - 100) * 0.5 + 40 + 50
else:
    charges = (units - 300) * 0.6 + 140 + 50
print("The charges is:", charges)
```

Output

Enter the number of units consumed: 125

The charges is: 102.5

31. **Write a program in Python to find and display income tax with the help of following rules:**

Monthly Salary	Income Tax
9000 or more	40% of monthly salary
7500-8999	30% of monthly salary
7499 or less	20% of monthly salary

Ans.
```
salary = int(input("Enter monthly salary: "))
if (salary >= 9000):
    itax = salary * 0.40
elif (salary >= 7500 and salary < 9000):
    itax = salary * 0.30
elif (salary <= 7499):
    itax = salary * 0.20
print("Income tax is:", itax)
```

Output

Enter monthly salary: 15000

Income tax is: 6000.0

32. **A small retail store is developing an inventory management system. They need a module that calculates the profit or loss for each item sold. Write a Python program that takes the cost price and selling price of an item as input and determines whether there is a profit, a loss, or no gain/loss. Ensure the program handles invalid inputs appropriately.** **Competency Based Que.**

Ans.
```
cost_price = float(input("Enter Cost
                          Price: "))
selling_price = float(input("Enter
                    Selling Price: "))
if cost_price < 0 or selling_price < 0:
    print("Invalid input! Prices cannot be
                              negative.")
elif selling_price > cost_price:
    profit = selling_price - cost_price
    print(f"Profit: {profit}")
elif selling_price < cost_price:
    loss = cost_price - selling_price
    print(f"Loss: {loss}")
else:
    print("No Profit, No Loss")
```

33. **A science education website wants to provide a simple temperature conversion tool for its users. Write a Python program that takes a temperature value and its**

unit (Celsius or Fahrenheit) as input and converts it to the other unit. Ensure the program handles invalid inputs appropriately.

Ans.
```
temperature = float(input("Enter
                        temperature value: "))
unit = input("Enter unit (C for Celsius,
      F for Fahrenheit): ").strip().upper()
if unit == "C":
    fahrenheit = (temperature * 9/5) + 32
    print(f"{temperature}°C is equal to
                         {fahrenheit:.2f}°F")
elif unit == "F":
    celsius = (temperature - 32) * 5/9
    print(f"{temperature}°F is equal to
                            {celsius:.2f}°C")
else:
    print("Invalid unit! Please enter 'C'
         for Celsius or 'F' for Fahrenheit.")
```

34. Write a Python program to input the marks of 5 subjects and print their sum and average. Also, find the grade according to given conditions:

Average	Grade
>=90 and <=100	A+
>=81 and <=90	A
>=71 and <=80	B+
>=61 and <=70	B
>=51 and <=60	C+
>=41 and <=50	C
>=0 and <=40	F

Ans.
```
print("Enter marks obtained in 5 subjects: ")
mark1 = int(input())
mark2 = int(input())
mark3 = int(input())
mark4 = int(input())
mark5 = int(input())
sum = mark1 + mark2 + mark3 + mark4 + mark5
average = sum  / 5
print("Total of marks:", sum)
print("Average:", average)
if (average > 91 and average <= 100):
  print("Your Grade is A+")
elif (average > 81 and average <= 90):
  print("Your Grade is A")
elif (average > 71 and average <= 80):
  print("Your Grade is B+")
elif (average > 61 and average <= 70):
  print("Your Grade is B")
elif (average > 51 and average <= 60):
  print("Your Grade is C+")
elif (average >= 41 and average <= 50):
  print("Your Grade is  C")
elif (average >= 0 and average <= 40):
  print("Your Grade is F")
else:
  print ("Strange Grade..!!")
```

Output

Enter marks obtained in 5 subjects:
95
88
92
89
90
Total of marks: 454
Average: 90.8
Your Grade is A+

35. Write a Python program to input some amount and calculate discount based on the amount and give rate. Also, display its output.

Average	Grade
0-5000	5%
5000-15000	12%
15000-25000	20%
above-25000	30%

Ans.
```
amount = int(input('Enter Sale Amount: '))
if amount <= 0:
    print('Invalid Amount')
      # No discount for invalid amounts
elif amount <= 5000:
    discount = amount * 0.05
      # 5%
elif 5000 < amount <= 15000:
    discount = amount * 0.12
      # 12%
elif 15000 < amount <= 25000:
    discount = amount * 0.2
      # 20%
else:
    discount = amount * 0.3
      # 30%
print('Discount:', discount)
print('Net Pay:', amount - discount)
```

Output

Enter Sale Amount: 10000
Discount: 1200.0
Net Pay: 8800.0

36. Explain the concept of loop control elements in the context of a `while` loop in Python. How do these elements work together to control the flow of a loop?

Ans. Loop control elements are essential components that govern the execution of a `while` loop in Python. They work together to determine when the loop starts, continues, and ultimately terminates.

Key Loop Control Elements

- **Initialization Expression** This expression initializes the loop variable before the loop begins. - It sets an initial value for the variable that will be used in the test expression.
- **Test Expression** This expression is evaluated at the beginning of each iteration. - If the expression evaluates to `True`, the loop body is executed. - If the expression evaluates to `False`, the loop terminates.
- **Loop Body** The loop body contains the statements that are executed repeatedly. - The statements within the loop body are indented to indicate their belonging to the loop.
- **Update Expression** This expression modifies the loop variable during each iteration. It ensures that the loop eventually terminates by changing the value of the test expression.

Example

```
count = 0                    # Initialization
while count < 5:             # Test expression
  print("Hello, world!")
  count += 1                 # Update expression
```

37. Write a Python program to generate and print:

(i) All prime numbers between 1 and 50.

(ii) Numbers in the sequence 5, 10, 15, ..., 50, but replace multiples of 10 with "X".

Ans. (i) Printing all prime numbers between 1 and 50

```
print("Prime numbers between 1 and 50:")
for num in range(2, 51):
    is_prime = True
    for i in range(2, int(num ** 0.5) + 1):
        if num % i == 0:
            is_prime = False
            break
    if is_prime:
        print(num, end=" ")
print("\n")
```

(ii) Printing the sequence 5, 10, 15, ..., 50 (Replacing multiples of 10 with "X")

```
print("Sequence with multiples of 10
replaced by 'X':")
for num in range(5, 51, 5):
    if num % 10 == 0:
        print("X", end=" ")
    else:
        print(num, end=" ")
```

38. Write a program to display a triangle of numbers using a for loop within a while loop.

Ans.

```
x = 1
while x <= 6:
  for y in range(1, x + 1):
    print(x, end="")
      print()
x = x + 1
```

Output

1
22
333
4444
55555
666666

39. Write a Python program to input the price of items and calculate the sales tax on 6%. Also, display its output.

Ans.

```
n = int(input("Enter the number of items
                    which you want to buy: "))
sub_total = 0
i = 1
while i <= n:
  item = int(input("Enter the price of an
                                    item: "))
  i = i + 1
  sub_total = sub_total + item
  sales_tax = sub_total * 0.06
  total = sub_total + sales_tax
print ("Sub total:", sub_total)
print ("Sales tax:", sales_tax)
print ("Amount including sales tax:", total)
```

Output

Enter the number of items which you want to buy:5
Enter the price of an item:120
Enter the price of an item:100
Enter the price of an item:350
Enter the price of an item:450
Enter the price of an item:840
Sub total: 1860
Sales tax: 1116.0
Amount including sales tax: 2976.0

Case Study Based Questions

Case Study 1

Looping is a powerful programming construct that allows us to repeatedly execute a block of code. Python provides two primary loop structures: `for` loops and `while` loops.

- **A `for` loop is used to iterate over a sequence of items, such as a list, tuple, or string. It's often used when we know the number of iterations in advance.**
- **A `while` loop repeatedly executes a block of code as long as a given condition is true. It's useful when we don't know the exact number of iterations beforehand.**

Based on the above information, answer the following questions.

(i) What is the purpose of a loop in Python?

(a) To execute a block of code repeatedly.
(b) To make decisions based on conditions.
(c) To define functions.
(d) To handle input and output.

(ii) Which loop is used to iterate over a sequence of items?

(a) while loop (b) for loop
(c) do-while loop (d) repeat-until loop

(iii) What is the condition for a while loop to continue execution?

(a) The loop variable must be less than a certain value.
(b) The loop variable must be greater than a certain value.
(c) The loop condition must evaluate to True.
(d) The loop condition must evaluate to False.

(iv) What is the difference between a for loop and a while loop?

(a) A for loop is used for definite iteration, while a while loop is used for indefinite iteration.
(b) A for loop is used for indefinite iteration, while a while loop is used for definite iteration.
(c) Both loops are used for the same purpose.
(d) None of the above.

(v) Which loop is more suitable for iterating over a list of items?

(a) while loop (b) for loop
(c) Both are equally suitable (d) Neither is suitable

(vi) Can a while loop execute indefinitely?

(a) Yes, if the loop condition is always true.
(b) No, a while loop always terminates after a fixed number of iterations.
(c) It depends on the specific implementation of the loop.
(d) None of the above.

Ans. (i) (a) To execute a block of code repeatedly
(ii) (b) for loop
(iii) (c) The loop condition must evaluate to True.
(iv) (a) A for loop is used for definite iteration, while a while loop is used for indefinite iteration.
(v) (b) for loop
(vi) (a) Yes, if the loop condition is always true.

Case Study 2

Consider the following program to find the number is even or odd with compound statement.

```
n = int(input("Enter a number: "))    #Line 1
print("The number is", __)            #Line 2
d = _____                             #Line 3
if d == _:                            #Line 4
  print("Remainder on division by 2 is:", d)
                                      #Line 5
  print("The number is an even number.")
                                      #Line 6
                                      #Line 7
_____
  print("Remainder on division by 2 is:",
 ________)                            #Line 8
  print("The number is an odd number.")
                                      #Line 9
```

Based on the above program, answer the following questions.

(i) Name the variable which will print by Line 2.

(a) d (b) n
(c) input (d) "Enter a number: "

(ii) Fill in the blank in Line 3.

(a) n / 2 (b) n * 2 (c) n % 2 (d) n - 2

(iii) Which value will be equal to d to satisfy the condition in Line 4?

(a) 1 (b) 2
(c) 0 (d) Any number

(iv) Fill in the blank in Line 7.

(a) if d == 1: (b) else:
(c) elif d == 1: (d) if d != 0:

(v) Which value will come to print to the odd number?

(a) 0 (b) 1 (c) n (d) d

Ans. (i) (b) n (ii) (c) n % 2
(iii) (c) 0 (iv) (b) else: (v) (d) d

SELF ASSESSMENT TEST

Multiple Choice Questions

1. for loop is also known as

(a) entry control loop (b) exit control loop
(c) Both (a) and (b) (d) None of these

2. Iterative statements evaluate the loop condition either.

(a) True (b) False
(c) Both (a) and (b) (d) None of these

3. Find the appropriate loop for the condition when a for loop is to be repeated 50 times.

(a) for i in range (0, 50, 1) : (b) for i in in range (1, 50, 1) :
(c) for i in range (0, 51, 1) : (d) for i in range (0, 1, 50) :

Fill in the Blanks

4. ________ is used to define code blocks in Python.

5. The ________ statement is used to exit a loop prematurely.

6. The ________ statement is used to skip the current iteration of a loop.

7. A loop within a loop is called a ________ loop.

8. ________ statements are used for decision-making in Python.

State Whether True or False

9. Indentation is optional in Python.

10. The break statement exits the current loop.

11. The continue statement skips the remaining code in the current iteration.

12. Nested loops cannot be used in Python.

13. The if-elif-else statement allows multiple conditions to be checked.

Assertion and Reason Based Questions

Assertion (A) and Reason (R) Type questions. Choose the correct option as:

(a) Both Assertion (A) and Reason (R) are true, and Reason (R) is the correct explanation of Assertion (A).
(b) Both Assertion (A) and Reason (R) are true, but Reason (R) is not the correct explanation of Assertion (A).
(c) Assertion (A) is true, but Reason (R) is false.
(d) Assertion (A) is false, but Reason (R) is true.

14. Assertion (A) Indentation is crucial in Python.
Reason (R) Indentation defines code blocks and ensures proper flow control.

15. Assertion (A) The break statement can be used to terminate a loop.
Reason (R) The break statement immediately exits the innermost loop.

16. Assertion (A) The continue statement exits the entire loop.
Reason (R) Python supports nested loops for complex iterations.

17. Assertion (A) Nested loops allow for complex iterations.
Reason (R) Nested loops are used when an inner loop needs to be executed multiple times for each iteration of an outer loop.

18. Assertion (A) Python loops always require a break statement to terminate.
Reason (R) Python's indentation rules enhance code readability.

Very Short Answer Type Questions

19. What is the smallest unit of execution in Python?

20. Write one difference between for loop and while loop.

21. The program execution starts with which statement?

Short Answer Type Questions

22. Find the syntax errors, if any, in the following program.

```
max = 0
a = int (input("Enter the value of a"))
b = int (input ("Enter the value of b"))
if (a>>b):
max = a
print (max):
```

23. What are the logical constructs used in for loop?

24. Write a program that accept a number and print cube of that number.

25. Write a program to find the sum of 3 numbers.

26. Is it necessary to write else with every if statement while writing nested if statements?

27. What will be the output?

(a)
```
if (44):
    print ("Forty four")
```

```
    else:
        print ("None")
(b)if (0):
        print ("Zero")
(c)if(10 == 5):
        print ("Equal")
    else:
        print("Not equal")
```

Long Answer Type Questions

28. Differentiate between if and if-else statements.

29. Give the purpose of iteration statement. What are the other names by which a iteration statement is referred to?

30. Describe a nested if statement.

31. Write a program that will allow an integer from 1 to 7 to be input and the name of the day of week corresponding to the integer to be output.

32. Write a program to input marks in five subjects. Find average and awards grades as per the following guidelines.

Percentage	Grade
90% and above	A
89% and 80%	B
79% and 70%	C
69% and 60%	D
59% and 50%	E
Less than 50%	Fail

33. Write Python program to sum the following series.

(i) $S=1+\frac{1}{2}+\frac{1}{3}+\frac{1}{4}+\frac{1}{5}+\frac{1}{6}+...+\text{n terms}$

(ii) $S=1+\frac{1}{1^2}+\frac{1}{2^3}+\frac{1}{3^4}+...+\text{ n terms}$

Case Study Based Questions

34. A ticket vending machine needs to determine the ticket price based on the customer's age. If the customer is under 12, the ticket price is half. If the customer is 65 or older, the ticket price is also half. Otherwise, the ticket price is full. The machine also needs to handle invalid inputs gracefully.

(i) Which flow control structure is most suitable for determining the ticket price based on age?
(a) for loop (b) while loop
(c) if-elif-else statement (d) break statement

(ii) To ensure the machine handles invalid age inputs, what type of flow control would be useful?
(a) continue statement (b) nested loops
(c) selection (d) repetition

(iii) If the machine needs to repeat the process until a valid age is entered, which flow control structure would be used?
(a) for loop (b) while loop
(c) break statement (d) continue statement

(iv) If the machine needs to stop the current transaction and start a new one if an error occurs, the machine will use:
(a) nested loops (b) continue statement
(c) break statement (d) if statements.

(v) The code blocks within the if-elif-else statements are defined by:
(a) Semicolons (b) Curly braces
(c) Indentation (d) Parentheses

Answers

1. (a) 2. (a) 3. (a) 4. Indentation
5. break 6. continue 7. nested 8. if-elif-else
9. False 10. True 11. True 12. False 13. True
14. (a) 15. (a) 16. (c) 17. (a) 18. (c)
34. (i) → (c), (ii) → (c), (iii) → (b), (iv) → (b), (v) → (c)

10
CHAPTER

In Python, strings are one of the most fundamental data types used to store and manipulate text. Whether you're working with user input, processing files, or displaying messages, understanding strings is essential for effective programming.

Strings

YOUR STUDY GOALS

YOUR PRACTICE GOAL

- Objective Type Questions (27 Qs ; MCQs, True or False, Fill in the Blanks, Assertion and Reason)
- Subjective Type Questions (46 Qs ; VSA, SA, LA)
- Case Study Based Questions-2

String is a sequence which is made up of one or more UNICODE characters. The character can be a letter, digit, whitespace or any other symbol.

In Python, we enclose strings within either single quotes (' ') or double quotes (" "). To create strings that span multiple lines, we use triple quotes (''' ''' or """ """).

e.g.
```
>>> a = '''Python
Programming
Language'''
>>> print (a)
Python
Programming
Language
```

Empty string can also be created in Python.

e.g.
```
>>> str = ' '
>>> print (str)
```

A string is an immutable data type. It means that the contents of the string cannot be changed after it has been created. An attempt to do this would lead to an error.

```
>>> str1 = "Hello World!"
    #if we try to replace character 'e' with 'a'
>>> str1[1] = 'a'
```

TypeError: 'str' object does not support item assignment.

10.1 Accessing Values in Strings

To access specific characters or parts of a string, we use indexing and slicing. Indexing uses square brackets [] with integer indices starting from 0.

Slicing uses a colon : to specify a range of indices.

For example, `s = "Python Language"`

It is called positive index

0	1	2	3	4	5	6	7	8	9	10	11	12	13	14
P	y	t	h	o	n		L	a	n	g	u	a	g	e
−15	−14	−13	−12	−11	−10	−9	−8	−7	−6	−5	−4	−3	−2	−1

It is called negative index

```
>>>s[6]
' '
>>>s[2 : 6]
'thon'
>>>s[5]
'n'
>>>s[-6]
'n'
>>>s[:6]
'Python'
>>>s[5:]
'n Language'
>>>s[: -3]
'Python Langu'
>>>s[-2:]
'ge'
>>>s[-2 : -6]
' '
>>>s[-7 : -3]
'angu'
```

If we try to access index out of the range or use decimal number, we will get errors.

```
>>> s[15]
Trackback (most recent call last):
File "<pyshell#14>", line 1, in <module>
   s[15]
IndexError : string index out of range
>>>s[4.5]
Trackback (most recent call last) :
File "<pyshell#15>", line 1, in <module>
   s[4.5]
TypeError : string indices must be integers
```

10.2 Traversing a String

Traversing a string means going through each character of the string one by one, typically from left end to the right end. This is a common technique used in many programming tasks that involve working with strings, character by character.

Python allows two ways to traverse a string are as follows

Using for loop

for statement can iterate over the elements of a sequence or string. It is used when you want to traverse all characters of a string.

e.g.
```
>>> sub = "COMPUTER"
>>> for i in sub:
     print (i, end = " ")
```

Output

C O M P U T E R

Or
```
>>> sub = "COMPUTER"
>>> for i in range (len(sub)):
         print (sub [i], '-', end = " ")
```

Output

C-O-M-P-U-T-E-R

Using while loop

A while loop can also be used to iterate over the characters of a string, but it requires more explicit index management.

e.g.
```
string = "Arihant, world!"
index = 0
while index < len(string):
    print(string[index], end = " ")
    index += 1
```

Output

Arihant, world !

10.3 String Operators

We can manipulate a string in different ways to use various operators. Here, we will discuss basic operators, comparison operators, membership operators, identity operators and slicing operators

Basic Operators

There are two basic operators in Python as + and *, As you know, + operator is used for addition and * operator is used for multiplication. But in Python, + operator is used for concatenation and * operator is used for replication.

These operators are as follows

String Concatenation Operator (+)

String concatenation is a very common operation in programming. It is used to merge or join two strings.

e.g.
```
s1 = 'Here'
s2 = 'Is'
```

```
s3 = 'Python'
s = s1 + s2 + s3
print (s)
```

Output

HereIsPython

e.g.
```
s1 = input("Enter first string:")
s2 = input("Enter second string:")
s = s1 + s2
print ("Concatenated string:", s)
```

Output

Enter first string: Python
Enter second string: Programming
Concatenated string: PythonProgramming

If you use + operator with integers, then it will add these values as

```
>>> c = 7 + 6
>>> print (c)
13
```

But if you take these integers as strings, then it will concatenate them as follows:

```
>>> c = '7' + '6'
>>> print (c)
76
```

When you take one value as integer and other as string and concatenate them with (+) operator, it will give an error as TypeError.

```
>>>C = '7' + 6
>>>print(C)
Trackback (most recent call last):
File "main.py", line 1, in <module>
  C = '7' + 6
TypeError : cannot concatenate 'str' and
                          'int' objects
```

String Replication Operator (*)

Sometimes we may be required to perform certain operations on string repetitively. To do this, a string replication operator is used. Asterisk sign (*) when used with a numeric data type it performs a multiplication operation. But when this sign is used with one string and one number it performs string replication operation.

e.g.
```
>>> a = 2 * "Hello"
>>> print (a)
HelloHello
```

Here, "Hello" shows the string and 2 shows the number of times that the string is to be replicated.

But if we use (*) operator with two integers, then it will perform multiplication on these numbers.

e.g.
```
>>> c = 7 * 4
>>> print (c)
28
```

When we take two strings with (*) operator, it will give error.

e.g.
```
>>> c = '7' * '4'
>>> print (c)
Trackback(most recent call last) :
  File "main.py", line 1, in <module>
    C = '7'*'4'
  TypeError : cannot multiply sequence by
  non-int of type 'str'
```

Comparison Operators

To compare two strings in Python, we use the same comparison operators as we do for numbers: ==, >, <, !=, <=, and >=. These operators check if two strings are equal, one is greater than the other, or if they are not equal. The comparison is based on the alphabetical order of the characters in the strings.

For example, "apple" is less than "banana" because 'a' comes before 'b' in the alphabet.

e.g.
```
>>> a = 'Python'
>>> b = 'PYTHON'
>>> a > b
True
```

e.g.
```
>>> a = 'Python'
>>> b = 'PYTHON'
>>> a == b
False
```

Membership Operators

Membership operators help us to check if a specific character or substring is present within a string. Python has two main membership operators

in Operator

The in operator is used to check if a specific value is present within a sequence like a string or a list. It returns True if the value is found, and False otherwise.

e.g.
```
>>> list1 = ['hi', 'hello', 'namaste',
                                'hiiii']

>>> 'hiii' in list1
False
>>> 'a' in 'apple'
True
```

not in Operator

The not in operator is the opposite of the in operator. It checks if a specific value is not present within a sequence like a string or a list. If the value is not found, it returns True; otherwise, it returns False.

e.g.
```
>>> list1 = ['hi', 'hello', 'namaste', 'hiiii']
>>> 'hiii' not in list1
True
>>> 'a' not in 'apple'
False
```

Identity Operators

Identity operators in Python are used to determine whether a value is of a certain class or type. They are usually used to determine the type of data which a certain variable contains.

Python has two main identity operators

is Operator

This operator returns True if both the operands point to the same memory location.

e.g.
```
>>> a = "abc"
>>> type(a) is str
True
>>> b = 23.5
>>> type(b) is int
False
```

is not Operator

This operator returns True if both the operands point to different memory location.

e.g.
```
>>> a = "abc"
>>> type(a) is not str
False
>>> b = 23.5
>>> type(b) is not int
True
```

Slicing Operators

String slicing is a powerful technique in Python that allows you to select a specific portion of a string by specifying the starting and ending positions.

Below are the operators used for slicing:

Operators	Syntax	Example

Basic Slicing	`string[start : end]`	`string = "Hello, World!"`
		`print(string[1 : 5])`
		Output "ello"

Omitting Indices	`string[: end]`
	string[start :]
		`print(string[:5])`
		Output "Hello"
		`print(string[6:])`
		Output "World!"

Step Sizing	`string[start:end:step]`	`print(string[0:10:2])`
		Output
		`"HloWr" (every other character)`

Negative Indexing	`string[-start : -end]`	`print(string[-6:-1])` **Output** "World"

10.4 Built-in String Methods

Python includes the following built-in methods to manipulate strings:

Method	Description	Example

len( )	Returns the length of the string.
	Syntax len(string)
		`>>>s = 'Python Program'`
		`>>> l = len(s)`
		`>>> print(l)`
		`14`

capitalize( )	This method is used to capitalize first character of a string.
	Syntax string.capitalize( )
		`>>> s = 'arihant'`
		`>>>s.capitalize()`
		`'Arihant'`
		`>>>'hello'.capitalize()`
		`'Hello'`
		`>>> 'how are you'.capitalize ()`
		`'How are you'`

title ( )	This method is used to convert the first character in each word to uppercase and remaining characters to lowercase in string and returns new string.
	Syntax str. title ( )
		`>>> str = 'Honesty is the best policy'`
		`>>> str1 = str.title ()`
		`>>> print (str1)`
		`Honesty 'Is' The Best Policy`

Method	Description	Example

lower( )	Converts all uppercase letters in string to lowercase.
	Syntax string.lower( )
		`>>>s = 'Python'`
		`>>>s.lower()`
		`'python'`
		`>>>s = 'PYTHON'`
		`>>>s.lower()`
		`'python'`

upper( )	This method is used to convert lowercase letters in string to uppercase.
	Syntax string.upper( )
		`>>>s = 'Hello'`
		`>>>s.upper()`
		`HELLO`
		`>>>s1 = 'Hello World'`
		`>>>s1.upper()`
		`'HELLO WORLD'`

count(str, start, end)	This method returns the number of occurrences of a substring in the given string.
	Syntax string.count(substring, start, end)
		`>>>s = 'He loves his books and his toys)`
		`>>>s.count ("his")`
		`2`
		`>>>s.count ("his", 0, 15)`
		`1`

find(str, start, end)	It returns the lower index of the substring if it is found in the given string. If it is not found, then it returns –1.
	Syntax string. find (substring, start, end)
		`>>>s = 'This is wow world'`
		`>>>s.find ('wow')`
		`8`
		`>>>s.find ('is')`
		`2`
		`>>>s.find ('the')`
		`-1`
		`>>>s.find ('is', 10, 15)`
		`-1`

rfind(str, start, end)	This method finds the last occurence of the specified value and returns – 1 if the value is not found.
	Syntax string. rfind (substring, start, end)
		`>>>s = "Hello, welcome to my world."`
		`>>>s = s.rfind("e", 5, 10)`
		`8`

index(str, start, end)	Same as find() method, but raises an exception if substring is not found.
	Syntax string.index(substring, start, end)
		`>>>s = 'This is world'`
		`>>>s.index ('is')`
		`2`
		`>>>s.index ('is', 10, 15)`
		`ValueError : substring not found`

endswith( )	Determines if a string or a substring endswith suffix; returns True, if so and False otherwise.
	Syntax string.endswith(suffix, start, end)
		`>>>s = 'This is wow world.'`
		`>>>s.endswith ('world.')`
		`True`
		`>>>s.endswith ('world')`
		`False`

startswith( )	Determines if a string or a substring of string starts with substring; returns True, if so and False otherwise.
	Syntax
	string.startswith(str, beg = 0, end = len (string))
		`>>>s = 'This is world'`
		`>>>s.startswith('This')`
		`True`
		`>>>s.startswith('is', 5, 8)`
		`True`
		`>>>s.startswith('is', 3, 5)`
		`False`

isalnum( )	Returns True if string has atleast 1 character and all characters are alphabetic and False otherwise.
	Syntax string.isalnum( )
		`>>>s = 'python'`
		`>>>s.isalnum ()`
		`True`
		`>>>s = ' '`
		`>>>s.isalnum ()`
		`False`
		`>>> s = 'program10'`
		`>>>s.isalnum()`

Method	Description	Example
		True >>>s = '5676' >>>s.isalnum() True
isalpha( )	Returns True if string has atleast 1 character and all characters are alphabetic and False otherwise. **Syntax** string.isalpha( )	>>>str = 'arihant' >>> str.isalpha() True >>>str = 'arihant2' >>>str.isalpha() False >>>str = ' ' >>> str.isalpha() False
isdigit( )	Returns True if string contains only digits and False otherwise. **Syntax** string.isdigit( )	>>>s = '54537' >>>s.isdigit() True >>>s1 = 'xyz534' >>>s1.is digit() False >>>s = ' ' >>>s.is digit() False
islower( )	Returns True if string has at least 1 case character and all case characters are in lowercase and False otherwise. **Syntax** string.islower( )	>>>s = 'python' >>>s.islower() True >>>s = 'Python' >>>s.islower() False >>>s = 'PYTHON' >>>s.islower() False
isupper( )	Returns True if string has atleast one case character and all case characters are in uppercase and False otherwise. **Syntax** string.isupper( )	>>>s = 'HELLO' >>>s.isupper() True >>>s = 'Hello' >>>s.isupper() False >>>s1 = 'DELHI6' >>>s1.isupper() True >>>s2 = '2345' >>>s2.isupper() False
isspace( )	Returns True if string contains only whitespace characters and False otherwise. **Syntax** string.isspace( )	>>>s = ' ' >>>s.isspace() True >>>s = 'How are you?' >>>s.isspace() False

Method	Description	Example
lstrip( )	This method is used to remove all leading whitespace in string. **Syntax** string. lstrip( )	>>>s = ‘ How are you?’ >>>s.lstrip() ‘How are you?’ >>>s1 = ‘ Hello ’ >>>s1.lstrip() ‘Hello ’ >>>s2 = ‘Hello’ >>>s2.lstrip (‘He’) ‘llo’
rstrip( )	Removes all trailing whitespace of string. **Syntax** string.rstrip( )	>>>s = ‘ Hello ’ >>>s.rstrip () ‘ Hello’ >>>s1 = ‘***Hello***’ >>>s1.rstrip (‘*’) ‘***Hello’

strip ( )	It returns a copy of the string with both leading and trailing characters removed (based on the string argument passed).
	Syntax
	string. strip ([chars])
		>>> str = ‘*** Health is wealth ***’
		>>> str1 = str.strip (‘*’)
		>>> print (str1)
		Health is wealth

replace(old str, new str)	Replaces all occurrences of old in string with new or at most max occurrences if max given **Syntax** string.replace(old, new[, max])	>>>s = ‘This is wow, time is great’ >>>s.replace (‘is’, ‘was’) ‘Thwas was wow, time was great’ >>>s.replace (‘is’, ‘was’, 2) ‘Thwas was wow, time is great’
join( )	This method is a string method that returns a string in which the elements of sequence have been joined by string separator. **Syntax** string.join(iterable)	>>>list1 = [‘H’, ‘E’, ‘L’, ‘L’, ‘O’] >>>s = ‘–’ >>>s1 = s.join(list1) >>>print(s1) H-E-L-L-O

partition ( )	This splits the string at the first occurrence of the separator and returns a tuple containing the part before separator, separator and the part after the separator. Here, separator is a string which is given has the argument.
	Syntax
	string. partition (separator)
		>>> str = ‘Honesty is the best policy’
		>>>print (str.partition (‘is’))
		(‘Honesty’, ‘is’, the best policy’)
		>>> print (str.partition (‘great’))
		(‘Honesty is the best policy’,‘’,‘’)

split( )	Splits string according to delimiter string and returns list of substring; split into at most num substrings if given **Syntax** string.split (“delimiter”, num)	>>>s = ‘11-This 12-is 13-wow’ >>>s.split() [‘11-This’, ‘12-is’, ‘13-wow’] >>>s.split (‘–’, 2) [‘11’, ‘This 12’, ‘is 13-wow’] >>>s.split (‘–’, 3) [‘11’, ‘This 12’, ‘is 13’, ‘wow’]
swapcase( )	This method is used to invert case for all letters in string. **Syntax** string.swapcase( )	>>>s = ‘This is Wow World’ >>>s.swapcase() ‘tHIS IS wOW wORLD’

istitle()	It returns True if the string is a titlecased string, False otherwise.
	Syntax string.istitle()
		>>> str = 'The Quick Brown Fox'
		>>> str1 = str.istitle()
		>>> print(str1)
		True

10.5 Programs

1. Python program to check whether entered string is palindrome or not.

Ans.
```
string = input("Enter the string :")
str1 = ""
for i in string:
    str1 = i + str1
print("String in reverse order :", str1)
if(string == str1):
    print("This is a palindrome string")
else:
    print("This is not a palindrome string")
```

Output

Enter the string : madam

String in reverse order : madam

This is a palindrome string

2. Python program to remove the characters of odd index values in a string.

Ans.
```
str1 = input("Enter the string:")
final = ""
for i in range (len(str1)):
    if i%2 == 0:
        final = final + str1[i]
print("Modified string is:", final)
```

Output

Enter the string:Learn Programming

Modified string is: LanPormig

3. Python program for following pattern.

```
*
* *
* * *
* * * *
* * * * *
* * * * * *
```

Ans.
```
str1 = "*"
a = " "
for i in range (6):
    a + = str1
    print(a)
```

4. Python program to remove the nth index character from a non-empty string.

Ans.
```
string = input("Enter the sring:")
n=int(input("Enter the index of the
                character to remove:"))
first = string[:n]
last = string[n + 1:]
print("Modified string:", first + last)
```

Output

Enter the sring:Programming

Enter the index of the character to remove:6

Modified string:Programing

5. Python program to form a new string made of the first 2 and last 2 characters from a given string.

Ans.
```
string1 = input("Enter string:")
cn = 0
for i in string1:
    cn = cn+1
new = string1[0:2] + string1[cn-2:cn]
print("Newly formed string is:")
print(new)
```

Output

Enter string : wonders world
Newly formed string is:
wold

Mind Map

STRINGS

String is a sequence which is made up of one or more UNICODE characters. The character can be a letter, digit, whitespace or any other symbol.

Accessing Values in Strings

To access specific characters or parts of a string, we use indexing and slicing. Indexing uses square brackets [] with integer indices starting from 0. Slicing uses a colon : to specify a range of indices.

- **Indexing** Accessing individual characters [e.g. S[0]]
- **Slicing** Extracting Substring [e.g. S[2:6]]
- **Negative indexing** [e.g. S[−1]]

Traversing a String

Traversing a string means going through each character of the string one by one, typically from left end to the right end.

Using for loop

e.g.

```
>>> sub = "COMPUTER"
>>> for i in sub:
        print (i, end = " ")
```

Using while loop

e.g.

```
string = "Arihant, world!"
index = 0
while index < len(string):
  print(string[index], end = " ")
  index += 1
```

Built-in String Methods

Methods	Syntax
len( )	len(string)
capitalize( )	string.capitalize( )
title ( )	string. title ( )
lower( )	string.lower( )
upper( )	string.upper( )
count(str,start, end)	string.count(substring, start, end)
find(str, start,end)	string. find (substring, start, end)
index(str, start, end)	string.index(substring, start, end)
isalpha( )	string.isalpha( )
isdigit( )	string.isdigit( )
islower( )	string.islower( )
isupper( )	string.isupper( )
strip ( )	string. strip ([chars])
join( )	string.join(iterable)

String Operators

Basic Operators

There are two basic operators in Python as + and *. + operator is used for concatenation and * operator is used for replication.

String Concatenation Operator (+)

e.g.

```
s1 = 'Here'
s2 = 'Is'
s3 = 'Python'
s = s1 + s2 + s3
print (s)
```

String Replication Operator (*)

e.g.

```
>>> a = 2 * "Hello"
>>> print (a)
HelloHello
```

Comparison Operators

To compare two strings in Python, we use the same comparison operators as we do for numbers: ==, >, <, !=, <=, and >=.

Membership Operators

Membership operators help us check if a specific character or substring is present within a string.

Python has two main membership operators- **in Operator, not in Operator.**

Identity Operators

Identity operators in Python are used to determine whether a value is of a certain class or type.

Python has two main identity operators - **is Operator, is not Operator.**

Slicing Operators

String slicing is a powerful technique in Python that allows you to select a specific portion of a string by specifying the starting and ending positions.

NCERT Folder

Exercise Questions

1. Consider the following string mySubject:

```
mySubject = "Computer Science"
```

What will be the output of the following string operations?

(i) `print(mySubject[0:len(mySubject)])`
(ii) `print(mySubject[-7:-1])`
(iii) `print(mySubject[::2])`
(iv) `print(mySubject[len(mySubject)-1])`
(v) `print(2*mySubject)`
(vi) `print(mySubject[::-2])`
(vii) `print(mySubject[:3] + mySubject[3:])`
(viii) `print(mySubject.swapcase())`
(ix) `print(mySubject.startswith('Comp'))`
(x) `print(mySubject.isalpha())`

Ans. (i) **Output** Computer Science

This traverses the string from the beginning to the end.

(ii) **Output** Scienc

This slices the string from the 7th character from the end to the 1st character from the end.

(iii) **Output** Cmue cec

This slices the string with a step size of 2, taking every other character.

(iv) **Output** e

This accesses the last character of the string.

(v) **Output** Computer ScienceComputer Science

This concatenates the string with itself.

(vi) **Output** eniSrtpo

This reverses the string and takes every other character.

(vii) **Output** Computer Science

This concatenates the first 3 characters with the remaining characters.

(viii) **Output** cOMPUTER sCIENCE

This swaps the case of each character.

(ix) **Output** True

This checks if the string starts with the substring 'Comp'.

(x) **Output** False

This checks if all characters in the string are alphabets.

2. Consider the following string myAddress:

```
myAddress = "WZ-1,New Ganga Nagar,New
Delhi"
```

What will be the output of following string operations :

(i) `print(myAddress.lower())`
(ii) `print(myAddress.upper())`
(iii) `print(myAddress.count('New'))`
(iv) `print(myAddress.find('New'))`
(v) `print(myAddress.rfind('New'))`
(vi) `print(myAddress.split(','))`
(vii) `print(myAddress.split(' '))`
(viii) `print(myAddress.replace('New','Old'))`
(ix) `print(myAddress.partition(','))`
(x) `print(myAddress.index('Agra'))`

Ans. (i) **Output** wz-1,new ganga nagar,new delhi

This converts all characters to lowercase.

(ii) **Output** WZ-1,NEW GANGA NAGAR,NEW DELHI

This converts all characters to uppercase.

(iii) **Output** 2

This counts the occurrences of the substring 'New'.

(iv) **Output** 5

This finds the first index of the substring 'New'.

(v) **Output** 21

This finds the last index of the substring 'New'.

(vi) **Output** ['WZ-1', 'New Ganga Nagar', 'New Delhi']

This splits the string at commas.

(vii) **Output** ['WZ-1, New', 'Ganga', 'Nagar, New', 'Delhi']

This splits the string into spaces.

(viii) **Output** WZ-1,Old Ganga Nagar,Old Delhi

This replaces all occurrences of 'New' with 'Old'.

(ix) **Output** ('WZ-1', ',', 'New Ganga Nagar,New Delhi')

This partitions the string at the first occurrence of the separator.

(x) **Output** ValueError: substring not found

The substring 'Agra' is not found in the string.

Programming Based Question

1. Write a program to input line(s) of text from the user until enter is pressed. Count the total number of characters in the text (including white spaces),total number of alphabets, total number of digits, total number of special symbols and total number of words in the given text. (Assume that each word is separated by one space).

Ans.

```
text = input("Enter your text (and hit
                                Enter): ")
```

```
char_count = 0
alpha_count = 0
digit_count = 0
symbol_count = 0
word_count = 1
for char in text:
    char_count += 1
    if char.isalpha():
        alpha_count += 1
    elif char.isdigit():
        digit_count += 1
    elif char.isspace():
        word_count += 1
    else:
        symbol_count += 1
print("Total characters:", char_count)
print("Total alphabets:", alpha_count)
print("Total digits:", digit_count)
print("Total symbols:", symbol_count)
print("Total words:", word_count)
```

Output

Enter your text (and hit Enter): Hello friends!!!
Total characters: 16
Total alphabets: 12
Total digits: 0
Total symbols: 3
Total words: 2

EXAM PATTERN QUESTIONS

Objective Type Questions

Multiple Choice Questions

1. String literals in Python are enclosed by

(a) double quotes (b) single quotes
(c) Both (a) and (b) (d) All of these

2. Consider a string variable named text that contains the phrase "Python Programming". How would you access the last character 'g' using its index position? Competency Based Que.

(a) text[17]
(b) text[18]
(c) text[-1]
(d) Both (a) and (c)

3. Which operator is used to repeat a string multiple times in Python?

(a) + (b) -
(c) * (d) /

4. Slice operation is performed on string with the use of

(a) ; (b) ,
(c) : (d) .

5. This method returns the length of the string

(a) len()
(b) length()
(c) l()
(d) leng()

6. This function converts all uppercase letters in string to lowercase letters.

(a) upper() (b) lower()
(c) isupper() (d) islower()

7. You have a string variable named sentence containing the value "apple,banana,cherry". You want to split this string into three parts using the comma (,) as the separator, preserving the separator itself. Which of the following Python expressions would achieve this, and what would be the resulting output? Competency Based Que.

(a) `sentence.partition(',') Output: ('apple', ',', 'banana,cherry')`
(b) `sentence.split(',') Output: ['apple', 'banana', 'cherry']`
(c) `sentence.partition(',') Output: (',', 'apple', 'banana,cherry')`
(d) `sentence.split(',') Output: ['apple', ',', 'banana', ',', 'cherry']`

Fill in the Blanks

8. The length of an empty string is ---________.

9. ________ is used to display the output in next line.

10. Triple quotes are used to represent _____ strings.

11. Using float for index results in ________.

12. Python compares the strings on the basis of _______

State Whether True or False

13. Traversing a string using a for loop in Python is always more efficient than using a while loop.

14. Negative indexing in Python allows you to access characters in a string from the end, starting with -1 for the last character.

15. The + operator can be used to concatenate both strings and numbers in Python.

16. The in operator can be used to check if a substring exists within a larger string.

17. The is operator returns True if two variables refer to the same memory location, regardless of their data types.

18. Slicing in Python, using the [start:end] notation, creates a new list containing the elements from the original list, including the element at the end index.

19. The join() method can only be used to concatenate strings within a list.

20. The max() function returns the maximum alphabetical character in a string, regardless of case.

Assertion and Reason Based Questions

Assertion (A) and Reason (R) Type questions. Choose the correct option as:

(a) Both Assertion (A) and Reason (R) are true, and Reason (R) is the correct explanation of Assertion (A).

(b) Both Assertion (A) and Reason (R) are true, but Reason (R) is not the correct explanation of Assertion (A).

(c) Assertion (A) is true, but Reason (R) is false.

(d) Assertion (A) is false, but Reason (R) is true.

21. Assertion (A) Strings in Python are immutable.

Reason (R) Once a string is created, its characters cannot be modified.

22. Assertion (A) The in operator can be used to check if a substring exists within a string.

Reason (R) The in operator returns True if the substring is found, otherwise False.

23. Assertion (A) Slicing is a technique to extract a portion of a string.

Reason (R) Slicing uses square brackets [] with colon : operator to specify the range of indices.

24. Assertion (A) The capitalize() method capitalizes the first character of a string.

Reason (R) It converts all other characters to lowercase.

25. Assertion (A) The split() method divides a string into a list of substrings based on a delimiter.

Reason (R) The delimiter is a character or sequence of characters that separates the substrings.

26. Assertion (A) The replace() method replaces all occurrences of a specific substring with another substring.

Reason (R) It returns a new string with the replacements.

27. Assertion (A) The join() method concatenates elements of a list into a string.

Reason (R) The delimiter used to join the elements is specified as an argument to the join() method.

Answers

1. (*c*) Both (a) and (b)
2. (*d*) Both (a) and (c)
3. (c) *
4. (*c*) :
5. (*a*) len()
6. (*b*) lower()
7. (*a*) sentence.partition(',') Output: ('apple', ',', 'banana,cherry')
8. zero/0
9. \n
10. multiline
11. TypeError
12. ASCII
13. False
14. True
15. False
16. True
17. True
18. False
19. False
20. False
21. (a) Both Assertion (A) and Reason (R) are true, and Reason (R) is the correct explanation of Assertion (A).
22. (a) Both Assertion (A) and Reason (R) are true, and Reason (R) is the correct explanation of Assertion (A).
23. (a) Both Assertion (A) and Reason (R) are true, and Reason (R) is the correct explanation of Assertion (A).
24. (a) Both Assertion (A) and Reason (R) are true, and Reason (R) is the correct explanation of Assertion (A).
25. (a) Both Assertion (A) and Reason (R) are true, and Reason (R) is the correct explanation of Assertion (A).
26. (a) Both Assertion (A) and Reason (R) are true, and Reason (R) is the correct explanation of Assertion (A).
27. (a) Both Assertion (A) and Reason (R) are true, and Reason (R) is the correct explanation of Assertion (A).

Subjective Type Questions

Very Short Answer Type Questions

1. What is string?

Ans. A sequence of characters is called string.

2. How to create an empty string?

Ans. string1=‘ ’

3. Are strings mutable or immutable?

Ans. Strings are immutable which means they cannot be changed after being created.

4. Which index number is used to represent the last character of a string?

Ans. -1

5. What is the primary purpose of string traversal?

Ans. To access each individual character within a string.

6. Observe the output

```
>>> s = 'Program'
>>> s [-2]
```

Ans. a

7. Find error to represent string.

```
s1 = Hello
```

Ans. Correct is:

```
s1 = "Hello"
```

8. If we try to access a character which is out of range of index, then which type of error will occur?

Ans. IndexError

9. What is the primary function of the + operator when used with strings in Python?

Ans. The primary function of the + operator is String concatenation (joining strings).

10. Write the output of given code.

```
s1 = 'Hello'
s2 = 'World'
s = s1+ s2
print (s)
```

Ans. HelloWorld

11. Observe the output

```
>>> c = '7' + 2
>>> print (c)
```

Ans. It will give TypeError because integer and string cannot be concatenate.

12. What do you mean by less than (<) operator?

Ans. Less than (<) operator checks if the left value (ASCII) is lesser than that on the right.

13. Write the output.

```
>>> x = 'Python'
>>> y = 'PYTHON'
>>> x < y
```

Ans. False

14. What is identity operator?

Ans. Identity operators in Python are used to determine whether a value is of a certain class or type.

15. Write the syntax of count() method in string.

Ans. string.count(substring, start, end)

16. Observe the output

```
>>> 'Program'.find('r')
```

Ans. 1

17. What is the use of isdigit() method in Python?

Ans. isdigit() method returns True, if string contains only digits and False otherwise.

18. Identify the Python string method that returns a lowercase version of a given string.

Ans. lower()

Short Answer Type I Questions

19. Can string literals span multiple lines? Also, give an example.

Ans. Yes, string literals can be span multiple lines. To write these strings triple quotes " " " or ' ' ' are used.

e.g.

```
>>>x = '''wonder
of
world'''
>>>print(x)
```

Output

wonder
of
world

20. How to access values in strings?

Ans. To access the individual element of a string, indexing is used. With the use of index operator [ ], we can access the values of strings. Python allows both positive and negative indexing for its sequence.

e.g. `string1="Hello world"`

It is called positive index

0	1	2	3	4	5	6	7	8	9	10
H	e	l	l	o		w	o	r	l	d
–11	–10	–9	–8	–7	–6	–5	–4	–3	–2	–1

It is called negative index

21. How can you traverse a string using for loop?

Ans. For statement can iterate over the elements of a sequence or string. It is used when you want to traverse all characters of string.

e.g.

```
>>>str="Program"
>>>for i in str:
        print(i)
```

Output

P
r
o
g
r
a
m

22. Explain how the asterisk operator (*) is used in Python to create a new string by repeating an existing string, and provide an example. **Competency Based Que.**

Ans. The asterisk operator (*) replicates a string a specified number of times. When used with a string and an integer n, it creates a new string that consists of the original string repeated n times.

e.g.
```
text = "Hello" * 2
print(text)
```

Output HelloHello

23. Describe the purpose and behavior of the == and in operators in Python, illustrating their usage with concise examples. **Competency Based Que.**

Ans. (i) **== Operator** The == operator compares the values (ASCII) of two operands. It returns True if the values are equal and False otherwise. It performs a case-sensitive comparison for strings.

e.g.
```
string1 = "Python"
string2 = "python"
print(string1 == string2)
```

Output False

(ii) **in Operator** The in operator checks if a value exists within a sequence (like a string, list, or tuple). It returns True if the value is found and False otherwise.

e.g.
```
text = "Programming"
print("gram" in text)
```

Output True

24. Find the output.

(i) 'are'.capitalize()

(ii) 'Hello'.endswith('lo')

(iii) 'How are you?'. find('a')

(iv) str=' '
str.isalpha()

Ans. (i) Are (ii) True
(iii) 4 (iv) False

25. Given a string, how can you determine if it is in title case? Define "title case" and provide an example of a string that is not in title case, explaining why. **Competency Based Que.**

Ans. A string is in title case if the first character of each word is uppercase, and all remaining characters are lowercase.

Example of a string NOT in title case:

"my name is Rahul"

This string is not in title case because the words "my", "name", and "is" do not start with uppercase letters. Only the word "Rahul" is correctly title cased.

26. Write the short note on

(i) isupper()

(ii) join()

Ans. (i) **isupper()** Returns True if string has atleast 1 cased character and all cased characters are in uppercase and False otherwise.

Syntax string.isupper()

(ii) **join()** Returns a string in which the elements of sequence have been joined by string separator.

Syntax string.join(iterable)

27. For each of the following tasks related to string manipulation in Python, identify the appropriate built-in function or method and briefly explain its purpose. **Competency Based Que.**

(i) Determine the number of characters in a given string.

(ii) Create a new string by removing any leading spaces from an existing string.

(iii) Find the character with the lowest ASCII value within a string.

Ans. (i) **len() function** It returns the number of characters (length) of the string.

(ii) **lstrip() method** It removes all leading whitespace characters (spaces, tabs, newlines) from the left side of the string, returning a new string.

(iii) **min() function** It returns the character with the lowest ASCII value from the string. If the string is empty, it raises a ValueError.

28. Predict the output.

(i) `'wonders'.center(12, '*')`

(ii) `'wonders25'.isalnum( )`

(iii) `'Hello1235'.isdigit()`

(iv) `'Hi Hello'.istitle()`

(v) `'This is nice'.endswith("nice")`

(vi) `"wonder".zfill(10)`

Ans. (i) '**wonders***'

(ii) True

(iii) False

(iv) True

(v) True

(vi) 0000wonder

Short Answer Type II Questions

29. **Write the short note on**

(a) **title ( )**

(b) **strip ( )**

Ans. (a) **title ( )** This method is used to convert the first character in each word to uppercase and remaining characters to lowercase in string and returns new string.

(b) **strip ( )** It returns a copy of the string with both leading and trailing characters removed (based on the string argument passed).

30. **Explain the behavior of the partition() method in Python when applied to a string. Specifically, discuss what happens when the separator is not found within the string, and provide the general syntax.**

Competency Based Que.

Ans. The partition() method is used to split a string into three parts based on the first occurrence of a specified separator. It returns a tuple containing:

1. The part of the string before the separator.
2. The separator itself.
3. The part of the string after the separator.

If the separator is not found within the string, the partition() method behaves as follows:

It returns a tuple where

- The first element is the original string itself.
- The second and third elements are empty strings.

General Syntax string.partition(separator)

31. **Predict the output and explain the reasoning behind each output, paying close attention to edge cases like negative indices and out-of-bounds access.**

Competency Based Que.

```
str = "Programming language"
```

(i) **str[3:5]** (ii) **str[-25]**

(iii) **str[-8]** (iv) **str[6:]**

Ans. (i) **Output** 'gr'

Reasoning Indexing starts at 0. [3:5] extracts characters from index 3 up to, but not including, 5.

(ii) **Output** IndexError: string index out of range

Reasoning Negative indexing starts from the end. -25 is out of bounds for a string of length 20.

(iii) **Output** 'T'

Reasoning Negative indexing counts from the end. -8 is the 8th character from the end.

(iv) **Output** 'mming language'

Reasoning [6:] extracts the substring starting from index 6 to the end.

32. **Write the program to print following pattern.**

```
#
# #
# # #
# # # #
```

Ans.

```
str1="#"
a = " "
for i in range (4):
    a+= str1
    print(a)
```

33. **Analyze the following code snippets and explain why one results in a TypeError and the other in a valid string concatenation. Provide the correct method to achieve string repetition instead of addition.**

Competency Based Que.

(i) a = 'A' + '2'

(ii) a = 'A' + 2

Ans. (i) a = 'A' + '2'

Output 'A2'

Explanation This code performs valid string concatenation. The + operator, when used with two strings, joins them together. Here, 'A' and '2' are both string literals, so they are concatenated to form the new string 'A2'.

(ii) a = 'A' + 2

Output TypeError: can only concatenate str (not "int") to str

Explanation This code results in a TypeError. The reason is that the + operator cannot directly concatenate a string ('A') with an integer (2). Python requires both operands of the + operator to be of the same data type when working with strings.

To achieve string repetition, you should use the * operator. This operator allows you to repeat a string a specified number of times.

e.g.
```
a = 'A' * 3
        # Repeat 'A' three times
print(a)   # Output: 'AAA'
```

34. **Find the output of given code.**

```
s='Hello'
s1 = '20'
s2 = 'World'
```

```
a = 4
b = 6
print(s + s2)
print (a + b + 16)
print (s1*a)
print(s*2)
print(s + s2 + s1)
```

Ans. HelloWorld

26

20202020

HelloHello

HelloWorld20

35. **Find the output.**

s = "Python Program"

(i) s[7] (ii) s[–4]

(iii) s[5:] (iv) s[:2]

(v) s[–1 : –4] (vi) s[1 : 4]

Ans. (i) 'P' (ii) 'g'

(iii) 'n Program' (iv) 'Py'

(v) ' ' (vi) 'yth'

Long Answer Type Questions

36. **Write a Python Program to called longest_word(sentence) that takes a string sentence as input and returns the longest word in that sentence. Assume that words are separated by spaces.**

Ans.

```
sentence = input("Enter a sentence: ")
words = sentence.split()
longest = ""
for word in words:
    cleaned_word = ''.join(char for char in
word if char.isalnum())
    if len(cleaned_word) > len(longest):
        longest = cleaned_word
print("Longest word:", longest)
```

37. **Find the output.**

str = "Computer Science"

(i) str[2]

(ii) str[–4]

(iii) str[5 : 7]

(iv) str[: 8]

(v) str[: –2]

(vi) str[–2 : –6]

(vii) str [2 :]

(viii) str[–20]

Ans. (i) 'm' (ii) 'e'

(iii) 'te' (iv) 'Computer'

(v) 'Computer Scien' (vi) ' '

(vii) 'mputer Science' (viii) IndexError

38. **Observe the code and write the output.**

(i) 'arihant publication'.capitalize()

(ii) 'arihant publication'.count('hant', 0, 10)

(iii) 'arihant publication'. endswith ('ion.')

(iv) 'Arihant Publication'.find('The')

(v) 'Arihant Publication'.index('cat')

(vi) 'Arihant Publication'.isalpha()

(vii) 'Arihant Publication'.isdigit()

(viii) 'Arihant Publication'.lower()

Ans. (i) 'Arihant publication' (ii) 1

(iii) False (iv) –1

(v) 13 (vi) False

(vii) False (viii) 'arihant publication'

39. **Consider the following code.**

```
string1=input("Enter string:")
cn = 0
for i in string1:
    cn = cn+1
new=string1[0:2]+string1[cn-2:cn]
print("Newly formed string is:")
print(new)
```

What will be the output when inputs are

(i) Program function (ii) Hello world

(iii) abbcba baccba (iv) abbbcac

Ans. (i) Pron (ii) Held

(iii) abba (iv) abac

40. **Consider the following code.**

```
str1=input("Enter string:")
final=" "
for i in range (len(str1)):
    if i % 2 ! = 0:
        final = final + str1[i]
    print("Modified string is:", final)
```

What will be the output when inputs are entered as

(i) Program (ii) Language

(iii) This is wow world

Ans. (i) rga (ii) agae

(iii) hsi o ol

41. **Python program to calculate the number of uppercase letters and lower case letters in a string.**

Ans.

```
str = input("Enter string:")
c1 = 0
c2 = 0
for i in str:
    if(i.islower()):
```

```
        c1 = c1+1
    elif(i.isupper()):
        c2 = c2+1
print("The number of lowercase
                characters is:")
print(c1)
print("The number of uppercase
                characters is:")
print(c2)
```

Output

Enter string:Python Program EASY
The number of lowercase characters is:
11
The number of uppercase characters is:
6

42. Explain the different string operators in Python. Discuss how each operator is used?

Ans. In Python, strings are sequences of characters, and there are several operators that let you work with and manipulate them. Here's a simple explanation of the key string operators and how they are used:

(i) **Concatenation (+)** The + operator is used to join two or more strings together.

Example:

```
result = "Hello" + " " + "World"
print(result) # Output: "Hello World"
```

(ii) **Repetition (*)** The * operator repeats a string a given number of times.

Example:

```
result = "abc" * 3
print(result) # Output: "abcabcabc"
```

(iii) **Membership (in, not in)** The in and not in operators check if a substring exists in a string.

Example:

```
result = "Hello" in "Hello, World" # True
result = "Python" not in "Hello, World" #
True
```

(iv) **Slicing ([start:end])** Slicing extracts a part of the string by specifying the start and end indices.

Example:

```
result = "Hello, World"[0:5]
print(result) # Output: "Hello"
```

(v) **Comparison (==, !=, <, >, etc.)** String comparison checks if two strings are equal or compares their order.

Example:

```
result = "apple" == "banana"  # False
result = "apple" < "banana"  # True
```

43. Python program to take in two strings and display the larger string without using built-in functions. Also, display its output.

Ans.

```
str1=input("Enter first string:")
str2=input("Enter second string:")
c1 = 0
c2 = 0
for i in str1:
    c1 = c1+1
for j in str2:
    c2 = c2+1
if(c1<c2):
    print("Larger string is:")
    print(str2)
elif(c1== c2):
    print("Both strings are equal.")
else:
    print("Larger string is:")
    print(str1)
```

Output

Enter first string:Program
Enter second string:Python
Larger string is:
Program

44. Find the output.

(i) **str = 'Hello'**
str1 = 'World'
str [–3]
str1 [–5]
str + str1
str1 [0]

(ii) **str = 'Hello'**
str1 = 'World'
str [–2 : –4]
str1 [: –6]
str*2
str1 [–7 :]

(iii) **str = 'Hello'**
str1 = 'World'
str [–2] + str1[4]
str1 [: –6] + str[0]
str1*3
str1 [–7 :] + str [3]

(iv) **str = 'Hello'**
str1 = 'World'
str [–2] + str1[4 : –1]
str1 [1 : –6] + str[0 : 4]
str1 + str
str1 [–7 : –10] + str[3:]

Ans. (i) 'l'
'W'
'HelloWorld'
'W'

(ii) ' '
' '
'HelloHello'
'World'

(iii) 'ld'
'H'
'WorldWorldWorld'
'Worldl'

(iv) 'l'
'Hell'
'WorldHello'
'lo'

45. If str1 = "Hello, world!" is a Python string, then:

(I) (A) **Explain how you would access and print the character at index 4 of the string str1.**

Or

(B) **Explain how you would use slicing to extract and print the substring "world" from str1.**

(II) (A) **Explain how you would traverse the string str1 using a for loop and print each character.**

Or

(B) **Explain how you would use the in operator to check if the substring "llo" is present in str1.**

Ans. (I) (A) Access the character at index 4 using str1[4]:

```
print(str1[4]) # Prints 'o'
```

Or

(B) Use slicing to extract "world" with str1[7:12]:

```
print(str1[7:12]) # Prints 'world'
```

(II) (A) Use a for loop to traverse and print each character in the string:

```
for char in str1: print(char)
```

Or

(B) Use the in operator to check if "llo" is in str1:

```
print("llo" in str1) # Prints True
```

46. **If str1 = "Python" and str2 = "Programming" are Python strings, then:**

(I) (A) **Explain the difference between using the + operator and the * operator with strings, providing examples using str1 and str2.**

Or

(B) **Explain how you would use the len() function to find the length of str2.**

(II) (A) **Explain how you would use the upper() method to convert str1 to uppercase.**

Or

(B) **Explain how you would use the split() method to split str2 into a list of words.**

Ans. (I) (A) The + operator concatenates strings, while the * operator repeats strings:

```
print(str1 + str2)
   # 'PythonProgramming'
print(str1 * 3)
   # 'PythonPythonPython'
```

Or

(B) Use the len() function to find the length of str2:

```
print(len(str2)) # Prints 11
```

(II) (A) Use the upper() method to convert str1 to uppercase:

```
print(str1.upper()) # 'PYTHON'
```

Or

(B) Use the split() method to split str2 into a list of words:

```
print(str2.split())
   # ['Programming']
```

Case Study Based Questions

Case Study 1

In Python, strings are sequences of characters. They are immutable, meaning they cannot be changed once created. To access individual characters or substrings, we use indexing and slicing. Indexing allows us to access a specific character by its position, while slicing allows us to extract a portion of the string. Python provides various string methods to manipulate and analyze text, such as upper(), lower(), capitalize(), find(), replace(), and many more.

Based on the above information, answer the following questions?

(i) **What is the correct way to define a string in Python?**

(a) string = "Hello" (b) string = 'Hello'
(c) Both (a) and (b) (d) None of these

(ii) **Which of the following is not a string method in Python?**

(a) upper() (b) lower()
(c) capitalize() (d) sqrt()

(iii) **What will be the output of the following code?**

```
str1 = "Hello, World!"
print(str1[6:])
```

(a) "Hello" (b) "World!"
(c) "World" (d) "Hello, World!"

(iv) **What is the output of the following code?**

```
text = "Python Programming"
print(text.upper())
```

(a) python programming
(b) PYTHON PROGRAMMING
(c) Python programming
(d) python Programming

(v) **How can you check if a substring exists within a string?**

(a) Using the in operator (b) Using the find() method
(c) Both (a) and (b) (d) None of these

(vi) **What does the replace() method do?**

(a) Replaces all occurrences of a substring with another substring.
(b) Removes a specific character from a string.

(c) Reverses the string.
(d) Splits a string into a list of substrings.

Ans. (i) (c) Both (a) and (b)
(ii) (d) sqrt()
(iii) (b) "World!"
(iv) (b) PYTHON PROGRAMMING
(v) (c) Both (a) and (b)
(vi) (a) Replaces all occurrences of a substring with another substring.

Case Study 2

Consider the following program to take in two strings and display the larger string without using built-in functions.

```
str1=input("Enter first string:")     #Line 1
str2=input("Enter second string:")    #Line 2
c1 = 0                                #Line 3
c2 = _                                #Line 4
for i in str1:                        #Line 5
    c1 = c1+1                         #Line 6
for j in str2:                        #Line 7
    c2 = c2+1                         #Line 8
if(__):                               #Line 9
    print("Larger string is:")        #Line 10
    print(str2)                       #Line 11
elif(__):                             #Line 12
    print("Both strings are equal.")  #Line 13
______                                #Line 14
    print("Larger string is:")        #Line 15
    print(__)                         #Line 16
```

Based on the above program, answer the following questions.

(i) **Which could be assigned to variable c2?**
(a) -1 (b) 1
(c) 0 (d) Any integer

(ii) **Which condition will be used in the if statement?**
(a) c1 > c2 (b) c1 < c2
(c) c1 == c2 (d) c1 != c2

(iii) **Which condition will be used in the elif statement?**
(a) c1 > c2 (b) c1 < c2
(c) c1 == c2 (d) c1 != c2

(iv) **Fill in the blank in Line 14.**
(a) if c1 > c2: (b) elif c1 == c2:
(c) else: (d) if c1 < c2:

(v) **What value will be printed in the last line?**
(a) str1 (b) str2
(c) c1 (d) c2

Ans. (i) (c) 0 (ii) (b) c1 < c2
(iii) (c) c1 == c2 (iv) (c) else:
(v) (a) str1

SELF ASSESSMENT TEST

Multiple Choice Questions

1. A sequence of characters is called
(a) string (b) tuple (c) list (d) dictionary

2. This method is used to capitalize first character of a string.
(a) capital() (b) capitalize()
(c) cap() (d) capitalized()

3. Which system is used for string replication?
(a) # (b) + (c) * (d) –

Fill in the Blanks

4. A sequence of characters is called a ________.
5. The ________ method is used to split a string into a list of substrings.
6. The ________ method is used to find the index of a substring in a string.
7. ________ is the process of accessing each character of a string.
8. The ________ method returns a copy of the string with all characters in lowercase.
9. ________ is the process of ensuring strings are encoded and decoded correctly.

State Whether True or False

10. Strings are mutable in Python.
11. The find() method returns -1 if the substring is not found.
12. String slicing creates a new string.
13. The replace() method modifies the original string.
14. Traversing a string means accessing each character in the string.
15. Python strings can only contain ASCII characters.

Assertion and Reason Based Questions

Assertion (A) and Reason (R) Type questions. Choose the correct option as:

(a) Both Assertion (A) and Reason (R) are true, and Reason (R) is the correct explanation of Assertion (A).
(b) Both Assertion (A) and Reason (R) are true, but Reason (R) is not the correct explanation of Assertion (A).
(c) Assertion (A) is true, but Reason (R) is false.
(d) Assertion (A) is false, but Reason (R) is true.

16. **Assertion (A)** String concatenation modifies the original strings.
Reason (R) Python's string methods offer powerful tools for text manipulation.

17. **Assertion (A)** The replace() method changes the original string in place.
Reason (R) String traversal allows access to individual characters.

18. **Assertion (A)** The find() method returns the first occurrence of a substring.
Reason (R) The find() method searches for the substring from left to right.

19. **Assertion (A)** String slicing creates a new string object.
Reason (R) String slicing extracts a portion of the original string without modifying it.

20. **Assertion (A)** String methods are used to manipulate strings.
Reason (R) String methods provide built-in functions for various string operations.

21. **Assertion (A)** Handling strings is essential for data processing.
Reason (R) Strings are used to represent text data, which needs to be processed correctly.

Very Short Answer Type Questions

22. How to represent negative index in string?
23. Write the output.

```
>>>a="Hello"
>>>a[-6]
```

24. Predict the output.

```
>>>a='2'+3
>>>print(a)
```

Short Answer Type Questions

25. How many operators are there in string? Name them.
26. What are comparison operators which used in string?
27. Write the short note on
(i) Greater than (>) operator.
(ii) Not equal to (!=) operator.
28. Predict the output.

```
>>>x="world"
>>>type(x)is str
>>>x * 2
```

29. Write the syntax for following built-in methods.

(i) center()

(ii) find()

(iii) rstrip

30. Find the error and explain them.

```
>>>a='wonders of world'
>>>a.index('of', 10, 20)
>>>a.find('of')
```

31. Find the output.

(i) 'program_25'.isalpha( )

(ii) '***Hello***'.lstrip('*')

(iii) 'Hello'.zfill(12)

Long Answer Type Questions

32. Write the names of string built-in methods for following.

(i) Performs both lstrip() and rstrip() on string.

(ii) Inverts case for all letters in string.

(iii) Splits strings at all newlines.

(iv) Returns minimum alphabetical character from the string.

33. Write a program to input a string and perform on it lstrip( ) and rstrip( ) methods.

34. Write a program to enter two strings and concate them using concatenation operator.

35. Write a program to enter a string and split the string at all newlines.

36. Write a program to input a string and find out of it to maximum and minimum alphabetical character.

Case Study Based Questions

37. A text analysis tool needs to process a large text file, count the occurrences of specific words, and identify the longest word in the file. The tool should also be able to handle different text encodings and remove punctuation.

(i) To read and process the text file, which Python data type would be most suitable?

(a) List (b) Tuple
(c) String (d) Dictionary

(ii) To count the occurrences of specific words, which string method would be useful?

(a) find()
(b) replace()
(c) count()
(d) split()

(iii) To remove punctuation from the text, which string operation would be most effective?

(a) String concatenation
(b) String slicing
(c) String replacement
(d) String traversal

(iv) To find the longest word, the tool needs to perform:

(a) String concatenation
(b) String slicing
(c) String traversal and comparison
(d) String formatting

(v) Handling different text encodings is part of:

(a) String methods
(b) Handling strings
(c) String operations
(d) Traversing a string

Answers

1. (a) 2. (b) 3. (c) 4. string 5. split()
6. find() 7. Traversing 8. lower()
9. Encoding 10. False 11. True 12. True
13. False 14. True 15. False 16. (d) 17. (d)
18. (a) 19. (a) 20. (a) 21. (a)
37. (i) → (c), (ii) → (c), (iii) → (c), (iv) → (c), (v) → (b)

11 CHAPTER

In this chapter, we will explore different types of errors in Python, debugging techniques, and tools that help troubleshoot and resolve issues efficiently.

▼ YOUR STUDY GOALS

11.1 Error Messages
11.2 Python Exception
11.3 Python Built-in Exceptions

▼ YOUR PRACTICE GOAL

- Objective Type Questions (21 Qs ; MCQs, True or False, Fill in the Blanks, Assertion and Reason)
- Subjective Type Questions (27 Qs ; VSA, SA, LA)
- Case Study Based Question-1

Debugging Programs

When a computer program doesn't work as expected, there's likely a mistake in the code, called a bug. Developers use debugging to carefully examine the code, piece by piece, to find and fix these bugs.

This helps to ensure the program works correctly and reliably. While debugging helps to identify and fix problems, testing is still necessary to make sure the program meets all its requirements.

11.1 Error Messages

An error message is a notification displayed by a computer or software program when something goes wrong. It's like a warning sign that alerts you to a problem.

A computer program error, caused by human mistakes in code or design, can lead to incorrect results or unexpected behavior.

Some common form of program errors are as given below

Compile-time Errors

All the errors that are detected and displayed by the compiler or interpreter are known as compile-time errors. Whenever the compiler displays an error, it will not be able to run.

It is therefore necessary that we fix all the errors so that we can successfully compile and run the program.

There are two categories of compile-time errors as follows

(i) Syntax errors
(ii) Semantic errors

Syntax Error

When a formal set of rules defined for writing a program in a particular language is not followed then error raised is known as syntax error.

Syntax errors occur when syntax rules of any programming language are violated.

Common Python syntax errors include

- Leaving out a keyword
- Putting a keyword in the wrong place
- Leaving out a symbol, such as a colon, comma or brackets
- Misspelling a keyword
- Incorrect indentation
- Empty block

For example,

```
def add_function( )
    msg = "How are you ?"
    print(msg)
    add_function( )
```

Here, Python is telling us that there's a mistake in the way we've written the code on the first line. The problem is that we forgot to put a colon (:) at the end of line 1 where we define the function.

If we fix that, we'll find another mistake. The lines inside the function aren't lined up correctly. They should all start at the same place to show that they belong together.

The correct code is

```
def add_function ():
    msg = "How are you ?"
    print (msg)
add_function ()
```

Semantic Error

This type of compile time error indicates an improper use of Python statements.

These errors occur when statements are not meaningful. The word "semantics" relates to the meaning of words, sentences or programs.

For example,

```
a = 10
b = 15
a + b = c
print (c)
```

Output

```
SyntaxError: can't assign to operator.
```

In the above code, the statement a + b = c will result in a semantic error as an expression cannot come on the left side of an assignment operator.

So, it will show an error message.

> **Mistake Alert**
>
> Some students might not pay attention to error messages, which can make it harder for them to find and fix problems in their code.

Run-time Errors

A run-time error occurs during a program's execution, after it has started running. It happens when the program encounters a situation it cannot handle, like dividing by zero or accessing invalid memory. These errors cause the program to abruptly stop or produce incorrect results. Debugging tools are often needed to identify and fix run-time errors.

Common Python run-time errors include

- Division by zero
- Performing an operation on incompatible types
- Using an identifier which has not been defined
- Accessing a list element, dictionary value or object attribute which does not exist
- Trying to access a file which does not exist

For example,

```
b = 0
a = 5
c = a / b
print ("The value of c is : ", c)
```

Output

```
ZeroDivisionError: integer division or module by zero
```

Here, this program will crash when it runs because you can't divide a number by zero.

Logical Errors

A logical error in programming occurs when a program runs without crashing but produces incorrect or unintended results. It happens due to flaws in the program's logic, such as incorrect conditions or calculations. These errors are difficult to detect because there are no syntax or runtime errors, and debugging requires careful testing.

Note *When a wrong formula is used to calculate any mathematical expression it gives logical error.*

Common Python logical errors include

- Using the wrong variable name
- Indenting a block to the wrong level
- Getting operator precedence wrong
- Making a mistake in a boolean expression

For example,

```
a = 7
b = 6
c = 5
avg = a * b * c/3
print(" The average is: ", avg)
```

Output

The average is 70.

The code should give us the answer 6, but it's actually giving 70. Even though the code looks right to the computer, there's a mistake in how we told it to calculate the average. We used the wrong formula.

The correct formula should be:

```
avg = (a + b + c) / 3
```

TEACHER TIP

Error messages are like hints that can help you find and fix problems in your code. Always pay attention to them and use them to figure out what's wrong.

Quick Test 1

1. Describe the process of "debugging" and why it's important for programmers.
2. Which of the following is NOT a type of runtime error in Python?
   (a) Division by zero (b) Index out of range
   (c) Syntax error (d) File not found
3. What is the difference between a syntax error and a semantic error?
4. Discuss the common types of runtime errors that can occur in Python programs and how to handle them.

11.2 Python Exception

An exception is like a roadblock in a program's journey. When this happens, the program stops and can't continue. To handle these roadblocks, we use exception handling. This helps us to deal with errors and unexpected situations in the program, which makes it more robust.

Exception Handling

Exception handling is a way to automatically deal with errors in a program. Many programming languages, including Python, have built-in tools for this. There are certain situations where errors are more likely to happen while the program is running.

When we try to read a file or get input from a user, things can sometimes go wrong.

For example, the file might be missing or the user might enter the wrong type of data. To handle these situations, we use a try-except block. We put the code that might cause an error in the try block. If an error occurs, the code in the except block will run, allowing us to handle the problem gracefully.

Syntax

```
try :
   {Run this code}
except:
   {Run this code if an exception occurs}
```

For example,

```
try:
   age = int (input ("Please enter your
                                     age: "))
   print (" I see that you are % d years
                              old . " % age)
except:
   print (" Hey, that was not a number !!")
```

Python will try to run the code inside the try block. If it encounters an error, it will stop running the try block and immediately jump to the except block. Any code that comes after the error in the try block will be skipped.

11.3 Python Built-in Exceptions

Python provides some basic exception classes which are already defined and can be used in generic cases.

Exception Class	Event
Exception	Base class for all exceptions.
ArithmeticError	Raised when numeric calculations fails.
AssertionError	Raised when Assert statement fails.
FloatingPointError	Raised when a floating point calculation fails.
ImportError	Raised when the imported module is not found.
IndexError	Raised when index of a sequence is out of range.
IndentationError	Raised when there is incorrect indentation.

Exception Class	Event
IOError	Raised when an input / output operation fails.
KeyboardInterrupt	Raised when the user interrupts program execution, generally by pressing Ctrl + C.
KeyError	Raised when the specified key is not found in the dictionary.
OverflowError	Raised when result of an arithmetic operation is too large to be represented.
NameError	Raised when an identifier is not found in the local or global namespace.
RuntimeError	Raised when a generated error does not fall into any category.
SyntaxError	Raised by parser when syntax error is encountered.
TypeError	Raised when a function or operation is applied to an object of incorrect type.
ValueError	Raised when a function gets argument of correct type but improper value.
ZeroDivisionError	Raised when division or module by zero takes place for all numeric types.
StopIteration	Raised when the next ( ) method of an iterator does not point to any object.
AttributeError	Raised in case of failure of attribute reference or assignment.
EOFError	Raised when there is no input from either raw_input ( ) or input ( ) function and the end of file is reached.

The finally block

The finally block in Python is used in exception handling and always executes, regardless of whether an exception occurs or not. It is typically used for cleanup actions like closing files or releasing resources.

Syntax

```
try:
    # block of code
    # this may throw an exception
finally:
    # block of code
    # this will always be executed
```

For example,

```
try:
    file1 = open ("Dairy.txt", "r")
    try:
        file1 . write ("Python Programming")
    finally:
        file1.  close ( )
        print (" Diary file closed")
except:
    print (" Error")
```

Output

Diary file closed

Error

Raising Exceptions

Raising an exception in Python is done using the raise keyword, which lets you manually trigger a specific exception to indicate an error or unwanted condition in the program.

Syntax

```
raise Exception_class, <value>
```

For example,

```
try:
    marks = int (input ("Enter the marks: "))
    if marks <30:
        raise ValueError
    else:
        print ("The marks are valid")
except ValueError:
    print ("The marks are not valid")
```

Output

Enter the marks: 25

The marks are not valid

Quick Test 2

1. What is the base class for all exceptions in Python?
2. Explain the concept of exception handling in Python. What are the key components involved?
3. How can you use the try-except block to handle exceptions in Python? Provide an example.
4. What is the purpose of the finally block in Python exception handling?

Mind Map

DEBUGGING PROGRAMS

Error Messages

An error message is a notification displayed by a computer or software program when something goes wrong.

Compile-time Errors

All the errors that are detected and displayed by the compiler or interpreter are known as compile-time errors. Whenever the compiler displays an error, it will not be able to run.

Syntax Error

When a formal set of rules defined for writing a program in a particular language is not followed then error raised is known as syntax error.

Semantic Error

These errors occur when statements are not meaningful. The word "semantics" relates to the meaning of words, sentences or programs.

Run-time Errors

Even if a program compiles and links without errors, it doesn't guarantee that it will run correctly. Sometimes, errors can occur while the program is running, leading to unexpected results or the program crashing. These are known as runtime errors.

Logical Errors

Sometimes, a program can run without crashing, but it still gives the wrong answer. This is because of logical errors, which are mistakes in the way the programmer has designed the program. These errors are the hardest to find and fix.

Exception Handling

Exception handling is a way to automatically deal with errors in a program

try-except Block

Syntax

```
  try :
    {Run this code}
 except:
    {Run this code if an
     exception occurs}
```

finally Block

Syntax

```
 try:
    # block of code
    # this may throw an
      exception
 finally:
    # block of code
    # this will always be
      executed
```

Raising Exceptions

Syntax

```
raise Exception_class,<value>
```

Python Built-in Exceptions

Exception Class	Event
Exception	Cause of Error
Arithmetic Error	Raised when numeric calculations fails.
Assertion Error	Raised when an assert statement fails.
Attribute Error	Raised when attribute assignment or reference fails.
EOF Error	Raised when the input() function hits end-of-file condition.
Floating Point Error	Raised when a floating point operation fails.
Import Error	Raised when the imported module is not found.
Index Error	Raised when the index of a sequence is out of range.
IO Error	Raised when an input/output operation fails.
Key Error	Raised when a key is not found in a dictionary.
Keyboard Interrupt	Raised when the user hits the interrupt key (Ctrl+C or Delete).
Name Error	Raised when a variable is not found in local or global scope.
Overflow Error	Raised when the result of an arithmetic operation is too large to be represented.
Runtime Error	Raised when an error does not fall under any other category.
Stop Iteration	Raised by next() function to indicate that there is no further item to be returned by iterator.
Syntax Error	Raised by parser when syntax error is encountered.
Indentation Error	Raised when there is incorrect indentation.
Type Error	Raised when a function or operation is applied to an object of incorrect type.
Value Error	Raised when a function gets an argument of correct type but improper value.
Zero Division Error	Raised when the second operand of division or modulo operation is zero.

EXAM PATTERN QUESTIONS

Objective Type Questions

Multiple Choice Questions

1. Errors are called as

(a) bugs (b) defects
(c) Both (a) and (b) (d) None of these

2. The process of identifying and fixing errors in a program is called:

(a) Compiling (b) Debugging (c) Testing (d) Executing

3. All the errors that are detected and displaced by the compiler or interpreter are known as

(a) Run time errors (b) Compile time errors
(c) Logical errors (d) None of these

4. Which of the following code snippets would prevent a Python program from being executed due to a syntax error? **Competency Based Que.**

(a) if x > 5 (b) print("Hello")
(c) for i in range(10): print(i) (d) All of the above

5. A program is running and encounters a problem that causes it to halt execution abruptly. Which of the following error types is most likely the cause? **Competency Based Que.**

(a) Run time (b) Compile time (c) Semantic (d) Syntax

6. _______ is a computer program used by programmers to test and debug a target program.

(a) Logical error (b) Runtime error
(c) Debugger (d) Break point

7. Which two activities are closely related and often go hand-in-hand in software development?

(a) Coding and Debugging
(b) Testing and Debugging
(c) Compiling and Linking
(d) Designing and Implementing

Fill in the Blanks

8. ___________ is an error in the code.

9. Compile time errors can _____ or _____.

10. Debugging is the process of finding error in a _____.

11. Logical error is due to some mistake in the _____.

12. A set of rules which give the meaning of a statement are _________.

State Whether True or False

13. A syntax error in Python will always prevent a program from running, even if the logic is correct.

14. A program that compiles without errors is guaranteed to run correctly and produce the desired output.

15. Indentation is crucial in Python and incorrect indentation can lead to syntax errors.

16. Logical errors are the easiest type of programming errors to find and fix because they always produce obvious incorrect output.

17. The finally block in Python is only executed if no exceptions occur within the corresponding try block.

Assertion and Reason Based Questions

Assertion (A) and Reason (R) Type questions. Choose the correct option as:

(a) Both Assertion (A) and Reason (R) are true, and Reason (R) is the correct explanation of Assertion (A).
(b) Both Assertion (A) and Reason (R) are true, but Reason (R) is not the correct explanation of Assertion (A).
(c) Assertion (A) is true, but Reason (R) is false.
(d) Assertion (A) is false, but Reason (R) is true.

18. Assertion (A) Debugging is a crucial step in software development.

Reason (R) Debugging helps to identify and fix errors in code, leading to more reliable and efficient software.

19. Assertion (A) Syntax errors are detected during the compilation process.

Reason (R) Syntax errors are caused by violations of the programming language's grammar rules.

20. Assertion (A) Runtime errors occur during the execution of a program.

Reason (R) Runtime errors are caused by logical errors in the code.

21. Assertion (A) A debugger is a tool used to identify and fix errors in code.

Reason (R) A debugger allows programmers to step through code execution line by line and inspect variables.

Answers

1. (c) Both (a) and (b)
2. (b) Debugging
3. (b) Compile time errors
4. (a) if x > 5
5. (a) Run time
6. (c) Debugger
7. (b) Testing and Debugging
8. Bug
9. syntax error, semantic errors
10. program
11. program logic
12. semantics
13. True
14. False
15. True
16. False
17. False
18. (a) Both Assertion (A) and Reason (R) are true, and Reason (R) is the correct explanation of Assertion (A).
19. (a) Both Assertion (A) and Reason (R) are true, and Reason (R) is the correct explanation of Assertion (A).
20. (c) Assertion (A) is true, but Reason (R) is false.
21. (a) Both Assertion (A) and Reason (R) are true, and Reason (R) is the correct explanation of Assertion (A).

Subjective Questions

Very Short Answer Type Questions

1. What do you mean by a bug?

Ans. An error, sometimes called 'a bug' is anything in the code that prevents a program from compiling and running correctly.

2. Define debugging in the context of software development. **Competency Based Que.**

Ans. Debugging is the process of identifying and removing errors (bugs) from a computer program.

3. How many types of compile-time errors?

Ans. There are two types of compile-time errors as follows.

(i) Syntax error (ii) Semantic error

4. Name the different types of errors.

Ans. (i) Syntax error (ii) Run-time error
(iii) Logical error

5. What do you mean by syntax of a program?

Ans. Syntax are the set of rules and regulations governing to the construction of a valid statement in a programming language.

6. What do you mean by syntax error ?

Ans. Errors which occur when the programming rules are violated called syntax errors.

7. What type of errors can be detected by a compiler?

Ans. Syntax error

8. Identify the type of error that occurs during program execution. **Competency Based Que.**

Ans. Run-time errors

9. When is the IndexError exception class used in a program ?

Ans. IndexError is raised when the index of a sequence is out of range.

10. Which exception class is used when the imported module is not found ?

Ans. ImportError

11. Write the syntax of raising exceptions.

Ans. raise Exception_class, <value>

12. Name the block in exception handling that guarantees execution regardless of whether an exception occurs.

Ans. Finally block **Competency Based Que.**

Short Answer Type I Questions

13. What is debugging?

Ans. Debugging is the process of finding and fixing errors in a program that cause it to malfunction or behave unexpectedly.

14. Differentiate between testing and debugging.

Ans. Differences between compile-time and run-time errors are as follows:

Feature	Testing	Debugging
Goal	To uncover errors within a software program.	To find the cause of errors and correct them within a software program.
Process	Running the software and observing its behavior.	Examining the code to understand its execution and identify the source of errors.
Outcome	A list of issues found (or confirmation that none were found).	Improved code where the identified errors have been removed or resolved.

15. What do you mean by compile-time error?

Ans. All the errors that are detected and displayed by the compiler or interpreter are known as compile-time errors. Whenever the compiler displays an error, it will not be able to run. It is therefore necessary that we fix all the errors so that we can successfully compile and run the program.

16. Identify and describe two distinct categories of errors that can prevent a program from compiling successfully.

Ans. Two major categories of compile-time errors are

(i) **Syntax errors** These are violations of the programming language's rules, like missing semicolons or incorrect keywords. The compiler can't understand the code's structure.

(ii) **Semantic errors** These happen when the code is grammatically correct but doesn't make logical sense, like using an undeclared variable or mismatched data types. The compiler understands the structure but can't execute it due to logical flaws.

17. Underline the syntax errors in the following program.

```
a = int(input(" Enter first number : ")
b = int(input(" Enter second number : "))
print(" a = ", a, end = "", "b = ", c)
c = a + b:
print d
```

Ans. The syntax errors are

```
a = int (input (" Enter first number : "))
b = int (input (" Enter second number : "))
print(" a = ", a, end = " ", "b = ", b)
c = a + b
print c
```

18. What are differences between compile-time and run-time errors?

Ans. Differences between compile-time and run-time errors are as follows:

Compile-time error	Run-time error
Compile-time errors are caught by the compiler, when we compile the program for error.	Run-time errors arise, when a program is in execution state.
For example, an incorrect syntax like missing paranthesis or semicolon.	*For example,* division by zero.

19. Differentiate between a logical error and syntax error. Also, give suitable examples of each in Python.

Ans. Differences between a logical error and syntax error are as follows:

Logical Error	Syntax Error
It occurs because of wrong implementation of logic.	It occurs when statements are wrongly written violating rules of the programming language.
With logical errors, the code is syntactically correct and compiler will not show any error message.	With syntax errors, the code is not syntactically correct and compiler will show the error messages.
It produces the output, but undesired.	It does not produce any output.
For example, if in place of (c = a * b); if by mistake (c = a + b); is written, it will be a logical error.	*For example,* if in place of if (a == b): if by mistake if (a == b), is written, it will be a syntax error.

20. The code given below will give an error on execution. Identify the type of the error and modify the code to handle such type of an error.

```
a = int(input(" Enter the value of a : "))
b = int(input(" Enter the value of b : "))
c = a/b
```

Ans. The error is run-time error

```
a = int(input("Enter the value of a:"))
b = int(input("Enter the value of b:"))
 if(b! = 0):
 c = a/b
```

21. Analyze the provided code snippet. Identify the line that will cause a run-time error and explain why that error occurs Competency Based Que.

```
a = int (input (" Enter a : "))
b = 0
c = a/b
```

Ans. The line c = a/b will cause a run-time error. This is because it attempts to divide the value of a by b, which is initialized to 0. Division by zero is an undefined mathematical operation and results in a ZeroDivisionError during program execution.

22. Define any two exception classes which are used in Python.

Ans. **KeyboardInterrupt** Raised when the user interrupts program execution, generally by pressing Ctrl + C.

OverflowError Raised when result of an arithmetic operation is too large to be represented.

Short Answer Type II Questions

23. Explain the difference between a syntax error and a semantic error in programming, providing an example of each.

Ans. Differences between syntax error and semantic error are as follows:

Feature	Syntax Error	Semantic Error
Nature of Error	Violation of the grammatical rules of the programming language	Code is grammatically correct, but doesn't make logical sense
Detection	Detected by the compiler or interpreter during the compilation or interpretation phase.	Not detected by the compiler; occurs during program execution (runtime)
Error Messages	Usually points to the exact location of the syntax error in the code.	Often harder to pinpoint; might lead to unexpected behavior or crashes
Examples	• Missing a semicolon or parenthesis • Misspelling a keyword • Incorrect indentation	• Using a variable before it's declared • Type mismatch (e.g., assigning a string to an integer variable) • Dividing by zero
Impact	Prevents the program from being executed.	Program runs but produces incorrect results or crashes

Example of Syntax Error

`print "Hello" (missing parentheses in Python 3) or a + b = c (attempting to assign a value to an expression).`

Example of Semantic Error

Using a variable before it has been declared or trying to assign a value of the wrong data type to a variable.

24. Describe what a runtime error is and give two common examples of runtime errors in Python.

Ans. A runtime error occurs during the execution of a program. These errors are not detected by the compiler or interpreter but arise when the program is running. They often cause the program to terminate abruptly.

Example 1: Division by zero (e.g., c = a / b where b is 0).

Example 2: Accessing a list element that doesn't exist (e.g., trying to access my_list[10] when my_list only has 5 elements).

25. Explain the purpose of exception handling in Python using a try-except block and provide a simple code example to illustrate its usage.

Ans. The purpose of exception handling in Python is to gracefully manage errors or unexpected situations that may occur during the execution of a program, preventing it from crashing. It allows the program to continue running even when errors arise, making it more robust. This is achieved using a try-except block.

try block: The code that might raise an exception is placed within the try block.

except block: If an exception occurs within the try block, the program immediately jumps to the except block, where the error is handled.

Code Example:

```
try:
age = int(input("Please enter your age: "))
print("I see that you are",age,"years
old.")
except ValueError:
    print("Hey, that was not a number!")
```

Long Answer Type Questions

26. What do you mean by logical errors?

Ans. In this case, the program does not give any error but still gives an incorrect output, it is due to logical errors. These errors occur due to mistakes of the programmer. This is the most difficult task to find and debug a logical error.

For example, when a wrong formula is used to calculate any mathematical expression it gives logical error.

Some Python logical errors include

- Using the wrong variable name
- Indenting a block to the wrong level
- Getting operator precedence wrong
- Making a mistake in a boolean expression

e.g.

```
a = 17
b = 11
c = 12
avg = (a * b)/(c +3)
print (" The average is : " , avg)
```

The above program, gives the result 12.4666667, but the expected output is 13.3333333.

Here is logical error that formula to find the average of numbers should be $avg = \frac{(a+b+c)}{3}$

27. Define the following exception classes.

(a) NameError **(b) RuntimeError**
(c) OverflowError **(d) IOError**

Ans. (a) **NameError** This error raised when a variable or function name is used that has not been defined or is out of scope. This often occurs when you try to access a variable that doesn't exist, or when you misspell a variable or function name.

e.g. `print(undefined_variable)`

(b) **RuntimeError** A broad class of exceptions that occur during runtime but don't fall into more specific categories like TypeError or ValueError. It's often raised when the interpreter encounters an unexpected condition or behavior.

e.g.
```
import math
math.sqrt(-1)
# Raises a ValueError, which is
          a subclass of RuntimeError
```

(c) **OverFlowError** This error raised when a calculation results in a value that is too large to be represented by the available data type. This often occurs when working with very large or very small numbers.

e.g.
```
import math
math.exp(1000)
# May raise an OverflowError
              depending on the system
```

(d) **IOError** Raised when an input/output operation fails. This can include errors related to reading from or writing to files, network sockets, or other input/output devices.

e.g.
```
f = open("nonexistent_file.txt", "r")
# Raises an IOError if the file
                 doesn't exist
```

Case Study Based Question

Case Study

Debugging is the systematic process of identifying, locating, and rectifying errors or bugs in computer programs or software. It involves analyzing code, testing inputs and outputs, and using debugging tools to pinpoint the exact cause of the issue.

Effective debugging is crucial for ensuring software quality, reliability, and performance. Common debugging techniques include using print statements, setting breakpoints, and utilizing a debugger to step through code execution.

By understanding the types of errors (syntax, runtime, and logical) and employing appropriate debugging strategies, developers can efficiently resolve issues and deliver high-quality software.

(i) What is a syntax error?
(a) An error in the logic of the code
(b) An error in the grammar or structure of the code
(c) An error that occurs during program execution
(d) An error caused by hardware malfunction

(ii) What is a runtime error?
(a) An error that occurs while the program is running
(b) An error in the design of the program
(c) An error in the input data
(d) An error in the compiler

(iii) What is a logical error?
(a) An error in the syntax of the code
(b) An error in the logic or algorithm of the code
(c) An error in the hardware of the computer
(d) An error in the operating system

(iv) Which of the following is a common debugging technique?
(a) Using comments
(b) Using print statements
(c) Using a text editor
(d) Using a web browser

(v) What is a debugger?
(a) A tool for writing code
(b) A tool for compiling code
(c) A tool for debugging code
(d) A tool for running code

(vi) What is the importance of debugging?
(a) To make code more efficient
(b) To make code more readable
(c) To ensure code quality and reliability
(d) To create more complex programs

(vii) Which of the following is a common debugging strategy?
(a) Divide and conquer
(b) Trial and error
(c) Guessing
(d) Ignoring the error

Ans. (i) (b) An error in the grammar or structure of the code
(ii) (a) An error that occurs while the program is running
(iii) (b) An error in the logic or algorithm of the code.
(iv) (b) Using print statements
(v) (c) A tool for debugging code
(vi) (c) To ensure code quality and reliability
(vii) (a) Divide and conquer

SELF ASSESSMENT TEST

Multiple Choice Questions

1. Which exception classes raised when a generated error does not fall into any category?

(a) RuntimeError
(b) TypeError
(c) KeyError
(d) AttributeError

2. Identify the syntax error from the following options

(a) Leaving out a keyword
(b) Division by zero
(c) Using the wrong variable name
(d) Trying to access a file which does not exist

3. Which type of compile time error indicates an improper use of Python statements?

(a) Syntax error
(b) Semantic error
(c) Logical error
(d) Express error

Fill in the Blanks

4. A ________ occurs when the program violates the rules of the programming language.

5. An error that occurs during the execution of a program is a ________ error.

6. ________ errors produce incorrect results without crashing the program.

7. The ________ block is used to ensure that code is always executed, regardless of whether an exception occurs.

8. The ________ statement is used to force an exception to occur.

9. ________ are used to handle errors in a structured way.

State Whether True or False

10. A SyntaxError occurs during runtime.

11. Logical errors cause a program to crash.

12. Exception handling allows a program to continue running after an error.

13. The finally block is executed only if an exception occurs.

14. Raising exceptions allows you to create custom error messages.

15. Compile time errors are found when the program is executing.

Assertion and Reason Based Questions

Assertion (A) and Reason (R) Type questions. Choose the correct option as:

(a) Both Assertion (A) and Reason (R) are true, and Reason (R) is the correct explanation of Assertion (A).
(b) Both Assertion (A) and Reason (R) are true, but Reason (R) is not the correct explanation of Assertion (A).
(c) Assertion (A) is true, but Reason (R) is false.
(d) Assertion (A) is false, but Reason (R) is true.

16. Assertion (A) Syntax errors are detected by the interpreter before execution.

Reason (R) Syntax errors violate the grammatical rules of the programming language.

17. Assertion (A) Logical errors are difficult to detect.

Reason (R) Logical errors do not cause the program to crash, but result in incorrect output.

18. Assertion (A) Exception handling improves program robustness.

Reason (R) Exception handling allows a program to gracefully handle runtime errors.

19. Assertion (A) The finally block is executed only when an exception is raised.

Reason (R) Debugging tools help identify and fix errors in code.

20. Assertion (A) Raising exceptions allows for custom error control.

Reason (R) Raising exceptions enables developers to create specific error messages and handle them appropriately.

Very Short Answer Type Questions

21. What do you mean by error in program?

22. Which type of error occurs in program when a number will be divided by zero?

23. Write the syntax of try_except block in Python.

24. What is meant by AttributeError exception class ?

Short Answer Type Questions

25. How can you stop debugging?

26. Distinguish between syntax error and semantic error.

27. The code is given below will give an error on execution. Identify the type of error and modify the code to handle such type of an error.

```
x = int (input (" Enter the value of x : "))
y = int (input (" Enter the value of y : "))
x = y + 10
d = x/y
```

28. Write some conditions which occur logical errors in Python.

29. What are the use of exception handling in Python?

30. Define two forms of program errors.

31. Explain run-time error with an example in Python.

Long Answer Type Questions

32. Explain the following terms.

(i) Exception (ii) EOFError

(iii) StopIteration (iv) ValueError

33. Write the output of the following code.

```
try:
    file2 = open ("File.txt" ,"r")
    try:
        file2.write ("Programming Langauge")
    finally:
        file2.close( )
        print("File closed")
except :
    print(" Error occurred ")
```

Case Study Based Questions

34. A data analysis script is designed to read a CSV file, perform statistical calculations, and output results. However, when processing large files, the script occasionally crashes with "ZeroDivisionError" and "FileNotFoundError." The script lacks proper exception handling.

(i) The "ZeroDivisionError" and "FileNotFoundError" are examples of which type of error?

(a) Syntax errors
(b) Compile-time errors
(c) Runtime errors
(d) Logical errors

(ii) To prevent the script from crashing, the developer should implement:

(a) Syntax correction
(b) Exception handling
(c) Logical correction
(d) Compile-time checks

(iii) Using a try-except block to catch and handle these errors is a form of:

(a) Raising exceptions
(b) Python build-in exceptions
(c) Exception handling
(d) The finally block

(iv) If the developer wants to ensure that the file is always closed, regardless of whether an exception occurs, they should use:

(a) try-except block (b) raise statement
(c) finally block (d) pass statement

(v) If the developer wants to force a specific error to occur during testing, they can use:

(a) try block (b) raise statement
(c) except block (d) finally block

Answers

1.	(a)	2.	(a)	3.	(a)	4.	Syntax error
5.	Runtime	6.	Logical	7.	Finally	8.	raise
9.	Exceptions			10.	False	11.	False
12.	True	13.	False	14.	True	15.	False
16.	(a)	17.	(a)	18.	(a)	19.	(d)
20.	(a)						

21. (i) → (c), (ii) → (b), (iii) → (c), (iv) → (c), (v) → (b)

12 CHAPTER

Lists

In Python, lists allow us to store multiple items in a single variable. For example, if you need to store the ages of all the students in a class, you can do this task using a list.

YOUR STUDY GOALS

12.1 Creating a List
12.2 Accessing Lists
12.3 Traversing a List
12.4 List Operators
12.5 List Operations
12.6 Build-in Functions
12.7 Programs

YOUR PRACTICE GOAL

- Objective Type Questions (27 Qs ; MCQs, True or False, Fill in the Blanks, Assertion and Reason)
- Subjective Type Questions (34 Qs ; VSA, SA, LA)
- Case Study Based Question-1

A list in Python is an ordered, mutable collection used to store multiple items. It can hold elements of different data types, including numbers, strings, or even other lists.

Lists are defined using square brackets [], and elements are accessed via their index. Because of their mutability, lists allow dynamic modifications like adding, removing, or updating elements.

12.1 Creating a List

In Python, lists can be created to put the elements in square brackets [ ]. The elements in the list are separated by the comma (,).

For example,
```
a = [34, 76, 11, 98]
b = ['s', 3, 6, 't']
c = [34, 0.5, 75]
d = [ ]
```

We can create different types of list in Python as follows:

(i) Empty List

Empty list can be created in Python using [ ] . It takes the truth value as false. Here is the two ways to create empty list as

```
>>>a = [ ]
>>>print (a)
```

Output [ ]

Or
```
>>>a = list ( )
>>>print (a)
```

Output [ ]

(ii) Mixed Data Types List

It can be created to place different data types such as integers, strings, double etc., into one list.

For example,

```
>>>a = ['Neha', 'Sharma', 25, 75, 6, 47]
>>>print(a)
```

Output

```
['Neha', 'Sharma', 25, 75, 6, 47]
```

(iii) Nested List

Nested lists are list objects where the elements in the lists can be lists themselves.

For example,

```
>>> A = ['Neha', 4, 1, [5, 23, 4], 98]
>> print (A)
```

Output

```
['Neha', 4, 1, [5, 23, 4], 98]
```

List A contains 5 elements while inner list contains 3 elements ([5, 23, 4]). List A is considered [5, 23, 4] as one element.

Lists are Mutable

In Python, lists are mutable. It means that the contents of the list can be changed after it has been created. #List list1 of colors

```
>>> list1 =
['Red','Green','Blue','Orange']
#change/override the fourth element of
list1
 >>> list1[3] = 'Black'
>>> list1 #print the modified list list1
['Red', 'Green', 'Blue', 'Black']
```

Creating List from an Existing Sequence

(a) **Using the list () Function** You can convert sequences like tuples or strings into lists.

Syntax

```
new_list_name = list (sequence / string)
    #Here, the sequence includes tuples,
lists etc.
```

For example,

```
my_tuple = (1, 2, 3)
my_list = list(my_tuple)
```

Output

[1, 2, 3]

(b) **Directly from input** You can create lists by taking input from the user.

For example,

```
# Creating an empty list
new_list = [ ]
# Numbers of elements as input
n = int (input ("Enter no. of elements ="))
#iterating till the range
for i in range (0, n):
  element = int (input ())
  #adding the element
  new_list.append (element)
print (new_list)
```

Output

Enter no. of elements = 4

12

10

'Arihant'

'Publications'

[1, 10, 'Arihant', 'Publications']

12.3 Accessing Lists

To access the list's elements, index number is used. Use the index operator [ ] to access the elements of a list. The index should be an integer. Index of 0 refers to first element, 1 refers to second element and so on. While the index of –1 refers to the last element, –2 refers to the second last element and so on.

For example,

```
l1 = [5, 7, 3, 4, 5, 6, 9, 0, 8]
```

It is called positive index

0	1	2	3	4	5	6	7	8
5	7	3	4	5	6	9	0	8
-9	-8	-7	-6	-5	-4	-3	-2	-1

It is called negative index

```
>>>l1 = [34, 87, 'Computer', 12, 'Python',
11, 76, 'Option']
>>>l1 [0]
34
>>>l1 [6]
76
>>>l1 [-4]
'Python'
>>>l1 [3]
12
```

```
>>>l1 [-3]
11
>>>l1 [8]
```

It will give an error as `IndexError: list index out of range`. Because it has 8 elements for which indexing are 0 to 7.

12.3 Traversing a List

Traversing a list is a technique to access an individual element of that list. It is also called iterate over a list.

There are multiple ways to iterate over a list in Python. These are as follows

Using for loop

The most common and easy way to traverse a list is with a for loop. For loop is used when you want to traverse each element of a list.

For example,

```
a = ['P', 'R', 'O', 'G', 'R', 'A', 'M']
for i in a:
  print (i, end = " ")
```

Output

P R O G R A M

Or

```
a = ['P', 'R', 'O', 'G', 'R', 'A', 'M']
for i in range (len(a)):
  print ((a [i]), end = "-")
```

Output

P-R-O-G-R-A-M

Program to display the elements of list

['P', 'Y', 'T', 'H', 'O', 'N']

in a separate line with their index number.

For example,

```
list1 = ['P', 'Y', 'T', 'H', 'O' 'N']
L1 = len (list1)
for i in range (L1):
   print ("Element :", list1 [i], "at index number", i)
```

Output

Element : P at index number 0

Element : Y at index number 1

Element : T at index number 2

Element : H at index number 3

Element : O at index number 4

Element : N at index number 5

Using while loop

A while loop can also be used to iterate over the elements of a list, but it requires more explicit index management.

For example,

```
list = ['A', 'r', 'i', 'h', 'a', 'n', 't']
index = 0
while index < len(list):
  print((list[index]), end = " ")
  index += 1
```

Output

A r i h a n t

12.4 List Operators

We can manipulate lists in different ways using various operators. These are as follows:

Comparison Operators

Comparison operators in Python are like scales that weigh two values and tell us if one is bigger, smaller, or equal to the other.

They use symbols like < (less than), > (greater than), == (equal to), != (not equal to), >= (greater than or equal to), and <= (less than or equal to). When we use these operators, they give us a True or False answer.

For example,

```
>>> a = [1, 2, 3, 4]
>>> b = [5, 2, 3, 4]
>>> a < b
True
```

For example,

```
>>> a = [2, 3, 4, 6]
>>> b = [2, [3,4], 6]
>>> c = [2, 3, 4, 6]
>>> a == b
False
>>> a == c
True
```

Membership Operators

These operators are used to find out whether a value is a member of a sequence such as string, list, tuple, dictionary etc. There are two types of membership operator as follows

(i) in operator

It evaluates True, if the value in the left operand appears in the sequence found in the right operand.

For example,

```
l1 = [45, 76, [3, 98], 6]
l2 = [60, [23, 43], 65]
for item in l1:
  if item in l2:
    print ("Exist")
else :
  print ("Not Exist")
```

Output

Not Exist

(ii) not in operator

It evaluates True, if the value in the left operand does not appear in the sequence found in the right operand.

For example,

```
a = 54
b = 87
list1 = [45, 65, 30, 78, 512, 87]
if (a not in list1):
  print ("a is NOT present in given
  list")
else :
  print ("a is present in given list")
if (b in list1):
  print ("b is present in given list")
else :
  print ("b is NOT present in given list")
```

Output

a is NOT present in given list
b is present in given list

12.5 List Operations

We can perform various operations on list in Python, some of them are describe below.

Concatenate Lists

The most conventional method to perform on the list concatenation, the use of (+) operator can easily add the whole of one list to other list and hence perform the concatenation.

Syntax `list = list1 + list2`

For example,

```
>>>l1 = [43, 56, 34]
>>>l2 = [22, 34, 98]
>>>l = l1 + l2
>>>l
[43, 56, 34, 22, 34, 98]
```

The (+) operator cannot add list with other type as number or string because this operator is used only with list types.

For example,

```
>>>l1 = [2, 5, 7]
>>>l = l1 + 5
Trackback (most recent call last) :
File "<pyshell#5>", line 1, in <module>
  l = l1 + 5
TypeError : can only concatenate list
                   (not "int") to list.
```

For example,

```
>>>l1 = [3, 2, 6]
>>>l = l1 + "Try"
Trackback (most recent call last):
File "<pyshell#1>", line 1, in <module>
l = l1 + "Try"
TypeError : can only concatenate list
                   (not "str") to list.
```

Replicating List

You can repeat the elements of the list using (*) operator. This operator is used to replicate the list.

Syntax `list = list1 * digit`

For example,

```
>>>l1 = [3, 2, 6]
>>>l = l1 * 2
>>>l
[3, 2, 6, 3, 2, 6]
```

Slicing of a List

If we want to display only a specific portion of the list, we use a technique called slicing. Slicing involves using the colon (:) symbol to indicate the range of elements we want to extract.

Below are the operators used for slicing:

Operators	Syntax	Example

Basic Slicing	`list[start : end]`	`list1 = [4, 3, 7, 6, 4, 9, 5, 0, 3, 2]`
		`print(list1 [2 : 5])`
		Output
		[7, 6, 4]

Omitting Indices	`string[: end]`
	`string[start :]`
		`print(list1[:5])`
		Output [4, 3, 7, 6, 4]
		`print(list1[3:])`
		Output [6, 4, 9, 5, 0, 3, 2]

Operators	Syntax	Example
Step Sizing	`string[start:end: step]`	`print(list1[1:10:3])` **Output** [3, 4, 0]
Negative Indexing	`string[-start : -end]`	`print(list1[-6:-1])` **Output** [4, 9, 5, 0, 3]

List Modification using Slicing

List can be modified after creating using slicing.

For example,

```
>>> l1 = [2, 4, "Try", 54, "Again"]
>>> l1[0:1] = [34, "Hello"]
>>> l1
[34, 'Hello', 4, 'Try', 54, 'Again']
>>> l1[4] = ["World"]
>>> l1
[34, 'Hello', 4, 'Try', ['World'], 'Again']
>>> l1[2] = "Hiiii"
>>> l1
[34, 'Hello', 'Hiiii', 'Try', ['World'], 'Again']
```

TEACHER TIP

Negative indices can be used to access elements from the end of the list.

12.6 Build-in Functions

Python has large number of build-in functions and methods that make programming easier. Some of them are follows:

Function	Description	Example
list()	Converts an iterable into a list. **Syntax** `list(sequence)`	`>>l=list("hello")` `>>l` `['h', 'e', 'l', 'l', 'o']`
append()	Adds an element to the end of a list. **Syntax** `list.append(item)`	`>>lst = [1, 2, 3]` `>>lst.append(4)` `>>lst` `[1, 2, 3, 4]`
extend()	Adds all elements from another sequence to the end of the list. **Syntax** `list.extend(list_2)`	`>>lst = [1, 2]` `>>lst.extend([3, 4])` `>>lst` `[1, 2, 3, 4]`
insert()	Inserts an element at a specified position. **Syntax** `list.insert(index, item)`	`>>lst = [1, 3]` `>>lst.insert(1,2)` `>>lst` `[1, 2, 3]`
sum()	Returns the sum of elements in a list. **Syntax** `sum(sequence)`	`>>lst = [1, 2, 3]` `>>sum(lst)` `6`
max()	Returns the largest element in a list. **Syntax** `max(sequence)`	`>>lst = [1, 3, 2]` `>>max(lst)` `3`
min()	Returns the smallest element in a list. **Syntax** `min(sequence)`	`>>lst = [1, 3, 2]` `>>min(lst)` `1`
len()	Returns the length (number of elements) in a list. **Syntax** `len(sequence)`	`>>lst = [1, 2, 3, 'hi']` `>>len(lst)` `4`
index()	Returns the index of the first occurrence of an element. **Syntax** `list.index(item)`	`>>lst = [1, 2, 3, 'Hello']` `>>lst.index('Hello')` `3`
count()	Returns the number of occurrences of an element in the list. **Syntax** `list.count(item)`	`>>lst = [1, 'New',2, 2, 3]` `>>lst.count(2)` `2`
reverse()	Reverses the elements of the list in place. **Syntax** `list.reverse()`	`>>lst = [1, 2, 3]` `>>lst.reverse()` `[3, 2, 1]`
pop()	Removes and returns an element at a specified index (default is the last element). **Syntax** `list.pop(index)`	`>>lst = [1, 2, 3, 78, 99]` `>>lst.pop(4)` `99` `Updated List: [1,2,3,78]`
remove()	Removes the first occurrence of a specified element. **Syntax** `list.remove(item)` If the item(argument)	`>>lst = [1, 3, 6]` `>>lst.remove(3)` `[1, 6]`
sort()	Sorts the elements of a list in place (ascending by default). **Syntax** `list.sort()` or `list.sort(reverse=True)`	`>>lst = [3, 1, 2]` `>>lst.sort()` `[1, 2, 3]`
sorted()	It takes a list as parameter and creates a new list consisting of the same elements arranged in sorted order. **Syntax** `list1.sorted(list2)`	`>> list1 = [23,45, 11,67,85,56]` `>> list2 = sorted(list1)` `>> list1` `[23,45,11,67,85,56]` `>> list2` `[11,23,45,56,67,85]`
clear()	Removes all elements from the list. **Syntax** `list.clear()`	`>>lst = [1, 2, 3]` `>>lst.clear()` `[]`

12.7 Programs

1. Find the Maximum, Minimum, and Mean of Numeric Values in a List.

Ans.
```
def find_stats(num_list):
  max_num = max(num_list)
  min_num = min(num_list)
  mean_num = sum(num_list) / len(num_list)
  return max_num, min_num, mean_num
numbers = [10, 25, 5, 30, 15]
max_val, min_val, mean_val
             = find_stats(numbers)
print("Maximum value is = :", max_val)
print("Minimum value is = :", min_val)
print("Mean is = :", mean_val)
```

2. Linear Search on a List of Numbers.

Ans.
```
def linear_search(num_list, target):
  for i in range(len(num_list)):
    if num_list[i] == target:
      return i
  return -1
numbers = [10, 25, 5, 30, 15]
target_value = 30
index = linear_search(numbers, target_value)
if index != -1:
  print(f"Target value {target_value}
                   found at index {index}")
else:
  print("Target value not found")
```

3. Counting the Frequency of Elements in a List.

Ans.
```
def count_frequencies(num_list):
  freq_dict = {}
  for num in num_list:
    if num in freq_dict:
      freq_dict[num] += 1
    else:
      freq_dict[num] = 1
  return freq_dict
numbers = [10, 25, 5, 30, 15, 10, 25, 5]
freq_dict = count_frequencies(numbers)
print(freq_dict)
Programs
```

4. Write a menu driven program to perform various list operations, such as:

- **Append an element**
- **Insert an element**
- **Append a list to the given list**
- **Modify an existing element**
- **Delete an existing element from its position**
- **Delete an existing element with a given value**
- **Sort the list in ascending order**
- **Sort the list in descending order**
- **Display the list.**

Ans.
```
# Menu driven program to do various list operations
myList = [22, 4, 16, 38, 13] # myList already has
                                       5 elements
while True:
  print("The list 'myList' has the following
                              elements:", myList)
  print("\nL I S T O P E R A T I O N S")
  print(" 1. Append an element")
  print(" 2. Insert an element at the desired
                                        position")
  print(" 3. Append a list to the given list")
  print(" 4. Modify an existing element")
  print(" 5. Delete an existing element by its
                                        position")
  print(" 6. Delete an existing element by its value")
  print(" 7. Sort the list in ascending order")
  print(" 8. Sort the list in descending order")
  print(" 9. Display the list")
  print(" 10. Exit")
  choice = int(input("ENTER YOUR CHOICE (1-10): "))
  # Append element
  if choice == 1:
    element = int(input("Enter the element to be
                                       appended: "))
    myList.append(element)
    print("The element has been appended.\n")
  # Insert an element at desired position
  elif choice == 2:
    element = int(input("Enter the element to be
                                       inserted: "))
    pos = int(input("Enter the position: "))
    if 0 <= pos <= len(myList):
      myList.insert(pos, element)
      print("The element has been inserted.\n")
    else:
      print("Invalid position.\n")
  # Append a list to the given list
  elif choice == 3:
    newList = input("Enter the elements separated
                   by commas (e.g. 1,2,3): ").split(',')
    newList = [int(x) for x in newList]
    myList.extend(newList)
    print("The list has been appended.\n")
  # Modify an existing element
  elif choice == 4:
```

```
        i = int(input("Enter the position of the
                                  element to be modified: "))
        if 0 <= i < len(myList):
            newElement = int(input("Enter the new
                                              element: "))
            oldElement = myList[i]
            myList[i] = newElement
            print(f"The element {oldElement} has been
                                              modified.\n")
        else:
            print("Position of the element is more than
                                  the length of the list.\n")
    # Delete an existing element by position
    elif choice == 5:
        i = int(input("Enter the position of the
                                  element to be deleted: "))
        if 0 <= i < len(myList):
            element = myList.pop(i)
            print(f"The element {element} has been
                                              deleted.\n")
        else:
            print("Position of the element is more than
                                  the length of the list.\n")
    # Delete an existing element by value
    elif choice == 6:
        element = int(input("Enter the element to be
                                              deleted: "))
        if element in myList:
            myList.remove(element)
            print(f"The element {element} has been
                                              deleted.\n")
        else:
            print(f"Element {element} is not present in
                                              the list.\n")
    # Sort the list in ascending order
    elif choice == 7:
        myList.sort()
        print("The list has been sorted in ascending
                                              order.\n")
    # Sort the list in descending order
    elif choice == 8:
        myList.sort(reverse=True)
        print("The list has been sorted in descending
                                              order.\n")
    # Display the list
    elif choice == 9:
        print("The list is:", myList)
    # Exit from the menu
    elif choice == 10:
        print("Exiting the program.")
        break
    else:
        print("Choice is not valid. Please enter a
                                  valid option (1-10).\n")
    # Pause to let the user read output
    input("Press any key to continue...")
```

5. Write a Python program to display all the common elements of two lists.

Ans.

```
list1 = []
num = int(input("Enter number of elements
                                   in List1: "))
for i in range(1, num+1):
    x = int(input("Enter element: "))
    list1.append(x)
list2 = []
num1 = int(input("Enter number of elements
                                   in List2: "))
for i in range(1, num1+1):
    y = int(input("Enter element: "))
    list2.append(y)
a_set = set(list1)
b_set = set(list2)
if (a_set & b_set):
  print("Common elements are:", a_set &
                                        b_set)
else:
  print("No common elements found")
```

6. Write a Python program to reverse a list in-place without creating a new list.

Ans.

```
def reverse_list(lst):
  lst.reverse()
  return lst
n = int(input("How many elements you want
                         to enter in a list? "))
my_list = []
for i in range(n):
  element = int(input("Enter the element: "))
  my_list.append(element)

print("Original List is:", my_list)
reversed_list = reverse_list(my_list)
print("List after reversing in place is:",
                                 reversed_list)
```

Mind Map

LISTS

Creating a List

We can create different types of list in Python as follows:

Empty List

```
>>>a = [ ]
>>>print (a)
Or
>>>a = list ( )
>>>print (a)
```

Mixed data Type List

```
>>>a = ['Neha', 'Sharma', 25, 75, 6, 47]
>>>print(a)
```

Nested List

```
>>> A = ['Neha', 4, 1, [5, 23, 4], 98]
>> print (A)
```

Note

In Python, lists are mutable. It means that the contents of the list can be changed after it has been created. #List list1 of colors

Accessing Lists

To access the list's elements, index number is used. Use the index operator [ ] to access the elements of a list. The index should be an integer. Index of 0 refers to first element, 1 refers to second element and so on.While the index of −1 refers to the last element, −2 refers to the second last element and so on.

```
>>>l1 = [34, 87, 'Computer', 12, 'Python', 11 ]
>>>l1 [0]
```

Output 34

Traversing a Lists

Traversing a list is a technique to access an individual element of that list. It is also called iterate over a list.

There are multiple ways to iterate over a list in Python.

Using for loop

```
a = ['P', 'R', 'O', 'G', 'R', 'A', 'M']
for i in a:
print (i, end = " ")
```

Using While loop

```
list = ['A', 'r', 'i', 'h', 'a', 'n', 't']
index = 0
while index < len(list):
print((list[index]), end = " ")
index += 1
```

List Operators

Comparison Operators

Comparison operators in Python are like scales that weigh two values and tell us if one is bigger, smaller, or equal to the other.

They use symbols like <, >, ==, != , >= , and <=

When we use these operators, they give us a True or False answer.

Membership Operators

These operators are used to find out whether a value is a member of a sequence such as string, list, tuple, dictionary etc. There are two types of membership operator as follows-

in operator, not in operator

List Operations

Concatenate Lists

Syntax list = list1 + list2

Replicating List

Syntax list = list1 * digit

Slicing of a List

If we want to display only a specific portion of the list, we use a technique called slicing. Slicing involves using the colon (:) symbol to indicate the range of elements we want to extract.

Built-in Functions

Methods	Syntax
list( )	list(squence)
append( )	list.append(item)
extend ( )	list.extend(list_2)
insert()	list.insert (index, item)
sum()	sum(sequence)
max()	max(sequence)
min()	min(sequence)
len()	len(sequence)
index()	list.index(item)
count()	list.count(item)
reverse()	list. reverse(item)
pop()	list. pop(item)
remove()	list. remove(item)
sort()	list.sort() or list.sort(reverse=True)
sorted()	list1.sorted(list2)
clear()	list.clear()

NCERT Folder

Exercise Questions

1. What will be the output of the following statements?

(i)
```
list1 = [12,32,65,26,80,10]
list1.sort()
print(list1)
```
(ii)
```
list1 = [12,32,65,26,80,10]
sorted(list1)
print(list1)
```
(iii)
```
list1 = [1,2,3,4,5,6,7,8,9,10]
print (list1[::-2])
print (list1[:3] + list1[3:])
```
(iv)
```
list1 = [1,2,3,4,5]
print (list1[len(list1)-1])
```

Ans. Output

(i) [10, 12, 26, 32, 65, 80]

(ii) [12, 32, 65, 26, 80, 10]

(iii) [10, 8, 6, 4, 2]

[1, 2, 3, 4, 5, 6, 7, 8, 9, 10]

(iv) 5

2. Consider the following list myList. What will be the elements of myList after the following two operations?

```
myList = [10,20,30,40]
```
(i) `myList.append([50,60])`

(ii) `myList.extend([80,90])`

Ans. (i) [10, 20, 30, 40, [50, 60]]

(ii) [10, 20, 30, 40, [50, 60], 80, 90]

3. What will be the output of the following code segment?

```
myList = [1,2,3,4,5,6,7,8,9,10]
for i in range(0,len(myList)):
  if i%2 == 0:
    print(myList[i])
```

Ans. Output

1

3

5

7

9

4. What will be the output of the following code segments?

(a)
```
myList = [1,2,3,4,5,6,7,8,9,10]
del myList[3:]
print(myList)
```
(b)
```
myList = [1,2,3,4,5,6,7,8,9,10]
del myList[:5]
print(myList)
```
(c)
```
myList = [1,2,3,4,5,6,7,8,9,10]
del myList[::2]
print(myList)
```

Ans. Output

(a) [1, 2, 3]

(b) [6, 7, 8, 9, 10]

(c) [2, 4, 6, 8, 10]

5. Differentiate between append() and extend()

Ans.

Feature	append()	extend()
Purpose	Adds a single element to the end of a list.	Adds all elements of an iterable (like another list, tuple, etc.) to the end of a list.
Argument Type	Any object (single element).	Any iterable object (list, tuple, set, string, etc.).
Effect on List	Increases the list's length by 1.	Increases the list's length by the number of elements in the iterable.
How Elements are Added	Adds the argument as a single element, even if it's a list itself.	Adds each element of the iterable individually.
Example	my_list = [1, 2, 3] my_list.append(4) print(my_list) # Output: [1, 2, 3, 4]	my_list = [1, 2, 3] my_list.extend([4, 5, 6]) print(my_list) # Output: [1, 2, 3, 4, 5, 6]

6. Consider a list:

```
list1 = [6,7,8,9]
```

What is the difference between the following operations on list1?

(a) `list1 * 2`

(b) `list1 *= 2`

(c) `list1 = list1 * 2`

Ans. (a) `list1 * 2`

Creates a new list This operation multiplies the list by 2, creating a new list that contains the original list repeated twice.

Does not modify the original list The original list1 remains unchanged.

e.g.
```
list1 = [6, 7, 8, 9]
new_list = list1 * 2
print(new_list)
[6, 7, 8, 9, 6, 7, 8, 9]
print(list1)
[6, 7, 8, 9]
```

(b) `list1 *= 2`

Modifies the original list This operation multiplies the list by 2 in-place, doubling the elements of the original list1.

Changes the original list The original list1 is now modified to contain the repeated elements.

e.g.
```
list1 = [6, 7, 8, 9]
list1 *= 2
print(list1)
[6, 7, 8, 9, 6, 7, 8, 9]
```

(c) `list1 = list1 * 2`

Assigns a new list to the variable This operation multiplies the list by 2, creating a new list, and then assigns this new list back to the variable list1.

Modifies the original list The original list1 is now replaced with the new, doubled list.

e.g.
```
list1 = [6, 7, 8, 9]
list1 = list1 * 2
print(list1)
[6, 7, 8, 9, 6, 7, 8, 9]
```

7. The record of a student (Name, Roll No., Marks in five subjects and percentage of marks) is stored in the following list:

```
stRecord =
['Raman','A-36',[56,98,99,72,69], 78.8]
```

Write Python statements to retrieve the following information from the list stRecord:

(a) Percentage of the student

(b) Marks in the fifth subject

(c) Maximum marks of the student

(d) Roll no. of the student

(e) Change the name of the student from 'Raman' to 'Raghav'

Ans. (a) `print(stRecord[3])`

(b) `print(stRecord[2][4])`

(c) `print(max(stRecord[2]))`

(d) `print(stRecord[1])`

(e) `stRecord[0] = 'Raghav'`

Programming Based Questions

1. Write a program to find the number of times an element occurs in the list.

Ans.
```
def count_occurrences(lst, element):
  count = lst.count(element)
  print(f"The element {element} occurs
                          {count} times.")
my_list = [1, 2, 3, 2, 1, 4, 2]
element_to_count = 2
count_occurrences(my_list,
                  element_to_count)
```

2. Write a program to read a list of n integers (positive as well as negative). Create two new lists, one having all positive numbers and the other having all negative numbers from the given list. Print all three lists.

Ans.
```
def separate_positive_negative(num_list):
  positive_list = []
  negative_list = []
  for num in num_list:
    if num > 0:
      positive_list.append(num)
    else:
      negative_list.append(num)
  return positive_list, negative_list
numbers = [1, -2, 3, -4, 5, -6]
positive, negative =
separate_positive_negative(numbers)
print("Original list:", numbers)
print("Positive numbers:", positive)
print("Negative numbers:", negative)
```

3. Write a function that returns the largest element of the list passed as parameter.

Ans.
```
def find_largest(num_list):
  return max(num_list)
numbers = [10, 25, 5, 30, 15]
largest = find_largest(numbers)
print("Largest number:", largest)
```

4. Write a function to return the second largest number from a list of numbers.

Ans.
```
def find_second_largest(num_list):
  largest = max(num_list)
  num_list.remove(largest)
  second_largest = max(num_list)
  return second_largest
numbers = [10, 25, 5, 30, 15]
second_largest =
         find_second_largest(numbers)
print("Second largest number:",
                   second_largest)
```

5. **Write a program to read a list of n integers and find their median.**

Note The median value of a list of values is the middle one when they are arranged in order. If there are two middle values then take their average.

Hint You can use an built-in function to sort the list

Ans.
```
def find_median(num_list):
  num_list.sort()
  n = len(num_list)
  if n % 2 == 0:
    median = (num_list[n//2 - 1] +
                                num_list[n//2]) / 2
  else:
    median = num_list[n//2]
  return median
numbers = [10, 25, 5, 30, 15]
median = find_median(numbers)
print("Median:", median)
```

6. **Write a program to read a list of elements. Modify this list so that it does not contain any duplicate elements, i.e., all elements occurring multiple times in the list should appear only once.**

Ans.
```
def remove_duplicates(lst):
  unique_list = []
  for num in lst:
    if num not in unique_list:
      unique_list.append(num)
  return unique_list
numbers = [1, 2, 3, 2, 1, 4, 2]
unique_numbers =
                remove_duplicates(numbers)
print("Unique numbers:", unique_numbers)
```

7. **Write a program to read a list of elements. Input an element from the user that has to be inserted in the list. Also input the position at which it is to be inserted. Write a user defined function to insert the element at the desired position in the list.**

Ans.
```
def insert_element(lst, element, position):
  lst.insert(position, element)
numbers = [1, 2, 3, 4, 5]
element_to_insert = 10
position_to_insert = 2
insert_element(numbers, element_to_insert,
                              position_to_insert)
print(numbers)
```

8. **Write a program to read elements of a list.**

(a) **The program should ask for the position of the element to be deleted from the list. Write a function to delete the element at the desired position in the list.**

(b) **The program should ask for the value of the element to be deleted from the list. Write a function to delete the element of this value from the list**

Ans.
```
def delete_element_by_position(lst,
                                  position):
  del lst[position]
def delete_element_by_value(lst, value):
  if value in lst:
    lst.remove(value)
  else:
    print("Element not found in the list.")
numbers = [1, 2, 3, 4, 5]
(a) position_to_delete = 2
    delete_element_by_position(numbers,
                                 position_to_delete)
    print(numbers)
(b) value_to_delete = 3
    delete_element_by_value(numbers,
    value_to_delete)
    print(numbers)
```

9. **Read a list of n elements. Pass this list to a function which reverses this list in-place without creating a new list.**

Ans.
```
def reverse_list(lst):
  lst.reverse()
numbers = [1, 2, 3, 4, 5]
reverse_list(numbers)
print(numbers)
```

EXAM PATTERN QUESTIONS

Objective Type Questions

Multiple Choice Questions

1. **Which value is used to represent the first index of the list?**

(a) 1 (b) 0 (c) -1 (d) a

2. **You have a list my_list = [10, 20, 30, 40, 50] and you need to retrieve the last element (50) without knowing the exact length of the list. Which of the following methods is the most efficient and direct way to achieve this?** **Competency Based Que.**

(a) my_list[len(my_list) - 1]
(b) my_list.pop()
(c) my_list[-1]
(d) my_list[4:5]

3. **Choose the output of the following Python code.**

```
l1 = list ()
print (l1)
```

(a) [] (b) () (c) [,] (d) Empty

4. **How do you create a true copy (a new, independent copy) of a Python list L1?**

(a) L2 = L1 (b) L2 = list(L1)
(c) L2.copy(L1) (d) It's not possible

5. **Suppose list**

```
l1 = [10, 20, 30, 40, 50, 60, 70]
print (l1[-3])
```

(a) 30 (b) 50 (c) 40 (d) Error

6. **Choose the output from the following code.**

```
list1 = ['A', 'R', 'I', 'H', 'A', 'N', 'T']
print (list1[7])
```

(a) T (b) N (c) A (d) Error

7. **You have a list data = [1, 2, 4, 5] and you need to insert the number 3 between 2 and 4. Which method would you use to achieve this?** **Competency Based Que.**

(a) data.extend(3) (b) data.append(3)
(c) data.insert(2, 3) (d) data.add(3)

8. **What is the output of the following Python code?**

```
L = ['A', 'r', 'i', 'h', 'a', 'n', 't']
print(len(L))
```

(a) 7 (b) 8
(c) 9 (d) None of these

Fill in the Blanks

9. Creating lists using L = [expression for variable in sequence] is called ________.

10. ______ method is used to add multiple elements to a given list.

11. [] indicates an ____ list.

12. The sort() function sorts the items of the list by default in ascending order and in ________.

13. ______ method is used to delete an element when its index is not known.

State Whether True or False

14. Lists in Python cannot be nested inside each other.

15. List comprehensions can be used to create a new list by filtering and transforming an existing list.

16. The clear() method removes all elements from the list and deletes the list itself.

17. Lists in Python can be directly compared for equality using ==.

18. Using the * operator on a list duplicates its elements.

19. Slicing a list with list[1:3] includes the elements at indexes 1 and 3.

20. The pop() method removes the first element from the list by default.

21. The insert() method in Python lists can add an element at a specific index.

Assertion and Reason Based Questions

Assertion (A) and Reason (R) Type questions. Choose the correct option as:

(a) Both Assertion (A) and Reason (R) are true, and Reason (R) is the correct explanation of Assertion (A).
(b) Both Assertion (A) and Reason (R) are true, but Reason (R) is not the correct explanation of Assertion (A).
(c) Assertion (A) is true, but Reason (R) is false.
(d) Assertion (A) is false, but Reason (R) is true.

22. **Assertion (A)** Lists in Python are homogeneous.

Reason (R) They can only store elements of the same data type.

23. **Assertion (A)** Lists in Python are mutable.

Reason (R) Elements of a list can be changed after the list is created.

24. **Assertion (A)** Negative indexing can be used to access elements from the end of a list.

Reason (R) The index -1 refers to the last element, -2 to the second last, and so on.

25. **Assertion (A)** Slicing can be used to extract a portion of a list.

Reason (R) It involves using the colon (:) operator to specify the start and end indices.

26. **Assertion (A)** The append() method adds an element to the beginning of a list.

Reason (R) It modifies the original list.

27. **Assertion (A)** The len() function returns the number of elements in a list.

Reason (R) It counts the number of items in the list.

Answers

1. (b) 0
2. (c) my_list[-1]
3. (a) []
4. (b) L2 = list(L1)
5. (b) 50
6. (d) Error
7. (c) data.insert(2, 3)
8. (a) 7
9. list comprehensions
10. extend()
11. empty
12. place
13. remove()
14. False
15. True
16. False
17. True
18. True
19. False
20. False
21. True
22. (d) Assertion (A) is false, but Reason (R) is true.
23. (a) Both Assertion (A) and Reason (R) are true, and Reason (R) is the correct explanation of Assertion (A).
24. (a) Both Assertion (A) and Reason (R) are true, and Reason (R) is the correct explanation of Assertion (A).
25. (a) Both Assertion (A) and Reason (R) are true, and Reason (R) is the correct explanation of Assertion (A).
26. (d) Assertion (A) is false, but Reason (R) is true.
27. (a) Both Assertion (A) and Reason (R) are true, and Reason (R) is the correct explanation of Assertion (A).

Subjective Type Questions

Very Short Answer Type Questions

1. What do you mean by list in Python ?

Ans. List is a type of container in data structures which is used to store multiple data at the same time.

2. Are lists mutable or immutable ?

Ans. Lists are mutable which means they can be changed after creation.

3. If my_list = ['a', 'b', 'c'], what is the index of 'a'?

Ans. 0

4. Write the syntax to create a list from an existing sequence.

Ans. new_list_name = list(sequence/string)

5. Write the output of the below code.

```
>>> l1 = list()
>>> print(l1)
```

Ans. []

6. If you need to look at every item in a list, what technique do you use?

Ans. Traversing

7. What is the use of the list() method?

Ans. The list() method takes sequence types and converts them to lists. This is used to convert a given tuple into a list.

8. Give the syntax for slicing a list's elements which are not consecutive.

Ans. sliced_list = list_name[start:stop:step]

9. What do you mean by the insert() method?

Ans. The insert() method is used to insert an element at a specified position in the list.

10. Define the min() function used in a list.

Ans. The min() function is used to return the minimum element out of the elements of a list.

```
min(list_name)
```

11. How to count the elements of a list?

Ans. list_name.count(element)

12. What sort() option arranges items from highest to lowest?

Ans. reverse=True

13. **Find the output.**

```
>>> l1 = [4, 3, 4, 5]
>>> l2 = [2, 6, 5, 4]
>>> l1 > l2
```

Ans. True

Short Answer Type I Questions

14. **What is a nested list ? Explain with an example.**

Or **Distinguish between string and list.**

Ans. Nested lists are list objects where the elements in the lists can be lists themselves.

For example,

```
list1 = [45, 43, 12, 'Math', 'Eng', [75,
                               34, 'A'], 5]
```

list1 contains 7 elements while inner list contains 3 elements. list1 is considered [75, 34, 'A'] as one element.

Or

Feature	String	List
Data Type	Immutable sequence of characters	Mutable sequence of items of any data type
Mutability	Cannot be changed after creation	Can be modified after creation (add, remove, change items)
Syntax	Enclosed in single (' ') or double (" ") quotes	Enclosed in square brackets ()
Iteration	Can iterate through individual characters	Can iterate through individual items
Operations	Concatenation (+), repetition (*), slicing, etc.	Append, insert, remove, sort, etc.
Example	"Hello"	[1, 2, 'a', 3.14]

15. **Observe the given list and find the answer of questions that follows.**

```
list1 = [45, 77, 87, "Next", "Try", 33, 43]
```

(i) list1[-2] (ii) list1[2]

Ans. (i) 33 (ii) 87

16. **What is the output of the below program?**

```
l2 = [75, 43, 40, 36, 28, 82]
l2.sort(reverse=True)
print(l2)
```

Ans. [82, 75, 43, 40, 36, 28]

17. **Find the errors.**

```
L1 = [2, 4, 5, 9]
L2 = L1 * 3
L4 = L1.pop(5)
L3 = L1 + 3
```

Ans. Error 1 L3 = L1 + 3 cannot add a list and an integer.

Error 2 L1.pop(5) tries to access an index out of range.

18. **Predict the output.**

```
L2 = [5, 4, 3, 1, 11]
print(L2.count(1))
print(L2.index(3))
print(L2.remove(11))
print(L2)
```

Ans. Output

1

2

None

[5, 4, 3, 1]

19. **Find the output.**

```
L = [3, 4, 53, 4, 0, 2, 4, 7, 29]
print(L[2:5])
print(L[::-1])
```

Ans. [53, 4, 0]

[29, 7, 4, 2, 0, 4, 53, 4, 3]

20. **Find the output of the given code.**

```
list1 = ["A", "R", "T", "H", "U", "R"]
for i in range(len(list1)):
  print(list1[i], end = " ")
```

Ans. A R T H U R

21. **Describe the outcome when you multiply a Python list by an integer. What does this operation achieve?**

Ans. Multiplying a Python list by an integer repeats its elements the specified number of times. It does not perform element-wise multiplication but creates a new list with repeated values.

e.g.
```
nums = [1, 2, 3] * 3
print(nums)
  # Output: [1, 2, 3, 1, 2, 3, 1, 2, 3]
```

22. **Consider the following list and answer the below questions:**

```
list1 = [89, 45, "Taj", "Qutub", 93, 42,
"Delhi", "Agra"]
```

(i) list1[5] (ii) "Qutab" not in list1

(iii) list1[-3] (iv) list1[9]

(v) list1[2:5] (vi) list1[-2:]

Ans. (i) 42 (ii) False

(iii) 42 (iv) IndexError (out of range)

(v) ["Taj", "Qutub", 93] (vi) ["Delhi", "Agra"]

23. **Predict the output.**

```
L1 = [3, 4, 5, 9, 11, 2, 27]
print(max(L1))
print(len(L1))
```

Ans. Output
27
7

24. **You have a list of numbers and need to find the index of the first occurrence of the number 5. Write a short Python code snippet that demonstrates how to do this using the appropriate list method.**

Ans.
```
my_list = [1, 2, 5, 3, 5]
index_of_5 = my_list.index(5)
print(index_of_5)
```
Output 2

Short Answer Type II Questions

25. **If L1 = [1, 2, 3, 2, 1, 2, 4, 2, ...] and L2 = [10, 20, 30, ...], then (Answer using built-in functions only)**

(I) (A) Write a statement to count the occurrences of 2 in L1.

Or

(B) Write a statement to remove the first occurrence of 1 from L1.

(II) (A) Write a statement to insert the number 5 at the third position in L2.

Or

(B) Write a statement to return the index of the first occurrence of 20 in L2.

Ans. (I) (A) count_of_2 = L1.count(2)
```
print(count_of_2)
```
Or

(B) L1.remove(1)
```
print(L1)
```
(II) (A) L2.insert(2, 5)
```
print(L2)
```
Or

(B) index_of_20 = L2.index(20)
```
print(index_of_20)
```

26. **If L1 = ['apple', 'banana', 'cherry', 'date', 'elderberry'] is a Python list, then:**

(I) (A) Explain how you would traverse the entire list L1 using a for loop and print each element.

Or

(B) Explain how you would access and print the element at index 2 of list L1.

(II) (A) Explain how you would traverse the list L1 using a while loop and print each element.

Or

(B) Explain how you would access and print the last element of list L1 without knowing its length beforehand.

Ans. (I) (A) Use a for loop to iterate over the list and print each element:
```
for item in L1: print(item)
```
(B) Access and print the element at index 2 using L1[2]:
```
print(L1[2])  # Prints 'cherry'
```
(II) (A) Use a while loop with an index counter to print each element:
```
index = 0; while index < len(L1):
          print(L1[index]); index += 1
```
(B) Access the last element using negative indexing L1[-1]:
```
print(L1[-1]) #Prints 'elderberry'
```

27. **(A) What is the result of the following Python code:**
```
my_list = [1, 2, 3]
my_list.append(4)
print(my_list)
```
Explain why you get this result.

Or

(B) Explain how you would create a list of squares of numbers from 1 to 5 using a list comprehension in Python.

Ans. (A) The result of the code is [1, 2, 3, 4].

The append() method adds the value 4 to the end of the existing list my_list. Therefore, after my_list.append(4), the list becomes [1, 2, 3, 4].

(B) To create a list of squares of numbers from 1 to 5 using a list comprehension:
```
squares = [x**2 for x in range(1, 6)]
print(squares)
```
Output [1, 4, 9, 16, 25]

Long Answer Type Questions

28. **You are developing a program that manages a dynamic list of tasks. This list needs to be flexible enough to allow for various types of modifications, including inserting new tasks at specific positions and integrating tasks from other lists.**

(i) Which Python list method is best for inserting a new task at a specific position? Explain its syntax and how it handles different insertion points. Provide a short code example.

(ii) Which Python list method is best for adding the contents of one task list to another? Explain its behavior and provide a short code example.

(iii) Briefly discuss the time complexity of these methods and suggest a scenario where an alternative data structure might be more efficient.

Ans. (i) Inserting an element at a specified position:

The insert() method is best.

Syntax `list.insert(index, element)`

Explanation Inserts element before the given index.

Example `tasks.insert(1, "New Task")`

(ii) Adding contents from one list to another:

The extend() method is best.

Explanation Appends all elements from one list to the end of another.

Example tasks.extend(additional_tasks)

(iii) Time Complexity and Alternatives:

insert() O(n) time complexity (n = elements after insertion).

extend() O(k) time complexity (k = length of added list).

Alternative If frequent insertions/deletions at both ends are needed, use a deque for O(1) time complexity.

29. Write a program to move all zeroes to the end of the list.

Ans.
```
list1 = [4, 7, 0, 9, 8, 0, 2, 0, 4, 9, 0]
count = 0
for i in range(len(list1)):
    if list1[i] != 0:
        list1[count] = list1[i]
        count += 1
while count < len(list1):
    list1[count] = 0
    count += 1
print("List after pushing all zeros to end
                                  of list:")
print(list1)
```

Output

List after pushing all zeros to end of list:

[4, 7, 9, 8, 2, 4, 9, 0, 0, 0, 0]

30. You are analyzing a Python list list1 that contains mixed data types, including a nested list.

```
list1 = [45, 65, "The", [65, "She", "He"],
90, 12, "This", 21]
```

(i) Explain how list1[3:4] works and what it returns. Why?

(ii) What value is returned by list1[4]? Explain.

(iii) What elements are included in list1[:7]? Why?

(iv) What is the result of list1[1:2] + list1[3:4]? Explain the steps.

Ans. (i) This slice extracts elements from index 3 up to (but not including) index 4. This includes only the element at index 3, which is the nested list [65, "She", "He"]. Therefore, it returns [[65, "She", "He"]].

(ii) This accesses the element at index 4, which is the fifth element in the list. This element is 90.

(iii) This slice extracts elements from the beginning of the list up to (but not including) index 7. It includes elements at indices 0 through 6. The result is [45, 65, "The", [65, "She", "He"], 90, 12, "This"].

(iv) **list1[1:2]** extracts the element at index 1, which is 65. Result: [65].

list1[3:4] extracts the nested list at index 3: [[65, "She", "He"]].

The + operator concatenates these two lists.

Result [65, [65, "She", "He"]].

31. You are tasked with developing a robust and efficient solution for analyzing numerical data entered by a user. This data represents a series of measurements, and your goal is to identify and report the third largest value.

Ans.
```
numbers = input("Enter numbers separated
                    by spaces: ").split()
    # Take input as a list of strings
numbers = [int(num) for num in numbers]
if len(numbers) < 3:
    print("Not enough values to determine
                 the third largest.")
else:
    numbers = list(set(numbers))
    numbers.sort(reverse=True)
    print("Third largest value:", numbers[2])
```

32. Write a Python program to find the odd and even numbers from entered list and display them in two different list.

Ans.
```
num = int(input("Enter number of
                         elements: "))
a = []
even = []
odd = []
for i in range(1, num+1):
    x = int(input("Enter element: "))
    a.append(x)
for y in a:
    if (y%2 == 0):
        even.append(y)
    else:
        odd.append(y)
print("The even list", even)
print("The odd list", odd)
```

33. Write a Python program to count positive and negative numbers in a list.

Ans.
```
num = int(input("Enter number of
                         elements: "))
x = []
for i in range(1, num+1):
    element = int(input("Enter element: "))
```

```
    x.append(element)
pos_count = 0
neg_count = 0
for i in x:
    if i > 0:
        pos_count += 1
    elif i < 0:
        neg_count += 1
print("Positive numbers in the list:",
                                    pos_count)
print("Negative numbers in the list:",
                                    neg_count)
```

34. Write a program to search a number entered by a user in a list of 100 numbers and then print the index position of that number. Now swap it with the number 10 places previous to it.

Ans.

```
searchlist = []
foundpos = -1
for i in range(100):
    searchlist.append(int(input("enter a
                                number")))
searchnum = int(input("enter the number to be
                                searched"))
for i in range(100):
  if (searchnum == searchlist[i]):
    foundpos = i
    break
if (foundpos == -1):
  print("Number not found")
else:
  print("Number found at", foundpos)
  a = searchlist[foundpos]
  searchlist[foundpos] = searchlist[foundpos - 10]
  searchlist[foundpos - 10] = a
  print("new list is", searchlist)
```

Case Study Based Question

Case Study

A Python list is a versatile data structure that allows you to store a collection of items. It's like a dynamic array, capable of holding elements of various data types, including integers, strings, and even other lists. Lists are mutable, meaning you can modify their contents after creation.

Based on the above information, answer the following questions.

(i) Which of the following is a correct way to create a list in Python?

(a) list1 = list() (b) list1 = [1, 2, 3, 4]
(c) Both (a) and (b) (d) None of these

(ii) Which of the following is true about Python lists?

(a) Lists are immutable.
(b) List size must be declared beforehand.
(c) List elements are stored contiguously in memory.
(d) The size(list1) function is used to find the size of a list.

(iii) Which of the following Python code snippets will result in an error?

(a) list1 = [] (b) list1 = [] * 3
(c) list1 = [2, 8, 7] (d) None of these

(iv) What is the output of the following code?

```
L = [1, 2, 3, 4, 5, [6, 7, 8]]
print(L[5])
```

(a) [6, 7, 8] (b) 6
(c) Error (d) None of these

(v) Consider the following list:

```
L1 = [10, 56, 23, 45, 55, 23, 11, 65, 47,
                                [15, 13], 75]
```

What will be the output of the following statement?

```
print(L1[::-3])
```

(a) [75, 65, 55, 56] (b) [75, 65, 55, 10]
(c) [75, 65, 55, 56, 10] (d) Error

(vi) Which of the following operations will sort a list in descending order?

(a) list_name.sort() (b) max(list_name)
(c) list_name.reverse() (d) list_name[-1]

Ans. (i) (c) Both (a) and (b)
(ii) (c) List elements are stored contiguously in memory.
(iii) (d) None of the above
(iv) (a) [6, 7, 8]
(v) (a) [75, 65, 55, 56]
(vi) (c) list_name.reverse ()

SELF ASSESSMENT TEST

Multiple Choice Questions

1. What is the output of following code?

```
list1=[4, 3, 7, 6, 4, 9, 5, 0, 3, 2]
l1=list1[1:10:3]
print(l1)
```

(a) [3, 7, 6] (b) [3, 4, 0]
(c) [3, 6, 9] (d) [7, 9,2]

2. Identify the output of following Python statement.

```
a = [[0, 1, 2], [3, 4, 5, 6]]
b=a [1] [2]
print (b)
```

(a) 2 (b) 1
(c) 4 (d) 5

3. Identify the output of following code.

```
list1 = [2, 3, 9, 12, 4]
list1.insert(4, 17)
list1.insert(2, 23)
print(list1 [-4])
```

(a) 4 (b) 9
(c) 12 (d) 23

Fill in the Blanks

4. An ordered, mutable sequence of elements is a _____.

5. The ________ method is used to insert an element at a specific index.

6. The ________ method is used to remove an element from a list by its index.

7. ________ is accessing each element of a list sequentially.

8. The ________ method reverses the order of elements in a list.

9. ________ lists enable creating data structures with multiple dimensions.

State Whether True or False

10. Lists are immutable in Python.

11. List slicing modifies the original list.

12. The insert() method adds an element to the end of a list.

13. Nested lists can contain lists of the same length only.

14. Passing a list as an argument to a function creates a copy of the list.

15. The reverse() method modifies the original list.

Assertion and Reason Based Questions

Assertion (A) and Reason (R) Type questions. Choose the correct option as:

(a) Both Assertion (A) and Reason (R) are true, and Reason (R) is the correct explanation of Assertion (A).
(b) Both Assertion (A) and Reason (R) are true, but Reason (R) is not the correct explanation of Assertion (A).
(c) Assertion (A) is true, but Reason (R) is false.
(d) Assertion (A) is false, but Reason (R) is true.

16. Assertion (A) Lists in Python are mutable.
Reason (R) Elements in a list can be modified after the list is created.

17. Assertion (A) List slicing creates a new list object.
Reason (R) List slicing extracts a portion of the original list without modifying it.

18. Assertion (A) The insert() method adds elements at a specified index.
Reason (R) The insert() method modifies the original list by adding elements at the given index.

19. Assertion (A) The sort() method returns a new sorted list without modifying the original.
Reason (R) List methods are built-in functions for list operations.

20. Assertion (A) Lists in Python can only store elements of the same data type.
Reason (R) List copying methods create independent copies of lists.

Very Short Answer Type Questions

21. Which type of data can be store in list?

22. Write an example of mixed data type list.

23. How to compare a list in Python ?

24. Write the syntax for finding the min element in list.

Short Answer Type Questions

25. What is the use of (*) operator in list?

26. Define the max ( ) function with an example.

27. Explain the parameters of given syntax.

```
l = list_name [Start : Stop : Step]
```

28. Find the errors.

```
L = [43, 47, 40, 72]
L1 = "L + Math"
L2 = L . extend (L1)
```

29. What is the output of below questions?

```
L = [45, 89, 74, 12, 9, 83]
```

(i) L. remove ( ) (ii) L. remove (12)

30. Predict the output.

```
L1 = [3, 2, 1]
L2 = [5, 9, 8]
print (L1 * L2)
print (L2.sort ( ))
print (L1.reverse( ))
```

31. Write a Python program to move all zeroes to the starting of the list.

32. Write a program to count the even numbers in a list.

Long Answer Type Questions

33. Write the best suited method's name for the following conditions.

(i) Remove the value from the list.
(ii) Sort the elements in descending order.
(iii) Calculate the sum of all the elements of list.
(iv) Return the minimum element out of elements.

34. Write the program to print second largest number from the list.

35. Write a program to find maximum and minimum sum of elements of list in a list. Also, display its output.

Case Study Based Questions

36. A library wants to create a system to track books that are currently checked out. The system should allow librarians to store book titles and the member IDs of those who borrowed them, identify overdue books, and calculate the total number of books checked out.

(i) Which Python data type would be most suitable for storing book titles and member IDs?
(a) Dictionary (b) Tuple
(c) String (d) List

(ii) To calculate the total number of books checked out, the system needs to perform:
(a) List sorting
(b) List traversal and counting
(c) List slicing
(d) List concatenation

(iii) To identify overdue books, the system should use:
(a) List sorting
(b) List concatenation
(c) List traversal and conditional checks
(d) List slicing

(iv) If the librarian wants to add a new book to the system, which list method would be used?
(a) sort()
(b) pop()
(c) append()
(d) remove()

(v) To store details for multiple copies of the same book, the system would use:
(a) Tuples
(b) Single list
(c) Dictionaries
(d) Nested lists

Answers

1. (b) 2. (d) 3. (b) 4. list 5. insert()
6. pop() 7. Traversing 8. reverse()
9. Nested 10. False 11. False 12. False 13. False
14. False 15. True 16. (a) 17. (a) 18. (a)
19. (d) 20. (d)
36. (i) → (d), (ii) → (b), (iii) → (c), (iv) → (c), (v) → (d)

13

CHAPTER

In Python, a tuple is a built-in data structure used to store an ordered, immutable collection of items.

▼ YOUR STUDY GOALS

13.1 Creating a Tuple in Python
13.2 Accessing Tuples
13.3 Traversing a Tuple
13.4 Tuple Operators
13.5 Tuple Operations
13.6 Packing and Unpacking Tuples
13.7 Built-in Methods
13.8 Deleting a Tuple
13.9 Programs

▼ YOUR PRACTICE GOAL

- Objective Type Questions (25 Qs ; MCQs, True or False, Fill in the Blanks, Assertion and Reason)
- Subjective Type Questions (33 Qs ; VSA, SA, LA)
- Case Study Based Questions-2

Tuples

A tuple is like a locked box that holds a bunch of things separated by commas (,). Once you put things in the box, you can't take them out or add new things. These things can be numbers, words, or even other boxes like this one. Tuples are great for storing information that you don't want to change, like a person's name and age.

Differences Between Tuple and List

Tuple	List
Elements of tuple are immutable	Elements of a list are mutable.
Tuples are declared in parentheses ( )	Lists are declared in square brackets [ ].
Iterating over the elements of a tuple is faster.	Iterating over a list is slower.
The list is better for performing operations, such as insertion and deletion.	A tuple data type is appropriate for accessing the elements.

13.1 Creating a Tuple in Python

To create a tuple in Python, put all the elements in a parentheses ( ), separated by commas. We can have tuples of the same type of data items as well as mixed types of data items.

```
A = (34, 76, 12, 90)
B = ('s', 3, 6, 'a')
C = (34, 0.5, 75)
D = ()
```

We can create different types of tuple in Python which are as follows:

Empty Tuple

An empty tuple, represented as (), is essentially a container with nothing inside.

It's considered false in logical operations, similar to the number 0.
There are two primary methods to create an empty tuple in Python.

```
>>> t = ()
>>> print (t)
()
```

Or

```
>>> t = tuple ()
>>> print (t)
()
```

Single Element Tuple

To create a single-element tuple, you must include a comma after the element, even if it's enclosed in parentheses. This is because Python might interpret a single element without a comma as an integer or expression.

e.g. (1) is interpreted as the integers 1, while (1,) is a tuple containing the integer 1.

Nested Tuple

Nested tuples are tuple objects where the elements in the tuples can be tuples themselves.

For example,

```
>>> t = ('Neha', 6, 9, (1, 4, 8), 'Rahul')
>>> print (t)
('Neha', 6, 9, (1, 4, 8), 'Rahul')
```

It contains 5 elements while the inner tuple contains 3 elements (1, 4, 8). Tuple will be considered (1, 4, 8) as one element.

Mixed Data Types Tuple

It can be created to place different data types such as integers, strings, double etc, into one tuple.

For example,

```
>>> t1 = ('Maths', 90, 89, 'English', 78.5)
>>> t1
('Maths', 90, 89, 'English', 78.5)
```

Creating Tuple from an Existing Sequence

(a) **Using the tuple () Function** You can convert sequences like strings or lists into tuples.

Syntax

```
new_tuple_name = tuple (sequence / string)
                #Here, the sequence includes string,
                                           lists etc.
```

For example,

```
my_list = [1, 2, 3]
my_tuple = tuple(my_list)
```

Output

(1, 2, 3)

Or

```
>>>T = "PROGRAM"
>>> T1 = tuple (T)
>>> T1
```

Output

('P', 'R', 'O', 'G', 'R', 'A', 'M')

(b) **Directly from input** You can create tuple by taking input from the user.

For example,

```
n = int(input("Enter the number of
                                elements: "))
t = ()
for i in range(n):
    element = input(f"Enter element : ")
    t += (element,)
print(t)
```

Output

Enter the number of elements: 2
Enter element : 10
Enter element : Anurag
('10', 'Anurag')

Mistake Alert

Students often make the mistake of trying to modify tuples, forgetting that they are immutable data structures.

13.2 Accessing Tuples

To get a specific item from a tuple, you use its index number. This is similar to how you access items in a list. The index starts from 0, so the first item has an index of 0, the second has an index of 1, and so on.

You can also use negative indices to access items from the end. For example, -1 refers to the last item, -2 to the second-to-last, and so on.

It is called positive index ↑

0	1	2	3	4	5	6	7	8
87	90	'Maths'	'English'	56	44	99	'Science'	23
–9	–8	–7	–6	–5	–4	–3	–2	–1

↓ It is called negative index

For example,

```
t1 = (87, 90, 'Maths', 'English', 56, 44,
99, 'Science', 23)
```

```
>>>t1[1]
90
>>>t1[- 2]
'Science'
>>>t1[7]
'Science'
>>>t1[4]
56
>>>t1[-3]
99
```

If we give index value out of range, then it will give error.

```
>>>t1[9]
Trackback (most recent call last) :
File "<pyshell#8>", line 1, in <module>
  t1[9]
IndexError : tuple index out of range.
```

If you give index number with decimal point, it will also give error.

```
>>>t1[4.5]
Trackback(most recent call last):
File"<pyshell#9>", line1, in <module>
  t1[4.5]
TypeError: tuple indices must be integers
or slices, not float.
```

13.3 Traversing a Tuple

Traversing a tuple is a technique to access an individual element of that tuple. It is also called iterate over a tuple.

There are multiple ways to iterate over a tuple in Python. These are as follows:

(i) Using for loop

The most common and easy way to traverse a tuple is with for loop. This method is used when you want to iterate all elements of a tuple.

For example,

```
t = ('P', 'Y', 'T', 'H', 'O', 'N')
for i in t:
  print (i, end = " ")
```

Output

PYTHON

Or

```
t = ('P', 'Y', 'T', 'H', 'O', 'N')
for i in range (len(t)):
  print (t[i], end = "-")
```

Output

P-Y-T-H-O-N

(ii) Using while loop

A while loop can also be used to iterate over the elements of tuple, but it requires more explicit index management.

For example,

```
my_tuple = (10, 20, 30, 40, 50)
index = 0
while index < len(my_tuple):
    print(my_tuple[index])
    index += 1
```

Output

10
20
30
40
50

13.4 Tuple Operators

We can manipulate lists in different ways using various operators. These are as follows:

Comparison Operators

A comparison operator in Python is also called Python relational operator (<, >, = =, ! =, > =, < =) that compares the values of two operands and returns True or False based on whether the condition is met.

Comparison operators for comparing tuples are as follows:

Operators	Description	Example

Less than (<)	It checks if the left value is lesser than that on the right.	`>>>a=(3, 5, 2, 7)`
		`>>>b=(3, 7, 0, 2)`
		`>>>a<b`
		`True`

Greater than (>)	It checks if the left value is greater than that on the right.	`>>>a=(4, 7, 2, 8)`
		`>>>b=(3, 7, (2), 8)`
		`>>>a>b`
		`True`

Less than or Equal to (<=)	It returns True only if the value on the left is either less than or equal to that on the right of the operator.	`>>>a=(0, 5, 1, 2)`
		`>>>b=(3, 4, 2, 5)`
		`>>>b<=a`
		`False`

Greater than or Equal to (>=)	It returns True only if the value on the left is greater than or equal to that on the right of the operator.	`>>>a=(4, 7, 2)`
		`>>>b=(2,(6,7), 4)`
		`>>>a>=b`
		`True`

Operators	Description	Example
Equal to (= =)	It returns True if the values on either side of the operator are equal.	`>>>a=(1,(2,3), 4)` `>>>b=(1,2,3,4)` `>>>a==b` `False`
Not equal to (!=)	It returns True if the values on either side of the operator are unequal.	`>>>a=(6, 7, 5)` `>>>b=(6, 4, 2)` `>>>a!=b` `True`

Membership Operators

These operators are used to check whether a value/variable exists in the sequence like string, list, tuples etc. These operators return True or False as per the conditions met.

Membership operators in Python are two types as follows:

(i) in Operator

This operator is used to check if a value exists in a sequence or not. It is exists in the sequence, then it will return True else it will return False.

For example,

```
tuple1 = (1,2,3,4,5)
tuple2 = (6,7,8,9)
for item in tuple2:
  print ("overlapping")
else:
  print ("not overlapping")
```

Output

not overlapping

(ii) not in Operator

This operator is the opposite of 'in' operator. So, if a value does not exist in the sequence then it will return a True else it will return a False.

For example,

```
x = 44
y = 30
tuple = (45, 65, 30, 78, 512)
if (x not in tuple):
  print ("x is NOT present in given tuple")
else:
  print ("x is present in given tuple")
if (y in tuple):
  print ("y is present in given tuple")
else:
  print ("y is NOT present in given tuple")
```

Output

x is NOT present in given tuple

y is present in given tuple

13.5 Tuple Operations

We can perform various operations on tuple in Python. Some of them are described below:

(i) Concatenate Tuples

To concatenate tuples, (+) operator is used in Python. This operator can easily add the whole of one tuple to other tuple and perform concatenation.

For example,

```
>>> t1 = (45, 65, 23, 9)
>>> t2 = (34, 23, 65)
>>> t = t1 + t2
>>> t
(45, 65, 23, 9, 34, 23, 65)
```

Concatenate operator (+) cannot add one tuple with other type as number or string. It will give error in such conditions.

For example,

```
>>>t1=(5, 3, 8, 3)
>>>t=t1+4
Trackback (most recent call last):
File "<pyshell # 5>", line1, in <module>
t=t1+4
TypeError : can only concatenate tuple
                    (not ''int'') to tuple
>>>t1=(4,5,3)
>>>t = t1 + "Hello"
Trackback (most recent call last):
File "<pyshell#6>", line1, in <module>
   t = t1 + "Hello"
TypeError: can only concatenate tuple
                      (not "str") to tuple
```

(ii) Replicate Tuple

You can repeat the elements of the tuple using (*) operator. This operator is used to replicate the tuple.

For example,

```
>>>t1=(4, 6, 2, 8)
>>>t=t1*3
>>>t
(4, 6, 2, 8, 4, 6, 2, 8, 4, 6, 2, 8)
```

This operator cannot multiply two tuples.

```
>>> t1 = (4, 6, 2, 8)
>>> t2 = (5, 0, 8)
>>> t = t1 * t2
>>> t
Trackback (most recent call last):
File "<pyshell#11>", line 1 , in <module>
t=t1*t2
TypeError : can't multiply sequence by
                    non-int of type 'tuple'.
```

(iii) Slicing Operators

Slicing is a technique used to extract a specific portion of a sequence, like a tuple. You can specify a starting point and an ending point (not inclusive) using the colon (:) operator. This will give you a new sequence containing the elements within that range.

Below are the operators used for slicing:

Operators	Syntax	Example

Basic Slicing	`tuple[start : end]`	`tuple1 = (4, 3, 7, 6, 4, 9, 5, 0, 3, 2)`
		`print(tuple1 [2 : 5])`
		Output (7, 6, 4)

Omitting Indices	`tuple[: end]`
	`tuple[start :]`
		`print(tuple1[:5])`
		Output (4, 3, 7, 6, 4)
		`print(tuple1[3:])`
		Output (6, 4, 9, 5, 0, 3, 2)

Step Sizing	`tuple[start:end:step]`	`print(tuple1[1:10:3])` **Output** (3, 4, 0)
Negative Indexing	`tuple[-start : -end]`	`print(tuple1[-6:-1])` **Output** (4, 9, 5, 0, 3)

13.6 Packing and Unpacking Tuples

In Python, tuples are collections of elements which are separated by commas. It packs elements or value together so; this is called packing. In other way, it is called unpacking of a tuple of values into a variable.

In packing, we put values together into a new tuple while in unpacking we extract those values into some single variables.

Syntax variable1, variable2, …, variableN = tuple_name

For example,

```
>>> tuple1 = (34, "Hello", 54, 89, "world")
```

To unpack the tuple, take variables equivalent to number of elements in that tuple.

```
>>> a, b, c, d, e = tuple1
```

Now, print individual variable which display the element of tuple.

```
>>> print (a)
34
>>> print (b)
Hello
>>> print (c)
54
>>> print (d)
89
>>> print (e)
world
```

13.7 Built-in Methods

In Python, tuple has large number of built-in functions which perform various operations and make the task easier.

Some of them are describe below:

Methods	Purpose	Syntax	Example

len()	Counts the number of elements in a tuple.	`len(tuple)`	`t1 = (45, "The", 67, 54, "That")`
			`print(len(t1))`
			Output 5

count()	Calculates the total occurrences of a given element in a tuple.	`tuple.count(element)`	`t1 = (10, 20, 40, 10, 50, 20, 10)`
			`print(t1.count(10))`
			Output 3

any()	Returns True if at least one element in the tuple is truthy (not False or 0), otherwise returns False.	`any(tuple)`	`t1 = (3, 6, 4)`
			`print(any(t1))`
			`Output: True`

max()	Returns the element with the maximum value in the tuple.	`max(tuple)`	`t1 = (34, 65, 77, 45, 87, 99, 90)`
			`print(max(t1))`
			Output 99

min()	Returns the elements with the minimum value in the tuple.	`min(tuple)`	`t1 = (34, 65, 77, 45, 87, 99, 90)`
			`print(min(t1))`
			Output 34

sorted()	Sorts the elements of the tuple in ascending order. Returns a new list.	`sorted(tuple)`	`t1 = (32, 45, 25, 33, 47)`
			`print(sorted(t1))`
			Output
			[25, 32, 33, 45, 47,]

Methods	Purpose	Syntax	Example

index()	Returns the index of the first occurrence of a specified element in the tuple.	`tuple.index(element)`	`t1 = (89, 9, "The", 23, "That")`
			`print(t1.index("The"))`
			Output 3
			`print(t1.index("Those"))`
			Output Raises a ValueError as "Those" is not in the tuple

tuple()	Converts strings and lists into tuple.	`tuple(list/string)`	`name = "NIHARIKA"`
			`print(tuple(name))`
			Output ('N', 'I', 'H', 'A', 'R', 'I', 'K', 'A')
			`num = [4, 6, 3, 7, 2, 4, 0, 7]`
			`print(tuple(num))`
			Output
			(4, 6, 3, 7, 2, 4, 0, 7)

sum()	Calculates the sum of all elements in a tuple. The elements must be numeric.	`sum(tuple)`	`marks = (78, 98, 80, 65, 75, 80)`
			`print("Total marks:",sum(marks))`
			Output
			Total marks: 476

reversed()	Returns an iterator that accesses the elements of a sequence in reverse order.	`reversed(sequence)`	`marks = (78, 98, 80, 65, 75, 80)`
			`t = reversed(marks)`
			`print(t)`
			Output
			`<reversed object at 0x00F49F70>`
			`for i in t:`
			`    print(i)`
			Output
			80, 75, 65, 80, 98, 78

13.8 Deleting a Tuple

Tuples are immutable and cannot be deleted, but deleting tuple entirely is possible by using the keyword "del".

For example,

```
t1 = (4,6,7,8,5,34,2)
print ("Tuple is :", t1)
del (t1)
print ("Tuple after deleting")
print (t1)
```

Output

Tuple is : (4,6,7,8,5,34,2)

Tuple after deleting

Trackback (most recent call last) :

File "<pyshell#6>", line 1, in <module>

print(t1)

NameError: name 't1' is not defined

13.9 Programs

1. Finding Minimum, Maximum, and Mean of Values in a Tuple

Ans.
```
my_tuple = (10, 25, 3, 15, 20)
# Find minimum
minimum = min(my_tuple)
print("Minimum value:", minimum)
# Find maximum
maximum = max(my_tuple)
print("Maximum value:", maximum)
# Calculate mean
mean = sum(my_tuple) / len(my_tuple)
print("Mean value:", mean)
```

2. Find Linear Search on a Tuple of Numbers

Ans.
```
my_tuple = (10, 25, 3, 15, 20)
target = 15
found = False
for i in range(len(my_tuple)):
    if my_tuple[i] == target:
        found = True
        index = i
        break
if found:
    print(f"Element {target} found at index {index}")
else:
    print("Element not found")
```

3. Counting the frequency of Elements in a Tuple

Ans.
```
my_tuple = (10, 25, 3, 15, 20, 10, 25, 3)
freq_dict = {}
for num in my_tuple:
    if num in freq_dict:
        freq_dict[num] += 1
    else:
        freq_dict[num] = 1
print("Frequency of each element:")
for num, count in freq_dict.items():
    print(f"{num}: {count}")
```

Mind Map

TUPLES

Tuple vs List

Tuple	List
• Elements of tuple are immutable.	• Elements of a list are mutable.
• Tuples are declared in parentheses ( ).	• Lists are declared in square brackets [ ].
• Iterating over the elements of a tuple is faster.	• Iterating over a list is slower.

Deleting Tuples

Tuples are immutable and cannot be deleted, but deleting tuple entirely is possible by using the keyword "del".

Traversing a Tuple

Using for Loop

```
t = ('P', 'Y', 'T', 'H', 'O', 'N')
for i in t:
print (i, end = " ")
```

```
t = ('P', 'Y', 'T', 'H', 'O', 'N')
for i in range (len(t)):
print (t[i], end = "-")
```

Using while Loop

```
my_tuple = (10, 20, 30, 40, 50)
index = 0
while index < len(my_tuple):
    print(my_tuple[index])
    index += 1
```

Creating a Tuple in Python

To create a tuple in Python, put all the elements in a parentheses ( ), separated by commas. We can create different types of tuple in Python which are as follows:

- Empty Tuple
- Single Element Tuple
- Nested Tuple
- Mixed Data Types Tuple

Tuple Operators

Comparison Operators

A comparison operator in Python is also called Python relational operator (<, >, = =, ! =, > =, < =) that compares the values of two operands and returns True or False based on whether the condition is met.

Membership Operators

These operators are used to check whether a value/variable exists in the sequence like string, list, tuples etc. These operators return True or False as per the conditions met. Membership operators in Python are two types: in , not in.

Accessing Tuples

To get a specific item from a tuple, you use its index number. This is similar to how you access items in a list. The index starts from 0, so the first item has an index of 0, the second has an index of 1, and so on.

Packing and Unpacking Tuples

In packing, we put values together into a new tuple while in unpacking we extract those values into some single variables.

Syntax variable1, variable2,…, variableN = tuple_name

Creating Tuple from an Existing Sequence

Using the tuple () Function

Example,

```
my_list = [1, 2, 3]
my_tuple = tuple(my_list)
```

Directly from Input

Example,

```
n = int(input("Enter the number of elements: "))
t = ()
for i in range(n):
    element = input(f"Enter element : ")
    t += (element,)
print(t)
```

Built-in Methods

Methods	Syntax
len()	len(tuple)
count()	tuple.count(element)
any()	any(tuple)
max()	max(tuple)
min()	min(tuple)
sorted()	sorted(tuple)
index()	tuple.index(element)
tuple()	tuple(list/string)
sum()	sum(tuple)
reversed()	reversed(sequence)

Tuple Operations

Concatenate Operations

```
>>> t1 = (45, 65, 23, 9)
>>> t2 = (34, 23, 65)
>>> t = t1 + t2
>>> t
```

Replicate Tuple

```
>>>t1=(4, 6, 2, 8)
>>>t=t1*3
>>>t
```

Slicing Operators

Slicing is a technique used to extract a specific portion of a sequence, like a tuple. You can specify a starting point and an ending point (not inclusive) using the colon (:) operator.

NCERT Folder

Exercise Questions

1. Consider the following tuples, tuple1 and tuple2:

```
tuple1 = (23,1,45,67,45,9,55,45)
tuple2 = (100,200)
```

Find the output of the following statements:

(i) `print(tuple1.index(45))`

(ii) `print(tuple1.count(45))`

(iii) `print(tuple1 + tuple2)`

(iv) `print(len(tuple2))`

(v) `print(max(tuple1))`

(vi) `print(min(tuple1))`

(vii) `print(sum(tuple2))`

(viii) `print(sorted(tuple1))`
`print(tuple1)`

Ans. Output

(i) 2 (ii) 3

(iii) (23, 1, 45, 67, 45, 9, 55, 45, 100, 200)

(iv) 2 (v) 67

(vi) 1 (vii) 300

(viii) [1, 9, 23, 45, 45, 45, 55, 67]
(23, 1, 45, 67, 45, 9, 55, 45)

2. "Lists and Tuples are ordered". Explain.

Ans. Lists and tuples are ordered collections means that the items in these collections have a specific order, and this order is maintained. For example, if you have a list of fruits: ["apple", "banana", "orange"], the order is important. The first fruit is "apple", the second is "banana", and the third is "orange". You can access these fruits by their position (index) in the list.

3. What advantages do tuples have over lists?

Ans. Tuples have a lot of advantages over a list, some of them are as follows:

- **Immutability** Tuples are immutable, meaning their contents cannot be changed after creation. This makes them safer and more reliable in certain scenarios, as accidental modifications are prevented.
- **Efficiency** Tuples are generally more memory-efficient than lists, especially for large datasets.
- **Hashability** Tuples can be used as keys in dictionaries, while lists cannot. This enables them to be used in various data structures and algorithms.
- **Readability** In some cases, using tuples can make code more readable and concise, especially when representing fixed data structures.

4. Prove with the help of an example that the variable is rebuilt in case of immutable data types.

Ans. When you modify an immutable data type like a tuple, a new tuple is created, and the original tuple remains unchanged. The variable is then reassigned to point to this new tuple.

e.g.
```
tuple1 = (1, 2, 3)
tuple2 = tuple1 + (4,)
print(tuple1)
print(tuple2)
```

Output

(1, 2, 3)

(1, 2, 3, 4)

In this example, tuple1 remains unchanged as tuples are immutable. When we add (4,) to it, a new tuple (1, 2, 3, 4) is created, and tuple2 is assigned to this new tuple.

5. TypeError occurs while statement 2 is running. Give a reason. How can it be corrected?

```
>>> tuple1 = (5)          #statement 1
>>> len(tuple1)           #statement 2
```

Ans. The error occurs because (5) is not considered a tuple. To create a single-element tuple, you need to add a comma after the element:

```
tuple1 = (5,)
  # Correct way to create a
                      single-element tuple
```

Now, len(tuple1) will correctly return 1.

6. With the help of an example show how you can return more than one value from a function.

Ans. In Python, functions can return multiple values by packing them into a tuple.

For example,

```
def calculate_circle_properties(radius):
      area = 3.14159 * radius * radius
    circumference = 2 * 3.14159 * radius
    return area, circumference
# Calling the function and unpacking the
                              returned values
radius = 5
area, circumference =
        calculate_circle_properties(radius)
print("Area:", area)
print("Circumference:", circumference)
```

Programming Based Questions

1. Write a program to read email IDs of n number of students and store them in a tuple. Create two new tuples, one to store only the usernames from the email IDs and second to store domain names from the email IDs. Print all three tuples at the end of the program. [Hint: You may use the function split()]

Ans.
```
n = int(input("Enter the number of
students: "))
email_ids = []
for i in range(n):
    email = input("Enter email ID {}:
                    ".format(i+1))
    email_ids.append(email)
email_tuple = tuple(email_ids)
usernames = []
domains = []
for email in email_tuple:
    username, domain = email.split('@')
    usernames.append(username)
    domains.append(domain)
username_tuple = tuple(usernames)
    #convert list tuple
domain_tuple = tuple(domains)
print("Email IDs:", email_tuple)
print("Usernames:", username_tuple)
print("Domains:", domain_tuple)
```

Output

Enter the number of students: 2
Enter email ID 1: Abc@gmail.com
Enter email ID 2: Xyz@musician.org
Email IDs: ('Abc@gmail.com', 'Xyz@musician.org')
Usernames: ('Abc', 'Xyz')
Domains: ('gmail.com', 'musician.org')

2. Write a program to input names of n students and store them in a tuple. Also, input a name from the user and find if this student is present in the tuple or not.

We can accomplish these by:

(a) writing a user defined function

(b) using the built-in function

Ans. (a) Using a User-Defined Function
```
def is_student_present(student_tuple,
                       name):
    for student in student_tuple:
        if student == name:
            return True
    return False
n = int(input("Enter the number of
                   students: "))
students = []
for i in range(n):
  name = input(f"Enter name of student
                           {i+1}: ")
  students.append(name)
student_tuple = tuple(students)
search_name = input("Enter the name to
                          search: ")
if is_student_present(student_tuple,
                     search_name):
  print(f"{search_name} is present in
                        the tuple.")
else:
  print(f"{search_name} is not present
                     in the tuple.")
```

Output

Enter the number of students: 2
Enter name of student 1: Anurag
Enter name of student 2: Abhishek
Enter the name to search: Abhishek
Abhishek is present in the tuple.

(b) Using the Built-in function in Operator
```
n = int(input("Enter the number of
                   students: "))
students = []
for i in range(n):
  name = input(f"Enter name of student
                           {i+1}: ")
  students.append(name)
student_tuple = tuple(students)
search_name = input("Enter the name to
                          search: ")
if search_name in student_tuple:
  print(f"{search_name} is present in
                        the tuple.")
else:
  print(f"{search_name} is not present
                     in the tuple.")
```

Output

Enter the number of students: 2
Enter name of student 1: Anurag
Enter name of student 2: Abhishek
Enter the name to search: Anurag
Anurag is present in the tuple.

EXAM PATTERN QUESTIONS

Objective Type Questions

Multiple Choice Questions

1. Which of the following is a collection of Python objects separated by commas and represented as (,)?

(a) List (b) Tuple
(c) Dictionary (d) String

2. Which of the following data types can be converted into a tuple using the tuple() function?

(a) List (b) String
(c) Dictionary (d) All of these

3. What is the output of the following code?

```
t1 = (70, 56, 'Hello', 22, 2, 'Hi', 'The',
                                   'World', 3)
print (t1[2:4])
```

(a) (56, 'Hello') (b) ('Hello', 22)
(c) ('Hello', 22,2) (d) (56, 'Hello', 22)

4. Is the following Python code valid?

```
>>> tup1 = (56, 25, 36, 15)
>>> result = tup1.update (4, )
```

(a) Yes, tup1=(56, 25, 36, 15,4) and result=(56, 25, 36, 15,4)
(b) Yes, tup1=(56, 25, 36,15) and result=(56, 25, 36, 15,4)
(c) No, because tuples are immutable
(d) No, because wrong syntax for update() method

5. What is the output of the following Python code?

```
my_tuple = (10, 20, 30, 40, 50)
print(my_tuple[2] + my_tuple.index(40))
```

(a) 42 (b) 43 (c) 33 (d) 45

6. What is the output of the following code?

```
t = (4, 0, 'Hello', 90, 'Two', ('One', 45),
                                      34, 2)
t1 = t[1] + t[-2]
print (t1)
```

(a) 34 (b) 38
(c) Hello34 (d) 45

7. What is the output of the following code?

```
t = (1, 2, 'Hello', 'The', 3, 4)
print (max(t))
```

(a) 'Hello' (b) 4
(c) 'The' (d) Error

8. Which of the following functions is not applicable to tuples in Python?

(a) append() (b) min()
(c) max() (d) count()

Fill in the Blanks

9. A ________ is an immutable sequence type in Python defined using parentheses.

10. Tuples in Python are indexed starting at ________.

11. The operation of joining two tuples together is known as ________.

12. Repeating the elements of a tuple is achieved using the ________ operator.

13. To check if an element exists in a tuple, the ________ keyword is used.

14. The built-in function ________ returns a new list containing the sorted elements of a tuple.

State Whether True or False

15. A tuple in Python is mutable.

16. Tuples support indexing, allowing you to access individual elements by their position.

17. The built-in function len() returns the number of elements in a tuple.

18. The tuple() function converts an iterable (such as a list) into a tuple.

19. The count() method on a tuple returns the first index of the specified element.

Assertion and Reason Based Questions

Assertion (A) and Reason (R) based questions. Mark the correct choice as

(a) Both (A) and (R) are true and (R) is the correct explanation for (A).
(b) Both (A) and (R) are true and (R) is not the correct explanation for (A).
(c) (A) is true and (R) is false.
(d) (A) is false but (R) is true.

20. **Assertion (A)** Tuples are immutable data structures in Python.

Reason (R) Once a tuple is created, its elements cannot be modified.

21. **Assertion (A)** Python provides built-in functions to work with tuples.

Reason (R) len(), max(), and min() are some of the functions used to manipulate tuples.

22. **Assertion (A)** Tuples can be used to store heterogeneous data.

Reason (R) Tuples can hold elements of different data types, such as integers, floats, strings, and even other tuples.

23. **Assertion (A)** Indexing is used to access individual elements in a tuple.

Reason (R) Each element in a tuple has an index, starting from 0.

24. **Assertion** Tuple unpacking is a technique to assign tuple elements to variables.

Reason It allows you to assign multiple values from a tuple to multiple variables in a single line.

25. **Assertion** Tuple slicing is used to extract a portion of a tuple.

Reason The colon (:) operator is used to specify the start and end indices of the slice.

Answers

1. (b) Tuple
2. (d) All of these
3. (b) ('Hello', 22)
4. (c) No, because tuples are immutable
5. (c) 33
6. (a) 34
7. (d) Error
8. (a) append()
9. tuple
10. 0
11. concatenation
12. * (repetition)
13. in
14. sorted
15. False
16. True
17. True
18. True
19. False
20. (a) Both (A) and (R) are true and (R) is the correct explanation for (A).
21. (a) Both (A) and (R) are true and (R) is the correct explanation for (A).
22. (a) Both (A) and (R) are true and (R) is the correct explanation for (A).
23. (a) Both (A) and (R) are true and (R) is the correct explanation for (A).
24. (a) Both (A) and (R) are true and (R) is the correct explanation for (A).
25. (a) Both (A) and (R) are true and (R) is the correct explanation for (A).

Subjective Questions

Very Short Answer Type Questions

1. What is tuple?

Ans. Tuple is a collection of Python objects separated by commas.

2. Are tuples mutable or immutable?

Ans. Tuples are immutable which means they cannot be changed after creation.

3. Which types of elements are stored in tuple?

Ans. Tuples hold a sequence of heterogeneous elements.

4. How to create an empty tuple?

Ans. Empty tuple can be created in Python using ( ).

e.g.

```
>>> t = tuple()
>>> print (t)
()
```

5. What do you mean by nested tuples?

Ans. Nested tuples are tuple objects where the elements in the tuples can be tuples themselves.

6. Write the syntax to create tuple from an existing sequence.

Ans. `new_tuple_name=tuple(sequence/string)`

7. Observe the output of giving code.

```
>>> t = ["T", "U", "P", "L", "E"]
>>> t2 = tuple (t)
>>> t2
```

Ans. ('T', 'U', 'P', 'L', 'E')

8. What is traversing a tuple in Python?

Ans. Traversing a tuple is a technique to access an individual element of that tuple.

9. What is the use of less than or equal to (<=) operator in tuple?

Ans. This operator returns True only if the value on the left is either less than or equal to that on the right of the operator.

10. Write the output of given code.

```
a = (2, 4, 3, 4)
b = (5, 8, 9)
t = a + b
print (t)
```

Ans. (2, 4, 3, 4, 5, 8, 9)

11. Riya made a tuple in Python. Now, she wants to display elements of tuple from beginning to a range. For this, which formula should she use?

Ans. [: Index]

12. Define len() method with respect to tuple in Python.

Ans. len() method is used to count the number of elements that present in the tuple.

Short Answer Type I Questions

13. Explain the mixed data types tuple with an example.

Ans. Mixed data types can be created to place different data types such as integers, strings, double etc into one tuple.

For example,

```
tuple1 = ('English', 90, 'Anurag', 'Noida',
                                    '99.5')
```

14. Observe the following tuple and answer the questions that follow.

```
tuple1 = ('English', 90, 'Anurag', 'Noida',
                                    '99.5')
```

(i) len(tuple1) (ii) tuple1[-3]

(iii) tuple1[3] (iv) tuple1[: 2]

Ans. (i) 5 (ii) 'Anurag'

(iii) 'Noida' (iv) ('English', 90)

15. Explain sum() method of tuple with an example.

Ans. sum() method is used to calculate the sum of elements of tuple. The elements of tuple must be integer.

```
Syntax sum (tuple_name)
```

For example,

```
>>> price = (100, 150, 95, 120, 80)
>>> sum(price)
545
```

16. How to traverse a tuple using for loop?

Ans. Refer to text on page no. 238 (Traversing a Tuple).

17. Observe the following tuples and answer the questions that follow.

```
t1 = (4, 7, 8, 9)
t2 = (0, 4, 3)
```

(i)
```
>>> t = t1 + t2
>>> print (t)
```

(ii)
```
>>> t = t1 * t2
>>> print (t)
```

Ans. (i) (4, 7, 8, 9, 0, 4, 3)

(ii) It gives TypeError because it can't multiply a sequence by non-int of type 'tuple'.

18. What do you mean by membership operators in Python?

Ans. Membership operators are used to check whether a value/variable exists in the sequence like string, list, tuple etc. These operators return True or False as per conditions met.

Membership operators are of two types as:

(i) in operator (ii) not in operator

19. Explain tuple slicing syntax with its parameters.

Ans. Syntax: tuple_name[start : stop : step]

Here,

- start integer where the slicing of the object starts
- stop integer until which the slicing takes place. The slicing stops at index stop -1.
- step integer value which determines the increment between each index for slicing.

20. Find the output of the given questions

```
t = (45, 76, 23, 'The', 89, ('This', 56),
(23, 'That'), 34)
```

(i) t[4]

(ii) t[2:10:3]

(iii) t[2] + t[-1]

Ans. (i) 89 (ii) (23,('This', 56)) (iii) 57

Short Answer Type II Questions

21. Distinguish between tuple and list.

Ans. Differences between tuple and list are as follows.

Tuple	List
Elements of a tuple are immutable	Elements of a list are mutable
Tuple is declared in parenthesis ()	List is declared in square brackets
Tuples cannot be changed after creation	Lists can be changed after creation
Iterating over the elements of a tuple is fast	Iterating over the elements of a list is slow

22. Write a Python program to find maximum and minimum elements in a tuple.

Ans.

```
tuple1 = (23, 45, -65, -45.20, 45.65, -24)
print("The tuple is:", tuple1)
```

```
mini = tuple1.index(min(tuple1))
maxi = tuple1.index(max(tuple1))
print("Maximum element in the tuple is:",
      max(tuple1), "at index number", maxi)
print("Minimum element in the tuple is:",
      min(tuple1), "at index number", mini)
```

23. Write the short note on the following terms.

(i) Tuple **(ii) in operator**

(iii) Equal to (= =) operator

Ans. (i) Tuple is a collection of Python objects separated by commas (,).

(ii) in operator is used to check if a value exists in a sequence.

(iii) Equal to (= =) operator returns True if the values on either side of the operator are equal.

24. Given a tuple of integers, write a program that calculates the sum of all odd numbers in the tuple.

Example:

If the tuple is (1, 2, 3, 4, 5, 6), the odd numbers are 1, 3, 5 and their sum is 9.

Ans.

```
numbers = (1, 2, 3, 4, 5, 6)
sum_odds = 0
for num in numbers:
    if num % 2 != 0:
        sum_odds += num
print("Sum of odd numbers:", sum_odds)
```

Long Answer Type Questions

25. Output the following statements

(i)
```
t1 = (25, 78, (45, (65, 89)), 90, (34, 8))
len(t1)
```

(ii)
```
t2 = (45, ('The', 78, ('This'), 67), 'The',
67, 67)
t2.count(67)
```

(iii)
```
t1 = (3,)
t2 = ()
t = t1 + t2
any(t)
```

(iv)
```
t3 = (87, 89, 56, 99, 75, 45, 100)
max (t3)
```

Ans. (i) 5 (ii) 2

(iii) True (iv) 100

26. Write a Python program to count the number of elements in a given range using traversal. Also write its output.

Ans.

```
c=0
r=80
tuple1=(10, 20, 30, 40, 50, 40, 40, 60, 70)
for x in tuple1:
    if x>=1 and x<=r:
        c+=1
print("Tuple:", tuple1)
print("Elements in a tuple:", c)
```

Output

Tuple: (10, 20, 30, 40, 50, 40, 40, 60, 70)

Elements in a tuple: 6

27. Find the output of the following code.

```
t = (4, (8, 0, 7))
print(t.count(0))
print(t[1][2])
print(t*2)
t1 = (4, 7, (2, 8))
print(len(t1))
print(t1[2])
print(t+t1)
```

Ans. Output

0

7

(4, (8, 0, 7), 4, (8, 0, 7))

3

(2, 8)

(4, (8, 0, 7), 4, 7, (2, 8))

28. Write a Python program to find the common elements in two tuples.

Ans.

```
tuple1 = (45, 87, 56, -78, 36, -12)
tuple2 = (65, 32, 45, -78, 36, -75)
a_set = set(tuple1)
b_set = set(tuple2)
if (a_set & b_set):
    print("Common elements are:", a_set &
b_set)
else:
    print("No common elements")
```

Output

Common elements are: {-78, 36, 45}

29. Write a Python program to calculate the sum and mean of the elements in a tuple.

Ans.

```
tuple1 = (23, 45, 20, 45, 65, 24)
print("The tuple is:", tuple1)
sum = 0
for num in range(len(tuple1)):
    sum = sum + tuple1[num]
mean = sum / num
print("SUM =", sum)
print("MEAN =", mean)
```

Output

The tuple is: (23, 45, 20, 45, 65, 24)

SUM = 222

MEAN = 44.4

30. Given a tuple of student marks, write a program to find and print the highest and lowest marks from the tuple.

Example:

For the tuple (67, 89, 45, 90, 76), the highest mark is 90 and the lowest mark is 45.

Ans.
```
marks = (67, 89, 45, 90, 76)
highest = marks[0]
lowest = marks[0]
for mark in marks:
        if mark > highest:
            highest = mark
    if mark < lowest:
        lowest = mark
print("Highest mark:", highest)
print("Lowest mark:", lowest)
```

31. Write a Python program to search a element with its index number.

Ans.
```
tuple1 = (12, 65, 78, -63, 2, 3, 78, -12)
x = int(input("Enter number to search:"))
found = False
for i in range(len(tuple1)):
    if tuple1[i] == x:
        found = True
        print("%d found at %dth position" %
                                            (x, i))
        break
if (found == False):
    print("%d is not in tuple" % x)
```

Output

Enter number to search: -63

-63 found at 3th position

32. Write a Python program to count the positive numbers and negative numbers in a tuple.

```
tuple1 = (23, -78, 65, 45, 30, -12, -65, -12)
pos_count, neg_count = 0, 0
for i in tuple1:
    if i > 0:
        pos_count += 1
    else:
        neg_count += 1
print("Positive numbers in the tuple:",
                                    pos_count)
print("Negative numbers in the tuple:",
                                    neg_count)
```

Output

Positive numbers in the tuple: 4

Negative numbers in the tuple: 4

33. Explain comparison operators with respect to tuple in Python.

Ans. Refer to text on page no. 238-239 (Comparison operators).

Case Study Based Questions

Case Study 1

Tuples are a fundamental data structure in Python, characterized by their immutability. This means that once a tuple is created, its elements cannot be modified. Tuples are ordered sequences, allowing access to elements through indexing. Each index in a tuple references a specific element.

Tuples support indexing and slicing operations, enabling the retrieval of individual elements or subsets of elements. The len() function is used to determine the number of elements within a tuple.

Python provides several built-in functions for working with tuples:

- **len(tuple)** Returns the number of elements in the tuple.
- **max(tuple)** Returns the largest element in the tuple.
- **min(tuple)** Returns the smallest element in the tuple.
- **tuple(iterable)** Converts an iterable (like a list or string) into a tuple.

(i) What is the nature of tuples in Python?

(a) Mutable (b) Immutable

(c) Both (a) and (b) (d) None of these

(ii) Which function is used to calculate the number of elements in a tuple?

(a) len(tuple) (b) count(tuple)

(c) size(tuple) (d) total(tuple)

(iii) How can you access individual elements within a tuple?

(a) By using their names

(b) By using their indices

(c) By using their positions

(d) By using their keys

(iv) **Can you modify the elements of a tuple after it's created?**
(a) Yes, using assignment
(b) Yes, using built-in functions
(c) No, tuples are immutable
(d) Only if the tuple is empty

(v) **What is the output of the following code:**
```
my_tuple = (1, 2, 3)
print(my_tuple[1])
```
(a) 1 (b) 2
(c) 3 (d) Error

Ans. (i) (b) Immutable
(ii) (a) len(tuple)
(iii) (b) By using their indices
(iv) (c) No, tuples are immutable
(v) (b) 2

Case Study 2

You are tasked with managing student records in a Python application using tuples. Each student record is represented as a tuple containing the student's name, age, and a nested tuple of their exam scores. All the student records are stored together in a single tuple called class_records.

Consider the following code snippet:
```
student1 = ("Amit", 15, (88, 92, 79))
student2 = ("Ravi", 16, (90, 85, 94))
student3 = ("Ronit", 15, (85, 87, 91))
class_records = (student1, student2, student3)
```
Based on the above information, answer the following multiple-choice questions:

(i) **Which of the following statements about the class_records tuple is TRUE?**
(a) class_records is mutable and can be modified after creation.
(b) class_records is immutable, meaning its contents cannot be changed once created.
(c) class_records is partially mutable; only its nested tuples can be modified.
(d) class_records can be modified, but its elements cannot be accessed using indexing.

(ii) **What is the result of the expression student1[2][1]?**
(a) 15 (b) 92
(c) (88, 92, 79) (d) "Amit"

(iii) **Which built-in function is used to determine the number of student records in class_records?**
(a) len(class_records)
(b) class_records.count()
(c) class_records.index()
(d) sum(class_records)

(iv) **Given the statement name, age, scores = student2, what will be the value of scores?**
(a) "Ravi"
(b) 16
(c) (90, 85, 94)
(d) The entire tuple student2

(v) **To access Ronit's third exam score, which of the following expressions is correct?**
(a) class_records[2][2][2]
(b) class_records[3][2][1]
(c) class_records[2][1][2]
(d) class_records[2][2][1]

Ans. (i) (b) class_records is immutable, meaning its contents cannot be changed once created.
(ii) (b) 92
(iii) (a) len(class_records)
(iv) (c) (90, 85, 94)
(v) (a) class_records[2][2][2]

SELF ASSESSMENT TEST

Multiple Choice Questions

1. Consider the declaration obj = (2, 'Hello', 3, 4). What will be the data type of obj?

(a) List (b) Tuple
(c) Dictionary (d) String

2. Choose the correct option with respect to Python.

(a) Both tuples and lists are immutable.
(b) Tuples are immutable while lists are mutable.
(c) Both tuples and lists are mutable.
(d) Tuples are mutable while lists are immutable.

3. Which of the following options will not result in an error when performed on tuples in Python where tupl=(5,2,7,0,3)?

(a) tupl[1]=2 (b) tupl.append(2)
(c) tupl1=tupl+tupl (d) tupl.sort()

Fill in the Blanks

4. The built-in function ________ returns the number of elements in a tuple.

5. The ________ function can be used to convert an iterable into a tuple.

6. The ________ method returns the number of times a specified element appears in a tuple.

7. The ________ method returns the first index at which a specified element is found in a tuple.

State Whether True or False

8. You can concatenate two tuples using the '+' operator.

9. Repeating the elements of a tuple is achieved by using the '*' operator.

10. The 'in' keyword can be used to test for membership in a tuple.

Assertion and Reason Based Questions

Assertion (A) and Reason (R) Type questions. Choose the correct option as:

(a) Both Assertion (A) and Reason (R) are true, and Reason (R) is the correct explanation of Assertion (A).
(b) Both Assertion (A) and Reason (R) are true, but Reason (R) is not the correct explanation of Assertion (A).
(c) Assertion (A) is true, but Reason (R) is false.
(d) Assertion (A) is false, but Reason (R) is true.

11. Assertion (A) Using the concatenation operator (+) with two tuples results in a new tuple containing all the elements of the original tuples.

Reason (R) Since tuples are immutable, concatenation does not modify the original tuples but creates a new tuple containing the combined elements.

12. Assertion (A) The repetition operator (*) can only be used with a tuple and an integer, and it creates a new tuple with the original tuple's elements repeated the specified number of times.

Reason (R) Python enforces that the second operand in the repetition operation must be an integer to determine the number of times the tuple should be repeated.

13. Assertion (A) Using slicing with a negative step, such as in tuple1[::-1], returns a new tuple with the elements in reverse order.

Reason (R) A negative step in slicing instructs Python to traverse the tuple in reverse order, effectively reversing the order of the elements in the resulting tuple.

Very Short Answer Type Questions

14. Tuple are immutable. Explain?

15. How to create single element tuple?

16. Write the output of given code.

```
>>> t=tuple ("HELLO")
>>> t
```

Short Answer Type Questions

17. What do you mean by unpacking tuples?

18. Which function is used to delete a tuple?

19. How to traverse a tuple using for ( ) loop?

20. What is tuple slicing?

21. Find the error.

```
t1=(2, 4, 5)
t2=(4, 3, 6)
t=t1*t2
```

22. Observe the following code and answer the questions that follow.

```
t=(45, 34, 43, ('Taj', 49), 21, 'Agra')
```

(i) t1=t[1 : 8 : 2]
(ii) t2 = t[: 4]
(iii) t2=t[2] + t[–2]

23. How to access a tuple in Python?

Long Answer Type Questions

24. Explain the following tuple built-in methods.

(i) reserved( ) (ii) sum( )
(iii) all ( ) (iv) tuple ( )

25. Find the output of following code.

```
a=(5, (7, 6, (0)))
print(a.count(6))
print (a[2][3])
print(a*3)
b=(7, 3, (4, 2))
print(len (b))
print(b[1])
print(a+b)
```

26. Write a python program to find element that second largest of a tuple's sequence.

27. Write a program that reverse a tuple of integers.

28. Write a program to find the sum and average of a given tuple.

Case Study Based Questions

29. Anurag is developing a Python application that uses configuration settings stored as tuples. Since these settings are read-only and sometimes complex, Anurag chooses tuples to prevent any accidental modifications. The configuration includes simple tuples, performs various operations like indexing and concatenation, uses tuple methods such as count() and index(), employs tuple assignment (unpacking), and even includes nested tuples for advanced settings.

Based on the above scenario, answer the following multiple-choice questions:

(i) Which of the following is the correct way to define a tuple in Python?

(a) {1, 2, 3} (b) [1, 2, 3]
(c) (1, 2, 3) (d) <1, 2, 3>

(ii) Anurag needs to access the second element from a tuple named config. Which of the following is the correct way to do so?

(a) config(2) (b) config[1]
(c) config{1} (d) config.index(2)

(iii) To determine how many times a particular value appears in a tuple settings, which method should Anurag use?

(a) settings.find() (b) settings.index()
(c) settings.count() (d) settings.len()

(iv) Which of the following correctly unpacks the tuple (10, 20, 30) into variables a, b, and c?

(a) a, b, c = (10, 20, 30)
(b) a = 10, b = 20, c = 30
(c) (a, b, c) = [10, 20, 30]
(d) a, b, c = {10, 20, 30}

(v) Consider a nested tuple config = ((1, 2), (3, 4)). Which expression correctly accesses the value 4?

(a) config[1][1] (b) config[0][1]
(c) config[1,1] (d) config[2][2]

Answers

1. (b) 2. (b) 3. (c) 4. len() 5. tuple()
6. count() 7. index() 8. True 9. True 10. True
11. (a) 12. (a) 13. (a)
29. (i) → (c), (ii) → (b), (iii) → (c), (iv) → (a), (v) → (a)

14

CHAPTER

A dictionary serves as a bridge between words and their meanings, helping us understand, learn and use language effectively.

▼ **YOUR STUDY GOALS**

▼ **YOUR PRACTICE GOAL**

- Objective Type Questions (23 Qs ; MCQs, True or False, Fill in the Blanks, Assertion and Reason)
- Subjective Type Questions (47 Qs ; VSA, SA, LA)
- Case Study Based Question-1

Dictionary

A dictionary in Python is like a real-world dictionary. It's a collection of words (keys) and their meanings (values). Each word is unique, and you can use it to find its meaning.

In Python, a dictionary also has unique keys, which are usually strings or numbers. Each key is paired with a value, which can be anything: a number, a word, a list, or even another dictionary. You can use the key to access its corresponding value.

14.1 Creating a Dictionary

To create a dictionary, you use curly braces {}. Inside the braces, each key-value pair is separated by a colon (:), and different pairs are separated by commas (,).

Syntax `dictionary_name = [key1 : value1, key2 : value2, …]`

For example,

```
>>> Employees = {"Abhi" : "Manager", "Manish" : "Project
Manager", "Aasha" : "Analyst", "Deepak" : "Programmer",
"Ishika" : "Tester"}
```

Here is the example of dictionary name Employees in which Employees names are stored as keys and their designation stored as values of respected keys.

Output

```
{'Abhi': 'Manager', 'Manish' : 'Project Manager', 'Aasha' :
'Analyst', 'Deepak' : 'Programmer', 'Ishika' : 'Tester'}
```

We can separate these dictionaries as follows

Key : Value Pair	Key	Value
"Abhi" : "Manager"	"Abhi"	"Manager"
"Manish" : "Project Manager"	"Manish"	"Project Manager"
"Aasha" : "Analyst"	"Aasha"	"Analyst"
"Deepak" : "Programmer"	"Deepak"	"Programmer"
"Ishika" : "Tester"	"Ishika"	"Tester"

We can also create empty dictionary.

For example, `dic1 = { }`

Dictionaries are also called **mappings or hashes or associative arrays.**

If you give list as key, then it will give Error

```
>>> dic = {[1, 2], "math"}
Trackback (most recent call last):
   File "<pyshell#7>", line 1, in <module>
      dic = {[1, 2], "math"}
TypeError : unhashable type : 'list'
```

Properties of Dictionary Keys

There are following points while using dictionary keys as follows.

(i) More than one entry per key is not allowed (no duplicate key is allowed).

(ii) Dictionaries' keys are case sensitive, same key name but with the different case are treated as different in Python.

(iii) The values in the dictionary can be of any type while the keys must be immutable like numbers, tuples or strings.

Mistake Alert

Students often forget to use quotation marks around string keys when creating dictionaries.

14.2 Accessing Elements from a Dictionary

In Python, to access the elements from a dictionary, keys are used. While in tuple and list, index is used to access the elements.

Syntax `dictionary_name[key]`

To access the respective value of key, that key has to given in square bracket with dictionary name.

For example,

```
>>>Employees ["Deepak"]
'Programmer'
>>>Employees ["Ishika"]
'Tester'
```

You can also give this as

```
>>>print ("Manish works as a", Employees
                                  ['Manish'])
Manish works as a Project Manager
```

If you give a key that does not exist in dictionary, then it will give error. So, before to access the value first ensure that key is available in dictionary or not.

```
>>>Employees ["Tushar"]
Trackback (most recent call last):
   File "<pyshell#11>", line1, in <module>
   Employees ["Tushar"]
KeyError : 'Tushar'
```

If you do not give any key with dictionary name, then it will give whole dictionary with different order.

For example,

```
>>>dic = {'1' : "Math", '2' : "Science",
                            '3' : "English"}
>>>dic
{'1' : 'Math', '3' : 'English', '2' :
                              'Science'}
```

14.3 Traversing a Dictionary

Traversing a dictionary means access each and every element of it. We can traverse a dictionary using for loop.

For example,

```
dic = {1 : "Math", 2 : "Science", 3 :
"English" 4 : "Music"}
```

There are multiple ways to iterate over (traversing) a dictionary in Python as follows.

(i) Iterate through All Keys

In above example, the order of subject number will change every time because the dictionary does not store keys in a particular order.

```
>>>print ("keys are")
>>>for i in dic :
       print(i)
```

Output

Keys are
1
2
3
4

(ii) Iterate through All Values

Again, in above example, the order of subjects are printed will change every time.

For example,

```
>>>print ("Values are")
>>>for i in dic:
       print(dic [i])
```

Output

Values are
Math
Science
English
Music

(iii) Iterate through All Keys Value Pairs

For example,

```
>>>print ("Keys :Values")
>>>for i in dic :
       print(i, ":", dic [i])
```

Output

Keys : Values

1 : Math	2 : Science
3 : English	4 : Music

Accessing Keys or Values Separately

You can access the keys or values of a dictionary separately.

- To access the keys in a dictionary named dict, you can use **dict.keys()**.
- To access the values, you can use **dict.values()**.

For example,

```
>>> dict = {1 : "Math", 2 : "Science", 3 : "English", 4 :
                                                   "Music"}
>>> dict.keys()
dict_keys([1, 2, 3, 4])
>>>dict.values()
dict_values(['Anurag', 'Sharma', 'Khushi', 'Deepika'])
```

You can also access the key-value pairs in a dictionary by using **dict.items()** method.

```
>>> dict = {1 : "Math", 2 : "Science", 3 : "English", 4 :
                                                   "Music"}
>>> dict.items()
dict_items([(1, 'Anurag'), (2, 'Sharma'), (3, 'Khushi'),
                                          (4, 'Deepika')])
```

14.4 Nested Dictionary

Nested dictionary means putting a dictionary inside another dictionary. It allows hierarchical data storage in key-value pair.

Syntax

```
Nested_dict = {'dictA' : {'key1' : 'value1'}, 'dictB' :
{'key2' : 'value2'}}
```

Here, the Nested_dict is a nested dictionary with the dictionary dictA and dictB. They are two dictionaries and each has its own key and value.

For example,

```
>>> Student = {112 : {'Name' : 'Anurag', 'Marks' : 490,
'Age' : 20}, 115 : {'Name' : 'Abhishek', 'Marks' : 480,
'Age' : 20}}
>>> Student
{112 : { 'Marks' : 490, 'Name' : 'Anurag', 'Age' : 20}, 115
: {'Marks' : 480, 'Age' : 20, 'Name' : 'Abhishek' }}
```

14.5 Adding Elements to Dictionary

In Python dictionary, adding elements in dictionary extend it with a single pair of values. One value at a time can be added to a dictionary by defining value along with the key.

Syntax `dictionary_name[key] = value`

For example,

```
>>> Teacher = {'Neha': 'Hindi', 'Akshay':
                        'Math', 'Parul': 'English'}
>>> Teacher['Nisha'] = 'Computer'
>>> Teacher
{'Akshay': 'Math', 'Nisha': 'Computer',
        'Neha': 'Hindi', 'Parul': 'English'}
```

You can also add elements into an empty dictionary by: dictionary_name[key] = value.

For example,

```
>>> dic = {}
>>> dic[1] = "Delhi"
>>> dic[2] = "Meerut"
>>> dic[3] = "Agra"
>>> dic[4] = "Chandigarh"
>>> dic
{1: 'Delhi', 2: 'Meerut', 3: 'Agra', 4:
                                   'Chandigarh'}
```

14.6 Updating Elements in a Dictionary

You can update elements that are already exist in a dictionary.

Syntax `dictionary_name [key] = value`

For example,

```
>>> Student = {11: 'Ashi', 12: 'Shivam',
13: 'Shrey', 14: 'Vicky'}
>>> Student[12] = 'Nishant'
>>> Student
{11: 'Ashi', 12: 'Nishant', 13: 'Shrey',
14: 'Vicky'}
```

If you enter a key that doesn't exist in the dictionary, it will add that key with the specified value.

```
>>> Student[15] = 'Kansal'
>>> Student
{11: 'Ashi', 12: 'Nishant', 13: 'Shrey',
14: 'Vicky', 15: 'Kansal'}
```

14.7 Deleting Elements from a Dictionary

These are following ways to delete elements from a dictionary as follows

(i) Using del Keyword

This keyword is used to delete a specific key-value pair from a dictionary.

Syntax `del dictionary_name[key]`

For example,

```
>>> Teacher = {"Name": "Ashi", "Subject":
        "Math", "Id": 2546, "Salary": 25000}
>>> del Teacher["Id"]
>>> Teacher
{'Name': 'Ashi', 'Subject': 'Math',
                              'Salary': 25000}
```

Note *If you try to delete a key that doesn't exist, it will raise a KeyError.*

```
>>> del Teacher["Age"]
Traceback (most recent call last):
  File "<pyshell#4>", line 1, in <module>
    del Teacher["Age"]
KeyError: 'Age'
```

(ii) Using pop() Method

This method removes a key-value pair and returns the removed value.

Syntax `dictionary_name.pop(key)`

For example,

```
>>> Teacher = {"Name": "Ashi", "Subject":
        "Math", "Id": 2546, "Salary": 25000}
>>> Teacher.pop("Id")
2546
>>> Teacher
{'Name': 'Ashi', 'Subject': 'Math',
                              'Salary': 25000}
```

An advantage of pop() over del is that you can provide a default value to be returned if the key is not found:

```
>>> Teacher.pop("Age", "Key not found in
dictionary")
'Key not found in dictionary'
```

14.8 in and not in Membership Operators

in and not in membership operators are used with dictionary. These operators check whether a specific key is present in dictionary or not. If it is present, then it will give True otherwise False.

Syntax

```
key in dictionary_name
key not in dictionary_name
```

For example,

```
>>> Employee = {'Id': 4598, 'Name':
            'Shubham', 'Dept': 'Programmer',
                              'Salary': 35000}
>>> 'Age' in Employee
False
>>> 'Id' in Employee
True
>>> 'Designation' not in Employee
True
```

Note These operators only work with keys, not values.

```
>>> 'Shubham' in Employee
False
```

To check if a value exists in a dictionary, you need to use the values() method:

```
>>> 'Shubham' in Employee.values()
True
```

14.9 Built-in Methods

Python has some built-in methods that dictionary objects can call. Some of them are described below.

Method	Description
len()	This method is used to return the total length of the dictionary. **Syntax** `len(dictionary_name)`
clear()	This method is used to remove the elements of the dictionary. It produces an empty dictionary. It will only delete elements, not a dictionary. It does not take any parameter and does not return any value. **Syntax** `dictionary_name.clear()`
get()	This method returns the value associated with a given key. If the key is not found, it returns a default value (None by default). **Syntax** `dictionary_name.get(key, value)`
keys()	This method returns a view object containing all the keys in the dictionary. **Syntax** `dictionary_name.keys()`
values()	This method returns a view object containing all the values in the dictionary. **Syntax** `dictionary_name.values()`
items()	This method returns a view object containing key-value pairs as tuples. **Syntax** `dictionary_name.items()`

dict()	This function is used to create a new dictionary. It can create an empty dictionary, a dictionary from another dictionary, or a dictionary from a sequence of key-value pairs.
	Syntax `dict()`
	`dict(mapping)`
	`dict(iterable)`

update()	This method updates a dictionary with key-value pairs from another dictionary or an iterable. **Syntax** `dictionary_name.update(other_dictionary)`
sorted()	This function returns a sorted sequence of the keys in the dictionary. **Syntax** `sorted(dictionary_name)` **Note** *If a dictionary contains both string and integer keys, it will raise a TypeError as they are not comparable.*
fromkeys()	This method creates a new dictionary from a given sequence of keys with a specified value. **Syntax** `dict.fromkeys(seq, value)`
copy()	This method returns a shallow copy of the dictionary. **Syntax** `dict.copy()`
popitem()	This method removes and returns an arbitrary key-value pair from the dictionary. **Syntax** `dict.popitem()`
setdefault()	This method returns the value of a key if it exists in the dictionary. If not, it inserts the key with a specified default value. **Syntax** `dict.setdefault(key[, default_value])`
max()	This method returns the maximum key from the dictionary. **Syntax** `max(dict)`
min()	This method returns the minimum key from the dictionary. **Syntax** `min(dict)`

14.10 Programs

1. Write a Program which counts the number of times a character appears in a given string using a dictionary.

Ans.
```
string = "Mississippi"
char_count = {}
for char in string:
    if char in char_count:
        char_count[char] += 1
    else:
        char_count[char] = 1
print(char_count)
```

Output

{'M': 1, 'i': 4, 's': 4, 'p': 2}

2. Write a Program to create a dictionary with names of employees, their salary and access them.

Ans.
```
employees = {
    "Arjun": 50000,
    "Bheem": 60000,
    "chaaru": 45000
}
# Accessing salary of an employee
print(employees["Bheem"])
# Printing all employee names and salaries
for name, salary in employees.items():
    print(f"{name}: {salary}")
```

Output

60000
Arjun: 50000
Bheem: 60000
chaaru: 45000

Mind Map

DICTIONARY

Creating a Dictionary

To create a dictionary, you use curly braces {}. Inside the braces, each key-value pair is separated by a colon (:), and different pairs are separated by commas (,).

Syntax dictionary_name = [key1 : value1, key2 : value2, …]

Accessing Elements from a Dictionary

In Python, to access the elements from a dictionary, keys are used.While in tuple and list, index is used to access the elements.

Syntax dictionary_name[key]

Modifying a Dictionary

Adding Elements to Dictionary

In Python dictionary, adding elements extend it with a single pair of values. One value at a time can be added to a dictionary by defining value along with the key.

Syntax dictionary_name[key]=value

Updating Elements to Dictionary

You can update elements that are already exist in a dictionary.

Syntax dictionary_name[key]=value

Deleting Elements from a Dictionary

Using del Keyword

Syntax del dictionary_name[key]

Using pop() Method

Syntax dictionary_name.pop(key)

Traversing a Dictionary

Iterate Through All Keys

```
>>>print ("keys are")
>>>for i in dic :
print(i)
```

Iterate Through All Values

```
>>>print ("Values are")
>>>for i in dic:
print(dic [i])
```

Iterate Through All Keys Values Pairs

```
>>>print ("Keys :Values")
>>>for i in dic :
print(i, ":", dic [i])
```

'in' and 'Not in' Membership Operators

in and not in membership operators are used with dictionary. These operators check whether a specific key is present in dictionary or not. If it is present, then it will give True otherwise False.

Syntax

key in dictionary_name

key not in dictionary_name

Built-in Methods

Methods	Syntax
len()	len(dictionary_name)
clear()	dictionary_name.clear()
get()	dictionary_name.get(key, value)
keys()	dictionary_name.keys()
values()	dictionary_name.values()
items()	dictionary_name.items()
update()	dictionary_name.update(other_dictionary)
sorted()	sorted(dictionary_name)
fromkeys()	dict.fromkeys(seq, value)
copy()	dict.copy()
popitem()	dict.popitem()
setdefault()	dict.setdefault(key[, default_value])
max()	max(dict)
min()	min(dict)

NCERT Folder

1. Consider the following dictionary stateCapital:

```
stateCapital =
{"AndhraPradesh":"Hyderabad",
"Bihar":"Patna","Maharashtra":"Mumbai",
"Rajasthan":"Jaipur"}
```

Find the output of the following statements:

(i) `print(stateCapital.get("Bihar"))`

(ii) `print(stateCapital.keys())`

(iii) `print(stateCapital.values())`

(iv) `print(stateCapital.items())`

(v) `print(len(stateCapital))`

(vi) `print("Maharashtra" in stateCapital)`

(vii) `print(stateCapital.get("Assam"))`

(viii)
```
del stateCapital["Rajasthan"]
print(stateCapital)
```

Ans. Output

(i) Patna

(ii) dict_keys(['AndhraPradesh', 'Bihar', 'Maharashtra', 'Rajasthan'])

(iii) dict_values(['Hyderabad', 'Patna', 'Mumbai', 'Jaipur'])

(iv) dict_items([('AndhraPradesh', 'Hyderabad'), ('Bihar', 'Patna'), ('Maharashtra', 'Mumbai'), ('Rajasthan', 'Jaipur')])

(v) 4

(vi) True

(vii) None

(viii) {'AndhraPradesh': 'Hyderabad', 'Bihar': 'Patna', 'Maharashtra': 'Mumbai'}

2. When to use a tuple or dictionary in Python. Give some examples of programming situations mentioning their usefulness.

Ans. Both tuples and dictionaries are fundamental data structures in Python, but they serve different purposes.

(i) **Tuples**

- Tuples are immutable means once created, tuples cannot be changed.
- Elements of tuples are stored in a specific order.
- Tuples are ordered sequences of elements

Example

A student's ID, name, and age can be stored as a tuple, as this information is unlikely to change:

```
student1 = (12345, "Alice Johnson", 20)
```

(ii) **Dictionaries**

- Dictionaries are mutable means elements can be added, removed, or modified.
- Elements of dictionaries are not stored in a specific order.
- Dictionaries are unordered collections of key-value pairs.

Example A student's grades in different subjects can be stored in a dictionary, as the number and names of subjects might vary:

```
student_grades = {"Math": 95, "Science":
88, "English": 92}
```

3. Write a Python program to find the highest 2 values in a dictionary.

Ans.
```
my_dict = {'a': 10, 'b': 25, 'c': 5, 'd':
                                30, 'e': 25}
  # Get a list of values
          values = list(my_dict.values())
  # Sort the values in descending order
                values.sort(reverse=True)
print("Highest 2 values:", values[:2])
```

4. Write a Python program to create a dictionary from a string.

Note Track the count of the letters from the string.

Sample string : 'w3resource'

Expected output : {'3': 1, 's': 1, 'r': 2, 'u': 1, 'w': 1, 'c': 1, 'e': 2, 'o': 1}

Ans.
```
string = 'w3resource'
char_count = {}
for char in string:
    if char in char_count:
        char_count[char] += 1
    else:
        char_count[char] = 1
print(char_count)
```

5. Write a program to input your friends' names and their Phone Numbers and store them in the dictionary as the key-value pair. Perform the following operations on the dictionary:

(a) Display the name and phone number of all your friends

(b) Add a new key-value pair in this dictionary and display the modified dictionary

(c) Delete a particular friend from the dictionary

(d) Modify the phone number of an existing friend

(e) Check if a friend is present in the dictionary or not

(f) Display the dictionary in sorted order of names

Ans.
```
friends = {}
while True:
    name = input("Enter friend's name
              (or type 'quit' to exit): ")
```

```
    if name.lower() == 'quit':
        break
    phone_number = input("Enter phone
                                    number: ")
    friends[name] = phone_number
```

(a) Display all friends and their phone numbers

```
print("\nAll friends and their phone
numbers:")
for name, number in friends.items():
    print(f"{name}: {number}")
```

(b) Add a new friend

```
new_name = input("\nEnter a new friend's
                                  name: ")
new_number = input("Enter the new
                  friend's phone number: ")
friends[new_name] = new_number
print("\nDictionary after adding a new
                               friend:")
for name, number in friends.items():
    print(f"{name}: {number}")
```

(c) Delete a friend

```
delete_name = input("\nEnter a friend's
                      name to delete: ")
if delete_name in friends:
    del friends[delete_name]
    print(f"\n{delete_name} has been
                               deleted.")
else:
    print(f"{delete_name} is not in your
                           friend list.")
```

(d) Modify a phone number

```
modify_name = input("\nEnter a friend's
    name to modify their phone number: ")
if modify_name in friends:
    new_number = input("Enter the new phone
                                 number: ")
    friends[modify_name] = new_number
    print(f"\n{modify_name}'s phone
                 number has been updated.")
else:
    print(f"{modify_name} is not in your
                             friend list.")
```

(e) Check if a friend is present

```
check_name = input("\nEnter a friend's
                         name to check: ")
if check_name in friends:
    print(f"{check_name} is in your friend
                                    list.")
else:
    print(f"{check_name} is not in your
                             friend list.")
```

(f) Display the dictionary in sorted order of names

```
sorted_friends =
sorted(friends.items())
print("\nSorted dictionary:")
for name, number in sorted_friends:
    print(f"{name}: {number}")
```

EXAM PATTERN QUESTIONS

Objective Type Questions

Multiple Choice Questions

1. What will be the output of the following Python code snippet?

```
d1 = {"Neha" : 86, "Yash" : 92}
d2 = {"Neha" : 86, "Yash" : 88}
d1 > d2
```

(a) True (b) False (c) Error (d) None

2. What will be the output of the following Python code?

```
Dic1 = {}
Dic1 [2] = 85
Dic1 [1] = [22, 23, 24]
print(Dic1[1][1])
```

(a) [22,23,24] (b) 23 (c) 22 (d) Error

3. What will be the output of the following Python code?

```
dic1 = {0 : 'One', 1 : 'Two', 2 : 'Three'}
for x, y in dic1:
    print(x, y)
```

(a) 0 1 2 (b) One Two Three
(c) 0 One 1 Two 2 Three (d) Error

4. What will be the output of the following Python code snippet?

```
d = {"Neha" : 140, "Paras" : 145}
print (list(d.keys()))
```

(a) ["Neha", "Paras"]
(b) ["Neha" : 140, "Paras" : 145]
(c) ("Neha", "Paras")
(d) ("Neha" : 140, "Paras" : 145)

5. **What will be the output of the following Python code snippet?**

```
dic1 = {1 : 'One', 2 : 'Two', 3 : 'Three'}
dic1 = {}
print (len(dic1))
```

(a) 1 (b) 0
(c) 3 (d) 2

6. **You have a dictionary student_grades = {'Alice': 85, 'Bob': 92}. You need to change Alice's grade to 90 and add a new student, Charlie, with a grade of 78.**

Which sequence of operations would correctly update the student_grades dictionary?

(a) student_grades['Alice'] = 90; student_grades.update({'Charlie': 78})
(b) student_grades.update({'Alice': 90, 'Charlie': 78})
(c) student_grades['Alice'] = 90; student_grades['Charlie'] = 78
(d) All of the above

7. **You want to count the occurrences of each letter in the word "banana".**

Which of the following dictionaries would be the correct output after counting the character frequencies?

(a) {'b': 1, 'a': 3, 'n': 2}
(b) {'a': 3, 'n': 2, 'b': 1}
(c) {'b': 1, 'a': 3, 'n': 2, 'c': 0}
(d) Either a or b

8. **You have a dictionary employee_salaries = {'John': 50000, 'Jane': 60000, 'Peter': 55000}.**

Which method would you use to get a list of all employee names (keys) in the dictionary?

(a) employee_salaries.values()
(b) employee_salaries.items()
(c) employee_salaries.keys()
(d) employee_salaries.get('John')

Fill in the Blanks

9. To add a new key-value pair to a dictionary or modify an existing one, you can use the syntax dictionary[key] = ______.
10. The ______ method removes all items from a dictionary.
11. The ______ method returns a copy of the dictionary.
12. The ______ method returns the value for the specified key if the key is in the dictionary. If not, it inserts the key with a specified value.
13. The ______ method returns a list of tuples, where each tuple is a key-value pair in the dictionary.

State Whether True or False

14. Dictionaries in Python are mutable, meaning you can change their contents after creation.
15. The keys() method returns a list of all keys in a dictionary.
16. The get() method will raise an error if the specified key is not found in the dictionary.
17. The popitem() method removes and returns an arbitrary key-value pair from the dictionary.
18. The len() function returns the number of key-value pairs in a dictionary.

Assertion and Reason Based Questions

Assertion (A) and Reason (R) based questions. Mark the correct choice as

(a) Both (A) and (R) are true and (R) is the correct explanation for (A).
(b) Both (A) and (R) are true and (R) is not the correct explanation for (A).
(c) (A) is true and (R) is false.
(d) (A) is false but (R) is true.

19. **Assertion (A)** Dictionaries are mutable data structures.

Reason (R) You can add, remove, or modify elements in a dictionary after it's created.

20. **Assertion (A)** Dictionaries are unordered.

Reason (R) The order of elements in a dictionary is not guaranteed.

21. **Assertion (A)** You can use the in operator to check if a key exists in a dictionary.

Reason (R) The in operator is used to check membership in dictionaries.

22. **Assertion (A)** Dictionaries can be nested.

Reason (R) A dictionary can contain other dictionaries as values.

23. **Assertion** You can iterate over the keys of a dictionary using a for loop.

Reason (R) The keys() method returns a view of the dictionary's keys.

Answers

1. (c) Error
2. (b) 23
3. (d) Error
4. (a) ["Neha", "Paras"]
5. (b) 0
6. (d) All of the above
7. (d) Either (a) or (b)
8. (c) employee_salaries.keys()
9. value
10. clear()
11. copy()
12. setdefault()
13. items()
14. True
15. False
16. False
17. True
18. True
19. (a) Both (A) and (R) are true and (R) is the correct explanation for (A).
20. (a) Both (A) and (R) are true and (R) is the correct explanation for (A).
21. (a) Both (A) and (R) are true and (R) is the correct explanation for (A).
22. (a) Both (A) and (R) are true and (R) is the correct explanation for (A).
23. (a) Both (A) and (R) are true and (R) is the correct explanation for (A).

Subjective Type Questions

Very Short Answer Type Questions

1. What is a dictionary?

Ans. Dictionary is an unordered collection of data values that stored the key : value pair instead of a single value as an element.

2. If you have a dictionary my_dict and you need to add a new key-value pair to it, can you directly modify my_dict or do you need to create a new dictionary?

Ans. You can directly modify my_dict.

3. Write the syntax to create a dictionary.

Ans. dictionary_name = {key1 : value1, key2 : value2, ...}

4. Can we create an empty dictionary?

Ans. Yes, we can create an empty dictionary.

For example, dic1 = {}

5. If you try to assign two different values to the same key in a dictionary, what will happen?

Ans. The second value will overwrite the first.

6. Which feature is used to access the elements from a dictionary?

Ans. Keys are used to access the elements from a dictionary.

7. What do you mean by traversing a dictionary?

Ans. Traversing a dictionary means accessing each and every element of it.

8. How many ways are there to iterate over a dictionary?

Ans. There are three ways to iterate over a dictionary as

(i) Iterate through all keys
(ii) Iterate through all values
(iii) Iterate through all keys value pairs

9. Write the output.

```
>>> dic = {'A' : 'One', 'B' : 'Two', 'C' :
'Three'}
>>> dic.keys()
```

Ans. dict_keys (['B', 'C', 'A'])

10. How to convert keys of a dictionary into a list?

Ans. list(dictionary_name.keys())

11. Riya made a dictionary. She wants to convert the values of the dictionary into lists. How can she do this?

Ans. list(dictionary_name.values())

12. Find the error and write correct code.

```
>>> dic = {}
>>> dic[Rahul] = (Computer)
```

Ans.

```
>>> dic = {}
>>> dic ['Rahul'] = 'Computer'
```

13. If you have a dictionary where one of the values is another dictionary, what is this structure called?

Ans. A nested dictionary.

14. Write the syntax to update elements in a dictionary.

Ans. dictionary_name[key] = value

15. What is the use of del keyword?

Ans. del keyword is used to delete the key that is present in the dictionary.

16. Find out the error and underline the error after correct it. `dictionary_name(key).pop`

Ans. `dictionary_name.pop(key)`

17. Give the output.

```
>>> dic = {'A' : 'One', 'B' : 'Two', 'C' :
'Three'}
>>> 'E' in dic
```

Ans. Output

False

18. **What will be the output?**

```
d = {"Ansh" : 18, "Varsha" : 20}
"Ansh" in d
```

Ans. True

19. **What will be the output?**

```
dic1 = {"Sahil" : 25, "Muskan" : 22}
dic2 = {"Sahil" : 26, "Muskan" : 23}
dic1 = dic2
```

Ans. False

20. **What will be the output?**

```
dic = ["Ansh" : 25, "Ritu" : 26]
dic['Ritu']
```

Ans. 26

Short Answer Type I Questions

21. **Write any two properties of dictionary keys.**

Ans. (i) Dictionaries keys are case sensitive, same key name but with the different case are treated as different keys in Python dictionaries.

(ii) The values in the dictionary can be of any type while the keys must be immutable like numbers, tuples or strings.

22. **How can you add the following data in an empty dictionary?**

Keys	Values
A	Agra
B	Bengaluru
C	Chennai
D	Delhi

Ans.

```
dic = {}
dic['A'] = 'Agra'
dic['B'] = 'Bengaluru'
dic['C'] = 'Chennai'
dic['D'] = 'Delhi'
```

23. **Find the output:**

```
Student = {1: 'Aman', 2: 'Bablu', 3: 'Chandan'}
Student[2] = 'Sahil'
print(Student)
Student[4] = 'Aasha'
print(Student)
```

Ans. {1: 'Aman', 2: 'Sahil', 3: 'Chandan'}

```
{1: 'Aman', 2: 'Sahil', 3: 'Chandan', 4: 'Aasha'}
```

24. **What is the advantage of the pop() method over the del keyword?**

Ans. The advantage of the pop() method over the del keyword is that it provides a mechanism to print the desired value if tried to remove a non-existing dictionary pair.

Syntax `dictionary_name.pop(key, "Text")`

25. **You are given a dictionary containing product names as keys and their prices as values. You need to write code to check if a specific product exists in the dictionary and, if it does, print its price.**

Write Python code to implement the above scenario. Explain the logic behind your approach.

Ans.

```
products = {"apple": 1.0, "banana": 0.5,
            "orange": 1.2}
product_to_check = "banana"
if product_to_check in products:
    print(f"The price of {product_to_check}
        is: {products[product_to_check]}")
else:
    print(f"{product_to_check} not found
        in the dictionary.")
```

26. **You have a dictionary my_dict = {'b': 2, 'a': 1, 'c': 3}. How would you obtain a sorted list of its keys without modifying the original dictionary? Explain the type of data returned.**

Ans. To obtain a sorted list of the keys in the dictionary my_dict = {'b': 2, 'a': 1, 'c': 3}, you can use the sorted() function. This function returns a sorted list of the dictionary keys without modifying the original dictionary.

```
my_dict = {'b': 2, 'a': 1, 'c': 3}
sorted_keys = sorted(my_dict.keys())
print(sorted_keys)
```

Type of Data Returned The sorted() function returns a list of keys sorted in ascending order. In this case, it will return ['a', 'b', 'c'].

27. **Find the output of the following code:**

```
my_dict = {'data1': 200, 'data2': 154,
           'data3': 277}
print(sum(my_dict.values()))
```

Ans. 631

28. **Find the output:**

```
dic = {'data1': 200, 'data2': 56, 'data3': 47}
result = 1
for key in dic:
    result = result * dic[key]
print(result)
```

Ans. 526400

29. **Predict the output:**

```
dic = {1: [45, 89, 65], 'A': (23, 45, 6)}
print(dic.keys())
print(dic.values())
```

Ans.

```
dict_keys([1, 'A'])
dict_values([[45, 89, 65], (23, 45, 6)])
```

30. Predict the output:

```
dic = {'a': 1, 'b': 2, 'c': 3, 'd': 4}
if 'a' in dic:
    del dic['a']
print(dic)
```

Ans. {'b': 2, 'c': 3, 'd': 4}

31. You have a dictionary student_grades with 7 key-value pairs. What will len(student_grades) return? Briefly explain why.

Ans. len(student_grades) will return 7.

The len() function, when used with a dictionary, counts the number of key-value pairs (items) present in the dictionary. Since student_grades has 7 key-value pairs, len() will return 7.

32. What is the use of the popitem() method in a dictionary?

Ans. The popitem() method in a dictionary helps to achieve a similar purpose.

It removes an arbitrary key-value pair from the dictionary and returns it as a tuple. There is an update for this method from Python version 3.7 only.

Syntax `dict.popitem()`

Short Answer Type II Questions

33. Given the dictionary d = {"Ansh": 18, "Varsha": 20}, explain the concept of dictionary keys in Python. Discuss the properties of dictionary keys, including their uniqueness and immutability.

Ans. In Python, a dictionary is a collection of key-value pairs. The keys in a dictionary are used to uniquely identify and access the associated values.

Properties of Dictionary Keys

1. **Uniqueness** Keys must be unique. If a key is repeated, the last value overwrites the previous one (e.g., d = {"Ansh": 18, "Varsha": 20}).
2. **Immutability** Keys must be immutable (e.g., strings, numbers, tuples) and cannot be changed after creation.
3. **Hashable** Keys must be hashable, meaning they can be used efficiently in hashing algorithms. Mutable types like lists cannot be keys.

34. What will be the output of this code

```
dic = {"Ansh": 25, "Ritu": 26}
keys_view = dic.keys()
keys_list = list(keys_view)
dic["Neha"] = 30
del dic["Ansh"]
print(keys_list)
print(list(keys_view))
```

Ans. ['Ansh', 'Ritu']

['Ritu', 'Neha']

35. Define the max() and min() functions in the context of Python dictionaries. Explain their behavior, syntax, and provide examples.

Ans. In Python, the max() and min() functions can be used with dictionaries to find the maximum or minimum key or value.

Syntax

```
max(dict)
min(dict)
```

Behavior

Without the key argument, max() and min() work with the dictionary keys.

With the key argument, they can compare dictionary values or use a custom rule for comparison.

Examples

```
d1 = {1: 'a', 3: 'b', 2: 'c'}; print(max(d1))
        # Output: 3
d2 = {'apple': 1, 'banana': 2}; print(min(d2))
        # Output: apple
```

36. Given a dictionary data with product IDs as keys and product details as values, write a Python function print_product_report(data) that iterates and prints a report including ID, name, price, quantity, and total value (price * quantity). Handle missing details with KeyError.

Ans.

```
def print_product_report(data):
    print("Product Report")
    for pid, details in data.items():
        try:
            name = details['name']
            price = details['price']
            qty = details['quantity']
            total_value = price * qty
            print(f"ID: {pid}, Name: {name},
             Price: ${price:.2f}, Qty: {qty},
                   Total: ${total_value:.2f}")
        except KeyError as e:
            print(f"Error: Missing
                  '{e.args[0]}' for ID {pid}")
Example Usage:
inventory =
{
    'A1': {'name': 'Laptop', 'price': 1200,
                         'quantity': 5},
    'B2': {'name': 'Mouse', 'price': 25,
                         'quantity': 20},
```

```
    'C3': {'name': 'Keyboard', 'price':
                        80}, # Missing 'quantity'
    'D4': {'name': 'Monitor', 'price': 300,
                              'quantity': 2}
}
print_product_report(inventory)
```

Output

Product Report

ID: A1, Name: Laptop, Price: $1200.00, Qty: 5, Total: $6000.00

ID: B2, Name: Mouse, Price: $25.00, Qty: 20, Total: $500.00

Error: Missing 'quantity' for ID C3

ID: D4, Name: Monitor, Price: $300.00, Qty: 2, Total: $600.00

37. Define the clear() method in the context of Python dictionaries. Explain its functionality, syntax, and provide a detailed example.

Ans. The clear() method in Python dictionaries is a built-in function that serves to remove all key-value pairs from a dictionary, effectively emptying it.

Functionality

When invoked, clear() modifies the dictionary object in place. It doesn't create a new dictionary; instead, it removes all existing elements from the original dictionary. The result is an empty dictionary {}.

Syntax

The syntax for using the clear() method is:

dictionary_name.clear()

Example

```
>>> dic = {1: "One", 2: "Two"}
>>> dic.clear()
>>> dic
{}
```

38. You have a dictionary student_grades = {'Alice': 85, 'Bob': 92, 'Charlie': 78}. Write a Python code snippet that iterates through this dictionary and prints each student's name along with their grade.

Ans.
```
student_grades = {'Alice': 85, 'Bob': 92,
'Charlie': 78}
for student, grade in
student_grades.items():
    print(f"{student}: {grade}")
```

Output Alice: 85

Bob: 92

Charlie: 78

39. You have three dictionaries representing product inventory from different stores: store1 = {'apple': 10, 'banana': 20}, store2 = {'orange': 15, 'grape': 25}, and store3 = {'kiwi': 30, 'mango': 35}. Write a Python function that takes these dictionaries as input and returns a single dictionary combining all the inventory items.

Ans.
```
def combine_inventories(store1, store2,
                        store3):
    # Combine all dictionaries into one
    combined_inventory = {**store1,
                         **store2, **store3}
    return combined_inventory
```

Example dictionaries

```
store1 = {'apple': 10, 'banana': 20}
store2 = {'orange': 15, 'grape': 25}
store3 = {'kiwi': 30, 'mango': 35}
result = combine_inventories(store1,
                             store2, store3)
print(result)
```

Output {'apple': 10, 'banana': 20, 'orange': 15, 'grape': 25, 'kiwi': 30, 'mango': 35}

40. Write a Python function multiply_numeric_values(data) that takes a dictionary data as input. The dictionary may contain a mix of different data types as values. The function should calculate and return the product of only the numeric values (integers, floats) present in the dictionary. If no numeric values are found, the function should return 1. Implement error handling to ignore non-numeric values.

Ans.
```
def multiply_numeric_values(data):
    result = 1
    has_numeric = False
    for value in data.values():
        if isinstance(value, (int, float)):
            result *= value
            has_numeric = True
    return result if has_numeric else 1
```

Example Usage:

```
dic = {'A': 50, 'B': 30, 'C': 20, 'D': 53,
'E': 'string'}
print(multiply_numeric_values(dic))
```

Output 1590000

Long Answer Type Questions

41. Write a Python program to split dictionary keys and values into separate lists.

Ans.
```
dic = {'A': 'Apple', 'B': 'Ball', 'C': 'Cat', 'D':
                          'Dog', 'E': 'Elephant'}
print("Original Dictionary:", str(dic))
# Split dictionary into keys and values
keys = dic.keys()
values = dic.values()
# Printing keys and values separately
print("keys:", str(keys))
```

```
print("values:", str(values))
```

Output

Original Dictionary: {'A': 'Apple', 'B': 'Ball', 'C': 'Cat', 'D': 'Dog', 'E': 'Elephant'}

keys: dict_keys(['A', 'B', 'C', 'D', 'E'])

values: dict_values(['Apple', 'Ball', 'Cat', 'Dog', 'Elephant'])

42. Write a short note on the following with an example:

(i) update() (ii) len()

Ans. (i) **update()** This method is used to update the dictionary with the elements from another dictionary object or from an iterable of key/value pairs.

Syntax

```
dictionary_name1.update(dictionary _name2)
```

For Example,

```
student = {"name": "Alice", "age":
                    20, "grade": "B"}
student.update({"age": 21, "grade":
                "A", "city":"New York"})
print(student)
```

Output

{'name': 'Alice', 'age': 21, 'grade': 'A', 'city': 'New York'}

(ii) **len()** This method is used to return the total length of the dictionary.

Syntax `len(dictionary_name)`

e.g.,

```
dic = {'A' : 'One', 'B' : 'Two', 'C' :
                    'Four', 'D' : 'Four'}
dic1 = {'A' : 'One', 'B' : 'Two', 'C' :
        'Four', 'D' : 'Four', 'E' : 'Five'}
dic.update(dic1)
print (dic)
a = len(dic)
print ('The length is' , a)
```

Output

{'A' : 'One', 'B' : 'Two', 'C' : 'Four', 'D' : 'Four', 'E' : 'Five'}

The length is 5

43. Write a Python program to remove a dictionary from a list of dictionaries:

Ans.
```
list1 = [{"id": 101, "data": "Happy"}, {"id": 102,
"data": "Birthday"}, {"id": 103, "data": "Vyom"}]
print("The original list is:")
for a in list1:
    print(a)
for i in range(len(list1)):
    if list1[i]['id'] == 103:
        del list1[i]
        break
print("List after deletion of
dictionary:")
for b in list1:
    print(b)
```

44. Analyze the code snippet x = {(1, 2): 1, (2, 3): 2} and print(x[(1, 2)]). Explain what data type is being used as keys in the dictionary x. Describe how Python accesses values in a dictionary using these keys. Predict the output of the print statement and justify your answer based on the properties of dictionaries and the provided code.

Ans. In the given code snippet x = {(1, 2): 1, (2, 3): 2} and print(x[(1, 2)]), a dictionary is created where the keys are tuples and the values are integers.

Data Type of Keys

The keys in the dictionary x are tuples. In this case, the keys are (1, 2) and (2, 3). Tuples are immutable data types in Python, which allows them to be used as dictionary keys.

Accessing Values in a Dictionary

Python accesses dictionary values using keys. When you access x[(1, 2)], Python looks for the key (1, 2) in the dictionary. Since the key (1, 2) exists, it retrieves the associated value, which is 1.

Predicted Output

The print statement print(x[(1, 2)]) will output: 1

45. Predict the output

(i)
```
dic = {}
dic[1] = 1
dic['1.0'] = 2
dic[1.0] = 4
sum = 0
for i in dic:
    sum += dic[i]
print(sum)
```

(ii)
```
dic = {}
dic[(1, 2, 4)] = 8
dic[(1, 2)] = 24
sum = 0
for i in dic:
    sum += dic[i]
print(sum)
print(dic)
```

Ans. (i) 6

(ii) 42

{(1, 2) : 24, (4, 2, 1) : 10, (1, 2, 4) : 8}

46. Write Python program to test if dictionary contains unique keys and values.

Ans.
```
dict1 = {'Nikunj': 1, 'Akshat': 2, 'Akansha': 3,
                                 'Manish': 1}
print("The original dictionary: "
                          + str(dict1))
```

```
flag = False
val = {}
for keys in dict1:
    if dict1[keys] in val:
        flag = True
        break
    else:
        val[dict1[keys]] = 1
print("Does dictionary contain repetition:
                                  " + str(flag))
```

47. Find the output of the given Python program to swap keys and values in dictionary.

```
old_dict = {'One' : 742, 'Two' : 145,
'Three' : 654, 'Four' : 321, 'Five' : 120,
'Six' : 365, 'Seven' : 459, 'Eight' : 449}
new_dict = dict([(value, key) for key,
value in old_dict.items()])
print("Original dictionary is:")
print(old_dict)
print()
print("Dictionary after swapping is:")
print("Keys:Values")
for i in new_dict:
    print(i, ":", new_dict[i])
```

Ans. Output

Original dictionary is:

{'One': 742, 'Two': 145, 'Three': 654, 'Four': 321, 'Five': 120, 'Six': 365, 'Seven': 459, 'Eight': 449}

Dictionary after swapping is:

Keys: Values
742 : One
145 : Two
654 : Three
321 : Four
120 : Five
365 : Six
459 : Seven
449 : Eight

Case Study Based Question

Case Study 1

A Python dictionary is a versatile data structure that stores data in key-value pairs. It's mutable, meaning you can add, remove, or modify elements after creation. Unlike lists and tuples, dictionaries are unordered, so the order of elements is not guaranteed. Dictionaries are defined using curly braces {} and are accessed using their keys. You can add new key-value pairs to a dictionary using the assignment operator =.

To access a value, you use the key within square brackets []. The keys(), values(), and items() methods allow you to iterate over the keys, values, or key-value pairs of a dictionary, respectively. Dictionaries offer efficient key-based access with a time complexity of O(1), making them a powerful tool for various data manipulation tasks.

(i) What is the primary characteristic of a Python dictionary?
(a) Ordered and immutable
(b) Unordered and mutable
(c) Ordered and mutable
(d) Unordered and immutable

(ii) Which of the following is used to define a dictionary in Python?
(a) Square brackets [] (b) Parentheses ()
(c) Curly braces {} (d) Angle brackets <>

(iii) How can you access a value in a dictionary?
(a) By its index (b) By its key
(c) By its position (d) By its order

(iv) What is the correct way to add a new key-value pair to a dictionary?
(a) dictionary[key] = value
(b) dictionary.add(key, value)
(c) dictionary.insert(key, value)
(d) dictionary.append(key, value)

(v) How can you iterate over the keys and values of a dictionary?
(a) Using a for loop with the items() method
(b) Using a for loop with the keys() method
(c) Using a for loop with the values() method
(d) All of the above

(vi) What is the time complexity of accessing a value in a dictionary by its key?
(a) O(n) (b) O(log n)
(c) O(1) (d) O(n^2)

Ans. (i) (b) Unordered and mutable
(ii) (c) Curly braces { }
(iii) (b) By its key
(iv) (a) dictionary[key] = value
(v) (d) All of the above
(vi) (c) O(1)

SELF ASSESSMENT TEST

Multiple Choice Questions

1. Suppose d = {"Rahul":40, "Riya":45}.

To obtain the number of entries in dictionary which command do we use?

(a) d.size() (b) len(d)
(c) size(d) (d) d.len()

2. Which of the following is not true about dictionary keys?

(a) More than one key is not allowed.
(b) Keys must be immutable.
(c) Keys must be integers.
(d) When duplicate keys encountered, the last assignment wins.

3. What will be the output of the following Python code?

```
a={1:5,2:3,3:4}
a.pop(3)
print(a)
```

(a) {1: 5}
(b) {1: 5, 2: 3}
(c) Error, syntax error for pop() method
(d) {1: 5, 3: 4}

Fill in the Blanks

4. A collection of key-value pairs is called a ________.

5. The ________ method returns a list of keys in a dictionary.

6. The ________ method returns a list of key-value pairs in a dictionary.

7. The ________ method adds or updates key-value pairs in a dictionary.

8. The ________ method removes a key-value pair from a dictionary.

9. The ________ function returns the number of key-value pairs in a dictionary.

State Whether True or False

10. Dictionaries are mutable.

11. Dictionary keys can be of any data type.

12. The values() method returns a list of keys in a dictionary.

13. The get() method returns the value for a given key, or a default value if the key is not found.

14. The clear() method removes a specific key-value pair from a dictionary.

15. sorted() method returns a new sorted dictionary.

Assertion and Reason Based Questions

Assertion (A) and Reason (R) Type questions. Choose the correct option as:

(a) Both Assertion (A) and Reason (R) are true, and Reason (R) is the correct explanation of Assertion (A).
(b) Both Assertion (A) and Reason (R) are true, but Reason (R) is not the correct explanation of Assertion (A).
(c) Assertion (A) is true, but Reason (R) is false.
(d) Assertion (A) is false, but Reason (R) is true.

16. Assertion (A) Dictionaries are mutable.

Reason (R) You can add, modify, or remove key-value pairs in a dictionary.

17. Assertion (A) The keys() method returns a list of values.

Reason (R) Dictionaries are mutable data structures.

18. Assertion (A) Dictionary keys must be immutable.

Reason (R) Dictionary keys are used for hashing, and mutable objects cannot be hashed.

19. Assertion (A) The update() method creates a new dictionary instead of modifying the existing one.

Reason (R) Dictionaries can store key-value pairs of different data types.

20. Assertion (A) The copy() method creates a shallow copy of a dictionary.

Reason (R) Changes to the copied dictionary do not affect the original dictionary.

Very Short Answer Type Questions

21. Read the code shown below and pick out the keys.

```
d = {"Sahil" : 25, "Muskan" : 22}
```

22. What will be the output?

```
d = {"Ansh" : 18, "Varsha" : 20}
"Varsha" in d
```

23. Write the syntax to traverse a dictionary.

Short Answer Type Questions

24. What will be the output?

```
dic = {'Ansh' : 25, 'Varsha' : 26}
print(list(dic.values()))
```

25. Which function is used to remove the first element of a set and the last element of a list?

26. Predict the output.

```
dic1 = {2 : (4, 5, 6), 'B' : [45, 3, 2]}
print (dic1.values())
print (dic1.keys())
```

27. Find the output.

```
dic = {'A' : 400, 'B' : 43, 'C' : 33}
print (sum (dic.values()))
```

28. Write the short note on pop() method.

29. Find out the error and correct it.

```
dic = {'One' : 1, 1 : 'One', 2 : 'Two', [1,
'One'] : 'Three'}
```

30. Find the errors.

```
s = "abbcdccba"
counter = {}
for i in s :
    counter [i] = counter [i] + 1
```

Long Answer Type Questions

31. Write a python program that checks if two same values in dictionary have different keys.

32. Write a Python program to create two dictionary and swap their values.

33. Write a Python program to create a dictionary and make two lists for dictionary keys and values.

34. Write a Python program to create dictionary of an Employee detail in which user add two keys after creation and delete one key after that.

35. Define any two functions which are used in dictionary.

Case Study Based Questions

36. A teacher wants to create a system to store and manage student information. The system should store student names, roll numbers, and grades. The teacher needs to access, modify, and traverse this information efficiently.

(i) Which Python data structure is most suitable for storing student information?

(a) List (b) Tuple
(c) Dictionary (d) Set

(ii) To access a student's grade using their roll number, the teacher should use:

(a) List indexing (b) Dictionary keys
(c) Tuple slicing (d) Set iteration

(iii) To add a new student's information to the system, the teacher would use:

(a) append()
(b) insert()
(c) Dictionary key assignment
(d) extend()

(iv) To get a list of all student roll numbers, the teacher should use:

(a) values() (b) items()
(c) keys() (d) get()

(v) To remove a student's information from the system, the teacher can use:

(a) popitem() or del (b) remove()
(c) discard() (d) clear()

Answers

1. (b) 2. (c) 3. (b) 4. Dictionary
5. keys() 6. items() 7. update() 8. pop()
9. len() 10. True 11. False 12. False 13. True
14. False 15. False 16. (a) 17. (d) 18. (a)
19. (d) 20. (c)
36. (i) → (c), (ii) → (b), (iii) → (c), (iv) → (c), (v) → (a)

15 CHAPTER

Python comes with a vast collection of built-in modules that provide essential functionalities, such as matematical operations (math) and generating random and static values.

▼ **YOUR STUDY GOALS**

15.1 Structure of a Python Module
15.2 Importing modules in a Python Program
15.3 Mathematical Module/Functions
15.4 Random Module/Functions
15.5 Statistics Module/Functions

▼ **YOUR PRACTICE GOAL**

- Objective Type Questions (24 Qs ; MCQs, True or False, Fill in the Blanks, Assertion and Reason)
- Subjective Type Questions (29 Qs ; VSA, SA, LA)
- Case Study Based Question-1

Introduction to Python Modules

We can think of a Python module as a special file that contains Python code. This code can include functions, classes, and variables.

It's like a toolbox with different tools to help us build Python programs. We save these modules with a .py extension. Modules make our code more organized and easier to manage. They allow us to break down our code into smaller, more manageable parts, which makes it easier to understand, debug, and reuse.

15.1 Structure of a Python Module

Structure of a Python module consists of different terms which are as follows:

- **doc string** It is useful for documentation purposes and always kept in triple quotes.
- **Variables** It is used for labels of data that consist in a program.
- **Classes** These are essentially a template to create objects.
- **Objects** These are instances of classes. Object is simply a collection of data (variables) and methods (functions).
- **Statements** These are logical instructions which can be read and executed by a Python interpreter.
- **Functions** It is a self-contained block of statements which are kept together to perform a specific task in a related manner.

15.2 Importing modules in a Python Program

To make use of the function in a module, you will need to import the module with an 'import' statement.

Once we import a module, we can directly use all the functions of that module.

Syntax `import module_name`

This gives us access to all the functions in the module(s). To call a function of a module, the function name should be preceded with the name of the module with a dot (.) as a separator.

In python, import statement can be used in two forms as below:

To Import Entire Module

To import the entire module, an import statement is used. Import statement is also used to import selecting modules.

Syntax `import module_name`

When we import a module, we're bringing it into our current program. which looks like module_name.function_name. This tells Python to look for the function_name inside the module_name.

e.g.
```
import math
print (math.sqrt (16))
```

Output

4.0

Here, math is a module which contains the function definition, variables, constants etc., related to mathematical functions.

sqrt () is a function which will find the square root of a number that is given in parentheses ().

To Import Selected Objects from a Module

When you import modules this way, you can refer to the functions by name rather than through dot notation.

Syntax `from module_name import object_name`

e.g.
```
from math import sqrt
print (sqrt (16))
```

Output

4.0

Here, math is a module and sqrt () is a function. Now, we do not need to use a math module with a function name, as math.sqrt().

e.g.
```
from random import randint
for i in range (5):
  print (randint (1, 20))
```

Output

4
10
3
7
9

To import Multiple objects

We can also import multiple objects in a single line. To import multiple objects, we can write the multiple objects or functions name using the comma (,) operator.

e.g., from math import sqrt, pi

To import All Objects of a Module

When you want to import all objects, you can use asterisk (*) symbol at last of keyword import.

Syntax `from module_name import *`

e.g. `from math import *`

Processing of import <module> Command

When import <module> is used, following things take place internally

- The code of the module which imported is interpreted and executed.
- When a module is imported, functions and variables defined in that module are now available to the program.
- To import module, same name as modules a new namespace is setup.

e.g. If you imported math module in your program, all objects and attributes of that module would be referred as

```
math.<object_name>
```

Processing of from <module> import <object> Command

When from <module> import <object> command is issued, following things take place internally

- The code of the module which imported is interpreted and executed.
- When a module is imported, only mentioned functions and variables are available to the program.
- In the current namespace, the imported definition is added because no new namespace is setup.

Mistake Alert

The student mistakenly left out the dot notation when accessing objects from imported modules, resulting in an error.

15.3 Mathematical Module/Functions

To access a wide range of mathematical functions, we need to import a special tool called the math module. This module provides tools to perform various calculations, like finding square roots, trigonometric functions, and more.

Some of the most popular mathematical functions are defined in math module as follows:

(i) sqrt ()

This function is used to find the square root of a specified expression or an individual number.

Syntax `math.sqrt(number)`

For example,

```
>>> import math
>>> s = math.sqrt(4)
>>> print(s)
2.0
>>> s1 = math.sqrt(15)
>>> print(s1)
3.872983346207417
>>> print(math.sqrt(0))
0.0
>>> print(math.sqrt(4.5))
2.1213203435596424
```

If you give a negative number as an argument, it will give an error.

```
>>> s2 = -4
>>> print(math.sqrt(s2))
Traceback (most recent call last):
  File "<pyshell#14>", line 1, in <module>
    print(math.sqrt(s2))
ValueError: math domain error
```

(ii) ceil()

This method returns the ceiling value of x, which is the smallest integer greater than or equal to x.

Syntax `math.ceil(x)`

For example,

```
>>> import math
>>> c = math.ceil(45.23)
>>> print(c)
46
>>> c1 = math.ceil(-76.89)
>>> print(c1)
-76
>>> a = 456.14
>>> print(math.ceil(a))
457
>>> x = math.pi
>>> print(math.ceil(x))
4
```

(iii) floor ()

The method is used to return a value which is less than or equal to a specific expression or value.

Syntax `math.floor (x)`

For example,

```
>>> import math
>>> f = math.floor (145.35)
>>> print (f)
145
>>>  b = -75.50
>>> print (math.floor (b))
-75
>>> x = math.pi
>>> print (math.floor (x))
3
```

(iv) pow ()

This method offers to compute the power of a number and hence can make the task of calculating power of a number easier. In this, two types to calculate power.

Pow (x, y) converts its arguments into float and then computes the power.

Syntax `pow (x, y)`

For example,

```
>>> import math
>>> x = 3
>>> y = 4
>>> print (pow (y, x))
64
```

```
>>> print (pow (7, 2))
49
>>> print (pow (-3, 2))
9
>>> print (pow (-4, 3))
-64
>>> print (pow (5, -2))
0.04
```

The pow(x, y, mod) function calculates x to the power of y, with an optional modulo mod, using a common numeric type for its arguments.

Syntax `pow (x, y, mod)`

For example,

```
>>> x = 4
>>> y = 3
>>> z = 10
>>> pow (x, y, z)
4
>>> pow (5, 3, 7)
6
>>> print (pow (6, 0, 2))
1
>>> pow(8, 3, 0)
Traceback (most recent call last):
  File "<pyshell#7>", line 1, in <module>
    pow(8, 3, 0)
ValueError: pow() 3rd argument cannot be 0.
```

(v) fabs()

This method returns the absolute value (positive value) of x.

Syntax `math.fabs (x)`

For example,

```
>>> import math
>>> x = -25
>>> math.fabs(x)
25.0
>>> print(math.fabs(65))
65.0
>>> print(math.fabs(-4.3))
4.3
```

(vi) sin()

This method returns the sine of the value passed as an argument. The value passed in this function should be in radians

Syntax `math.sin(x)`

For example,

```
>>> import math
>>> x = 65
>>> math.sin(x)
0.8268286794901034
>>> print(math.sin(5.3245521))
-0.8184069203707078
>>> a = math.pi
>>> x = a/4
>>> math.sin(x)
0.7071067811865475
```

(vii) cos()

This method returns the cosine of value passed as argument. The value passed in this function should be in radians

Syntax `math.cos(x)`

For example,

```
>>> import math
>>> x = 9
>>> math.cos(x)
-0.9111302618846769
>>> math.cos(0)
1.0
>>> math.cos(-4)
-0.6536436208636119
>>> a = math.pi
>>> math.cos(a) / 2
-0.5
```

(viii) tan()

This method returns the tangent of value passed as argument. The value passed in this function should be in radians

Syntax `math.tan(x)`

For example,

```
>>> import math
>>> x = 30
>>> math.tan(x)
-6.405331196646276
>>> math.tan(0)
0.0
>>> math.tan(90)
-1.995200412208242
>>> print(math.tan(-5))
3.380515006246586
```

(ix) pi

It is a mathematical constant, the ratio of the circumference of a circle to its diameter.

Syntax `math.pi`

For example,

```
>>> import math
>>> math.pi
3.1415926...
```

(x) e

It is a mathematical constant.

Syntax `math.e`

For example,

```
>>> import math
>>> math.e
2.71828182846
```

15.4 Random Module/Functions

Python offers a random module that can generate random numbers. These random modules depend on a pseudo random number that generates function random() and this number generates a random float number between 0.0 and 1.0.

Some random functions are describe below

(i) random()

This method is used to generate a float random number less than 1 and greater than or equal to 0. This function does not require any arguments.

Syntax `random.random()`

For example,

```
>>> import random
>>> print(random.random())
0.7358047613841759
```

(ii) randint()

This method is one of the methods that handle random numbers. It has two parameters start and end which generate an integer between start and end (including both).

Syntax `random.randint(start, end)`

For example,

```
>>> import random
>>> print(random.randint(10, 50))
34
>>> print(random.randint(5, 70))
19
>>> print(random.randint(-80, -20))
-20
>>> print(random.randint(-12, 60))
35
```

(iii) randrange()

This method returns a random selected element from the range created by the start, stop and step arguments. The value of start is 0 by default. Similarly, the value of step is 1 by default.

Syntax `random.randrange(start, stop, step)`

For example,

```
>>> import random
>>> print(random.randrange(10, 100, 5))
70
>>> print(random.randrange(20, 30, 10))
20
>>> print(random.randrange(-50, -20, 10))
-30
>>> print(random.randrange(-10, 0, 4))
-6
```

15.5 Statistics Module/Functions

Python is a great tool for working with numbers and statistics. To use its powerful statistical functions, we need to import a special module named statistics. This module lets us do calculations like finding mean, medians, and mode. However, this module is only available in Python version 3.4 and later.

Some statistics functions are as follow

(i) mean()

It returns the simple arithmetic mean of data which can be a sequence or iterator. Arithmetic mean is the sum of data divided by the number of data sets.

Syntax `statistics.mean(data_set)`

For example,

```
>>> import statistics
>>> list = [45, 78, 21, 32, 45, 56]
>>> statistics.mean(list)
46.16666666666664
>>> list = [-14, 25, -32, -12, 0, 65]
>>> statistics.mean(list)
5.333333333333333
>>> t = (14, 14, 12, 32, 78)
>>> statistics.mean(t)
30.0
>>> t1 = (-12, -23, 45, -20, 16)
>>> statistics.mean(t1)
4.0
>>> l1 = [1, 2, 2, 3, 4, 5, 6, -8]
>>> statistics.mean(l1)
```

```
1.2
>>> statistics.mean()
Traceback (most recent call last):
  File "<pyshell#11>", line 1, in <module>
    statistics.mean()
TypeError: mean() missing 1 required
positional argument: 'data'
```

(ii) median()

This function calculates the middle value of the arithmetic data in iterative order. If there are an odd number of values, median() returns the middle value. If there are an even number of values it returns an average of two middle values.

Syntax `statistics.median(data_set)`

For example,

```
>>> import statistics
>>> list = [12, 54, 89, 65, 78]
>>> statistics.median(list)
65
>>> list1 = [45, -12, -65, 78, 0]
>>> statistics.median(list1)
0
>>> t = (78, 98, 23, -32, 8.6, -9)
>>> statistics.median(t)
15.8
```

(iii) mode()

This function returns the number with the maximum number of occurrences.

Syntax `statistics.mode(dataset)`

For example,

```
>>> import statistics
>>> list=[45, 89, 45, 78, 65, 32, 45, 66]
>>> statistics.mode(list)
45
>>> list1=[4, 5, 6, 5, 7, 0, 6, 5, 98, 4, 5,
                                          6, 5]
>>> statistics.mode(list1)
5
>>> t=(-45, -89, 0, -89, 36, -86, -36)
>>> statistics.mode(t)
-89
```

When two numbers have the same occurrence of numbers then it will give an error.

```
>>> list2=[-45, -89, 0, -89, 36, -36, -36]
>>> statistics.mode(list2)
Traceback (most recent call last):
  File "<pyshell#27>", line 1, in <module>
    statistics.mode(list2)
  File "C:\Python34\lib\statistics.py",
                              line 434, in mode
    'no unique mode; found %d equally
                  common values' % len(table)
Statistics.StatisticsError: no unique
          mode; found 2 equally common values
```

TEACHER TIP

Try creating your own small modules to practice organizing code and using dot notation to access objects within them.

Mind Map

PYTHON MODULES

Structure of a Python Module

Structure of a Python Module Consist of Different Terms

- doc string
- Variables
- Functions
- Classes
- Statements
- Objects

Importing Modules in a Python Program

To make use of the function in a module, you will need to import the module with an 'import' statement.

Syntax import module_name

- **To Import Entire Module**
  Syntax import module_name
- **To Import Selected Objects from a Module**
  Syntax from module_name import object_name
- **To import Multiple objects**
  Syntax from module_name import obj1, obj2
- **To import All Objects of a Module**
  Syntax from module_name import *

Statistics Module/Functions

mean()

Syntax statistics.mean(data_set)

median()

Syntax statistics.median(data_set)

mode()

Syntax statistics.mode(data_set)

Mathematical Module/Functions

Common Functions

- **sqrt ()**
  Syntax math.sqrt(number)
- **ceil()**
  Syntax math.ceil(x)
- **floor ()**
  Syntax math.floor (x)
- **pow ()**
  Syntax pow (x, y)
- **fabs()**
  Syntax math.fabs (x)

Trignometric Functions

- **sin ()**
  Syntax math.sin(x)
- **cos()**
  Syntax math.cos(x)
- **tan ()**
  Syntax math.tan (x)

Mathematical Functions

- **pi**
  Syntax math.pi
- **e**
  Syntax math.e

Random Module/ Functions

random()

Syntax random.random()

randint()

Syntax random.randint(start, end)

randrange()

Syntax random.randrange(start, stop, step)

EXAM PATTERN QUESTIONS

Objective Type Questions

Multiple Choice Questions

1. Which module is used for sqrt () to find the square root of a number?

(a) random (b) square root
(c) math (d) statistics

2. Identify the correct output.

```
print (pow(-3, 2))
```

(a) 9 (b) -9
(c) 8 (d) - 8

3. You are creating a Python module to organize code for a game. Which of the following elements could you include in this module?

(a) A function to calculate the player's score
(b) A class to represent game characters
(c) A variable to store the game's difficulty level
(d) All of the above

4. Identify the correct output of

```
>>> import math
>>> f = math.floor (145.35)
>>> print (f)
```

(a) 146 (b) 145 (c) 145.3 (d) 145.4

5. Which of the following is an incorrect import statement?

(a) import module_name
(b) from module_name import object_name
(c) import object_name from module_name
(d) import module_name as alias

6. What will be the output of the following Python code?

```
random.randrange(0,91,5)
```

(a) 10 (b) 18 (c) 79 (d) 95

7. You want to use all the functions and variables defined in a module named "utilities" without specifying each one individually. Which import statement would you use?

(a) import utilities (b) from utilities import *
(c) import utilities.* (d) from utilities import all

8. Which function can generate even random numbers within a specific range?

(a) randrange() (b) random()
(c) randint() (d) None of these

Fill in the Blanks

9. To use the square root function from the math module, you can write math._______.

10. The random._______ function returns a random integer between two specified numbers (inclusive).

11. The statistics._______ function calculates the average of a list of numbers.

12. To import the cos function from the math module directly, you can use the statement from math import _______.

13. The random._______ function returns a randomly selected element from a range created by the start, stop, and step arguments.

State Whether True or False

14. The import math statement makes all functions within the math module directly accessible without using the module name as a prefix.

15. The random.random() function returns a random integer within a specified range.

16. The statistics.mode() function returns the most common data point from a dataset.

17. The from math import pi statement imports the entire math module.

18. The math.fabs() function returns the absolute value of a floating-point number.

Assertion and Reason Based Questions

Assertion (A) and Reason (R) based questions. Mark the correct choice as

(a) Both (A) and (R) are true and (R) is the correct explanation for (A).
(b) Both (A) and (R) are true and (R) is not the correct explanation for (A).
(c) (A) is true and (R) is false.
(d) (A) is false but (R) is true.

19. Assertion (A) The import math statement imports the entire math module.
Reason (R) This allows access to all functions and constants defined within the math module.

20. **Assertion (A)** The from math import sqrt statement imports the sqrt function from the math module.

Reason (R) This allows direct use of the sqrt function without the math. Prefix.

21. **Assertion (A)** The random() function in the random module generates a random float between 0.0 and 1.0.

Reason (R) It returns a pseudo-random number.

22. **Assertion (A)** The randint() function in the random module generates a random integer within a specified range.

Reason (R) It takes two arguments: the lower and upper bounds of the range.

23. **Assertion (A)** The mean() function in the statistics module calculates the arithmetic mean of a data set.

Reason (R) It sums up all the values in the data set and divides by the number of values.

24. **Assertion (A)** The mode() function in the statistics module finds the most frequent value in a data set.

Reason (R) It returns the value that occurs most often.

Answers

1. (c) math
2. (a) 9
3. (d) All of the above
4. (b) 145
5. (c) import object_name from module_name
6. (a) 10
7. (b) from utilities import *
8. (a) randrange()
9. sqrt()
10. randint()
11. mean()
12. cos
13. randrange()
14. False
15. False
16. True
17. False
18. True
19. (a) Both (A) and (R) are true and (R) is the correct explanation for (A).
20. (a) Both (A) and (R) are true and (R) is the correct explanation for (A).
21. (b) Both (A) and (R) are true and (R) is not the correct explanation for (A).
22. (a) Both (A) and (R) are true and (R) is the correct explanation for (A).
23. (a) Both (A) and (R) are true and (R) is the correct explanation for (A).
24. (a) Both (A) and (R) are true and (R) is the correct explanation for (A).

Subjective Type Questions

Very Short Answer Type Questions

1. The output of the following code is either 1 or 2. State whether this statement is true or false.

```
import random
random.randint (1, 2)
```

Ans. True

2. What is the output of the given code?

```
import random
random.choice (20, 30, 3)
```

Ans. There is a syntax error and correct code is random.choice ([20, 30, 3])

3. Predict the output.

```
import random
random.choice ([15.5, 156.9, 76])
```

Ans. Either 15.5, 156.9 or 76

4. If you have a set of related functions you want to reuse in multiple Python scripts, what would you create?

Ans. A module.

5. What is the output of the function given below?

```
import random
random.choice ('MOST')
```

Ans. Either M, O, S and T

6. How do you randomly rearrange the elements of a list in place?

Ans. random.shuffle()

7. How can you randomly select an integer from the sequence 0, 1, 2, 3, 4 using random.choice?

Ans. random.choice(range(5))

8. Which function is equivalent to random. randint (4, 7)?

Ans. 4 + random. randrange (4) on return any one of 4, 5, 6 and 7.

9. Which type of elements are accepted by random.shuffle()?

Ans. lists

10. What is return by math.floor (-20.0)?

Ans. 20

11. How to import modules in Python?

Ans. Modules can be imported using the import keyword.

Short Answer Type I Questions

12. What will be the output of the given code?

```
import random
random.randrange (1, 100, 10)
```

Ans. 91

The output of this code can be any value which is a multiple of 10, plus 1. Hence a variable like 11, 21, 31, 41,...91 can be output. Also, the value should necessarily be between 1 and 100.

13. What is return by the following code?

(i) **math.ceil(8.7)** (ii) **math.floor(9.5)**

Ans. (i) 9 (ii) 9

14. Write the short note on

(i) **ceil()** (ii) **floor()**

Ans. (i) ceil() method returns a ceiling value of x i.e, the smallest integer not less than x.

Syntax `math.ceil(x)`

(ii) **floor()** method is used to return a value which is less than or equal to a specific expression or value.

Syntax `math.floor(x)`

15. What is the output of the given code?

(i) **int(math.pow(5, 3))**

(ii) **print(math.pow(5, 3))**

(iii) **int(pow(5, 3, 4))**

Ans. (i) 125 (ii) 125.0 (iii) 1

16. You need to simulate rolling a standard six-sided die. How would you generate a random integer between 1 and 6 (inclusive) in Python?

Ans. To generate a random integer between 1 and 6 (inclusive), you would use the random.randint(1, 6) function.

This function takes two arguments, the lower and upper bounds of the desired range, and returns a random integer within that range. In this case, it would return a random integer between 1 and 6, including both 1 and 6 as possibilities.

17. You need to calculate the cosine of an angle in your Python program. How would you do this using the math module?

Ans. First, you need to import the math module using the statement import math. This makes all the functions and constants defined within the math module available for use in your code

- Then, you can use the math.cos() function to calculate the cosine of the angle. Remember that the math.cos() function expects the angle to be in radians. If your angle is in degrees, you'll need to convert it to radians first using the math.radians() function.
- For example, to calculate the cosine of 30 degrees

```
import math
angle_degrees = 30
angle_radians = math.radians
                    (angle_degrees)
cosine = math.cos(angle_radians)
print(cosine)
    # Output: 0.8660254037844386
```

18. What is the statistics module in Python? How can you use its functions?

Ans. The statistics module in Python provides various functions to perform statistical calculations on numerical data. To use these functions, you first need to import the module:

```
import statistics
```

Here are some of the common functions:

- **mean()** Calculates the arithmetic mean of a data set.

```
mean_value = statistics.mean
                    ([1, 2, 3, 4, 5])
```

- **median()** Calculates the median of a data set.

```
median_value = statistics.median
                    ([1, 2, 3, 4, 5, 6, 7])
```

- **mode()** Calculates the mode (most frequent value) of a data set.

```
mode_value = statistics.mode
                    ([1, 2, 3, 2, 1, 2, 3])
```

19. What is the significance of modules in programming?

Ans. Modules are essentially self-contained units of code that encapsulate specific functionalities. They offer several advantages in programming:

1. **Code Organization** Modules help in breaking down complex programs into smaller, more manageable chunks. This improves code readability and maintainability.
2. **Reusability** Once a module is created, it can be reused in different projects, saving development time and effort.
3. **Modularity** Modules promote modular programming, where different components of a program can be developed and tested independently.
4. **Namespace Management** Modules create separate namespaces, preventing naming conflicts between variables and functions in different parts of the code.
5. **Code Sharing** Modules can be shared and distributed among developers, facilitating collaboration and knowledge sharing.

Short Answer Type II Questions

20. Predict the Output

```
import math
x = 2.5
y = -3.8
print(math.ceil(x))
print(math.floor(y))
print(math.pow(2, 3))
```

Ans. Output

3

-4

8.0

21. Explain the difference between import math and from math import sqrt. Provide an example of how you would use the sqrt function in each case.

Ans. import math Imports the full module; functions are accessed with math.function().

Example `import math; print(math.sqrt(25))`

Output 5.0

from math import sqrt Imports only sqrt; it can be used directly.

Example `from math import sqrt; print(sqrt(25))`

Output 5.0

Comparison import math avoids name conflicts but requires math. prefix. Whereas from math import sqrt makes calls shorter but may cause name conflicts.

22. Predict the Output:

```
import random
random.seed(42)
print(random.randint(1, 10))
print(random.random())
print(random.randrange(0, 10, 2))
```

What will be the output of this code snippet?

Ans. Output:

2

0.6394267984578837

4

23. Explain the difference between mean, median, and mode from the statistics module.

Measure	Definition	Formula / Method	Example Output	Best Used For
Mean	The average of all values.	Sum of values ÷ Total count	mean([2, 4, 6, 8]) → 5.0	Numerical data where outliers are not a concern.
Median	The middle value of a sorted dataset.	Middle value (or avg. of two middle values if even count)	median ([1, 3, 5, 7, 9]) → 5	Skewed data where extreme values exist.
Mode	The most frequently occurring value.	Most common value in the dataset	mode([1, 2, 2, 3, 4]) → 2	Categorical or repeated numerical data.

24. Explain the purpose of the math.fabs() and math.pow() functions. Provide examples of when you would use each of these functions in a real-world scenario.

Ans. math.fabs(x) Returns the absolute value of x (a float). Used when you need the magnitude of a number regardless of its sign (e.g., calculating distance).

math.pow(x, y) Returns x raised to the power of y (a float). Used for exponentiation (e.g., calculating compound interest).

Examples `math.fabs(-5.2)` returns 5.2.
`math.pow(2, 4)` returns 16.0.

Long Answer Type Questions

25. Predict the output.

```
import math
print ("cos:", math.cos (1.047197551))
print ("sin:", math.sin (0.523598775))
print ("tan:", math.tan (0.463647609))
print ("degree:", math.degrees (3.1415926))
print ("radian:", math.radians (180))
```

Ans. Output

cos : 0.5000000001702586

sin : 0.4999999994818579

tan : 0.49999999999899236

degree : 179.99999692953102

radian : 3.141592653589793

26. What is the output of the given code?

```
import statistics
from fractions import Fraction as F
from decimal import Decimal as D
a = statistics.mean([11, 2, 13, 14, 44])
b = statistics.mean([F(8, 10), F(11, 20),
                     F(2, 5), F(28, 5)])
c = statistics.mean([D("1.5"), D("5.75"),
                     D("10.625"), D("2.375")])
print ("Simple mean:", a)
print ("Fraction mean:", b)
print ("Decimal mean:", c)
```

Ans. Output

Simple mean: 16.8
Fraction mean: 147/80
Decimal mean: 5.0625

27. Predict the output?

```
import statistics
list = [5, 2, 5, 6, 1, 2, 6, 7, 2, 6, 3, 5, 5]
x = statistics.mean(list)
print (x)
y = statistics.median(list)
print (y)
z = statistics.mode(list)
print (z)
```

Ans. Output

4.230769230769231
5
5

28. Define the random module in Python.

Ans. Refer to text on page no. 274 (Random Module/Functions).

29. How does the import <module> command work behind the scenes?

Ans. When you use the import <module> command, here's what happens internally:

1. **Interpretation and Execution** Python first interprets and executes the code within the imported module. This means any functions or variables defined in the module are created.
2. **Making Objects Available** After execution, Python makes these functions and variables accessible to the program that imported the module.
3. **Namespace Creation** A new namespace is created for the imported module. This namespace shares the same name as the module itself. This namespace helps to avoid naming conflicts with objects in your current program.

Case Study Based Question

Case Study 1

Python modules are self-contained units of code that encapsulate specific functionalities. They promote code organization, reusability, and modularity. When a module is imported, its code is executed, and its objects (functions, variables, classes) become accessible to the importing script.

However, it's important to manage namespaces carefully to avoid naming conflicts. Using dot notation with the module name is crucial when accessing objects from a module imported using the import <module> syntax.

(i) What is the primary purpose of Python modules?
(a) To organize code into reusable units.
(b) To make code more complex.
(c) To slow down program execution.
(d) To hide code from the user.

(ii) When a module is imported, what happens to its code?
(a) It is copied into the current script.
(b) It is executed and its objects are made available.
(c) It remains unchanged and inaccessible.
(d) It is deleted from the system.

(iii) Why is namespace management important when using modules?
(a) To prevent naming conflicts between objects.
(b) To make code more difficult to understand.
(c) To increase the size of the program.
(d) To slow down program execution.

(iv) What is the correct way to access a function my_function from a module named my_module?
(a) my_function()
(b) module_name.my_function()
(c) import my_function()
(d) from my_function import my_module

(v) Which of the following is NOT a benefit of using modules in Python?
(a) Improved code readability.
(b) Increased code complexity.
(c) Enhanced code reusability.
(d) Better code organization.

Ans. (i) (a) To organize code into reusable units.
(ii) (b) It is executed and its objects are made available.
(iii) (a) To prevent naming conflicts between objects.
(iv) (b) module_name.my_function()
(v) (b) Increased code complexity.

SELF ASSESSMENT TEST

Multiple Choice Questions

1. Which module is used for pow() to find the power of a number?

(a) random (b) math

(c) statistics (d) power

2. To include the use of functions which are present in the statistics library, we must use the option

(a) statistics.h (b) import statistics

(c) import.statistics (d) statistics.statistics

3. The value passed in sin() should be in

(a) degree (b) meter

(c) inch (d) radian

Fill in the Blanks

4. The ________ module provides functions for mathematical calculations.

5. The ________ function generates a random integer within a given range.

6. The ________ module provides functions for statistical calculations.

7. The ________ function returns the mean of a list of numbers.

8. The ________ statement is used to import specific functions from a module.

9. The ________ function returns the absolute value of a number.

State Whether True or False

10. The math module provides functions for statistical calculations.

11. The random module can generate both integer and floating-point random numbers.

12. The statistics module includes trigonometric functions.

13. You can import specific functions from a module using the from statement.

14. The ceil() function rounds a number down to the nearest integer.

15. random.random() generates a random integer.

Assertion and Reason Based Questions

Assertion (A) and Reason (R) Type questions. Choose the correct option as:

(a) Both Assertion (A) and Reason (R) are true, and Reason (R) is the correct explanation of Assertion (A).

(b) Both Assertion (A) and Reason (R) are true, but Reason (R) is not the correct explanation of Assertion (A).

(c) Assertion (A) is true, but Reason (R) is false.

(d) Assertion (A) is false, but Reason (R) is true.

16. Assertion (A) The math module is primarily used for generating random numbers.

Reason (R) Python modules provide a way to organize and reuse code.

17. Assertion (A) The random module can generate random integers.

Reason (R) The random module includes functions like randint() and randrange().

18. Assertion (A) The statistics module is used for calculating statistical measures.

Reason (R) The statistics module includes functions like mean(), median(), and mode().

19. Assertion (A) The from statement is used to import all functions from a module.

Reason (R) The from module import * syntax allows importing all functions.

20. Assertion (A) The ceil() function always rounds a number down to the nearest integer.

Reason (R) Modules are used to extend the functionality of Python.

Very Short Answer Type Questions

21. What is the output of the given code?

```
import random
random.choice (50, 100, 10)
```

22. The output of the following code is either 10 or 20, state whether this statement is True or False.

```
import random
random.randint (10, 20)
```

Short Answer Type Questions

23. What is mean by import statement?

24. **Predict the output.**

```
import random
random.choice ([3.4, 8.3, 2])
```

25. **What will be the output of the given code?**

```
import random
random.randrange (10, 200, 20)
```

26. **What is return by following code?**

(i) `int (math.pow (4, 2))`

(ii) `print (math.pow (4, 2))`

(iii) `print (math.pow (4, 3, 2))`

27. **What is the output of the given code?**

```
from random import shuffle
a = ['This', 'That', 'These', 'Those',
'They']
shuffle (a)
print (a)
```

28. **Predict the output of the given code.**

(i) `math.ceil (9.6)`

(ii) `math.floor (9.4)`

(iii) `math.floor (-9.4)`

29. **Write the short note on sin () method.**

Long Answer Type Questions

30. **Predict the output.**

```
import math
print ("ceil:", math.ceil (8.65))
print ("fabs:", math.fabs (8.65))
print ("fabs:", math.fabs (-8.65))
print ("floor:", math.floor (-8.65))
print ("pow:", math.pow (5, 4))
print ("round:", round  (7.654265))
print ("round:", round (7.654265, 2))
print ("sqrt:", math.sqrt (289))
```

31. **What is return by the following code?**

```
import math
print ("cos:", math.cos (42.3651))
print ("sin:", math.sin (1))
print ("tan:", math.tan (0))
print ("degree:", math.degrees (3.14))
print ("radian:", math.radians (90))
```

32. **What is the output of the given code?**

```
import statistics
list1 = [23, 45, 3, 5, 6, 7, 12, 32, 11, 22,
8, 45]
a = statistics. mean (list1)
print (a )
b = statistics.median (list1)
print (b)
c = statistics.mode (list1)
print (c)
```

33. **Define the statistics module in Python.**

Case Study Based Questions

34. **A data analyst needs to create a Python tool to analyze a dataset. The tool should calculate the mean, median, and mode of the data, as well as generate random samples for testing purposes.**

(i) **To calculate the mean, median, and mode of the data, which module should the analyst import?**

(a) math (b) random
(c) statistics (d) os

(ii) **To generate random integers within a specific range, the analyst should use which function from the random module?**

(a) random() (b) randrange()
(c) sqrt() (d) ceil()

(iii) **To calculate the median of a list of numbers, the analyst can use:**

(a) statistics.mean() (b) statistics.mode()
(c) statistics.median() (d) math.sqrt()

(iv) **To import only the mean() and mode() functions from the statistics module, the analyst should use:**

(a) import statistics
(b) from statistics import *
(c) from statistics import mean, mode
(d) import mean, mode from statistics

(v) **To generate a random floating-point number between 0 and 1, the analyst should use which function from the random module?**

(a) randint() (b) randrange()
(c) random() (d) fabs()

Answers

1. (b) 2. (b) 3. (d) 4. math 5. randint()
6. statistics 7. mean() 8. From.import 9. abs
10. False 11. True 12. False 13. True 14. False
15. False 16. (d) 17. (a) 18. (a) 19. (d)
20. (d)
34. (i) → (c), (ii) → (b), (iii) → (c), (iv) → (c), (v) → (c)

16

CHAPTER

This chapter explores the relationship between society, law and ethics focusing on how they guide human behavior and decision making.

▼ YOUR STUDY GOALS

16.1 Digital Footprints
16.2 Digital Society and Netizens
16.3 Data Protection
16.4 Cyber Crime
16.5 Cyber Safety
16.6 Malware: Threats to Computer Security
16.7 Information Technology Act (IT Act)
16.8 E-Waste Management
16.9 Technology and Society

▼ YOUR PRACTICE GOAL

- Objective Type Questions (40 Qs ; MCQs, True or False, Fill in the Blanks, Assertion and Reason)
- Subjective Type Questions (43 Qs ; VSA, SA, LA)
- Case Study Based Questions-2

Society, Law and Ethics

Cyber ethics is about behaving safely and responsibly online. It's like a set of rules to keep everyone safe on the internet. By understanding the dangers of harmful and illegal online activities, we can protect ourselves and others.

Cyber ethics is not just about technology; it's about how we use technology and how it affects us as individuals and as a society. It's about the right and wrong of using computers, and the laws and rules we need to keep everyone safe and fair.

16.1 Digital Footprints

A digital footprint is all the information you leave behind when you use the internet. It's like a trail of breadcrumbs that shows where you've been online.

This includes everything from your social media posts and online purchases to your browsing history and location data. By understanding your digital footprint, you can be more aware of your online privacy and security.

Types of Digital Footprint

Digital footprints can be divided into two main types.

1. **Active Digital Footprint** This refers to the information you choose to share online. Every time you post something on social media or comment on a blog, you're creating an active digital footprint.

   Example Social media posts, Blog entries, Comments on forums or articles.

2. **Passive Digital Footprint** This refers to the information collected about you without your knowledge or consent. It's generated by your online activities and is often tracked by websites and apps.

   Example Cookies, Metadata, Analytics data

Importance of Understanding Digital Footprints

It's essential to be aware of your digital footprint to protect yourself for several reasons:

- **Privacy** Knowing what information is available online can help you protect your privacy.
- **Reputation** Your digital footprint can influence how others perceive you, such as potential employers or educational institutions.
- **Online Safety** Recognizing the types of data collected can help you make informed decisions about sharing information online.

16.2 Digital Society and Netizens

As technology continues to shape our world, we increasingly rely on digital tools for everyday tasks. From socializing and shopping to learning and working, the internet has become an integral part of our lives.

However, with this digital transformation comes the responsibility to be a responsible digital citizen. This means being aware of online etiquette, respecting others, and using technology ethically. By understanding and practicing these principles, we can create a positive and inclusive online environment.

Net Etiquettes

Net etiquette is about behaving politely and respectfully online. Here are some pointers to follow for good online behavior:

1. **Be Kind and Respectful** Treat others online with the same respect you'd show in person. Avoid using hurtful language or engaging in cyberbullying.
2. **Be Ethical** Respect copyright laws and give credit to others' work. Avoid plagiarism and ensure you cite sources appropriately.
3. **Think Before You Click** Consider the impact of your posts. Once something is online, it's difficult to remove.
4. **Take Responsibility** Own up to your mistakes and apologize sincerely.
5. **Protect Your Privacy** Be cautious about sharing personal information. Respect the privacy of others.
6. **Communicate Clearly** Use clear language and avoid sarcasm or humor that might be misunderstood.
7. **Engage Positively** Contribute to online discussions in a constructive way. Offer support and encouragement.

Digital Communication Etiquettes

Digital communication, which includes email, texting, and social media, has made it easier to connect with others.

However, it's important to use these tools respectfully and effectively. Here are some of the key etiquettes to follow:

(A) Be Efficient

- **Respect Time** Respond promptly to important messages. Understand that not everyone can reply instantly.
- **Conserve Data** Avoid large file attachments. Use cloud storage for sharing large files.

(B) Be Respectful

- **Maintain Courtesy** Be polite and constructive in all your online interactions, regardless of the platform.
- **Avoid Aggression** Refrain from using offensive language or engaging in personal attacks.

(C) Be Reliable

- **Build Trust** Be mindful of your online contributions. A positive online reputation can enhance your credibility.
- **Be Thoughtful** Contribute meaningfully to discussions and forums.

Social Media Etiquettes

Social media has become a major part of our lives, letting us connect with people around the world. Platforms like Facebook, Twitter, and Instagram allow us to share our thoughts and experiences.

But with this increased connection, it's important to be respectful and responsible online.

Here are some essential etiquettes to follow:

1. Protect Your Privacy

- **Strong Passwords** Create complex passwords and change them regularly.
- **Be Selective with Friends** Only accept friend requests from people you know and trust.
- **Verify Information** Be cautious of fake news and misinformation. Verify information before sharing.

2. Be Responsible

- **Think Before You Post** Consider the potential consequences of your online actions.
- **Respect Privacy** Ask for permission before sharing photos or stories of others.
- **Be Kind and Respectful** Treat others with kindness and avoid negative behavior.

16.3 Data Protection

Data protection is about keeping our personal information safe and secure. This means we should have control over our information, deciding who can access it and for what purpose. Essentially, data protection empowers individuals to make informed choices about their personal information.

Consequences of Data Breaches

- **Security Risks** Your personal information could be exposed to hackers and cybercriminals.
- **Data Loss** You may lose important documents, photos, or financial information.
- **Malware Infection** Your devices could be infected with viruses or malware.
- **Financial Loss** You may become a victim of identity theft or fraudulent activities.
- **Reputational Damage** Your personal reputation could be spoiled.

Protecting Your Personal Data

- **Strong Passwords**: Use strong, unique passwords for all your online accounts.
- **Secure Wi-Fi** Use strong Wi-Fi passwords and avoid public Wi-Fi for sensitive activities.
- **Be Mindful Online** Avoid sharing personal information on social media and be cautious of suspicious emails and links.
- **Regular Updates** Keep your software and operating systems up-to-date with the latest security patches.
- **Use Security Software** Install reliable antivirus and anti-malware software.
- **Data Encryption** Encrypt sensitive data to make it harder for unauthorized individuals to access.
- **Secure Data Disposal** Shred physical documents containing personal information and securely delete digital files.

Intellectual Property Right (IPR)

Intellectual property (IP) refers to creations of the mind, such as inventions, literary and artistic works, designs, and symbols.

These creations are protected by law, granting exclusive rights to their owners. These rights allow creators to control how their work is used and to benefit from their creations. Common types of IP rights include:

(a) **Copyright** protects original creative works, such as books, music, films, paintings, and sculptures. As soon as a work is created, it is automatically copyrighted.

This means that the creator has exclusive rights to reproduce, distribute, perform, display, and adapt their work.

(b) **Patent** protects inventions, such as new products or processes. Unlike copyright, patents require a formal application and approval process.

Once granted, a patent gives the inventor exclusive rights to their invention for a limited period, typically 20 years.

(c) **Trademark** is a distinctive sign, such as a word, phrase, symbol, design, or logo, that identifies and distinguishes the goods or services of one business from those of others. It prevents others from using a similar mark that could confuse consumers.

The protection of intellectual property rights of individuals lead to the following features.

(i) It encourages people to create new software as well as helps them to improve the existing applications.

(ii) An environment is provided for innovative thoughts and technologies.

(iii) Provides the assurity of good returns, people and businesses invest in the national economy.

Violation of IPR

Violation of Intellectual property Rights (IPR) means infringement of the exclusive rights or someone uses someone else's copyrighted, patented, or trademarked work without permission.

This includes various forms of violations:

1. **Plagiarism** is the act of copying someone else's work or ideas and claiming them as your own. This dishonest practice not only disrespects the original creator but can also have serious consequences in academic and professional settings.
2. **Copyright infringement** happens when someone uses a copyrighted work, like a song, book, or movie, without the permission of the copyright owner. This can include copying, distributing, or performing the work without authorization.
3. **Trademark infringement** occurs when someone uses a trademark that is identical or confusingly similar to a registered trademark. This can mislead consumers and harm the reputation of the brand owner.

TEACHER TIP

Plagiarism involves using someone else's work without proper attribution.

Copyright infringement occurs when someone uses copyrighted material without permission or payment.

Quick Test 1

1. What is net etiquettes, and why is it important?
2. What are some practical steps to protect your digital footprint?
3. What are the challenges of digital communication, and how can we overcome them?
4. What steps can individuals take to protect their personal data?
5. Explain the concept of intellectual property rights.
6. What are the different types of intellectual property rights, and how are they protected?

Software Licensing

A software license is a legal agreement that outlines the terms and conditions for using software. It grants users certain rights, such as the ability to install and use the software, but also imposes limitations, such as restrictions on copying or distributing the software. These licenses typically include information about warranties, disclaimers, and the software provider's liability.

Benefits of Using Licensed Software

- Using Unlicensed Software Against the Law
- The Right Software License Can Save our Money
- We can Receive Around-The-Clock License Support

Types of Public Licenses

Public licenses are legal tools that allow creators to share their work with others while specifying how it can be used.

Two of the most common public licenses are Creative Commons (CC) and GNU General Public License (GPL). Understanding these licenses is important for both creators and users in the digital age.

1. Creative Commons (CC)

Creative Commons licenses allow creators to share their work, such as websites, music, and literature, with others while still maintaining some control over how their work is used.

Features of Creative Commons (CC)

- **Free to Share** CC-licensed works can be shared and distributed without permission.
- **Flexible Use** Creators can choose how their work can be used, whether it's for personal or commercial purposes.
- **Encourages Creativity** CC licenses promote collaboration and the creation of new works.

2. GNU General Public License (GPL)

The GNU General Public License (GPL) is a software license that ensures software remains free for users. It allows users to run, study, share, and modify the software, fostering an open-source approach to software development.

Features of GPL

- **Free to Modify** Users can modify the source code of GPL-licensed software to suit their needs.

- **Share Modifications** Any modifications made to the software must also be shared under the GPL license.
- **Commercial Use** GPL-licensed software can be distributed for free or for a fee.

Free and Open Source Software (FOSS)

Free and Open-Source Software (FOSS) is software that is freely available and allows users to access and modify its source code. This means anyone can use, study, share, and improve the software. FOSS relies on a large community of developers who collaborate to create and maintain the software.

Popular examples of FOSS include

- **Operating Systems** Linux-based operating systems like Ubuntu and Fedora.
- **Productivity Tools** LibreOffice, a free and open-source office suite, and Mozilla Firefox, a widely used web browser.

16.4 Cyber Crime

Cybercrime refers to criminal activities that involve computers and networks. These crimes can range from hacking into computer systems to using the internet for malicious purposes like spreading malware or stealing personal information.

Cybercriminals may target individuals, businesses, or even governments, causing significant financial and reputational damage. The financial industry is a prime target for cybercrime due to the vast amounts of sensitive financial data stored and transmitted electronically. Cybercriminals often exploit vulnerabilities in banking systems to steal money, credit card information, and other valuable assets.

There are the most common cyber crimes as follows

Hacking

Hacking involves illegally accessing computer systems or networks. Hackers use their technical skills to exploit vulnerabilities and gain unauthorized access to sensitive information or resources.

Types of Hackers

(a) **Ethical Hackers (White Hat Hackers)** Ethical hackers use their skills to identify and report vulnerabilities in systems. They work with organizations to improve security and protect against malicious attacks.

(b) **Non-Ethical Hackers (Black Hat Hackers or Crackers)** Black hat hackers exploit vulnerabilities to steal data, damage systems, or cause other harm. They often engage in illegal activities for personal gain or malicious intent.

Phishing and Fraud Emails

Phishing is a cybercrime where attackers use deceptive tactics to trick individuals into revealing sensitive personal information, such as passwords and credit card numbers. They often do this by sending fraudulent emails or directing victims to fake websites that mimic legitimate ones.

Common Methods of Phishing

1. Email Spoofing

- Fake emails are sent to deceive users into thinking they are from legitimate sources.
- These emails often mimic the look and feel of real organizations.
- Be cautious of suspicious URLs and email addresses.

2. Phone Calls and Text Messages

- Fraudulent calls and text messages can also be used to trick users into revealing personal information.
- Be alert of unexpected requests for sensitive information.

How to Avoid Phishing

- Verify the sender's email address and URL.
- Be cautious of unsolicited requests.
- Avoid clicking on suspicious links or downloading attachments from unknown sources.
- Never share personal information over unsecured platforms.

Cyber Bullying

Cyberbullying involves using technology to harass, threaten, or embarrass others online. It's a serious issue that can have harmful consequences for victims, especially young people. While cyberbullying is a growing concern, many countries are enacting laws to combat this crime and protect individuals from online harassment.

The following are just a few examples

- Making fun of another use in an internet chat room.
- Posting offensive messages on a user's facebook or Myspace page.

Cyber Trolls or Cyber Trolling

Trolling is a form of online harassment where individuals intentionally post offensive or provocative comments to upset others. Trolls often target specific individuals or groups, aiming to provoke emotional responses and disrupt online communities. This behavior can have serious consequences for victims, including emotional distress and social isolation.

Ransomware

Ransomware is a type of cyberattack where malicious software encrypts a victim's files, making them inaccessible. Cybercriminals then demand a ransom payment to decrypt the files. In some cases, they may also threaten to leak sensitive information if the ransom is not paid.

Ransomware can infect systems in following ways

- **Malicious Websites** Visiting compromised or poorly secured websites can lead to ransomware infections.
- **Untrusted Downloads** Downloading software from unreliable sources can introduce ransomware to your system.
- **Phishing Emails** Opening malicious email attachments can trigger ransomware attacks.
- **Malicious Ads** Clicking on harmful advertisements can infect your device with ransomware.

Quick Test 2

1. What are the benefits of using licensed software?
2. What are the advantages and disadvantages of open-source software compared to proprietary software?
3. What are the key differences between Creative Commons and GPL licenses?
4. How can individuals protect themselves from cybercrime?
5. Explain the concept of phishing and how to avoid phishing attacks.
6. What is ransomware, and how does it work?

16.5 Cyber Safety

Cyber safety is about using technology safely and responsibly. It involves understanding the potential risks associated with online activities, such as cyberbullying, hacking, and ransomware, and taking steps to protect ourselves and others. Various approaches to cyber safety is founded

- Maintaining a positive approach about the many benefits brought by technologies.
- Encouraging the public to identify the risks associated with ICT.
- Putting in place strategies to minimise and manage risks.
- Recognising the importance of effective teaching and learning programmes.

Safely Browsing the Web

By using a combination of preventative measures and making good choices online you can stay safe when browsing the web. Following are the some precautions for web browsing

Before you Start : Update your Software

Exploiting e-mail and web browsing applications is the most common way hackers and malware try to gain access to devices and your information. Protect yourself before you start browsing the web by making sure that all softwares are up-to-date.

Protect your Web Browser

You can adjust the settings in your web browser to work in a more or less secure way. Most web browsers will give you warnings when they detect you visiting a malicious website.

Pay attention to these warnings, they can help protect you from malware, phishing and identity theft.

Learn more about the Security Settings on your Browser

Settings and security models are different for each browsers, visit the following vendor websites to learn more about the security settings in your browser

- Internet Explorer
- Mozilla Firefox
- Google Chrome
- Opera

Identity Protection while using Internet

Our personal information, like our name, address, and financial details, defines our identity and should be protected. When we share this information online, we trust that it will be used responsibly.

However, there's a risk of identity theft, where malicious actors can misuse our personal information for fraudulent activities. This can lead to significant financial and emotional harm.

Websites Track You Online in Many Ways

Tracking is generally used by advertising networks to build up detailed profiles for pinpoint ad-targeting even tracking down users for special purpose such as affecting their political choices. The type of information is compiled through your web page usage patterns for tracking you.

This include the following

(i) **IP Address** Your IP address is a unique identifier that can reveal your approximate geographic location.

(ii) **Cookies** Websites use cookies, small text files stored on your device, to track your browsing habits and preferences.

Cookies can be of the following types:

- **First-Party Cookies** These are created by the website you're visiting. They store information like your login credentials and preferences.
- **Third-Party Cookies** These are created by third-party advertisers and track your browsing behavior across different websites. They often lead to targeted advertising.

(iii) **HTTP Referrer** This information tells websites where you came from, helping them understand user behavior and traffic sources.

(iv) **Super Cookies** These persistent cookies can track your browsing activity across multiple devices, making it difficult to maintain privacy.

(v) **User Agent** Your user agent string reveals information about your browser and operating system, allowing websites to tailor their content and ads.

Solution to Protect the Identity When Websites Track You Online

All the above things leak your identity information to websites. The most common solution to this is using private browsing or anonymous browsing on the Internet.

(i) **Private Browsing** Use incognito or private browsing mode to prevent your browser from storing your browsing history, cookies, and other data.

(ii) **Proxy Servers** Mask your IP address by routing your internet traffic through a proxy server.

(iii) **Virtual Private Networks (VPNs)** Encrypt your internet traffic and hide your IP address, providing a higher level of privacy and security.

(iv) **Anonymous Browsers** Use browsers like Tor to browse the web anonymously, protecting your identity and location.

Confidentiality of Information

Confidentiality protects sensitive information from unauthorized access. It ensures that only authorized individuals can view and use the data. This is achieved through various methods, such as restricting access to authorized users, using strong passwords, and employing encryption techniques to scramble data.

Best practices used to ensure confidentiality are as follows

(i) Use a firewall wherever possible.

(ii) Control browsers setting to block tracking.

(iii) Browse privately wherever possible.

(iv) Be careful while posting on the Internet.

(v) Ensure safe sites while entering crucial information.

(vi) Carefully handle e-mail.

(vii) Do not give sensitive information on wireless networks.

(viii) Avoid using public computers to make sure the following thinks.

- Browse privately.
- Do not save your login details.
- Never save passwords while using public computer.
- Disable the feature that store passwords.
- Properly logout before leaving public computer.
- Clear history and cookies.

16.6 Malware: Threats to Computer Security

Malware stands for **malicious software.** It is a broad term that refers to a variety of malicious programs that are used to damage computer system, gather sensitive information, or gain access to private computer systems.

Malware is an unwanted software that any unauthorized person wants to run on your computer. These are known as security threats. It includes computer viruses, worms, trojan horses, rootkits, spyware, adware etc.

Some of them are described below

VIRUS

VIRUS stands for Vital Information Resources Under Siege. Computer Viruses are small programs that can negatively affect the health of your computer. It obtains control of a PC and directs it to perform unusual and often destructive actions.

Virus copies itself and attaches itself to other programs which further spread the infection. The virus can affect or attack any part of the computer software such as the boot block, operating system, system areas, files and application program.

On the other hand, it is also true that not all computer problems are caused by computer viruses. This could be caused by other things such as an error (bug) or misconfiguration of software or hardware. For example, Bomber, Whale, OneHaff, KoKo, Eliza etc.

Some common viruses are tabulated below

Year	Name
1971	Creeper
1982	Elk Cloner
1988	The Morris Internet Worm
1999	Melissa
2000	I Love You
2001	Code Red
2003	SQL Slammer
2003	Blaster
2004	Sasser
2010	Stuxnet
2011	Trojan
2012	Rootkit
2014	Generic PUP
2014	Net Worm

Effects of Virus

There are many different effects that viruses can have on your computer, depending on the types of virus. Some viruses can

(i) monitor what you are doing.
(ii) slow down your computer's performance.
(iii) destroy all data on your local disk.
(iv) affect on computer networks and the connection to Internet.
(v) increase or decrease memory size.
(vi) create more than one partitions.

Trojan

A Trojan, or Trojan Horse, is a non-self-replicating type of malware which appears to perform a desirable function but instead facilitates unauthorized access to the user's computer system. Trojans do not attempt to inject themselves into other files like a computer virus. Trojan horses may steal information, or harm their host computer systems. Trojans may use drive-by downloads or install via online games or Internet-driven applications in order to reach target computers. Unlike viruses, Trojan horses do not replicate themselves.

For example, Beast, Sub7.Zeus, ZeroAccess Rootkit etc.

Adware

Adware is software that displays unwanted advertisements on your computer or mobile device. These ads can pop up as banners, windows, or even change your browser's homepage.

Often, adware sneaks onto your system bundled with free software, and its purpose is to generate revenue for its creators by showing you ads. It can slow down your device and sometimes lead to further security risks.

16.7 Information Technology Act (IT Act)

As the internet has become increasingly prevalent, so too have cybercrimes like hacking, phishing, and online fraud. To combat these threats, many countries have enacted laws to protect personal information and ensure the safety of internet users.

Introduction to IT Act 2000

The Information Technology Act of 2000 (IT Act) is an Indian law that recognizes electronic transactions and facilitates electronic communication. It aims to promote electronic commerce by providing a legal framework for online activities, including electronic filing of documents with government agencies. The IT Act of 2000, originally consisting of 94 sections, covers the entire nation of India. It applies to both Indian citizens and foreigners who commit cybercrimes involving Indian computer systems or networks.

The IT Act was amended in 2008 to introduce provisions related to cybercrime, including penalties for sending offensive messages and engaging in cyber terrorism. However, some sections of the amended Act, particularly Section 66A, were later challenged and deemed unconstitutional by the Supreme Court of India.

Objective of IT Act

- To stop computer crime and protect the privacy of Internet users.
- To make more power to IPO, RBI and Indian evidence Act for restricting electronic crime.
- To give legal recognition for keeping books of accounts by bankers and other companies in electronic form.
- To give legal recognition to digital signatures for accepting any agreement via computer.
- To provide facility of filing documents online relating to school admission or registration in employment exchange.
- To give legal recognition to any transaction which is done by electronic way or use of the Internet.

Scope of IT Act

- IT Act 2000 is not applicable on the attestation for making will of anybody. Physical attestation by two witnesses in must.
- Attestation for giving power of attorney of property is not possible via electronic record.
- A contract of sale of any immovable property.
- IT Act 2000 is not applicable on the attestation for creating trust via electronic way. Physical attestation is must.

Features of IT Act 2000

- It helps to promote E-Commerce.
- It includes a high penalty for cyber crime.
- It provides filing online forms.
- It enhances the corporate business.

16.8 E-Waste Management

E-waste (Electronic waste) comprises the electronic products that are no longer useful to us. Electronic waste may also be defined as discarded computers, office electronic equipment, entertainment electronics devices, mobile phones, television sets and refrigerators. This includes used electronics which are destined for reuse, resale, salvage, recycling or disposal.

E-waste management has become a significant problem due to the technical process we have gained in the last century.

E-Waste Disposal Process

E-waste is categorized by the government of India under the broad class of hazardous waste. Within E-waste, there are several categories such as large and small household appliances, electrical and electronic toys and sporting tools, computer and related equipment.

Composition of E-Waste

E-waste, consisting mainly of metals and plastics, also contains hazardous substances like heavy metals and harmful chemicals. These substances, often found in components like circuit boards and cooling systems, can have detrimental environmental impacts, including ozone layer depletion and climate change. The diverse nature of electronic devices makes it difficult to categorize their specific material composition.

The E-waste management involves proper recycling and recovery of the disposed material. The recycle and recovery includes the following unit operations:

Dismantling

- Disassembling electronic devices to separate valuable components from hazardous materials.
- Removing reusable parts and hazardous substances.

Segregation

- Sorting materials into different categories (ferrous metals, non-ferrous metals, plastics, etc.) for recycling.
- Shredding materials to facilitate separation.

Refurbishment and Reuse

- Repairing and reconditioning reusable electronic devices.

Recycling and Recovery

- Recycling valuable materials like metals and plastics.
- Recovering precious metals from electronic components.

Treatment and Disposal

- Safely disposing of hazardous materials like CFCs, PCBs, and mercury.

- Treating and disposing of non-recyclable waste in an environmentally responsible manner.

Advantages of E-Waste Recycling

If you have electronic items which have stopped working and as good as waste matters, it is a good idea to opt for E-waste recycling. The key advantages are:

- **Conservation of Natural Resources** Recycling reduces the need for raw materials, saving energy and minimizing environmental impact.
- **Environmental Protection** Proper recycling prevents hazardous substances from entering the environment.
- **Job Creation** The recycling industry creates jobs and boosts the economy.
- **Landfill Reduction** Recycling reduces the amount of waste sent to landfills.
- **Cost Savings** Recycling can save money by reducing the need for new materials and energy.

Disadvantages of E-Waste Recycling

Some disadvantages of E-waste recycling are as follows:

- **Increased Energy Consumption and Pollution** The recycling process itself can consume energy and generate pollution, especially during transportation and processing.
- **Environmental Risks from Improper Handling** Improper handling of waste during recycling can lead to environmental contamination.
- **Lower Quality of Recycled Products** Recycled products may not always meet the same quality standards as new products, especially if they contain recycled materials with potential contaminants.

16.9 Technology and Society

ICT (Information and Communication Technology) are general purpose technologies whose value and impact arise primarily from their use in other economic and social sectors.

Three capabilities are especially important for economic and social development as

- Enable greater efficiency in economic and social processes.
- Enhance the effectiveness of co-operation between stakeholders.
- Increase the volume and range of information available to people, businesses and governments.

Societal Issues by Technology

- **Lack of social skills** Frequency of interacting personally has been reduced much thus kids and teenagers are deprived of basic social manner.
- **Poor sleeping habit** Endorsing online activities have affected the sleeping pattern of people.
- **Addiction** Addiction of technology is no less than the drug addiction.
- **Depression** Dependence on technology and less interaction with fellow human beings can lead to depression.
- **Lack of privacy** People are opening up their private space by giving their information on social sites giving rise to criminal activities.

Cultural Changes Induced by Technology

- **Online shopping** Use of online shopping has changed the culture of going out to the market and buying goods.
- **Home delivery of foods** Online home delivery of foods have changed the culture of going out for dinner or lunch with family and also the culture of home cooked food.
- **Social media** Social media has changed the culture of going to a friend's place to have a chitchat.

Quick Test 3

1. How can you protect your privacy while browsing the internet?
2. What are the different types of cookies and how do they affect your privacy?
3. What is the importance of keeping your software and browser up-to-date?
4. Define malware and discuss the different types of malware attacks.
5. What are the environmental impacts of improper e-waste disposal?
6. How has technology impacted our daily lives and social interactions?

Mind Map

SOCIETY, LAW AND ETHICS

Digital Footprints

A digital footprint is all the information you leave behind when you use the internet. It's likea trail of breadcrumbs that shows where you've been online.

Active Digital Footprint

This refers to the information you choose to share online.

Example Social media posts, Blog entries, Comments on forums or articles.

Passive Digital Footprint

This refers to the information collected about you without your knowledge or consent.

Example Cookies, Metadata, Analytics data

Cyber Safety

Cyber safety is about using technology safely and responsibly. It involves understanding the potential risks associated with online activities, such as cyberbullying, hacking, and ransomware, and taking steps to protect ourselves and others.

01 Safely Browsing the Web
02 Identity Protection while using Internet
03 Confidentiality of Information

Data Protection

Data protection is about keeping our personal information safe and secure. This means we should have control over our information, deciding who can access it and for what purpose.

Consequences of Data Breaches

- Reputational Damage
- Financial Loss
- Data Loss
- Security Risks
- Malware Infection

Protecting Your Personal Data

- Strong Passwords
- Secure Wi-Fi
- Secure Data Disposal
- Be Mindful Online
- Data Encryption
- Regular Updates
- Use Security Software

Intellectual Property Right (IPR)

Intellectual property (IP) refers to creations of the mind, such as inventions, literary and artistic works, designs, and symbols.

Common types of IP rights:

- Copyright
- Patent
- Trademark

Violation of IPR

- Copyright infringement
- Trademark infringement
- Plagiarism

Software License

A software license is a legal agreement that outlines the terms and conditions for using software.

Types of Public Licenses

Public licenses are legal tools that allow creators to share their work with others while specifying how it can be used.

- Creative Commons (CC)
- GNU General Public License (GPL)

Free and Open Source Software (FOSS)

Public licenses are legal tools that allow creators to share their work with others while specifying how it can be used.

Digital Society and Netizens

Net Etiquettes

Net etiquette is about behaving politely and respectfully online. Here are some pointers to follow for good online behavior:

01 Be Kind and Respectful
02 Be Ethical
03 Think Before You Click
04 Take Responsibility
05 Protect Your Privacy
06 Communicate Clearly
07 Engage Positively

Digital Communication Etiquettes

Digital communication, which includes email, texting, and social media, has made it easier to connect with others. Here are some of the key etiquettes to follow:

- Be Efficient
- Be Respectful
- Be Reliable

Social Media Etiquettes

Social media has become a major part of our lives, letting us connect with people around the world. Platforms like Facebook, Twitter, and Instagram allow us to share our thoughts and experiences.

Here are some essential etiquettes to follow:

- Protect Your Privacy
- Be Responsible

Cyber Crime

There are the most common cyber crimes as follows

- Hacking
- Ransomware
- Phishing and Fraud Emails
- Cyber Bullying
- Cyber Trolls or Cyber Trolling

Information Technology Act (IT Act)

The Information Technology Act of 2000 (IT Act) is an Indian law that recognizes electronic transactions and facilitates electronic communication.

E-Waste Management

Electronic waste comprises the electronic products that are no longer useful to us. This includes used electronics which are destined for reuse, resale, salvage, recycling or disposal.

Malware

Malware, or Malware Software, is any program or file that's intentionally harmful to a computer, network or server. e.g., Virus, Trojan, Adware.

NCERT Folder

In-text Questions

1. Can your digital footprints be used to judge your attitude and work ethics?

Ans. Yes, digital footprints reflect online behavior, interactions, and activities, which can be analyzed to judge a person's attitude and work ethics.

2. As a digital citizen, list various services that you avail online.

Ans. Online banking, social media, e-commerce, email, cloud storage, streaming services, and online learning platforms.

3. Is having the same password for all your accounts on different websites safe?

Ans. No, using the same password increases the risk of multiple accounts being compromised if one gets hacked.

4. Suppose someone's email password is 'tecnnology' which is weak. Can you suggest a stronger password?

Ans. Yes, a stronger password could be T3cH#n0l0gy@123, combining uppercase, lowercase, numbers, and special characters.

5. Why should we always mention the source from which we got an idea or used resources (text, image, audio, video, etc.) to prepare a project or a write-up?

Ans. To give proper credit, avoid plagiarism, and respect intellectual property rights.

6. How can you unsubscribe from a mail group or block an email sender?

Ans. Click the "Unsubscribe" link at the bottom of the email or use the "Block" or "Report Spam" option in your email settings.

Exercise Questions

1. After practicals, Atharv left the computer laboratory but forgot to sign off from his email account. Later, his classmate Revaan started using the same computer. He is now logged in as Atharv. He sends inflammatory email messages to few of his classmates using Atharv's email account. Revaan's activity is an example of which of the following cyber crime? Justify your answer.

(a) Hacking (b) Identity theft
(c) Cyber bullying (d) Plagiarism

Ans. (b) Identity theft

2. Rishika found a crumpled paper under her desk. She picked it up and opened it. It contained some text which was struck off thrice. But she could still figure out easily that the struck off text was the email ID and password of Garvit, her classmate. What is ethically correct for Rishika to do?

(a) Inform Garvit so that he may change his password.
(b) Give the password of Garvit's email ID to all other classmates.
(c) Use Garvit's password to access his account.

Ans. (a) Inform Garvit so that he may change his password

3. Suhana is down with fever. So she decided not to go to school tomorrow. Next day, in the evening she called up her classmate, Shaurya and enquired about the computer class. She also requested him to explain the concept. Shaurya said, "Mam taught us how to use tuples in python". Further, he generously said, "Give me some time, I will email you the material which will help you to understand tuples in python". Shaurya quickly downloaded a 2-minute clip from the Internet explaining the concept of tuples in python. Using video editor, he added the text "Prepared by Shaurya" in the downloaded video clip. Then, he emailed the modified video clip to Suhana. This act of Shaurya is an example of:

(a) Fair use (b) Hacking
(c) Copyright infringement (d) Cyber crime

Ans. (c) Copyright infringement

4. After a fight with your friend, you did the following activities. Which of these activities is not an example of cyber bullying?

(a) You sent an email to your friend with a message saying that "I am sorry".
(b) You sent a threatening message to your friend saying "Do not try to call or talk to me".
(c) You created an embarrassing picture of your friend and uploaded on your account on a social networking site.

Ans. (b) You sent a threatening message to your friend saying "Do not try to call or talk to me".

5. Sourabh has to prepare a project on "Digital India Initiatives". He decides to get information from the Internet. He downloads three web pages (webpage 1, webpage 2, webpage 3) containing information on Digital India Initiatives. Which of the following steps taken by Sourabh is an example of plagiarism or copyright infringement. Give justification in support of your answer.

(a) He read a paragraph on " Digital India Initiatives" from webpage 1 and rephrased it in his own words. He finally pasted the rephrased paragraph in his project.

(b) He downloaded three images of " Digital India Initiatives" from webpage 2. He made a collage for his project using these images.

(c) He downloaded "Digital India Initiative" icon from web page 3 and pasted it on the front page of his project report.

Ans. (c) He downloaded "Digital India Initiative" icon from web page 3 and pasted it on the front page of his project report.

6. Match the following:

Column A	Column B
(i) Plagiarism	(a) Fakers, by offering special rewards or money prize asked for personal information, such as bank account information.
(ii) Hacking	(b) Copy and paste information from the Internet into your report and then organise it.
(iii) Credit card fraud	(c) The trail that is created when a person uses the Internet.
(iv) Digital Foot Print	(d) Breaking into computers to read private emails and other files.

Ans. (i) → (c), (ii) → (d), (iii) → (a), (iv) → (b)

7. You got the below shown SMS from your bank querying a recent transaction. Answer the following:

(a) Will you SMS your pin number to the given contact number?

(b) Will you call the bank helpline number to recheck the validity of the SMS received?

Ans. (a) No, I will not SMS my pin number to the given contact number.

(b) Yes, I will call the bank helpline number to recheck the validity of the SMS received.

8. Preeti celebrated her birthday with her family. She was excited to share the moments with her friend Himanshu. She uploaded selected images of her birthday party on a social networking site so that Himanshu can see them. After few days, Preeti had a fight with Himanshu. Next morning, she deleted her birthday photographs from that social networking site, so that Himanshu cannot access them. Later in the evening, to her surprise, she saw that one of the images which she had already deleted from the social networking site was available with their common friend Gayatri. She hurriedly enquired Gayatri "Where did you get this picture from?". Gayatri replied "Himanshu forwarded this image few minutes back".

Help Preeti to get answers for the following questions. Give justification for your answers so that Preeti can understand it clearly.

(a) How could Himanshu access an image which I had already deleted?

(b) Can anybody else also access these deleted images?

(c) Had these images not been deleted from my digital footprint?

Ans. (a) Once an image is uploaded to a social media platform, it can be easily downloaded and shared by others, even if you delete it later. This is because the image is stored on the platform's servers and can be accessed by anyone who has the link.

(b) Yes, anyone who has access to the image, either through a direct link or a shared copy, can view it. This highlights the importance of being cautious about what you share online, as once something is shared, it can be difficult to completely remove it.

(c) No, the images were not completely deleted from your digital footprint. While you deleted them from the social media platform, copies may still exist on other devices or servers.

Additionally, once an image is shared online, it can be re-shared and spread widely, making it difficult to control its distribution.

9. The school offers wireless facility (wifi) to the Computer Science students of Class XI. For communication, the network security staff of the school have a registered URL schoolwifi.edu. On 17 September 2017, the following email was mass distributed to all the Computer Science students of Class XI. The email claimed that the password of the students was about to expire. Instructions were given to go to URL to renew their password within 24 hours.

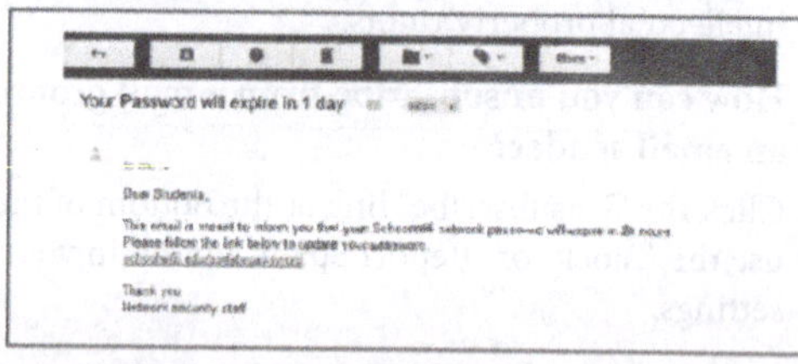

(a) Do you find any discrepancy in this email?

(b) What will happen if the student will click on the given URL?

(c) Is the email an example of cyber crime? If yes, then specify which type of cyber crime is it. Justify your answer.

Ans. (a) Yes, the given link in question is different from the link shown in email

(b) If the student will click on the URL then maybe it's possible that viruses or malware and other things come into the device of his system.

(c) Yes, an email is an example of Cyber Crime. It is a type of email spoofing, here In a spoofing attack, a hacker or malicious individual impersonates another user or device on a network, duping users or systems into believing they are legitimate or authentic.

10. You are planning to go for a vacation. You surfed the Internet to get answers for the following queries:
(a) Weather conditions
(b) Availability of air tickets and fares
(c) Places to visit
(d) Best hotel deals
Which of your above mentioned actions might have created a digital footprint?

Ans. When you surf the internet to get answers for the queries like weather conditions, availability of air tickets and fares, places to visit, best hotel deals, you leave a digital footprint. The websites you visit, the searches you perform, and the content you view online all contribute to your digital footprint.

11. How would you recognise if one of your friends is being cyber bullied?
(a) Cite the online activities which would help you detect that your friend is being cyber bullied?
(b) What provisions are in IT Act 2000, (amended in 2008) to combact such situations.

Ans. (a) I'll recognize my friend as follow:
- **Changes in behavior** Increased anxiety, depression, or withdrawal from social activities.
- **Avoidance of technology** Reluctance to use devices or social media.
- **Physical signs** Difficulty sleeping, changes in appetite, or physical complaints.
- **Direct evidence** Screenshots of harassing messages or posts.

(b) Provisions are in IT Act 2000, (amended in 2008) to combact such situations are as follow:
- **Section 66A** Punishes the sending of offensive messages through communication services.
- **Section 67** Deals with publishing or transmitting obscene material in electronic form.

12. Write the differences between the following
(a) Copyrights and Patents
(b) Plagiarism and Copyright infringement
(c) Non-ethical hacking and Ethical hacking
(d) Active and Passive footprints
(e) Free software and Free and open source software

Ans. (a) **Copyrights vs. Patents** Copyrights protect original works of authorship, while patents protect inventions and innovations.

(b) **Plagiarism vs. Copyright Infringement** Plagiarism involves copying someone else's work without attribution, while copyright infringement involves using copyrighted material without permission.

(c) **Non-Ethical Hacking vs. Ethical Hacking** Non-ethical hackers exploit vulnerabilities for malicious purposes, while ethical hackers identify and report vulnerabilities to improve security.

(d) **Active Footprints vs. Passive Footprints** Active footprints are intentionally created by user actions, while passive footprints are collected without user awareness.

(e) **Free Software vs. Free and Open-Source Software** Free software emphasizes the freedom to use, study, share, and modify software, while free and open-source software (FOSS) adds the requirement of open source code.

13. If you plan to use a short text from an article on the web, what steps must you take in order to credit the sources used?

Ans. To credit sources, you can use in-text citations (e.g., "According to Smith (2023)") and a reference list at the end of your work.

14. When you search online for pictures, how will you find pictures that are available in the free public domain. How can those pictures be used in your project without copyright violations?

Ans. To find free-to-use images, you can search for images with a Creative Commons license. These images can be used without copyright restrictions as long as you follow the specific terms of the license.

15. Describe why it is important to secure your wireless router at home. Search the Internet to find the rules to create a reasonably secure password. Create an imaginary password for your home router. Will you share your password for home router with following people. Justify your answer.
(a) Parents **(b) Friends**
(c) Neighbours **(d) Home Tutors**

Ans. Securing your home router is crucial to protect your network and personal information. A strong password should be a combination of uppercase and lowercase letters, numbers, and symbols.
- **Share password with** Parents
- **Don't share password with** Friends, Neighbors, Home Tutors

Sharing your password with others can compromise your network security.

16. List down the steps you need to take in order to ensure
(a) your computer is in good working condition for a longer time.
(b) smart and safe Internet surfing.

Ans. (a) To maintain your computer's health and security:
- **Regular updates** Keep your operating system and software updated.
- **Antivirus software** Use a reliable antivirus program.
- **Firewall** Enable your firewall to protect your network.

- **Strong passwords** Create strong, unique passwords for your accounts.
- **Backup data** Regularly back up your important files.
- **Safe browsing** Avoid suspicious websites and downloads.

(b) **Don'ts** Never visit websites that are not trustworthy. Install pirated software.
Go for free and unlicensed antivirus software.
Do's Install a purchased copy of a good antivirus software with a strong firewall in it.

17. What is data privacy? Websites that you visit collect what type of information about you?

Ans. Data privacy refers to the protection of personal information. Websites collect information like your IP address, browsing history, and preferences to personalize ads and content.

18. In the computer science class, Sunil and Jagdish were assigned the following task by their teacher.

(a) Sunil was asked to find information about "India, a Nuclear power". He was asked to use Google Chrome browser and prepare his report using Google Docs.

(b) Jagdish was asked to find information about "Digital India". He was asked to use Mozilla Firefox browser and prepare his report using Libre Office Writer.=

What is the difference between technologies used by Sunil and Jagdish?

Ans. The primary difference lies in the software and hardware used. Sunil used Google Chrome and Google Docs, both developed by Google, while Jagdish used Mozilla Firefox and LibreOffice Writer, both open-source software.

19. Cite examples depicting that you were a victim of following cyber crime. Also, cite provisions in IT Act to deal with such a cyber crime.

(a) Identity theft (b) Credit card account theft

Ans. (a) If someone uses your personal information to open credit accounts or commit fraud, it's identity theft.

(b) If your credit card information is stolen and used for unauthorized purchases, it's credit card fraud.

20. Neerja is a student of Class XI. She has opted for Computer Science. Neerja prepared the project assigned to her. She mailed it to her teacher. The snapshot of that email is shown below.

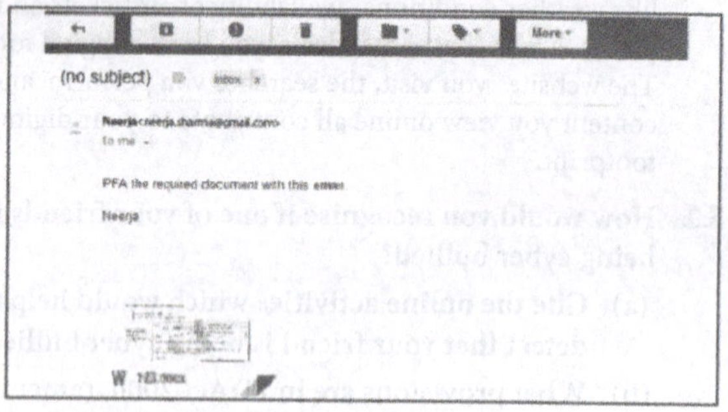

Find out which of the following email etiquettes are missing in it. Justify your answer.

(a) Subject of the mail (b) Formal greeting
(c) Self-explanatory terms (d) Identity of the sender
(e) Regards

Ans. The given email lacks proper etiquette in several aspects:

(a) A clear and concise subject line is missing, which is essential for grabbing the recipient's attention.

(b) A formal greeting like "Dear Sir/Madam" or "Hello Sir/Madam" is absent, making the email appear less professional.

(c) The email body lacks clarity and uses terms that might not be easily understood by the recipient.

(e) A respectful closing like "Sincerely," "Regards," or "Best Regards" is missing.

EXAM PATTERN QUESTIONS

Objective Type Questions

Multiple Choice Questions

1. What is a digital footprint?

(a) A physical mark left on a digital device
(b) The trail of data left behind from online activities
(c) A virus affecting digital devices
(d) A software used for tracking user activities

2. Which of the following is an example of an active digital footprint?

(a) Websites visited without logging in
(b) Emails sent to a friend
(c) Data collected by search engines without user consent
(d) Browsing history stored automatically

3. Why is it difficult to completely erase digital footprints?
(a) Because data is permanently stored in the local device
(b) Because users do not have control over server-stored data
(c) Because digital footprints do not exist in reality
(d) Because all online activities are automatically erased

4. Which of the following best describes the role of a responsible netizen?
(a) Sharing personal information to enhance social networking
(b) Practicing safe, ethical, and legal use of digital technology
(c) Encouraging cyberbullying to gain popularity online
(d) Downloading copyrighted materials for personal use without permission

5. Why is it important to "respect data limits" in digital communication?
(a) To ensure emails are read quickly without distractions
(b) To prevent unnecessary delays in receiving responses
(c) To optimize bandwidth usage and avoid sending large attachments
(d) To allow people to send unlimited content without restrictions

6. Which of the following actions violates social media etiquettes?
(a) Using strong passwords and changing them frequently
(b) Befriending unknown people without verifying their authenticity
(c) Fact-checking information before sharing it online
(d) Avoiding the upload of sensitive content to maintain privacy

7. How can one effectively deal with an Internet troll?
(a) Engage in an argument to defend personal opinions
(b) Report them but also respond with counterarguments
(c) Ignore their comments to prevent further escalation
(d) Share their inflammatory messages to warn others

8. .... is the kind of firewall that is connected between the device and the network connecting to the Internet.
(a) Hardware firewall
(b) Software firewall
(c) Stateful inspection firewall
(d) Microsoft firewall

9. Which of the following scenarios best describes a case of trademark infringement?
(a) Using someone else's copyrighted book passages in a research paper without citing the source
(b) Selling a product under a brand name that closely resembles an already registered brand
(c) Downloading and using a copyrighted image in a blog post without permission
(d) Copying a patented formula and claiming it as a new invention

10. .... of the following is NOT a method for protecting sensitive data?
(a) Encryption (b) Authentication
(c) Open access publication (d) Secure transmission

11. A pharmaceutical company develops a new drug formula and wants to ensure no other company can manufacture it for 20 years. What should they apply for?
(a) Copyright (b) Trademark
(c) Patent (d) Plagiarism license

12. A student copies text from an online article into their project without mentioning the source. Which of the following terms best describes this action?
(a) Copyright infringement (b) Trademark violation
(c) Plagiarism (d) Patent breach

13. They are hackers and their main motive is to gain financial profit by doing cyber crimes. Who are "they" referred to here?
(a) White hat hackers (b) Black hat hackers
(c) Hactivists (d) Gray hat hackers

14. How does ransomware typically prevent users from accessing their data?
(a) By deleting system files and corrupting the operating system.
(b) By modifying the user's login credentials and locking them out of their accounts.
(c) By encrypting files and demanding a ransom to restore access.
(d) By flooding the system with unnecessary requests, causing it to crash.

15. A user receives an email claiming to be from their bank, asking them to verify their account details by clicking on a link. The email contains the bank's official logo and formatting. This is an example of:
(a) Ransomware attack (b) Phishing attack
(c) Malware attack (d) Ethical hacking

16. In .... type of cybercrime can an attacker use stolen personal data to obtain medical treatment or drugs under a victim's name?
(a) Financial identity theft (b) Medical identity theft
(c) Criminal identity theft (d) Banking fraud

17. Which of the following is NOT a provision under the Indian Information Technology Act, 2000?
(a) Legal recognition of electronic records and digital signatures

(b) Establishment of Cyber Appellate Tribunal for resolving cyber crime disputes
(c) Authorization of unlimited data collection by private companies without user consent
(d) Guidelines for processing, storage, and transmission of sensitive information

18. Under the IT Act, 2000, which of the following cyber crimes is punishable?
(a) Using another person's password without their consent
(b) Sharing personal data online with the owner's permission
(c) Sending an email without an attachment
(d) Browsing publicly available information on the internet

19. Which of the following element make E-Waste hazardous in nature?
(a) Lead (b) Glass (c) Plastic (d) Iron

Fill in the Blanks

20. The practice of following appropriate behavior while communicating online, including being polite, precise, and respectful of time, is known as __________.

21. The illegal use of someone else's registered brand name or logo for commercial purposes is termed __________.

22. A __________ is a type of malicious program that appears legitimate but actually performs harmful activities when executed.

23. The IT Act of India was enacted in the year __________ to provide legal recognition for electronic transactions and curb cyber crimes.

24. Browsing the internet safely includes checking for __________ in a website URL to ensure a secure connection.

25. Using strong passwords, enabling two-factor authentication, and avoiding public Wi-Fi for financial transactions are essential measures for __________.

26. The form of online harassment where individuals are repeatedly targeted with harmful or offensive messages is called __________.

27. Improper disposal of electronic waste can release toxic substances like __________, which harm the environment and human health.

28. In digital spaces, ensuring inclusivity by designing assistive technologies for people with disabilities is crucial to addressing __________ issues.

State Whether True or False

29. Cybercrime includes only financial fraud and data theft.

30. Hacking and ethical hacking are the same, as both involve accessing computer systems.

31. Adware is a type of malware that displays unwanted advertisements but does not pose any security risk.

32. Proper e-waste management involves reusing, recycling, and safely disposing of old electronic devices.

33. The Information Technology (IT) Act in India does not cover cybercrimes related to identity theft.

34. Gender bias and accessibility issues in technology can create barriers for some users.

35. Assistive technologies, like screen readers and voice recognition, help individuals with disabilities use computers more efficiently.

Assertion and Reason Based Questions

Assertion (A) and Reason (R) based questions. Mark the correct choice as

(a) Both (A) and (R) are true and (R) is the correct explanation for (A).
(b) Both (A) and (R) are true and (R) is not the correct explanation for (A).
(c) (A) is true and (R) is false.
(d) (A) is false but (R) is true.

36. Assertion (A) Cybercrime is a growing concern in today's digital age.
Reason (R) The increasing use of the internet has led to a rise in cyberattacks and data breaches.

37. Assertion (A) Phishing is a type of cyberattack that uses deceptive tactics to steal personal information.
Reason (R) Phishing attacks often involve sending fraudulent emails that mimic legitimate sources.

38. Assertion (A) E-waste can have a significant negative impact on the environment.
Reason (R) E-waste contains hazardous materials that can contaminate soil and water.

39. Assertion (A) Intellectual Property Rights (IPR) are legal rights granted to inventors and creators. Reason: IPR protects original works of authorship, inventions, and distinctive brand identifiers.

40. Assertion (A) Cyberbullying is a form of bullying that takes place online.
Reason (R) Cyberbullying involves the use of electronic communication to bully a person, typically by sending messages of an intimidating or threatening nature.

Answers

1. (b) The trail of data left behind from online activities
2. (b) Emails sent to a friend
3. (b) Because users do not have control over server-stored data
4. (b) Practicing safe, ethical, and legal use of digital technology
5. (c) To optimize bandwidth usage and avoid sending large attachments
6. (b) Befriending unknown people without verifying their authenticity
7. (c) Ignore their comments to prevent further escalation
8. (a) Hardware firewall
9. (b) Selling a product under a brand name that closely resembles an already registered brand
10. (c) Open access publication
11. (c) Patent
12. (c) Plagiarism
13. (b) Black hat hackers
14. (c) By encrypting files and demanding a ransom to restore access.
15. (b) Phishing attack
16. (b) Medical identity theft
17. (c) Authorization of unlimited data collection by private companies without user consent
18. (a) Using another person's password without their consent
19. (a) Lead
20. Communication Etiquettes
21. Trademark infringement
22. Trojan
23. 2000
24. HTTPS
25. Cyber Safety
26. Cyber Bullying
27. Lead and Mercury
28. Accessibility and Gender Issues
29. False
30. False
31. False
32. True
33. False
34. True
35. True
36. (a) Both (A) and (R) are true and (R) is the correct explanation for (A).
37. (a) Both (A) and (R) are true and (R) is the correct explanation for (A).
38. (a) Both (A) and (R) are true and (R) is the correct explanation for (A).
39. (a) Both (A) and (R) are true and (R) is the correct explanation for (A).
40. (a) Both (A) and (R) are true and (R) is the correct explanation for (A).

Subjective Type Questions

Very Short Answer Type Questions

1. Rohan joins an online discussion group. How should he behave to ensure respectful communication?

Ans. Follow netiquette – respect others' views and communicate politely.

2. Write any two risk of using weak passwords.

Ans. (i) Accessing the bank account

(ii) Sending e-mails in your name

3. Rahul notices a rise in online fraud cases in his city. What could be the possible reasons?

Ans. (i) Widespread use of computers

(ii) Increased broadband access

(iii) Financial gains from cybercrimes

4. Write any one point to prevent the hacking.

Ans. Create a complex password to prevent the hacking.

5. Which measure is used to avoid online scam?

Ans. Do not click on any link in a mail that tells you to change any of your password or security code.

6. Meera receives threatening messages on social media from an unknown person. What is this an example of?

Ans. Cyberbullying – using technology to harass or threaten someone.

7. What are social networking sites?

Ans. A social networking service is an online service, platform or site that focuses on facilitating the building of social networks or social relations among people. The most popular sites are currently Facebook, Twitter etc.

8. What do you mean by cyber safety?

Ans. Cyber safety refers to practices and measures taken to protect users from online threats like hocking, phishing, cyberbullying and malware.

9. What is the use of IP address to identify the device?

Ans. IP address is a unique address of your device when you connect to internet from your IP address, a website can determine your rough geographical location.

10. Name the solution to protect the identity when website track you online.

Ans. (i) Incognito browsing (ii) Proxy
(iii) Virtual Private Network (VPN)

11. Define a program which control traffic flow between two networks.

Ans. A firewall is a computer program that controls traffic flow between two networks.

12. What is the purpose of digital certificate?

Ans. The purpose of a digital certificate is to guarantee that the individual sending the message really is who he or she claims to be.

13. Which type of malware appears harmless?

Ans. A trojan horse is a malware program that appears harmless (like text editor) but actually performs malicious functions.

14. Which term is used to refer to viruses, worms, trojan horse, spyware etc?

Ans. Malware is a general terms used to refer to viruses, worms, trojan horse, spyware etc.

15. What do you mean by computer viruses?

Ans. Computer viruses are malicious code that cause damage of data and files on a system.

16. What is the method to get rid of viruses?

Ans. Antivirus is the method to get rid of viruses.

17. Write three harmful effects which is delivered by trojan horse.

Ans. (i) Opening up a security hole
(ii) Spreading itself via e-mail
(iii) Deleting and damaging files

18. Explain program which eats up entire memory.

Ans. A worm is a self-replicating program, which eats up the entire disk space or memory.

Short Answer Type I Questions

19. Give any two criteria for distribution of OSS.

Ans. (i) The program must include source code and allows distribution with source code as well as a compiled form.
(ii) The license shall not restrict any party from selling or giving away the software distribution containing programs from several different sources.

20. Define password and also give the name of its two modes.

Ans. A password is an unspaced sequence of characters used to determine that a computer user requesting access to a computer system is really that particular user.

There are two common modes of password as follows
(i) Weak password (ii) Strong password

21. What are the major factors behind plagiarism?

Ans. Following are the major factors about the reasons behind plagiarism :
(i) Being lazy
(ii) Lack of enforcement
(iii) Fear of failure
(iv) Not having enough knowledge
(v) Lack of management skills

22. Rahul received an email claiming he won a lottery, but to claim the prize, he was asked to provide his bank details. Later, he found unauthorized transactions in his account. What kind of cyber crime has Rahul experienced, and how can he prevent it? Competency Based Que.

Ans. Rahul has experienced phishing, a type of cyber crime where fraudsters trick users into revealing sensitive information. To prevent it, he should avoid clicking on suspicious links and never share personal details online.

23. Neha started receiving threatening messages on social media from an unknown person. The messages made her feel unsafe, and the person kept creating new accounts to contact her even after she blocked them. What is this type of online harassment called, and what should Neha do? Competency Based Que.

Ans. This is cyber stalking, where someone repeatedly harasses or threatens a person online. Neha should report the stalker to the platform, block them, and inform the authorities if the threats continue.

24. Posing as someone else online and using his/her personal/financial information for shopping online or posting something is a common type of cyber crime these days. Competency Based Que.

(i) What are such types of cyber crimes collectively called?

(ii) What measures can you take to stop these?

Ans. (i) Online fraud
(ii) The measures to stop these frauds may include:
- A monitoring official body that ensures that sanctity of E-commerce company and delivery of goods/services as promised.
- Strong security mechanism by the E-commerce site and payment gateways to prevent stealing of crucial information.

25. Explain confidentiality of information.

Ans. Refer to text on page 290. (Confidentiality of Information).

26. Privacy is the protection of personal information given online. In E-commerce, it is related to a company's policies on the use of user data.
(i) Why is the above given statement important?
(ii) What is the need to safeguard the user privacy?

Ans. (i) It is important for the safeguard of user privacy online.
(ii) Online world is an open world and thus the personal information of a user must not be available openly, as it may be misused. Thus, it is very important and highly needed to safeguard user privacy.

27. Write four symptoms of a malware attack.

Ans. Some primary indications of a malware attack are
(i) A program disappears from the computer even though you did not intentionally remove the program.
(ii) An antivirus program cannot be installed on the computer, or the antivirus program will not run.
(iii) You see unusual error messages.
(iv) You cannot print items correctly.

28. How can a virus is harmful for the computer system?

Ans. Virus causes damage to the data and files of a computer system. It can affect or attack any part of the computer software such as boot block, operating system, system areas, files and various application programs.

29. Give three guidelines to prevent the virus attack.

Ans. Three guidelines to prevent the virus attack are as follows:
(i) Avoid to open unexpected e-mail attachments and downloads from unreliable sources. Resist the urge to double click everything in your mailbox.
(ii) In stable reliable antivirus, scanning software and download its updates regularly.
(iii) Scan files downloaded from the Internet or other external sources.

30. If your computer attacked by a trojan horse, what damage it may cause?

Ans. If computer attacked by a trojan horse, it can
(i) Steal passwords (ii) Copy sensitive data
(iii) Carry out any other harmful operations etc.

31. Explain the digital form of signature.

Ans. Digital signature is an electronic form of a signature that can be attached to an electronically transmitted message and used to authenticate the identity of a sender.

Short Answer Type II Questions

32. "You should use the internet ethically". Justify this in detail

Ans. Justification for Using the Internet Ethically:
1. **Protects Privacy** Ethical internet use ensures personal and sensitive information is not misused or leaked.
2. **Prevents Cybercrimes** Responsible behavior helps in reducing cyberbullying, hacking, and fraud.
3. **Maintains Credibility** Sharing accurate information builds trust and prevents misinformation.
4. **Respects Intellectual Property** Using copyrighted content with permission or proper citation prevents plagiarism.
5. **Ensures Safe Online Environment** Ethical behavior promotes a respectful and inclusive digital space.
6. **Avoids Legal Consequences** Ethical internet use prevents legal actions related to cybercrimes and copyright violations.
7. **Encourages Positive Digital Footprint** Responsible actions online shape a good reputation for future opportunities.

33. Aditi is a college student who frequently uses social media and online platforms for academic discussions. One day, she receives a message from an unknown person asking for her personal details, including her address and phone number, claiming to be from a scholarship program. She is unsure whether to share this information. Based on cyber ethics guidelines, what should Aditi do in this situation? Explain which ethical principles apply here and why. **Competency Based Que.**

Ans. Aditi should not share her personal details with an unknown person because it could be a scam or phishing attempt. The following cyber ethics principles apply to this situation:
1. **Confidentiality** Aditi should keep her personal and sensitive information private and not share it with strangers online. Sharing such details could lead to identity theft or misuse.
2. **Honesty & Credibility** Legitimate scholarship programs usually communicate through official channels. Aditi should verify the sender's credibility before taking any action.
3. **Respect for Privacy** She should be cautious about her own privacy and that of others. Just as she wouldn't want someone else to misuse her information, she should be aware of online threats.
4. **Professionalism** Aditi should report such messages to the concerned authority (like her college administration or cybersecurity cell) and block the sender instead of engaging with them.
5. **Communication Etiquette** If she chooses to reply, she should be polite but firm in declining to share personal details without proper verification.

34. Rohan recently created a new bank account and was asked to set a secure password for online banking. He wants to ensure his password is strong enough to prevent hacking attempts. What guidelines should Rohan follow while creating his password? **Competency Based Que.**

Ans. Rohan should follow these password security guidelines:

1. **Use a mix of characters** Combine uppercase and lowercase letters, numbers, and symbols.
2. **Avoid common words and patterns** Do not use easily guessed passwords like "password123" or "abcd5678".
3. **Keep it unique** Use a different password for each account and avoid reusing old passwords.
4. **Do not include personal information** Avoid using birthdays, phone numbers, or names in passwords.
5. **Make it long and complex** A strong password should be at least 12-16 characters long.

By following these guidelines, Rohan can protect his banking details from unauthorized access.

35. List some advantages and disadvantages of social networking sites.

Ans. Advantages of social networking sites

(i) **Connectivity** The main advantage of the social media is connectivity. People from anywhere can connect with anyone.

(ii) **Updates** The main advantage of the social media is that you update yourself from the latest happenings around the world.

(iii) **Awareness** Social media also create awareness and innovate the way people live. It is the social media which has helped people discover new and innovative stuffs that can enhance personal lives.

Disadvantages of social networking site

(i) **Hacking** Personal data and privacy can easily be hacked and shared on the Internet, which can make financial losses and loss to personal life.

(ii) **Cyber bullying** This is the use of technology like the Internet, e-mail, cell phones, social media or picture to harass, threaten or target a person.

(iii) **Glamorizes Drugs and Alcohol** One of the disadvantages of the social media is that people start to follow others who are drug and share their views and videos on the web.

36. List the guidelines to avoid plagiarism.

Ans. To avoid plagiarism, follow these guidelines:

1. **Use Your Own Words** Write in your own language and style.
2. **Cite Sources Properly** Give credit to the original author using proper citations.
3. **Paraphrase Correctly** Rephrase ideas in your own words while retaining the original meaning.
4. **Use Quotation Marks** Enclose direct quotes within quotation marks and cite the source.
5. **Include a Reference List** List all sources used in a bibliography or reference section.
6. **Avoid Copy-Pasting** Do not copy content from the internet or books without attribution.
7. **Use Plagiarism Checkers** Verify your work using online plagiarism detection tools.
8. **Understand Fair Use** Follow guidelines for using copyrighted material legally.

37. What are the penalties for cyber crime?

Ans. There are a wide range of potential penalties. Some computer crimes have minor penalties associated with them, while more serious crimes can impose significant fines and lengthy prison sentences.

(i) Fines Fines for a conviction of various computer and Internet crimes range widely. A misdemeanor conviction can result in relatively minor fines.

(ii) Jail or Prison A person convicted of certain Internet or computer crimes may also face a jail or prison sentence. The most serious crimes, such as possessing child pornography, can result in a prison sentence of 20 years or more.

(iii) Probation Probation sentences for computer crimes are also possible as either individual penalties or in addition to jail or fines. Probation terms can differ widely, but typically last atleast one year and require the person on probation to not commit more crimes, maintain employment, report to a probation officer and pay all court costs and fines.

Long Answer Type Questions

38. Explain the rules for good netiquette.

Ans. Below are the rules to follow for good netiquette :

(i) Avoid posting offensive comments online.

(ii) Never spam others by sending large amounts of unsolicited E-mail.

(iii) Don't troll people in web forums or website comments by repeatedly annoying them.

(iv) Don't use offensive language.

(v) Do not trust other when you are new.

(vi) Avoid replying to negative comments with more negative comments.

(vii) Stick the topic when posting in online forums or when commenting on photos or videos such as YouTube or Facebook comments.

39. Raj is an entrepreneur who recently launched his online store. He noticed an increase in online frauds, hacking attempts, and phishing scams. He wants to understand why cybercrimes are rising and how he can protect his business. What factors contribute to the rise of cybercrimes, and what steps can Raj take to enhance cybersecurity?

Ans. The rise in cybercrimes is influenced by several factors:

1. **Increasing Internet Penetration** More people and businesses are using the internet, making them potential targets for cybercriminals.

2. **Technological Advancements** Rapid developments in technology introduce new vulnerabilities that hackers can exploit.
3. **Lack of Cybersecurity Awareness** Many individuals and businesses do not have sufficient knowledge to protect themselves from threats.

To enhance cybersecurity, Raj should:

- Regularly update software and security patches.
- Educate employees about phishing and online fraud.
- Implement strong authentication measures, such as multi-factor authentication (MFA).
- Use secure payment gateways and encrypted transactions.

40. Write the various ways from which to avoid being stalked on social media.

Ans. There are various ways from being stalked on social media

- **Hide your contracts** You should hide your contacts because a stalker may try to reach out to a friend of yours in order to get close to you.
- **Use security features** Keep your computer free from threats or breaches in security by installing safety software and a firewall.
- **Disable geotagging** It can be dangerous because a stalker can known where you are. So geotagging should be disable.
- **Make your profile private** Always make your profile private, to protect yourself from a stalker, set your setting to only share information.
- **Delete an old account** You should delete your old account that are inactive.

41. How to protect the identity while using internet?

Ans. To protect your identity online, consider the following tips:

- **Strong, Unique Passwords** Create strong, unique passwords for each of your online accounts. Avoid using easily guessable information like birthdays or pet names.
- **Beware of Phishing Attacks** Be cautious of suspicious emails, messages, or phone calls that ask for personal information.
- **Secure Wi-Fi Networks** Use strong passwords for your home Wi-Fi network and avoid using public Wi-Fi for sensitive activities.
- **Privacy Settings** Review and adjust the privacy settings on your social media accounts to limit the amount of personal information you share.
- **Be Mindful of What You Share Online** Think twice before sharing personal information, such as your home address or phone number, on public platforms.
- **Use Two-Factor Authentication** Enable two-factor authentication whenever possible to add an extra layer of security to your accounts.
- **Keep Software Updated** Regularly update your operating system and software to protect against vulnerabilities.
- **Use Antivirus Software** Install and keep your antivirus software up-to-date to protect your device from malware.
- **Be Wary of Public Wi-Fi** Avoid accessing sensitive information on public Wi-Fi networks, as they are often less secure.

42. Explain the online identity verification methods.

Ans. Online identity verification methods are crucial for ensuring the security and trust in digital interactions. Here are some common methods:

- **Knowledge-Based Authentication (KBA)** Uses personal questions or past addresses but can be vulnerable to social engineering.
- **Document Verification** Verifies government-issued IDs like passports or driver's licenses against official databases.
- **Biometric Verification** Uses fingerprints, facial recognition, or voice authentication; highly secure but requires special hardware.
- **Device-Based Verification** Analyzes device details like IP address and browser fingerprint; less reliable for shared devices.
- **Two-Factor Authentication (2FA)** Requires two identification forms (e.g., password + OTP), enhancing security.
- **Continuous Authentication** Monitors user behavior (typing patterns, location) to detect anomalies.

43. What are the specific usage rules that can help you to protect yourself on social networking sites?

Ans. There are various tips, with the help of these you can protect yourself on social networking sites as:

- **Limit Personal Information** Avoid sharing sensitive details that hackers can use to access your accounts.
- **Be Cautious with Links** Even if sent by a friend, verify links before clicking as their account may be compromised.
- **Choose Friends Wisely** Identity thieves may create fake profiles to steal your information.
- **Directly Access Websites** Always type the website URL instead of clicking links from emails to avoid phishing scams.
- **Think Before You Post** Anything shared online is permanent, so be mindful of your content.
- **Customize Privacy Settings** Control who can view your personal information.
- **Use Unique Passwords** Avoid using the same password for multiple accounts to reduce security risks.
- **Be Wary of Third-Party Apps** Cybercriminals may use them to steal your data.

Case Study Based Questions

Case Study 1

The word 'plagiarism' comes from the Latin word 'plagiarius,' which means kidnapping. Plagiarism refers to the act of copying another person's ideas, words, or work and pretending they are our own. It can be intentional or accidental, such as copying data from someone else's computer without permission and redistributing it. Some common reasons behind plagiarism include:

- **Fear of failure**
- **Lack of knowledge**
- **Laziness**
- **Lack of enforcement**
- **Competition**
- **Poor management skills**

Based on the above information, answer the following multiple-choice questions:

(i) What is the meaning of the Latin word 'plagiarius'?

(a) Copying (b) Writing
(c) Kidnapping (d) Stealing

(ii) Which of the following is a guideline to avoid plagiarism?

(a) Copy from multiple sources
(b) Provide proper citations and references
(c) Use others' work without permission
(d) Remove the author's name before copying

(iii) Which of the following is NOT a reason behind plagiarism?

(a) Fear of failure (b) Lack of knowledge
(c) Hard work and honesty (d) Competition

(iv) What is the term used when someone copies another person's work without giving credit?

(a) Citation (b) Paraphrasing
(c) Plagiarism (d) Referencing

(v) Can the intention behind plagiarism be malicious?

(a) Yes
(b) No
(c) Only in academic writing
(d) Only if it's accidental

Ans. (i) (c) Kidnapping
(ii) (b) Provide proper citations and references
(iii) (c) Hard work and honesty
(iv) (c) Plagiarism
(v) (a) Yes

Case Study 2

If someone comes up with a new idea, that idea becomes their intellectual property. Intellectual Property (IP) is a legal concept that grants exclusive rights to creations of the mind. These include musical, literary, and artistic works, discoveries and inventions, as well as words, phrases, symbols, and designs. Intellectual Property Rights (IPR) provide legal protection to owners over their creative works. Common types of IPR include copyright, trademarks, patents, industrial design rights, trade dress, and in some jurisdictions, trade secrets.

Based on the above information, answer the following multiple-choice questions:

(i) What is the full form of IPR?

(a) International Property Rights
(b) Intellectual Property Rights
(c) Internal Product Regulation
(d) Intellectual Patent Registration

(ii) Artistic works such as novels, poems, and paintings are protected under which type of Intellectual Property Rights?

(a) Patent (b) Trademark
(c) Copyright (d) Trade secrets

(iii) How can Intellectual Property Rights (IPR) be controlled?

(a) By ignoring copyrights and trademarks
(b) By granting exclusive rights through legal protections
(c) By allowing free use of all creations
(d) By keeping ideas secret and unpublished

(iv) For how many years does a patent protect an invention?

(a) 5 years (b) 10 years
(c) 20 years (d) Lifetime

(v) Which Intellectual Property Right protects a word, name, or design used for branding a product or company?

(a) Copyright (b) Trademark
(c) Patent (d) Industrial design rights

Ans. (i) (b) Intellectual Property Rights
(ii) (c) Copyright
(iii) (b) By granting exclusive rights through legal protections
(iv) (c) 20 years
(v) (b) Trademark

SELF ASSESSMENT TEST

Multiple Choice Questions

1. **Charlene is an artist. She displays her artwork on the Internet using her website to attract buyers. One day while browsing the Internet she discovers that another artist has displayed her painting portraying it as his own. Which rights of Charlene was infringed?**
   (a) Digital Privacy Rights
   (b) Intellectual Property Rights
   (c) Digital Property Rights
   (d) Intellectual Privacy Rights
2. **Shreya told her friend Princy about a term that, "It is the study of ethics pertaining to computers, encompassing user behaviour and what computers are programmed to and how this affects individuals and society". What is it?**
   (a) Cyber ethics (b) Plagiarism
   (c) Netiquette (d) Hacking
3. **Which of the following refers to attempt to gain information from undisclosed areas?**
   (a) Hacking (b) Knowledge
   (c) Etiquette (d) Plagiarism

Fill in the Blanks

4. **______ is an exclusive legal right granted to an inventor for a certain period, preventing others from making, using, or selling the invention without permission.**
5. **The unauthorized use or reproduction of another's work without proper credit is known as ______.**
6. **A ______ license allows creators to share their work with the public while still retaining some rights.**

State Whether True or False

7. **Eavesdropping in cybersecurity refers to secretly listening to private conversations over a network.**
8. **Phishing attacks often use fake emails or messages to trick users into revealing sensitive information.**
9. **Ransomware is a type of malware that deletes data from a system permanently.**
10. **Cyberbullying refers only to direct messages and does not include public posts or comments.**
11. **Using a VPN (Virtual Private Network) can help improve online safety by encrypting internet traffic.**

Assertion and Reason Based Questions

Assertion (A) and Reason (R) Type questions. Choose the correct option as:

(a) Both Assertion (A) and Reason (R) are true, and Reason (R) is the correct explanation of Assertion (A).
(b) Both Assertion (A) and Reason (R) are true, but Reason (R) is not the correct explanation of Assertion (A).
(c) Assertion (A) is true, but Reason (R) is false.
(d) Assertion (A) is false, but Reason (R) is true.

12. **Assertion (A)** Malware can damage hardware components of a computer.
    Reason (R) Viruses and Trojans can manipulate the software but cannot directly harm physical components.
13. **Assertion (A)** Proper disposal of e-waste is essential to reduce environmental damage.
    Reason (R) E-waste contains toxic substances like lead and mercury that can contaminate soil and water.

Very Short Answer Type Questions

14. **What do you mean by worms?**
15. **What different types of threats are available to computer security?**
16. **What is the role of proxy to protect the identity, when website track you online?**
17. **How can we detect the malware?**
18. **Name the most common cyber crime.**
19. **What are the controls of intellectual property rights?**
20. **Write the forms of software piracy.**

Short Answer Type Questions

21. **Write the guidelines to set the password.**
22. **What do you mean by eavesdropping?**
23. **What is the use of identity verification?**
24. **Which types of laws are used to stop software piracy?**
25. **What do you mean by creative common license?**
26. **Explain the popular social networking sites.**
27. **How to safely browsing the web?**
28. **What measures are used to safeguard user privacy?**

Long Answer Type Questions

29. What do you mean by firewall ? Explain its types.

30. What are the specific usage rules to protect yourself on social networking sites?

31. What is the use of identity protection while using Internet?

32. Explain online fraud. How to ensure safe sites while entering crucial information?

33. Define the following terms.
(i) Trojan horse (ii) Spyware
(iii) Virus attack (iv) Worm

34. Explain the network security protocols.

Case Study Based Question

35. Phishing is a type of cyber attack in which attackers fraudulently acquire sensitive information like passwords and credit card details by pretending to be a trustworthy person or organization. Victims usually receive malicious emails or text messages that appear to be from a bank, government office, or other trusted entity.

These messages often create a sense of urgency or fear, tricking victims into clicking a fraudulent link that leads to a fake website. Once victims enter their login credentials, the attackers steal the information to commit identity theft, empty bank accounts, or sell personal data on the black market.

Based on the above information, answer the following multiple-choice questions:

(i) What is phishing?
(a) A type of online fraud to steal personal information
(b) A method of cooking
(c) A type of computer hardware
(d) A way to protect sensitive data

(ii) Is phishing done only through email?
(a) Yes, only through email
(b) No, it can also be done through text messages and phone calls
(c) No, it is only done through social media
(d) No, it is only done through websites

(iii) How can you report a phishing or suspicious email?
(a) Ignore it and delete it
(b) Click the link to check if it is real
(c) Report it to the organization being impersonated or to cybersecurity authorities
(d) Forward it to your friends

(iv) If you fall for a phishing scam, what should you do to limit the damage?
(a) Change your passwords immediately
(b) Report the scam to your bank or relevant authorities
(c) Monitor your bank account for suspicious activity
(d) All of the above

(v) Email authentication can help protect against phishing attacks. True or False?
(a) True (b) False

Answers

1. (d) 2. (a) 3. (a) 4. Patent
5. Plagiarism 6. Creative commons
7. True 8. True 9. False 10. False 11. True
12. (d) 13. (a)
35. (i) → (a), (ii) → (b), (iii) → (c), (iv) → (d), (v) → (a)

Practical List of Python Programming

AIM 1. Input a welcome message and display it.

Procedure

```
message = input("Enter a welcome message: ")
print("Your message:", message)
```

```
Output                                   Clear
Enter a welcome message: hello
Your message: hello

=== Code Execution Successful ===
```

AIM 2. Input two numbers and display the larger / smaller number.

Procedure

```
num1 = int(input("Enter first number: "))
num2 = int(input("Enter second number: "))
larger = max(num1, num2)
smaller = min(num1, num2)
print("Larger number:", larger)
print("Smaller number:", smaller)
```

```
Output                                   Clear
Enter first number: 45
Enter second number: 89
Larger number: 89
Smaller number: 45

=== Code Execution Successful ===
```

AIM 3. Input three numbers and display the largest / smallest number.

Procedure

```
num1 = int(input("Enter first number: "))
num2 = int(input("Enter second number: "))
num3 = int(input("Enter third number: "))
largest = max(num1, num2, num3)
smallest = min(num1, num2, num3)
print("Largest number:", largest)
print("Smallest number:", smallest)
```

```
Output                                   Clear
Enter first number: 68
Enter second number: 54
Enter third number: 29
Largest number: 68
Smallest number: 29

=== Code Execution Successful ===
```

AIM 4. Generate the following patterns using nested loops:

Pattern-1	Pattern-2	Pattern-3
*	12345	A
**	1234	AB
***	123	ABC
****	12	ABCD
*****	1	ABCDE

Procedure **Pattern-1**

```
rows = int(input("Enter the number of rows: "))
for i in range(1, rows + 1):
    for j in range(i):
        print("*", end="")
    print()
```

```
Output                                    Clear
Enter the number of rows: 4
*
**
***
****

=== Code Execution Successful ===
```

Pattern-2

```
rows = int(input("Enter the number of rows: "))
for i in range(rows, 0, -1):
    for j in range(1, i + 1):
        print(j, end="")
    print()
```

```
Output                                    Clear
Enter the number of rows: 5
12345
1234
123
12
1

=== Code Execution Successful ===
```

Pattern-3

```
rows = int(input("Enter the number of rows: "))
for i in range(1, rows + 1):
    for j in range(i):
        print(chr(65 + j), end="")
    print()
```

```
Output                                    Clear
Enter the number of rows: 5
A
AB
ABC
ABCD
ABCDE

=== Code Execution Successful ===
```

AIM 5. **Write a program to input the value of x and n and print the sum of the following series:**

- $1 + x + x^2 + x^3 + x^4 + \ldots x^n$
- $1 - x + x^2 - x^3 + x^4 - \ldots x^n$
- $x + \frac{x^2}{2} + \frac{x^3}{3} + \frac{x^4}{4} + \ldots \frac{x^n}{n}$
- $x + \frac{x^2}{2!} + \frac{x^3}{3!} + \frac{x^4}{4!} + \ldots \frac{x^n}{n!}$

Procedure

```
import math
x = float(input("Enter the value of x: "))
n = int(input("Enter the value of n: "))
# Series 1: 1 + x + x^2 + x^3 + ... + x^n
sum1 = sum(x**i for i in range(n + 1))
print("Sum of Series 1:", sum1)
# Series 2: 1 - x + x^2 - x^3 + x^4 - ... + x^n
sum2 = sum((-1)**i * x**i for i in range(n + 1))
print("Sum of Series 2:", sum2)
# Series 3: x + x^2/2 + x^3/3 + x^4/4 + ... + x^n/n
sum3 = sum((x**i) / i for i in range(1, n + 1))
print("Sum of Series 3:", sum3)
# Series 4: x + x^2/2! + x^3/3! + x^4/4! + ... + x^n/n!
sum4 = sum((x**i) / math.factorial(i) for i in range(1, n + 1))
print("Sum of Series 4:", sum4)
```

Output Clear

```
Enter the value of x: 4
Enter the value of n: 3
Sum of Series 1: 85.0
Sum of Series 2: -51.0
Sum of Series 3: 33.33333333333333
Sum of Series 4: 22.666666666666664

=== Code Execution Successful ===
```

AIM 6. **Determine whether a number is a perfect number, an Armstrong number or a palindrome.**

Procedure

```
num = int(input("Enter a number: "))
# Checking Perfect Number
sum_of_factors = 0
for i in range(1, num):
    if num % i == 0:
        sum_of_factors += i
if sum_of_factors == num:
    print(num, "is a Perfect Number.")
else:
    print(num, "is NOT a Perfect Number.")
# Checking Armstrong Number
temp = num
```

```
digits = [int(d) for d in str(temp)]
power = len(digits)
armstrong_sum = 0
for d in digits:
    armstrong_sum += d ** power
if armstrong_sum == num:
    print(num, "is an Armstrong Number.")
else:
    print(num, "is NOT an Armstrong Number.")
# Checking Palindrome
num_str = str(num)
reversed_num = num_str[ : : -1]
if num_str == reversed_num:
    print(num, "is a Palindrome.")
else:
    print(num, "is NOT a Palindrome.")
```

```
Output                                   Clear
Enter a number: 153
153 is NOT a Perfect Number.
153 is an Armstrong Number.
153 is NOT a Palindrome.
Enter a number: 99
99 is NOT a Perfect Number.
99 is NOT an Armstrong Number.
99 is a Palindrome.
Enter a number: 28
28 is a Perfect Number.
28 is NOT an Armstrong Number.
28 is NOT a Palindrome.
```

AIM 7. Input a number and check if the number is a prime or composite number.

Procedure

```
num = int(input("Enter a number: "))
if num <= 1:
    print(num, "is neither Prime nor Composite.")
else:
    count = 0
    for i in range(2, num):
        if num % i == 0:
            count += 1
            break
    if count == 0:
        print(num, "is a Prime Number.")
    else:
        print(num, "is a Composite Number.")
```

```
Output                                   Clear
Enter a number: 7
7 is a Prime Number.
Enter a number: 16
16 is a Composite Number.
```

AIM 8. Display the terms of a Fibonacci series.

Procedure
```
num = int(input("Enter the number of terms: "))
a, b = 0, 1
for _ in range(num):
    print(a, end=" ")
    a, b = b, a + b
print()
```

```
Output                                        Clear
Enter the number of terms: 5
0 1 1 2 3

=== Code Execution Successful ===
```

AIM 9. Compute the greatest common divisor and least common multiple of two integers.

Procedure
```
import math
a = int(input("Enter first number: "))
b = int(input("Enter second number: "))
# Compute GCD using math.gcd()
gcd = math.gcd(a, b)
# Compute LCM using the formula: LCM(a, b) = (a * b) / GCD(a, b)
lcm = (a * b) // gcd
print("GCD of", a, "and", b, "is:", gcd)
print("LCM of", a, "and", b, "is:", lcm)
```

```
Output                                        Clear
Enter first number: 4
Enter second number: 8
GCD of 4 and 8 is: 4
LCM of 4 and 8 is: 8

=== Code Execution Successful ===
```

AIM 10. Count and display the number of vowels, consonants, uppercase, lowercase characters in string.

Procedure
```
text = input("Enter a string: ")
vowels = consonants = uppercase = lowercase = 0
vowel_chars = "AEIOUaeiou"
for char in text:
    if char.isalpha():
        if char in vowel_chars:
            vowels += 1
        else:
            consonants += 1
        if char.isupper():
            uppercase += 1
        elif char.islower():
            lowercase += 1
# Display results
print("Vowels:", vowels)
print("Consonants:", consonants)
```

```
print("Uppercase letters:", uppercase)
print("Lowercase letters:", lowercase)
```

```
Output                                                Clear
Enter a string: Arihant
Vowels: 3
Consonants: 4
Uppercase letters: 1
Lowercase letters: 6

=== Code Execution Successful ===
```

AIM 11. Input a string and determine whether it is a palindrome or not; convert the case of characters in a string.

Procedure

```
text = input("Enter a string: ")
if text == text[::-1]:
    print("The string is a Palindrome.")
else:
    print("The string is NOT a Palindrome.")
converted_text = text.swapcase()
print("Converted case string:", converted_text)
```

```
Output                                                Clear
Enter a string: Arihant
The string is NOT a Palindrome.
Converted case string: aRIHANT
Enter a string: madam
The string is a Palindrome.
Converted case string: MADAM
```

AIM 12. Find the largest/smallest number in a list/tuple

Procedure

```
numbers = [12, 45, 78, 23, 56, 81, 4]
largest = max(numbers)
smallest = min(numbers)
print("Largest number:", largest)
print("Smallest number:", smallest)
```

```
Output                                                Clear
Largest number: 81
Smallest number: 4

=== Code Execution Successful ===
```

AIM 13. Input a list of numbers and swap elements at the even location with the elements at the odd location.

Procedure

```
numbers = list(map(int, input("Enter numbers separated by space: ").split()))
for i in range(0, len(numbers) - 1, 2):
    numbers[i], numbers[i + 1] = numbers[i + 1], numbers[i]
print("List after swapping:", numbers)
```

```
Output                                                Clear
Enter numbers separated by space: 2 4 6 8 10
List after swapping: [4, 2, 8, 6, 10]

=== Code Execution Successful ===
```

AIM 14. **Input a list/tuple of elements, search for a given element in the list/tuple.**

Procedure

```
elements = input("Enter elements separated by space: ").split()
search_element = input("Enter the element to search: ")
if search_element in elements:
    print(search_element, "is present in the list at index",
elements.index(search_element))
else:
    print(search_element, "is not present in the list.")
```

```
Output                                              Clear
Enter elements separated by space: 2 4 5 6 10
Enter the element to search: 5
5 is present in the list at index 2

=== Code Execution Successful ===
```

AIM 15. **Create a dictionary with the roll number, name and marks of n students in a class and display the names of students who have marks above 75.**

Procedure

```
n = int(input("Enter the number of students: "))
students = {}
for _ in range(n):
    roll_no = input("Enter Roll Number: ")
    name = input("Enter Name: ")
    marks = int(input("Enter Marks: "))
    students[roll_no] = {"name": name, "marks": marks}
# Display students with marks above 75
print("\nStudents with marks above 75:")
for student in students.values():
    if student["marks"] > 75:
        print(student["name"])
```

```
Output                                              Clear
Enter the number of students: 2
Enter Roll Number: 01
Enter Name: Shruti
Enter Marks: 99
Enter Roll Number: 02
Enter Name: Priyanka
Enter Marks: 75

Students with marks above 75:
Shruti

=== Code Execution Successful ===
```

SAMPLE QUESTION PAPER 1

A Highly Simulated Sample Question Paper for CBSE Class XI Examination

COMPUTER SCIENCE

Time : 3 Hours **Max. Marks : 70**

General Instructions

1. This question paper contains 37 questions.
2. All questions are compulsory. However, internal choices have been provided in some questions. Attempt only one of the choices in such questions.
3. The paper is divided into 5 Sections- A, B, C, D and E.
4. Section A consists of 21 questions (1 to 21). Each question carries 1 Mark.
5. Section B consists of 7 questions (22 to 28). Each question carries 2 Marks.
6. Section C consists of 3 questions (29 to 31). Each question carries 3 Marks.
7. Section D consists of 4 questions (32 to 35). Each question carries 4 Marks.
8. Section E consists of 2 questions (36 to 37). Each question carries 5 Marks.
9. All programming questions are to be answered using Python Language only.
10. In case of MCQ, text of the correct answer should also be written.

SECTION A

21 × 1 = 21

1. State True or False.
Runtime errors in Python are also known as compile time errors.

2. Identify the output of the following code snippet

```
x = 10
y = 5
print(x > 5 and y < 10)
# Output: ?
```

(a) True (b) False
(c) 10 (d) 5

3. Python interpreters are available for operating system(s)

(a) Windows (b) MacOS
(c) Both (a) and (b) (d) None of these

4. What will be the output of the following Python code snippet?

```
python
CopyEdit
d1={"Neha":86, "Yash":92}
d2={"Neha":86, "Yash":88}
d1 > d2
```

(a) True (b) False (c) Error (d) None

5. What will be printed by the following code?

```
d = {"name": "Alice", "age": 25}
print([d"name"])
```

6. What will be the output of the following Python code?

```
Dicl={}
Dicl[2]=85
Dicl[1]=[22,23,24]
print(Dicl[1][1])
```

(a) [22,23,24] (b) 23 (c) 22 (d) Error

7. Which of the following errors will result in the abnormal termination of the program?

(a) Run time (b) Compile time
(c) Semantic (d) Syntax

8. What is cyber security?

(a) Provides security against malware
(b) Provides security against cyber-terrorists
(c) Protects a system from cyber attacks
(d) All of the above

9. Two inputs A and B of NAND gate have 0 as output, if

(a) A is 0 (b) B is 0
(c) Both are zero (d) Both are 1

10. Write the missing statement to complete the following code:

```
numbers = [3, 1, 4, 1, 5, 9, 2, 6, 5, 3]
max_num = ________ # Fill in the blank to find the maximum number
print("The maximum number is:", max_num)
```

11. State whether the following statement is True or False:
Slicing a string creates a new string object.

12. Find the output of the following code.

```
i = 1
while(i<5):
    print(i)
    i=i*2
```

(a) 1 (b) 1 2 4
(c) 1 2 3 4 (d) 1 2 4 3

13. What is the result of the OR operation between the binary numbers 1010 and 1100?

14. Write the output.

```
>>> x='Python'
>>> y='PYTHON'
>>> x<y
```

(a) True (b) False
(c) Error (d) None

15. Which of the following is a collection of Python objects separated by commas and represent as (,)?

(a) List (b) Tuple
(c) Dictionary (d) String

16. They are hackers and their main motive is to gain financial profit by doing cyber crimes.

Who are "they" referred to here?

(a) White hat hackers
(b) Black hat hackers
(c) Hactivists
(d) Gray hat hackers

17. In binary language, each letter of the alphabet, each number and each special character is made up of a unique combination of

(a) 8 bytes (b) 8 KB
(c) 8 characters (d) 8 bits

18. ________ are the most obvious kind of constants.

(a) Keywords (b) Literals
(c) Variables (d) Identifiers

19. Explain the concept of type conversion in Python.

Directions (Q. Nos. 20 and 21) are Assertion (A) and Reason (R) based questions. Mark the correct choice as

(a) Both A and R are True and R is the correct explanation for A.
(b) Both A and R are True and R is not the correct explanation for A.
(c) A is True but R is False.
(d) A is False but R is True.

20. Assertion (A) The intellectual property of people are protected by IPR.

Reason (R) Plagiarism is the illegal publish or use of someone else's work in one's own name.

21. Assertion (A) Python codes do not require curly braces { } for making blocks.

Reason (R) Python uses indentation for grouping statements in a block.

SECTION B

7×2=14

22. What is the difference between primary memory and secondary memory in a computer system? Explain with examples.

23. Write four symptoms of a malware attack.

24. (I) Write the dual of the boolean expression. (A+0).(A.1.A')

Or Find the complement of the following boolean function. F1 = A.B'+C'.D'

(II) State the distributive laws of boolean algebra. How do they differ from the distributive laws of ordinary algebra?

Or What do you mean by boolean algebra?

25. Identify the correct output(s) of the following code def check_numbers():

```
    nums = [10, 20, 30, 40, 50]
    nums.pop(2)
    nums.append(100)
    return sum(nums)
result = check_numbers()
print(result)
```

(a) 250 (b) 230
(c) 210 (d) 200

26. What will be the output of the following Python code snippet?

```
dic1={1:'One',2:'Two',3:'Three'}
dic1={}
print(len(dic1))
```

27. (I) (A) What type of loop should be used to iterate over a fixed range of numbers where the range is predefined and the number of iterations is known beforehand?

Or (B) What type of loop should be used when you want to continue iterating until a condition is met, and you do not know the number of iterations in advance?

(II) (A) What Python operator is used to check whether a value exists in a sequence such as a list or string?

Or (B) What Python operator is used to compare the identity of two objects to see if they refer to the same object in memory?

28. **(A)** What is the role of Intellectual Property Rights (IPR) in protecting digital content?

Or

(B) Define cybercrime and explain at least two common types of cybercrime, such as hacking and phishing.

SECTION C

3×3=9

29. **(A)** What are the major factors about the reasons behind plagiarism?

Or **(B)** Explain the guidelines about cyber ethics.

30. **(A)** Define Boolean logic and explain the truth tables for the AND, OR, and NOT operations.

Or

(B) Explain the concept of ASCII and Unicode encoding schemes. How do they differ in representing characters?

31. **(A)** Predict the output of the following Python code:

```
def check_numbers():
    num_list = [1, 2, 3, 4, 5]
    for num in num_list:
        if num % 2 == 0:
            print("Even")
        else:
            print("Odd")
    return len(num_list)
result = check_numbers()
print("List Length:", result)
```

What will be the output of the code?

Or

(B) Predict the output of the following Python code:

```
x = 10
y = 20
if x < y:
    if x == 10:
        print("Condition 1")
    else:
        print("Condition 2")
else:
    print("Condition 3")
```

What will be the output of the code?

SECTION D

4×4=16

32. **(A)** Predict the output of the following Python code:

```
words = ["apple", "banana", "cherry", "date"]
new_words = [word.upper() for word in words
                                 if "a" in word]
print(new_words)
print("-".join(new_words))
print(len(new_words))
print(new_words[1][2])
```

Or

(B) Predict the output of the following Python code:

```
my_tuple = (10, 20, [30, 40], (50, 60))
my_tuple[2].append(50)
print(my_tuple)
my_dict = {"A": [1, 2, 3], "B": (4, 5, 6)}
my_dict["A"].append(4)
print(my_dict)
print(sum(my_dict["B"]))
```

33. Which list built-in methods are best suited for the following conditions?

1. Removes and returns the last element from a list.
2. Returns the index of the first occurrence of a given element in a list.
3. Sorts the elements of a list in ascending order permanently.
4. Merges elements of two lists into a single list.

34. **(A)** To display all variables and their data types from a Python program where different types of variables (integer, float, string, list, tuple, dictionary) are used.

(B) To display only those numbers from a list that are divisible by both 3 and 5.

Or

(A) To find and display the largest of three given numbers using conditional statements.

(B) To generate and display the first 10 numbers in the Fibonacci series using a loop.

35. Consider the following list and answer the below questions

```
l1=[89,45,"Taj","Qutub",93,42,"Minar","Delhi","Agra"]
```

(i) l1[5:]

(ii) "Qutab" not in l1

(iii) l1[-3]

(iv) l1[9]

SECTION E

2×5=10

36. Amit is worried about the rising incidents of cybercrimes, such as hacking, phishing, and ransomware attacks. He wants to ensure that his data and online activities are secure.

Write a brief guide for Amit, covering the following:

1. What is phishing, and how can he recognize phishing attempts?
2. What are ransomware attacks, and what steps can Amit take to avoid falling victim to ransomware?

3. Explain two basic practices Amit should follow to ensure cyber safety and protect his identity online.

37. ABC Corporation is developing a software application for managing customer feedback. The application needs to process and format customer comments, check for certain patterns in the comments, and display the formatted result.

As a Python developer, you need to implement the following features:

(I) Suggest an appropriate data type for storing customer comments and justify your choice.

(II) Which string operation would you recommend to check if a given comment starts with "Great" and why?

(III) Write a Python expression to remove any leading and trailing spaces from a given comment.

(IV) Identify and fix the issue in the following code snippet:

```
comment = "This is a great product!     "
formatted_comment = comment.strip()
print(formatted_comment)
```

(V) (A) Write a Python program using a loop to count how many times the word "excellent" appears in a customer's comment.

Or (B) What method would you use to split a customer comment into a list of words? Write a sample code to demonstrate this.

SAMPLE QUESTION PAPER 2

A Highly Simulated Sample Question Paper for CBSE Class XI Examination

COMPUTER SCIENCE

Time : 3 Hours **Max. Marks : 70**

General Instructions

See Sample Question Paper 1

SECTION A

21 × 1 = 21

1. State True or False.

Every if statement must be followed by an else or else-if statement.

2. What will be the output of the following Python code?

```
dicl = {0: 'One', 1: 'Two', 2: 'Three'}
for x, y in dicl.items():
    print(x, y)
```

(a) 012 (b) One Two Three
(c) 0 One 1 Two 2 Three (d) Error

3. Which of the following operator operates on a single variable?

(a) NOT (b) AND (c) OR (d) XOR

4. What will be the output of the following Python code snippet?

```
students = {"Aarav": 98, "Siya": 95, "Kabir": 92}
print(tuple(students.keys()))
```

(a) ["Aarav", "Siya", "Kabir"]
(b) ("Aarav", "Siya", "Kabir")
(c) {"Aarav", "Siya", "Kabir"}
(d) ("Aarav": 98, "Siya": 95, "Kabir": 92)

5. What will be the output of the following Boolean logic expression?

```
A = 1
B = 0
C = 1
Output = (A AND B) OR (A AND C)
print(Output)
```

6. What will be the output of the following Python code ?

```
t1 = (70, 56, 'Hello', 22, 2, 'Hi', 'The', 'World', 3)
print(t1[-7:-5])
```

(a) (56, 'Hello') (b) ('Hello', 22)
(c) ('Hello', 22, 2) (d) (56, 'Hello', 22)

7. This function converts all uppercase letters in a string to lowercase letters.

(a) upper() (b) lower()
(c) isupper() (d) islower()

8. Which of the following elements make E-Waste hazardous in nature?

(a) Lead (b) Glass (c) Plastic (d) Iron

9. **A hexadecimal can be represented by**
(a) three binary bits
(b) four binary bits
(c) six binary bits
(d) eight binary bits

10. **Write the missing statement to complete the following code:**

```
numbers = [10, 20, 30, 40, 50]
total = 0
for num in numbers:
______ # Add each number to total
print("Sum of numbers:", total)
```

11. **State whether the following statement is True or False: "Phishing is a cybercrime where attackers trick individuals into providing sensitive information by pretending to be a trustworthy entity, often through emails or fake websites."**

12. **What will be the output of the following code?**

```
my_tuple = (5, 10, 15, 20)
my_list = list(my_tuple)
my_list.append(25)
print(len(my_tuple), end='#')
print(len(my_list), end='%')
```

(a) 4#5% (b) 5#4%
(c) 4#4% (d) 5#5%

13. **What is the purpose of the Information Technology (IT) Act?**

14. **What will be the output of the following code?**

```
my_dict = {'apple': 12, 'banana': 15, 'cherry': 70}
my_dict.update({'banana': 80, 'grape': 14})
print(len(my_dict), end='#')
print(my_dict['banana'], end='%')
```

(a) 4#80% (b) 3#15%
(c) 4#15% (d) 3#80%

15. **In complex number, a + ib, where b represents as**
(a) real part (b) imaginary part
(c) special part (d) None of these

16. **Python is based on**
(a) ABC language (b) Modula 3
(c) Both (a) and (b) (d) None of these

17. **Which of the following is/are Python syntax error?**
(a) Leaving out a keyword (b) Misspelling a keyword
(c) Incorrect indentation (d) All of the above

18. **These statements enable a program with a cyclic flow of logic**
(a) Sequence (b) Compound
(c) Single (d) Iterative

19. **Explain system software.**

Directions (Q20 and Q21) are Assertion(A) and Reason(R) based questions. Mark the correct choice as:
(a) Both A and R are true and R is the correct explanation for A
(b) Both A and R are true and R is not the correct explanation for A
(c) A is True but R is False
(d) A is False but R is True

20. **Assertion (A) An operating system manages hardware resources and provides a user interface to interact with the computer.**
Reason (R) The operating system acts as a bridge between the user and the hardware, enabling the execution of application software.

21. **Assertion (A) A list can be a key of a dictionary.**
Reason (R) A list is a mutable data type.

SECTION B

7×2=14

22. **Observe the following tuple and answer the questions that follow.**

```
t1= (76, 56, 'Harish', 'Ansh', 98, (45, 34), 'Muskan')
```

(i) len(t1)
(ii) t1[-6]
(iii) t1[3]
(iv) t1[: 2]

23. **Construct logical expressions to represent the following conditions:**
(i) A number is greater than or equal to 50 but less than 100.
(ii) A binary number is divisible by 4 or a hexadecimal number is greater than or equal to A (decimal 10).

24. **Observe the given list and find the answer of questions that follows.**
(I) list1=[45, 77, 87, 'Next', 'Try', 33, 43]
(i) list1 [-2] (ii) list1 [2]

Or

Define packing and unpacking tuples.

(II) Observe the given list and find the answer to the questions that follow:
list1=[12, 34, 56, 'Python', 'Java', 78, 90]
(i) list1[-3] (ii) list1[1:4]

Or

Define indexing and slicing in lists.

25. **What is e-waste management? Discuss the importance of proper disposal of electronic gadgets.?**

26. Explain the functions of an operating system and describe its role in managing hardware and software resources.?

27. (I) Which feature is used to access the elements from a dictionary?

Or

Give the output.

```
dic = {'A': "One", 'B': "Two", "C": "Three"}
'E' in dic
```

(II) What is used to remove an item from a dictionary in Python?

Or

Give the output:

```
dic = {'X': 10, 'Y': 20, 'Z': 30}
dic.pop('Y')
print(dic)
```

28. (A) Define phishing and explain how it can affect individuals and organizations.

Or

(B) What are some important measures for cyber safety while browsing the internet?

SECTION C

3×3=9

29. (A) Define the number system and explain how the conversion from binary to decimal is performed.

Or

(B) Explain De Morgan's laws in Boolean algebra with examples.

30. (A) Using someone else's work without permission or proper attribution, such as copying text, images, or software, is a violation of intellectual property rights.

(i) What is plagiarism?

(ii) What are the consequences of copyright infringement?

(iii) What measures can be taken to prevent plagiarism and copyright infringement?

Or

(B) Posing as someone else online and using his/her personal/financial information for shopping online or posting something is a common type of cyber crime these days.

(i) What is cyber crime?

(ii) What are such types of cyber crimes collectively called?

(iii) What measures can you take to stop these?

31. (A) Predict the output of the following Python code:

```
import math
import random
result = math.pow(3, 2)
random_num = random.randint(1, 10)
print(f"Power result: {result}")
print(f"Random number: {random_num}")
```

What will be the output of the code?

Or

(B) Predict the output of the following Python code:

```
import statistics
data = [5, 10, 15, 20, 25]
mean_value = statistics.mean(data)
print(f"Mean of the list: {mean_value}")
```

What will be the output of the code?

SECTION D

4×4=16

32. (A) Predict the output of the following Python code:

```
my_tuple = (12, 15, 20, 25)
new_tuple = tuple(x * 2 for x in my_tuple
                        if x % 5 == 0)
print(new_tuple)
print("-".join(map(str, new_tuple)))
print(len(new_tuple))
print(new_tuple[0] * 2)
```

Or

(B) Predict the output of the following Python code:

```
my_dict = {"A": 100, "B": 200, "C": 300}
my_dict["D"] = 400
print(my_dict)
my_dict["A"] = 150
print(my_dict)
```

33. Which dictionary built-in methods are best suited for the following conditions?

1. Adds a new key-value pair to the dictionary.
2. Removes an item from the dictionary based on the key.
3. Returns a list of all keys in the dictionary.
4. Returns a list of all values in the dictionary.

34. (A) To find the number of vowels in a given string.

(B) To remove all whitespaces from a string.

Or

(A) To check if a given number is a prime number.

(B) To print the multiplication table of a given number using loops.

35. (i) What will be the output of the following code using the math module?

```
import math
print(math.ceil(4.7))
```

(ii) What will be the output of the following code using the random module?

```
import random
print(random.choice([1, 2, 3, 4, 5]))
```

(iii) What will be the output of the following code using the statistics module?

```
import statistics
data = [2, 4, 6, 8, 10]
print(statistics.median(data))
```

(iv) What will be the output of the following code using the math module?

```
import math
print(math.fabs(-10))
```

SECTION E

2 × 5 = 10

36. **Amit is an active social media user and is concerned about the impact of his online presence. He wants to make sure he follows proper digital etiquettes and maintains a positive online image.**

Write a brief guide for Amit, covering the following:

1. **What are net etiquettes? How can Amit ensure that he communicates respectfully and responsibly online?**
2. **What are social media etiquettes, and what steps should Amit take to avoid negative consequences when interacting on social media platforms?**
3. **Explain two basic practices Amit should follow to ensure his online activities are ethical and respectful towards others.**

37. **XYZ Electronics is planning to set up an online order management system for its customers. The system will need to process orders, track inventory, and generate invoices. As a software engineer, you need to design and implement a simple solution for the system, considering the following points:**

(I) Suggest an appropriate data type for storing the order quantity and justify your choice.

(II) Which data type would you use to store the customer name and why?

(III) Write a Python expression to calculate the total cost of an order, considering the price of a single item and the quantity ordered.

(IV) Identify and fix any potential errors in the following code snippet:

```
order_quantity = input("Enter the order
quantity: ")
item_price = 20.5
total_cost = order_quantity * item_price
print("Total cost:", total_cost)
```

(V) (A) What type of loop would you recommend to process all orders in a list of orders (with each order as a dictionary containing order details)? Justify your choice.

Or

(B) Write a Python program that uses an if-else statement to check if the quantity of items in an order is valid (greater than 0). If the quantity is invalid, display an error message.

SAMPLE QUESTION PAPER 3

A Highly Simulated Sample Question Paper for CBSE Class XI Examination

COMPUTER SCIENCE

Time : 3 Hours

Max. Marks : 70

General Instructions

See Sample Question Paper 1

SECTION A

21 × 1 = 21

1. **State True or False:**

The max() function returns the smallest alphabetical character from the string based on ASCII values.

2. **What is the output of the following code?**

```
t = (4.0, "Hello", 90, 'Two', ('One', 45), 34, 2)
t1=t[1] + t[-2]
print(t1)
```

(a) 34 (b) 38 (c) Hello34 (d) TypeError

3. **What will be the output of the following Python code?**

```
random.randrange(0,91,5)
```

(a) 10 (b) 18

(c) 79 (d) 95

4. **What will be the output of the following Python code snippet?**

```
s = "Arihant Publication"

print(s.upper())
```

(a) "Arihant Publication"

(b) "ARIHANT PUBLICATION"

(c) "arihant publication"

(d) "aRIHANT pUBLICATION"

5. **What will be the output of the following Boolean logic expression?**

```
X = 1
Y = 0
Z = 0
Output = (X OR Y) AND (X AND (NOT Z))
print(Output)
```

(a) 0 (b) 1

(c) True (d) False

6. **Which of the following methods is used to insert an element at a specified position in a list in python?**

(a) insert() (b) add()

(c) append() (d) put()

7. **What is the output of the following Python code snippet?**

```
string = "Hello, World!"
print(string.split(","))
```

(a) ["Hello", "World!"] (b) ["Hello,", "World!"]

(c) ["Hello"] (d) ["World!"]

8. **While surfing on internet if your geo location is turned on, than it makes**

(a) Active digital footprint

(b) Passive digital footprint

(c) Active footprint

(d) Passive footprint

9. **The octal system**

(a) needs less digits to represent a number than in the binary system

(b) needs more digits to represent a number than in the binary system

(c) needs the same number of digits to represent a number as in the binary system

(d) needs the same number of digits to represent a number as in the decimal system

10. **Write the missing statement to complete the following code:**

```
sentence = "Python is amazing"
count_a = 0
for char in sentence:
    ____________ # Count occurrences of 'a'
print("Number of times 'a' appears:", count_a)
```

11. **State whether the following statement is True or False.**

"E-waste should be disposed of in regular household trash bins."

12. **What will be the output of the following code?**

```
my_list = [2, 4, 6, 8]
my_tuple = tuple(my_list)
my_list.insert(2, 10)
print(len(my_tuple), end='#')
```

```
print(len(my_list), end='%')
```
(a) 4#5% (b) 5#4%
(c) 4#4% (d) 5#5%

13. What is the purpose of a copyright in Intellectual Property Rights (IPR)?

14. What will be the output of the following code?
```
count = 0
for i in range(2, 10, 2):
    count += i
print(count, end='#')
print(len(range(2, 10, 2)), end='%')
```
(a) 20#4% (b) 10#5%
(c) 20#5% (d) 10#4%

15. All the errors that are detected and displaced by the compiler or interpreter are known as
(a) Run time errors
(b) Compile time errors
(c) Logical errors
(d) None of the above

16. while loops are called as
(a) entry control loops (b) exit control loops
(c) Both (a) and (b) (d) None of these

17. Is the following Python code valid?
```
>>>tupl=(56, 25, 36, 15)
>>> result=tupl.update(4)
```
(a) Yes, tup1 = (56, 25, 36, 15, 4) and result = (56, 25, 36, 15, 4)
(b) Yes, tup1 = (56, 25, 36, 15) and result = (56, 25, 36, 15, 4)
(c) No, because tuples are immutable
(d) No, because wrong syntax for update() method

18. How can you check if a string contains a specific substring in Python?
(a) Using the contains() method
(b) Using the in Keyword
(c) Using the search() function
(d) Using the hasSubstring() method

19. What is the function of the CPU in a computer system?

Directions (Q20 and Q21) are Assertion(A) and Reason(R) based questions. Mark the correct choice as:
(a) Both A and R are true and R is the correct explanation for A
(b) Both A and R are true and R is not the correct explanation for A
(c) A is True but R is False
(d) A is False but R is True

20. Assertion (A) A dictionary value can be accessed by its index.

Reason (R) A dictionary is not ordered by indexes.

21. Assertion (A) Binary is the most fundamental number system used in computers.

Reason (R) Binary uses only two digits, 0 and 1, which can be easily represented by electronic switches (on/off).

SECTION B

7 × 2 = 14

22. Distinguish between tuple and list.

23. (i) Write the equivalent boolean expression for the following logic circuit.

(ii) Give the dual of (A.B' + C.A')D

24. (I) What is the output of below questions?

l2 = [75, 43, 40, 36, 28, 82]

(i) l2.sort()

(ii) l2.sort(reverse = True)

Or

Define the replicating lists with an example.

(II) What is the output of the below code?

l1 = [10, 20, 30, 40, 50]

(i) l1.append(60)

(ii) l1.insert(2, 25)

Or

Define list concatenation with an example.

25. Give three guidelines to prevent the virus attacks?

26. Explain the different types of memory in a computer system and describe their role.

27. (I) Which operator is used to check equality between two values in Python?

Or

Give the output:
```
x = 10
y = 10.0
print(x == y)
```
(II) What is used to convert a string to an integer in Python?

Or

Give the output:
```
x = "123"
y = int(x)
print(y)
```
28. (A) Define plagiarism and explain how it can impact individuals and organizations.

Or

(B) What are the key differences between copyright and trademark, and how do they protect intellectual property?

SECTION C

3 × 3 = 9

29. (A) Define the functions of an Operating System and explain its role in managing hardware and software resources.

Or

(B) Explain truth tables for the AND, OR, and NOT operations in Boolean logic. How are they used in logic circuits?

30. (A) Improper disposal of electronic waste can lead to environmental pollution and health hazards.

(i) What is e-waste?

(ii) What are the potential environmental risks of improper e-waste disposal?

(iii) What measures can be taken for proper e-waste management?

Or

(B) Gender and disability issues need to be addressed while teaching and using computers in society.

(i) What are the key challenges faced by individuals with disabilities in accessing technology?

(ii) How can technology be made more inclusive for people with disabilities?

(iii) What is the role of computers in promoting gender equality in education and the workplace?

31. (A) Predict the output of the following Python code:

```
sentence = "hello world"
uppercase_sentence = sentence.upper()
split_sentence = sentence.split()
print(f"Uppercase: {uppercase_sentence}")
print(f"Split sentence: {split_sentence}")
```

What will be the output of the code?

Or

(B) Predict the output of the following Python code:

```
text = "   Python programming is fun!   "
stripped_text = text.strip()
count_python = text.count("Python")

print(f"Stripped text: '{stripped_text}'")
print(f"Count of 'Python': {count_python}")
```

SECTION D

4 × 4 = 16

32. (A) Predict the output of the following Python code:

```
numbers = [5, 10, 15, 20, 25]
sum_of_numbers = 0
for num in numbers:
    if num % 2 == 0:
        sum_of_numbers += num
    else:
        sum_of_numbers -= num
print(sum_of_numbers)
```

What will be the output of the code?

Or

(B) Predict the output of the following Python code:

```
count = 0
while count < 5:
    print(f"Count: {count}")
    count += 1
else:
    print("Loop finished.")
```

What will be the output of the code?

33. Which string built-in methods are best suited for the following conditions?

1. Joins a list of strings into a single string, with a specified separator.
2. Replaces all occurrences of a substring with a new substring in the string.
3. Checks if the string ends with a specific substring.
4. Counts how many times a substring appears in the string.

34. (A) To find the maximum and minimum numbers in a list of integers.

(B) To find the sum of all even numbers in a list using a loop.

Or

(A) To check if a given string is a palindrome.

(B) To reverse the characters of a given string and display the result.

35. Write a python Program to print the following pattern according to the user's choice:

SECTION E

2 × 5 = 10

36. Rohit is concerned about the increasing threats of cybercrime and malware attacks. He wants to make sure he takes the necessary precautions to protect himself and his devices.

Write a brief guide for Rohit, covering the following:

1. What is hacking, and how can Rohit protect his personal information and devices from hackers?
2. What is malware, and what steps can Rohit take to protect his computer from viruses, trojans, and adware?

3. Explain the importance of identity protection while browsing the web and the measures Rohit should take to safeguard his identity online.

37. XYZ Tech is planning to design a software solution for managing product prices and categories. The system will need to store product data efficiently and perform various operations on it. As a software engineer, you need to design a simple solution, considering the following points:

(I) Suggest an appropriate data type for storing the prices of products and justify your choice.

(II) Which data type would you use to store the product category (e.g., Electronics, Apparel) and why?

(III) Write a Python expression to calculate the average price of all products in a tuple of product prices.

(IV) Identify and fix any potential errors in the following code snippet:

```
product_prices = (200, 350, 500, 450)
total_price = product_prices[0] +
product_prices[1] + product_prices[2]
print("Total price:", total_price)
```

(V) (A) What type of tuple operation would you recommend to find the maximum and minimum prices from a tuple of product prices? Justify your choice.

Or

(B) Write a Python program that checks if a given product price exists in a tuple. If it exists, display the position (index) of the price in the tuple.

Answers

Sample Question Paper - 1

1. False **2.** (a) **3.** (c) **4.** (c) **5.** Syntax error **6.** (b) **7.** (a) **8.** (d) **9.** (d)
10. max(numbers) **11.** True **12.** (b) **13.** 1110 **14.** (b) **15.** (b) **16.** (b) **17.** (d) **18.** (b)
19. Type Conversion in Python refers to converting one data type into another. **20.** (b) **21.** (a)

Sample Question Paper - 2

1. False **2.** (c) **3.** (a) **4.** (b) **5.** 1 **6.** (b) **7.** (b) **8.** (a) **9.** (b) **10.** total+=num
11. True **12.** (a)
13. The Information Technology (IT) Act aims to provide legal recognition to electronic transactions, combat cybercrime, and ensure data security in digital communications.
14. (a) **15.** (b) **16.** (c) **17.** (d) **18.** (d)
19. System software is a set of programs that manage hardware and provide a platform for running application software.
20. (a) **21.** (d)

Sample Question Paper - 3

1. False **2.** (d) **3.** (a) **4.** (b) **5.** 1 **6.** (a) **7.** (a) **8.** (b) **9.** (a)
10. if char =='a':
count_a+=1
11. False **12.** (a)
13. The purpose of copyright in IPR is to protect the original works of authors, granting them exclusive rights to use and distribute their creations.
14. (a) **15.** (b) **16.** (a) **17.** (c) **18.** (b)
19. It processes instructions, performs calculations, and manages information. **20.** (d) **21.** (a)